SECOND EDITION

Issues in Feminism

An Introduction to Women's Studies

Sheila Ruth

Southern Illinois University–Edwardsville

Mayfield Publishing Company
Mountain View, California • London • Toronto

Copyright © 1990 by Mayfield Publishing Company
Copyright © 1980 by Houghton Mifflin Company,
Issues in Feminism: A First Course in Women's Studies

Library of Congress Cataloging-in-Publication Data

Issues in feminism : an introduction to women's
studies / [compiled by] Sheila Ruth. — 2nd ed.
        p.   cm.
    Includes bibliographical references.
    ISBN 0-87484-937-3 : $25.00
    1. Feminism—United States.   2. Women's
    studies—United States.
    I. Ruth, Sheila.
    HQ1426.I853   1990   90-5537
    305.42'0973—dc20   CIP

Manufactured in the United States of America
10 9 8 7 6 5 4 3

Mayfield Publishing Company
1240 Villa Street
Mountain View, California 94041

Sponsoring editor, Franklin C. Graham; production
editor, Wendy Calmenson, The Book Company;
manuscript editor, L. Jay Stewart; cover designer,
Ingbritt Christensen. The text was set in 9/11
Palatino by Thompson Type and printed on 50#
Finch Opaque by Banta Company.

Once again
To the people who have loved me . . .

George and Mary Sack
Michael Allaband
Amity Ruth
Mary Helen Osborne

Contents

Preface

When I was first preparing *Issues in Feminism* in 1978, I wrote:

> *Women's studies was born out of the women's movement, which was born out of the concrete experience, realities, and possibilities of women's lives. No matter how much a part of the traditional, "respectable" university the research, faculty, or students of women's studies become, we never lose sight of our beginnings or continuing rootedness in women's liberation, because it is the rootedness in its issues that gives impetus and meaning to our work.*
>
> *Those of us engaged in what is currently called women's studies (research and learning in a feminist context) have come along different routes, yet almost without exception each of us is here because at some time in our personal history we have specifically experienced events or ideas that have propelled us into a reappraisal of our lives as women. Generally it was the power of those experiences and the shock of the appraisal that created in us the desire and the commitment to know more about women, womanhood, and the consequences of gender definition.*

In the years since this book's beginnings, a great deal has changed: society has changed; women's studies has changed; I have changed.

The eighties have been the decade of the reactionary. In national politics and in social attitudes, progressive liberalism has been forced into retrenchment, and feminists find ourselves in an environment that *seems* overtly more accepting but is actually more hostile. More women work than ever before, are in the professions, have educations, and have seen some small improvements in income. It is more respectable not to marry, or to be a single parent, and "liberated women" are fixtures in television series. Yet, E.R.A. was defeated in 1982 and is rarely heard of today; affirmative action for women has been all but destroyed after the Reagan years, and we are losing ground in reproductive autonomy. Many women are increasingly poor. Worse, our young people are for the most part apolitical, and many young women—perhaps most—believe that feminism is beside the point, all important battles having been settled.

Nonetheless, the seeds of the activism of the sixties were sown in the fifties, and perhaps our losses in the eighties will shock more women back into action in the coming decade. If that is to be so, women's studies is faced with a vast responsibility.

In this decade of retrenchments, the fortunes of women's studies have been mixed. On the one hand, we have grown. More than two-thirds of American colleges and universities have women's studies programs, a growing number with graduate offerings. The National Women's Studies Association, founded in 1977, now has over 3,000 members, a journal of its own, growing influence. In the late 1970's, careful women did not profess an interest in feminist scholarship until they had received tenure, and ambitious women avoided the field altogether. Today there are chairs in women's studies, joint appointments, and visiting lectureships. Women's studies today has luminaries, canons, "schools of thought," and a vast literature.

Let us not be mistaken, however, about our "place." We still live on the margin. Many programs continue to survive on the voluntary overwork of their faculty; many ambitious young academics still think it prudent to avoid association with us, and we have had only the slightest impact on the traditional content or the traditional faculty of the traditional disciplines.

For those of us involved in women's studies, our growth presents a two-edged sword. On the one hand, we have matured and grown in sophistication, having developed language, terminology and concepts that help us to be more accurate in our analyses. We have opened up new areas of investigation. Very important, we are sensitizing ourselves to our own blind spots, sharpening our awareness regarding diversity among women and regarding the complexity of our subject. As women's studies has survived now over twenty years, we are seeing second-generation feminist scholars, many of whom have been attracted to women's studies by the power of our scholarship and our classrooms rather than by direct experience in the women's movement.

On the other hand, although few would not delight in our growth, we must continue to be wary: sophistication must not be allowed to degenerate into the vacuity we deplore in other fields. Today's young scholars must be encouraged to anchor their work firmly in the world outside the classroom. Today, as in the past, if we lose our rootedness in the women's movement, in concrete social action, we will lose not only our passion, but our heart and our meaning.

As time and society and women's studies have moved along, so have I. Women's studies is 20ish. I am 50ish. Having been instructed by my work and my colleagues (dare I use the word *sisters*?), I am losing some of my blind spots. I am becoming, for example, keenly aware of my own particularity—a white, middle class, professional, midwesterner

crusted around a working class, Jewish, loner Bronx kid. I understand better what that enables me to say and what I should leave for others to say. I tend to be more careful in my speech, measuring, qualifying. I have given up what Mary Helen Osborne calls "certitude"; I know how much I don't know. I hope that is reflected in this new edition.

What has not altered is my passionate belief in the women's movement, in the need for social change, in the possibilities of the future. I am still an unregenerate feminist rooted, by choice, in the spirit of (dare I use the word?) women's liberation. I hope that, too, is reflected in this new edition.

This book is designed for beginners in feminism and women's studies, for those who have not yet had the experience of recognition and reappraisal, or who have had it only in the most inchoate way. The text and readings included here not only impart information but seek as their foremost goal to precipitate in the reader an awareness of the self versus gender definition. This is a primer in the most exact sense: it is directed at the prime, the spring, the level of consciousness out of which come the need and the decision to know. It aims to engage students by revealing the gender issues imbedded in the most familiar facets of life—family relationships, work, education, media, religion, popular culture. The ideas presented here comprise a first course in women's studies that is first both logically and existentially.

The experiences we have, the awarenesses we develop, and the manner in which we develop them are rarely ordered according to the patterns of academic disciplines. Reality, after all, is not disciplinary. Neither is this book, since it attempts, at least in part, to present ideas as life might. The readings are interdisciplinary, ranging across many fields of study and chosen to reveal issues in their interrelatedness. I have not necessarily selected the most recent pieces, the most erudite, or even the most reputable. I brought together statements from past and present that are representative of the prevailing notions that have had terrific impact on the lives of women (and hence men). These readings, diverse as they are, go together. They have been selected for their collective power to provide a picture of the pattern of ideas about women. The readings are meant to educate in the broadest sense; not only to bring students face to face with their experience now, but also to provide them with a context, the sources of current beliefs in the ideas of the distant and not so distant past.

The theme of this book in both text and readings is twofold. First, in order to understand ourselves and our world we must be aware of all the notions regarding women, from the academic to the popular, from the scientific to the pseudoscientific, from the complex to the simplistic and from the thoughtful to the downright silly. Second, understanding can emerge only from critical analysis grounded in a sensitivity to even the homeliest events of our day-to-day lives.

After a short discussion of the nature of women's studies, we begin with an explication of the major themes of sex-role arrangements—the images of male and female ideals, the roles and expectations of gender as they have been expressed in various aspects of our culture and as they criss-cross with class, race, ethnicity, sexual identity, and other social categories that have resulted in extraordinary discrimination. We begin with these images, the Mars and Venus ideals, because in a variety of cultural forms they are at the root of social beliefs and attitudes toward the sexes. They have great explanatory value, both for the traditionalist, as justification for current behaviors, and for the feminist, as a schema to be explored. Then, following the presentation of some classic theories of why gender bifurcation and asymmetry exist, the images of ideal masculinity and femininity are traced through their appearances in such pertinent and affecting aspects of life as family, sexuality, education, work and politics. Here, in the parts of our life we feel most deeply, the images are revealed in all their distortion and power. I hope that if students can recognize the destructive potential of the traditional images and stereotypes in their own lives, they will seek alternatives.

Although what follows covers a range of areas, from psychology to economics, from politics to anthropology, its place is primarily in the humanities. The driving questions in the issues presented are:

What does this mean? How does this affect the quality of our lives? What would be better? Why does it matter?

If there is a discipline involved in the book, it is philosophy. Its process is to pose questions, articulate varying responses, assess them, set the stage for further questions, and so on—the Socratic approach, all in the quest for knowledge. Its consequence is growth in wisdom and spirit. Nonetheless, what we will be doing here is women's studies, a nondisciplinary, multidisciplinary, counterdisciplinary feminist exploration of the conditions of our lives, where we ourselves set the boundaries of what may be asked and of what we may ultimately do with the answers we devise.

To complete a project like *Issues in Feminism* requires many kinds of help and support. I am grateful to many colleagues who have reviewed the manuscript and offered guidance and suggestions, especially Joseph J. Arpad, California State University at Fresno; Susan Arpad, California State University at Fresno; Anne M. Butler, Utah State University; Carol Coburn, University of Kansas; Joan Hagman, Concordia College; Annis H. Hopkins, Arizona State University; Louis Levesque-Lopman, Regis College; and Betty C. Safford, California State University at Fullerton.

Special thanks go to my Chair, Thomas Paxson, for allowing me to organize my time so that I could be alone so much; to John Scott Millar and Diane Elaine Whitley Dudding—through all my endless requests they never stopped smiling; to Kim Blankenship—it is customary to say that without the help of so-and-so, the work would never have been done, and in Kim's case, it is true; to Mary Helen Osborne, whose wit, energy, humor, and warmth have fed a hungry soul; to Amity for her "go-get-em, Mom"'s; and to Michael, who hung in, gave me space, made appointments to see me when possible, and prepared feasts of many kinds.

—Sheila Ruth

1

An Introduction to Women's Studies

What Is "Women's Studies"?

In the middle to late 1960s, a scattering of courses focusing on feminist issues began to appear on college campuses. In 1970 the terms *women's studies* or *feminist studies* were first used to refer to them. Against strong resistance, two or three courses developed into thousands of courses, into programs, into a whole new educational and intellectual enterprise.

According to a study by Florence Howe, in 1980 university faculty were teaching more than twenty thousand such courses in institutions all over the country.[1] Programs existed on all levels of study from the undergraduate minor to the doctorate. We can also expand the extent and size of women's studies if we consider the thousands of noncredit courses offered through extension and continuing education programs and those offered in other countries.

In 1977 the number of people involved in feminist research had grown so large and their interests were so diverse that it became necessary to establish some formal means of communication and support. In January of that year, delegates from institutions all over the country participated in the founding of the National Women's Studies Association. By 1987 it had roughly three thousand members![2]

For contemporary university education and for some high schools, women's studies is a fact of life. But what is the nature of this new enterprise? What precisely does it do?

Because women's studies is still very young—only about twenty years old—it is difficult to suggest an absolute definition. Scholars are just beginning to articulate and explain the challenging new insights and methods that are developing within the field. Women's studies is a field that has few models; it consciously rejects many traditional forms of inquiry, concepts, and explanatory systems; at the same time, it is developing traditions and authorities of its own.

You will learn in this chapter how feminist researchers are discovering that the historically accepted theories and explanations—even the methods of pursuing knowledge—are rife with prejudice and misunderstandings about women in particular and humanity in general. Committed to pursuing tolerance in methodology and interpretation so we can avoid the danger of creating more rigid principles of research, as feminist thinkers, we are extremely hesitant to impose limits on the work of others who seek to restore balance and find clarification. Therefore, we place a high value on freedom and self-determination. Ideologically, and often temperamentally, we are suspicious of hierarchies and structures of control whether in social relations or intellectual pursuits. Self-disciplined freedom and cooperative efforts, we believe, are more apt to produce constructive results in most endeavors.

Thus, most of us try to support and be open to ideas and approaches different from our own.

You will see that openness and freedom from prejudice is not easy to attain, and the work is far from complete. Serious errors have occurred. Among the *isms* with which we have struggled are racism, ethnocentrism, heterosexism, classism, ageism. Yet we are becoming more sophisticated in our analyses. As we grow, we encompass and integrate more diverse perspectives, enlarge our understanding, and become more accurate.

For all these reasons—the newness of feminist research, the hesitancy to embrace constricting standards, and the unusually strong desire for tolerance, experimentation, and growth—the ideas, methods, curricula, and theories of women's studies exhibit great diversity and resist easy definition. Those of us now working in women's studies have called it variously a process, a field of inquiry, a critical perspective, a center for social action, and/or the academic arm of the women's movement. It is all of these and more.

The "Study of Women"

For centuries, women have been "studied." Aristotle concluded that we were "misbegotten males," conceived instead of men when the winds were not propitious. Aquinas decided that since women were at least necessary for procreation, God had not after all made some terrible mistake in creating us. Freud determined the vengeful, castrating, penis-envying character of us all, and the philosopher Karl Stern theorized about our "nonreflective," cosmically tied life of nature.[3]

Such concepts in the past study of women reflect the nature of most of these studies: They were carried on almost exclusively by men working together in institutions and disciplines absolutely closed to women. An examination of the many traditional works on women reveals certain characteristics:

- Women are generally looked *at*; we rarely did our own looking and still more rarely were we asked for our opinions or expressions concerning our own experience. Those expressions that women have offered have tended to be ignored or debunked unless they reinforced existing beliefs.

- Women are generally "studied" in a separate section or subsection of a work, as though we were some kind of extra appendage or anomaly, not readily understood within the general context of the inquiry. In Aristotle's *Politics,* for example, following a discussion of human excellence is a separate section asking whether women as well as men might have "excellence," and if so, in what this excellence might consist.[4] (He decided that women are admirable when obedient and silent.) An *Introduction to Islam*[5] contains fifteen chapters describing the fundamental beliefs and practices of the "people" of the religion. One chapter is entitled, "The Muslim Woman." As we might expect, no chapter exists on "the Muslim man."

- Professional and academic studies of women reflect the prejudices and attitudes that exist in the wider culture. Without women's own perspectives and statements to balance and uncover the historical fund of ignorance and superstition surrounding our lives, conventional (misogynist) wisdom has been carried into research by so-called authorities on the subject, has hardened into accepted theories, and has ultimately become science. As science, these myths about women have been used to justify all sorts of oppression from witch hunts to clitoridectomy.

Until recently, the accepted studies of women from primitive times to the present have examined women as if we were senseless, semihuman creatures unable to speak for ourselves; we have been prodded, dissected, categorized and filed, researched and resolved. No wonder the traditional products of the "study of women" are distorted and counterproductive.

Such an approach to understanding women's lives necessarily produces poor information. Reverse the gender, treating the male as the adjunct of humanity instead of the female. Can you imagine a history of westward expansion containing a chapter on the pioneer husband or the pioneer male? Or how would you evaluate an analysis of masculine attitudes on impotence that was researched and written entirely by women based on their observations alone and with no input from men?

Women's Studies and Feminism

What transforms the "study of women" into women's studies is reflected in the terms themselves. In the "*study of women*," women are objects; in *women's studies*, we are subjects.

Women's studies has a feminist base. Feminists do not agree among themselves on one all-inclusive and universally acceptable definition of the term *feminism*. Depending on a number of factors, *feminism* can mean different things and have a variety of functions. We shall see later that several different theories of feminism exist, and considerable discussion centers on what it means to be a feminist, what goals feminism should have, and how feminists should behave. Feminism may be a perspective, a world view, a political theory, a spiritual focus, or a kind of activism. Actually, one learns best what feminism means by listening to the statements of women who perceive themselves to be feminists and by understanding how they respond to events and conditions.

Just how much range in meaning there can be for the term is reflected in this partial list of the definitions of "Feminism" as reported in Cheris Kramarae and Paula A. Treichler's *Feminist Dictionary*:[6]

"May be defined as a movement seeking the reorganization of the world upon a basis of sex-equality in all human relations; a movement which would reject every differentiation between individuals upon the ground of sex, would abolish all sex privileges and sex burdens, and would strive to set up the recognition of the common humanity of woman and man as the foundation of law and custom."

Theresa Billington-Greig, "Feminism and Politics," *The Contemporary Review*, Nov. 1911

". . . has as yet no defined creed . . . [Is] the articulate consciousness of mind in women . . . in its different forms of expression."

"The Freewoman" 1911, *Votes for Women*

"Feminism at heart is a massive complaint. Lesbianism is the solution. . . . Until all women are lesbians there will be no true political revolution. No feminist per se has advanced a solution outside of accommodation to the man."

Jill Johnston, *Lesbian Nation*, 1973

"Begins but cannot end with the discovery by an individual of her self-consciousness as a woman. It is not, finally, even the recognition of her reasons for anger, or the decision to change her life, to go back to school, to

leave a marriage. . . . Feminism means finally that we renounce our obedience to the fathers and recognize that the world they have described is not the whole world. . . . Feminism implies that we recognize fully the inadequacy for us, the distortion, of male-created ideologies, and that we proceed to think, and act, out of that recognition."

Adrienne Rich, *Of Woman Born*, 1976

"A method of analysis as well as a discovery of new material. It asks new questions as well as coming up with new answers. Its central concern is with the social distinction between men and women, with the fact of this distinction, with its meanings, and with its causes and consequences."

Juliet Mitchell and Anne Oakley, *The Rights and Wrongs of Women*, 1976

"Is a mode of analysis, a method of approaching life and politics, a way of asking questions and searching for answers, rather than a set of political conclusions about the oppression of women."

Nancy Hartsock, "Feminist Theory and the Development of Revolutionary Strategy," in Zillah Eisenstein, *Capitalist Patriarchy and the Case for Socialist Feminism*, 1979

"Feminism is the political theory and practice to free all women; women of color, working-class women, poor women, physically challenged women, lesbians, old women, as well as white economically privileged heterosexual women. Anything less than this is not feminism, but merely female self-aggrandizement."

Barbara Smith in Cherríe Moraga and Gloria Anzaldúa, *This Bridge Called My Back*, 1981

"Is a commitment to eradicating the ideology of domination that permeates Western culture on various levels—sex, race, and class, to name a few—and a commitment to reorganizing U.S. society, so that the self-development of people can take precedence over imperialism, economic expansion, and material desires."

Bell Hooks, *Ain't I a Woman*, 1981

"Is an entire world view or gestalt, not just a laundry list of 'women's issues.' Feminist theory provides a basis for understanding every area of our lives, and a feminist perspective can affect the world politically, culturally, economically, and spiritually."

Charlotte Bunch, *Learning Our Way*, 1983

"Third World feminism is about feeding people in all their hungers."

Cherríe Moraga, *Loving in the War Years*, 1983

From Alice Walker we have the strong, jubilant definition of a *"womanist,"* a variation on the term *feminist.*

Womanist 1. From womanish. *(Opp. of "girlish," i.e., frivolous, irresponsible, not serious.) A black feminist or feminist of color. From the black folk expression of mothers to female children, "You acting womanish," i.e., like a woman. Usually referring to outrageous, audacious, courageous or* willful *behavior. Wanting to know more and in greater depth than is considered "good" for one. Interested in grown-up doings. Acting grown up. Being grown up. Interchangeable with another black folk expression: "You trying to be grown." Responsible. In charge. Serious.*

2. Also: A woman who loves other women, sexually and/or nonsexually. Appreciates and prefers women's culture, women's emotional flexibility (values tears as natural counterbalance of laughter), and women's strength. Sometimes loves individual men, sexually and/or nonsexually. Committed to survival and wholeness of entire people, male and female. Not a separatist, except periodically, for health. Traditionally universalist, as in: "Mama, why are we brown, pink, and yellow, and our cousins are white, beige, and black?" Ans.: "Well, you know the colored race is just like a flower garden, with every color flower represented." Traditionally capable, as in: "Mama, I'm walking to Canada and I'm taking you and a bunch of other slaves with me." Reply: "It wouldn't be the first time."

3. Loves music. Loves dance. Loves the moon. Loves the Spirit. Loves love and food and roundness. Loves struggle. Loves the Folk. Loves herself. Regardless.

4. Womanist is to feminist as purple to lavender.[7]

Notwithstanding our diversity, certain beliefs, values, and attitudes are common to all feminists. These might be articulated as follows to set a context for comprehending the rich variety of feminist/womanist thought.

- *Feminism* means literally *"womanism."* As feminists we value women, not in the hypocritical fashion of centuries of male-dominated cultures in which women were valued for the work they could produce, the price they could bring, or the services they could render; nor do we value women provided they behave according to some externally imposed set of requirements. Rather we value women in and of themselves, as ends in themselves, and for themselves.

- As feminists we value the fact of being women as highly as we value the fact of being human. We do not accept the cultural images of women as incompetent, petty, irresponsible, or weak. In contrast, we affirm our capacities to be strong, capable, intelligent, successful, ethical human beings. Many of us believe that our history and special forms of experience have set the conditions for making us particularly "excellent" human beings.

- As feminists we value autonomy for ourselves as individuals and for women as a group. We mean to develop the conditions that will enable us to control our own political, social, economic, and personal destinies.

- As feminists we reject attitudes that regard the traditionally ascribed masculine characteristics of aggression, power, and competition as good and desirable and the ascribed feminine characteristics of compassion, tenderness, and compromise as weak and ridiculous. We tend to reject both the practice of separating human qualities into two categories—one of them for men and one for women—and the valuing of one of those categories above the other. Instead we recognize that all such characteristics may appear in either sex, and we evaluate each of them on its own merit.

- As feminists we understand that the majority of beliefs and attitudes regarding women both in our own culture and in most other cultures are false or wrongheaded, based on myth, ignorance, and fear. It is necessary to replace inaccurate myth with reality and ignorance with knowledge about women created by women, first for women and finally for all people.

- As feminists we point out that for centuries we have been denied our rights as citizens and as human beings. The right to vote, the right to earn a substantive living commensurate with effort, the freedom to determine whether to bear children—the denial of these and other freedoms constitute concrete instances of oppression. We recognize that women possess persistent strength and spirit in the face of such oppression and are optimistic about the possibilities of change. Many of the qualities developed by women in the face of denial are precious and unique.

It is this feminist base—on the one hand, a realization that women's reality has been distorted, on the other, a positive and affirming stance toward women and womanhood—that transforms the "study of women" into women's studies. Women's studies might have been called feminist studies, and in some institutions it is; but some feminist educators have argued that this term is strategically unwise since it evokes resistance from entrenched and powerful antifemale forces within institutions.

Women's programs, both academic and nonacademic—even after twenty years of excellence—are often met with derision or intolerance. The same forces that limit the freedom, status, and power of women in the wider society limit women within academe. For reasons we shall explore in this book, a prowoman stance is very threatening to traditional attitudes and structures. The very word *feminism* carries fearful connotations for many people and evokes a defensive response.

Remarks that the student of women's studies may encounter express that defensive posture.

- "Are you taking that stuff?! What are you, a *libber*?"

- "Women's studies? What good is that going to do you?"

- "Since you've been reading that stuff you've been hard to get along with. I don't want to hear any more about it."

Faculty hear the same kind of comments, cast a little differently.

- "Feminism is biased. How do you expect to teach a course like that fairly? You can't be objective."

- "You were hired to teach political science, not waste your time getting sidetracked on trivia. *Women in Politics* is just too esoteric a course for this department to spend resources on."

- "Women's studies! Are you kidding? When are we going to get a men's studies program?"

- "We've got to get back to basics. Women's studies is just a faddish temporary trend."

Although women constitute more than half the human population, serious examination of women's world and its implications for all humanity is simply not perceived to be meaningful and important from a male-centered perspective. Feminist contentions that both women and the wider society are being deprived of female power are not seen as valid; the argument is dismissed just as women are often dismissed. Rarely do the fruits of feminist research find their way from women's studies into the wider curriculum or the classrooms of other instructors, a situation that becomes a point of frustration for women's studies student and teacher alike.

Some researchers contend that certain areas of investigation directly relevant to women's lives may be pursued without a political perspective or a sex-theoretical stance: the female endocrine system, for example, or human reproduction. Such subjects, it is argued, are simply factual. It does not matter whether they are pursued by feminists or nonfeminists. Their content, being neutral in this respect, might be considered women's studies, but not feminist studies.

Feminist theoreticians in every field, however, are convinced that no purely factual studies exist. The way knowledge has been ordered, the methods of asking and answering questions, and the constructs used to understand data have all developed within a framework of male bias. Even an apparently true statement like the following becomes problematic from a feminist perspective: "The Renaissance took place during the fourteenth, fifteenth, and sixteenth centuries." A feminist historian illustrates the effect of a woman-oriented perspective on this traditionally accepted, so-called historical truth.

A young specialist in the Renaissance spoke to the obvious but unasked question, "Did women have a renaissance?" Her response was a jolt, for she suggested that the bourgeoisification of Italian society deprived women of power, created a patriarchal culture, and, in general, set women back in their quest for human liberty and autonomy. So what "renaissance" can be considered? What is progress, after all, if the transformation to a modern social order is achieved at the expense of half a population?

Such questions would never have been asked within the context of traditional political and economic history, nor would they emerge in ordinary considerations of intellectual "revolutions." The Renaissance becomes problematic only as a question of social history, and it is precisely that field with which the women's movement has merged to create a wholly new way to regard the human past.[8]

It is still a matter of argument whether truly neutral investigations with respect to sex orientation are possible. Perhaps a continuum of neutrality to non-neutrality is more the case. Our developing conceptual tools will resolve this question. Whatever the resolution, though, the framework of the enterprise itself must be feminist.

An interesting development of the last few years has been the growth of two new fields, offshoots of women's studies: men's studies and gender studies. Prompted by the insights and new perspectives of feminist scholarship, some male scholars have begun to rethink the nature of masculinity, much as women have been analyzing the meanings of femininity and womanhood.

As Harry Brod explains, the new critique of the social constructions of manhood contains two main themes:

An acceptance of the obvious fact that most scholarship, in the conventional sense, has been about men, and the contention that such scholarship, in perhaps a more significant sense, has not really been about men at all. In my attempt to make "The Case for Men's Studies," I offer the following formulation:

> *While seemingly about men, traditional scholarship's treatment of generic man as the human norm in fact systematically excludes from consideration what is unique to men qua men. The overgeneralization from male to generic human experience not only distorts our understanding of what, if anything, is truly generic to humanity but also precludes the study of masculinity as a specific male*

experience, rather than a universal paradigm for human experience. The most general definition of men's studies is that it is the study of masculinities and male experiences as specific and varying social-historical-cultural formations. Such studies situate masculinities as objects of study on a par with femininities, instead of elevating them to universal norms.

Men's studies questions assumptions that have passed beyond the horizons of usual scholarly inquiry to bring them back under critical purview. These assumptions about masculinity are so widely shared that they cease to appear as assumptions.[9]

Gender studies, as one might expect, is an umbrella enterprise said to encompass both fields of research, women's studies and men's studies. Now certainly it is time that maleness and men's behavior be investigated in the same critical way as femaleness and by men as well as by women. Better understanding of men as men and the resultant changes in men's behavior and values can only accelerate the evolution of humane societies. Furthermore, it is natural that feminist insight should spur men to look into their own lives. Men's studies has real value and can complement feminist critique.

Some women's studies scholars are justifiably concerned, however, about the development of gender studies programs. Although women's studies is gender scholarship, not all gender scholarship can be or should be thought of as women's studies. Women's studies is and must be feminist. Gender studies may not be. If women's studies allows itself to be absorbed into gender studies, will it lose its feminist-activist foundations? Will its themes and goals be diluted or co-opted by men's interests under the guise of "universal" concerns, as they are in the wider curriculum and society? Might its women scholars and teachers, its methodologies, and its structures likewise be co-opted or displaced?

Bias in Academe

Bias—which means prejudice, the absence of objectivity—derives from a term that means oblique, slanted, not standard or true, off-center. Bias implies some kind of distortion, usually unconscious. It is ironic that the enterprise of women's studies should be charged with bias.

When it is argued that feminist thinkers and women's studies are biased, at least two things are being said: (1) that feminists hold a set of beliefs that is somehow off-center, askew from "the truth"; and (2) that either we are unaware of having a distorted perspective, or we deliberately intend to impose slanted views on unsuspecting and vulnerable minds.

Feminism is perceived as a skewing of reality. Feminists would argue, however, that it is the traditional male-defined image of reality that is skewed.

Centuries ago discerning thinkers in science, theology, and philosophy recognized the fallacy of mistaking the part for the whole. In philosophy and theology, it was perceived that to mistake human values and perspectives for universal ones was to be misled in analyses of God and reality. This mistake was called *anthropocentrism,* and cautious thinkers learned to avoid it. More recently, social scientists have become aware of the dangers of *ethnocentrism,* the practice of imposing the standards of one's own culture on another. *Egocentrism,* whether conceptual (as when an individual assumes that others see reality as he or she does) or ethical, also distorts understanding. The error lies in assuming that one's own special perspective or world view is the true and only one, applicable everywhere to everyone or everything. Universally acknowledged to be fallacious, all such isms are guarded against—all, that is, except the most pervasive and distorting ism of all: *masculine-ism* or *masculism* (sometimes called *androcentrism*).

Masculism, as practiced in our culture, has many facets. We shall explore them in Chapter 2. Here we need only say that masculism is in part the mistaking of male perspectives, beliefs, attitudes, standards, values, and perceptions for all human perceptions. Masculism is pervasive in our culture except for feminist challenge, and it is most frequently unconscious.

In almost every culture, the tools and conditions necessary for learning and analysis, the means of communication, and the forms of legitimization of knowledge have been jealously and effectively kept from women. In some societies, the artifacts of history, the symbols of religious significance, and the activities of power are all secreted in a special hut, the men's hut, taboo to women. In other cultures, men speak a private language that the women of the tribe are forbidden to utter; in that language, the policies of the tribe are decided. In our own culture, disfranchisement was effected in an analogous way. Reading and studying were deemed dangerous for women, contributing to discontent and rebellion against our "natural" roles as wives and helpmates. Too much learning, it was said, would drain the energies necessary for us to produce children. Mathematics and science were particularly dangerous. They might rob women of a meek and gentle loveliness. Women were not supposed to have the stomach or the wit for politics. Such views have functioned as justifications for denying women the education, tools, and power to sustain ourselves and to direct society.

Women have been barred from the possibility of contributing all we can to the acknowledged intellectual and scientific world view. That has been reserved for men, who are in control of the academic disciplines, the universities, the learned societies, the presses, and the research foundations. With women virtually excluded from the intellectual power centers, the (male) minority opinion has been fallaciously equated with all that could be said. The male establishment has, in essence, appropriated reality for itself. Men have dominated the wider society. Their needs and goals have become official social goals. In learning, male thought has become official thought. The male stance has become the official human stance.

Consider, for example, the following analysis of the concept of respect by Joel Feinberg, a contemporary philosopher (italics added):[10]

> *In olden days, when power and authority went hand in hand . . . the scale of respect was one with the scales of power and status. This was the background against which the earliest moralists could begin demanding that respect be shown to various classes of the* deserving weak, *too. Hence our rude and unimpressed ancestors were urged to "show respect" for women, for the aged, for the clergy. . . . Christianity gave dignity even to the meek and humble. Respect could then be extended to the aged, to women, to the clergy. . . .*
>
> *To see a woman as having dignity now is to see her as in a moral position to make claims against* our *conduct, even though she may lack physical or political power over us. Certain minimal forms of consideration are her due, something she has coming, and can*

rightfully claim, even when she is in no position to make demands in the gunman sense. Insofar as we think of her that way we have respect for her . . . and insofar as she shares this image of herself she has self-respect.[11]

As I read this argument from my woman's perspective, I think: Indeed! And would any *man* in such a position—weak, meek, humble, and without power—perceive himself with self-respect? Who is this author to speak for me? And who are the *we* (*us, our*) of whom Feinberg speaks? He is a philosopher addressing philosophers. But he could not mean that only philosophers grant respect in this fashion. (Besides, I am a philosopher). No, Feinberg is analyzing the concept of respect as it is used, given, and granted in society, among people. Which people? Society surely must include women. Do women grant respect that way? Am I part of that *we, us*? I certainly do not perceive women and our worthiness that way. Generic *we*? Rather not. This is a mental involution impossible for me to make without self-alienation.

Feinberg's essay and his use of *we* (*us, our*) in juxtaposition to the term *women* is only one example among many of a world view that constitutes humanity as male and relegates women to the status of out-group. Comfortable and confident that ''we boys'' are ''we everyone,'' Feinberg exhibits the masculist usurpation of universality. The usurpation is conveniently masked by the linguistic device of generic *man* and is so generally accepted that it has become invisible to the naked (that is, nonfeminist) eye. For example, a film entitled *Why Man Creates* (1968), produced for the Kaiser Corporation and ostensibly an inquiry into the nature and motivation of *human* creativity, is composed of sequences in which scientists, artists, inventors, and symbols are all male; women appear only as wives, foils, or subjects of art. *The Uncommitted: Alienated Youth in Modern American Society* (1960), a sociopsychological study by Kenneth Keniston based on profiles of alienated young people, contained not one female profile, yet purported to be a study of alienated *youth*. The jacket of the book stated that ''Mr. Keniston starts from an intensive study of alienated *youth*, asking why a group of talented and privileged young *men* should reject . . .'' (italics added). An advertisement describes a work entitled *The States of Human Life: A Biography of Entire Man* (1974)

as follows: ''In this study of the career of *the individual*, the age-grades are considered as escarpments. . . . The perspective of *the individual* . . . shifts radically as *he* grows from infancy to young *manhood* and from maturity to old age'' (italics added). In another example, a modern logic textbook asks the supposedly general reader, ''She won't give you a date?'' Finally, the Constitution of the United States had declared, ''We the people,'' although at the time women had been totally disfranchised. The examples are endless.

The conceptual confusing of *human* and *male* historically and in the present in all disciplines and inquiries is so pervasive as to be the rule rather than the exception. Feminist criticism is revealing male bias, not creating a female one, as charged. Women's studies seeks to be the prophylactic of bias, not the cause.

The Goals of Women's Studies

Among the goals of women's studies is to uncover masculist bias in the history of knowledge as well as to create new knowledge and new values through positive research into women's experience. Women's studies seeks:

- to change women's sense of ourselves, our self-image, our sense of worth and rights, our presence in the world;

- to change women's aspirations based on an increased sense of self-confidence and self-love, to allow women to create for ourselves new options in our own personal goals as well as in our commitments and/or contributions to society;

- to alter the relations between women and men, to create true friendship and respect between the sexes in place of ''the war between the sexes'';

- to give all people, women and men, a renewed sense of human worth, to restore to the center of human endeavors a love for beauty, kindness, justice, and quality in living;

- to erase from the world all the representations of unwholesome, illegitimate power of one group over another: sexism, racism, heterosexism, classism, and so on;

- to end the race toward the destruction of the planet;

- to reaffirm in society the quest for harmony, peace, and humane compassion.

Such goals may appear presumptuous or at least not obviously related to the study of women's lives. But feminists have found that the movement that began in the concrete events of women's daily lives has implications that reach to the very foundations and structure of all life.

The Enfranchisement of Women in the University

Earlier, in the discussion of bias, reference was made to the exclusion of women from all the powerful policymaking institutions of our society and culture. That women all over the world should not have won suffrage until the turn of the century (New Zealand being first in 1893) is an indication of our exclusion from power in other areas of public life.

Until the end of the nineteenth century—except for the lowest paid, lowest status jobs—most women anywhere in the world had little access to economic independence. Within the family, they had small power over their possessions, their work, or their reproductive capacities. Legally they were at the mercy of male judges, lawyers, jurors, and laws. Women of any race or class found the doors of institutions of higher education barred to them. Oberlin was the first American college to admit women, in 1833, but its earliest programs for women were largely composed of home economics, religion, and other "female" subjects.

Today, because it is illegal to bar women from admission to any public educational institution on the basis of sex, we are entering universities and professional schools in increasing numbers, although still disproportionately in terms of race and ethnicity. One would think, therefore, that women's lives, priorities, and values on campus would be significantly enhanced and that the institutions, too, would reflect the results of our particular input. But strong forces both within women and within institutions impel women to be absorbed into the male world view rather than to create a new one. The masculine perspective in education; the preponderance of male faculty, administrators, textbooks, and curricular materials; the pressures of husband care and child care; the conflicts between women's family roles and educational needs; the general contempt for women's views all conspire to allow women on campus only a physical presence, not a powerful intellectual/spiritual influence or full participation.

Certainly it is a major goal of women's studies to reverse discriminatory conditions in the educational system, and campus feminists engage in a number of activities to accomplish this end. Besides increasing the university community's awareness of the conceptual issues, we are often involved in activities directed toward changing policies in administration that have direct bearing on women's abilities to attend school—policies regarding admissions, affirmative action, financial assistance, health facilities, sexual harrassment, child-care programs, part-time attendance, scheduling, and more. Feminist faculty, in or outside of women's studies, move for fairer decisions on salaries, promotion, and hiring, and we work toward increasing women's participation in decision making by seeking important administrative or committee appointments. The intent is to create balance and to eradicate the historical accumulation of masculist control.

Women have the right to full educational and professional opportunity, and this is the primary reason for ending university discrimination. But there is another reason as well, also profound and far-reaching.

The Restoration of Humane Commitments

It has already been pointed out that education and learning have historically been the private preserve of men; that today, knowledge and the formation of knowledge are largely in the hands of men; and that masculism distorts conceptualization. But as we shall see in Chapter 2, masculism goes well beyond conceptual bias, beyond the universalization of male perspectives in thought, to a universalization of male perspectives and attitudes in values and behavior.

Masculism is not only the cause of misinterpretations of women's nature, it is also the reflection, the expression of an almost universal abhorrence for women themselves and for a whole set of characteristics historically ascribed to women in Western culture: sensitivity, acquiescence, compassion, compromise, aesthetic sensibility. These qualities, though officially regarded with respect, are actually considered appropriate only in women. In men, except in special circumstances and in measured amounts, they are generally regarded with contempt. The complementary qualities have been prescribed for and encouraged in men—strength, competitiveness, power, emotional reserve, the warrior virtues—and these are the qualities expected in the public sphere. In any environment dominated by men, the warrior virtues are likely to prevail. The university is no exception.

For the last decade, educators have been decrying a growing dehumanization in universities, a waning of aesthetic and ethical commitment. Students and faculty alike question the university's mission; we fear our absorption into the wider technocracy, shudder at the absence of meaningfulness and at the "cash mentality" among us. Some speak of a moral crisis or a failure of vision.

Of course something *is* wrong, and we can look to many factors involved. But as we shall see, the androcentric university is a microcosm of the wider society, and its character defects reflect those of society.

Universities are products of the cultures that provide the individuals who people them and the ideas that govern them. In turn, by contributing to society the leaders of government, industry, art, and communication and by bequeathing to society scientific and social theories or inventions and discoveries, the universities help to mold and direct cultural attitudes and consciousness. An exchange of authority takes place between society and the halls of knowledge.

It can be easy to lose sight of the tremendous impact of much that is said and done in academe. What researchers and professors have learned and created in their institutions is passed on to their students, who in turn pass it to others through their work—in business, in government, in every phase of social life. The theories and arguments developed in lunchrooms and offices become tomorrow's "science," the "truths" that ultimately govern legal policy, psychotherapeutic techniques, media expression, and finally social behavior. If the truths of academe, developed in a masculist environment, seem to reflect and reinforce the warrior qualities, it is small wonder.

Consider the tone of university experience. It is not difficult to see that human compassion and car-

ing, personal sensitivity, authenticity, love, and openness are not highly prized in formal education. Even talk of such things tends to embarrass people, to make them uneasy. Academic language is distant, cold, rife with jargon. Instructional faculty combat with administrators. Professors bore and bombard their students with disconnected facts not clearly relevant to life experience. Students are wary of participation in class or intimacy with one another. Courses and programs die and are born and die again, fitting students (however poorly) to meet the requirements of industry or government but rarely giving them the tools to live well. Academe is not typically a loving, caring environment.

It is, however, competitive, sometimes ruthless. Students learn to be "successful." Faculty spar at intellectual gatherings, guard their positions, and compete for salary, status, and power. We are all reluctant to reveal our feelings and admit vulnerability. The warrior virtues prevail in contemporary education, blotting out the humane, a condition becoming increasingly obvious.

Human Redefinition and Social Values

Many feminists believe that women's reclamation of ourselves and our power may bring about a whole new way of being, a redefinition of human values. I agree but have to point out that such an idea must be based on a belief that is much debated—the idea that women are somehow in a special position with regard to value and better able to make ethical or humane judgments than most or many men.

For centuries, culminating in the Victorian period, a certain kind of woman—one removed from or rising above her carnal nature—was thought to be especially sacred, especially like the Virgin Mary, a mother of the generations, a keeper of morality. In the nineteenth century, enshrined within the family, middle-class women were charged with the responsibility for maintaining human morality by keeping their own lives "pure," by investing the young with a love for virtue, and by creating a home where it could flourish. Women were to furnish society with a place and experience apart from the harsh realities of work and government.

The image of woman as keeper of morality was, however, double-edged. As we shall see in Chapter

3, it was based on all kinds of myths and misconceptions; and it placed impossible burdens on women, denying them their own freedom and requiring them to maintain public morality when they had no power to do so. Feminists quite rightly reject this image.

That women may be especially predisposed to human virtue carries yet another assumption that is problematic—that women and men really are by nature different, at least in this respect. The contention that women and men are constitutionally different has been used as the main justification for rigid role distinctions and female subordination for centuries, and feminists have taken great pains to gather evidence against it.

Yet the belief that women may be in a special position with regard to value, better able to make humane judgments, is not necessarily based on the concepts described above. Rather it may be based on one or more of the following arguments: (1) in our culture women are trained and encouraged to develop caring or nurturing values and aesthetic sensibilities; (2) women's position outside the realms of power has also kept us from being fully absorbed into the psychodynamics of power and warrior values; (3) women's history of oppression and denial makes us especially sensitive to the abuses of power and domination; (4) the concrete realities of women's lives—the creation of life, the intimate connection with rites of passage, the maintenance of the necessities of living—give us different perspectives on what is valuable and important in existence.

From infancy onward, women's lives are suffused with the affective (that is, feeling, experiential, noncognitive) aspects of living. Considerations of beauty, tenderness, warmth, compassion, and love have been prescribed to be the special province of women. No doubt society's motivation was *not* to make women especially humane, but to make us excellent servants. Nonetheless, our intimate relationship with the nonwarrior (or antiwarrior) virtues, our inculcated avoidance of domination together with our intact intellectual capacities may indeed render women especially insightful in matters of human value.

Women, particularly feminist women, hold a key to new perspectives on society. If new goals, values, and visions are to be infused into society, we must win for women access to all the centers of power and policy, from science and industry to art and communication. This is a major goal of women's studies.

Changes in Lifestyles and Self-Concepts

Nothing goes deeper in one's personal awareness or has more far-reaching implications for the whole of one's existence than her or his sexual identity. This accounts in part for the great resistance to feminism; it also accounts for the impact feminist learning and consciousness-raising have on students. Propelled into self-examination by the intensity of the search and the research, women and men alike report changes in attitudes and lifestyles that represent tremendous emotional, intellectual, spiritual, and professional growth.

Consciousness-raising means what it says: It raises the level of consciousness, of awareness one has about the feelings, behaviors, and experiences surrounding sex roles. The woman who learns how much of her personal being emanates from her social and political status as a woman must ask herself how much of that being she wants to keep, how much she wants to change, what she might want to change, and how she plans to do it. Bewilderment, surprise, pain, joy, anger, and love accompany this growth.

Feminist instructors and students alike have been chided about consciousness-raising in women's studies courses. It has been argued that consciousness-raising (1) makes the courses "soft"; (2) belongs in the women's movement, not in school; (3) is not a legitimate part of formal university education; (4) is brainwashing; and (5) sometimes causes great anguish with which some students are unable to cope.

You will discover as you read this book that women's studies is anything but soft. You will find that consciousness-raising occurs as a result of new insights and innovative ideas. Rather than brain-*washing*, raised consciousness comes as a result of brain-*opening*.

Consciousness-raising can be painful. Yet pain is not in itself something to avoid at all times for there are two kinds of pain—destructive and constructive. Destructive pain is suffered in a no-win situation. Embedded in the status quo, it leads to no benefits, no improvements. It just hurts. Such pain is best avoided. Constructive pain differs dramatically. It is like the physical distress we feel when we decide to get our bodies in shape after some disuse. Our muscles ache; we strain and groan, but we grow stronger. Much the same thing happens when we grow emotionally or spiritually. Our insights, memories, and feelings—not accustomed to such use—may cause us pain. Our new sense of autonomy and freedom, and the attendant responsibility, may make us anxious. We hurt, but we grow stronger. Emotional and spiritual strength are necessary to well-being.

Consider some of the comments taken from the journals of students in an introductory course in women's studies:

- "I feel like a ton of bricks has been lifted off my shoulders. I finally found me. For the first time in my life I really looked at myself and said, 'I like you!' I decided that there is only one companion that you can count on all through your life— yourself. If I don't like me, who will? I took a full survey of myself and decided what I liked and what *I* would like to change, not because I wanted to look good in someone else's eyes, but because I wanted to look good in *my* own eyes. I feel so free, happy; like I could lick the world. This is the way I want to stay—this is the way I always want to feel. And I will because I like me."

- "I have more pride; I am more confident in myself as a woman. I used to wonder if my womanhood would be a slight handicap. I now realize it is my strongest asset!"

- "While we were talking about fear and pain being all a part of growing, I found a great deal of consolation because I had felt both. . . . It took a while, but I now realize that all the things I learned and have become aware of will not allow me to keep silent. Also, those feelings of understanding and support will never really be left behind because I'll carry those feelings inside of me forever."

The Terms and Techniques of Women's Studies

Women's Studies must be pursued on its own terms if it is to maintain its integrity. Although the integration of feminist perspectives and insights into the

regular curriculum is an ultimate goal of most feminist educators, the absorption of women's studies into the masculist domain is not something we seek. That might involve a loss of the unique configuration of methods and approaches we have developed. The feminist classroom typically differs from others, and feminist research bears the mark of its status outside the mainstream.

Feminist Pedagogy

Feminist faculty, like any others, gather information and ideas and impart them to students. Often they do this in traditional ways: they lecture, lead group discussions, show films, assign term papers, and give exams. Just as often, however, they opt for other procedures, sometimes unorthodox.

Feminist faculty frequently diverge from their colleagues in attitudes, experiences, or methods. Many of us have come to academe from the learning laboratories of social action outside the university— from counterculture organizations, from consciousness-raising and feminist groups, from political parties and equal rights agencies. Out of these experiences we have learned the strength of the entrenched power structures. Others of us, having lived within the established system and, having tried its regular channels and found them resistant, have learned the same lesson in another way. Experiencing life, as philosopher Mary Daly puts it, "on the boundaries of patriarchal space,"[12] we have developed modes that are often in juxtaposition to traditional academic etiquette.

Although women's studies is beginning to generate some kinds of formal credentials, for the most part one enters this field as thinkers entered any field centuries ago—through experience and self-directed research. We have few models on which to style our activities. The criterion for our methods is productivity.

The result of these factors and others is a highly innovative, spontaneous, and authentic modus operandi. In a feminist classroom, one is apt to find group projects, small-group discussions, self-directed or student-directed study, credit for social change activities or for life experience, contracts or self-grading, diaries and journals, even meditation or ritual. Noticeable in a feminist classroom are two factors not typical in college classrooms: an acceptance of, and even emphasis on, the personal-affective element in learning; and a warm, human relationship among persons in the class, students and teacher. Having rejected the commitment to inappropriate or unnecessary reserve, feminist teachers are no longer at pains to maintain the manly aura of distance—from their work or from one another. Recognizing, too, that hierarchical structures can belie what is common to female experience, feminist faculty often seek alternatives to the traditional student-teacher dichotomy.

The Interdisciplinary Nature of Women's Studies

Almost all women's studies programs, curricula, and analyses are interdisciplinary. For the most part, the programs have avoided separating into discrete departments. Although this has raised some serious practical problems—of funding, staffing, and scheduling, for example—it serves important purposes. Some of these are pragmatic, having to do with survival in the institution, professional flexibility for instructors, and the like; but the most important reasons for the interdisciplinary structure of women's studies are philosophical.

Feminist theorists have found that insights into the elements of women's lives and their effects on the progress of humanity do not sensibly divide into the traditional academic disciplines. Understanding, for example, how the concept *human nature* is distorted by the omission of women from the subject requires sophisticated knowledge of history, sociology, psychology, linguistics, philosophy, and other fields. Feminist analysis requires global knowledge.

Sensitized by our own investigations, many feminists have gone on to challenge the entire departmental or disciplinary structure as it exists today. Some of us suggest that the division of knowledge into neat areas with boundaries that ought not to be crossed is analogous to (and possibly derived from) the warrior behavior of separating land into territories that then must be justified and guarded. Intellectual boundaries, we may argue, are not only artificial; they are destructive.

Feminist theoreticians, then, recognizing the importance of global knowledge and not typically given to territorial competition, are at least interdisciplinary—I tend to think of us as counterdisciplinary. Elizabeth Janeway, feminist educator, comments:

Women have both history and reality on their side. Our knowledge of the world as it is is really quite formidable, broadly based, aware of detail, and not afraid to make connections between areas which the traditionally minded see as separate. Our experience makes us interdisciplinary. Well, this is a most useful and needed ability in a fragmented society, and particularly in an educational system where the trend for years has been to know more and more about less and less. Research is valuable—if it is used; and to be used, it must be allowed to connect with other research and, even more, with everyday life.[13]

The Scope of Women's Studies

Given what has been said about the global nature of feminist research, you can see how broad a scope women's studies must have. It ranges across history, psychology, art, economics, literature, philosophy, sociology, political science, biology, mathematics, law, and on through every area called an academic discipline. Of course, no one can be conversant with the details of all fields, but the study of women's experience requires some sophistication in each.

Thus, women's studies investigators must be multifaceted in perspectives, yet there is specialization as well. A feminist psychologist is a psychologist with a woman orientation. She pursues her work with a feminist perspective and challenges the sexist bias and beliefs in her field, often, though not always, focusing on issues most pertinent to women. As a feminist philosopher, I have the traditional interests in metaphysics, ethics, and epistemology, but I add to their study my special feminist awareness. I might, for example, challenge the validity of Hobbes's argument that life is "a war of all against all," wondering whether this may be so for men (warriors?) but perhaps not so for women. I question the traditionally accepted basic assumptions of philosophy, its definition of *objectivity,* for example, and its relationship to prescribed male emotional reserve. But beyond a feminist analysis of traditional questions, I am involved in raising other questions crucial for women. What does the term *matriarchy* imply for utopian visions? How does a notion of God as female change theology (the*al*ogy?). What does my woman's understanding of the dehumanizing effect of rape tell me about the ethical implications of physical integrity?

Some Basic Concepts

This book is primarily about women, our experience, history, present situation, and future. It is about men too, insofar as men's lives affect women. When we say that we are going to talk about women and men, when we use the words *woman, man, female, male, feminine, masculine,* what do we mean? What is a woman or a man? What possible different meanings do the terms *feminine* or *masculine* involve?

Perhaps the questions seem odd, their answers obvious. Yet it will become increasingly clear that such words as *woman, man, female,* or *male* are used in a variety of ways; they connote all sorts of meanings, and therefore have wide-ranging implications—psychological, political, social, and so on. Unless this is understood, one is apt to encounter a great deal of confusion in the analyses of sex roles.

To inquire into what it is to be a woman or a man, one must understand that various contexts exist in which to formulate definitions and make analyses, and though these may impinge on one another, their viewpoints are not the same. For example, the fact that females bear offspring (a biological aspect of womanhood) may be partly responsible for the kind of work a woman engages in (a cultural aspect), and that may have tremendous bearing on her status (political and social aspects). Furthermore, to understand that arrangements of these variables change from culture to culture (an anthropological aspect), it is necessary to know which economic and historical factors affect the others and how.

Before we continue, certain terms and concepts should be clearly understood because they are essential tools of our analysis. These are: *sex, gender, role, stereotype,* and *ideal.*

Sex is a term used by social scientists and biologists to refer to certain biological categories, female and male. Identification of sex is based on a variety of factors including chromosomal patterns, hormonal makeup, and genital structure. The determination of sex is considerably more complex than is generally understood, but it is the least ambiguous of the five concepts we are considering.

Gender, on the other hand, is a social, not a physiological, concept. *Femininity* and *masculinity,* the terms that denote one's gender, refer to a complex set of characteristics and behaviors prescribed for a particular sex by society and learned through the socialization experience. For example, femininity (female gender) for certain groups of women in our culture requires passivity, fragility, and proclivities for nurturance. A little girl—given dolls to play with, prohibited from engaging in wild play, dressed in frilly or constricting clothing, and rebuked for so-called unladylike behavior—is reinforced in those behavior patterns here called feminine, and she learns to be passive, fragile, and nurturing.

The exact relation between sex and gender is controversial. Some argue that sexual characteristics are fixed in nature and account for gender and role arrangements; others sharply disagree. (This is part of what is called the "nature/nurture controversy.") Lionel Tiger, for example, argues that "leadership" or "dominance" is a characteristically male trait in animal as well as in human communities.[14] He contends that the trait is inheritable, therefore biological, and thus accounts for the dominance of men over women in human society. In other words, dominance or submission are biological (sexual) characteristics that account for the gender prescription of passivity in women and aggressiveness in men. Tiger is challenged by those who point to the tremendous variation of behavior and arrangements both in the animal kingdom and in different societies. These commentators argue that the observed malleability and diversity of behavior imply a loose association between sex and gender.[15]

Gender is composed of a set of socially defined character traits. *Role* is composed of a pattern of behaviors prescribed for individuals playing a certain part in the drama of life. The sociologist Theodore R. Sarbin defined role as "the organized actions of a person in a given position."[16] For example, the role of teacher in our society requires such actions as imparting knowledge to students, attending classes, counseling, or grading papers; it might also include certain attitudes, values, and even appearance.

In almost every society, females and males on the basis of their sex are assigned separate and specific roles, the sex roles. Varying from culture to culture, and within a culture by a variety of factors (class, religion, race, age, and so on), the sex roles are made up of a set of expected behaviors with accompanying gender traits. The role of a middle-class white female in our society includes playing with dolls, helping mother, getting married, having children, doing housekeeping, being sexy, typing, and so on. Many of these behaviors in their turn form other role configurations. Marrying, for example, requires that one be a wife, which entails another whole set of behaviors. The role of a woman, then, includes a series of subroles such as daughter, wife, mother, office worker, and so on. In this book, we shall be largely concerned with analyses of sex roles, their nature, composition, effects, and implications.

Stereotype is a concept related to role, yet distinct. Defined by one author as a "picture in our heads,"[17] a stereotype is a composite image of traits and expectations pertaining to some group (such as teachers, police officers, Jews, or women)—an image that is persistent in the social mind though it is somehow off-center or inaccurate. Typically, the stereotype is an overgeneralization of characteristics that may or may not have been observed in fact. Often containing a kernel of truth that is partial and thus misleading, the stereotype need not be self-consistent, and it has a remarkable resistance to change by new information; to wit, Lippmann's following remark:

> If the experience contradicts the stereotype, one of two things happens. If the man is no longer plastic, or if some powerful interest makes it highly inconvenient to rearrange his stereotypes, he pooh-poohs the contradiction as an exception that proves the rule, discredits the witness, finds a flaw somewhere, and manages to forget it. But if he is still curious and open-minded, the novelty is taken into the picture, and allowed to modify it. Sometimes, if the incident is striking enough, and if he has felt a general discomfort with his established scheme, he may be shaken to such an extent as to distrust all accepted ways of looking at life, and to expect that normally a thing will not be what it is generally supposed to be.[18]

Not all stereotypes are pejorative, but many are. One stereotype image of a feminist is a woman incapable of fulfilling the traditional role requirements for femininity, unable to "catch a man," homely, dirty, aggressive, strident, shrill, sexually promiscuous (or frigid or a lesbian or all three), unkempt, ill-clothed, middle or upper middle class, childish, making speeches, carrying banners, and burning underwear. It is this image that is meant when clearly feminist women demur, "Now, I'm no libber,

but . . ." Many feminists are not middle class or white or college educated. Feminists wear a variety of costumes and have differing sexual codes and identities. Stereotypes can have wide-ranging effects on both the stereotyped group and those with whom the members of the group interact. Stereotypes can and do direct behavior.

An *ideal* is much like a stereotype. It, too, is a "picture in our heads"; it is resistant to change, frequently inconsistent, generally fits a very few, and is frequently based on false information. But the ideal contains only traits the society deems desirable. It functions as a standard and a goal, such as a "lady" or "the American girl."

All of these concepts are involved in the analyses of women's experience. Feminist investigators ask: What are the biological, physiological, and anatomical characteristics that distinguish women from men, and what are their implications? How are the sexes inherently different in makeup and behavior? What are the major psychological factors in women's lives; which, if any, are based on femaleness per se, and which come as a consequence of women's role in this and other societies? Since women's lives are apt to be markedly different across economic, educational, or racial lines, what traits or qualities, if any, can be said to characterize the category of women in general? How and why do they operate? How are the perceived female ideals different from the perceived stereotypes? What is their origin? How do they affect the daily lives of women in particular and people in general? In the following chapters, we shall be using the concepts of sex, gender, role, stereotype, and ideal to explore these and other questions.

Notes

[1]Florence Howe, "The Power of Education," in *Women's Studies in the Curriculum* (Winston-Salem, NC: Salem College, 1983), p. 24, quoted in Catharine R. Stimpson with Nina Kressner Cobb, *Women's Studies in the United States* (New York: Ford Foundation, 1986), p. 4.

[2]Mariam Chamberlain, "Enriching the Curriculum: Women's Studies." *Thought and Action: The NEA Higher Education Journal* IV, no. 2 (Fall 1988): 24.

[3]In Karl Stern, *The Flight from Woman* (New York: Farrar, Straus & Giroux, 1965), pp. 21–22.

[4]Aristotle, *Politics* Book 1, Chap. 13, 1259b–1260a.

[5]Muhammad Hamidullah, *Introduction to Islam*, 2nd ed. Paris: Centre Culturel Islamique, 1968. (c/o The Mosque, Place Puits de l'Ermite, Paris, France.)

[6]Cheris Kramarae and Paula Treichler with the assistance of Ann Russo, *A Feminist Dictionary*. New York: Pandora Press, 1985, pp. 158–160, passim. Copyright © Cheris Kramarae and Paula A. Treichler, 1985. Reprinted with permission of Unwin Hyman Ltd.

[7]"Womanist" from *In Search of Our Mothers' Gardens*. New York: Harcourt Brace Jovanovich, 1983, pp. xi–xii. Copyright © 1983 by Alice Walker. Reprinted by permission of Harcourt Brace Jovanovich Inc.

[8]Bari Watkins, "Women and History," in *Women on Campus: The Unfinished Liberation*, ed. *Change Magazine* Editors (New York: *Change Magazine*, 1975).

[9]Harry Brod, "Introduction," *The Making of Masculinities: The New Men's Studies*. Boston: Allen & Unwin, 1987, p. 2.

[10]Some of the following discussion is included in my paper, "Methodocracy, Misogyny, and Bad Faith: Sexism in the Philosophic Establishment," *Metaphilosophy* 10, No. 1 (January 1979): 48–61.

[11]Joel Feinberg, "Some Conjectures About the Concept of Respect," *Journal of Social Philosophy*, 3, No. 2 (April 1973): 1–3.

[12]Mary Daly, *Beyond God the Father* (Boston: Beacon Press, 1973).

[13]Elizabeth Janeway, "Women on Campus: The Unfinished Liberation," in *Women on Campus*, ed. by *Change Magazine* Editors (New York: *Change Magazine*, 1975), p. 27.

[14]Lionel Tiger, *Men in Groups* (New York: Random House, 1969).

[15]See, for example, Margaret Mead, *Sex and Temperament in Three Primitive Societies* (New York: Morrow, 1935).

[16]Theodore R. Sarbin, "Role Theory," in *Handbook of Social Psychology*, ed. Gardner Lindzey (Reading, Mass.: Addison-Wesley, 1954), I, 225.

[17]Walter Lippmann, *Public Opinion* (New York: Harcourt, Brace, 1922).

[18]Ibid., p. 100.

A New Angle of Vision

Gerda Lerner

Noted historian Gerda Lerner is the author of several books, including The Female Experience *(1979),* The Majority Finds Its Past *(1979), and* A Death of One's Own. *She is a past president of the Organization of American Historians and currently teaches at the University of Wisconsin-Madison as Robinson-Edwards Professor of History.*

Here Lerner explains why examining the world from only one perspective, men's, is distorting. We require both perspectives—women's and men's— ultimately integrated, to view reality more accurately, to see with greater enrichment, and to transform consciousness.

Excerpted from Gerda Lerner, "A New Angle of Vision," in *The Creation of Patriarchy*. New York: Oxford University Press, 1986, pp. 11–14. © 1986 Gerda Lerner. Used by permission of Oxford University Press, Inc., and the author.

As WE UNDERTAKE THIS EXPLORATION, HOW ARE we, then, to think of women-as-a-group? Three metaphors may help us see from our new angle of vision:

In her brilliant 1979 article, Joan Kelly spoke of the new "doubled vision" of feminist scholarship:

> . . . woman's place is not a separate sphere or domain of existence but a position within social existence generally. . . . *[F]eminist thought is moving beyond the split vision of social reality it inherited from the recent past. Our actual vantage point has shifted, giving rise to a new consciousness of woman's "place" in family and society. . . . [W]hat we see are not two spheres of social reality (home and work, private and public), but two (or three) sets of social relations.*[1]

We are adding the female vision to the male and that process is transforming. But Joan Kelly's metaphor needs to be developed one step further: when we see with one eye, our vision is limited in range and devoid of depth. When we add to it the single vision of the other eye, our range of vision becomes wider, but we still lack depth. It is only when both eyes see together that we accomplish full range of vision and accurate depth perception.

The computer provides us with another metaphor. The computer shows us a picture of a triangle (two-dimensional). Still holding that image, the triangle moves in space and is transformed into a pyramid (three-dimensional). Now the pyramid moves in space creating a curve (the fourth dimension), while still holding the image of the pyramid and the triangle. We see all four dimensions at once, losing none of them, but seeing them also in their true relation to one another.

Seeing as we have seen, in patriarchal terms, is two-dimensional. "Adding women" to the patriarchal framework makes it three-dimensional. But only when the third dimension is fully integrated and moves with the whole, only when women's vision is equal with men's vision, do we perceive the true relations of the whole and the inner connectedness of the parts.

Finally, another image. Men and women live on a stage, on which they act out their assigned roles, equal in importance. The play cannot go on without both kinds of performers. Neither of them "contributes" more or less to the whole; neither is marginal or dispensable. But the stage set is conceived, painted, defined by men. Men have written the play, have directed the show, interpreted the meanings of the action. They have assigned themselves the most interesting, most heroic parts, giving women the supporting roles.

As the women become aware of the difference in the way they fit into the play, they ask for more equality in the role assignments. They upstage the men at times, at other times they pinch-hit for a missing male performer. The women finally, after considerable struggle, win the right of access to equal role assignment, but first they must "qualify." The terms of their "qualifications" are again set by the men; men are the judges of how women measure up; men grant or deny admission. They give preference to docile women and to those who fit their job-description accurately. Men punish, by ridicule, exclusion, or ostracism, any woman who assumes the right to interpret her own role or—worst of all sins—the right to rewrite the script.

It takes considerable time for the women to understand that getting "equal" parts will not make them equal as long as the script, the props, the stage setting, and the direction are firmly held by men. When the women begin to realize that and cluster together between the acts, or even during the performance, to discuss what to do about it, this play comes to an end.

Looking at the recorded History of society as though it were such a play, we realize that the story of the performances over thousands of years has been recorded only by men and told in their words. Their attention has been mostly on men. Not surprisingly, they have not noticed all the actions women have taken. Finally, in the past fifty years, some women have acquired the training necessary for writing the company's scripts. As they wrote, they began to pay more attention to what women were doing. Still, they had been well trained by their male mentors. So they too found what men were doing on the whole more significant and, in their desire to upgrade the part of women in the past, they looked hard for women who had done what men did. Thus, compensatory history was born.

What women must do, what feminists are now doing, is to point to that stage, its sets, its props, its director, and its scriptwriter, as did the child in the fairy tale who discovered that the emperor was naked, and say, the basic inequality between us lies within this framework. And then they must tear it down.

What will the writing of history be like when that umbrella of dominance is removed and definition is shared equally by men and women? Will we devalue the past, overthrow the categories, supplant order with chaos?

No—we will simply step out under the free sky. We will observe how it changes, how the stars rise and the moon circles, and we will describe the earth and its workings in male and female voices. We may, after all, see with greater enrichment. We now know that man is not the measure of that which is human, but men and women are. Men are not the center of the world, but men and women are. This insight will transform consciousness as decisively as did Copernicus's discovery that the earth is not the center of the universe. We may play our separate parts on the stage, sometimes exchanging them or deciding to keep them, as it works out. We may discover new talent among those who have always been living under the umbrella of another's making. We may find that those who had previously taken upon themselves the burden of both action and definition may now have more freedom for playing and experiencing the pure joy of existence. We are no more under an obligation to describe what we will find than were the explorers sailing to the distant edge of the world, only to find that the world was round.

We will never know unless we begin. The process itself is the way, is the goal.

Notes

[1] Joan Kelly, "The Doubled Vision of Feminist Theory: A Postscript to the 'Women of Power' Conference," *Feminist Studies* 5: no. 1 (Spring 1979):221–22.

The Myth of the Male Orgasm

Bette-Jane Raphael

Bette-Jane Raphael, author of Can This Be Love? And Other Quandaries of Love in the Eighties *(1985), has been senior editor for* Viva *magazine and for* Working Woman.

Here Raphael presents with wonderful humor the absurdity of research and theories based on myth, false assumptions, and misplaced objectivity. Parodying Freud and other "experts" who presume to explain and describe the female sexual experience from their armchairs, so to speak, she shows what nonsense might have been produced if the tables had been turned and all that we knew about male sexuality (or, for that matter, male anything) had been created by women looking at men.

Is there such a thing as male orgasm? For decades, scientists have argued about it, written tracts about it, philosophized about it, and, in more recent years, conducted countless studies. But as Dr. Mary Jane Grunge, president of SMOS (the Society for Male Orgasmic Studies), said in her opening statement of the society's ninth annual cookout: "We still don't know."

But do we? Recent findings by Dr. Fern Herpes and her colleague, Dr. Lavinia Shoot, indicate that the mystery is at last on the brink of being unmasked. Working under a grant from NASA, which was disturbed by the cleaning bills for its last Apollo mission, Dr. Herpes and Dr. Shoot conducted a study of 300 middle-class men between the ages of 14 and 23. Their findings seem to indicate that not only is there a male orgasm, there may actually be two distinct kinds!

While 43 percent of the men in the Herpes/ Shoot study were found to have trouble attaining orgasm consistently, or did not attain orgasm at all, and while another 4½ percent had no opinion, a whopping 50½ percent (four men fell asleep during their interviews, which accounts for the other two percent) admitted they had two distinctly different kinds of orgasms. After careful questioning, psychological testing, and physical examinations, Dr. Herpes came to the following conclusion (Dr. Shoot came to a different conclusion and left in a huff): there are two types of male orgasm. For purposes of clarification, Dr. Herpes called these penile orgasm and the spherical orgasm.

Of the two orgasms, Dr. Herpes hypothesizes that the spherical orgasm is the more mature. "Men who are enamored of their penises, who see their penises as the seat of all sexual pleasure, are just a bunch of babies. I hate them. Only the spherically oriented male can be thought of as mature because he can identify with the female to a much greater extent than the penile-oriented

19

male. Thus the former's identification with his balls, which are the closest thing he has to female breasts."

Dr. Shoot, who consented to speak in rebuttal to Dr. Herpes, had this to say: "That woman is crazy. Men don't have two types of orgasm. They just think they do. My own findings reveal that they don't even have one kind of orgasm. Actually, there is no such thing as the male orgasm. What passes for orgasm in the male is really a mild form of St. Vitus dance. This afflicts more than 55 percent of the male population in this country, and if Herpes wasn't so hipped on orgasm she'd admit she's wrong. But as far as she's concerned, *everything* is orgasm!"

It should be noted that Dr. Amelia Leviathan is in close agreement with Dr. Shoot. She too believes that what passes for male orgasm is actually a disease. But contrary to Dr. Shoot, she believes the affliction is actually a form of epilepsy localized in the groin. She feels she proved this in her much publicized recent study of 100 male rats, 50 of whom had epilepsy. The epileptic rats, Dr. Leviathan found, could mate with the female rats, even if the female rats didn't want to. The nonepileptic rats just sat around exposing themselves.

Confusing the question of male orgasm even further is Dr. Jennifer Anis, who conducted a study of nearly 700 married males in their late 20s and 30s. According to the results of her study, the issue of male orgasmic or nonorgasmic capacity is clouded by the fact that many men simulate orgasm in order to please their partners. Nearly 25 percent of the men in the Anis group admitted they had at some time in their marriage faked orgasm either because they were tired, or because they knew their partners would be hurt if they didn't climax, or because they had headaches.

Nearly half the men in the Anis study had mild to severe orgasmic difficulties. (It was this group, incidentally, whose psychologial profiles appeared in Dr. Anis's widely acclaimed paper, "The Prostate, the Penis, and You-oo," wherein it was revealed that all the orgasmically troubled men shared a common fear of their mothers' cuticles, a hatred of Speedwriting ads in subways, and a horror of certain kinds of peaked golf hats.) What has not been revealed until now, however, is that a great many of these men lead perfectly satisfactory sex lives *without* orgasm, a finding which would seem to put to rest the theory that men must achieve orgasm in order to enjoy sex.

Well, if men can enjoy sex without orgasm, can they also become fathers without achieving climax? Here again the answer is by no means clear. Dr. Herpes and Dr. Shoot, of course, disagree. Dr. Shoot says yes, they can, if they think they can. Dr. Herpes says no, not unless they have either a penile or a spherical orgasm. Dr. Anis believes they can fake it.

Lastly there is the question of the multiple orgasm. Do men have them? Unfortunately, here we are still very much in the dark. The only person ever to do research in this area was Dr. Helen Hager-Bamf, in 1971. From January through April of that year, Dr. Hager-Bamf personally tested more than 3,000 randomly selected men for duration and number of orgasms. Tragically dead at the age of 28, she never recorded her findings.

So where do we stand? Is there such a thing as male orgasm? Can men enjoy sex without it? Is a low orgasmic capacity psychologically or physiologically induced? To quote Dr. Grunge at her recent press conference, "Who knows?"

Perhaps the answers are not as important as the fact that the questions are finally being taken seriously. So that, someday, the boy who sells shoes, the young fellow in upholstery, and the man who sews alligators on shirts will no longer have to walk around in perplexity, confused and unnerved by the myth of the male orgasm.

When that day arrives, perhaps male sexuality will come out of the bathroom and into the bedroom where it belongs.

Women

Jessie Bernard

*Sociologist Jessie Bernard, born in 1903, received her
Ph.D. at Washington University in St. Louis in 1935.
She was the first woman professor at Princeton
University (1959–60) and today is professor emerita at
Pennsylvania State University. She holds honorary
degrees from six universities and numerous prizes and
awards. Professor Bernard gave the opening address at
International Women's Year. She is the author of
several books, including* The Female World *(1981),*
Self-Portrait of a Family *(1978),* The Future of
Motherhood *(1974),* The Future of Marriage
(1972), and Academic Women *(1964).*

*In the following selection, Bernard makes it clear
that the terms* woman *and* man *are not simple
concepts: Each in its turn denotes groups of people
often tremendously different from some members of
their own category and yet similar to members of
the other. In her explanations of the meaning and
applications of sex, gender, and role with regard to the
definition of the word* woman, *Bernard articulates the
difficulties in developing adequate categorizations and
types for analysis, describes the errors and pitfalls that
have characterized such work in the past, and shows
how stereotypic expectations have imbedded themselves
in social scientific research.*

*Female and male are to some extent ambiguous
categories; feminine and masculine are much more so.
An abundance of evidence from anthropology,
sociology, and other fields attests to the variability of
gender definition within and across cultures. Traits
expected of women in one culture (passivity or obesity,
for example) may be repugnant in others. Men of the
Middle East are expected to be openly affectionate with
one another; in contrast, American men are required to
be reserved. What all of this implies, of course, is that
manhood and womanhood, femininity and
masculinity, are not absolute, cosmically ordained
realities, unchanging and unchangeable; they are at
least in part, if not in toto, socially defined patterns
and arrangements. Hence these concepts are open to
critique on many grounds including utility,
productiveness, justice, and esthetics.*

The Mark of Eve

Despite universal recognition of differences
among women, whatever their causes, women as
everyone knows, are women.[1] Still, Ruth Useem,
a sociologist, once commented on the inadequacy
of the single mark she had to make on all documents asking for "sex." All she could do was
check the F box. But she knew that this "mark of
Eve" told the reader very little about her. There
were so many kinds of F: F_1, F_2, . . . F_n, and yet
there was no way to let the reader know which
one she was.[2]

Her comment was by no means trivial, face-
tious, or irrelevant to policy, for the "mark of Eve"
a woman makes in the F box ascribes a status to
her that is quite independent of her qualities as an
individual. Every other mark she makes on that
or any other documents will be evaluated in terms
of that mark. Assumptions will be made about her
on the basis of it. Privileges, responsibilities, prerogatives, obligations will be assigned on the basis of it also. Policy will rest on it. A great deal
rides on that one mark, for it refers to the most
fundamental differentiation among human beings. But it leaves out differences among the Fs
themselves, as important as the similarities. Yet,
though there are few bodies of lore and literature
more extensive than that on the nature of differences between men and women, there are few
less extensive than those on the nature of differences among women themselves.

The Visibility Gap

In the age of innocence, moving picture producers
made it very clear to us at the very outset of
a picture who were the good guys and who the

bad. The good guys wore white hats. In nineteenth-century melodramas the villain wore an identifying mustache so that we knew he was going to foreclose the mortgage unless the beautiful daughter capitulated to his advances. In Greek drama there were appropriate masks to inform us about the characters.

Despite our dependence on visual cues, however, there is always a visibility gap. The outer mark does not tell us all there is to know about the person inside. The same mark stamps a wide variety of people. Not all the farmers who bore the mark of Cain killed grazers and herders. A wide variety of men bore that mark. A wide variety of people inhabit the bodies of women (as also, of course, the bodies of men as well). For women are not interchangeable parts.

$F_1, F_2, \ldots F_n$

Whatever the differences may be between M and F, and whatever the origin of these differences may be, they are matched and in some cases exceeded by differences among women themselves. A woman may in many ways be more like the average man than she is like another woman. A very considerable research literature undergirds the fact that there are extensive differences among women in such sociologically relevant variables as interests, values, and goals. These differences have to be taken into account when dealing with programs or policies involving women.

Two polar types turn up with singular consistency in the research literature on women, whether the point of view is sociological or psychological.[3] Alice Rossi assigned the terms ''pioneer'' and ''housewife'' to these types, using the term ''traditional'' for those who fell in between (Rossi, 1965, pp. 79–80). Another team of researchers called the polar types ''homemaking-oriented'' and ''career-oriented'' (Hoyt and Kennedy, 1958). Another researcher spoke of ''creative intellectual'' when referring to a type that corresponded to pioneer or career-oriented (Drews, 1965). Eli Ginzberg and his associates found women they called ''supportive,'' who corresponded roughly to the housewife or home-oriented subjects in the other studies, and ''influential'' women who resembled the pioneer type (Ginzberg, 1966). The existence of such types can scarcely be challenged.

The exact numerical population size of these several types is not important, for it doubtless changes over time and is certainly changing today. In the recent past, however, one of the striking facts that emerged from the studies was the agreement they showed with respect to the incidence of the several types in different samples. At the high school senior level, 7 to 8 percent of the ''creative intellectuals'' had the drive to achieve the lifestyle they desired. Among college freshmen, 8 percent fell into the career-oriented category. Among college graduates, 7 percent were pioneers. Among women who had done graduate work, 10 percent were living an influential lifestyle. At Cornell, 8 percent of a sample of women in 1950 and 6 percent of a sample in 1952 showed high career orientation (Goldsen, 1960, p. 136). At Vassar, however, also in the 1950's, two-thirds answered ''true'' to the statement ''I would like a career'' (Freedman, 1967, p. 136). In context, this answer was interpreted by Caroline Bird to mean ''career'' in a secondary sense. Perhaps more indicative of a pioneer orientation was the answer to the statement ''I enjoy children,'' which elicited a negative in 8 percent of the women. That the Vassar women were changing rapidly was suggested by Caroline Bird, who noted that the classes of 1964 to 1966 voted for ''career with as little time out for family as possible'' and that there was even a notable rise in the number of girls who said they were pursuing a ''career period'' (Bird, 1968, p. 184). The proportion in all the samples who fell into the housewife or home-making or supportive category was consistently about a fifth or a fourth. It is interesting to compare this figure with the proportion, about 18 percent, of college women who, a generation ago, were reported by Lewis M. Terman to be greatly interested in the domestic arts (Terman and Miles, 1936, pp. 209–210).

It would require considerably more focused research to pinpoint with greater accuracy and precision the relative incidence of the several types and the reasons that explain these proportions. Equally important would be research to document trends in such incidence. My own reading of current trends is that one of the most drastic shake-ups in the social order today is the breaking up of old blocs and their re-forming into new configurations. Yesterday's data no longer reflect the current scene. In 1969 a national sample of youth showed 10 percent of the young women to be radical reformers and 17.1 percent moderate reformers (Yankelovich, 1969).

The characterization of the pioneer (or career-oriented or creative intellectual or influential) type varied with the interests of the researchers; but here, too, there was notable convergence. Among the high-school girls, the creative intellectuals tended to be more receptive than other girls to the new, to growth, and to change; they were less conventional and conforming. Among college students, those who fell into the pioneer or career-oriented category tended to show up in all the studies as different from other college women. The Kansas State career-oriented freshmen were higher on "endurance" and "achievement" than the homemaking-oriented women and lower on "succorance" and "heterosexuality"—in the sense of being interested in attracting young men, not as contrasted with homosexuality (Hoyt and Kennedy, 1968). Rossi's housewives characterized themselves as dependent; they showed strong nurturance toward the young; they were socially rather than occupationally competitive. In contrast, the pioneers were less dependent, less nurturant, more egalitarian; they valued the world of ideas more. They characterized themselves as dominant and occupationally competitive (the married less so than the single). Ginzberg's women with the influential lifestyle were characterized by a striving for autonomy; they found their major sources of gratification in the social significance of their work and the personal relations involved in it. In both the Rossi and the Ginzberg samples, the women in the pioneer or influential category were far more likely to be working (70 percent in both samples) and less likely to be married; the reverse was true for the housewives and supportive women. At Cornell, it was found that the career-oriented women were more likely than the family-oriented women to be nonconformists with "a certain irreverence for rules and conventions" (Freedman, 1967, p. 140). At Vassar, years of careful research yielded this picture of career-oriented students:

> Students who say "true" to "I would like a career" are somewhat more intellectual, unconventional, independent (perhaps rebellious), and flexible in thinking and outlook. They are also somewhat more alienated or isolated socially. [At Cornell, career women engaged in just as many extracurricular activities as other women and were just as likely to associate with men (Goldsen, 1960, p. 54).] It is interesting to observe that these differences are most pronounced [among

> seniors]. Results for the Ethnocentrism Scale . . . are in line with findings of other studies which demonstrate that attitudes toward the role and behavior of women are likely to accord with attitudes toward members of outgroups or "underprivileged" groups. Individuals, including women themselves, who hold somewhat stereotyped views of Negroes or foreigners, for example, are likely to adhere to traditional or rather fixed notions of what is appropriate activity for women (Freedman, 1967, p. 140).

The explanations of such differences among women also vary according to the researchers' predilections. One team of psychologists is satisfied by a pattern of "needs." Career-oriented women, they believe, are motivated by one or more of four such needs: to establish one's worth through competitive behavior or achievement, to know intellectually and understand ("intraception"), to accomplish concrete goals (endurance), and to avoid relations with men (heterosexuality). The homemaking women are motivated by needs of affection and acceptance (succorance) (Hoyt and Kennedy, 1958). But another psychologist is quite agnostic: "Psychology has nothing to say about what women are really like, what they need and what they want, essentially, because psychology does not know" (Weisstein, 1969, p. 78). Sociologists and social psychologists tend to look to socialization variables to interpret the difference. Since career orientation may change with age and experience, it is hazardous to put too much credence in any analysis that makes it depend on personality variables, which are presumably quite stable. Such an approach, in any event, still leaves the genesis of the needs themselves to be explained.

Whatever the incidence and whatever the explanation, telescoping all these women into the single F box blots out a great deal of sociologically important diversity. In many situations F_1 may have more in common with M_1 than with any of the other Fs. Rank, for example, is more important than sex in many situations. A princess has more in common with a prince than with a domestic; a professional woman often has more in common with a colleague than with a cleaning woman; an heiress with an heir than with a woman receiving welfare payments. Sometimes F_i and F_j have not only different but opposing points of view, each seeing the other as a threat either to a vested interest or to opportunity for achievement. The wife of a workingman may not agree with the woman worker on the principle of equal pay for equal work; she believes her husband should get more because he has to support his family. (Perhaps the only thing that all Fs have in common as yet is the concern that adequate gynecological, obstetrical, and pediatric services be widely available, and that public toilet facilities be supplied with emergency equipment.)

It would, then, be more in line with the facts of life if, instead of compressing all women into the single F category, the diversity among them could be recognized by allowing for F_1, F_2, . . . F_n. Thus the woman who says she is content to devote her life to the traditional pattern of homemaking could be differentiated from the woman who is willing to settle for nothing less than the complete gamut—marriage, children, and a career. . . .

Sex

If both the layman and the scientist have underplayed the differences among women, they have tended to overplay the differences between females and males. A great deal of the work of running the world rests on making simple classificatory decisions. Into which category does X fall? Y? or Z? Which rules apply? Anything, therefore, that simplifies this process by predecision is welcomed by administrators and executives and copers in general. Sex is such a predecision-maker. F goes here, M there: so much easier than having to study each case individually to decide on its merits where it belongs, which rule to apply. It is such a simple, straightforward, ineffable, easily applied criterion that it has rarely been challenged.

But new research issuing from clinic and laboratory is beginning to shake our old naiveté about sex. We now know that, far from being a simple, straightforward, genetically determined phenomenon, sex has at least three components—chromosomal, hormonal, anatomical—and conceivably more. Although for most people these three components are matched to produce a clear-cut male or female individual, such is not always the case. There can be mistakes. These "errors of the body" have alerted us to some of the anomalies possible in the sphere of sexuality. When all goes normally, as it usually does, the M and F boxes fit very well to distinguish males and females. They can accommodate almost everyone. But things do not always go normally. Some-

times a genetic F is masculinized hormonally *in utero* with the result that anatomical anomalies confuse gender assignment at birth; or a genetic M is not masculinized *in utero*, making gender equivocal. Such errors are rare and turn up so infrequently that relatively little is yet known about them; they are so rare that, once they are recognized, we can disregard them in any analysis of large-scale sociological phenomena.[4] Their major relevance for our discussion here is the lesson they teach with respect to the relative contribution of biological, social, cultural, and sociological factors to gender.

With the exception of those who are victims of "errors of the body" there is no overlap between male and female populations. They are categorically different. Still it is interesting to note that, different though the equipment at their disposal may be, they respond quite similarly to the same stimuli. Estrogens and androgens, for example, have the same effect on both sexes, making for greater or less sexual motivation, greater or less aggressiveness (Hamber and Lunde, 1966). This suggests that the two sexes also respond about the same way to other kinds of stimuli—psychological and social. What is important are the kinds of stimuli they are subjected to. Interesting also is the finding that creative personalities, whether housed in female or in male bodies, have similar personality characteristics.

Gender

Gender refers to the complex of traits that determine whether one checks the M or the F box. It is, to be sure, inextricably related to sex, but "the two realms, sex and gender, are not at all inevitably bound in anything like a one-to-one relationship, but each may go in its quite independent way" (Stoller, 1968, pp. vii–ix). Sex is a biological fact; gender, though based on biology, is a social-cultural-sociological-psychological fact. Gender consists of gender identity and gender role (Stoller, 1968, p. 92): the first a social and psychological phenomenon; the second, a cultural and sociological and interactional one.

Gender identity begins in the hospital delivery room. As soon as an infant is born it is, on the basis of anatomical cues, assigned a gender which is well established by age two. The infant's life course is almost sealed by that act; for it is primarily this gender assignment rather than anatomy, or even heredity, that, in Freud's terminology, is destiny. Almost every decision made by the outside world about this child is going to take this assignment into account. Every structured relationship will be defined in terms of it, and the child will accept it in most cases.

Gender Identity

Scarcely a woman alive would have any hesitation about marking the proper F or M box. A woman knows she is a female. The whole matter of gender identity would probably never have occurred to a woman; it looks to her like a man-made problem manufactured by male psychoanalysts, illustrating the sexism that modern women are protesting against. This sexism of psychoanalysts is nowhere better portrayed than in their inability to understand how women could possibly have any sense of femaleness without something like a phallus to prove to themselves that they were women. An inverted phallus or vagina was invoked to solve the riddle. It has been a major contribution of recent gender research to show it does not take a vagina, notoriously lacking in sensitivity, to confer gender identity on females. Breasts and menstruation serve quite adequately to remind them that they are female, strange as it may seem to a breastless nonmenstruating individual. To psychoanalysts, the muscle that daily (and, in youth, hourly) reminds males of their sex seemed the sine qua non of gender identity; a creature lacking it must be only a defective male. The results of this thinking showed up in therapy; "It is possible that the analyst's view of a successful analysis may be skewed if he feels he has reached the core of a woman's femininity when he has been able to get her to share with equanimity his belief that she is really an inferior form of male" (Stoller, 1968, p. 63).

Actually a woman's gender identity is firm, even, in some cases, if her heredity or anatomy is not. In Table 1 for example, three women are discussed who would unhesitatingly mark the F box; they have female gender identity (numbers 2, 3, and 5). But both their heredities and their anatomies differ. One (number 3) has female heredity and external anatomy but no vagina. One (number 2) has female heredity but, as a result of masculinization *in utero*, male-appearing genitalia; female gender was assigned to her at birth and despite the anatomical anomaly she finds the F box acceptable. A third woman (number 5) has neuter heredity and anomalous anatomy; but, assigned female gender at birth, she, too, has no problem with the F box. Such

women may be unhappy about their inadequate or flawed sexuality, but their gender identity is unimpaired; they feel like women and unequivocally check the F box. All are F even though either their heredity or their anatomy does not conform to F specifications.

Such cases show the independence of gender identity from either heredity or anatomy. They illustrate its social nature: "those aspects of sexuality that are called gender are . . . learned postnatally" (Stoller, 1968, p. xiii) primarily from the mother but also from the father, siblings, and friends.

Cases number 1 and 2 also illustrate the social nature of gender identity or the acceptance of the gender assigned at birth. In both cases the infants were genetically females but in both cases the external genitalia, according to which gender is assigned, had been masculinized *in utero* and were therefore anomalous. In the case of one of the children (number 2), the diagnosis of sex was correct and the child was assigned female gender and reared as a female. In the other (number 1), the diagnosis was incorrect and the child was assigned male gender and reared as a male. The first became as feminine as other little girls, the other a masculine little boy. Same sex heredity, same prenatal "error," but different gender assignment and hence different gender identity.

Gender is so thoroughly bred into the infant by the world around it and becomes so much a part of its identity that even if the assignment is later discovered to be an error, it is almost impossible to change. Despite the discovery that the individual is genetically a male, he continues to have female gender identity.

All these findings warn us against taking the M and F boxes too much for granted. Gender identity does not apparently always just come naturally. It has to be learned. And there is no one-to-one relationship between it and sex.

The emphasis on the social and acquired nature of gender identity does not rule out a biological component, for "if the first main finding of [recent research] is that gender identity is primarily learned, the second is that there are biological forces that contribute to this" (Stoller, 1968, p. xiii). Sometimes, for reasons not yet clear, gender assignment does not "take," as in cases 4, 6, 7, and 8. The resulting phenomena curb any dogmatism we may show with respect to our knowledge of sex and gender. The nature of the biological component involved in gender is still

Table 1 Deviances illustrating the equivocal relation of gender identity to heredity and anatomy

Genetic sex	Internal anatomy	External anatomy	Gender assignment	Gender identity
1. Female	Female	Equivocal	Male	Male
2. Female	Female	Equivocal	Female	Female
3. Female	Defective	Female	Female	Female
4. Female	Female	Female	Female	Male
5. Neuter (XO)	Defective	Female	Female	Female
6. Equivocal (XXY)	Female	Male	Male	Female
7. Male	Male	Equivocal	Female	Male
8. Male	Male	Equivocal	Male	Female

1. "Money and the Hampsons . . . describe two children masculinized *in utero* by excessive adrenal androgens, both biologically normal females, genetically and in their internal sexual anatomy and physiology, but with masculinized external genitalia. The proper diagnosis having been made, one child was raised unequivocally as a female . . . ; she turned out to be as feminine as other little girls" (p. 57).

2. "The other, not recognized to be female, was raised without question as a male . . . and became an unremarkably masculine little boy" (p. 57).

3. "The patient is a 17-year-old, feminine, attractive, intelligent girl who appeared anatomically completely normal at birth, but behind whose external genitalia there was no vagina or uterus. Her parents, having no doubts, raised her as a girl, and female and feminine is what she feels she is" (p. 56).

4. "These people, living permanently as unremarkably masculine men, are biologically normal females and were so recognized as children . . . Among those I know one is an expert machine tool operator, another an engineering draftsman, another a research chemist. Their jobs are quiet, steady, and unspectacular; their work records as men are excellent. They are sociable, not recluses, and have friendships with both men and women. Neither their friends nor their colleagues at work know they are biologically female. They are not clinically psychotic" (pp. 194, 196).

5. "[She] is a person as biologically neuter as a human can be, chromosomally XO . . . And yet when she was first seen at age 18 . . . she was quite unremarkably feminine in her behavior, dress, social and sexual desires, and fantasies, indistinguishable in these regards from other girls . . . Her gender identity is not based on some simple biological given, such as endocrine state. It comes from the fact that she looked like a girl . . . Given the anatomical prerequisites to the development of her femininity, it set in motion the complicated process that results in gender identity" (p. 22).

6. ". . . born an apparently normal male, . . . the boy's body became feminized" (p. 77).

7. "A child . . . at birth was found to be an apparently normal female and so was brought up as a girl for fourteen years . . . A physical examination [at adolescence] raised doubts shortly to be confirmed. . . . The inquiry . . . revealed that although the external genitalia looked the same as those of a normal girl of her age, she was in fact a chromosomally normal male" (pp. 67, 69).

8. "This patient . . . was male in anatomical appearance. However, as far back as memory goes, he was extremely feminine. . . . Hospitalized as a result of hepatitis, he was discovered to be genetically and anatomically male" (p. 75).

Source: Data from Robert J. Stoller, *Sex and Gender, on the Development of Masculinity and Femininity* (Science House, New York, 1968).

an open question. Beach calls it an unresolved issue (Beach, 1965, p. 565) and Stoller confesses that the evidence is equivocal, "so we must leave this subject without any sense of its having been settled" (Stoller, 1968, p. 85). For this reason as well as for the reason that sexual anomalies are so rare, the strictly biological factors in gender are given no further attention here. Although they teach us a great deal about the normal aspects of sex and gender, they cannot be invoked in sociological analyses. Further discussion would distort the picture by overemphasizing rare exceptions.

Although the etiological contribution of biological factors to gender identity may be equivocal and often irrelevant, the indirect or derivative contribution of biological factors cannot be denied. In the crucial years when both F and M are working out their mature identities, they are producing different reactions in one another. She produces an erection in him; another boy does not. His touch on her breasts thrills her; another girl's does not. She wants him to caress her; she does not want another girl to. Being reacted to by others as F is different from being reacted to by them as M. And the reaction to F is different from the reaction to M. She can receive him, he cannot receive her. It does not take a sophisticated analysis in terms of symbolic interactionism to see that the different effect each has *on* the other and the different reaction each has *to* the other will produce different conceptions of the self in both M and F. These differences are ultimately biological but, like the functional basis for differences (to be discussed later), in a derived rather than in a direct sense.

Gender Role

Along with gender assignment goes a constellation of traits suitable for characterizing the gender. When illustrating or demonstrating the gender identity of patients, Stoller gives such evidence of feminine gender identity as wanting babies and having a great interest in clothes, cooking, sewing, makeup, ornamentation, and the like (Stoller, 1968, pp. 21–22). These are clearly not all the product of heredity nor of anatomy. They are traits that our society labels feminine.

Some of the specific contents or traits that constitute masculine or feminine gender may vary from place to place and time to time. In Iran, for example, some of the traits that we develop as parts of feminine gender are included in the pattern for masculine gender and vice versa:

> In Iran . . . men are expected to show their emotions. . . . If they don't, Iranians suspect they are lacking a vital human trait and are not dependable. Iranian men read poetry; they are sensitive and have well-developed intuition and in many cases are not expected to be too logical. They are often seen embracing and holding hands. Women, on the other hand, are considered to be coldly practical. They exhibit many of the characteristics we associate with men in the United States. A very perceptive Foreign Service officer who had spent a number of years in Iran once observed, "If you think of the emotional and intellectual sex roles reversed from ours, you will do much better out here." . . . Fundamental beliefs like our concepts of masculinity and femininity are shown to vary widely from one culture to the next (Hall, 1963, p. 10).[5]

The specific contents of masculinity and femininity vary with time also; people worry over the "masculinization of women" and the "feminization of men." The Victorian contents of feminine gender included weakness, helplessness, fragility, delicacy,

and even ill health. Clark Vincent has pointed out how ill-fitting the traditional contents of gender roles are today for both F and M. On tradition-oriented tests, modern middle-class women tend to test low; middle-class men, on the other hand, "tend to score high on femininity when items are included which formerly described the more dependent, intuitive, sensitive, 'peacemaking' role of the female in a tradition-oriented society" (Vincent, 1966, p. 199).

Gender specifications vary not only with time and place but also with the researcher or scientist who reports them. One survey of the literature on the feminine character concluded that "there is hardly any common basis to the different views. The difficulty is not only that there is disagreement on specific characteristics [of feminine gender] and their origin, but that even when there is agreement the emphasis is laid on absolutely different attributes" (Klein, 1946, p. 164).

The most widely recurrent traits attributed to women in western societies have been passivity, emotionality, lack of abstract interests, greater intensity of personal relationships, and an instinctive tenderness for babies (Klein, 1946, p. 164). The test of masculinity-femininity includes such items as passivity, disinclination for physical violence, sensitivity to personal slights and to interpersonal relations, lack of concern for abstractions, and a positive attitude toward culturally defined esthetic experience.

If femaleness and maleness are categorical, non-overlapping, the same cannot be said with respect to femininity and masculinity. Here the overlap can be considerable (Figure 1). Traits denominated as feminine show up in men, and those denominated as masculine show up in women.[6] Here the distinction between *typical* and *characteristic* is important. The typical is the average or the modal. And for many traits, where the overlap is great, the average woman and the average man may not be very different. But when women and men do differ, they differ in characteristic ways, women "characteristically" in one direction, men in another. By and large, women tend to differ in the direction of passivity, nurturance, nonviolence, and men in the direction of aggression, dominance, and violence. The tendency of most societies is to pull women in one direction and men in the other, so that very often the distributions are skewed (Figure 2). For the convenience of managers and copers, it would be ideal if femininity and masculinity were as categorically clear-cut as femaleness

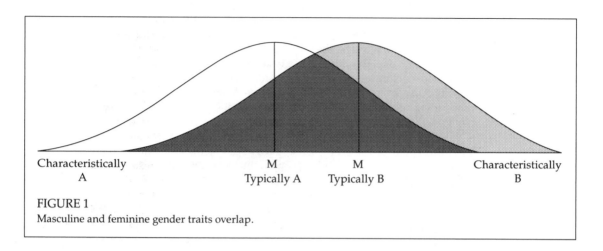

Characteristically
A

M
Typically A

M
Typically B

Characteristically
B

FIGURE 1
Masculine and feminine gender traits overlap.

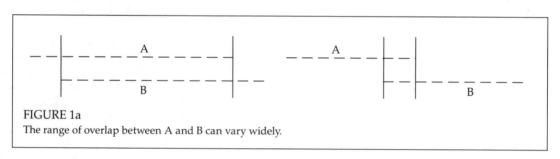

FIGURE 1a
The range of overlap between A and B can vary widely.

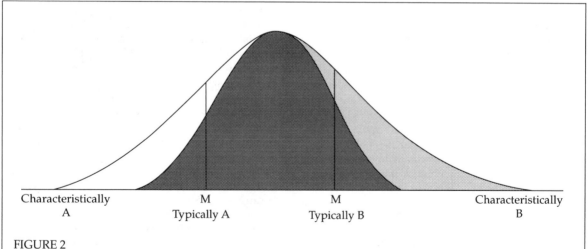

Characteristically
A

M
Typically A

M
Typically B

Characteristically
B

FIGURE 2
Skewed distributions of gender traits. *The socialization process has pulled A and B in different directions so that the distributions are skewed in a desired direction.*

and maleness; it would save them a great deal of trouble if all females were characteristically feminine and all males were characteristically masculine. But the fact is that they aren't. The important thing is not, therefore, whether or not "women" are *z*-er than "men," or "men" *v*-er than "women," but whether Mary is *z*-er than John, or John *v*-er than Mary.

Viola Klein has traced the conceptualization of sex differences through three stages, beginning with Aristotle's category of feminine traits which led him to conclude that femininity was a "kind of natural defectiveness." According to this conceptualization, women are underdeveloped beings with the external attributes of human beings but lacking individuality, intellectual ability, or character. A second stage granted that women were not inferior men but simply different, complementary, inverse. This point of view flourished at the end of the nineteenth and beginning of the twentieth centuries. The third, current, conceptualization sees personality traits as products of functional roles (Klein, 1946, pp. 169–170).

Despite the enormous amount of ink that has been spilled in clearly specifying the nature of psychological gender differences, the conclusion seems to be that it is not so much *what* is defined as masculine or feminine as that such distinctions are made at all. It makes no difference whether pink is for girls and blue for boys, emotionality for girls and rationality for boys, or the other way round. What does make a difference is that a difference is made. It is not the explanations offered for the existence of differences (inherent, acquired, functional, structural) but the fact that there is something to explain. It is the bifurcation by sex that is the fundamental fact. The traits, functions, and work assigned to each part of the bifurcation are secondary; the bifurcation itself is what is primary.

Sex has inevitable structural concomitants and consequences. The structural components that operate differentially on the sexes are both horizontal and vertical; the world women live in tends to be different, and it is usually secondary to the world of men.

The Sphere of Women

Once an individual has been assigned a gender, he (or she) is thereafter relegated to the world or sphere designed for those with his (or her) gender. Even when the work of both women and men was in the home, they lived in different worlds: there was a sphere for men and a sphere for women. Even today there is a woman's world recognized by almost everyone and thoroughly exploited by the mass media. It has quite a different structure from the world of men.

These worlds can be described in terms of several dimensions or variables that those sociologists who follow Talcott Parsons have found useful in describing social systems. Five such dimensions have been encapsulated in terms of five pairs of variables. A community can, first of all, make one's position rest on what one *does* or on what one *is*; it can be the result of achievement or of ascription. Second, the expectations that parties in any relationship share may be specific or diffuse. Duties, obligations, and responsibilities may be defined specifically and contractually, or they may be left unspecified. If they are specified, each party knows precisely what is expected of him and of others; nothing more can be demanded than what is specified, and nothing less can be supplied. The accountant may not be asked to run the computer, the lawyer to run the elevator. If they are left diffuse, there is a rather amorphous, blurred set of expectations that leave precise limits undefined. A friend may be expected to lend money, arrange a date, or share a record collection. Third, a community can require that all relationships be governed by general universalistic principles, or it can permit them to be governed by particularistic personal loyalties and obligations tailored to the particular individuals involved. Fourth, it can permit behavior to be oriented toward furthering one's own interests, or it can require that actions be oriented toward a larger group or the collectivity as a whole, regardless of individual wishes. Finally, the community can admit a wide range of relationships in which there is a minimum of affect or emotional gratification (in which relationships are neutral), or it can allow a wide range of relationships in which affectivity or emotional gratification plays a large part. It is clear that a society in which the first of each of these five pairs of variables prevails will be quite different from one in which the second of each does.

These dimensions or ways of patterning the variables have been used to describe communities or societies of different kinds. For example, ascription, diffuseness, particularism, collectivity-orientation, and affectivity have been used to describe preliterate societies. The first three pairs of dimensions have been used to characterize developing countries as contrasted with modern ones; the degree to which they approached achievement, specificity, and universalistic characteristics has been taken as a measure of modernization (Hoselitz, 1964).

It is not too fanciful to view the gender world or sphere in which women live as characterized, like a preliterate society, by ascription, diffuseness, particularism, collectivity-orientation, and affectivity. In effect, to view women as inhabiting an underdeveloped, if not a primitive, world.

The first step has been taken when feminine gender is ascribed to the female infant. A lifelong train of consequences then ensues. She is thereafter dealt with on the basis of what she is—a woman—rather than on what she does, on her (feminine) qualities rather than on her performance, just as reported for preliterate cultures.

Once this assignment and consequent ascription have been made, a woman is consigned to a world or "sphere" in which her relationships are diffuse rather than specific or contractual. Even in a work situation where presumably relations are contractual and specific, the secretary has diffuse expectations to live up to, such as the variegated services expected of an "office wife" or "girl Friday." The sphere of women is expected to be characterized by particularistic morality more than by universalistic morality, by intense personal loyalty more than by principles. Women are to protect their children even when the children are delinquents or criminals, to do everything they can for those near and dear to them rather than be blindly just or impartial. On the job, women, as part of their supportive function, are expected to be more loyal to their employers than are men. One reads from time to time that men have reported wrongdoing on the part of their employers; one rarely reads that women have. The "developed" country that men inhabit almost forces them to undercut one another to get ahead. In the women's sphere, women are expected to be oriented toward the larger group or the collectivity and to make sacrifices for it. We know that in marriage it is wives who make more of the adjustments; it is taken for granted that mothers make sacrifices for their children; it is expectable that if necessary, the daughter rather than the son will sacrifice marriage to take care of elderly parents. Yet the pursuit of self-interest is almost a virtue in the world men inhabit.

In using this form of "pattern-variable" it is essential to make perfectly clear that the personal char-acteristics of the individuals involved are not the focus of attention; it is rather the shared expectations built into the situation. A social system leads to certain kinds of behavior on the part of its members regardless of their personal qualities or traits. We tend thereafter to attribute to the individuals the qualities expected in them by the system. For example, Freud tells us that the superego of women "is never as inexorable, as impersonal, as independent of its emotional origins as we require it to be in men [affectivity]. Character-traits which critics of every epoch have brought up against women—that they show less sense of justice than men . . . that they are more often influenced in their judgments by their feelings of affection or hostility [particularism]—all these would be amply accounted for by the modification in the formation of their super-ego" (Freud, 1925, pp. 257–258). In terms of the pattern-variable frame of reference, Freud is saying that in women's world affectivity rather than affective neutrality is the expectation, and particularistic rather than universalistic morality. The expectation of this particular pattern in the world of women imposes it on them.

Spock offers specific examples of how such expectations are realized in the modal personality types of men and women. Women, he tells us, become indignant when legal logic results in an unfair decision. "Her husband says, 'Don't you see that the law *has* to take this position, even if it occasionally causes injustice?'" (Spock, 1970). The feminine modal personality type does not. That is not the logic of her (particularistic) world. Her perch is in a particularistic world, his in a universalistic one. They do not see the same things.

There are those who bemoan the passing of the ascriptive, diffusely defined, particularistic, collectivity-oriented, and affective pattern, who believe that a great loss was suffered when it gave way to an achievement-oriented, contractual, specifically defined, universalistic, and affectively neutral pattern. This judgment may have some validity. Still, so long as half of the population inhabits a world patterned one way and the other half another world, the first is at a disadvantage. . . .

Notes

[1]There is, interestingly, less consensus with respect to the term *lady*. In Victorian times a lady was a special kind of person, refined, circumspect, noble, virtuous, sexless, well

behaved, and well mannered. Both the term and the concept went out of fashion in the twentieth century. Modern women did not want to be ladies; to be called "ladylike" came to be something to be resented. It has been with some surprise, therefore, that I have noted a return to the use of this term, even by fellow social scientists in research conferences. They speak of research subjects as "ladies," as though at a loss of what else to call women.

[2]In my book, *The Sex Game,* I used the concept of subsexes as a ploy to emphasize the importance of such intrasex differences among both women and men.

[3]It is important always to note the date of any research on women. The era of the feminine mystique, from the end of the war through the 1950s, exerted a powerful influence on what women thought and felt.

[4]Female anomalies are especially rare, being only one-third to one-eighth as common as male anomalies (Stoller, 1968, p. 197).

[5]Margaret Mead also made a great deal of the cultural contents of gender, which she labeled *temperament* (Mead, 1925).

[6]In a sample of 604 men and 696 women in the general population, Terman found both men and women in the range of scores on masculinity-femininity from -80 to $+60$; but above 60 there were no women and below -99 there were no men (Terman, 1936, p. 72).

References

Adler, Alfred
1924 *The Practice and Theory of Individual Psychology* (London: Kegan Paul).

Beach, Frank
1965 "Retrospect and Prospect," *Sex and Behavior* (New York: Wiley).

Bernard, Jessie
1945 "Observation and Generalization in Cultural Anthropology," *American Journal of Sociology,* 50, pp. 284–291.

———
1968 *The Sex Game* (Englewood Cliffs, N.J.: Prentice-Hall).

Bird, Caroline
1968 *Born Female: The High Cost of Keeping Women Down* (New York: McKay).

Drews, Elizabeth Monroe
1965 "Counseling for Self-Actualization in Gifted Girls and Young Women," *Journal of Counseling Psychology,* 12 (Summer), pp. 167 ff.

Eells, John S., Jr.
1964 "Women in Honors Programs: Winthrop College,"

in Philip I. Mitterling (ed.), *Needed Research on Able Women in Honors Programs, College, and Society* (New York: Columbia University Press).

Freedman, Mervin
1967 *The College Experience* (San Francisco: Jossey-Bass).

Freud, Sigmund
1961 "Some Psychological Consequences of the Anatomical Distinction between the Sexes," *Collected Works,* Standard edition, Vol. 19 (London: Hogarth Press). This paper was originally published in 1925.

Ginzberg, Eli, et al.
1966 *Life Styles of Educated Women* (New York: Columbia University Press).

Goldsen, Rose K., et al.
1960 *What College Students Think* (New York: Van Nostrand).

Hacker, Helen
1951 "Women as a Minority Group," *Social Forces,* 30 (Sept.), pp. 60–66.

Hall, Edward T.
1963 *The Silent Language* (Greenwich: Premier Books).

Hamberg, David A., and Donald T. Lunde
1966 "Sex Hormones in the Development of Sex Differences in Human Behavior," in Maccoby, Eleanor (ed.), *The Development of Sex Differences* (Stanford, Calif.: Stanford University Press), Chapter 1.

Hoselitz, Bert F.
1964 "Social Stratification and Economic Development," *International Social Science Journal,* 16 (2); also "Social Structure and Economic Growth," *Economia Internationale,* 6 (Aug. 1953).

Hoyt, Donald P,, and Carroll E. Kennedy
1958 "Interest and Personality Correlates of Career-Motivated and Homemaking-Motivated College Women," *Journal of Counseling Psychology,* 5 (Spring), 44–49.

Klein, Viola
1946 *The Feminine Character* (New York: International Universities Press).

Mead, Margaret
1935 *Sex and Temperament in Three Primitive Societies* (New York: Morrow).

Riesman, David
1964 "Introduction," in Jessie Bernard, *Academic Women* (University Park: Pennsylvania State University Press).

Rossi, Alice
1965 "Who Wants Women in the Scientific Professions?" in Jacqueline A. Mattfeld and Carol G. Van Aken (eds.), *Women and the Scientific Professions* (Cambridge: M. I. T. Press).

Spock, Benjamin
    1970 "Decent and Indecent" (*McCall*, 1970). This citation from *Washington Post*, Feb. 5.

Stoller, Robert J.
    1968 *Sex and Gender* (New York: Science House).

Terman, Lewis M., and C. C. Miles
    1936 *Sex and Personality: Studies in Masculinity and Femininity* (New York: McGraw-Hill).

Vaerting, Mathilde, and Mathias Vaerting
    1923 *The Dominant Sex, A Study in the Sociology of Sex Differences* (London: Allen and Unwin).

Vincent, Clark
    1966 "Implications of Change in Male-Female Role Expectations for Interpreting M-F Scores," *Journal of Marriage and the Family*, 28 (May), 196–199.

Weisstein, Naomi
    1969 "Kinder, Kuche, Kirche as Scientific Law: Psychology Constructs the Female," *Motive*, 19 (March-April), 78–85.

Yankelovich, Daniel
    1969 *Generations Apart* (Columbia Broadcasting Company).

Black Women: Shaping Feminist Theory

Bell Hooks

Bell Hooks (Gloria Watkins), born in Kentucky, is currently associate professor of English and women's studies at Oberlin College. She is the author of Talking Back: Thinking Feminist, Thinking Black, Ain't I A Woman, *and* Feminist Theory: From Margin to Center.

Black women, Hooks explains, have a special vantage point from which to view, critique, and enrich both our society and feminist theory. Living on the edge develops a particular way of seeing—unique, sustaining, and strengthening to "our sense of self and our solidarity." The feminist movement cannot succeed until it can incorporate the diverse perspectives of women on the margin.

Bell Hooks, *Feminist Theory: From Margin to Center.* Boston: South End Press, 1984, pp. 1–15.

FEMINISM IN THE UNITED STATES HAS NEVER emerged from the women who are most victimized by sexist oppression; women who are daily beaten down, mentally, physically, and spiritually—women who are powerless to change their condition in life. They are a silent majority. A mark of their victimization is that they accept their lot in life without visible question, without organized protest, without collective anger or rage. Betty Friedan's *The Feminine Mystique* is still heralded as having paved the way for contemporary feminist movement—it was written as if these women did not exist. Friedan's famous phrase, "the problem that has no name," often quoted to describe the condition of women in this society, actually referred to the plight of a select group of college-educated, middle and upper class, married white women—housewives bored with leisure, with the home, with children, with buying products, who wanted more out of life. Friedan concludes her first chapter by stating: "We can no longer ignore that voice within women that says: 'I want something more than my husband and my children and my house.'" That "more" she defined as careers. She did not discuss who would be called in to take care of the children and maintain the home if more women like herself were freed from their house labor and given equal access with white men to the professions. She did not speak of the needs of women without men, without children, without homes. She ignored the existence of all nonwhite women and poor white women. She did not tell readers whether it was more fulfilling to be a maid, a babysitter, a factory worker, a clerk, or a prostitute, than to be a leisure class housewife.

She made her plight and the plight of white women like herself synonymous with a condition affecting all American women. In so doing, she deflected attention away from her classism, her racism, her sexist attitudes towards the masses of

American women. In the context of her book, Friedan makes clear that the women she saw as victimized by sexism were college-educated, white women who were compelled by sexist conditioning to remain in the home. She contends:

> It is urgent to understand how the very condition of being a housewife can create a sense of emptiness, non-existence, nothingness in women. There are aspects of the housewife role that make it almost impossible for a woman of adult intelligence to retain a sense of human identity, the firm core of self or "I" without which a human being, man or woman, is not truly alive. For women of ability, in America today, I am convinced that there is something about the housewife state itself that is dangerous.

Specific problems and dilemmas of leisure class white housewives were real concerns that merited consideration and change, but they were not the pressing political concerns of masses of women. Masses of women were concerned about economic survival, ethnic and racial discrimination, etc. When Friedan wrote The Feminine Mystique, more than one-third of all women were in the work force. Although many women longed to be housewives, only women with leisure time and money could actually shape their identities on the model of the feminine mystique. They were women who, in Friedan's words, were "told by the most advanced thinkers of our time to go back and live their lives as if they were Noras, restricted to the doll's house by Victorian prejudices."

From her early writing, it appears that Friedan never wondered whether or not the plight of college-educated, white housewives was an adequate reference point by which to gauge the impact of sexism or sexist oppression on the lives of women in American society. Nor did she move beyond her own life experience to acquire an expanded perspective on the lives of women in the United States. I say this not to discredit her work. It remains a useful discussion of the impact of sexist discrimination on a select group of women. Examined from a different perspective, it can also be seen as a case study of narcissism, insensitivity, sentimentality, and self-indulgence which reaches its peak when Friedan, in a chapter titled, "Progressive Dehumanization," makes a comparison between the psychological effects of isolation on white housewives and the impact of confinement on the self-concept of prisoners in Nazi concentration camps.

Friedan was a principal shaper of contemporary feminist thought. Significantly, the one-dimensional perspective on women's reality presented in her book became a marked feature of the contemporary feminist movement. Like Friedan before them, white women who dominate feminist discourse today rarely question whether or not their perspective on women's reality is true to the lived experiences of women as a collective group. Nor are they aware of the extent to which their perspectives reflect race and class biases, although there has been a greater awareness of biases in recent years. Racism abounds in the writings of white feminists, reinforcing white supremacy and negating the possibility that women will bond politically across ethnic and racial boundaries. Past feminist refusal to draw attention to and attack racial hierarchies suppressed the link between race and class. Yet class structure in American society has been shaped by the racial politic of white supremacy; it is only by analyzing racism and its function in capitalist society that a thorough understanding of class relationships can emerge. Class struggle is inextricably bound to the struggle to end racism. Urging women to explore the full implication of class in an early essay, "The Last Straw," Rita Mae Brown explained:

> Class is much more than Marx's definition of relationship to the means of production. Class involves your behavior, your basic assumptions about life. Your experience (determined by your class) validates those assumptions, how you are taught to behave, what you expect from yourself and from others, your concept of a future, how you understand problems and solve them, how you think, feel, act. It is these behavioral patterns that middle class women resist recognizing although they may be perfectly willing to accept class in Marxist terms, a neat trick that helps them avoid really dealing with class behavior and changing that behavior in themselves. It is these behavioral patterns which must be recognized, understood, and changed.

White women who dominate feminist discourse, who for the most part make and articulate feminist theory, have little or no understanding of white supremacy as a racial politic, of the psychological impact of class, of their political status within a racist, sexist, capitalist state.

It is this lack of awareness that, for example, leads Leah Fritz to write in *Dreamers and Dealers*, a discussion of the current women's movement published in 1979:

> *Women's suffering under sexist tyranny is a common bond among all women, transcending the particulars of the different forms that tyranny takes.* Suffering cannot be measured and compared quantitatively. *Is the enforced idleness and vacuity of a "rich" woman, which leads her to madness and/or suicide, greater or less than the suffering of a poor woman who barely survives on welfare but retains somehow her spirit? There is no way to measure such difference, but should these two women survey each other without the screen of patriarchal class, they may find a commonality in the fact that they are both oppressed, both miserable.*

Fritz's statement is another example of wishful thinking, as well as the conscious mystification of social divisions between women, that has characterized much feminist expression. While it is evident that many women suffer from sexist tyranny, there is little indication that this forges "a common bond among all women." There is much evidence substantiating the reality that race and class identity creates differences in quality of life, social status, and lifestyle that takes precedence over the common experience women share—differences which are rarely transcended. The motives of materially privileged, educated, white women with a variety of career and lifestyle options available to them must be questioned when they insist that "suffering cannot be measured." Fritz is by no means the first white feminist to make this statement. It is a statement that I have never heard a poor woman of any race make. Although there is much I would take issue with in Benjamin Barber's critique of the women's movement, *Liberating Feminism*, I agree with his assertion:

> *Suffering is not necessarily a fixed and universal experience that can be measured by a single rod: it is related to situations, needs, and aspirations. But there must be some historical and political parameters for the use of the term so that political priorities can be established and different forms and degrees of suffering can be given the most attention.*

A central tenet of modern feminist thought has been the assertion that "all women are oppressed." This assertion implies that women share a common lot, that factors like class, race, religion, sexual preference, etc. do not create a diversity of experience that determines the extent to which sexism will be an oppressive force in the lives of individual women. Sexism as a system of domination is institutionalized, but it has never determined in an absolute way the fate of all women in this society. Being oppressed means the *absence of choices*. It is the primary point of contact between the oppressed and the oppressor. Many women in this society do have choices (as inadequate as they are), therefore exploitation and discrimination are words that more accurately describe the lot of women collectively in the United States. Many women do not join organized resistance against sexism precisely because sexism has not meant an absolute lack of choices. They may know they are discriminated against on the basis of sex, but they do not equate this with oppression. Under capitalism, patriarchy is structured so that sexism restricts women's behavior in some realms even as freedom from limitations is allowed in other spheres. The absence of extreme restrictions leads many women to ignore the areas in which they are exploited or discriminated against; it may even lead them to imagine that no women are oppressed.

There are oppressed women in the United States, and it is both appropriate and necessary that we speak against such oppression. . . . However, feminist emphasis on "common oppression" in the United States was less a strategy for politicization than an appropriation by conservative and liberal women of a radical political vocabulary that masked the extent to which they shaped the movement so that it addressed and promoted their class interests.

Although the impulse towards unity and empathy that informed the notion of common oppression was directed at building solidarity, slogans like "organize around your own oppression" provided the excuse many privileged women needed to ignore the differences between their social status and the status of masses of women. It was a mark of race and class privilege, as well as the expression of freedom from the many constraints sexism places on working class women, that middle class white women were able to make their interests the primary focus of feminist movement and employ a rhetoric of commonality that made their condition synonymous with "oppression." Who was there to demand a change in vocabulary? What other group of women in the United States had the same access to universities, publishing houses, mass media, money? Had middle class black women begun a movement in which they had labeled themselves "oppressed," no one would have taken them seriously. Had they established public forums and given speeches about their "oppression," they would have been criticized and attacked from all sides. This was not the case with white bourgeois feminists for they could appeal to a large audience of women, like themselves, who were eager to change their lot in life. Their isolation from women of other class and race groups provided no immediate comparative base by which to test their assumptions of common oppression. . . .

. . . As more and more women acquired prestige, fame, or money from feminist writings or from gains from feminist movement for equality in the work force, individual opportunism undermined appeals for collective struggle. Women who were not opposed to patriarchy, capitalism, classism, or racism labeled themselves "feminist." Their expectations were varied. Privileged women wanted social equality with men of their class; some women wanted equal pay for equal work; others wanted an alternative lifestyle. Many of these legitimate concerns were easily co-opted by the ruling capitalist patriarchy. . . .

Feminists in the United States are aware of the contradictions. Carol Ehrlich makes the point in her essay, "The Unhappy Marriage of Marxism and Feminism: Can It Be Saved?," that "feminism seems more and more to have taken on a blind, safe, nonrevolutionary outlook" as "feminist radicalism loses ground to bourgeois feminism," stressing that "we cannot let this continue":

Women need to know (and are increasingly prevented from finding out) that feminism is not about dressing for success, or becoming a corporate executive, or gaining elective office; it is not being able to share a two career marriage and take skiing vacations and spend huge amounts of time with your husband and two lovely children because you have a domestic worker who makes all this possible for you, but who hasn't the time or money to do it for herself; it is not opening a Women's Bank, or spending a weekend in an expensive workshop that guarantees to teach you how to become

assertive (but not aggressive); it is most emphatically not about becoming a police detective or CIA agent or marine corps general.

But if these distorted images of feminism have more reality than ours do, it is partly our own fault. We have not worked as hard as we should have at providing clear and meaningful alternative analyses which relate to people's lives, and at providing active, accessible groups in which to work.

. . . The ideology of "competitive, atomistic liberal individualism" has permeated feminist thought to such an extent that it undermines the potential radicalism of feminist struggle. The usurpation of feminism by bourgeois women to support their class interests has been to a very grave extent justified by feminist theory as it has so far been conceived. (For example, the ideology of "common oppression.") Any movement to resist the co-optation of feminist struggle must begin by introducing a different feminist perspective—a new theory—one that is not informed by the ideology of liberal individualism.

The exclusionary practices of women who dominate feminist discourse have made it practically impossible for new and varied theories to emerge. Feminism has its party line and women who feel a need for a different strategy, a different foundation, often find themselves ostracized and silenced. . . .

. . . My persistent critique has been informed by my status as a member of an oppressed group, experience of sexist exploitation and discrimination, and the sense that prevailing feminist analysis has not been the force shaping my feminist consciousness. This is true for many women. There are white women who had never considered resisting male dominance until the feminist movement created an awareness that they could and should. My awareness of feminist struggle was stimulated by social circumstance. Growing up in a Southern, black, father-dominated, working class household, I experienced (as did my mother, my sisters, and my brother) varying degrees of patriarchal tyranny, and it made me angry—it made us all angry. Anger led me to question the politics of male dominance and enabled me to resist sexist socialization. Frequently, white feminists act as if black women did not know sexist oppression existed until they voiced feminist sentiment. They believe they are providing black women with "the" analysis and "the" program for liberation. They do not understand, cannot even imagine, that black women, as well as other groups of women who live daily in oppressive situations, often acquire an awareness of patriarchal politics from their lived experience, just as they develop strategies of resistance (even though they may not resist on a sustained or organized basis).

These black women observed white feminist focus on male tyranny and women's oppression as if it were a "new" revelation and felt such a focus had little impact on their lives. To them it was just another indication of the privileged living conditions of middle and upper class white women that they would need a theory to inform them that they were "oppressed." The implication being that people who are truly oppressed know it even though they may not be engaged in organized resistance or are unable to articulate in written form the nature of their oppression. These black women saw nothing liberatory in party line analyses of women's oppression. Neither the fact that black women have not organized collectively in huge numbers around the issues of "feminism" (many of us do not know or use the term) nor the fact that we have not had access to the machinery of power that would allow us to share our analyses or theories about gender with the American public negate its presence in our lives or place us in a position of dependency in relationship to those white and nonwhite feminists who address a larger audience.

The understanding I had by age thirteen of patriarchal politics created in me expectations of the feminist movement that were quite different from those of young, middle class, white women. When I entered my first women's studies class at Stanford University in the early 1970s, white women were revelling in the joy of being together—to them it was an important, momentous occasion. I had not known a life where women had not been together, where women had not helped, protected, and loved one another deeply. I had not known white women who were ignorant of the impact of race and class on their social status and consciousness (Southern white women often have a more realistic perspective on racism and classism than white women in other areas of the United States). I did not feel sympathetic to white peers who maintained that I could not expect them to have knowledge of or understand the life experiences of black women. Despite my back-

ground (living in racially segregated communities), I knew about the lives of white women, and certainly no white women lived in our neighborhood, attended our schools, or worked in our homes.

When I participated in feminist groups, I found that white women adopted a condescending attitude towards me and other nonwhite participants. The condescension they directed at black women was one of the means they employed to remind us that the women's movement was "theirs"—that we were able to participate because they allowed it, even encouraged it; after all, we were needed to legitimate the process. They did not see us as equals. They did not treat us as equals. And though they expected us to provide firsthand accounts of black experience, they felt it was their role to decide if these experiences were authentic. Frequently, college-educated black women (even those from poor and working class backgrounds) were dismissed as mere imitators. Our presence in movement activities did not count, as white women were convinced that "real" blackness meant speaking the patois of poor black people, being uneducated, streetwise, and a variety of other stereotypes. If we dared to criticize the movement or to assume responsibility for reshaping feminist ideas and introducing new ideas, our voices were tuned out, dismissed, silenced. We could be heard only if our statements echoed the sentiments of the dominant discourse.

Attempts by white feminists to silence black women are rarely written about. All too often they have taken place in conference rooms, classrooms, or the privacy of cozy living room settings, where one lone black woman faces the racist hostility of a group of white women. From the time the women's liberation movement began, individual black women went to groups. Many never returned after a first meeting. Anita Cornwall is correct in "Three for the Price of One: Notes from a Gay Black Feminist," when she states, ". . . sadly enough, fear of encountering racism seems to be one of the main reasons that so many black women refuse to join the women's movement." Recent focus on the issue of racism has generated discourse but has had little impact on the behavior of white feminists towards black women. Often the white women who are busy publishing papers and books on "unlearning racism" remain patronizing and condescending when they relate to black women. This is not surprising given that frequently their discourse is aimed solely in the direction of a white audience and the focus solely on changing attitudes rather than addressing racism in a historical and political context. They make us the "objects" of their privileged discourse on race. As "objects," we remain unequals, inferiors. Even though they may be sincerely concerned about racism, their methodology suggests they are not yet free of the type of paternalism endemic to white supremacist ideology. Some of these women place themselves in the position of "authorities" who must mediate communication between racist white women (naturally they see themselves as having come to terms with their racism) and angry black women whom they believe are incapable of rational discourse. Of course, the system of racism, classism, and educational elitism remain intact if they are to maintain their authoritative positions.

In 1981 I enrolled in a graduate class on feminist theory where we were given a course reading list that had writings by white women and men, one black man, but no material by or about black, Native American Indian, Hispanic, or Asian women. When I criticized this oversight, white women directed an anger and hostility at me that was so intense I found it difficult to attend the class. When I suggested that the purpose of this collective anger was to create an atmosphere in which it would be psychologically unbearable for me to speak in class discussions or even attend class, I was told that they were not angry. *I* was the one who was angry. Weeks after class ended, I received an open letter from one white female student acknowledging her anger and expressing regret for her attacks. She wrote:

> *I didn't know you. You were black. In class after a while I noticed myself, that I would always be the one to respond to whatever you said. And usually it was to contradict. Not that the argument was always about racism by any means. But I think the hidden logic was that if I could prove you wrong about one thing, then you might not be right about anything at all.*

And in another paragraph:

> *I said in class one day that there were some people less entrapped than others by Plato's picture of the world. I said I thought we, after fifteen years of education, courtesy of the ruling class, might be more entrapped than others who had not received a start in life so close*

to the heart of the monster. My classmate, once a close friend, sister, colleague, has not spoken to me since then. I think the possibility that we were not the best spokespeople for all women made her fear for her self-worth and for her Ph.D.

Often in situations where white feminists aggressively attacked individual black women, they saw themselves as the ones who were under attack, who were the victims. During a heated discussion with another white female student in a racially mixed women's group I had organized, I was told that she had heard how I had "wiped out" people in the feminist theory class, that she was afraid of being "wiped out" too. I reminded her that I was one person speaking to a large group of angry, aggressive people; I was hardly dominating the situation. It was I who left the class in tears, not any of the people I had supposedly "wiped out."

Racist stereotypes of the strong, superhuman black woman are operative myths in the minds of many white women, allowing them to ignore the extent to which black women are likely to be victimized in this society and the role white women may play in the maintenance and perpetuation of that victimization. In Lillian Hellman's autobiographical work *Pentimento*, she writes, "All my life, beginning at birth, I have taken orders from black women, wanting them and resenting them, being superstitious the few times I disobeyed." The black women Hellman describes worked in her household as family servants, and their status was never that of an equal. Even as a child, she was always in the dominant position as they questioned, advised, or guided her; they were free to exercise these rights because she or another white authority figure allowed it. Hellman places power in the hands of these black women rather than acknowledge her own power over them; hence she mystifies the true nature of their relationship. By projecting onto black women a mythical power and strength, white women both promote a false image of themselves as powerless, passive victims and deflect attention away from their aggressiveness, their power (however limited in a white supremacist, male-dominated state), their willingness to dominate and control others. These unacknowledged aspects of the social status of many white women prevent them from transcending racism and limit the scope of their understanding of women's overall social status in the United States.

Privileged feminists have largely been unable to speak to, with, and for diverse groups of women because they either do not understand fully the interrelatedness of sex, race, and class oppression or refuse to take this interrelatedness seriously. Feminist analyses of woman's lot tend to focus exclusively on gender and do not provide a solid foundation on which to construct feminist theory. They reflect the dominant tendency in Western patriarchal minds to mystify woman's reality by insisting that gender is the sole determinant of woman's fate. Certainly it has been easier for women who do not experience race or class oppression to focus exclusively on gender. Although socialist feminists focus on class and gender, they tend to dismiss race or they make a point of acknowledging that race is important and then proceed to offer an analysis in which race is not considered.

As a group, black women are in an unusual position in this society, for not only are we collectively at the bottom of the occupational ladder, but our overall social status is lower than that of any other group. Occupying such a position, we bear the brunt of sexist, racist, and classist oppression. At the same time, we are the group that has not been socialized to assume the role of exploiter/oppressor in that we are allowed no institutionalized "other" that we can exploit or oppress. (Children do not represent an institutionalized other even though they may be oppressed by parents.) White women and black men have it both ways. They can act as oppressor or be oppressed. Black men may be victimized by racism, but sexism allows them to act as exploiters and oppressors of women. White women may be victimized by sexism, but racism enables them to act as exploit-ers and oppressors of black people. Both groups have led liberation movements that favor their interests and support the continued oppression of other groups. Black male sexism has undermined struggles to eradicate racism just as white female racism undermines feminist struggle. As long as these two groups or any group defines liberation as gaining social equality with ruling class white men, they have a vested interest in the continued exploitation and oppression of others.

Black women with no institutionalized "other" that we may discriminate against, exploit, or oppress often have a lived experience that directly challenges the prevailing classist, sexist, racist social structure and its concomitant ideology. This lived experience may shape our consciousness in such a way that our world view differs from those who have a degree of privilege (however relative within the existing system). It is essential for continued feminist struggle that black women recognize the special vantage point our marginality gives us and make use of this perspective to criticize the dominant racist, classist, sexist hegemony as well as to envision and create a counterhegemony. I am suggesting that we have a central role to play in the making of feminist theory and a contribution to offer that is unique and valuable. The formation of a liberatory feminist theory and praxis is a collective responsibility, one that must be shared. Though I criticize aspects of feminist movement as we have known it so far, a critique which is sometimes harsh and unrelenting, I do so not in an attempt to diminish feminist struggle but to enrich, to share in the work of making a liberatory ideology and a liberatory movement.

Constitution: Preamble and Statement of Purpose

National Women's Studies Association (NWSA)

The National Women's Studies Association was founded in 1977. The current formulation of its constitution, adopted in 1982, shows the close association between the women's movement and women's studies and between a social process, its values and goals, and an intellectual or academic enterprise. Clearly we can see why women's studies has been called "the academic arm of the women's movement."

Presented and passed at the February 1982 Meeting of the Coordinating Council (CC), passed at the Delegate Assembly (DA) in June 1982, and ratified by the membership in September 1982. Reprinted with permission of the National Women's Studies Association.

Preamble

The National Women's Studies Association was formed to further the social, political, and professional development of Women's Studies throughout the country and the world, at every educational level and in every educational setting. To this end, this organization is committed to being a forum conducive to dialogue and collective action among women dedicated to feminist education and change.

Women's Studies owes its existence to the movement for the liberation of women; the feminist movement exists because women are oppressed. Women's Studies, diverse as its components are, has at its best shared a vision of a world free from sexism and racism. Freedom from sexism by necessity must include a commitment to freedom from national chauvinism; class and ethnic bias; anti-Semitism, as directed against both Arabs and Jews; ageism; heterosexual bias— from all the ideologies and institutions that have consciously or unconsciously oppressed and exploited some for the advantage of others. The development of Women's Studies in the past decade, the remarkable proliferation of programs that necessitated this Association, is a history of creative struggle to evolve knowledge, theory, pedagogy, and organizational models appropriate to that vision.

Women's Studies is the educational strategy of a breakthrough in consciousness and knowledge. The uniqueness of Women's Studies has been and remains its refusal to accept sterile divisions between academy and community, between the growth of the mind and the health of the body, between intellect and passion, between the individual and society.

Women's Studies, then, is equipping women not only to enter society as whole and productive human beings, but to transform the world to one that will be free of all oppression. This Constitution reaffirms that commitment.

I. Purpose

Because

—Feminist education is a process deeply rooted in the women's movement and remains accountable to that community;

—Feminist aims include the elimination of oppression and discrimination on the basis of sex, race, age, class, religion, ethnicity, and sexual orientation, as well as other barriers to human liberation inherent in the structure of our society;

—Feminist education is not only the pursuit of knowledge about women, but also the development of knowledge for women, a force which furthers the realization of feminist aims;

Therefore

—The National Women's Studies Association actively supports and promotes feminist education, and supports the persons involved in that effort, at any educational level and in any educational setting.

I

Consciousness: Concepts, Images, and Visions

AS WE EXPLORE THE TOPICS IN THIS BOOK, WE WILL consider womanhood in all its perspectives—biological, social, political, and philosophical. We begin in this part with *sexual consciousness*—the abstract, symbolic, sometimes prelingual elements of our sexual reality. Meanings, associations, expectations, images, stereotypes, and ideals of both sexes form the framework, the underpinnings, the "mind set" of sexual reality, which in large part directs and determines our social-sexual behavior. *We* begin here because much of *it* begins here.

We will examine first in Chapter 2 the dynamics of patriarchy, the male-identified, male-governed, masculist society in which we live. It is both the setting in which traditional (male-identified) images of womanhood were created and the foil against which our new, woman-identified ideals are being forged. In Chapters 3 and 4 we will explore images of women, patriarchal stereotypes and ideals, as well as feminist affirmations. The discussion of consciousness will close in Chapter 5 with an analysis of some of the theories and explanations for the asymmetrical relations of the sexes.

2

The Dynamics of Patriarchy

Conceptions of Patriarchy

The terms *patriarchy* and *matriarchy* can have a variety of meanings. Since the suffix *-archy* literally means "the rule of," patriarchy means literally *the rule of the fathers* and matriarchy, *the rule of the mothers*. The traditional use of the terms in social science, particularly anthropology, has intended a meaning close to this literal sense: In this context, a patriarchy is a society in which formal power over public decision and policy-making is held by adult men; a matriarchy is then a society in which policy is made by adult women.

Many contemporary anthropologists argue that although there have been, and still are, societies that are matrilineal (societies in which descent is traced through the females) and matrilocal (in which domicile after marriage is with the wife's family), little if any evidence shows that true matriarchies, societies ruled by women, ever existed. Yet the concept of matriarchy flourishes in feminist theory.

Such a circumstance can be confusing unless it is realized that feminists can use the terms *patriarchy* and *matriarchy* in various ways. Depending on context, the terms may be scientific (as above), political, philosophic, or even poetic. In feminist thought, matriarchy can mean not only the rule of women (any women), but also the rule of what historically has been taken to be the fe-male principle, or the rule of feminist ideals. Patriarchy, then, would refer not simply to a society where men hold power, but rather to a society ruled by a certain kind of men wielding a certain kind of power—a society that reflects the underlying values of the traditional male ideal. Thus feminists frequently use *patriarchy* to denote a culture whose driving ethos is an embodiment of masculist ideals and practices.

Feminists argue that we in contemporary Western culture inhabit a patriarchy, both in the anthropological and in the political, feminist sense. Patriarchy, then, has determined almost entirely the nature and quality of our society, its values and priorities, the place and image of women within it, and the relation between the sexes. Thus, to comprehend our lives and experiences, we must understand the dynamics of patriarchy—what it is and how it works. To do this, we must ask the following questions:

- Since patriarchy is an embodiment of the masculist ideal, what is that ideal; how is it derived from the traditional picture of ideal masculinity?

- What are the underlying themes of that ideal; how and why do they actually function in the real world?

- What is the effect of the ideal—on men, on women, and on society in general?

Let us begin with a discussion of the nature of the male ideal, its content and imperatives. We can then burrow deeper, examining its underlying dynamic, to reveal the hidden prescriptions of contemporary masculinity, its implications and effects.

The Male Ideal

We must begin with a caution that we are examining masculinity and the male ideal, and not the concept of human excellence. Because our masculist society has historically perceived men to be the only fully and primarily human creatures, and because—as we saw in Chapter 1—the concepts *human* and *male* have frequently been confused, the concept of the human ideal has been similarly confused with that of the masculine. This blurring of concepts has led to a good deal of misunderstanding and mischief.

The "Human" and the "Male": A Preliminary Distinction

When I have asked students (women and men alike) to suggest people whom they believed represented human ideals, they have named Mahatma Gandhi, Abraham Lincoln, Martin Luther King, Jr., Jesus, and other great-hearted individuals. When I have asked them to suggest "ideal men," they have again listed Gandhi, Lincoln, King, and Jesus, but the same lists have also included such names as Tom Cruise, John Wayne, and Indiana Jones. Even the students were perplexed by the range and disparity of their choices. What, they asked, accounts for this confusion?

The students were confused by the ambiguity surrounding the term *man*, which can mean in our language either *human* or *male*. Such usage, feminists point out, derives from the ancient masculist presumption that humanity and masculinity are one and the same and that excellence in humanity is therefore the same as excellence in masculinity. By such reasoning, if a man enhances his masculine qualities, he must also be enhancing his "human" qualities; and as he develops excellence in human character, so must he as well, become more "manly." Recognizing this ambiguity, we can understand why the terms *male ideal* and *ideal man* might not be distinguished and thus how Tom Cruise and Mahatma Gandhi might appear on the same list.

Until feminists crystalized the problem, researchers had given precious little consideration to

the masculine element distinct from the human. But once the simple fact is realized that *human* and *masculine* are not the same, it is evident that ideal masculinity and ideal humanity are different, too, and that no sense can be made of either one until they are separated and compared.

The intellectual community has spent considerable energy identifying the qualities of human excellence. Philosophers of classical antiquity included intelligence, independence, temperance, honesty, courage, responsibility, altruism, justice, and rationality in their vision. Modern authors have added more characteristics, particularly the affective traits, such as humor, compassion, and sensibility. Now, to fully comprehend the male ideal, we must ask how these qualities of human excellence are related to the imperatives of masculinity. Which of them are retained and which discarded? How are they adapted to the masculine image, and how are they changed? In a conflict between masculine and human ideals, which takes precedence for most men? Under what conditions? These are questions that must be explored if we are to understand more than superficially what contemporary images of masculinity mean to men and ultimately to women.

The Masculine Ideal

Consider the men, real or fanciful, who have come to be known as masculine heroes in our culture. Figures like Babe Ruth, Tarzan, the Lone Ranger, Mr. T, Joe Namath, Rambo, Magnum P.I., Rooster Cogburn, Axel Foley are the personalities that have had enduring appeal to large audiences of both sexes.

An examination of these images begins to reveal the qualities of today's ideal male. Typically, our hero exhibits many of the classical traits of human excellence, adapted though they may be to contemporary circumstances: He is intelligent, competent, courageous, honest (at least with the "right" people), healthy, and strong. Responsible and persevering, he pursues right as he sees it and lets no one deter him from his course: That is, he has spirit or backbone. Thus from the shores of Iwo Jima to the hills of Montana, soldier or cowboy or rugged ex-fighter-come-home, John Wayne gets the job done. Not an intellectual, though natively intelligent, he always knows just how to make things come out right. Fearless in the face of danger, he speaks truth to his adversaries—Indians, captors, crooks, towns-people—and always triumphs.

It becomes apparent that our image of the ideal male is not fully drawn using the classical qualities of intelligence, honesty, courage, and so on. Added dimensions transform the ideal man from the merely human to the masculine: The contemporary hero is (1) sexual and (2) tough, that is, violent in a socially approved way. (As we shall see later on, these two factors—sex and violence—coalesce.)

For the most part, the masculine heroes in our culture can be grouped into just a few categories: soldiers (warriors), cops and detectives (warriors against crime), cowboys (pioneer warriors against bad guys, Indians, warriors of the untamed environment), tough doctors (warriors against disease, ignorance, or the hospital administration), and rough but basically good crooks (warriors against . . . fill in the blanks). Our hero may be handsome or rugged, young or graying or bald, a good guy or a good bad guy, a learned professional or a street-educated bum, but one thing is certain—he is tough in a special and desirable way: He isn't afraid of pain; he doesn't shun a "necessary" fight; he can't be pushed; he perseveres in his will; he wins. Taciturn or talkative, he doesn't mince (words or movement), and whether in a lab coat or a three-piece suit, like the "Incredible hulk," he communicates the untamed animal within, under control but nonetheless operating.

The Warrior Imperative

Masculinity, manhood, is symbolized by the astro-logical symbol ♂, which represents Mars, the ancient god of war. That is no accident, for the heart and essence of the masculine ideal is the warrior image. The true male, the "man's man," the virile, exciting hero is a warrior, regardless of what he battles. Without the aura of the fighter, a man may be important or powerful, or even humanly excellent, but he will not be masculine in the traditional sense. Indiana Jones is a scholar, a professor, successful in his profession, intelligent, capable. He is quiet, one might even say reserved and conservative. He is transformed into a symbol of potent masculinity, however, by the alter character within: the fearless, never defeated, unorthodox, knock-'em-down, shoot-'em-up, get-the-girl wise guy. Ford plays the same character in *Witness* in a different

venue: a competent, successful cop who succeeds because he is tough, relentless in a fight, breaks rules when he chooses, gives them what for, and gets the girl.

From *Robocop* to *L.A. Law,* the male heroes are fighters. Aggressive—sometimes downright truculent and even violent—they epitomize the ideal of the primal warrior, the prototype of pure masculinity. In the words of Marc Feigen Fasteau, a lawyer and feminist, ". . . men are brought up with the idea that there *ought* to be some part of them, under control until released by necessity, that thrives on [violence]. This capacity, even affinity, for violence, lurking beneath the surface of every real man, is supposed to represent the primal, untamed base of masculinity."[1]

But a proclivity for violence, though necessary, is not in itself a sufficient characterization of the warrior-hero. Within the ideal lies a further, hidden prescription. It is the reverse side of the coin: the "real" man must never exhibit the complementary characteristics, those qualities that would render him unfit for battle—delicacy, sensitivity, fastidiousness, pity, emotionality, fearfulness, need, tenderness toward other men, and certain other humane traits. These are exactly the qualities reserved for women, expected and required of women, and symbolized by ♀, the sign of Venus, goddess of life. The masculine ideal is *all* "man," *all* Mars, *none* of Venus. Ultimately, it comes to this: The warrior virtues together with the negation of their complement (the affective qualities) compose the patriarchal ideal of masculinity.

Patriarchal Ideal of Masculinity

Warrior Virtues	*Not-Male (Complement)*
aggressiveness	passivity
courage	timidity
physical strength and health	fragility and delicacy
self-control and emotional reserve	expressiveness
perseverance and endurance	frailty
competence and rationality	emotionality
independence	needfulness
self-reliance, autonomy	dependence
individuality	humility
sexual potency	chastity, innocence or receptivity

The ideal patriarchal male must be not only brave, but never-timid; not only independent, but never-needful; not only strong, but never-weak. Committed to victory in battle, which is his first priority, he is a man of constraint and restraint, for violent emotions of any kind might deter him from his rationally designed course or strategy. For this man, control over himself and his needs or feelings is perceived to be the key to control over events.

The contemporary superhero is supersexed; yet with all the emphasis on potency (as a sign of strength and power), the version of sex presented by this masculist imperative is devoid of sensuality. According to the precepts of Mars, the warrior must not involve himself with commitments other than success; nor can he allow himself the luxury of compliance, of shared control or surrender—to himself or to his partner. If feeling must be denied—if sensitivity, delicacy, and needfulness are prohibited—then surely an experience as profoundly emotional and affective as full sensuality must also be denied. Instead of yielding to the affective self, as implied by sensuality, the warrior hero must fight another battle, treating sex as war (between the sexes), making conquests and gaining victories. Even the contemporary vision of the sexual expert is more a matter of a "mission accomplished" than of shared delight. *Cheers* hero Sam Malone (Ted Danson) drives women mad with his rugged good looks and his adolescent charm, yet we can see that his own involvement is less than complete; even when "in love," he is distant, ambivalent, frequently exploitative.

Malone is an interesting character, because he represents a bridge between the formal image of ideal masculinity (perfectly represented by John Wayne) and another of its aspects—culturally subliminal, slightly illicit, and only grudgingly acknowledged—the good guy who is so bad or the guy who is good because he's so bad, sharply characterized by such images as Charles Bronson in *Death Wish* or James Bond, 007.

The official portrait of the perfect man, à la Wayne, depicts a man accomplished and successful, a warrior, a fighter in socially approved arenas, strong, powerful, and dominating, fully controlled, emotionally detached, logical, orderly, duty-bound, and committed to the "right" side. He is law-abiding (for the most part) and motivated by the altruis-

tic values of his society. He is, in the strictest sense, a hero.

Malone, and a score of others quite like him—Crocodile Dundee, Axel Foley (Beverly Hills Cop), Rocky, for example—represents a uniquely 1980s variation on the theme, halfway between the classic strong man and the contemporary "new man." On the outside, this man is tough, cool, slick, proud; he is hot stuff. He charms women, takes what he wants, does what he likes, fights the system. As far as women are concerned, as one undergraduate woman put it, "he's a dick, but it's okay, because he's actually only half a dick (which is sexy) and half not a dick." That is, under the traditional masculist exterior roams a character more appealing (at least to this young woman), the boy inside the man—playful, sensitive, confused, needy, messing up by the numbers, ("a tear not quite on the cheek"). He is Star Man, an advanced being, yet a baby; Rocky, oh so tough but oh so dependent on his lady; Dundee, king of the outback, wielder of big knife, who cannot fathom a bidet; Malone, jock and lady killer, brought down by his attraction to the wrong (bright, independent, educated, but safely goofy) woman.

Actually, although very '80s, this is not a new image. In the '30s and '40s, Jimmy Stewart, Cary Grant, and Clark Gable played this type very well. The '80s element is the degree of tension between the two poles and perhaps also the sheer immaturity of the personalities depicted.

On the far end resides the darker aspect of maleness, the character who is most defined by the martial ideals—the tough, hard, uncompromising, totally controlled warrior-man. On the "good" side of this role is James Bond, sex symbol of the seventies. He strayed a bit: he beat women (but only those of the other side), he killed (with a license), he was "b-a-a-a-d." In the eighties, he was replaced by Bronson's character or by Rambo—more savage, less controlled, less suave, reflecting perhaps the frustrations of their decade. These men are released from the rules of civilization by the unconscionable crimes of the enemy. That is, with "justification" they kill without quarter, pleasure themselves with the fruits of their fury, and bring order out of chaos with brute force, as a proper warrior should.

But what happens when the justification dissolves or the control goes awry? Then we have the monster-sergeant of *Platoon*, who is just a shade away from his acceptable counterpart.

The dark side of the masculine imperative is an alliance between violence, sexuality, a certain baseness, and mischief, pointedly manifest in events like the one during the Viet Nam war described here:

> . . . *some of the GIs who conducted the My Lai massacre raped women before they shot them. The day after that "mission," an entire platoon raped a woman caught fleeing a burning hut. And a couple of days later a helicoptor door gunner spotted the body of a woman in a field. She was spread-eagled, with an Eleventh Brigade patch between her legs. Like a "badge of honor," reported the gunner. "It was obviously there so people would know the Eleventh Brigade had been there."*[2]

Machismo: Bad Is Good

Under the gloss of the classic heroic ideal is a hidden agenda, a group of themes and imperatives spawned by the warrior ideal and containing the underlying realities of patriarchal manliness. They take precedence over, or transform, the classical values, and they constitute the concrete fleshing out of the abstract formal ideal. The word for this aspect of masculinity is *machismo*.

Machismo is the Latin-American word for the mystique of "manliness." It denotes a configuration of attitudes, values, and behaviors clearly articulated by a Michael Jackson hit on MTV: "I'm bad," he sings joyfully, bumping his hips and groin sexually. All the associations are made: masculinity, genitalia, bad . . . desirable.

The machismo element of masculinity is that of the bad boy, of mischief that can and sometimes does slip into downright evil. This configuration is not an aberration, peripheral to masculinity. It is essential to it. Encouraged by parents ("Trouble, trouble, trouble, isn't he *all* boy?"), tolerated in school, and enhanced by sports, military traditions, and many rites of passage—for example, the bachelor dinner, Friday night with the boys, or "sowing wild oats"—machismo is real and present. Although its expression may vary with class, race, or location, it forms an important part of the male world view, for its alternative is the sissy or goody-two-shoes, an object of ridicule and rejection.

Though the expression and the intensity of mischief may vary, the components are relatively stable.

General Naughtiness; Breaking the Rules El Macho does what he chooses, often the opposite of what is required. Christian society requires certain attitudes of temperance; el Macho drinks too much, spends too much, gambles, and engages in excessive and/or illicit sex. In extreme, he may steal or kill; in polite society, he swears and fools around. The point of the behavior is in the fact of breaking the rules; too much concern for submission is clearly effeminate. Michael Douglas is evil but fascinating and sexy in the film *Wall Street*.

Violence El Macho thrives on it. Mere fighting does not satisfy this requirement, but blood-and-guts confrontations, or at least a willingness to accept them. Cockfighting, boxing, and hand-to-hand infantry combat are perceived as male pursuits. El Macho Minor plays football, brawls with the guys in the tavern, tells war stories, or initiates fraternity brothers with a paddle. El Macho Major carries a switchblade and is not afraid to use it.

Sexual Potency Machismo is a cultural image, a human type, but it is a sexual identity as well. Potency—defined as the ability to have sex often and as rapidly as possible, to impregnate with ease—is tightly integrated into the other components described. Violence and sexuality are *not* juxtaposed in this context. Instead, they are different facets of the same thing. El Macho uses his sex like a weapon. In street language you "deck 'em and dick 'em," you "tear off a piece," or "bang 'em" or "hit 'er"—all intensely violent metaphors. In extreme, one rapes or gang-bangs; ordinarily, one simply exploits or insults.

Contempt for Women Since masculinity requires a commitment to Mars and an aversion to Venus, it is hardly surprising that el Macho should be contemptuous of Venus's earthly manifestations: women. The official macho attitude requires that women—in their delicacy, dependence, timidity, gullibility, and softness—be used and enjoyed, like a peach plucked from a tree and just as easily discarded. A young man told me that his father advised him to practice the four f's: "Find 'em, feel 'em, fuck 'em, and forget 'em." Contempt blossoms into hatred: Women are stupid, dangerous, wheedling. The only exceptions are those who cannot be contemplated as sexual partners—mothers and sisters, for example, or nuns.

The women's movement reserves the word *macho* for behavior and attitudes expressive of these values wherever they appear. He who even jokingly brags of his macho orientation (and there are those who do) either misunderstands what he says or deserves the misapprobation he receives, for it is this aspect of the masculine imperative that transforms an inadequate lifestyle (the martial hero) into a destructive one.

The Male Role in the Twentieth Century

In a book that includes a variety of writings on the male role, Deborah S. David and Robert Brannon have translated these concepts into the concrete imperatives of masculinity for the contemporary Western man.[3] They contend that four major themes underlie required behavior for men and boys. These themes appear early in life, function powerfully in the socialization process, and pervade the masculine conceptual environment.

1. "No sissy stuff"—the rejection of any of the characteristics reserved for femininity, either in the male's own behavior or in other men. This includes the fear of being labeled a sissy and the discomfort in female environments, the rejection of vulnerability, and the flight from close male friendships.

2. "The Big Wheel"—the quest for wealth, fame, success, and signs of importance.

3. "The Sturdy Oak"—the aura of confidence, reliability, unshakable strength and toughness. "I can handle it."

4. "Give 'em hell"—the enjoyment and expression of aggression, violence, and daring.[4]

The Effects of Patriarchy

Thus, a two-part image of masculinity characterizes our culture: on the one hand, the warrior hero, a compilation of classical ideals and warrior qualities; on the other hand, the machismo syndrome, the undercurrent of mischief, composed of a predilection for violence, intemperate and exploitative sex, and recklessness.

The commandments of Mars are:

Dominate and control—people, events, objects.
Succeed at any cost. Never admit defeat or error.
Control your emotions. Avoid strong feelings.
Strive for distance—from others and from self.
Banish needfulness (called "weakness").
Be contemptuous of needfulness in others.
Guard against the female within and without.
Protect your image (or ego).

Add the machismo orientation:

Exhibit a kind of reckless unconcern for rules.
Embrace violence.
Place sexuality in a power context.

Such are the imperatives of the masculine ideal in our patriarchy.

As we explore and observe the imperatives of the masculine mystique, it is essential to remember that we are dealing with an image, an ideal, or a stereotype. The image functions as a standard; it does not represent any individual or even a group of individuals. Although a man may strive to meet the requirements of the image, he cannot become the image in reality any more than a woman can in reality become all that is implied by the title "playmate of the year."

The sexual stereotypes, in this case the masculine ideal, function as social norms and mores in the culture. These are, as the sociologist William G. Sumner showed, values and attitudes that begin dimly somewhere in the past, become so habitualized that they take on an aura of cosmic validity, and ultimately become so imbedded in the social fabric that they cannot allow for deviation or rejection.[5] They are usually perceived not as social rules but as enduring truths and realities. Learned through the process of socialization, mores—including sex-role prescriptions—are internalized by individuals and become extremely powerful determinants of behavior. As David and Brannon's discussion points out, the young boy learns truculence as a value for men the same way he learns that Americans eat beef but not horse meat. The picture of ideal manhood is presented to him as a required model, not as a choice.

Yet a variety of factors affect a male's response to the model—how strongly it is presented to him, the successes (or failures) he has within it, the values that are juxtaposed to it, the alternative lifestyle he learns and tries, and many more. One way or another, by adoption, rejection, or adaptation, each male must reckon with these idealized images of masculinity. Insofar as he internalizes the masculine imperatives, he will exhibit its characteristics, will try to control others with them, and will be controlled by them.

The sex-role prescriptions function in this way: Although they are male expressions, they are in large part independent of individual men; and although men may benefit or suffer from them and have a stake in maintaining or ending them, men as social beings are nevertheless subject to them, as are women.

Men Under Patriarchy

Men are not the greatest victims of patriarchy (as I have heard it said), but they are certainly victimized. If the sex roles, both female and male, are destructive, as feminists believe they are, then men as well as women are afflicted.

One might hypothesize that any externally imposed role model would create difficulties. After all, any prescriptive set of behaviors and values will inevitably contain elements contrary to existing patterns and "natural" inclinations in individuals. What makes these sex roles particularly difficult and conflictive, however, is their tremendous scope, the intensity of feelings surrounding them, their inflexibility, and the aspects of one's identity that they affect.

A role model for a pop musician, let us say, requires certain standards of competence with music and with instruments. It also prescribes other activities and values related to the work, such as mobility and a willingness to hustle for engagements. Going a little deeper, one expects as well a particular personal style. If the pop musician fails to meet these

expectations, the penalty for deviation may adversely affect his or her musical career, but it is unlikely to be extreme beyond that point. That is, it is unlikely to imply diminution of the player's very being and human worth.

But deviation from the sex roles has just that effect. In our culture, and possibly for all people, the sense of one's sexual identity and of one's sexual desirability are powerful components of the sense of self and self-worth. Accordingly, deviation from sexual norms incurs severe penalties, not only from others but often from oneself as well. In other words, the inability or even the refusal to meet sex-role prescriptions, for whatever reason, creates serious conflicts for the individual. Whether in terms of adapting to the culture and the society or in terms of resolving inner confusion, the person who deviates from gender expectations experiences real difficulty.

In a genuine way, then—and in several respects—men in a patriarchy experience a painful situation.[6] Certainly, should a man fail to adopt the masculine role expectations, either by default (because he cannot meet them) or by choice (because he rejects them on principle), he must confront and resolve both the social traumas and the conflicts within himself. People will punish him for his deviation, through rejection, ostracism, ridicule, or more formidable signs of hostility. Because he is not a "man's man" or a "real" man, he is apt to find himself ill received both in traditional male environments and among many traditional women. Male students who do not submit to the masculine mold have described their surprise at being rejected not only by men (as they expected) but also by women, who consider them unmanly or unattractive as sexual partners.

If the pain of rejection from without is hard to bear, so is the pain of rejection from within. From childhood on, from our membership in the culture, we carry with us beliefs and attitudes extremely difficult to change. Even after we have deliberately altered our opinions and behaviors in the light of a better considered and more rationally chosen set of ideals, the old, internalized value judgments continue in force, thwarting our resolve through doubt and self-contention and raising both anxieties and emotional turmoil. Breaking habits is hard; breaking these ancient and heavily prescribed habits of thought, feeling, and action is particularly hard. While part of the person opts for a new style, the other part rejects it. The result is inner war.

The problems entailed in rejecting traditional gender ideals are obvious; they are much the same problems involved in trying to reject any highly valued cultural norm. The problems that follow *accepting* the patriarchal image are far less obvious because they are so fully integrated into the culture, yet they are considerably more severe in their effects. The supermale image of masculinity is not a human image; machismo is not humane. The masculine mystique is directly at odds with a good portion of the classical and Christian ideals of human excellence; it is at odds with many of the known components of mental health; and it is certainly at odds with many elements that both philosophers and social scientists believe are essential to human happiness.

The classical ideal, although inadequate because it fails to treat the affective qualities of human life, still includes a certain tranquillity of spirit born of temperance, a strong commitment to the rights and needs of other individuals through social order, and thoughtful ethical awareness and responsibility. It is an ideal of intelligent, rational behavior, and although it contains a goodly element of physical strength, courage, and spirit, it is not given to violence per se, or pugnacity as an end in itself.

The Christian ideal, too, is one of temperance and tranquillity. With greater emphasis on peace and gentleness than the classic ideal, it is yet disciplined and highly concerned with law.

But the masculine mystique—particularly the machismo component—values violence, recklessness, intemperance, exploitativeness, and aggressive pursuit of success at all costs. Surely the man raised under the imperatives of both the classical and the martial visions suffers considerable conflict. Since our society officially teaches him the traditional or classical virtues and at the same time requires the martial, he is asked to exhibit incompatible qualities and behaviors; to love his neighbor or brother but to carry a bayonet; to be charitable and loving but to also succeed in business; to be a responsible father and husband but to prove his potency through untrammeled sex. To be pulled between contradictory values and requirements is not unusual in our changeable, diverse so-

ciety. In fact, some social commentators suggest that the most important capacity for people in the coming era will be the capacity to change and adapt. But the martial imperative is such that it denies men the means to adapt in a substantive, meaningful, integrative way.

Adaptation and growth, as well as change at the spiritual and emotional level, requires a great deal of reflection, introspection, self-awareness, self-criticism, and emotional integrity. To flourish under conditions of stress and change, one must be capable of understanding one's feelings and accepting them, of seeking and using assistance, and of nurturing an enduring internal sense of self. But these very capacities are denied by the masculist male ideal. The proper warrior has neither the time nor the patience for reflection and introspection. His imperative is direct action. He perceives thinking as effete and equates it with indecisiveness.

And feelings? We all "know" that big boys don't cry. They also don't get scared and don't need anyone to help them. Although the martial virtue of emotional reserve refers primarily to feelings not convenient for a warrior—such as fear, anguish, grief, and hurt—the truly "manly" man is expected to exhibit reserve in all feelings. Anger and lust might be acceptable, but even these ought never to operate spontaneously, independent of plan, for they must not interfere with success. Even the so-called positive emotions—humor, love, joy—must be controlled lest they interfere with duty. (Have we not been regaled with tales of foolish men who forsook their commitments for love and were dashed into dishonor? Think of *Anthony and Cleopatra* or *Of Human Bondage*.) Young boys are trained early not to feel—to "take it like a man" and to "keep a stiff upper lip."

The key word in this image is *distance*—from the self, from one's feelings and needs, from other men, and from women. The perfect warrior trusts no one and has one loyalty: the battle and its success. He succeeds or he is worthless. In business, in science or argumentation, in relationships or encounters, or in sex, a man under patriarchy must win or set himself to winning. That is why weakness is contemptible—the weak (the needful, the feeling, or the tender) do not win (that is, dominate, control, overwhelm). A man must push, strive, never let up, and loathe himself if he fails.

Where Mars triumphs, men are shorn of their affective elements, impelled toward distance and truculence, and robbed of many precious experiences of life and self. They find themselves consigned to an arena of striving, pressure, anxiety, and threat. They must content themselves with the prescribed fruits of patriarchal success—status, power, and public praise. In such a context, even pleasure is transitory and shallow. Not a happy prospect. But happiness, in terms that Aristotle or Plato or Buddha might understand—an ongoing, profound experience—is not the issue for the warrior. He has no time for that kind of experience. He is too busy winning.

This is not a wholesome picture, to be sure. Men who pursue the macho ideal indeed lose a good deal in life, yet we must not be blind to a harsh reality: They hold a tremendous advantage in power, privilege, and position. And because masculist men have the presiding power in society, their perspectives and values, including the martial ideal, permeate our culture. These have become, in fact, the guiding ethos of much social behavior. That is why, feminists argue, we inhabit a patriarchy.

Social Priorities in Patriarchy

This discussion has shown that the essential element of the masculine ideal is warrior aggressiveness. The rationale is as follows: "Since this is a violent world, the man of the world must be violent." It is rarely proposed that the world is violent because the ideal man of the world is violent. Feminists, however—both female and male—have suggested just that.

Shulamith Firestone, Andrea Dworkin, Gloria Steinem, Brian Easlea, and countless others have commented on the principle of violence in our patriarchal culture. Some argue that this element of masculism is the root of all the other destructive forces that plague us: war, racism, rape, and environmental abuse. Mary Daly, a feminist theologian, philosopher, and educator, argues that all of these problems are manifestations of the "phallocentric" commitment to power and domination (of people, events, and things). She calls the configuration of power through violence "phallic morality," and sees it expressed through "The Most Unholy Trinity: Rape, Genocide, and War."[7] If Daly's language seems extreme or exceptional, her thesis is not.

Sexism, Masculism, and Patriarchy

Before going on, let us pause to review and order some important concepts. Sexism, masculism, and patriarchy are related, as we have seen, but the terms may not always be used interchangeably.

Sexism is a way of seeing the world in which differences between males and females, actual or alleged, are perceived as profoundly relevant to important political, economic, and social arrangements and behavior. To understand more readily the base meaning of the term *sexism*, consider some human factor not typically perceived as relevant to such arrangements and substitute it for sex differences—for example, hair color. Thus, hairism is a way of seeing the world in which differences in hair color are perceived as profoundly relevant to important political, economic, and social arrangements and behavior. In that case, ego identities, social roles, work assignments, rights and obligations, and human relationships would all be determined in large measure by the color of one's hair.

It seems absurd, doesn't it? After all, the color of one's hair has nothing to do with one's functioning in society. Hair color as a sociopolitically relevant trait is recognized as absurd because in our culture there are no claims that it is related in any way to other traits that *are* important to social function, such as intelligence, character, competence, maturity, and responsibility.

Sexism belongs to this class of concepts. Under sexism, claims are made that functionally relevant traits such as character, competence, and so on are related to, and in fact determined by, one's biological sexual identity: Males are intelligent, responsible, courageous; females are emotional, dependent, and flighty; hence males rather than females are suited to authority.

Of course, the maintenance of such claims does not constitute the full meaning of sexism. For if that were the case, sexism would simply be a logistic for ordering social functions that were evaluated as neutral. Men and women would be perceived as different, therefore having different things to do, but they and their activities would still be held to be of equal worth and consideration. The argument would be much like this: Bananas and apples are different and respectively go better with certain foods, but neither fruit is judged superior to the other. In fact, many sexists claim that this is precisely what they do believe about sexual arrangements. However, their claim is false.

The essence of sexism (and of racism, nativism, heterosexism, and similar prejudices) is its inherent evaluative element. The term *sexism* may appear to be neutral, and some maintain that women, too, may be sexist (that is, female chauvinistic), but that is not the way sexism functions in our society. "Separate but equal" is a lie between the races; "complementary but equal" is a lie between the sexes, for functioning sexists believe, maintain, require, and insist that men are superior to women in every way that matters. Both a dichotomy of sexual characteristics and a negative judgment about women (misogyny) are essential features of our culture's particular brand of sexism, *masculism*.

Masculism (or *androcentrism*) is the elevation of the masculine, conceptually and physically, to the level of the universal and the ideal. It is the valuing of men above women. It is, as well, an honoring of a male principle (conceived of as Mars, a warring configuration of qualities) above the female (conceived of as Venus, a serving and nurturing configuration). Some feminists have referred to this honoring of the male and the male principle as phallic worship or *phallocentrism* because male identity in a martial context is so intricately bound up with and expressed through their sexuality, more specifically, genital sexuality.

Women Under Patriarchy

Masculism in a political context is *patriarchy*. A consideration of the condition of women under patriarchy will fill the remainder of this book, but some general remarks are appropriate here because the misogynist, patriarchal treatment of women and womanhood is the quintessence of masculism, its culmination and fullest expression.

If masculism is at heart the worship of Mars and the embracing of phallic morality to the exclusion of its complement, then the rejection of Venus and the rejection of the traits symbolized by her—love, beauty, tenderness, or acquiescence—as well as the rejection of woman, her earthly manifestation, becomes logical and predictable. No "real man" may tolerate—within himself, at least—the tender qualities. He must deny himself any tendency toward

them, any personal experience of them. Instead, these traits must be projected outward; the complement of his masculine character is settled on his sexual complement, woman: "I am man; she is woman. I am strong; she is weak. I am tough; she is tender. I am self-sufficient; she is needful."

Woman serves this important function in patriarchy: As the negative image of man, his complement, she is the receptacle of all the traits he cannot accept in himself, yet cannot, as a *human* being, live without. The image of Woman contains that element of humanity ripped from Man—an element she keeps for him, still in the world, available when and where needed, but sufficiently distant to avoid interfering with business. Yet even as negation, woman's place is not safe. As man must flee from the Venus principle within himself, as he must hold that configuration in contempt, so he must hold woman in contempt as well, for *in patriarchy* she is the incarnation of Venus and nothing else. The outcome of this arrangement for man is ambivalence. He is both drawn to and repelled by patriarchal woman. Although she represents love, tenderness, compassion, nurturance, passion, beauty, and pleasure, she is also, fashioned by him, the composite of all the reasons why these traits were banned for men: She is weak, emotional, dependent, imprudent, incompetent, timid, and undependable.

Woman's place, then, as we shall see in detail in Chapter 3, is precarious and unstable. She is the object of love and hate, fascination and horror. As Venus, she carries traits that are at once beautiful and terrible, seductive and dangerous; hence she may be held and tolerated by men but only so long as she serves and is controlled, like feelings within. Adored and reviled, worshiped and enslaved, the image of woman as well as her "place" is the natural outcome of masculist values and needs. More than a convenience (which it is), the subordination of women is a necessity in patriarchy. Economically, politically, biologically, and psychologically, it is the foundation on which the entire structure rests.

Notes

[1] Marc Feigen Fasteau, *The Male Machine* (New York: McGraw-Hill, 1974), p. 144.

[2] Lucy Komisar, "Violence and the Masculine Mystique," *Washington Monthly*, 2, No. 5 (July 1970), 45.

[3]Deborah S. David and Robert Brannon, eds., *The Forty-Nine Percent Majority: The Male Sex Role* (Reading, MA: Addison-Wesley, 1976).

[4]Ibid., pp. 13–35.

[5]William G. Sumner, *Folkways* (Boston: Ginn and Co., Publishers, 1907).

[6]In Chapter 3 you will see that women face many of the same problems, cast differently, that men face in dealing with their sex roles.

[7]Mary Daly, *Beyond God the Father* (Boston: Beacon Press, 1973), ch. 4.

Men as "Gendered Beings"

Michael S. Kimmel and Michael Messner

Sociologist Michael S. Kimmel teaches courses on gender and social theory at State University of New York at Stony Brook. His books include Changing Men: New Directions in Research on Men and Masculinity *(1987) and* Men Confronting Pornography. *Michael Messner teaches sociology in the Program for the Study of Women and Men in Society at the University of Southern California. He has authored* Sport, Man and the Gender Order: Critical Feminist Perspectives *with D. F. Sabo (1989) and is working on a second book on sports and gender, tentatively titled* Masculinity and Sports: The Lives of Male Athletes *(forthcoming, Beacon Press).*

Kimmel and Messner explain that although men as well as women come to know themselves "through the prism of gender," for men that prism is generally invisible, and they often view themselves as society does: human, generic person. Since the women's movement, some men are beginning to examine themselves as males, *as gendered beings, and they are studying the effects of their masculinity on society.*

BUT WHAT DOES IT MEAN TO EXAMINE MEN "AS men"? Most courses in a college curriculum are about men, aren't they? But these courses routinely deal with men only in their public roles, so we come to know and understand men as scientists, politicians, military figures, writers, and philosophers. Rarely, if ever, are men understood through the prism of gender.

But listen to some male voices from some of these "ungendered" courses. Take, for example, composer Charles Ives, debunking "sissy" types of music; he said he used traditional tough guy themes and concerns in his drive to build new sounds and structures out of the popular musical idiom (cf. Wilkinson, 1986: 103). Or architect Louis Sullivan, describing his ambition to create "masculine forms": strong, solid, commanding respect. Or novelist Ernest Hemingway, retaliating against literary enemies by portraying them as impotent or homosexual.

Consider also political figures, such as Cardinal Richelieu, the seventeenth-century French First Minister to Louis XIII, who insisted that it was "necessary to have masculine virtue and do everything by reason" (cited in Elliott, 1984: 20). Closer to home, recall President Lyndon Baines Johnson's dismissal of a political adversary: "Oh him. He has to squat to piss!" Or his boast that during the Tet offensive in the Vietnam War, he "didn't just screw Ho Chi Minh. I cut his pecker off!"

Democrats have no monopoly on unexamined gender coloring their political rhetoric. Richard Nixon was "afraid of being acted upon, of being inactive, of being soft, or being thought impotent, of being dependent upon anyone else," according to his biographer, Bruce Mazlish. And don't forget Vice-President George Bush's revealing claim that in his television debate with Democratic challenger Geraldine Ferraro he had "kicked ass."

(That few political pundits criticized such unapologetic glee concerning violence against women is again indicative of how invisible gender issues are in our culture.) Indeed, recent political campaigns have revolved, in part, around gender issues, as each candidate attempted to demonstrate that he was not a "wimp" but was a "real man." (Of course, the few successful female politicians face the double task of convincing the electorate that they are not the "weak-willed wimps" that their gender implies in the public mind while *at the same time* demonstrating that they are "real women.")

These are just a few examples of what we might call gendered speech, language that uses gender terms to make its case. And these are just a few of the thousands of examples one could find in every academic discipline of how men's lives are organized around gender issues, and how gender remains one of the organizing principles of social life. We come to know ourselves and our world through the prism of gender. Only we act as if we didn't know it.

Fortunately, in recent years, the pioneering work of feminist scholars, both in traditional disciplines and in women's studies, and of feminist women in the political arena has made us aware of the centrality of gender in our lives. Gender, these scholars have demonstrated, is a central feature of social life, one of the central organizing principles around which our lives revolve. In the social sciences, gender has now taken its place alongside class and race as the three central mechanisms by which power and resources are distributed in our society, and the three central themes out of which we fashion the meanings of our lives.

We certainly understand how this works for women. Through women's studies courses and also in courses about women in traditional disciplines, students have explored the complexity of women's lives, the hidden history of exemplary women, and the daily experiences of women in the routines of their lives. For women, we know how gender works as one of the formative elements out of which social life is organized.

The Invisibility of Gender: A Sociological Explanation

Too often, though, we treat men as if they had no gender, as if only their public personae were of interest to us as students and scholars, as if their interior

experience of gender was of no significance. This became evident when one of us was in a graduate seminar on Feminist Theory several years ago. A discussion between a white woman and a black woman revolved around the question of whether their similarities as women were greater than their racial differences as black and white. The white woman asserted that the fact that they were both women bonded them, in spite of their racial differences. The black woman disagreed.

"When you wake up in the morning and look in the mirror, what do you see?" she asked.

"I see a woman," replied the white woman.

"That's precisely the issue," replied the black woman. "I see a black woman. For me, race is visible every day, because it is how I am not privileged in this culture. Race is invisible to you, which is why our alliance will always seem somewhat false to me."

Witnessing this exchange, Michael Kimmel was startled. When *he* looked in the mirror in the morning, he saw, as he put it, "a human being: universally generalizable. The generic person." What had been concealed—that he possessed both race and gender—had become strikingly visible. As a white man, he was able not to think about the ways in which gender and race had affected his experiences.

There is a sociological explanation for this blind spot in our thinking: the mechanisms that afford us privilege are very often invisible to us. What makes us marginal (unempowered, oppressed) are the mechanisms that we understand because those are the ones that are most painful in daily life. Thus, white people rarely think of themselves as "raced" people, rarely think of race as a central element in their experience. But people of color are marginalized by race, and so the centrality of race is both painfully obvious and urgently needs study. Similarly, middle-class people do not acknowledge the importance of social class as an organizing principle of social life, largely because for them class is an invisible force that makes everyone look pretty much the same. Working-class people, on the other hand, are often painfully aware of the centrality of class in their lives. [Interestingly, upper-class people are often more aware of class dynamics than are middle class people. In part, this may be the result of the emphasis on status within the upper class, as lineage, breeding, and family honor take center stage. In part, it may also be the result of a peculiar marginalization of the upper class in our society, as in the overwhelming number of television shows and movies that are ostensibly about just plain (i.e., middle-class) folks.]

In this same way, men often think of themselves as genderless, as if gender did not matter in the daily experiences of our lives. Certainly, we can see the biological sex of individuals, but we rarely understand the ways in which *gender*—that complex of social meanings that is attached to biological sex—is enacted in our daily lives. For example, we treat male scientists as if their being men had nothing to do with the organization of their experiments, the logic of scientific inquiry, or the questions posed by science itself. We treat male political figures as if masculinity were not even remotely in their consciousness as they do battle in the political arena.

References

Brod, Harry, ed.
 1987 *The Making of Masculinities*. Boston: Allen and Unwin.

Carrigan, Tim, Bob Connell, and John Lee
 1985 "Toward a New Sociology of Masculinity" in *Theory and Society*, 5(14).

Chodorow, Nancy
 1978 *The Reproduction of Mothering*. Berkeley: University of California Press.

Connell, R. W.
 1987 *Gender and Power*. Stanford, CA: Stanford University Press.

David, Deborah, and Robert Brannon, eds.
 1976 *The 49% Majority*. Reading, MA: Addison-Wesley.

Elliott, J. H.
 1984 *Richelieu and Olivares*. New York: Cambridge University Press.

Epstein, Cynthia Fuchs
 1986 "Inevitability of Prejudice" in *Society*, Sept./Oct.

Farrell, Warren
 1975 *The Liberated Man*. New York: Random House.

Feigen-Fasteau, Marc
 1974 *The Male Machine*. New York: McGraw-Hill.

Gilder, George
 1986 *Men and Marriage*. Gretna, LA: Pelican Publishers.

Gilligan, Carol
 1982 *In a Different Voice*. Cambridge, MA: Harvard University Press.

Goldberg, Steven
 1975 *The Inevitability of Patriarchy*. New York.

———.
 1986 "Reaffirming the Obvious" in *Society*. Sept./Oct.

Hearn, Jeff
 1987 *The Gender of Oppression*. New York: St. Martin's Press.

Hrdy, Sandra Blaffer
 1981 *The Woman That Never Evolved*. Cambridge, MA: Harvard University Press.

Kimmel, Michael S., ed.
 1987 *Changing Men: New Directions in Research on Men and Masculinity*. Newbury Park, CA: Sage Publications.

Mead, Margaret
 1935 *Sex and Temperament in Three Primitive Societies*. New York: McGraw-Hill.

Pleck, Joseph
 1981 *The Myth of Masculinity*. Cambridge, MA: M.I.T. Press.

——— and Elizabeth Pleck, eds.
 1980 *The American Man*. Englewood Cliffs, NJ: Prentice-Hall.

——— and Jack Sawyer, eds.
 1974 *Men and Masculinity*. Englewood Cliffs, NJ: Prentice-Hall.

Tiger, Lionel, and Robin Fox
 1984 *The Imperial Animal*. New York: Holt, Rinehart & Winston.

Trivers, Robert
 1972 "Parental Investment and Sexual Selection" in *Sexual Selection and the Descent of Man* (B. Campbell, ed.). Chicago: Aldine Publishers.

Wilkinson, Rupert
 1986 *American Tough: The Tough Guy Tradition and American Character*. New York: Harper and Row.

Wilson, E. O.
 1976 *Sociobiology: The New Synthesis*. Cambridge, MA: Harvard University Press.

Patriarchy, Scientists, and Nuclear Warriors

Brian Easlea

Brian Easlea received a doctorate in mathematical physics from London University in 1961 and, during the 1960s, taught nuclear physics in various countries. He later studied the history, philosophy, and social studies of science which he taught at Sussex University until 1987. He has published on issues relating to both capitalism and science, and gender and science.

Lest anyone believe that masculism, martial values, or patriarchy is either not real or not important, this frightening piece should bring them up short. Easlea shows that the present "masculinity of science" may very well kill us. What is more, he offers an alternative perspective.

From Michael Kaufman, *Beyond Patriarchy*. Toronto: Oxford University Press, 1987.

IN A LECTURE AT THE UNIVERSITY OF CALIFORNIA in 1980, the Oxford historian Michael Howard accused the world's scientific community, and particularly the Western scientific community, of an inventiveness in the creation and design of weapons that has made, he believes, the pursuit of a "stable nuclear balance" between the superpowers virtually impossible. At the very least, he found it curious that a scientific community that had expressed great anguish over its moral responsibility for the development of the first crude fission weapons "should have ceased to trouble itself over its continuous involvement with weapons-systems whose lethality and effectiveness make the weapons that destroyed Hiroshima and Nagasaki look like clumsy toys."[1] On the other hand, in the compelling pamphlet *It'll Make a Man of You: A Feminist View of the Arms Race*, Penny Strange expresses no surprise at the militarization of science that has occurred since the Second World War. While acknowledging that individual scientists have been people of integrity with a genuine desire for peace, she tersely states that "weapons research is consistent with the attitudes underlying the whole scientific worldview" and that she looks forward to "an escape from the patriarchal science in which the conquest of nature is a projection of sexual dominance."[2] My aim in this article is to explore the psychological attributes of patriarchal science, particularly physics, that contribute so greatly to the apparent readiness of scientists to maintain the inventive momentum of the nuclear arms race.

My own experiences as a physicist were symptomatic of the problems of modern science. So I begin with a brief account of these experiences followed by a look at various aspects of the masculinity of science, particularly physics, paying special attention to the ideology surrounding the concept of a scientific method and to the kinds of sexual rhetoric used by physicists to describe both their "pure" research and their contributions to weapons design. I conclude with some thoughts on the potential human integrity of a life in science—once patriarchy and its various subsystems have become relics of history.

A Personal Experience of Physics

Growing up in the heart of rural England, I wanted in my early teens to become a professional bird-watcher. However, at the local grammar school I was persuaded that boys who are good at mathematics become scientists: people just don't become bird-watchers. I did in fact have a deep, if romantic, interest in physics, believing that somehow those "great men" like Einstein and Bohr truly understood a world whose secrets I longed to share. So I went to University College London in 1954 to study physics and found it excruciatingly boring. But I studied hard and convinced myself that at the postgraduate level it would be different if only I could "do research"—whatever that mysterious activity really was. It didn't seem remarkable to me at the time that our class consisted of some forty men and only three or four women. At that time, I was both politically conservative and politically naive, a situation not helped by the complete absence of any lectures in the physics curriculum on "science and society" issues.

In my final year it was necessary to think of future employment. Not wanting to make nuclear weapons and preferring to leave such "dirty" work to other people, I considered a career in the "clean and beautiful" simplicity of the electronics industry. I came very close to entering industry but in the end, to my great happiness, was accepted back at University College to "do research" in mathematical physics. It was while doing this research that I was to begin my drift away from a career in physics.

One event in my graduate years stands out. As an undergraduate I had only twice ever asked about the nature of reality as presented by modern physics, and both times the presiding lecturer had ridiculed my question. However, one day a notice appeared announcing that a famous physicist, David Bohm, together with a philosopher of science were inviting physics students to spend a weekend in a large country house to discuss fundamental questions of physics. That weekend was an enlightening experience that gave me the confidence to believe that physics was not solely a means for manipulating nature or a

path to professional mundane achievement through the publication of numerous, uninteresting papers, but ideally was an essential part of human wisdom.

In the early 1960s, while I was on a two-year NATO Fellowship at the Institute of Theoretical Physics in Copenhagen, the first cracks and dents began to appear in my worldview. I met scientists from around the world, including the Soviet Union, who engaged me in animated political discussions. With a group of physicists I went on a ten-day tour of Leningrad and Moscow and, equipped with a smattering of Russian, I left the group to wander about on my own and kept meeting people who, at this high point of the Cold War, implored me to believe that Russia wanted peace. I couldn't square this image of Russia and the Russian people with what I had become accustomed to in Britain and would soon be exposed to while teaching at the University of Pittsburgh.

It seemed to be a world gone mad: my new university in Pittsburgh awarded honorary degrees to Werner von Braun, the former Nazi missile expert, and to Edward Teller, the father of the H-bomb. The Cuban blockade followed; Kennedy, Khrushchev, and physics were going to bring about the end of the world. I kept asking myself how the seemingly beautiful, breathtaking physics of Rutherford, Einstein, Heisenberg, and Niels Bohr had come to this.

New experiences followed which deepened my frustration with physics and increased my social and philosophic interests. University appointments in Brazil gave me a first-hand experience with the type of military regime that the United States so liked to support to save the world from communism. In the end I returned to the University of Sussex, where I taught "about science" courses to non-science students and "science and society" courses to science majors.

The more I learned, the more I became convinced that the reason physics was so misused and the reason the nuclear arms race existed was the existence of capitalist societies, principally the United States, that are based on profit making, permanent war economies, and the subjugation of the Third World. My pat conclusion was that if capitalism could be replaced by socialism, human behavior would change dramatically. But I felt uneasy with this belief since oppression and violence had not first appeared in the world in the sixteenth century. As the years went by and the feminist movement developed, I came to explore the profound psychological connections between the discipline of physics and the world of the warriors—connections that are ultimately rooted in the social institutions of patriarchy. That is the focus of this paper.

The Masculinity of Physics

Indisputably, British and American physics is male-dominated. In Britain in the early 1980s, women made up only 4 percent of the membership of the Institute of Physics, and in the United States women made up only 2 percent of the faculty of the 171 doctorate-awarding physics departments.[3] This male domination of physics has obviously not come about by chance; not until recently have physicists made serious attempts to encourage women to study the discipline and enter the profession. Indeed, in the first decades of the twentieth century strenuous attempts by physicists to keep women out of their male preserve were not unknown. Symbolic of such attempts in the 1930s was that of no less a man than the Nobel laureate Robert Millikan, who in 1936 wrote to the President of Duke University questioning the wisdom of the University's appointment of a woman to a full physics professorship.[4] As the statistics amply demonstrate, the male domination of physics continues despite publicized attempts by physicists to eliminate whatever prejudice still exists against the entry of women into the profession.

A second aspect of the masculinity of physics is that the men who inhabit this scientific world—particularly those who are successful in it—behave in culturally masculine ways. Indeed, as in other hierarchical male-dominated activities, getting to the top invariably entails aggressive, competitive behavior. Scientists themselves recognize that such masculine behavior, though it is considered unseemly to dwell upon it, is a prominent feature of science. The biologist Richard Lewontin even goes so far as to affirm that "science is a form of competitive and aggressive activity, a contest of man against man that provides knowledge as a side-product."[5] Although I wouldn't agree with Lewontin that knowledge is a mere "side-product" of such competition, I would, for example, agree with the anthropologist Sharon Traweek, who writes that those most prestigious of physicists—the members of the high-energy physics "community"—display the highly masculine behavioral traits of "aggressive individualism, haughty self-confi-

dence, and a sharp competitive edge."[6] Moreover, Traweek's verdict is supported by the remarks of the high-energy physicist Heinz Pagels, who justifies such masculine behavior by explaining that a predominant feature in the conduct of scientific research has to be intellectual aggression, since, as he puts it, "no great science was discovered in the spirit of humility."[7] Scientists, then, physicists included, behave socially in a masculine manner.

A third aspect of the masculinity of physics is the pervasiveness of the ideology and practice of the conquest of nature rather than a human goal of respectful interaction and use. Although, of course, many attitudes (including the most gentle) have informed and continue to inform the practice of science, nevertheless a frequently stated masculine objective of science is the conquest of nature. This was expressed prominently by two of the principal promoters and would-be practitioners of the "new science" in the seventeenth century, Francis Bacon and René Descartes, the former even claiming that successful institutionalization of his method would inaugurate the "truly masculine birth of time." Although modern scientists usually attempt to draw a distinction between "pure" and "applied" science, claiming that pure science is the attempt to discover the fundamental (and beautiful) laws of nature without regard to possible application, it is nevertheless widely recognized that it is causal knowledge of nature that is sought, that is, knowledge that in principle gives its possessors power to intervene successfully in natural processes. In any case, most "pure" scientists know very well that their work, if successful, will generally find application in the "conquest of nature." We may recall how the first investigators of nuclear energy wrote enthusiastically in the early years of the twentieth century that their work, if successful, would provide mankind with an almost limitless source of energy. Both the "pure" and the technological challenges posed by the nucleus proved irresistible: the nucleus was there to be conquered and conquest was always incredibly exciting. Even in today's beleaguered domain of nuclear power for "peaceful" purposes, the ideology and practice of the conquest of nature has not disappeared. Thus, rallying the troops in 1979 at the twenty-fifth anniversary of the formation of the UK Atomic Energy Authority, the physicist chairman of the Authority, Sir John Hill, said that we will be judged "upon our achievements and not upon the plaintive cries of the faint-hearted who have lost the courage and ambitions of our forefathers, which made mankind the master of the earth."[8]

The masculine goal of conquest undoubtedly makes its presence felt in our images of nature and beliefs about the nature of reality; this constitutes a fourth aspect of the masculinity of physics and of science in general. That which is to be conquered does not usually emerge in the conqueror's view as possessing intrinsically admirable properties that need to be respected and preserved. Much, of course, could be written on specific images of nature, particularly with respect to "pure" and "applied" research objectives, and the subject does not lend itself to obvious generalizations. Nevertheless, it is clear that from the seventeenth century onwards, natural philosophers, men of science, and scientists tended to see the "matter" of nature as having no initiating, creative powers of its own (a point of view maintained only with some difficulty after the development of evolutionary theory in the nineteenth century). The historian of science, R. S. Westfall, is certainly not wrong when he writes that "whatever the crudities of the seventeenth century's conception of nature, the rigid exclusion of the psychic from physical nature has remained as its permanent legacy."[9] No matter what the cognitive arguments in favor of science's generally reductionist conception of "matter" and nature, it is clear that a nature that is seen as "the mere scurrying of matter to and fro" is a nature not only amenable to conquest but also one that requires no moral self-examination on the part of its would-be conqueror. "Man's place in the physical universe," declared the Nobel laureate physical chemist (and impeccable Cold-War warrior) Willard Libby, "is to be its master . . . to be its king through the power he alone possesses—the Principle of Intelligence."[10]

A fifth aspect of the masculinity of physics lies in the militarization the discipline has undergone in the twentieth century. Optimistically, Francis Bacon had expressed the hope in the seventeenth century that men would cease making war on each other in order to make collective warfare on nature. That hope has not been realized, nor is it likely to be. We may, after all, recall C. S. Lewis's opinion that "what we call Man's power over nature turns out to be a power exercised by some men over other men [and women] with nature as its instrument."[11] In the overall militarization of science that has occurred largely in this century and that was institutionalized during and after the Second World War, physics and its associated disciplines have indeed been in the forefront. For example, in a courageous paper to the *American Journal of Physics*, the physicist E. L. Woollett reported that at the end of the 1970s some 55 percent of physicists and astronomers carrying out research and development in the United States worked on projects of direct military value and he complained bitterly that physics had become a largely silent partner in the nuclear arms race.[12] It is estimated that throughout the world some half million physical scientists work on weapons design and improvement. As the physicist Freeman Dyson has reported, not only is the world of the scientific warriors overwhelmingly male-dominated but he sees the competition between physicists in weapons creation, allied to the (surely masculine) thrill of creating almost limitless destructive power, as being in large part responsible for the continuing qualitative escalation of the nuclear arms race.[13] Moreover, competition between weapons physicists is still a powerful motivating force in the nuclear arms race. Commenting on the rivalry at the Livermore Weapons Laboratory between two physical scientists, Peter Hagelstein and George Chapline, as to who would be the first to achieve a breakthrough in the design of a nuclear-bomb-powered X-ray laser, the head of the Livermore "Star Wars" Group, Lowell Wood, alleged: "It was raw, unabashed competitiveness. It was amazing—even though I had seen it happen before . . . two relatively young men . . . slugging it out for dominance in this particular technical arena."[14] And he then went on to agree with Richard Lewontin's unflattering description of motivation throughout the world of science:

> I would be very surprised if very many major scientific endeavors, maybe even minor ones, happen because a disinterested scientist coolly and dispassionately grinds away in his lab, devoid of thoughts about what this means in terms of competition, peer esteem, his wife and finally, prizes and recognition. I'm afraid I'm sufficiently cynical to think that in excess of 90 percent of all science is done with these considerations in mind. Pushing back the frontiers of knowledge and advancing truth are distinctly secondary considerations.[15]

One might, no doubt naively, like to believe that male scientists do not compete among themselves for the privilege of being the first to create a devastating new weapon. That belief would certainly be quite wrong.

Given such a sobering description of the masculine world of physics in Britain and North America, it isn't altogether surprising if girls, whose gender socialization is quite different from that of boys, are reluctant to study physics at school. What's more, it is in no way irrational, as British science teacher Hazel Grice points out, for girls to reject a subject that appears to offer "as the apex of its achievement a weapon of mass annihilation."[16]

Scientific Method for Scientists and Warriors

One common description of physics is that it is a "hard," intellectually difficult discipline, as opposed to "soft" ones, such as English or history. The hard-soft spectrum spanning the academic disciplines is, of course, well-known, and within the sciences themselves there is also a notorious hard-soft spectrum, with physics situated at the hard end, chemistry somewhere toward the middle, biology toward the soft end, and psychology beyond. Insofar as mind, reason, and intellect are (in a patriarchy) culturally seen as masculine attributes, the hard-soft spectrum serves to define a spectrum of diminishing masculinity from hard to soft.

But what is held to constitute intellectual difficulty? It seems that the more mathematical a scientific discipline, the more intellectually difficult it is believed to be and hence the "harder" it is. Mathematics not only makes a discipline difficult, it seems: it also makes it rigorous; and the discipline is thus seen to be "hard" in the two connecting senses of difficult and rigorous. The fact that physics, and especially theoretical physics, makes prodigious use of sophisticated mathematics no doubt contributes to their enviable position at the masculine end of the hard-soft spectrum. It is perhaps of more relevance, however, that mathematics and logical rigor are usually seen as essential components of the "scientific method" and it is the extent to which a discipline is able to practice the "scientific method" that determines its ultimate "hardness" in the sense of intellectual difficulty, the rigor of its reasoning, and the reliability and profundity of its findings. Physics, it is widely believed, is not only able to but does make excellent use of the "scientific method," which thus accounts for its spectacular successes both in the understanding of physical processes and in their mastery. While, of course, all the scientific disciplines aspire to practice the "scientific method," it is physics and related disciplines that are held to have succeeded best.

But does such a procedure as the "scientific method" really exist? If it does, it is deemed to enjoy masculine rather than feminine status insofar as it rigorously and inexorably arrives at truth about the natural world and not mere opinion or wishful thinking. Such a method must therefore, it seems, be ideally characterized by logically rigorous thinking aided by mathematics and determined by experimental, that is, "hard" evidence with no contamination by feminine emotion, intuition, and subjective desires. "The scientific attitude of mind," explained Bertrand Russell in 1913, "involves a sweeping away of all other desires in the interests of the desire to know—it involves the suppression of hopes and fears, loves and hates, and the whole subjective emotional life, until we become subdued to the material, able to see it frankly, without preconceptions, without biases, without any wish except to see it as it is."[17] Such a view of the scientific method remains incredibly influential. In 1974 the sociologist Robert Bierstedt could confirm that "the scientist, *as such*, has no ethical, religious, political, literary, philosophical, moral, or marital preferences. . . . As a scientist he is interested not in what is right or wrong, or good and evil, but only in what is true or false."[18] Numerous examples could be given. Emotion, wishful thinking, intuition, and other such apparent pollutants of cognition are held to betray and subvert the objectivity of the scientific method, which is the hard, ruthless application of logic and experimental evidence to the quest to understand and master the world. Thus while the philosopher of science Hans Reichenbach could tell the world in 1951 that "the scientific philosopher does not want to belittle the value of emotions, nor would he like to live without them" and that the philosopher's own life could be as passionate and sentimental as that of any literary man, nevertheless the truly scientific philosopher "refuses to muddle emotion and cognition, and likes to breathe the pure air of logical insight and penetration."[19] Perhaps that is why the Nobel laureate physicist, Isidor Rabi, then eighty-four years of age, could confide in the early 1980s to Vivian Gornick that women were temperamentally unsuited to science, that the female nervous system was "simply different." "It makes it impossible for them to stay with the thing," he explained. "I'm afraid there's no use quarrelling with it, that's the way it is."[20]

Now the view of successful "scientific method" as masculine logic, rigor, and experimentation necessarily untainted and uncontaminated with feminine emotion, intuition, and wishful thinking is completely and hopelessly wrong. Such a scientific method is as elusive as "pure" masculinity. If nothing else, the invention of theories demands considerable intuition and creative imagination, as every innovative scientist knows and often has proclaimed. Does this therefore mean that the masculine "objectivity" of scientific method is intrinsically compromised? The philosopher of science, Carl Hempel, explains that it doesn't, since "scientific objectivity is safeguarded by the principle that while hypotheses and theories may be freely invented and *proposed* in science [the so-called context of discovery], they can be *accepted* into the body of scientific knowledge only if they pass critical scrutiny [the context of justification], which includes in particular the checking of suitable test implications by careful observation and experiment."[21] Alas for this typical defense of scientific objectivity, for ever since the work of Thomas Kuhn in his 1962 essay *The Structure of Scientific Revolutions*, it is generally accepted that no hard and fast distinction can be readily drawn between such a feminine context of discovery and a masculine context of justification.[22]

For this is what seems to be at issue. Not only does the notion of scientific objectivity appear to entail a clear-cut distinction between the masculine investigator and the world of "feminine" or "female" matter, within the psyche of the masculine investigator there also appears to be a pressing need to establish an inviolable distinction between a masculine mode of "hard," rigorous reasoning determined by logic and experimental evidence and, should it operate at all, a feminine mode characterized by creative imagination, intuition, and emotion-linked preferences. However, such clear-cut distinctions neither exist nor are possible in scientific practice, no matter how much the masculine mode appears paramount in normal research. What certainly does exist (although not uniformly so) is a very impassioned commitment to deny an evaluative subjective component to scientific practice; we may see such a mas-

culine commitment as stemming from an emotional rejection and repudiation of the feminine within masculine inquiry. In other words, the impassioned claim that there exists an unemotional, value-free scientific method (or context of justification) may be interpreted as an emotional rejection and repudiation of the feminine and, if this is so, it would mean that scientific practice carried out (supposedly) in an "objective," value-free, unemotional way is in fact deeply and emotionally repressive of the feminine. This is a hornets' nest with all kinds of implications, but it may help to explain why much of modern science has, I shall argue, been embraced so uncritically by a society that is misogynistic and, in the case of the war industries, misanthropic as well. It is partly because patriarchal science is fundamentally antifeminine that its practitioners are psychologically vulnerable to the attractions of the "defense" industry.

We learn from Freeman Dyson that the world of the warriors, which comprises military strategists, scientists, and Pentagon officials, is ostentatiously defined by a "deliberately cool," quantitative style that explicitly excludes "overt emotion and rhetoric"—it is a style modelled on "scientific method" and directly opposed to, for example, the "emotional," "anecdotal" style of the anti-nuclear campaigner Helen Caldicott, whose arguments, according to Dyson, the warriors find unacceptable even when they manage to take them seriously.[23] For her part, Helen Caldicott believes that great rage and hatred lie suppressed behind the seemingly imperturbable, "rational" mask of scientific military analysis.[24] The military historian Sue Mansfield has posed the problem at its starkest: the stress placed in the scientific world on "objectivity" and a quantitative approach as a guarantee of truth, together with the relegation of emotions to a peripheral and unconscious existence, has, she maintains, carried "from its beginnings in the seventeenth century the burden of an essential hostility to the body, the feminine, and the natural environment."[25]

Sexual Rhetoric by Scientists and Warriors

The stereotype of the sober male scientist dispassionately investigating the properties of matter with, obviously, not a single sexual thought in mind is singularly undermined by the extent to which scientists portray nature as female in their informal prose, lectures, and talks. Indeed, according to the historian of science, Carolyn Merchant, the most powerful image in Western science is "the identification of nature with the female, especially a female harbouring secrets."[26] Physicists often refer to their "pure" research as a kind of sexual exploration of the secrets of nature—a female nature that not only possesses great subtlety and beauty to be revealed only to her most skilful and determined admirers and lovers, but that is truly fearsome in her awesome powers.

"Nature," wrote the high-energy physicist Frank Close in the *Guardian*, "hides her secrets in subtle ways." By "probing" the deep, mysterious, unexpectedly beautiful submicroscopic world, "we have our eyes opened to her greater glory."[27] The impression is given of a non-violent, male exploration of the sexual secrets of a mysterious, profoundly wonderful female nature. From the end of the nineteenth century to the middle 1980s, such sentiments have frequently been expressed by famous physicists. Thus, addressing the annual meeting of the British Association in 1898, the physicist Sir William Crookes announced to his audience, "Steadily, unflinchingly, we strive to pierce the inmost heart of nature, from what she is to reconstruct what she has been, and to prophesy what she yet shall be. Veil after veil we have lifted, and her face grows more beautiful, august, and wonderful, with every barrier that is withdrawn."[28]

But no matter how many veils are lifted, ultimately the fearsome and untameable "femaleness" of the universe will remain.[29] Even if female nature is ultimately untameable, scientific research and application can reveal and make usable many of nature's comparatively lesser secrets. It is striking how successful scientific research is frequently described in the language of sexual intercourse, birth, and claims to paternity in which science or the mind of man is ascribed the phallic role of penetrating or probing into the secrets of nature—with the supposed hardness of successful scientific method now acquiring an obvious phallic connotation. Accounts of the origins of quantum mechanics and nuclear physics in the first decades of the twentieth century illustrate this well. In 1966 the physicist, historian, and philosopher of science, Max Jammer, admiringly announced that those early achievements of physicists in quantum mechanics clearly showed "how far man's intellect can penetrate into the secrets of na-

ture on the basis of comparatively inconspicuous evidence"; indeed, Victor Weisskopf, Nobel laureate, remembers how the physicists at Niels Bohr's institute were held together "by a common urge to penetrate into the secrets of nature."[30] While Frederick Soddy was already proudly convinced by 1908 that "in the discovery of radioactivity . . . we had penetrated one of nature's innermost secrets,"[31] it was Soddy's collaborator in those early years, Sir Ernest Rutherford, who has been adjudged by later physicists and historians to have been the truly masculine man behind nuclear physics' spectacular advances in this period. Referring to Rutherford's triumphant hypothesis in 1911 that the atom consisted of an extremely concentrated nucleus of positively charged matter surrounded by a planetary system of orbiting electrons, one of Rutherford's assistants at the time, C. G. Darwin, later wrote that it was one of the "great occurrences" of his life that he was "actually present half-an-hour after the nucleus was born."[32] Successful and deep penetration, birth, and ensuing paternity: these are the hallmarks of great scientific advance.

At first sight it might seem that there is little untoward in such use of sexual, birth, and paternity metaphors, their use merely demonstrating that nuclear research, like scientific research in general, can be unproblematically described by its practitioners as a kind of surrogate sexual activity carried out by male physicists on female nature. However, not only did all the early nuclear pioneers (Rutherford included) realize that enormous quantities of energy lay waiting, as it were, to be exploited by physicists—"it would be rash to predict," wrote Rutherford's collaborator, W. C. D. Whetham, "that our impotence will last for ever"[33]—but, ominously, some of the sexual metaphors were extremely aggressive, reminding one forcibly of the ideology of (masculine) conquest of (female) nature. Indeed, since Rutherford's favorite word appears to have been "attack," it does not seem startling when one of the most distinguished physicists in the United States, George Ellery Hale, who was convinced that "nature has hidden her secrets in an almost impregnable stronghold," wrote admiringly to Rutherford in astonishingly military-sexual language. "The rush of your advance is overpowering," he congratulated him, "and I do not wonder that nature has retreated from trench to trench, and from height to height, until she is now capitulating in her inmost citadel."[34]

The implications of all this were not lost on everyone. Well before the discovery of uranium fission in 1939, the poet and Cambridge historian Thomas Thornely expressed his great apprehension at the consequences of a successful scientific assault on nature's remaining nuclear secrets:

Well may she start and desperate strain,
To thrust the bold besiegers back;
     If they that citadel should gain,
What grisly shapes of death and pain
May rise and follow in their track![35]

Not surprisingly, just as military scientists and strategists have adopted the formal "scientific style" of unemotional, quantitative argument, so they also frequently make informal use of sexual, birth, and paternity metaphors in their research and testing. Now, however, these metaphors become frighteningly aggressive, indeed obscene: military sexual penetration into nature's nuclear secrets will, the metaphors suggest, not only shake nature to her very foundations but at the same time demonstrate indisputable masculine status and military paternity. We learn that the first fission bomb developed at the Los Alamos laboratory was often referred to as a "baby"—a baby boy if a successful explosion, a baby girl if a failure. Secretary of War Henry Stimson received a message at Potsdam after the successful Trinity test of an implosion fission weapon which (after decoding) read:

Doctor has just returned most enthusiastic and confident that the little boy [the uranium bomb] is as husky as his big brother [the tested plutonium bomb]. The light in his eyes discernible from here to Highhold and I could have heard his screams from here to my farm.[36]

Examples are abundant: the two bombs (one uranium and one plutonium) exploded over Japanese cities were given the code names "Little Boy" and "Fat Man"; a third bomb being made ready was given the name "Big Boy." Oppenheimer became known as the Father of the A-Bomb and indeed the National Baby Institution of America made Oppenheimer its Father of the Year. Edward Teller, publicly seen as the principal physicist behind the successful design of the first fusion weapon or H-bomb, seemingly takes pains in his memoirs to draw readers' attention to the fact that it was a "phallic" triumph on his part.[37] After the enormous blast of the first H-bomb obliterated a Pacific island and all its life, Teller sent a triumphant telegram to his Los Alamos colleagues, "It's a boy."[38] Unfortunately for Teller, his paternity status of "Father of the H-Bomb" has been challenged by some physicists who claim that the mathematician Stanislaw Ulam produced the original idea and that all Teller did was to gestate the bomb after Ulam had inseminated him with his idea, thus, they say, making him the mere Mother.

Following the creation of this superbomb, a dispute over two competing plans for a nuclear attack against the Soviet Union occurred between strategists in the RAND think tank and the leading generals of the Strategic Air Command (SAC) of the U.S. Air Force. In a circulated memorandum the famous strategist Bernard Brodie likened his own RAND plan of a limited nuclear strike against military targets while keeping the major part of the nuclear arsenal in reserve to the act of sexual penetration but with withdrawal before ejaculation; he likened the alternative SAC plan to leave the Soviet Union a "smoking radiating ruin at the end of two hours" to sexual intercourse that "goes all the way."[39] His colleague Herman Kahn coined the term "wargasm" to describe the all-out "orgastic spasm of destruction" that the SAC generals supposedly favored.[40] Kahn's book On Escalation attempts, like an elaborate scientific sex manual, a precise identification of forty-four (!) stages of increasing tension culminating in the final stage of "spasm war."[41] Such sexual metaphors for nuclear explosions and warfare appear to be still in common use. In 1980 General William Odom, then a military adviser to Zbigniew Brzesinski on the National Security Council, told a Harvard seminar of a strategic plan to release 70 to 80 percent of America's nuclear megatonnage "in one orgasmic whump,"[42] while at a London meeting in 1984, General Daniel Graham, a former head of the Defense Intelligence Agency and a prominent person behind President Reagan's Strategic Defense Initiative, brought some appreciative chuckles from his nearly all-male audience in referring to all-out nuclear "exchange" as the "wargasm."[43]

What is one to make of such metaphors and in particular of an analogy that likens ejaculation of semen during sexual intercourse (an act, one hopes, of mutual pleasure and possibly the first stage in the creation of new life) with a nuclear bombardment intended to render a huge country virtually lifeless, perhaps for millenia to come? And what conception of pleasure was foremost in Kahn's mind when he coined the term "wargasm"—surely the most obscene word in the English language—to describe what he sees as the union between Eros and Thanatos that is nuclear holocaust? I find such comparisons and terminology almost beyond rational comment. Simone de Beauvoir's accurate observation that "the erotic vocabulary of males" has always been drawn from military terminology becomes totally inadequate.[44] Brodie's and Kahn's inventiveness has surely eclipsed Suzanne Lowry's observation in the *Guardian* that "'fuck' is the prime hate word" in the English language.[45] Indeed, given the sexual metaphors used by some of the nuclear warriors, one can understand Susan Griffin's anguished agreement with Norman Mailer's (surprising) description of Western culture as "drawing a rifle sight on an open vagina"—a culture, Griffin continues, "that even within its worship of the female sex goddess hates female sexuality."[46] We may indeed wonder why a picture of Rita Hayworth, "the ubiquitous pinup girl of World War II," was stenciled on the first atomic bomb exploded in the Bikini tests of 1946.[47]

Unconscious Objectives of Patriarchy and Patriarchal Physics

There has been much analysis of the Catholic Church's dichotomization of women into two steeotypes: the unattainable, asexual, morally pure virgin to which the Christian woman could aspire but never reach and the carnal whore-witch representing uncontrollable sexuality, depravity, wickedness, and the threat of universal chaos and disorder. During the sixteenth and seventeenth centuries such a fear and loathing of women's apparent wickedness came to a head in the European witch craze that was responsible for the inquisition and execution of scores of thousands of victims, over 80 percent of them female. A major historian of the witch craze, H. C. E. Midelfort, has noted that "one cannot begin to understand the European witch craze without recognizing that it displayed a burst of misogyny without parallel in Western history."[48]

Whatever the causes of the European witch craze, what may be particularly significant is that it coincided with the first phase of the scientific revolution,

the peak of the witch craze occurring during the decades in which Francis Bacon, René Descartes, Johannes Kepler, and Galileo Galilei made their revolutionary contributions. In *one* of its aspects, I believe that the scientific revolution may be seen as a secularized version of the witch craze in which sophisticated men either, like Francis Bacon, projected powerful and dangerous "femaleness" onto nature or, like René Descartes, declared nature to be feminine and thus totally amenable to manipulation and control by (the mind of) man. We recall how Simone de Beauvoir declared that woman is seemingly "represented, at one time, as pure passivity, available, open, a utensil"—which is surely Descartes's view of "feminine" matter—while "at another time she is regarded as if possessed by alien forces: there is a devil raging in her womb, a serpent lurks in her vagina, eager to devour the male's sperm"—which has more affinity to Francis Bacon's view of "female" matter.[49] Indeed, Bacon likened the experimental investigation of the secrets of "female" nature to the inquisition of witches on the rack and looked forward to the time when masculine science would shake "female" nature to her very foundations. It is, I believe, the purified natural magical tradition advocated by Bacon (with considerable use of very aggressive sexual imagery) that contributed in a major way to the rise of modern science. Believing firmly in the existence of the secrets of nature that could be penetrated by the mind of man, Bacon predicted that eventually the new science would be able to perform near miracles. And indeed the momentous significance of the scientific revolution surely lies in the fact that, unlike the rituals of preliterate societies which in general failed to give their practitioners power over nature (if this is what they sought), the male practitioners of modern science have been rewarded with truly breathtaking powers to intervene successfully in natural phenomena (we have become blasé about the spectacular triumphs of modern science, but what a near miracle is, for example, a television picture). Bacon's prediction that the new science he so passionately advocated would inaugurate the "truly masculine birth of time" and eventually shake nature to her very foundations has been triumphantly borne out by the achievements of modern physics and the sad possibility of devastating nature with environmental destruction, nuclear holocaust, and nuclear winter.

Clearly modern science possesses what might be called a rational component. In this article I am taking for granted the fact that modern science produces knowledge of nature that "works" relative to masculine (and other) expectations and objectives and that the intrinsic interest and fascination of scientific inquiry would render a non-patriarchal science a worthy and central feature of a truly human society. What I am here concerned with is the "truly masculine" nature of scientific inquiry involving the discipline's would-be rigid separation between masculine science and "female" nature and the possibility of an underlying, if for the most part unconscious, hostility to "dangerous femaleness" in the minds of some, or many, of its practitioners—a hostility presumably endemic to patriarchal society. A case can be made—and has been both by Carolyn Merchant and myself—that a powerful motivating force, but not the only one, behind the rise of modern science was a kind of displaced misogyny.[50] In addition a case can be made that a powerful motivating force behind some (or much) modern science and particularly weapons science is a continuation of the displaced misogyny that helped generate the scientific revolution.

Certainly a counterclaim is possible that modern science might have had some misogynistic origins, but that this has no relevance today. In disagreement with such a counterclaim, however, it can be plausibly argued that the industrialized countries have remained virulently misogynistic, as seen in the prevalence of violence practiced and depicted by men against women. If there is indeed a link between misogyny, insecure masculinity, and our conceptions of science, particularly weapons science, then we are given a way to understand why nuclear violence can be associated in warriors' minds with sexual intercourse and ejaculation. Moreover, not only does Sue Mansfield suggest that at a deep level the scientific mentality has carried from its inception in the seventeenth century "the burden of an essential hostility to the body, the feminine, and the natural environment," but she also points out that, if human life survives at all after a nuclear holocaust, then it will mean the total restoration of the power of arm-bearing men over women. This leads her to make a significant comment that "though the reenslavement of women and the destruction of nature are not conscious goals of our nuclear stance, the language of

our bodies, our postures, and our acts is a critical clue to our unexamined motives and desires."[51]

Of course, at the conscious level the scientific warrior today can, and does, offer a "rational" explanation for his behavior: his creation of fission and fusion weapons, he maintains, has made the deliberate starting of world war unthinkable and certainly has preserved peace in Europe for the last forty years. Whatever financial gain comes his way is not unappreciated but is secondary to the necessity of maintaining his country's security; likewise whatever scientific interest he experiences in the technological challenge of his work is again secondary to the all-important objective of preserving the balance of terror until world statesmen achieve multilateral disarmament. While well-known arguments can be made against the coherence of such a typical rationalization, what I am suggesting is that at a partly conscious, partly unconscious, level the scientific warrior experiences not only an almost irresistible need to separate his (insecure) masculinity from what he conceives as femininity but also a compulsive desire to create the weapons that unmistakably affirm his masculinity and by means of which what is "female" can, if necessary and as a last resort, be annihilated. (And it must be noted that scientific warriors can be supported by women or even joined by female warriors in their largely unconscious quest to affirm masculine triumph over the feminine and female.)

Conclusion

Looking over the history of humanity—the "slaughter-bench of history" as Hegel called it—I feel compelled to identify a factor—beyond economic and territorial rationales—that could help explain this sorry escalation of weaponry oppression, and bloodshed. It seems to me of paramount importance to try to understand why men are generally the direct oppressors, oppressing other men and women, why in general men allow neither themselves nor women the opportunity to realize full humanity.

While the political scientist Jean Bethke Elshtain may well be correct when she writes skeptically that no great movement will ever be fought under the banner of "androgyny," I suggest that it could well be fought under the banner of "a truly human future for everyone."[52] And that would entail the abolition of the *institutionalized* sexual division of labor. Men and women must be allowed the right to become complete human beings and not mutilated into their separate masculine and feminine gender roles. At the same time, I agree with Cynthia Cockburn when she writes in her book *Machinery of Dominance* that "men need more urgently to learn women's skills than women need to learn men's" and that "the revolutionary step will be to bring men down to earth, to domesticate technology and reforge the link between making and nurturing."[53]

In such a world "education" could not remain as it is now in Britain and the United States (and elsewhere). Certainly there would be no "physics" degree as it exists today, although there would be studies that would eventually take "students" to the frontiers of research in "physics." Needless to say, such an educational system would not be male-dominated (or female-dominated), it would not institutionalize and reward socially competitive aggressive behavior, and there would be no objective in "physics" education of the "conquest of nature," although it would certainly recognize the need to find respectful, ecologically sound ways of making use of nature. Moreover, images of nature would, I suspect, undergo some profound changes (with probably major changes to some theories as well), and clearly in a truly human world there would be no militarization of physics. As for the "scientific method," this would be recognized to be a somewhat mysterious activity, perhaps never completely specifiable, certainly an activity making use of the full range of *human* capacities from creative intuition to the most rigorous logical reasoning.

As for sexual imagery, that would surely thrive in the new truly human activity of scientific research, given that sexual relations—deprived of the hatred that now so greatly distorts sexuality—would continue to provide not only much of the motivation but also the metaphors for describing scientific activity (and much else). Consider, for example, the language of a woman who was awarded just about every honor the discipline of astrophysics could bestow (but only after she spent years challenging blatant sexism and discrimination). The images invoked by Cecilia Payne-Gaposchkin are more directly erotic than the "equivalent" sexual imagery used by male scientists and physicists (not to mention their frequent aggressive imagery); her language was of her friendship, her love, her delight, her ecstasy with the world of "male" stars and galaxies. Writing of nature as female, Payne-Gaposchkin advises her fellow researchers: "Nature has always had a trick of surprising us, and she will continue to surprise us. But she has never let us down yet. We can go forward with confidence,

> *Knowing that nature never did betray*
> *The heart that loved her.*"[54]

But it was an embrace of relatedness that Payne-Gaposchkin had sought and which had given her great satisfaction throughout her life, the satisfaction arising, in the words of Peggy Kidwell, from a sustained impassioned, loving endeavor "to unravel the mysteries of the stars."[55] In a truly human world, the principal purpose and result of science, as Erwin Schrödinger once said, will surely be to enhance "the general joy of living."[56]

Notes

I am most grateful to Michael Kaufman for his extremely skillful pruning of a very long manuscript.

[1] Michael Howard, "On Fighting a Nuclear War," in Michael Howard, *The Causes of War and Other Essays* (London: Temple Smith, 1983), 136.

[2] Penny Strange, *It'll Make a Man of You* (Nottingham, England: Mushroom Books with Peace News, 1983), 24–5.

[3] These statistics are taken from *Girls and Physics: A Report by the Joint Physics Education Committee of the Royal Society and the Institute of Physics* (London, 1982), 8, and Lilli S. Hornig, "Women in Science and Engineering: Why So Few?" *Technology Review* 87 (November/December, 1984), 41.

[4] See Margaret W. Rossiter, *Women Scientists in America: Struggles and Strategies to 1940* (Baltimore: Johns Hopkins University Press, 1982), 190–1.

[5] Richard Lewontin, "'Honest Jim' Watson's Big Thriller, about DNA," Chicago *Sun Times*, 25 Feb. 1968, 1–2, reprinted in James D. Watson, *The Double Helix . . . A New Critical Edition*, edited by Gunther S. Stent (London: Weidenfeld, 1981), 186.

[6] Sharon Traweek, "High-Energy Physics: A Male Preserve," *Technology Review* (November/December, 1984), 42–3; see also her *Particle Physics Culture: Buying Time and Taking Space* (1987), forthcoming.

[7] Heinz Pagels, *The Cosmic Code: Quantum Physics as the Language of Nature* (London: Michael Joseph, 1982), 338.

[8]Sir John Hill, "The Quest for Public Acceptance of Nuclear Power," *Atom*, no. 273 (1979): 166–72.

[9]Richard S. Westfall, *The Construction of Modern Science* (1971; Cambridge: Cambridge University Press, 1977), 41. It should be noted, however, that quantum mechanics is essentially an antireductionist theory; see, for example, the (controversial) book by Fritjof Capra, *The Tao of Physics* (London: Fontana, 1976).

[10]Willard Libby, "Man's Place in the Physical Universe," in John R. Platt, ed., *New Views of the Nature of Man* (Chicago: University of Chicago Press, 1965), 14–15.

[11]C. S. Lewis, *The Abolition of Man* (1943; London: Geoffrey Bles, 1946), 40.

[12]E. L. Woollett, "Physics and Modern Warfare: The Awkward Silence," *American Journal of Physics* 48 (1980): 104–11.

[13]Freeman Dyson, *Weapons and Hope* (New York: Harper and Row, 1984), 41–2.

[14]William J. Broad, *Star Warriors: A Penetrating Look into the Lives of the Young Scientists Behind Our Space Age Weaponry* (New York: Simon and Schuster, 1985), 204.

[15]*Ibid.*

[16]Hazel Grice, letter to the *Guardian*, 9 Oct. 1984, 20.

[17]Bertrand Russell, "Science in a Liberal Education," the *New Statesman* (1913) reprinted in *Mysticism and Logic and Other Essays* (Harmondsworth: Penguin, 1953), 47–8.

[18]Robert Bierstedt, *The Social Order* (1957; New York: McGraw-Hill, 1974), 26.

[19]Hans Reichenbach, *The Rise of Scientific Philosophy* (1951; Berkeley and Los Angeles: California University Press, 1966), 312.

[20]Vivian Gornick, *Women in Science: Portraits from a World in Transition* (New York: Simon and Schuster, 1984), 36.

[21]Carl Hempel, *Philosophy of Natural Science* (Englewood Cliffs, N.J.: Prentice-Hall, 1966), 16.

[22]See, for example, Imre Lakatos and Alan Musgrave, eds., *Criticism and the Growth of Knowledge* (Cambridge: Cambridge University Press, 1970), Sandra Harding, "Is Gender a Variable in Conceptions of Rationality? A Survey of Issues," *Dialectica: International Journal of Philosophy of Knowledge* 36 (1982): 225–42, and Harry M. Collins, ed., special issue of *Social Studies of Science* 11 (1981): 3–158, "Knowledge and Controversy: Studies of Modern Natural Science."

[23]Freeman Dyson, *Weapons and Hope*, 4–6.

[24]Helen Caldicott, "Etiology: Missile Envy and Other Psychopathology," in her *Missile Envy: The Arms Race and Nuclear War* (New York: William Morrow, 1984).

[25]Sue Mansfield, *The Gestalts of War: An Inquiry into Its Origins and Meaning as a Social Institution* (New York: Dial Press, 1982), 224.

[26]Carolyn Merchant, "Isis' Consciousness Raised," *Isis* 73 (1982): 398–409.

[27]Frank Close, "And now at last, the quark to top them all," the *Guardian*, 19 July 1984, 13, and "A shining example of what ought to be impossible," the *Guardian*, 8 Aug. 1985, 13.

[28]Sir William Crookes, quoted in E. E. Fournier d'Albe, *The Life of Sir William Crookes* (London: Fisher Unwin, 1923), 365.

[29]See, for example, the physicist Paul Davies's account of "black holes," "naked singularities," and "cosmic anarchy" in his *The Edge of Infinity: Naked Singularities and the Destruction of Space-time* (London: Dent, 1981), especially 92–3, 114, 145.

[30]Max Jammer, *The Conceptual Development of Quantum Mechanics* (New York: McGraw-Hill, 1966), 61, and Victor Weisskopf, "Niels Bohr and International Scientific Collaboration," in S. Rozenthal, ed., *Niels Bohr: His Life and Work as Seen by His Friends and Colleagues* (Amsterdam: North Holland, 1967), 262.

[31]Frederick Soddy, *The Interpretation of Radium* (London, 1909), 234.

[32]C. G. Darwin quoted in A. S. Eve, *Rutherford* (Cambridge: Cambridge University Press, 1939), 199, 434.

[33]W. C. D. Whetham, *The Recent Development of Physical Science* (London: Murray, 1904), 242.

[34]G. E. Hale quoted in Helen Wright, *Explorer of the Universe: A Biography of George Ellery Hale* (New York: Dutton, 1966), 283, and in A. S. Eve, *Rutherford*, 231.

[35]"The Atom" from *The Collected Verse of Thomas Thornely* (Cambridge: W. Heffer, 1939), 70–1, reprinted in John Heath-Stubbes and Phillips Salmon, eds., *Poems of Science* (Harmondsworth: Penguin, 1984), 245.

[36]Richard G. Hewlett and Oscar E. Anderson, *A History of the United States Atomic Energy Commission* (Pennsylvania State University Press, 1962), vol. 1, *The New World, 1939–1946*, 386.

[37]Edward Teller with Allen Brown, *The Legacy of Hiroshima* (London: Macmillan, 1962), 51–3.

[38]Edward Teller, *Energy from Heaven and Earth* (San Francisco: W. H. Freeman, 1979), 151. See also Norman Moss, *Men Who Play God* (Harmondsworth: Penguin, 1970), 78. For general detail see my *Fathering the Unthinkable: Masculinity, Scientists and the Nuclear Arms Race* (London: Pluto Press, 1983), ch. 3.

[39]Bernard Brodie's memorandum is referred to by Fred Kaplan in *The Wizards of Armageddon* (New York: Simon and Schuster, 1983), 222. I have not seen the text of Brodie's memorandum. The chilling phrase "smoking, radiating ruin at the end of two hours" comes from a declassified Navy memorandum on a SAC briefing held in March 1954;

see David Alan Rosenberg, "'A Smoking Radiating Ruin at the End of Two Hours': Documents on American Plans for Nuclear War with the Soviet Union 1954–55," *International Security* 6 (1981/82), 3–38.

[40] Herman Kahn, *On Escalation: Metaphors and Scenarios* (London: Pall Mall, 1965), 194.

[41] Note that Gregg Herken in *Counsels of War* (New York: Knopf, 1985), 206, writes that Bernard Brodie objected to Herman Kahn's "levity" in coining the term "wargasm."

[42] Quoted in Thomas Powers, "How Nuclear War Could Start," *New York Review of Books*, 17 Jan. 1985, 34.

[43] Roger Hutton, (personal communication) who attended the meeting when researching the Star Wars project.

[44] Simone de Beauvoir, *The Second Sex* (1949; Harmondsworth: Penguin, 1972), 396.

[45] Suzanne Lowry, "O Tempora, O Mores," the *Guardian*, 24 May 1984, 17.

[46] Susan Griffin, *Pornography and Silence: Culture's Revenge Against Nature* (London: Women's Press, 1981), 217.

[47] Paul Boyer, *By the Bomb's Early Light: American Thought and Culture at the Dawn of the Atomic Age* (New York: Pantheon, 1985), 83.

[48] H. C. E. Midelfort, "Heartland of the Witchcraze: Central and Northern Europe," *History Today* 31 (February 1981): 28.

[49] Simone de Beauvoir, *The Second Sex*, 699.

[50] See, for example, Carolyn Merchant, *The Death of Nature: Women, Ecology and the Scientific Revolution* (San Francisco: Harper and Row, 1980), and my *Science and Sexual Oppression: Patriarchy's Confrontation with Women and Nature* (London: Weidenfeld, 1981), ch. 3 and *Fathering the Unthinkable*, ch. 1.

[51] Sue Mansfield, *The Gestalts of War*, 223.

[52] Jean Bethke Elshtain, "Against Androgyny," *Telos* 47 (1981), 5–22.

[53] Cynthia Cockburn, *Machinery of Dominance* (London: Pluto Press, 1985), 256–7.

[54] Katherine Haramundanis, ed., *Cecilia Payne-Gaposchkin: An Autobiography and Other Recollections* (Cambridge: Cambridge University Press, 1984), 237.

[55] *Ibid.*, 28.

[56] "Science, Art and Play," reprinted in E. C. Schrödinger, *Science, Theory and Man* (New York: Dover, 1957), 29; see, for example, Euan Squires, *To Acknowledge the Wonder: The Story of Fundamental Physics* (Bristol: Adam Hilger, 1985).

Dividing Lines: Men's Response to Women's Demands for Equality and Power

Anthony Astrachan

Anthony Astrachan has been a prize-winning foreign correspondent for the Washington Post *and a senior editor of* Geo *magazine and* Medical Economics. *He reports that his interest in men's responses to women's demands for equality and power began when he married a talented reporter for the* Washington Post *and saw the paper transform her into a housewife in its own eyes, his first example of the male denial of female competence and transformation of professional women into traditional figures that he describes in* How Men Feel, *the book from which this selection is taken.*

There is, of course, as much divrsity among men as there is among women, and that is expressed in the way each man responds to feminist insights and demands. Astrachan describes differences in men's reactions based on several variables, such as class, race and sexual preference.

Class

The class of gender crosses the boundaries of class defined by income, education, and power. Where the political and psychological dimensions intersect, men and women are indeed class enemies at many moments in their lives. (The oppressed class always sees the struggle more clearly than the dominant; so far, women have seen this more clearly than men.) But the human condition is that these enemies must love each other and often do.

The ways they love each other, the ways through this contradiction, this paradox, vary according to the familiar categories of class. Income and education do affect men's feelings about women's demands for independence and equality. So does power. Men treat women as equals more easily when they are sure of themselves and their money and power, or when questions of power are diffuse.

Blue-collar men feel the contradiction between their physical power and their place at the bottom of the male hierarchy, and they are more obvious than men in other classes about their need to treat women as underlings to compensate. They are more honest, or quicker to voice their anger and their fear, about changes in the balance of power and in sex roles, at work and at home. They find it harder than men with higher incomes and more education to overcome the traditions of their culture that prohibit treating women as equals, but some do so; at least one market researcher finds that blue-collar men express fewer traditional and macho values than stereotypes suggest, that some express higher expectations of intimacy and emotional support in relationships with women than middle-class men do.[1] This sometimes translates from talk into action. Lower-income men in my small sample and in advertising surveys sometimes do more housework than middle-class men, I suspect for the simple reason that their wives work but they still can't afford maids.

Middle-class and upper-class men are more affected by the psychotherapy subculture and by commercial trends, both forces that make some try, and others pretend to try, to understand and accept what women are doing. A higher proportion of middle-class men than either blue-collar or upper-class men is genuinely supportive of women at work. A higher proportion is also more likely to take a real share in, or real responsibility for, child care and housework. In both cases it's still a small minority that reaches the stage of association. Many upper-class men talk about their devotion to equality, but few give it in business management and only slightly more in the professions. In both groups their economic, command, and prestige power is real and they don't want to lose it. They are probably sincere when they talk about equality in their personal lives, and the proportion who treat their wives as equals, while small, may be as great as in the middle-class. But with upper-class men, I can't escape the feeling that it's more a matter of principle than practice because they hire maids and nannies, almost always female.

Middle-class and upper-class men, I found in my interviews, are more likely than blue-collar men to sense that there is something wrong about our effort to monopolize power, to keep women powerless. (It's harder for blue-collar men because they are further from real power.) Part of it is cognitive dissonance between our preaching democracy, human rights, and social mobility, and our practicing a kind of power politics that transforms gender and race into class. But I think our sense of wrong goes deeper than that. We know that mastery produces satisfaction, that competence means power and self-esteem. Conversely, we know that failure in mastery produces dissatisfaction, which turns into rage. We know that powerlessness, which we have made congruent with incompetence, is synonymous with low self-respect. We restrict women's mastery and deny them power even as they force us to recognize their competence.

Race

The black experience of the gender revolution is different from white and Hispanic for several reasons. Black women have been working outside the home for so many generations that the idea of women in the workplace was not as revolutionary for them or their men as it was for other groups. Black women in general are still at the bottom of the economic ladder, but the proportion with better education, higher-status jobs, and higher salaries than men have is higher than it is among whites. This means the balance of economic and work power between men and women did not shift as dramatically for blacks as for others in recent years. Black women have been heading families in larger proportions for at least sixty years, so the balance of power at home did not shift so dramatically there either. In addition, the women's movement originated in and focused on the white middle class; it was the creation of white women whom many blacks see as a threat to black progress. So it did not touch black women as deeply as white, did not stimulate them to offer as many challenges as quickly to black men as white women did to white men.

Despite this, the balance at work and home for blacks *has* been affected by the changes of the past fifteen years. Many black men identify with women's demands as an outgrowth of the civil rights movement. The proportion who strongly resist women's demands is probably greater than the proportion of whites, however, if only because they are more conscious of how little power they have and are therefore more sensitive to every erosion in it. Many middle-class black men think they see women with money and power all around them, and they are often more intensely hostile than their white counterparts. Many black women have come to recognize what they see as a double oppression, racial and sexual. So do many black men, like the Atlanta banking consultant who said, "Men have no control now, and they're looking for control. . . . You can't deal with your boss because he's white, and you can't control the home place because your wife is making as much as you do."[2]

Among poorer blacks, many men simply do not "feel like a man" because of their inability to find a good job, earn good money, and do even half the providing for a family. They may feel impotent (and sometimes turn sexually impotent), or they may abandon the families they start and then feel even less like a man. They may displace their anger and resentment from the economy and the white world onto women—and all the more so when they see black women who earn decent money and provide single-handedly for families. The men's economic disability has many causes. Thomas Sowell, an economist, and William Wilson, a sociologist, are black conservatives who argue that the psychological legacy of the past is more important than anything in the society as a whole in blacks' failure to advance economically. Most blacks who have looked at the problem disagree, blaming continuing racial discrimination, real if not always intentional, visible in an array of facts:[3] black men show greater increases in rates of chronic disease and mental illness than white men. Blacks are imprisoned at a rate four or five times higher than whites (and prison is not a place that trains men in sensitivity to women). The unemployment rate for black men officially is twice as high as the rate for white men and in fact may be much worse than that. (There is nearly a one-to-one correspondence in the increase in unemployment among black men and the increase in female-headed families over the years, according to Walter Allen, a sociologist at the University of Michigan.) Government welfare programs give no money to mothers and children if there is a man in the house. Yet many black men continue to maintain a connection with children even when they abandon the family in form or in reality—a sign that it may be possible to draw them into one of the main channels for men's participation in the gender revolution.

Hispanic attitudes resemble whites' more than blacks' because the place of *la mujer* was so unquestionably in the home that the movement of women into the workplace was a dramatic change for Latins as it was for Anglos, indeed even more revolutionary in most Hispanic communities than in the majority society. The myth that women are not in the labor force persisted far longer for Chicanas than for Anglos, though today the proportions for all women sixteen and over are similar. Hispanic men and women both insist that Latin machismo and the importance of the family are often misunderstood by Anglos, but their more accurate versions still emphasize the traditional importance of the father and the confinement of the mother to home, even if she demonstrates real strength there. A Hispanic woman who achieves an income or occupational level higher than her husband's arouses more agony in her spouse than occurs in any other ethnic group. Mexican-Americans often go on to say that the rebellion

against the forces of machismo and family by Chicana women has created a change that may be greater in the long run than the changes among Anglos. But the forces of change are attenuated by the Hispanic birthrate, 75 percent higher than that of the rest of the population (25.5 births per thousand compared with 14.7 for non-Hispanics), with a higher percentage born to women under twenty, which keeps more women from finishing high school and from finding better jobs. The birthrate of course reflects Catholic doctrine, but it also reflects the belief of many, perhaps most Hispanic males that manhood is demonstrated by the number of children a man has. My impression is that while the dynamics of power change among Hispanics resemble the Anglos', the proportion and the intensity of male resistance approaches the blacks'.

Region

I did the interviews for this book in cities and suburbs in four regions to make sure I did not fall into the trap of identifying any one place with the whole country. They were the East (New York and Washington), the Midwest (Chicago, Detroit, and two smaller cities), the South (Atlanta, Dallas, and two smaller cities), and California (Los Angeles and the San Francisco Bay area). My impressions reflect the conclusions of experts on the census data that the United States is becoming ever more homogeneous in many respects, though diversity is growing in others. I found the highest percentage of opponents of change in the South and a greater proportion in the Midwest than on the two coasts. There was a higher percentage of supporters in the East and West, but the Midwest came close to them in the proportion of pragmatics. I can't prove, but I imagine, that my impressions reflect such facts as the increasing similarity of all regions in education and per capita income, or the higher proportion of older people in the South. And the census data, of course, say nothing about differences in cultural values among the regions.

My overriding impression was that none of the differences was significant. Ambivalents were the biggest single group in every region. Anger, fear, and anxiety and relief, admiration, and identification can be found with equal ease or difficulty around the country.

Age and Stages of Growth

I did not find, as some of my friends expected, that older men uniformly tend to resist and younger men to support what women are doing, as though revolution depended primarily upon youth. It's true that men in their twenties today grew up with feminism in the air they breathed, and with an informality between the sexes that has many causes besides feminism. Many of them are freer of sex-role stereotypes than older men are. In surveys they profess more support for the equality of women than do older men or the male population as a whole, and a few studies say that (in much smaller proportions) they are more likely to live up to their professions. It's also true that men in their sixties are often more devoted to, or more the prisoner of, the habits that go with the old stereotypes. But in every season of a man's life from his twenties through his fifties, I found opponents, ambivalents, pragmatists, and supporters.

Looking at men under thirty, I found more who speak in terms of equality than those in any other age group, of equality within marriage and equality for women at work. But there are just as many in this group who assume power or privilege as there are true egalitarians. Many expect their wives to have careers, for instance, but also expect those careers to take second place to their own. Many become angry or fearful when they compete against women in the workplace. The under-thirties are traditional in tending to start relationships and initiate sex more often than the women they know, as the few women I interviewed confirm. They are often unsure how to treat single women and more cautious—from fear or anxiety—about marriage, so they postpone it. (The proportion of men between twenty-five and twenty-nine who are single grew from 23 to 38 percent between 1960 and 1984.[4]) But young men are better able to say no to a woman's initiative than are their elders, and better able to maintain nonsexual friendships with women.

There are also some who reject tradition without moving toward equality—young men who seem ready to let women assume the kind of dominance that used to be male. I met two who talked about being househusbands; half-consciously they expect their wives to support them in a mirror image of the old wage-earner ethic, and they have no idea how much labor is involved in child raising. Three had little idea of how they wanted to earn a living, little

concept of a career—like women before the recent changes. They are no doubt responding to the changes women are making, but hardly in an egalitarian fashion.

The most traditional of the under-thirties are blue-collar men for whom the factory is the place where they pass from the worlds of home and school, which they see as being run by women, to a world run by men. A woman personnel manager in the heavy equipment plant mentioned in Chapter 5, who dealt every day with the workers, saw this, and I heard her thought echoed in many men's conversations. She said:

> Women who come to work in the factory are violating not only the man's sense of family but his sense of order in the world. Look at the world the man-child grows up in: up to the eighth grade it's run almost entirely by women—his mother and his teachers. Even in high school, there are a lot of women teachers—and the girl students affect the boys, whether they behave themselves or go wild. Graduation from high school and coming to work in the plant is graduation from a woman's world and coming into a man's world. When they see a woman at work on the line, it looks like, "Oh, Lord, here comes Mother back again."

Many of these men, even though they grew up in a world much influenced by feminist ideas, still see women primarily as sex objects, not as fellow workers. Many are more self-centered and less helpful than their elders to any peer; they give less support to women on the job than some older men who are uncomfortable with the female presence but have been conditioned both to help their buddies and to help ladies. And, as the personnel manager saw, many younger men think of the shop as the first place they will be members of a male world. Not all blue-collar men under thirty are like this, but many are—enough to remind people not to jump to conclusions or ignore the intersection of age with class.

Many men in their thirties, men born between 1945 and 1955, were closer to what had been predicted: old enough to have acquired traditional attitudes but young enough to have felt the impact of feminist charges and changes. Some tried to respond positively. Others were too unsure of themselves to resolve questions in a way that satisfied them or the women in their lives. Women looking at young men and at the thirties group often complain that they are getting neither what they asked nor the positive supports that accompanied the denial of equality in the old system.

Men in their late thirties and men in their forties were often in the position of marrying a homemaker and celebrating their tenth anniversary with a career woman. Some of these marriages ended in divorce, and the men in those that lasted probably struggled even harder to master the changing rules of the game. A *Ms.* magazine collective described both: "Some men who ran this gauntlet did not feel thanked enough. Some men who resisted change felt punished, angry, and occasionally guilty." That jibes completely with my interviews. *Ms.* added a point I didn't hear often, but which I find easy to believe: "Those feelings, once hidden, now surface as pained concern for the failures of feminism."[5]

Men under forty provide the members of two groups who have achieved prominence in the media, yuppies and new men. Both occupy a bigger place in middle-class consciousness than they do in the population. Yuppies acount for only 4 percent of the baby boom, the seventy-six million people between the ages of twenty-one and thirty-nine. This figure comes from an advertising agency measure of the consumer population; what could be more appropriate? J. Walter Thompson U.S.A. defines yuppies as people in this age group who combine higher education (five years, on the average) and high income (a median of $39,100).[6] Despite the *u* for "urban" in yuppie, the agency finds that 56 percent of them live in the suburbs and only one in six is female. This figure may say more about their employers than about the yuppies themselves, but it provides an important reason for my observation that yuppies are unlikely to treat women as equals: they don't meet them as peers in large numbers.

Yuppies, by definition, are devoted to acquisitive and career pursuits, and appear (to me, at least) to be more selfish and narcissistic than the population as a whole. This may give them additional reason to postpone marriage and treasure the freedom of the single state. No doubt it also affects their behavior in marriage; I suspect that much of what I read about remodeling houses and finding new recipes for wholesome dishes reflects a yuppie attempt to substitute material ventures for some of the psychological effort needed to build intimacy and make a marriage last. I wonder if this makes for a more egalitarian marriage—it might, if the spouse were of the same kind—or a less. The first yuppies are now turning forty, and their behavior may change as they enter middle age and become more capable of thinking about others and integrating the masculine and feminine in themselves.

Thompson defines another 16 percent of the baby boom age group as would-bes, people with the same education as yuppies and presumably with yuppie values, but a median income of only $15,000—teachers, clergy, social workers, paramedics, college instructors. There's obviously considerable overlap between Thompson's would-bes and my service occupations, and a much higher proportion of would-bes than yuppies are women. Those two facts should make more of the male would-bes treat women as equals.

When I'm asked about yuppies, however, I think not only about that low 4 percent proportion of the baby boomers, but also of the downward mobility of the whole generation, including elite workers, workers, and housewives. Real after-tax income for families headed by a person aged twenty-five to thirty-four declined 2.3 percent between 1961 and 1982. The combined take-home pay of a two-earner couple in this age group is probably less than what each of their respective fathers earned on his own at the same age.[7] Now, that's a good reason for having no, or fewer, children. But—thinking back to my expectations of a group with a high proportion of women and a lot of service jobs—a man may not treat his wife as an equal if he earns no more than she does; it may only fuel his anger and his anxiety.

The new man is someone whom feminists, social scientists, and advertisers all search for. Barbara Ehrenreich describes the prototype as twenty-five to forty years old, single, affluent, and living in a city, "for it is among such men that the most decisive break in the old masculine values is occurring."[8] (I disagree on the single and I have doubts about the affluent.) He is usually able to choose his clothes, decorate his apartment, and cook for himself—abilities that certainly distinguish him from traditional man, even if, as Ehrenreich says, he uses these skills to demonstrate his class status. They also enable him to stay independent of the women who used to take care of his domestic needs, and he does indeed tend to avoid commitment, in the current phrase. "Sensitivity" is a touchstone for the new man, who claims that he knows how to be "in touch with his feelings." Ehrenreich has her doubts. "Quite possibly," she says, "as sensitivity has spread, it has lost its moorings in the therapeutic experience and come to signify the heightened receptivity associated with consumerism: a vague appreciation that lends itself to aimless shopping."

That fits with marketing definitions of the new man. Playboy Marketing Services describes him as single, separated, divorced, widowed, living with someone who works or married with a working wife, and making purchasing decisions. It estimated in 1984 that 64.9 percent of all men meet this definition, rather different from my estimate of 5 to 10 percent who genuinely support women's demands for independence and equality.[9] (See Chapter 17.) Advertising agencies describe him similarly, in terms of his willingness to do household chores (described in Chapter 9) and his propensity to make brand choices of products used in those chores, but they put him at 13 to 22 percent of all men.

All the surveys agree that men under thirty-five were more likely to show new-man characteristics than those over thirty-five. As I've said, I'm not so sure.

Hyatt & Esserman Research Associates did a poll for *Good Morning America* in 1980 that put the proportion of new men at 19 percent. They asked forty questions and defined the new man in terms of responses to the three that created the greatest division of opinion among the 752 men interviewed. The new man disagreed with the statement, "If women have children at home under six years of age, they should not work." He agreed that "when women marry, it's fine for them to keep their maiden names." And he agreed that "if both parents work, the wife and husband should take turns to stay home when the kids are sick."[10]

But two thirds of *all* men in the Hyatt & Esserman survey disagreed with the statement, "A man should never cry in public," and six out of seven agreed that men can be just as good at changing diapers as women. Those figures show how men in general have been affected by change. They are evidence for my feeling that it will be hard to reverse the revolution. But neither they nor the 19 percent of Hyatt & Esserman's definition of new men are going to make the revolution succeed. That will take another kind of man, or this kind of new man after he has gone

through or been put through profound struggle with himself and society.

Some new men are certainly over thirty-five, even over forty. Older men do seem to find it harder than younger men to accept women on the job, but there are so many exceptions to this that I mention it only with reluctance. I found several older men who were genuinely supportive of women's demands for equality and choice. It takes a man who is relatively sure of his own competence, his own achievement, and his own masculinity to feel and behave positively about the changes women are making. Not every successful man is positive about these changes; many hate them as denials of their own lives and values, their own manhood. But a large proportion of those men who do like what women are doing are successful in their own terms. That means many of them are middle-aged.

Older men who are egalitarian and younger men who aren't don't constitute a historical anomaly as much as they illustrate the process of adult development that Daniel Levinson outlined.[11] A young man in his twenties, in early adulthood, is striving to take his place in the world as an adult male. He is apt to try to control or repress the feminine in himself. That often makes it harder for him to respond to women making changes, whom he sees as competing for places as adult "males." A man in his late thirties usually makes an intense effort to achieve a more senior, "manly" position in the world. That often makes him neglect or repress the feminine in himself and also makes him more hostile to women engaged in the same effort. In the forties, the period of the mid-life transition and the famous mid-life crisis, a man becomes more able to integrate the masculine and feminine in himself—and, if he is not too much the victim of tradition, more able to accept and support women's efforts to achieve independence and choice.

Homosexual Men

Many homosexuals, particularly gay activists, talk in convincing and fascinating detail about the ways that the women's movement gave them courage to do two things: come out of the closet, and free themselves from the sexist culture in which they grew up. The two are intimately connected, but not identical; most gay men learn to accept and enjoy their sexual preferences before they discover the emptiness of conventional ideas of masculinity. Individual women inspired individual men to raise their consciousness (as happened to many straight men). Women's openness about sex encouraged gay men to be open about their sex lives. The collective militancy of the women's movement provided a model for the gay rights movement. The increasing numbers of gay men who have experienced these things identify strongly with women's demands for equality and independence. Steve Borst, an actor, spoke to me about both the personal and political aspects:

> There was one woman, there was an enormous amount of love between me and her. It was through her consciousness, her struggle to perceive herself as a valid human being who didn't have to put up with heckling in the street and the vagaries of relationships with men and things like that, that I began to understand my situation and apply those principles to my gayness as something that was part of my self, that could make me stronger as a person and in society. And there's a political level on which something like this happened to numbers of gay men. The development of the civil rights movements in this country started with blacks, went to women, then to gays, it was a progression from visibility to invisibility. The blacks were the most visible to straight white males, the women were harder for men to see, and before Stonewall in 1969 [the riot over police harassment that is usually considered the start of the gay liberation movement], the gays were invisible. Now we're visible, to ourselves and to everybody else.

Friendships like Borst's with straight women are very important to gay men. They seldom have deep friendships with straight men. Friendships with other gay men face problems and tensions similar to those of nonsexual friendships between heterosexual men and women: they might become sexual, which changes the nature of love and trust. Seymour Kleinberg believes from his own and others' experience that "the richest, least infantile, and most moral relationships gay men form are with women."[12] Both are struggling to realize their refusal to conform to the demands of traditional society. "Abandoning arbitrarily assigned, restrictive, sexual role-playing . . . she frees the male from an equally restrictive, equally arbitrary opposite role," John Rechy says, elaborating

on the idea.[13] Women who have such friendships testify that the gay men neither patronize them nor treat them as objects as most straight men do.

Other gays say that it was their discovery, or rather their realization and fulfillment, of their homosexuality that enabled them to transcend traditional sex roles, to give up the efforts they had made since childhood to be "masculine" in the sense of repressing emotion or believing in "the system of leaders and followers," to "free the sister in ourselves" (an old slogan of the Gay Liberation Front).[14] They don't attribute this to friendship with a woman or the example of the women's movement. But a consciousness they think has been raised only through gayness still makes them identify with the changes of the gender revolution.

Gays learn early that they constitute an oppressed class, as women do. A few connect their oppression directly to their sexuality, which gives them something in common with a radical feminist like Ellen Willis. Kleinberg quotes a man who considered "the prodigality of gay promiscuity" as "a compensation for the injustices society has wished on us." Kleinberg says this struck him as more than mere defiance because it "implies that sexual obsession is not devoted exclusively to sensual pleasure but is much involved with an individual's sense of powerlessness."[15] Few straight men have reached an equivalent insight, which I think deserves to be included in revolutionary philosophy.

Homosexuals who give the women's movement credit for the start of their own liberation say that gays with other views probably make up a majority. Some compensate for their oppression by trying to dominate lesbians in gay activist groups, or women in their workplaces, acting very much like blue-collar workers or neurotically insecure men of any class in searching for people they can define as inferior—and finding women. An advertising man told me, "We want to be the equals of straight men, and if that means screwing women—figuratively—we'll do it."

Some gays would not care if they ever saw another woman. Some are clones who have adopted one variety or another of macho look, whether rigid Wall Street or heavy leather, and oppressive images of physical strength, sexual violence, and dominance. These two groups overlap; "the macho gesture is prominent in those gay bars and resorts where women are entirely absent," Kleinberg notes. He offers another important insight:

The homosexuals who adopt images of masculinity, conveying their desire for power and their belief in its beauty, are in fact eroticizing the very values of straight society that have tyrannized their own lives. . . . The perversity of imitating their oppressors guarantees that such blindness will work itself out as self-contempt. . . .

While straight men define their ideas from a variety of sources (strength, achievement, success, money), two of those sources are always their attitudes toward women and toward paternity. It is no coincidence that the same decade that popularized liberation for women and announced that the nuclear family was a failure also saw men return to a long-haired, androgynous style. If straight men are confused about their maleness, what is the dilemma for gay men, who rarely did more than imitate these ideas?[16]

Kleinberg sees gays as tending toward one or another of two alternatives: the macho life, or a species of feminism that derives from recognition of "the common oppression" of homosexuals and women. Both tendencies show that sexual preference does not insulate a man from the forces of change or the question of gender power. Gay men are participants in the revolution and the fight against it, and they, like straight men, must pay the costs even or especially when they struggle to make it work.

Notes

[1]Barbara Ehrenreich, "A Feminist's View of the New Man," New York *Times Magazine*, 20 May 1984, and "Blue-Collar Lovers and Allies," *Ms.*, September 1985.

[2]Diane Weathers, "A New Black Struggle," *Newsweek*, 27 August 1979.

[3]See Ronald Smothers, "Concern for the Black Family: Attention Now Turns to Men," New York *Times*, 31 December 1983.

[4]Census Bureau figures quoted in Alvin P. Sanoff et al., "The American Male," *U.S. News & World Report*, 3 June 1985.

[5]Nancy Chodorow et al., "Feminism 1984: Taking Stock on the Brink of an Uncertain Future," *Ms.*, January 1984.

[6]The study also lists elite workers, 3 percent of the total, with a median income of $34,852 but no higher education, and workers, 55 percent of the total, with no higher education and a median income of $10,036. Housewives and students account for the remaining 22 percent. Bert Metter and Peter Kim, "The New American Consumer" (Unpublished study by J. Walter Thompson U.S.A., New York, 1985).

[7]Bureau of Labor Statistics and Census Bureau data quoted in Phillip Longman, "The Downwardly Mobile Baby Boomers," *The Wall Street Journal*, 12 April 1985.

[8]Ehrenreich, "New Man."

[9]Anthony Astrachan, "Overview: Marketing to Men," *Advertising Age*, 4 October 1984.

[10]Ibid.

[11]Daniel Levinson, *The Seasons of a Man's Life* (New York: Alfred A. Knopf, 1978).

[12]Seymour Kleinberg, *Alienated Affections: Being Gay in America* (New York: St. Martin's Press, 1980).

[13]John Rechy, *The Sexual Outlaw* (New York: Dell, 1977). Two books describe friendship between women and gay men: Rebecca Nahas and Myra Turley, *The New Couple: Women and Gay Men* (New York: Seaview, 1979); and John Malone, *Straight Women/Gay Men: A Special Relationship* (New York: Dial, 1981).

[14]Jeff Keith, "My Own Men's Liberation" (Article distributed at a Men and Masculinity Conference).

[15]Kleinberg, *Alienated Affections*.

[16]Ibid.

3

Images of Women in Patriarchy: The Masculist-Defined Woman

The "Naming" of Women

. . . It is necessary to grasp the fundamental fact that women have had the power of naming *stolen from us. We have not been free to use our own power to name ourselves, the world, or God. The old naming was not the product of dialogue—a fact inadvertently admitted in the Genesis story of Adam's naming the animals and the women. Women are now realizing that the universal imposing of names by men has been false because partial. That is, inadequate words have been taken as adequate. . . .*

To exist humanly is to name the self, the world, and God. . . .

Mary Daly[1]

In a society where men have controlled the conceptual arena and have determined social values as well as the structure of institutions, it is not surprising that women should have lost the power of *naming,* of explaining and defining for ourselves the realities of our own experience. In a patriarchal culture, men define (explain, analyze, describe, direct) the female just as they define nearly everything else. The issue is not only that men perceive women from masculine per-

spectives, but also that given the nature of socialization, all members of society—including women—perceive the female from the prevailing masculine perspective.

The Male Identification of Women

It is argued by many feminists, and properly so, that women—sometimes directly, often indirectly—have had considerable impact on the structure and quality of society.[2] In primitive times women were very likely the inventors of pottery, food preservation, and other "domestic" technology; hence they probably also originated early forms of social organization. As teachers of the young, women have always done much to form the individual attitudes and values within the community, and our personal influence on one another and on men has long been recognized (although often maligned).

But informal networks and personal power are not social power, and the influence that women do wield is frequently deflected and counterbalanced—often distorted—by the subordinate and peripheral place we have been assigned in society. The attitudes and values we teach, the influences we mean to effect are often alien to us, originating not in our own perspectives but in sources we have inherited and internalized. We learn our roles and their attendant behaviors from mothers who themselves were bent to the yoke as we are meant to be. We attend male-dominated schools and universities. We read books, manuals, and bibles written by men for male ends. We learn about and care for our bodies through male physicians, institutions, and medical societies. We are exhorted and chastised by male priests. We model ourselves after images presented in media controlled almost entirely by men, who publish the newspapers and magazines, manage the advertising agencies, produce and direct films, and determine fashion trends in the great couture houses of Europe. Finally, through societally cultivated dependency, we place ourselves in the position of bartering our self-definition for "protection."

The naming of women has been effected by men primarily through control of the social institutions that determine behavior and attitudes. As social beings subject to those institutions, we have commonly (although not without exception) adopted the images wrought by that naming, often unaware that the ideals and visions we live by are of our own creation. From our first breath—from our entry into a world of pink and white ruffles; of dolls and docility; of behaving like a lady; of loving strokes for submission, quiet, and gentility; of cutout dolls in wedding gowns and Barbie dolls that develop breasts; of cheering on the sidelines; of applause for being picked; of frowns for "tomboy" activities, assertiveness, intelligence, and independence—from that earliest time before we can even question, we absorb an environment that teaches us a vision of femininity so pervasive and complete that it appears real; it appears to be our own.

> Being good at what was expected of me was one of my earliest projects . . .
>
> Girls were different from boys, and the expression of that difference seemed mine to make clear. Did my loving, anxious mother, who dressed me in white organdy pinafores and Mary Janes and who cried hot tears when I got them dirty, give me my first instruction? Of course. Did my doting aunts and uncles with their gifts of pretty dolls and miniature tea sets add to my education? Of course. But even without the appropriate toys and clothes, lessons in the art of being feminine lay all around me, and I absorbed them all: the

> fairy tales that were read to me at night, the brightly colored advertisements I pored over in magazines before I learned to decipher the words, the movies I saw, the comic books I hoarded, the radio soap operas I happily followed whenever I had to stay in bed with a cold. I loved being a little girl, or rather I loved being a fairy princess, for that was who I thought I was.
>
> Susan Brownmiller[3]

By the time we are old enough, wise enough, and angry enough to discard this vision, the seed planted in our infancy and constantly tended has so taken root—becomes so integral a part of us—that to reject it has almost the force of rejecting ourselves. Such is the meaning of saying that it is easier to fight an external enemy than one who has "outposts in your head."[4]

The alien definition of women, even more extreme than it first appears, goes beyond merely the producing and imposing of foreign images, beyond women's accepting these images as our own; it proceeds all the way to our accepting the status of not only less-than-standard humanity but of less-than-standard *being*, of "otherness."[5] "Otherness," in existentialist terms, is a social-moral as well as a personal-psychological assignment of women to the role of a less than primary, less than completely worthy human being. Otherness defines women as the "other half" of humanity, the half that helps, that *assists* in the work of society whether by staying out of the way or by relieving the primary beings of chores that would impede their work or by procreating. Otherness defines woman as satellite, adjunct, alter to man, but not as an end in herself. It accounts for woman being tuned to a servant consciousness, to *care for* before being *cared for*, to keep to the background in a place of her own, to yield to man's will, which is valued in itself directly *for* the world whereas she is only *in* the world. It accounts for women being told not to take jobs away from men, as if the jobs were somehow the cosmically ordained property of men. It accounts for wanting sons and deeming daughters less valuable.

Woman Identification Versus Male Identification: The Alternatives

The woman created in and by the male perspective is called by the women's movement the *male-identified woman*. The alternative, the woman-identified woman, is surely a feminist vision. She is a person who indeed understands herself to be subject (self), not object (other); she respects both her womanhood and her humanity; she takes her direction and definition from values that are her own, born of her own self-perceived qualities and goals as well as those of other women; she contributes to society that which she takes to be meaningful and does so in her own way.

Such a woman is only now evolving. In a patriarchal environment, hostile as it is to assertive, self-defined women, the processes of woman identification and of growth toward that new identity are perplexing, confusing, and arduous. The new images that feminists are laboring to draw are necessarily influenced by the struggle in which we are engaged.

What we shall see, then, in this chapter and the next, is a contest of visions: on the one hand, the male-identified ideals and masculist stereotypes; on the other, feminist responses and affirmations. The pictures created—primarily of women but affecting all humanity—are intricately interwoven by circumstance, race, class, nationality, religion, sexuality, age, and a host of factors, yet they are so different from masculist ideals as to entail two separate realities: patriarchal perspective and feminist consciousness.

Ideals and Images: The Masculist Definition

It is an extraordinary fact of women's lives that for centuries, across space and time and from culture to culture, women have been consistently treated with ambivalence, misogyny, and subordination.[6] These constant themes in the naming of women by patriarchal societies may find different expressions and may vary in intensity and effect, but they recur almost universally.

Although many have formed a variety of hypotheses, ranging from the scientific to the religious and from the accepting to the vehemently opposed, the origins and causes of women's subordination have never been definitely explained. Certain things are clear, however. The masculist images of women and the roles that these images support are socially constructed to create a situation very convenient for men in many ways. The patriarchal definitions of femininity provide the masculist with excellent rationales for the uses to which women have been put as well as granting potent sociopsychological advantages. The female role of helpmeet, for example, follows "naturally" from the patriarchal definition of women's nature; it provides men with tremendous privilege, power, and pleasure. Women are expected to serve men physically, taking care of their homes, property, clothing, or persons; economically, doing countless jobs for which women are ill paid or not paid at all; sexually, as wives, mistresses, or prostitutes; and reproductively, assuring men of paternity through female chastity. Because women do the "shitwork" of society (as the movement refers to all the work men do not wish to do), men are freed to spend their time on socially valued activities for which they receive all kinds of material and psychological rewards. From this use of women, men accrue extra time, energy, and power.

The image of woman as man's complement offers an extremely effective support mechanism for the masculist self-image: The softer, weaker, and more dependent the woman is, the stronger and more powerful the man appears; the more a servant the woman, the more a master the man. And the more the woman withdraws into home and gentility, the more the arenas of government and industry are left to the iron grasp of warriors and warrior values.

The misogynist picture of women as substandard—not quite human, incompetent, petty, evil, and lacking in responsibility and moral aptitude—stands as clear justification to the masculist for our subordination and suffering. After all, since we cause all the trouble in the world and instigate misfortune and disaster (Eve taking the apple, Pandora opening the box), it is natural and fitting that we should be punished for our deeds and controlled, lest we do further harm.

> *". . . in sorrow thou shalt bring forth children; and thy desire shall be to thy husband, and he shall rule over thee."*
>
> (Genesis 3:16)

Patriarchal society has indeed been well served by these masculist images; it behooves us to understand them. Although neither the origin or cause of these images can be traced definitively, feminists have proposed cogent conjectures that help clarify the issue.

Ambivalence: An Undercurrent

The images of women in our culture are fraught with contradiction: Woman is the sublime, the perfect, the beautiful; she is the awful, the stupid, the contemptible. She is the mother of god as well as the traitor of the garden. She is the tender young creature man marries and protects as well as the treacherous, manipulative sneak who tricked him into a union he never sought. Keeper of virtue, she is yet a base and petty creature, incapable of rational moral judgment, cosmically wise, concretely stupid. Explicitly or implicitly, women are represented as having dual natures, of being all that is desirable, fascinating, and wonderful yet also being extremely destructive and dangerous. Ambivalence toward a whole range of real and alleged female powers (birth, menstruation, seduction, intuition) expresses itself in a subliminal patriarchal belief that women have a great deal of "big magic," very much worth having but destined to go awry if not controlled and subdued.

No doubt, a variety of sources for such attitudes exist, but, feminists argue, we must understand them all within this important context: In patriarchy, images of women—like other conceptualizations—have been male created. The stereotypes of women, contradictory and conflicting, are male projections. As such, we must understand them as outward expressions of male attitudes. The dichotomy in the representation of women, therefore, is a strong indication of extreme ambivalence on the part of men.

In literature, psychology, philosophy, or religion, one comes face to face, again and again, with the ambivalence men feel toward women. They seek her, the eternal feminine. They want and desire her, but oh so much the worse for them! Men are exhorted by the stronger and more stoic among them to beware the lures and entrapments of females. In the first century A.D., Paul proclaimed the dangers of sin, sex, and uncontrolled women (all related). Centuries later, in language altered for "science," yet reminiscent of primitive mythology—toothed vaginas and grasping spiders—Freud offered the same caution.

Students of many disciplines try to account for the origin and cause of these attitudes. Certain sociologists, for example, have pointed out that ambivalence is typical of feelings experienced by any dominant group toward those it colonizes or exploits—a mixture of need and contempt, guilt, anger, and fear.

Many anthropologists, tracing a long history of male fear of women, place great emphasis on attitudes toward female regenerative powers and organs, so magical, so powerfully important and stirring, yet so utterly female and both mysterious and alien to men. Anthropologists such as H. R. Hays, Wolfgang Lederer, and Joseph Campbell point to the frequency of myths crediting the *first* birth to a man (like Adam). They point to menstrual taboos and blood magic, and they postulate that men feel strong envy for a power that they themselves can never have.

Psychologists, from classical times to the present, have pointed to male fears surrounding the sex act—fear of impotence, detumescence, vaginal containment, and other, more abstract matters, such as absorption by the partner, possession, or even castration. That the act of intercourse[7] is simultaneously perceived as a most desirable and also a fearful or dangerous experience may account for male ambivalence, in the view of many psychologists.[8]

That all these factors contribute to ambivalence is likely the case, yet I, as well as many other feminists, am more apt to seek the major source of masculist attitudes to women or womanhood in the intricate, primal dimensions of men's own gender identity, in the values and imperatives of the martial ideal.

Masculinity as defined in patriarchy, you remember, requires men to repudiate in themselves most of the affective components of human experience: It is imprudent to feel. It is very difficult, however, not to acknowledge feeling, and as a result at least two major facets of life are thrown into severe conflict for men—sex and an entire configuration of experience we may call *the tender*. These conflicts have direct bearing on male attitudes toward women.

Although it is surely true that the sex act is surrounded with certain fears and danger, I contend that it is not intercourse itself that provides the greatest conflict, but rather what sex represents. It is not the mechanical act of sex that has usually been presented as the great source of "sin" but rather the *enjoyment* of the act, the surrender to sex; it is sensuality and its attendant implications—fun, caprice, relaxation, nonstriving. Whether the language be religious (Paul warning against sin and damnation) or psychological (Freud fretting about the id and sublimation), sensuality and pleasure have been consistently presented as the foe of duty, the primary value of the martial ideal. The message is always the same: A man has a choice between duty (manhood) and indulgence (sensuality, pleasure, and self). If he chooses the former, he gains pride, identity, praise, and worthiness; if he chooses the latter, all he may expect is dissipation and disgrace.

For the masculist, *woman* and *sex* are nearly synonymous terms. The rejection of sensuality necessitates, then, a rejection of the object and instigator of sensuality—woman. If sex evokes mixed feelings—of approach and avoidance—most certainly woman must evoke the same feelings.

But the problem does not end here. The ambivalence goes further. Besides sensuality and pleasure, the warrior must also expunge from his character the parts of himself that either express vulnerability or render him vulnerable—fear, sensitivity, need, desire, grief, hurt, trust, and all the other traits, qualities, and feelings that are part of the tender. Because the tender is not allowable in men but is impossible to live without, patriarchy splits this element off from men and instead invests it in women, where men may enjoy it in greater safety. Yet even in this externalized form, the tender remains a danger that each man must guard against because he knows—though he would probably deny it—how easily he might yield to it, how much he wishes to yield.

In this light, we can understand male contempt for women's "emotionalism" as a rejection of emotions within; ridicule of female timidity as flight from timidity within; hatred of the woman without as fear of the woman within. The ambivalence, then, that men feel toward women is something we can understand, at least in part, as a displaced expression of an inner conflict so frustrating and frightening that it cannot be contained but must instead be projected outward, onto women.

That we should be the recipients of all these "bad" feelings is not surprising; it is common for minorities or out-groups to serve as scapegoats for the masters. But that we should function as the object of this particular displaced ambivalence is even more to be expected: We are, after all, the male-identified symbol of the entire configuration the male is required to excise.

Man has ordained woman as the carrier of all he dare not entertain in himself—and he hates her for it. It is as if mankind has said to woman: "Woman—be tenderness, be nurture, be vulnerability, be laughter, play, and fun for me, because I cannot be these things myself"; but then "You are all the things the great Mars has deemed evil and dangerous; and therefore you are evil and dangerous."

Misogyny: The Expression

Attitude is easily converted into judgment: *woman is desirable* is quickly transformed into *woman is good; woman is frightening* readily becomes *woman is bad.*

Misogyny—the hatred or distrust of women—is an integral part of masculism and patriarchy. Veiled by chivalry or a mythic masking of female roles (called *mystification* in the women's movement), it is nonetheless a potent force in the relations of men and women—and readily apparent should the veil or mask be rent even slightly. It is misogyny that underlies not only rape, invective, and abuse but also beauty contests, work segregation, menstrual taboos, mother-in-law jokes, "old bag" themes, patronizing etiquette, and current sexual mores.

Misogyny includes the beliefs that women are stupid, petty, manipulative, dishonest, silly, gossipy, irrational, incompetent, undependable, narcissistic, castrating, dirty, overemotional, unable to make altruistic or moral judgments, oversexed, undersexed, and a host of other ugly things. Such beliefs culminate in attitudes that demean our bodies, our abilities, our characters, and our efforts and so imply that we must be controlled, dominated, subdued, abused, and used, not only for male benefit but for our own. St. Jerome, Freud, the Rolling Stones, and numerous others have all agreed that when it comes to punishment women need it and love it.

The image of woman as victim is nowhere more acutely portrayed than in *Story of O,*[9] originally published in France and described by reviewers variously as "pornographic," "political,"[10] or "mystical"[11]—undoubtedly, all three. The plot is simple: O is a young woman subjected by her lover and his comrades to continual sadosexual torture and humiliation unto death, all of which (vividly portrayed in "erotic" images) both O and her lover willingly, consciously, even joyfully, accept as proof of O's love as well as punishment for her "wantonness'' (any little bits of self-assertion). During the course of the book, O is transformed from an individual to a totally degraded, totally pliant, totally selfless (in the worst sense) creature—a sexual garbage pail, for "love."

Many feminists have pointed out that what is important about the book is not the plot but the theme, as it is interpreted and responded to by its commentators. Jean Paulhan, in a prefacing essay significantly titled "Happiness in Slavery," describes the "mystical" theme in these familiar terms:

At last a woman who admits it![12] *Who admits what? Something that women have always refused till now to admit (and today more than ever before). Something that men have always reproached them with: that they never cease obeying their nature, the call of their blood, that everything in them, even their minds, is sex. That they have constantly to be nourished, constantly washed and made up, constantly beaten. That all they need is a good master, one who is not too lax or kind: for the moment we make any show of tenderness they draw upon it, turning all the zest, joy, and character at their command to make others love them. In short, that we must, when we go to see them, take a whip along.*[13]

Paulhan praises woman's uniqueness, her greater "understanding" born of childlikeness, her more primitive decency, requiring "nothing less than hands tied behind the back . . . the knees spread apart and bodies spread-eagled, than sweat and tears."[14] The other "official" commentator, Mandiargues, proposes that the theme is "the tragic flowering of a woman."[15]

Such talk is important. It is not simply an aberration but rather the expression of a vital and common principle of masculism: that woman is most adored, most exquisite, most revered when she is sufficiently selfless to be martyred. In O, self-effacement that would be repulsive in men, inimical to all the classical values of human excellence, is deemed mystically beautiful, fulfilling, and sacrificial. The Sacred Principle of Victimization[16] means that women are more conveniently exploitable and indeed more sexually exciting when they are stripped not only of clothing but also of power, strength, assertiveness, and sense of self. Should one doubt the relevance of such an attitude here and today, consider how titillating men find the newspaper stories of rape, the torture-murders of *True Detective Magazine*, the bent-over beauties in *Hustler* magazine, and the tough sex of current movies and rock videos. Because women are bad, they must be punished. Misogyny earns women torture of one kind or another.[17]

Stereotypes: Good Women and Bad

The ultimate ambivalence finally expresses itself in the ultimate bifurcation into good women and bad. The judgments of good and bad, like the images themselves, are male projections, resting not only on the extent to which any woman meets the specifications of her role requirements or adheres to the standards set for her but also on a particular male's needs and his attitudes toward that role configuration at some moment in time. That is, an image may be judged good at one time and bad at another, depending on its serviceability to those making the judgment. As the image is judged, so is the woman expressing that image. Meeting the complex imperatives of femininity is a tenuous affair at best.

All male-identified ideals of women rest on one basic presupposition: that women are and ought to be completely defined and understood within their biological capacities, sexual or reproductive. These capacities determine our "place" in the world, and we are only "good," one way or another, when we are (willingly or unwillingly) in that place. Should we instead stray—particularly through our own assertiveness but even by accident—then we are bad women and can only be redeemed if we are returned to our proper sphere.

In patriarchy, for women, "anatomy is destiny," and our physical capacities determine for us two separate and often conflicting roles—that of procreator-mother and that of sexual partner.[18] The "good" woman, then, each in a different sense, is she who serves, either in the capacity of excellent mother or of excellent mistress or both.

Mother: The Primary Ideal

The Marian image, Mother, nurture incarnate, is patriarchy's most positive image for women. This lady, charged ostensibly with the care of the young, is the complement of male power—she is tenderness, fragility, love, charity, loyalty, submission, and sacrifice. Carrier of man's seed, she is the essence of purity, totally absorbed in the activities and qualities of caring. Serene and satisfied within her role, placing the needs of her charges above her own, she busies herself with feeding them, watching over them, making them happy. Intuitive, cosmically linked with lunar cycles, she has special powers and therefore little need for rationality.

> *Just as in sexual physiology the female principle is one of receiving, keeping and nourishing—woman's specific form of creativeness, that of motherhood, is tied up with the life of nature, with a* non-reflective *bios. . . . Indeed, the four-week cycle of ovulation, the rhythmically alternating tides of fertility . . . the nine months of gestation . . . ties woman deeply to the life of nature, to the pulse beat of the cosmos.*[19]

> *I think, perhaps, that insofar as insight—the seeing into, the throwing of light into darkness, the intellectual illumination—aims at greater self-awareness and a more conscious functioning, it belongs into the mode or sphere of male development. The eternal feminine, static, perfect in itself, does not and need not develop. What any given woman does not know about it, insight therapy cannot ever teach her. Insight therapy, even in women, can only address itself to the masculine aspect. A given woman, through insight, can become more aware and more conscious, but not more feminine—although the balance of male and female within her may at times be shifted through insight which enables her to place less stress on male modes of functioning; in that case a covered-up femininity may emerge: but only as much of it as was there in the first place.* One *is a woman, one* learns *to be a man. Therapeutic theories stressing insight deal primarily with men because only men—and the masculine aspects of women—can be approached by and can utilize insight.*[20]

Womanhood, it would seem then, is closer to nature than manhood, more compelling as well as more disastrous if denied. One might wonder (and feminists do) how anything so "natural" and "instinctive" *could* be denied. Yet according to theory it sometimes is, and then not only do women themselves suffer, but the whole world goes topsy-turvy; it is askew, even in danger. Men lose their manhood, children become psychotic, society dissolves, and the natural order is disturbed!

In the language of the women's movement, the mothering role is *mystified,* covered over with a whole set of myths, fantasies, and images that hide many realities of the role and the person who lives it.

Playmate: The Illicit Ideal

Mother is the *official* good woman of the Western world. But another kind of "good" woman exists, good in a different sense, good in an elbow-in-the-rib or slightly déclassé kind of way—a sexy, naughty, fun-loving lady: the playmate.

The Marian image, the classic model of femininity in the West, born out of the fear and loathing of sex and sensuality rampant in the early Christian church, is pointedly asexual: pure, chaste, and virginal, despite marriage, wifehood, and childbirth. The good woman in this image, the Mother, is an asexual or even antisexual ideal, too pure for carnality. Sex is beneath her. She is patient, enduring, dutiful, submissive, and nurturing, *and she doesn't play around.* She's not supposed to, and she doesn't want to, not even with her husband. Hence her converse, the Playmate.

For the playmate, playing around is a *raison d' être.* She is built "to take it" and to give it. You can tell by the seductive, compliant look in her eyes, the parted lips, the knowing smile, the receptive, open posture of her opulent young body. But the playmate is no ordinary whore. She is interesting (bright enough to be companionable but not too bright to be uncooperative or threatening). She is independent (able to take care of herself but needful enough to succumb to male power). She is choosy (nobody wants something that anyone can have). She is even a little aggressive, a little dangerous—enough to make her a worthy trophy.

"There are two kinds of girls," a saying goes, "the kind you bring home to Mother and the kind you bring home to Father." Each has an attendant schema of responses and rewards. The playmate is for playing, for fun, not for seriousness and heavy obligation. She has waived her claims to adulation from afar. She isn't chaste so one need not hide "baser" motivations and appetites. Since she's not timid or naive, one needn't be solicitous or protective. She's worldly wise—no need for protocol, courtship, and protestations of love. Having opted out of "purity" and the category of the primary

ideal, she has abandoned the status and prerogatives of the "official" good woman. Mother and
playmate, lady and tramp, Mary and Eve, the dichotomy—familiar in novels, movies, and sermons—creates tension that puts women in a bind.

The Wife

It should be obvious by now that the two female
ideals, perfect mother and perfect mistress, are incompatible. No one can be chaste, submissive,
timid, needful, innocent, loyal, tender, and serene
and *at the same time* sexually wise, perky, naughty,
independent, and so on. Yet that is exactly the position into which middle-class American patriarchy
places women, for to be both Mary/Mother and
Playmate is the prescribed role and image of the
ideal woman—girlfriend, roommate, date, or wife.
Like the "hell of a woman" in a popular song lyric,
she is supposed to be all things to her hell of a man:
not just *act* all things, but *be* them—"woman, baby,
witch, lady." It's a difficult game, for even if she
wins, she loses—her identity, her self-concept, her
sense of autonomy, cohesion, and direction. It is a
schizophrenic setup.

The Dichotomy Dichotomizes: The Misogynist Flip

All that effort, and as often as not, it doesn't even
work. Each of us may indeed choose between a life
modeled on Mary or a life modeled on Playmate,
settling for the rewards of either role. We may even
manage to negotiate the tricks and turns of playing
both, but that still cannot guarantee us undying
love.

Circumstances arise over which none have control and in which Mary, the Playmate, or even Hell-
uvawoman may become a pain in the neck, an object of contempt, a creature to be avoided. Reflected
visions, after all, ultimately depend on the minds of
those who reflect. And the extent to which any of
these roles is prized (and consequently the woman
playing it praised) depends on how well it serves
the function for which it was created and how long
that function endures. Mary is desirable to one
seeking nurture, understanding, and mothering (for
himself or his children). But she rapidly becomes a
nuisance when that same man sets out to find exu-

berant or illicit sex. The playmate is fun when playing is what he wants, but she is an unsuitable
companion at the company dinner.

Each ideal is subject to a "serviceability" factor:
The status of the role itself, its value and meaning,
and even the language used to refer to it can shift
radically as its utility shifts or its context changes.
She who is "the little woman" in church becomes
"the old lady" at the bar; she who was seen as "a
good old girl" in graduate school may be seen as "a
slut" when he joins the club.

Within a single moment, depending on changing
attitudes or interests, the image may shift—good
becomes bad, bad becomes good. The nurturing
Mary becomes the old ball and chain, and very easily her innocence becomes stupidity; her chastity,
frigidity; her nurture, suffocation; her loyalty, im-
prisonment; her beauty, vanity; her earthiness, carnality; her children, obligation. The Playmate
becomes Eve, the Traitor of the Garden, she who is
trouble, and contempt mushrooms into hatred.

> *And I have found a woman more bitter than death,*
> *who is the hunter's snare, and her heart is a net, and*
> *her hands are bonds. . . .*
>
> *More bitter than death, again, because that is natural*
> *and destroys only the body; but the sin which arose*
> *from woman destroys the soul . . . bodily death is an*
> *open and terrible enemy, but woman is a wheedling*
> *and secret enemy.*[21]

This serviceability factor in women's role manifests more clearly than all the rest—including the
images that allege to portray her—that under patriarchy women's lives are meant to be lived not for
ourselves, but for men's needs, and our cultural images are defined by that fact. The major factor in the
flip from good to bad (that is, serviceable to not serviceable) is the matter of intrusiveness into male affairs; it has to do with women's self-assertion, self-
direction, and will. It is important to have Mary; it is
fun to have playmates—just so long as neither get
in the way. When a woman moves toward her own
needs, gets "pushy," or stands in the way of *his*
wishes, Mary becomes the Ball and Chain (alias the
Wif'nkids), and the Playmate becomes the Bitch.

As you look at the following chart, remember
that any or all of these images may be perceived or
expected from any one woman, sometimes at the
same time.

BASIC FEMALE STEREOTYPES

	Nonsexual	Sexual
	The Virgin Mary/Mother-Wife:	*The Playmate/Lover:*
Serviceable	chaste, pure, innocent, good proper-looking, conservative, matronly nurturing, selfless, loving, gentle, "mother of his children" submissive, pliable, receptive compromising, tactful, loyal fragile, needful, dependent feeling, nonrational, aesthetic, spiritual understanding, supportive	sensuous, sexually wise, experienced sexy, "built," stylish satisfying, eager, earthy, mysterious, slightly dangerous sexually receptive, agreeable, "game" challenging, exciting independent, carefree, "laid back" bright, fun-loving, playful, carnal responsive, ego-building
	The Old Ball and Chain/Wif'nkids:	*Eve/The Witch-Bitch Temptress:*
Nonserviceable	frigid, sexually uninteresting frumpy or slatternly cloying, suffocating, obligating incapable of decision, changeable, scatterbrained dumb, passive nagging, shrewish, harping helpless, burdensome overemotional, irrational, unreasonable shrewd, manipulative, sneaky	promiscuous, bad coarse, vulgar, trampy tempting, leads one into sin and evil undiscriminating she's "anybody's" bitchy, demanding, selfish; she "asks for it" immoral, makes trouble thoughtless, sinful, evil immodest, unladylike

Variations on the Theme: Ethnic Overlay

Since the men who make up and direct the patriarchy in which we live are mostly white, Christian, and middle class, it is not surprising that the primary models of womanhood in our society are markedly WASP. Across racial, ethnic, and class lines, one composite image prevails. The fragile, pale-skinned Madonna and the saucily tanned Playmate with flowing blond hair are clearly white, Christian images not even marginally attainable for the very large segment of the female population who are members of racial or ethnic subgroups. Yet, viable or not, these images continue to function as models, held up to us either as ideals we must strain to copy in whatever meager way possible or as evidence of our inferiority.

The WASP quality of the cultural ideal puts minority women—black, Chicana, Jew, or other—in an even more constricted double bind. Not only are we subject to all the usual contradictions of the bifurcated female image—sexual/nonsexual, good/bad—but we must also deal with a second set of problems compounded and enlarged by our particular ethnic status and circumstances. Oppressed as women, oppressed again as minorities, we are expected to choose between loyalties, between liberations. Caught between minority men's anger at WASP behavior and their unconscious acceptance of WASP ideals, minority women "cannot win for losing": If we strain to meet prevailing standards, we are selling out; if we do not, we are unattractive.

Whichever way we choose to go, however we resolve the cultural loyalties, the issue of our own self-image also arises. The traditional minority woman, as any other, seeks desirability as a mate, seeks the whole range of social approbation that comes of being thought "beautiful," of meeting current standards of beauty. Should those standards be even farther removed from her real self than they are from other women, she must either work harder to meet them, risking proportionately deeper self-alienation, or she must accept defeat and wrestle with an intense sense of inferiority.

I vividly remember, as an adolescent Jewish girl of the 1950s—hooked on Marilyn Monroe and Ava Gardner, Debbie Reynolds and Liz Taylor—how I fretted at my unfashionably curly hair, trying tire-lessly to straighten its resilient black locks. I remember, too, staring enviously at my *shiksa* girlfriends' straight noses. Anything, I thought, even being old, would be better than having this awful bumpy nose. At nineteen, I had it "fixed."

For the Jewish women who fix their noses, for the black women who straighten their hair, for the millions of us who attempt or contemplate "corrections" to body and character that must ever remain inadequate, there must always be a severe sense of either deceit or defeat. The experience is more than self-diminishing; it is crushing.

Although ideals and models rarely vary from one group to another, the pejorative stereotypes, born of particular history and circumstance, admit of a good deal of variation and adjustment. For example, the Jewish woman, as a woman, may still function as the old ball and chain or the bitch temptress; but she may, as well, be placed within some other disparaging categories, exotic variations on the traditional themes. The young Jewish woman who is ethnically identified and hence esteemed by the Jewish community (and therefore *less* desirable to her male compatriots for the reasons pointed out above) is known as "the nice Jewish girl"—the NJG. Her more chic, less ethnically identified counterpart, the Jewish american princess (the JAP) is disparaged precisely because she avoids the social pitfalls of ethnic identification and strives so diligently to meet the WASP model. In either case, the racist, masculist mythology will ultimately turn both women into the Jewish Mother—aggressive, brassy, domineering, suffocating, unwholesomely self-inclined. If she cares too little, she's a shrew; if she cares too much, she's sick. Finally, any Jewish woman may be typed the "pushy Jewish broad," projecting onto her female self all the worst traits of the Jewish stereotype—a classic example of how an image, created by an external dominant group and internalized within the minority group, is applied to women by any men, in and out of the group, and even by women themselves.

Just as entangled in the dilemma of ethnic identification is the black woman, bound on one hand by white images of black women and on the other by black images of white women. For men, black or white, who adopt the traditional WASP models, the black woman functions both as a symbol of racial difference and as the usual receptacle of misogyny.

Pejorative images of her only intensify the traditional dichotomies.

In the black context, the Mother-Nurturer gone wrong is not only the frigid nuisance, the nag of white society; she is also the destroyer of the race—the matriarch of the Moynihan Report, who controls the family, castrates the black man by displacing him as head of the household, and thereby contributes to the destruction of black manhood, the family unit, and black pride.[22] Rather than being prized and lauded, the strength, resiliency, and independence developed in the black woman through centuries of hardship are in true masculist style deflected and turned against her.

These same traits—strength and assertiveness—are the very ones that mark the black version of Eve. In the black context, Eve is still the Playmate gone awry, only worse. Here we have the Hot Black Bitch, an image obviously constructed by the white overlord, yet at least partially reflected in the black community as well. Whereas the white playmate is naughty, her stereotypic black counterpart is depicted as without morals, without limits, sexually voracious, undiscriminating, and hard as nails, her behavior and character placing her completely outside the bounds of chivalry and masculine protection.

Each woman can and should analyze the particular version of the stereotype applicable to her background. This is certain: Whatever the ethnic, racial, and class variations, however the images are adapted and reflected, they all are born of masculist experience to serve masculist needs. They have little to do with women's undistorted natures.

Effects of the Stereotype

The patriarchal images of women—whether sexual or nonsexual, working class or middle class, black or white—have a common denominator. They all say that women as human beings are substandard: less intelligent; less moral; less competent; less able physically, psychologically, and spiritually; small of body, mind, and character; often bad or destructive. The images argue that we have done little in society (besides reproduce) to earn our keep; that we have made only small contribution to culture, high or low, yet always push for more than we deserve. Sometimes cute or adorable, sometimes consoling, but only in a controlled context, we are pleasant baubles to have around. In any other guise, we are a nuisance at best, a disaster at worst.

These and other stereotypical images of women work to destroy us. In their positive aspects, they are impossible to meet; in the negative, they are deprecatory and ugly, flourishing in the minds of women who are forced to live them. Functioning in large part as social norms, they have great power to direct attitudes and behavior among the group stereotyped as well as in the larger community. The tragedy of the female stereotype is that it impels women not only to appear substandard but also to become substandard; it moves to form us into the loathed monster. If the work of the stereotype be done, we are reduced to the weak, hapless creatures required by social lore, living in the mold, even experiencing ourselves according to the myth.

Limited experience, opportunity, and education, deemed appropriate for beings who must not become "too smart for our own good"; restrictive clothing and play, tailored for our more "alluring" and refined bodies; disapproval for behavior (sports, for example, competition, and assertiveness) that might strengthen body or character; suitors who require subservience and fragility; adolescent girlfriends straining to become "desirable" women; parents prompting us to marriage or marriageability; these and countless other experiences and influences combine to make us believe the myth and copy the model.

The model requires that we be pretty, gentle, and kind; we can become pretty, gentle, and kind. The model, however, also requires that we be silly, weak, and incompetent. Are we not required then to become silly, weak, and incompetent? Haven't we often tried? Then as we work to fit the mold and exhibit the expected traits, we reinforce the stereotype and so perpetuate the cycle and give "truth" to the lie. And if the lie be true, then everything follows. Because women are incompetent and weak, we must be protected, set apart, and given a safe "place," guarded by "our" men. Since we are petty and evil, unable to get along even with each other, we must be controlled for the good of ourselves and society. We deserve the contempt in which we are held.

Clearly, to live in the shadow of such attitudes is intolerable, even when they are hidden by chivalry or mystification, even when they are temporarily suspended for our good behavior. Life and personhood defined within such constraints is necessarily distorted, out of phase with even the barest elements of emotional and physical health, spiritual transcendence, and joy. But the misery brought on by these ideals extends beyond the psychological and spiritual elements of life. Because we are speaking here only about images, we have not yet raised the issue of more concrete oppression—poverty and physical abuse.

In the following chapter we will examine feminist responses to these images, feminist insights into the nature and effects of patriarchal stereotypes, the struggles women experience in freeing themselves, and the alternative, woman-identified images we are forging in the struggle.

Notes

[1]Mary Daly, *Beyond God the Father* (Boston: Beacon Press, 1973), p. 8.

[2]See, for example, Mary R. Beard, *Woman as Force in History* (New York: Macmillan, 1946). Some contemporary feminists make this argument from a cross-cultural perspective, pointing out that "power" is a highly complex notion that varies within and across social groups. See also Gerda Lerner's selection from *The Creation of Patriarchy* in Chapter 5.

[3]Susan Brownmiller, *Femininity* (New York: Fawcett Columbine, 1984), pp. 13–14.

[4]Sally Kempton's terminology in "Cutting Loose," *Esquire*, July 1970, p. 57.

[5]The treatment of "otherness" relative to women is most typically associated with the French existentialist philosopher Simone de Beauvoir, who developed the concept in her landmark work, *The Second Sex*, ed. and trans. H. M. Parshley (New York: Knopf, 1953).

[6]There is a school of feminists who question the thesis of the universal subordination of women within patriarchal culture. They contend that women's power in some societies is different but real; hence, subordination is a term not universally applicable. I am not of this opinion.

[7]For an interesting analysis of the meaning of the relation of carnality and femaleness for men, see Beauvoir, *The Second Sex*, chap. IX.

[8]Whether there are oedipal components to male fear of sex I hesitate to conjecture, although others have. Certainly it ought to be considered but in another, wider study of this problem.

[9]Pauline Réage, *Story of O*, trans. Sabine d'Estré (New York: Grove Press, 1965).

[10] Andrea Dworkin, *Woman Hating* (New York: E. P. Dutton & Co., 1974), pp. 55–63.

[11] André Pieyre de Mandiargues, "A Note on *Story of O*," in Réage, *Story of O*, p. xvi.

[12] It is a sport among the readers and commentators of *Story of O* to guess at the sex of its author (who uses a pen name). Actually it matters little whether it was written by a man or a woman; the book is the expression of one fully steeped in the perspectives and values of masculism, and, as I have pointed out, these are not gender specific.

[13] Jean Paulhan, "Happiness in Slavery," in Réage, *Story of O*, p. xxv.

[14] Ibid., p. xxviii.

[15] Mandiargues, "A Note," ibid., p. vii.

[16] The idea that victimization per se is an essential principle of female excellence in patriarchy appeared in Andrea Dworkin's *Woman Hating* (New York: E. P. Dutton & Co., 1974).

[17] Some of this discussion appeared in Sheila Ruth, "Sexism, Patriarchy, and Feminism: Toward an Understanding of Terms" (Paper delivered at Pioneers for Century III Conference, Cincinnati, Ohio, March 1976).

[18] "Anatomy is destiny," argued Sigmund Freud. For the female, he contended, the body, its makeup and potential, determines personality and character in a far more definitive way than is true for men.

[19] Karl Stern, *The Flight from Woman* (New York: Farrar, Straus & Giroux, 1964), pp. 21–22.

[20] Wolfgang Lederer, *The Fear of Women* (New York: Grune & Stratton, 1968), pp. 269–70. Note that Beauvoir argued just the opposite in *The Second Sex*, that one is "not born, but becomes a woman."

[21] K. Kramer and J. Sprenger, *Malleus Maleficarum*, trans. M. Summers (London: Arrow Books, 1971), p. 112.

[22] Daniel Patrick Moynihan, *The Negro Family: The Case for National Action*, U.S. Department of Labor, Office of Policy Planning and Research, 1965. Moynihan wrote this analysis of black needs and problems for the president of the United States, thereby launching many of the economic programs of the sixties. Moynihan argued that "In essence, the Negro community has been forced into a matriarchal structure, which . . . imposes a crushing burden on the Negro male, and in consequence on a great many Negro women as well" (p. 29).

Know Your Enemy

Robin Morgan

An award-winning poet, political theorist, and feminist activist, Robin Morgan is the author of ten books. For twenty years a leader of this wave of feminism in the United States, she is a founder of the New York Women's Law Center, the Feminist Women's Health Network, the National Battered Women's Refuge Network, the Feminist Writer's Guild, and the National Rape Crisis Center Network, among others. A contributing editor to Ms.*, she received the Front Page Award for Distinguished Journalism in 1981 as well as the Wonder Woman Award for International Peace and Understanding in 1982. She compiled and edited the now-classic anthology* Sisterhood Is Powerful *in 1970, and in 1984 did the same with* Sisterhood Is Global: The International Women's Movement Anthology. *Active in the international women's movement for fifteen years, she is a cofounder of the Sisterhood is Global Institute—the first international feminist think tank. Her writing has been translated into seven languages, and she has traveled widely, lecturing and organizing. In 1986 she spent more than six weeks in the Middle East, investigating the conditions of women in Palestinian refugee camps. Currently chair of the New York State Hands Across America Committee for Justice and Empowerment, she has recently completed her eleventh book,* The Demon Lover, *which Norton published in February 1989.* Ms. *Morgan lives in New York City.*

The quotations in ''Know Your Enemy'' speak for themselves: they say misogyny is old, real, powerful, very much with us. They will probably continue to evoke the horror, anger, and will to action that they have since first published.

Robin Morgan, ''Know Your Enemy'' from *Sisterhood Is Powerful*. New York: Vintage, 1970.

Know Your Enemy: A Sampling of Sexist Quotes

The glory of a man is knowledge, but the glory of a woman is to renounce knowledge.

—Chinese proverb

Do not trust a good woman, and keep away from a bad one.

—Portugese proverb

Women are sisters nowhere.

—West African proverb

Whenever a woman dies there is one quarrel less on earth.

—German proverb

Never trust a woman, even though she has given you ten sons.

—Chinese proverb

In childhood a woman must be subject to her father; in youth, to her husband; when her husband is dead, to her sons. A woman must never be free of subjugation.

—*The Hindu Code of Manu, V*

I thank thee, O Lord, that thou hast not created me a woman.

—Daily Orthodox Jewish Prayer (for a male)

There is a good principle which created order, light, and man, and an evil principle which created chaos, darkness, and woman.

—Pythagoras

We may thus conclude that it is a general law that there should be naturally ruling elements and elements naturally ruled . . . the rule of the freeman over the slave is one kind of rule; that of the male over the female another . . . the slave is entirely without the faculty of deliberation; the female indeed possesses it, but in a form which remains inconclusive . . .

—Aristotle (*Politics*)

If thy wife does not obey thee at a signal and a glance, separate from her.

—*Sirach* 25:26

When a woman thinks . . . she thinks evil.

—Seneca

Creator of the heavens and the earth, He has given you wives from among yourselves to multiply you, and cattle male and female. Nothing can be compared with Him.

—*Holy Koran of Islam*

And the rib, which the Lord God had taken from man, made he a woman and brought her unto the man. And Adam said, This is now bone of my bone, and flesh of my flesh; she shall be called Woman, because she was taken out of Man.

—*Genesis* 2:22–23

How can he be clean that is born of a woman?

—*Job* 4:4

Suffer women once to arrive at an equality with you, and they will from that moment become your superiors.

—Cato the Elder, 195 B.C.

Let the women learn in silence with all subjection . . . I suffer not a woman to usurp authority over men, but to be in silence.

—St. Paul

Wives, submit yourselves unto your husbands . . . for the husband is the head of the wife, even as Christ is the head of the church.

—*Ephesians* 5:23–24

The five worst infirmities that afflict the female are indocility, discontent, slander, jealousy, and silliness . . . Such is the stupidity of woman's character, that it is incumbent upon her, in every particular, to distrust herself and to obey her husband.

—*Confucian Marriage Manual*

God created Adam lord of all living creatures, but Eve spoiled it all.

—Martin Luther

All witchcraft comes from carnal lust, which is in women insatiable.

—Kramer and Sprenger, Inquisitors (*Malleus Maleficarum*, c. 1486)

A man in general is better pleased when he has a good dinner than when his wife talks Greek.

—Samuel Johnson

The whole education of women ought to be relative to men. To please them, to be useful to them, to make themselves loved and honored by them, to educate them when young, to care for them when grown, to counsel them, to console them, and to make life sweet and agreeable to them—these are the duties of women at all times and what should be taught them from their infancy.

—Jean Jacques Rousseau

Women have no moral sense; they rely for their behavior upon the men they love.

—La Bruyere

Most women have no characters at all.

—Alexander Pope

I never knew a tolerable woman to be fond of her own sex.

—Jonathan Swift

*Man for the field and woman for the hearth:
Man for the sword and for the needle she:
Man with the head and woman with the heart:
Man to command and woman to obey;
All else confusion.*

—Alfred, Lord Tennyson

Men are men, but Man is a woman.

—G. K. Chesterton

Nature intended women to be our slaves . . . they are our property; we are not theirs. They belong to us, just as a tree that bears fruit belongs to a gardener. What a mad idea to demand equality for women! . . . Women are nothing but machines for producing children.

—Napoleon Bonaparte

To men a man is but a mind. Who cares what face he carries or what he wears? But woman's body is *the woman.*

—Ambrose Bierce

Regard the society of women as a necessary unpleasantness of social life, and avoid it as much as possible.

—Count Leo Tolstoy

A woman who is guided by the head and not the heart is a social pestilence: she has all the defects of the passionate and affectionate woman, with none of her compensations; she is without pity, without love, without virtue, without sex.

—Honoré de Balzac

And a woman is only a woman but a good cigar is a smoke.

—Rudyard Kipling

Women have great talent, but no genius, for they always remain subjective.

—Arthur Schopenhauer

One must have loved a woman of genius to comprehend the happiness of loving a fool.

—Talleyrand

If the feminine abilities were developed to the same degree as those of the male, her (woman's) maternal organs would suffer and we should have a repulsive and useless hybrid.

—P. J. Moebius (German scientist, 1907)

The great question that has never been answered, and which I have not yet been able to answer despite my thirty years of research into the feminine soul, is: What does a woman want?

—Sigmund Freud

The woman's fundamental status is that of her husband's wife, the mother of his children.

—Talcott Parsons

Man's superiority *will be shown, not in the fact that he has enslaved his wife, but that* he *has made her free.*

—Eugene V. Debs

Women should receive a higher education, not in order to become doctors, lawyers, or professors, but to rear their offspring to be valuable human beings.

—Alexis Carrel, *Man, the Unknown*

Woman as a person enjoys a dignity equal with men, but she was given different tasks by God and by Nature which perfect and complete the work entrusted to men.

—Pope John XXIII

It would be preposterously naive to suggest that a B.A. can be made as attractive to girls as a marriage license.

—Dr. Grayson Kirk (former President, Columbia University)

Women, in general, want to be loved for what they are and men for what they accomplish. The first for their looks and charm, the latter for their actions.

—Theodor Reik

My secretary is a lovable slave.

—Morris Ernst, attorney, on the 50th Anniversary of his having hired Paula Gross, secretary.

Women are usually more patient in working at unexciting, repetitive tasks . . . Women on the average have more passivity in the inborn core of their personality . . . I believe women are designed in their deeper instincts to get more pleasure out of life—not only sexually but socially, occupationally, maternally—when they are not aggressive. To put it another way I think that when women are encouraged to be competitive too many of them become disagreeable.

—Dr. Benjamin M. Spock, *Decent and Indecent*

Women? I guess they ought to exercise Pussy Power.

—Eldridge Cleaver, 1968

AND

A woman's place is in the home/Housewives are such dull people/Women's talk is all chatter/Intelligent women are emasculating/If you're so smart why aren't you married/Can you type?/Working women are unfeminine/A smart woman never shows her brains/It is a woman's duty to make herself attractive/All women think about are clothes/Women are always playing hard to get/No man likes an easy woman/Women should be struck regularly, like gongs/Women like to be raped/Women are always crying about something/Women don't understand the value of a dollar/Women executives are castrating bitches/Don't worry your pretty little head about it/Dumb broad/It is glorious to be the mother of all mankind/A woman's work is never done/Women are only interested in trapping some man/A woman who can't hold a man isn't much of a woman/Women hate to be with other women/Women are always off chattering with each other/Some of my best friends are women . . .

Whether Woman Should Have Been Made in the First Production of Things

St. Thomas Aquinas

St. Thomas Aquinas (1227–1274), medieval philosopher and theologian, was named the official philosophic authority of the Catholic Church by Pope Leo XIII in 1879. His reasoning forms the basis of Catholic doctrine and pervades much of Protestant theology as well. As such, it has exerted tremendous influence on Western culture and hence on women's lives. Through the church, Aquinas's ideas continue in importance today, having their effect on arguments regarding contraception and abortion, women's place in the priesthood, women's role in the family, women's role in the economy, and so on.

In the following discussion, Aquinas asks whether one could say that because women are defective and sinful (more so than men) they ought not to have been created in the first innocent beginning of things by an all-perfect God. Certainly, women should have been created, he replies, for nature decrees that men must have "helpers," not in cultural works, but in reproduction. That is, women are necessary as biological assistants.

Aquinas was known for his reconciliation of Christian doctrine with the philosophy of Aristotle, increasingly important in the thirteenth century. The philosopher he refers to in his opening remarks is Aristotle, who theorized that "females are weaker and colder in nature, and we must look upon the female character as being a sort of natural deficiency" (De Generatione Animalium, IV, 6, 775a 15). Aristotle's analysis of woman as "misbegotten male" is one of a whole genre of theories, popular through the centuries, treating womanhood as a partial or defective instance of manhood.

St. Thomas Aquinas. *Summa Theologicae.*

Question XCII
The Production of Woman

First Article
Whether Woman Should Have Been Made in the First Production of Things?

We proceed thus to the First Article:—

Objection 1. It would seem that woman should not have been made in the first production of things. For the Philosopher says that the *female is a misbegotten male.*[1] But nothing misbegotten or defective should have been in the first production of things. Therefore woman should not have been made at that first production.

Obj. 2. Further, subjection and limitation were a result of sin, for to the woman was it said after sin (*Gen.* iii. 16): *Thou shalt be under the man's power;* and Gregory says that, *Where there is no sin, there is no inequality.*[2] But woman is naturally of less strength and dignity than man, *for the agent is always more honorable than the patient*, as Augustine says.[3] Therefore woman should not have been made in the first production of things before sin.

Obj. 3. Further, occasions of sin should be cut off. But God foresaw that woman would be an occasion of sin to man. Therefore He should not have made woman.

On the contrary, It is written (*Gen.* ii. 18): *It is not good for man to be alone; let us make him a helper like to himself.*

I answer that, It was necessary for woman to be made, as the Scripture says, as a *helper* to man; not, indeed, as a helpmate in other works, as some say,[4] since man can be more efficiently helped by another man in other works; but as a helper in the work of generation. This can be made clear if we observe the mode of generation

95

carried out in various living things. Some living things do not possess in themselves the power of generation, but are generated by an agent of another species; and such are those plants and animals which are generated, without seed, from suitable matter through the active power of the heavenly bodies. Others possess the active and passive generative power together, as we see in plants which are generated from seed. For the noblest vital function in plants is generation, and so we observe that in these the active power of generation invariably accompanies the passive power. Among perfect animals, the active power of generation belongs to the male sex, and the passive power to the female. And as among animals there is a vital operation nobler than generation, to which their life is principally directed, so it happens that the male sex is not found in continual union with the female in perfect animals, but only at the time of coition; so that we may consider that by coition the male and female are one, as in plants they are always united, even though in some cases one of them preponderates, and in some the other. But man is further ordered to a still nobler work of life, and that is intellectual operation. Therefore there was greater reason for the distinction of these two powers in man; so that the female should be produced separately from the male, and yet that they should be carnally united for generation. Therefore directly after the formation of woman, it was said: *And they shall be two in one flesh* (Gen. ii. 24).

Reply Obj. 1. As regards the individual nature, woman is defective and misbegotten, for the active power in the male seed tends to the production of a perfect likeness according to the masculine sex; while the production of woman comes from defect in the active power, or from some material indisposition, or even from some external influence, such as that of a south wind, which is moist, as the Philosopher observes.[5] On the other hand, as regards universal hu-

man nature, woman is not misbegotten, but is included in nature's intention as directed to the work of generation. Now the universal intention of nature depends on God, Who is the universal Author of nature. Therefore, in producing nature, God formed not only the male but also the female.

Reply Obj. 2. Subjection is twofold. One is servile, by virtue of which a superior makes use of a subject for his own benefit; and this kind of subjection began after sin. There is another kind of subjection, which is called economic or civil, whereby the superior makes use of his subjects for their own benefit and good; and this kind of subjection existed even before sin. For the good of order would have been wanting in the human family if some were not governed by others wiser than themselves. So by such a kind of subjection woman is naturally subject to man, because in man the discernment of reason predominates. Nor is inequality among men excluded by the state of innocence, as we shall prove.[6]

Reply Obj. 3. If God had deprived the world of all those things which proved an occasion of sin, the universe would have been imperfect. Nor was it fitting for the common good to be destroyed in order that individual evil might be avoided; especially as God is so powerful that He can direct any evil to a good end.

Notes

[1] *De Gener. Anim.*, II, 3 (737a 27).

[2] *Moral.*, XXI, 15 (PL 76, 203).

[3] *De Genesi ad Litt.*, XII, 16 (PL 34, 467).

[4] Anonymously reported by St. Augustine, *De Genesi ad Litt.*, IX, 3 (PL 34, 395).

[5] Aristotle, *De Gener. Anim.*, IV, 2 (766b 33).

[6] Q.96, a.3.

Femininity

Sigmund Freud

*The Austrian psychologist Sigmund Freud (1856–
1939) was one of the earliest theorists and probably the
most influential in the areas of clinical psychology and
psychoanalysis. Although extraordinarily creative and
insightful as ground-breaker in a new dimension, his
work has been severely criticized for its ethnocentricity,
its lack of objective verification (or perhaps even
verifiability), and more recently, its thorough sexism.
Freud's theories on the nature of women's psychology
include the following themes: (1) that for women,
anatomy is destiny—more so than for men, women's
lives and personalities are prescribed by their biological
and reproductive nature; (2) that women are not only
fundamentally different from men in character but
inferior to them physically (in sexual capacity and
equipment), emotionally (in stability and control),
and ethically (in the sense of honesty and justice).*

*The essay reprinted here (written about 1933) is
Freud's most famous treatise on femininity. It was at
one time (until quite recently—into the forties or
fifties) the official word on female psychology.
Although Freud and this analysis have been challenged
roundly from all quarters, its themes are still highly
influential and pervade much of both contemporary
clinical and popular thought.*

LADIES AND GENTLEMEN,[1]—ALL THE WHILE I AM
preparing to talk to you I am struggling with an
internal difficulty. I feel uncertain, so to speak, of
the extent of my licence. It is true that in the
course of fifteen years of work psycho-analysis
has changed and grown richer; but, in spite of
that, an introduction to psycho-analysis might
have been left without alteration or supplement.
It is constantly in my mind that these lectures are
without a *raison d'être*. For analysts I am saying
too little and nothing at all that is new; but for you
I am saying too much and saying things which
you are not equipped to understand and which
are not in your province. I have looked around for
excuses and I have tried to justify each separate
lecture on different grounds. The first one, on the
theory of dreams, was supposed to put you back
again at one blow into the analytic atmosphere
and to show you how durable our views have
turned out to be. I was led on to the second one,
which followed the paths from dreams to what is
called occultism, by the opportunity of speaking
my mind without constraint on a department of
work in which prejudiced expectations are fighting to-day against passionate resistances, and I
could hope that your judgement, educated to tolerance on the example of psycho-analysis, would
not refuse to accompany me on the excursion. The
third lecture, on the dissection of the personality,
certainly made the hardest demands upon you
with its unfamiliar subject-matter; but it was impossible for me to keep this first beginning of an
ego-psychology back from you, and if we had
possessed it fifteen years ago I should have had
to mention it to you then. My last lecture, finally,
which you were probably able to follow only by
great exertions, brought forward necessary corrections—fresh attempts at solving the most important conundrums; and my introduction would
have been leading you astray if I had been silent
about them. As you see, when one starts making
excuses it turns out in the end that it was all inevitable, all the work of destiny. I submit to it, and I
beg you to do the same.

To-day's lecture, too, should have no place in an introduction; but it may serve to give you an example of a detailed piece of analytic work, and I can say two things to recommend it. It brings forward nothing but observed facts, almost without any speculative additions, and it deals with a subject which has a claim on your interest second almost to no other. Throughout history people have knocked their heads against the riddle of the nature of femininity—

Häupter in Hieroglyphenmützen,
Häupter in Turban und schwarzem Barett,
Perückenhäupter und tausend andre
Arme, schwitzende Menschenhäupter. . . .[2]

Nor will *you* have escaped worrying over this problem—those of you who are men; to those of you who are women this will not apply—you are yourselves the problem. When you meet a human being, the first distinction you make is 'male or female?' and you are accustomed to make the distinction with unhesitating certainty. Anatomical science shares your certainty at one point and not much further. The male sexual product, the spermatozoon, and its vehicle are male; the ovum and the organism that harbours it are female. In both sexes organs have been formed which serve exclusively for the sexual functions; they were probably developed from the same [innate] disposition into two different forms. Besides this, in both sexes the other organs, the bodily shapes and tissues, show the influence of the individual's sex, but this is inconstant and its amount variable; these are what are known as the secondary sexual characters. Science next tells you something that runs counter to your expectations and is probably calculated to confuse your feelings. It draws your attention to the fact that portions of the male sexual apparatus also appear in women's bodies, though in an atrophied state, and vice versa in the alternative case. It regards their occurrence as indications of *bisexuality*,[3] as though an individual is not a man or a woman but always both—merely a certain amount more the one than the other. You will then be asked to make yourselves familiar with the idea that the proportion in which masculine and feminine are mixed in an individual is subject to quite considerable fluctuations. Since, however, apart from the very rarest cases, only one kind of sexual product—ova or semen—is nevertheless present in one person, you are bound to have doubts as to the decisive significance of those elements and must conclude that what constitutes masculinity or femininity is an unknown characteristic which anatomy cannot lay hold of.

Can psychology do so perhaps? We are accustomed to employ 'masculine' and 'feminine' as mental qualities as well, and have in the same way transferred the notion of bisexuality to mental life. Thus we speak of a person, whether male or female, as behaving in a masculine way in one connection and in a feminine way in another. But you will soon perceive that this is only giving way to anatomy or to convention. You cannot give the concepts of 'masculine' and 'feminine' *any* new connotation. The distinction is not a psychological one; when you say 'masculine', you usually mean 'active', and when you say 'feminine', you usually mean 'passive'. Now it is true that a relation of the kind exists. The male sex-cell is actively mobile and searches out the female one, and the latter, the ovum, is immobile and waits passively. This behaviour of the elementary sexual organisms is indeed a model for the conduct of sexual individuals during intercourse. The male pursues the female for the purpose of sexual union, seizes hold of her and penetrates into her. But by this you have precisely reduced the characteristic of masculinity to the factor of aggressiveness so far as psychology is concerned. You may well doubt whether you have gained any real advantage from this when you reflect that in some classes of animals the females are the stronger and more aggressive and the male is active only in the single act of sexual union. This is so, for instance, with the spiders. Even the functions of rearing and caring for the young, which strike us as feminine *par excellence*, are not invariably attached to the female sex in animals. In quite high species we find that the sexes share the task of caring for the young between them or even that the male alone devotes himself to it. Even in the sphere of human sexual life you soon see how inadequate it is to make masculine behaviour coincide with activity and feminine with passivity. A mother is active in every sense towards her child; the act of lactation itself may equally be described as the mother suckling the baby or as her being sucked by it. The further you go from the narrow sexual sphere the more obvious will the 'error of superimposition'[4] become. Women can display great activity in various directions, men are not able to live in company with their own kind unless they develop a large amount of passive adaptability. If you now tell me that these facts go to prove precisely that both men and women are bisexual in the psychological sense, I shall conclude that you have decided in your own minds to make 'active' coincide with 'masculine' and 'passive' with 'feminine'. But I advise you against it. It seems to me to serve no useful purpose and adds nothing to our knowledge.[5]

One might consider characterizing femininity psychologically as giving preference to passive aims. This is not, of course, the same thing as passivity; to achieve a passive aim may call for a large amount of activity. It is perhaps the case that in a woman, on the basis of her share in the sexual function, a preference for passive behaviour and passive aims is carried over into her life to a greater or lesser extent, in proportion to the limits, restricted or far-reaching, within which her sexual life thus serves as a model. But we must beware in this of underestimating the influence of social customs, which similarly force women into passive situations. All this is still far from being cleared up. There is one particularly constant relation between femininity and instinctual life which we do not want to overlook. The suppression of women's aggressiveness which is prescribed for them constitutionally and imposed on them socially favours the development of powerful masochistic impulses, which succeed, as we know, in binding erotically the destructive trends which have been diverted inwards. Thus masochism, as people say, is truly feminine. But if, as happens so often, you meet with masochism in men, what is left to you but to say that these men exhibit very plain feminine traits?

And now you are already prepared to hear that psychology too is unable to solve the riddle of femininity. The explanation must no doubt come from elsewhere, and cannot come till we have learnt how in general the differentiation of living organisms into two sexes came about. We know nothing about it, yet the existence of two sexes is a most striking characteristic of organic life which distinguishes it sharply from inanimate nature. However, we find enough to study in those human individuals who, through the possession of female genitals, are characterized as manifestly or predominantly feminine. In conformity with its peculiar nature, psycho-analysis does not try to describe what a woman is—that would be a task it could scarcely perform—but sets about enquiring how she comes into being, how a woman develops out of a child with a bisexual disposition. In recent times we have begun to learn a little about

this, thanks to the circumstance that several of our excellent women colleagues in analysis have begun to work at the question. The discussion of this has gained special attractiveness from the distinction between the sexes. For the ladies, whenever some comparison seemed to turn out unfavourable to their sex, were able to utter a suspicion that we, the male analysts, had been unable to overcome certain deeply-rooted prejudices against what was feminine, and that this was being paid for in the partiality of our researches. We, on the other hand, standing on the ground of bisexuality, had no difficulty in avoiding impoliteness. We had only to say: 'This doesn't apply to *you*. You're the exception; on this point you're more masculine than feminine.'

We approach the investigation of the sexual development of women with two expectations. The first is that here once more the constitution will not adapt itself to its function without a struggle. The second is that the decisive turning-points will already have been prepared for or completed before puberty. Both expectations are promptly confirmed. Furthermore, a comparison with what happens with boys tells us that the development of a little girl into a normal woman is more difficult and more complicated, since it includes two extra tasks, to which there is nothing corresponding in the development of a man. Let us follow the parallel lines from their beginning. Undoubtedly the material is different to start with in boys and girls: it did not need psycho-analysis to establish that. The difference in the structure of the genitals is accompanied by other bodily differences which are too well known to call for mention. Differences emerge too in the instinctual disposition which give a glimpse of the later nature of women. A little girl is as a rule less aggressive, defiant and self-sufficient; she seems to have a greater need for being shown affection and on that account to be more dependent and pliant. It is probably only as a result of this pliancy that she can be taught more easily and quicker to control her excretions: urine and faeces are the first gifts that children make to those who look after them, and controlling them is the first concession to which the instinctual life of children can be induced. One gets an impression, too, that little girls are more intelligent and livelier than boys of the same age; they go out more to meet the external world and at the same time form stronger object-cathexes. I cannot say whether this lead in development has been confirmed by exact observations, but in any case there is no question that girls cannot be described as intellectually backward. These sexual differences are not, however, of great consequence: they can be outweighed by individual variations. For our immediate purposes they can be disregarded.

Both sexes seem to pass through the early phases of libidinal development in the same manner. It might have been expected that in girls there would already have been some lag in aggressiveness in the sadistic-anal phase, but such is not the case. Analysis of children's play has shown our women analysts that the aggressive impulses of little girls leave nothing to be desired in the way of abundance and violence. With their entry into the phallic phase the differences between the sexes are completely eclipsed by their agreements. We are now obliged to recognize that the little girl is a little man. In boys, as we know, this phase is marked by the fact that they have learnt how to derive pleasurable sensations from their small penis and connect its excited state with their ideas of sexual intercourse. Little girls do the same thing with their still smaller clitoris. It seems that with them all their masturbatory acts are carried out on this penis-equivalent, and that the truly feminine vagina is still undiscovered by both sexes. It is true that there are a few isolated reports of early vaginal sensations as well, but it could not be easy to distinguish these from sensations in the anus or vestibulum; in any case they cannot play a great part. We are entitled to keep to our view that in the phallic phase of girls the clitoris is the leading erotogenic zone. But it is not, of course, going to remain so. With the change to femininity the clitoris should wholly or in part hand over its sensitivity, and at the same time its importance, to the vagina. This would be one of the two tasks which a woman has to perform in the course of her development, whereas the more fortunate man has only to continue at the time of his sexual maturity the activity that he has previously carried out at the period of the early efflorescence of his sexuality.

We shall return to the part played by the clitoris; let us now turn to the second task with which a girl's development is burdened. A boy's mother is the first object of his love, and she remains so too during the formation of his Oedipus complex and, in essence, all through his life. For a girl too her first object must be her mother (and the figures of wet-nurses and foster-mothers that merge into her). The first object-cathexes occur in attachment to the satisfaction of the major and simple vital needs,[6] and the circumstances

of the care of children are the same for both sexes. But in the Oedipus situation the girl's father has become her love-object, and we expect that in the normal course of development she will find her way from this paternal object to her final choice of an object. In the course of time, therefore, a girl has to change her erotogenic zone and her object—both of which a boy retains. The question then arises of how this happens: in particular, how does a girl pass from her mother to an attachment to her father? or, in other words, how does she pass from her masculine phase to the feminine one to which she is biologically destined?

It would be a solution of ideal simplicity if we could suppose that from a particular age onwards the elementary influence of the mutual attraction between the sexes makes itself felt and impels the small woman towards men, while the same law allows the boy to continue with his mother. We might suppose in addition that in this the children are following the pointer given them by the sexual preference of their parents. But we are not going to find things so easy; we scarcely know whether we are to believe seriously in the power of which poets talk so much and with such enthusiasm but which cannot be further dissected analytically. We have found an answer of quite another sort by means of laborious investigations, the material for which at least was easy to arrive at. For you must know that the number of women who remain till a late age tenderly dependent on a paternal object, or indeed on their real father, is very great. We have established some surprising facts about these women with an intense attachment of long duration to their father. We knew, of course, that there had been a preliminary stage of attachment to the mother, but we did not know that it could be so rich in content and so long-lasting, and could leave behind so many opportunities for fixations and dispositions. During this time the girl's father is only a troublesome rival; in some cases the attachment to her mother lasts beyond the fourth year of life. Almost everything that we find later in her relation to her father was already present in this earlier attachment and has been transferred subsequently on to her father. In short, we get an impression that we cannot understand women unless we appreciate this phase of their pre-Oedipus attachment to their mother.

We shall be glad, then, to know the nature of the girl's libidinal relations to her mother. The answer is that they are of very many different kinds. Since they persist through all three phases of infantile sexuality, they also take on the characteristics of the different phases and express themselves by oral, sadistic-anal and phallic wishes. These wishes represent active as well as passive impulses; if we relate them to the differentiation of the sexes which is to appear later—though we should avoid doing so as far as possible—we may call them masculine and feminine. Besides this, they are completely ambivalent, both affectionate and of a hostile and aggressive nature. The latter often only come to light after being changed into anxiety ideas. It is not always easy to point to a formulation of these early sexual wishes; what is most clearly expressed is a wish to get the mother with child and the corresponding wish to bear her a child—both belonging to the phallic period and sufficiently surprising, but established beyond doubt by analytic observation. The attractiveness of these investigations lies in the surprising detailed findings which they bring us. Thus, for instance, we discover the fear of being murdered or poisoned, which may later form the core of a paranoic illness, already present in this pre-Oedipus period, in relation to the mother. Or another case: you will recall an interesting episode in the history of analytic research which caused me many distressing hours. In the period in which the main interest was directed to discovering infantile sexual traumas, almost all my women patients told me that they had been seduced by their father. I was driven to recognize in the end that these reports were untrue and so came to understand that hysterical symptoms are derived from phantasies and not from real occurrences. It was only later that I was able to recognize in this phantasy of being seduced by the father the expression of the typical Oedipus complex in women. And now we find the phantasy of seduction once more in the pre-Oedipus prehistory of girls; but the seducer is regularly the mother. Here, however, the phantasy touches the ground of reality, for it was really the mother who by her activities over the child's bodily hygiene inevitably stimulated, and perhaps even roused for the first time, pleasurable sensations in her genitals.[7]

I have no doubt you are ready to suspect that this portrayal of the abundance and strength of a little girl's sexual relations with her mother is very much overdrawn. After all, one has opportunities of seeing little girls and notices nothing of the sort. But the objection is not to the point. Enough can be seen in the children if one knows how to look. And besides, you should consider how little of its sexual wishes a child can bring to preconscious expression or communicate at all. Accordingly we are only within our rights if we study the residues and consequences of this emotional world in retrospect, in people in whom these processes of development had attained a specially clear and even excessive degree of expansion. Pathology has always done us the service of making discernible by isolation and exaggeration conditions which would remain concealed in a normal state. And since our investigations have been carried out on people who were by no means seriously abnormal, I think we should regard their outcome as deserving belief.

We will now turn our interest on to the single question of what it is that brings this powerful attachment of the girl to her mother to an end. This, as we know, is its usual fate: it is destined to make room for an attachment to her father. Here we come upon a fact which is a pointer to our further advance. This step in development does not involve only a simple change of object. The turning away from the mother is accompanied by hostility; the attachment to the mother ends in hate. A hate of that kind may become very striking and last all through life; it may be carefully overcompensated later on; as a rule one part of it is overcome while another part persists. Events of later years naturally influence this greatly. We will restrict ourselves, however, to studying it at the time at which the girl turns to her father and to enquiring into the motives for it. We are then given a long list of accusations and grievances against the mother which are supposed to justify the child's hostile feelings; they are of varying validity which we shall not fail to examine. A number of them are obvious rationalizations and the true sources of enmity remain to be found. I hope you will be interested if on this occasion I take you through all the details of a psycho-analytic investigation.

The reproach against the mother which goes back furthest is that she gave the child too little milk—which is construed against her as lack of love. Now there is some justification for this reproach in our families. Mothers often have insufficient nourishment to give their children and are content to suckle them for a few months, for half or three-quarters of a year. Among primitive peoples children are fed at their mother's breast for two or three years. The figure of the wet-nurse who suckles the child is as a rule merged into the mother; when this has not happened, the reproach is turned into another one—that the nurse, who fed the child so willingly, was sent away by the mother too early. But whatever the true state of affairs may have been, it is impossible that the child's reproach can be justified as often as it is met with. It seems, rather, that the child's avidity for its earliest nourishment is altogether insatiable, that it never gets over the pain of losing its mother's breast. I should not be surprised if the analysis of a primitive child, who could still suck at its mother's breast when it was already able to run about and talk, were to bring the same reproach to light. The fear of being poisoned is also probably connected with the withdrawal of the breast. Poison is nourishment that makes one ill. Perhaps children trace back their early illnesses too to this frustration. A fair amount of intellectual education is a prerequisite for believing in chance; primitive people and uneducated ones, and no doubt children as well, are able to assign a ground for everything that happens. Perhaps originally it was a reason on animistic lines. Even to-day in some strata of our population no one can die without having been killed by someone else—preferably by the doctor. And the regular reaction of a neurotic to the death of someone closely connected with him is to put the blame on himself for having caused the death.

The next accusation against the child's mother flares up when the next baby appears in the nursery. If possible the connection with oral frustration is preserved: the mother could not or would not give the child any more milk because she needed the nourishment for the new arrival. In cases in which the two children are so close in age that lactation is prejudiced by the second pregnancy, this reproach acquires a real basis, and it is a remarkable fact that a child, even with an age difference of only 11 months, is not too young to take notice of what is happening. But what the child grudges the unwanted intruder and rival is not only the suckling but all the other signs of maternal care. It feels that it has been dethroned, despoiled, prejudiced in its rights; it casts a jealous hatred upon the new baby and develops a grievance against the faithless mother which often finds expression in a disagreeable change in its behaviour. It becomes 'naughty', perhaps, irritable and disobedient and goes back on the advances it has made towards controlling its excretions. All of this has been very long familiar and is accepted as self-

evident; but we rarely form a correct idea of the strength of these jealous impulses, of the tenacity with which they persist and of the magnitude of their influence on later development. Especially as this jealousy is constantly receiving fresh nourishment in the later years of childhood and the whole shock is repeated with the birth of each new brother or sister. Nor does it make much difference if the child happens to remain the mother's preferred favourite. A child's demands for love are immoderate, they make exclusive claims and tolerate no sharing.

An abundant source of a child's hostility to its mother is provided by its multifarious sexual wishes, which alter according to the phase of the libido and which cannot for the most part be satisfied. The strongest of these frustrations occur at the phallic period, if the mother forbids pleasurable activity with the genitals—often with severe threats and every sign of displeasure—activity to which, after all, she herself had introduced the child. One would think these were reasons enough to account for a girl's turning away from her mother. One would judge, if so, that the estrangement follows inevitably from the nature of children's sexuality, from the immoderate character of their demand for love and the impossibility of fulfilling their sexual wishes. It might be thought indeed that this first love-relation of the child's is doomed to dissolution for the very reason that it is the first, for these early object-cathexes are regularly ambivalent to a high degree. A powerful tendency to aggressiveness is always present beside a powerful love, and the more passionately a child loves its object the more sensitive does it become to disappointments and frustrations from that object; and in the end the love must succumb to the accumulated hostility. Or the idea that there is an original ambivalence such as this in erotic cathexes may be rejected, and it may be pointed out that it is the special nature of the mother-child relation that leads, with equal inevitability, to the destruction of the child's love; for even the mildest upbringing cannot avoid using compulsion and introducing restrictions, and any such intervention in the child's liberty must provoke as a reaction an inclination to rebelliousness and aggressiveness. A discussion of these possibilities might, I think, be most interesting; but an objection suddenly emerges which forces our interest in another direction. All these factors—the slights, the disappointments in love, the jealousy, the seduction followed by prohibition—are, after all, also in operation in the relation of a *boy* to his mother and are yet unable to alienate him from the maternal object. Unless we can find something that is specific for girls and is not present or not in the same way present in boys, we shall not have explained the termination of the attachment of girls to their mother.

I believe we have found this specific factor, and indeed where we expected to find it, even though in a surprising form. Where we expected to find it, I say, for it lies in the castration complex. After all, the anatomical distinction [between the sexes] must express itself in psychical consequences. It was, however, a surprise to learn from analyses that girls hold their mother responsible for their lack of a penis and do not forgive her for their being thus put at a disadvantage.

As you hear, then, we ascribe a castration complex to women as well. And for good reasons, though its content cannot be the same as with boys. In the latter the castration complex arises after they have learnt from the sight of the female genitals that the organ which they value so highly need not necessarily accompany the body. At this the boy recalls to mind the threats he brought on himself by his doings with that organ, he begins to give credence to them and falls under the influence of fear of castration, which will be the most powerful motive force in his subsequent development. The castration complex of girls is also started by the sight of the genitals of the other sex. They at once notice the difference and, it must be admitted, its significance too. They feel seriously wronged, often declare that they want to 'have something like it too', and fall victim to 'envy for the penis', which will leave ineradicable traces on their development and the formation of their character and which will not be surmounted in even the most favourable cases without a severe expenditure of psychical energy. The girl's recognition of the fact of her being without a penis does not by any means imply that she submits to the fact easily. On the contrary, she continues to hold on for a long time to the wish to get something like it herself and she believes in that possibility for improbably long years; and analysis can show that, at a period when knowledge of reality has long since rejected the fulfilment of the wish as unattainable, it persists in the unconscious and retains a considerable cathexis of energy. The wish to get the longed-for penis eventually in spite of everything may contribute to the motives that

drive a mature woman to analysis, and what she may reasonably expect from analysis—a capacity, for instance, to carry on an intellectual profession—may often be recognized as a sublimated modification of this repressed wish.

One cannot very well doubt the importance of envy for the penis. You may take it as an instance of male injustice if I assert that envy and jealousy play an even greater part in the mental life of women than of men. It is not that I think these characteristics are absent in men or that I think they have no other roots in women than envy for the penis; but I am inclined to attribute their greater amount in women to this latter influence. Some analysts, however, have shown an inclination to depreciate the importance of this first instalment of penis-envy in the phallic phase. They are of opinion that what we find of this attitude in women is in the main a secondary structure which has come about on the occasion of later conflicts by regression to this early infantile impulse. This, however, is a general problem of depth psychology. In many pathological—or even unusual—instinctual attitudes (for instance, in all sexual perversions) the question arises of how much of their strength is to be attributed to early infantile fixations and how much to the influence of later experiences and developments. In such cases it is almost always a matter of complemental series such as we put forward in our discussion of the aetiology of the neuroses.[8] Both factors play a part in varying amounts in the causation; a less on the one side is balanced by a more on the other. The infantile factor sets the pattern in all cases but does not always determine the issue, though it often does. Precisely in the case of penis-envy I should argue decidedly in favour of the preponderance of the infantile factor.

The discovery that she is castrated is a turning-point in a girl's growth. Three possible lines of development start from it: one leads to sexual inhibition or to neurosis, the second to change of character in the sense of a masculinity complex, the third, finally, to normal femininity. We have learnt a fair amount, though not everything, about all three.

The essential content of the first is as follows: the little girl has hitherto lived in a masculine way, has been able to get pleasure by the excitation of her clitoris and has brought this activity into relation with her sexual wishes directed towards her mother, which are often active ones; now, owing to the influence of her penis-envy, she loses her enjoyment in her phallic sexuality. Her self-love is mortified by the comparison with the boy's far superior equipment and in consequence she renounces her masturbatory satisfaction from her clitoris, repudiates her love for her mother and at the same time not infrequently represses a good part of her sexual trends in general. No doubt her turning away from her mother does not occur all at once, for to begin with the girl regards her castration as an individual misfortune, and only gradually extends it to other females and finally to her mother as well. Her love was directed to her *phallic* mother; with the discovery that her mother is castrated it becomes possible to drop her as an object, so that the motives for hostility, which have long been accumulating, gain the upper hand. This means, therefore, that as a result of the discovery of women's lack of a penis they are debased in value for girls just as they are for boys and later perhaps for men.

You all know the immense aetiological importance attributed by our neurotic patients to their masturbation. They make it responsible for all their troubles and we have the greatest difficulty in persuading them that they are mistaken. In fact, however, we ought to admit to them that they are right, for masturbation is the executive agent of infantile sexuality, from the faulty development of which they are indeed suffering. But what neurotics mostly blame is the masturbation of the period of puberty; they have mostly forgotten that of early infancy, which is what is really in question. I wish I might have an opportunity some time of explaining to you at length how important all the factual details of early masturbation become for the individual's subsequent neurosis or character: whether or not it was discovered, how the parents struggled against it or permitted it, or whether he succeeded in suppressing it himself. All of this leaves permanent traces on his development. But I am on the whole glad that I need not do this. It would be a hard and tedious task and at the end of it you would put me in an embarrassing situation by quite certainly asking me to give you some practical advice as to how a parent or educator should deal with the masturbation of small children.[9] From the development of girls, which is what my present lecture is concerned with, I can give you the example of a child herself trying to get free from masturbating. She does not always succeed in this. If envy for the penis has provoked a powerful impulse against clitoridal masturbation but this nevertheless refuses to give way, a violent struggle for liberation ensues in which the girl, as it were, herself takes over the role of her deposed mother and gives expression to her entire dissatisfaction with her inferior clitoris in her efforts against obtaining satisfaction from it. Many years later, when her masturbatory activity has long since been suppressed, an interest still persists which we must interpret as a defence against a temptation that is still dreaded. It manifests itself in the emergence of sympathy for those to whom similar difficulties are attributed, it plays a part as a motive in contracting a marriage and, indeed, it may determine the choice of a husband or lover. Disposing of early infantile masturbation is truly no easy or indifferent business.

Along with the abandonment of clitoridal masturbation a certain amount of activity is renounced. Passivity now has the upper hand, and the girl's turning to her father is accomplished principally with the help of passive instinctual impulses. You can see that a wave of development like this, which clears the phallic activity out of the way, smooths the ground for femininity. If too much is not lost in the course of it through repression, this femininity may turn out to be normal. The wish with which the girl turns to her father is no doubt originally the wish for the penis which her mother has refused her and which she now expects from her father. The feminine situation is only established, however, if the wish for a penis is replaced by one for a baby, if, that is, a baby takes the place of a penis in accordance with an ancient symbolic equivalence. It has not escaped us that the girl has wished for a baby earlier, in the undisturbed phallic phase: that, of course, was the meaning of her playing with dolls. But that play was not in fact an expression of her femininity; it served as an identification with her mother with the intention of substituting activity for passivity. *She* was playing the part of her mother and the doll was herself: now she could do with the baby everything that her mother used to do with her. Not until the emergence of the wish for a penis does the doll-baby become a baby from the girl's father, and thereafter the aim of the most powerful feminine wish. Her happiness is great if later on this wish for a baby finds fulfilment in reality, and quite especially so if the baby is a little boy who brings the longed-for penis with him.[10] Often enough in her combined picture of 'a baby from her father' the emphasis is laid on the baby and her father left unstressed. In this way the ancient masculine wish for the possession of a penis is still faintly visible through the femininity now achieved. But perhaps we ought rather to recognize this wish for a penis as being *par excellence* a feminine one.

With the transference of the wish for a penis-baby on to her father, the girl has entered the situation of the Oedipus complex. Her hostility to her mother, which did not need to be freshly created, is now greatly intensified, for she becomes the girl's rival, who receives from her father everything that she desires from him. For a long time the girl's Oedipus complex concealed her pre-Oedipus attachment to her mother from our view, though it is nevertheless so important and leaves such lasting fixations behind it. For girls the Oedipus situation is the outcome of a long and difficult development; it is a kind of preliminary solution, a position of rest which is not soon abandoned, especially as the beginning of the latency period is not far distant. And we are now struck by a difference between the two sexes, which is probably momentous, in regard to the relation of the Oedipus complex to the castration complex. In a boy the Oedipus complex, in which he desires his mother and would like to get rid of his father as being a rival, develops naturally from the phase of his phallic sexuality. The threat of castration compels him, however, to give up that attitude. Under the impression of the danger of losing his penis, the Oedipus complex is abandoned, repressed and, in the most normal cases, entirely destroyed, and a severe super-ego is set up as its heir. What happens with a girl is almost the opposite. The castration complex prepares for the Oedipus complex instead of destroying it; the girl is driven out of her attachment to her mother through the influence of her envy for the penis and she enters the Oedipus situation as though into a haven of refuge. In the absence of fear of castration the chief motive is lacking which leads boys to surmount the Oedipus complex. Girls remain in it for an indeterminate length of time; they demolish it late and, even so, incompletely. In these circumstances the formation of the super-ego must suffer; it cannot attain the strength and independence which give it its cultural significance, and feminists are not pleased when we point out to them the effects of this factor upon the average feminine character.

To go back a little. We mentioned as the second possible reaction to the discovery of female castration the development of a powerful masculinity complex. By this we mean that the girl refuses, as it were, to recognize the unwelcome fact and, defiantly rebellious, even exaggerates her previous masculinity, clings to her clitoridal activity and takes refuge in an identification with her phallic mother or her father. What can it be that decides in favour of this outcome? We can only suppose that it is a constitutional factor, a greater amount of activity, such as is ordinarily characteristic of a male. However that may be, the essence of this process is that at this point in development the wave of passivity is avoided which opens the way to the turn towards femininity. The extreme achievement of such a masculinity complex would appear to be the influencing of the choice of an object in the sense of manifest homosexuality. Analytic experience teaches us, to be sure, that female homosexuality is seldom or never a direct continuation of infantile masculinity. Even for a girl of this kind it seems necessary that she should take her father as an object for some time and enter the Oedipus situation. But afterwards, as a result of her inevitable disappointments from her father, she is driven to regress into her early masculinity complex. The significance of these disappointments must not be exaggerated; a girl who is destined to become feminine is not spared them, though they do not have the same effect. The predominance of the constitutional factor seems indisputable; but the two phases in the development of female homosexuality are well mirrored in the practices of homosexuals, who play the parts of mother and baby with each other as often and as clearly as those of husband and wife.

What I have been telling you here may be described as the prehistory of women. It is a product of the very last few years and may have been of interest to you as an example of detailed analytic work. Since its subject is woman, I will venture on this occasion to mention by name a few of the women who have made valuable contributions to this investigation. Dr. Ruth Mack Brunswick [1928] was the first to describe a case of neurosis which went back to a fixation in the pre-Oedipus stage and had never reached the Oedipus situation at all. The case took the form of jealous paranoia and proved accessible to therapy. Dr. Jeanne Lampl-de Groot [1927] has established the incredible phallic activity of girls towards their mother by some assured observations, and Dr.

Helene Deutsch [1932] has shown that the erotic actions of homosexual women reproduce the relations between mother and baby.

It is not my intention to pursue the further behaviour of femininity through puberty to the period of maturity. Our knowledge, moreover, would be insufficient for the purpose. But I will bring a few features together in what follows. Taking its prehistory as a starting-point, I will only emphasize here that the development of femininity remains exposed to disturbance by the residual phenomena of the early masculine period. Regressions to the fixations of the pre-Oedipus phases very frequently occur; in the course of some women's lives there is a repeated alternation between periods in which masculinity or femininity gains the upper hand. Some portion of what we men call 'the enigma of women' may perhaps be derived from this expression of bisexuality in women's lives. But another question seems to have become ripe for judgement in the course of these researches. We have called the motive force of sexual life 'the libido'. Sexual life is dominated by the polarity of masculine-feminine; thus the notion suggests itself of considering the relation of the libido to this antithesis. It would not be surprising if it were to turn out that each sexuality had its own special libido appropriated to it, so that one sort of libido would pursue the aims of a masculine sexual life and another sort those of a feminine one. But nothing of the kind is true. There is only one libido, which serves both the masculine and the feminine sexual functions. To it itself we cannot assign any sex; if, following the conventional equation of activity and masculinity, we are inclined to describe it as masculine, we must not forget that it also covers trends with a passive aim. Nevertheless the juxtaposition 'feminine libido' is without any justification. Furthermore, it is our impression that more constraint has been applied to the libido when it is pressed into the service of the feminine function, and that—to speak teleologically—Nature takes less careful account of its [that function's] demands than in the case of masculinity. And the reason for this may lie—thinking once again teleologically—in the fact that the accomplishment of the aim of biology has been entrusted to the aggressiveness of men and has been made to some extent independent of women's consent.

The sexual frigidity of women, the frequency of which appears to confirm this disregard, is a phenomenon that is still insufficiently understood. Sometimes it is psychogenic and in that case accessible to influence; but in other cases it suggests the hypothesis of its being constitutionally determined and even of there being a contributory anatomical factor.

I have promised to tell you of a few more psychical peculiarities of mature femininity, as we come across them in analytic observation. We do not lay claim to more than an average validity for these assertions; nor is it always easy to distinguish what should be ascribed to the influence of the sexual function and what to social breeding. Thus, we attribute a larger amount of narcissism to femininity, which also affects women's choice of object, so that to be loved is a stronger need for them than to love. The effect of penis-envy has a share, further, in the physical vanity of women, since they are bound to value their charms more highly as a late compensation for their original sexual inferiority.[11] Shame, which is considered to be a feminine characteristic *par excellence* but is far more a matter of convention than might be supposed, has as its purpose, we believe, concealment of genital deficiency. We are not forgetting that at a later time shame takes on other functions. It seems that women have made few contributions to the discoveries and inventions in the history of civilization; there is, however, one technique which they may have invented—that of plaiting and weaving. If that is so, we should be tempted to guess the unconscious motive for the achievement. Nature herself would seem to have given the model which this achievement imitates by causing the growth at maturity of the pubic hair that conceals the genitals. The step that remained to be taken lay in making the threads adhere to one another, while on the body they stick into the skin and are only matted together. If you reject this idea as fantastic and regard my belief in the influence of lack of a penis on the configuration of femininity as an *idée fixe*, I am of course defenceless.

The determinants of women's choice of an object are often made unrecognizable by social conditions. Where the choice is able to show itself freely, it is often made in accordance with the narcissistic ideal of the man whom the girl had wished to become. If the girl has remained in her attachment to her father—that is, in the Oedipus complex—her choice is made according to the paternal type. Since, when she turned from her mother to her father, the hostility of her ambivalent relation remained with her mother, a choice of this kind should guarantee a happy marriage. But very often the outcome is of a kind that presents a general threat to such a settlement of the conflict due to ambivalence. The hostility that has been left behind follows in the train of the positive attachment and spreads over on to the new object. The woman's husband, who to begin with inherited from her father, becomes after a time her mother's heir as well. So it may easily happen that the second half of a woman's life may be filled by the struggle against her husband, just as the shorter first half was filled by her rebellion against her mother. When this reaction has been lived through, a second marriage may easily turn out very much more satisfying.[12] Another alteration in a woman's nature, for which lovers are unprepared, may occur in a marriage after the first child is born. Under the influence of a woman's becoming a mother herself, an identification with her own mother may be revived, against which she had striven up till the time of her marriage, and this may attract all the available libido to itself, so that the compulsion to repeat reproduces an unhappy marriage between her parents. The difference in a mother's reaction to the birth of a son or a daughter shows that the old factor of lack of a penis has even now not lost its strength. A mother is only brought unlimited satisfaction by her relation to a son; this is altogether the most perfect, the most free from ambivalence of all human relationships.[13] A mother can transfer to her son the ambition which she has been obliged to suppress in herself, and she can expect from him the satisfaction of all that has been left over in her of her masculinity complex. Even a marriage is not made secure until the wife has succeeded in making her husband her child as well and in acting as a mother to him.

A woman's identification with her mother allows us to distinguish two strata: the pre-Oedipus one which rests on her affectionate attachment to her mother and takes her as a model, and the later one from the Oedipus complex which seeks to get rid of her mother and take her place with her father. We are no doubt justified in saying that much of both of them is left over for the future and that neither of them is adequately surmounted in the course of development. But the phase of the affectionate pre-Oedipus attachment is the decisive one for a woman's future: during it preparations are made for the acquisition of the characteristics with which she will later fulfil her role in the sexual function and perform her invaluable social tasks. It is in this identification

too that she acquires her attractiveness to a man, whose Oedipus attachment to his mother it kindles into passion. How often it happens, however, that it is only his son who obtains what he himself aspired to! One gets an impression that a man's love and a woman's are a phase apart psychologically.

The fact that women must be regarded as having little sense of justice is no doubt related to the predominance of envy in their mental life; for the demand for justice is a modification of envy and lays down the condition subject to which one can put envy aside. We also regard women as weaker in their social interests and as having less capacity for sublimating their instincts than men. The former is no doubt derived from the dissocial quality which unquestionably characterizes all sexual relations. Lovers find sufficiency in each other, and families too resist inclusion in more comprehensive associations.[14] The aptitude for sublimation is subject to the greatest individual variations. On the other hand I cannot help mentioning an impression that we are constantly receiving during analytic practice. A man of about thirty strikes us as a youthful, somewhat unformed individual, whom we expect to make powerful use of the possibilities for development opened up to him by analysis. A woman of the same age, however, often frightens us by her psychical rigidity and unchangeability. Her libido has taken up final positions and seems incapable of exchanging them for others. There are no paths open to further development; it is as though the whole process had already run its course and remains thenceforward insusceptible to influence—as though, indeed, the difficult development to femininity had exhausted the possibilities of the person concerned. As therapists we lament this state of things, even if we succeed in putting an end to our patient's ailment by doing away with her neurotic conflict.

That is all I had to say to you about femininity. It is certainly incomplete and fragmentary and does not always sound friendly. But do not forget that I have only been describing women in so far as their nature is determined by their sexual function. It is true that that influence extends very far; but we do not overlook the fact that an individual woman may be a human being in other respects as well. If you want to know more about femininity, enquire from your own experiences of life, or turn to the poets, or wait until science can give you deeper and more coherent information.

Notes

[1][This lecture is mainly based on two earlier papers: 'Some Psychical Consequences of the Anatomical Distinction between the Sexes' (1925*j*) and 'Female Sexuality' (1931*b*). The last section, however, dealing with women in adult life, contains new material. Freud returned to the subject once again in Chapter VII of the posthumous *Outline of Psycho-Analysis* (1940*a* [1938]).]

[2]Heads in hieroglyphic bonnets,
Heads in turbans and black birettas,
Heads in wigs and thousand other
Wretched, sweating heads of humans. . . .
     (Heine, *Nordsee* [Second Cycle, VII, 'Fragen'].)

[3][Bisexuality was discussed by Freud in the first edition of his *Three Essays on the Theory of Sexuality* (1905*d*). The passage includes a long footnote to which he made additions in later issues of the work.]

[4][I.e., mistaking two different things for a single one. The term was explained in *Introductory Lectures*, XX.]

[5][The difficulty of finding a psychological meaning for 'masculine' and 'feminine' was discussed in a long footnote added in 1915 to Section 4 of the third of his *Three Essays* (1905*d*), and again at the beginning of a still longer footnote at the end of Chapter IV of *Civilization and its Discontents* (1930*a*).]

[6][Cf. *Introductory Lectures*, XXI.]

[7][In his early discussions of the aetiology of hysteria Freud often mentioned seduction by adults as among its commonest causes (see, for instance, Section I of the second paper on the neuro-psychoses of defence (1896*c*), and Section II (*b*) of 'The Aetiology of Hysteria' (1896*c*). But nowhere in these early publications did he specifically inculpate the girl's father. Indeed, in some additional footnotes written in

1924 for the *Gesammelte Schriften* reprint of *Studies on Hysteria*, he admitted to having on two occasions suppressed the fact of the father's responsibility. He made this quite clear, however, in the letter to Fliess of September 21, 1897 (Freud, 1950*a*, Letter 69), in which he first expressed his scepticism about these stories told by his patients. His first published admission of his mistake was given several years later in a hint in the second of the *Three Essays* (1905*d*), but a much fuller account of the position followed in his contribution on the aetiology of the neuroses to a volume of Löwenfeld (1906*a*). Later on he gave two accounts of the effects that this discovery of his mistake had on his own mind—in his 'History of the Psycho-Analytic Movement' (1914*d*), and in his *Autobiographical Study* (1925*d*), (Norton, 1963). The further discovery which is described in the present paragraph of the text had already been indicated in the paper on 'Female Sexuality' (1931*b*).]

[8][See *Introductory Lectures*, XXII and XXIII.]

[9][Freud's fullest discussion of masturbation was in his contributions to a symposium on the subject in the Vienna Psycho-Analytical Society (1912*f*).]

[10][See below.]

[11][Cf. Section II of 'On Narcissism' (1914*c*).]

[12][This had already been remarked upon earlier, in 'The Taboo of Virginity' (1918*a*).]

[13][This point seems to have been made by Freud first in a footnote to Chapter VI of *Group Psychology* (1921*c*). He repeated it in the *Introductory Lectures*, XIII, and in Chapter V of *Civilization and its Discontents* (1930*a*). That exceptions may occur is shown by the example above.]

[14][Cf. some remarks on this in Chapter XII (D) of *Group Psychology* (1921*c*).]

I Am Unclean . . .

H. R. Hays

The novelist and anthropologist H. R. Hays studied at Cornell and Columbia and has taught at the University of Minnesota, Fairleigh Dickinson, and Southampton. He is the author of several works in social anthropology: From Ape to Angel, In the Beginnings, Children of the Raven, *and* The Kingdom of Hawaii.

The Dangerous Sex, *from which this selection is taken, is described by Frederic Wertham as "a long overdue and well-documented study of man's inhumanity to woman." Through an examination of the beliefs, customs, and mores of cultures from the primitive to the present, Hays chronicles the hostility and cruelty with which men have treated women and seeks reasons in male fears and ignorance. The chapter reprinted here describes the highly prevalent treatment of woman as dirty, woman as cosmically dangerous. The biological processes of women have "big magic"; they are fraught with serious consequences and thus surrounded by "big scare." Interestingly, the theme of male fear of women, not a new or uncommon idea, is increasingly a factor in analyses of male-female relations.*

H. R. Hays. *The Dangerous Sex*. N.Y.: Putnam's Sons, 1964.

WHEN MENSTRUATING, A SURINAM NEGRO woman lives in solitude. If anyone approaches her, she must cry out, "I am unclean."

The notion that women's sexual processes are impure is worldwide and persistent; the magical fear of menstrual blood is particularly intense. In the first place, the fact that blood flows from the female genitals at regular intervals sets women off from the other sex and gives them the exceptional properties of mana in a world in which men set the norm. The taboos which surround the first menstruation are particularly severe. The phenomenon itself is frequently explained as a supernatural wound, the result of an attack by a bird, a snake or a lizard. The origin of the female genital as a result of castration or sadistic attack is also illustrated in myths concerning the creation of women. Since male fantasy is dominant in human institutions, a very early time is often referred to in which there were only men and no women. The Negritos of the Malay Peninsula maintain there was once an ancestral creator entity, the monitor lizard. Since his contemporaries were all men, the lizard caught one of them, cut off his genitals and made him into a woman who became the lizard's wife and the ancestor of the Negritos. When Christopher Columbus discovered the Indians inhabiting Haiti, whom he named Caribs, he left a friar among them as a missionary. Friar Pane recorded a story concerning the Indian ancestors who had no women yet felt they should have some. One day they observed certain creatures who were falling out of the trees or hiding in the branches. These alien beings had no sex organs whatsoever. The Carib ancestors bound them and tied woodpeckers to them in the proper place. The birds pecked out the desired sexual orifices. Not only do we have here the theme of women being created by castration appearing on opposite sides of the world but, significantly enough, the image of the vulva as a wound also occurs in the fantasies of male psychoanalytical patients.

New Guinea carvings show images of women

with a crocodile attacking the vulva, a hornbill plunging its beak into the organ or a penislike snake emerging from it. On the one hand there is the idea of castration and on the other an image of the female genital being created by a sadistic attack by the penis, symbolized by lizard, bird beak, or snake. The mysterious and dangerous nature of the wound is uppermost in primitive tradition.

Blood in all of its manifestations is a source of mana. In the case of menstrual blood the ancient ambivalence is in evidence with the harmful aspect predominating. The dangers of contact and contagion are so great that women are nearly always secluded or forced to reside apart during their monthly periods. Special huts are built for them by the Bakairi of Brazil, the Shuswap of British Columbia, the Gauri of northern India, the Veddas of Ceylon, and the Algonkian of the North American forest. From this it can be seen that the custom covers the globe.

Then, too, a sort of fumigating sometimes takes place. Siberian Samoyed women step over fires of burning reindeer skin. They must also refrain from cooking food for their men. Among the Nootka of the Canadian northwest coast, at her first period a girl is given her private eating utensils and must eat alone for eight months. The Chippewa girl also eats alone, cannot cross a public road or talk to any man or boy. Eskimo girls at their first period are taboo for forty days. They must sit crouching in a corner, their faces to the wall, draw their hoods over their heads, let their hair hang over their faces and only leave the house when everyone else is asleep. Hermann Ploss describes a still more curious segregation practiced by the Australians of Queensland. The girl is taken to a shady place. Her mother draws a circle on the ground and digs a deep hole into which the girl must step. "The sandy soil is then filled in, leaving her buried up to the waist. A woven hedge of branches or twigs is set around her with an opening toward which she turns her face. Her mother kindles a fire at the opening, the girl remains in her nest of earth in a squatting posture with folded arms and hands resting downward on the sand heap that covers her lower limbs."

We are not told how long she must remain in the condition of the heroine of Beckett's play, *Happy Days*, but it is evident that the soil is supposed to purify or nullify her dangerous condition.

Among the Dogon of East Africa the menstrual taboo is so strong that a woman in this condition brings misfortune to everything she touches. Not only is she segregated in an isolated hut and provided with special eating utensils, but if she is seen passing through the village a general purification must take place. The Wogeo of South Australia believe that if a man has contact with a menstruating woman he will die from a wasting disease against which there is no remedy whatsoever.

The Hindus observe an endless number of prohibitions during the first three days of a woman's period. She must not weep, mount a horse, an ox or an elephant, be carried in a palanquin or drive in a vehicle.

In Hebrew tradition the menstruating woman is forbidden to work in a kitchen, sit at meals with other people, or drink from a glass used by others. Any contact with her husband is a sin and the penalty for intercourse during her period is death for both. Indeed the misfortunes which men suffer when they break the menstrual taboo vary but they are always severe. A Uganda Bantu woman by touching her husband's effects makes him sick; if she lays a hand on his weapons, he will be killed in the next fight. The natives of Malacca believe that coitus, or even contact, will cause the man to lose his virility.

The prohibitions which we have just been discussing occur in ancient or primitive cultures. Menstrual anxiety, however, is so deeply ingrained in the male psyche that it lingers in folk tradition. The peasants of eastern Europe believe that a woman must not bake bread, make pickles, churn butter or spin thread during her period or all will go wrong. Here, of course, is a survival of the idea that food is particularly susceptible to the deadly contagion. In Silesian folklore women during their periods are forbidden to plant seedlings or work in the garden. The Roman author Pliny tells us that contact of menstruous women with new wine or ripe fruit will sour both. The same author provides us with examples of ambivalence: "Hailstorms, whirlwinds and lightnings even will be scared away by a woman uncovering her body while her courses are upon her. . . . Also if a woman strips herself naked while she is menstruating and walks around a field of wheat, the caterpillars, worms, beetles and other vermin will fall off the ears of corn [wheat]. Algonkian women walk around a cornfield for the same reason. Menstrual blood is also thought to cure leprosy and is actually by European peasants sometimes put into a man's coffee as a love charm. In Russian folklore it is said to cure warts and birthmarks. These instances are enough to show that the basic principle of ambivalent mana is involved. The overwhelming amount of evidence proves, however, that men do not envy the female ability to menstruate but fear it.

An example cited by Havelock Ellis shows that even in the late nineteenth century educated men were not free of this superstition. In 1891 a British doctor, William Goodell, wrote that he had to shake off the tradition that women must not be operated upon during their periods. "Our forefathers from time immemorial have thought and taught that the presence of a menstruating woman would pollute solemn religious rites, would sour milk, spoil the fermentation in wine vats, and much other mischief in a general way." Ellis also cites several instances of violinists who were convinced that the strings of their instruments continually broke while their wives were indisposed.

Even Hermann Ploss and Max Bartels in their gynecological and anthropological work *Woman*, first published in Germany in 1905, wrote: "But it seems very doubtful whether these superstitions and traditions will ever be eradicated. They are far too deeply and far too widely ramified in the mind and emotions of humanity."

It will be seen that all the basic predispositions to anxiety are involved. Women by their recurring supernatural wound are set apart as aliens from the male norm. Sensitivity to contact and contagion is aroused and the symbol of the whole complex is blood, the powerful magic liquid on which life depends.

But menstruation is not the only female process which is surrounded with precautions. Pregnancy and childbirth, although the focus of various ideas, again arouse anxiety connected with blood, impurity and contagion. In addition, the production of a live being from a woman's body undoubtedly endows her with the supernatural properties of mana. In most cases the woman must be segregated or else she must give birth alone in the forest as among the Negritos, some east coast African Negroes, the Kiwai Papuans and the Guaná of Paraguay. The Hottentots of South Africa, the Tahitians, the Todas of India and the Gilyaks of the island of Sakhalin are among those who build a special hut or tent.

The misfortunes brought about by pregnancy and childbirth parallel those of menstruation. Among the Indians of Costa Rica, a woman pregnant for the first time infects the whole neighborhood; she is blamed for any deaths which may occur and her husband is obliged to pay damages. Cape Town Bantu males believe that looking upon a lying-in woman will result in their being killed in battle. Some Brazilian Indians are sure that if the woman is not out of the house during childbirth weapons will lose their power. The Sulka of New Britain feel that in addition men will become cowardly and taro shoots will not sprout. A purification ceremony consists of chewing ginger, spitting it on twigs which are held in the smoke of a fire, and repeating certain charms. The twigs are then placed on the taro shoots, on weapons, and over doors and on roofs.

Those who aid the parturient woman are also sure to be infected by the contagion. Garcilaso de la Vega, the chronicler of the ancient Incas, wrote that no one must help a woman in childbirth, and any who did would be regarded as witches. Among the Hebrews the midwife was regarded as unclean. The whole concept of "lying in"—only recently dispelled by new medical theories requiring the new mother to be up and about as soon as possible—which was rationalized as necessary for the woman to regain her strength, originated in magical precautions, as is clearly shown by the extreme length of time during which primitive women were sequestered and by the ceremonies carried out to purify them. To cite a few examples: The time varied from forty days, among the Swahili of Africa, to two months among the Eskimo or two to three months in Tahiti. Significantly enough, the period was longer after the birth of a girl in India, among the Hebrews, among many New Guinea tribes, the Masai of West Africa, and the Cree Indians of North America.

An example of purification ceremonies is the bathing of Hebrew women in special bathhouses in which both menstruating and parturient women were cleansed. After her time of sequestration was over, the Hebrew woman was required to send a lamb and a dove to the priest as sacrifices. The Pueblo Indians treat the purification more lyrically. Five days after the child is born, its mother is ceremonially washed. She then walks in the retinue of a priest to view the sunrise, throwing up cornflowers and blowing them about in the air.

In accordance with the feeling that the exceptional is imbued with mana, miscarriage, being more abnormal than ordinary birth, is regarded with particular apprehension. The African Bantu consider it a cause of drought. They also believe that if a woman succeeds in aborting herself and at once has sexual relations with a man his death will follow.

The samplings just given are selected from a wealth of evidence which demonstrates that the male attitude toward female sexual functions is basically apprehensive; women, in short, are dangerous. Taboos and fears of contagion, however, are not limited to the physical crises in their lives. When we investigate the ideas of contact still further, a host of activities requires avoidance of women in general.

Since nutrition is one of the basic needs of human beings, and food is brought into contact with the body, it is not surprising that food and eating are universally involved with magical precautions. Women being intrinsically dangerous, their relation to food is a psychological problem. We have already cited food and eating taboos in relation to menstruation. Among preliterates and in ancient civilizations it is the rule rather than the exception that women do not eat with their husbands. Although in later periods the idea that the dominant male must be served first also enters the picture, the germ of the custom is certainly the notion that female impurity will contaminate a man's food and do him harm. Throughout Africa men and women eat separately, and the same is true of many South American tribes. In Melanesia and Polynesia the same segregation is observed. The Todas, those hill people of India who have already been cited, also observe the taboo, as do the sophisticated Hindus. If the wife of one of the Hindus were to touch his food it would be rendered unfit for his use. The same precaution was widespread in North America. The early traveler and artist George Catlin said he never saw Indians and squaws eating together. Henry Rowe Schoolcraft, the first American anthropologist, when he was an Indian agent among the Chippewa, married a half-Indian girl. Although his wife had been educated in England and helped him collect Algonkian folklore and her dark-skinned mother prevented a border incident by mediating between her people and the whites, the mother's conservatism was so intense that she could never be persuaded to eat with her son-in-law.

The two exclusive male activities of hunting and fighting are also very often associated with avoidance of women. Nothing is closer to man's maleness than his weapons and his hunting gear. In Tahiti, women are prohibited from touching weapons and fishing apparatus. In Queensland the natives throw away their fishing lines if women step over them, and elsewhere a woman is forbidden to step over objects, because in so doing the woman's sex passes over them and they are thus exposed to the seat of contagion. (When a Maori warrior wishes to absorb the phallic magic of a powerful chief, he crawls between his legs.) A Dakota Indian's weapons must not be touched by a woman and women of the Siberian hunting tribes must abide by the same taboo. If a woman touches a Zulu's assegai, he cannot use it again.

Cattle among the southern Bantu are an important form of male ego expression and in this case they are taboo to women. If women touch them the beasts will fall ill. Fighting cocks among the Malay are treated in the same way. This taboo, however, among the Bantu does not apply to girls who have not yet reached puberty or to old women who have passed the menopause, proving conclusively that it is the female sexual mana which is thought to do the damage.

The necessity of abstaining from intercourse with women before undertaking the chase and warfare has sometimes been explained as a fear of the debilitating effect of what is considered the weaker sex. Indeed it is often so rationalized by the primitives themselves. That this is a late addition is indicated by the fact that fasting often accompanies the ritual surrounding hunting and war and fasting can scarcely be construed as a method of conserving strength.

Sexual abstinence before war and hunting is practiced all over Polynesia and in many parts of Melanesia. The headhunters of Assam, in India, are particularly strict in observing this taboo. In one case the wife of a headman spoke to her husband, unaware that he was returning with a group of warriors who had taken trophy heads. When she learned what she had done she was so disturbed that she grew sick and died. In British Columbia and other areas of North America which were inhabited by the hunting tribes, the taboo against contact with women before hunting or fighting was carefully observed. The Huichol of Mexico did so, and explained that a deer would never enter the snare of a man who was sleeping with his wife. It would simply look at the trap, snort "pooh, pooh" and go away. Throughout Africa continence and avoidance were observed before war and hunting. Women were forbidden to approach the Zulu army except (as in the case of cattle) for old women past the menopause, because such women "have become men."

The hunting taboo can be exaggerated to the extent that the Bangalas of equatorial Africa remain continent while they are making nets to capture wild pigs and the Melanesian of the Torres Straits refrain from intercourse during the mating season of turtles (an important food), in a curious defiance of the principles of mimetic magic.

Most extreme of all is the taboo which functions on the principle that since the name is a part of the individual, its use will affect his well-being. The Bantu women of Nyasaland do not speak their husband's names or any words that may be synonymous. A Warramunga woman of Australia may not mention the ordinary name of a man, which she knows, and in addition he has a secret name which she does not even know. Similarly the Hindus, whom we have continually cited as taboo ridden, do not allow a woman to mention her husband's name. She must speak of him as the "man of the house" or "father of the household" and if she dreams of his name this will result in his untimely death.

The tiny Bushmen, who are one of the oldest peoples and who support life by the simplest of hunting and gathering techniques, exemplify nearly all of the avoidances we have been discussing. Men and women sit on different sides of their crude shelters of woven twigs or grasses—if a man occupies a woman's place he will become impotent. When a man sets out to shoot an eland or a giraffe, he must avoid intercourse or the poison on his arrows will lose its power. A Bushman woman gives birth secretly in the bush. If a man inadvertently steps over the spot he will lose his ability to hunt.

A Bushman myth emphasizes the alienation of the two sexes almost in terms of their being different tribes. In the early times men and women lived apart, the former hunting animals exclusively, the latter pursuing a gathering existence. Five of the men, who were out hunting, being careless creatures, let their fire go out. The women, who were careful and or-

derly, always kept their fire going. The men, having killed a springbok, became desperate for means to cook it, so one of their number set out to get fire, crossed the river, and met one of the women gathering seeds. When he asked her for some fire, she invited him to the feminine camp. While he was there she said, "You are very hungry. Just wait until I pound up these seeds and I will boil them and give you some." She made him some porridge. After he had eaten it, he said, "Well, it's nice food so I shall just stay with you." The men who were left waited and wondered. They still had the springbok and they still had no fire. The second man set out, only to be tempted by female cooking, and to take up residence in the camp of the women. The same thing happened to the third man. The two men left were very frightened. They suspected something terrible had happened to their comrades. They cast the divining bones but the omens were favorable. The fourth man set out timidly, only to end by joining his comrades. The last man became very frightened indeed and besides by now the springbok had rotted. He took his bow and arrows and ran away.

On the other side of the world, among the Pueblo and Zuñi Indians, myths which tell of the emergence of their forefathers from the ground also divide the sexes into two camps, although in this case the women are portrayed as less efficient than the men in their attempts to reach the upper world. In these traditional stories such matters as sex and marriage are completely ignored, the sexes are viewed as groups living apart, a theme which may be a reflection of the periodic segregation of women.

The earliest types of religion at any rate codify male anxiety by proclaiming that women shall remain inactive for a considerable portion of their lives. The same religious sanctions prohibit them from participating in many human activities, partly excluding them from the human condition. And all the evidence points to the fact that this situation began with the simplest types of group association, in all probability as far back as the Paleolithic.

Despite these barriers of alienation and fear, the sex drive after all does insure reproduction. The act of procreation, however, arouses still another type of ambivalence which affects the status of women and substantiates the view that the conditions of man's development as a social being prevent him from ever taking eros for granted.

References

Cazeneuve, Jean
    1958 *Les rites et la condition humaine*. Paris.

Crawley, Ernest
    1960 *The Mystic Rose*. (Meridian) New York.

Ellis, Havelock
    1901–1928 *Studies in the Psychology of Sex*, Vol. I. Philadelphia.

Hays, H. R.
    1963 *In the Beginnings*. New York.

Ploss, Hermann, and Bartels, M. C. A. and P. R. A.
    1935 *Woman: An Historical, Gynaecological and Anthropological Compendium*, 3 Vols. London.

Woman as "Other"

Simone de Beauvoir

*French existentialist Simone de Beauvoir (1908–1986)
is one of the most important figures of the women's
movement in the twentieth century.* The Second
Sex *was one of the earliest inquiries into the social
construction of "femininity" and sparked a great deal
of debate. Beauvoir was a political activist all her life
and participated in the women's movement in France
during the second wave.*

Le Deuxième Sexe (The Second Sex) *was
published in France in 1949 and in the United States
in 1953, a time and climate hospitable neither to
feminist scholarship nor to activism. Coming at a time
of transition for the women's movement, between the
social-psychological debates of the twenties and thirties
and the liberation movement of the sixties, the book
was a work of great creativity and courage. Broad in
range and at times complex in argument, it covers
issues in philosophy, biology, psychology, sociology,
anthropology, education, politics, history, and more.
The unifying theme is summarized by H. M. Parshley
in the translator's preface:*

> *. . . Since patriarchal times women have in general
> been forced to occupy a secondary place in the
> world in relation to men, a position comparable in
> many respects with that of racial minorities in spite
> of the fact that women constitute numerically at
> least half of the human race, and further that this
> secondary standing is not imposed of necessity by
> natural "feminine" characteristics but rather by
> strong environmental forces of educational and
> social tradition under the purposeful control of
> men. This, the author maintains, has resulted in
> the general failure of women to take a place of
> human dignity as free and independent existents,
> associated with men on the plane of intellectual and
> professional equality, a condition that not only has
> limited their achievement in many fields but also
> has given rise to pervasive social evils and has had
> a particularly vitiating effect on the sexual
> relations between men and women.*

*Beauvoir's thesis is not new and was not new in
1949, but it had been ignored, and her treatment of it
was unique. Today, she has been faulted for being
nonpolitical in her orientation, not sufficiently
concerned with remedy, and at times even sexist in her
perspective. Although that may be true of the work in
its present context, it was a criticism far less applicable
in its day, and the book was widely read.*

*As a philosophy, existentialism emphasizes direct
experience, feeling, awareness, choice, commitment,
and honesty. It strives for living "authentically," being
true to one's own values and insights, living fully and
freely, taking responsibility for one's actions,
sharpening one's understanding, and ultimately
moving beyond the confines of the brute here and now
as determined by the concrete social environment. In
this, one is said to strive for* transcendence. *A major
theme of* The Second Sex *is that women's peripheral
existence denies them the chance for transcendence.*

*In the following selection, Beauvoir analyzes the
female condition of* otherness *or* alterity. *It is
natural, she argues, for people—either individually or
collectively—to understand their existence in terms of
a fundamental duality: I (Self) and things not myself
(Other). The mature adult juxtaposes her or his own
needs and perceptions against those of others,
understanding at the same time that the other person
is doing so as well. To me, I am Self, you are Other;
but to you, you are Self, I am Other. I realize and
accept this as so. Beauvoir terms the equality of claims
to Self and Otherness from different perspectives*
reciprocity. *She points out, however, that the typical
reciprocity of claims to Selfness does not obtain
between women and men. Men perceive themselves as
Self and women as Other. That is as it should be. The
problem Beauvoir emphasizes is that women too
perceive men as Self (as subject) and themselves as
Other. Commonly, neither men nor women recognize
the reciprocity of Selfness for women.*

From THE SECOND SEX by Simone de Beauvoir,
translated and edited by H. M. Parshley. Copyright
1952 by Alfred A. Knopf, Inc. Reprinted by permission
of the publisher.

A MAN WOULD NEVER GET THE NOTION OF WRITING A book on the peculiar situation of the human male.[1] But if I wish to define myself, I must first of all say: "I am a woman"; on this truth must be based all further discussion. A man never begins by presenting himself as an individual of a certain sex; it goes without saying that he is a man. The terms *masculine* and *feminine* are used symmetrically only as a matter of form, as on legal papers. In actuality the relation of the two sexes is not quite like that of two electrical poles, for man represents both the positive and the neutral, as is indicated by the common use of *man* to designate human beings in general; whereas woman represents only the negative, defined by limiting criteria, without reciprocity. In the midst of an abstract discussion it is vexing to hear a man say: "You think thus and so because you are a woman"; but I know that my only defense is to reply: "I think thus and so because it is true," thereby removing my subjective self from the argument. It would be out of the question to reply: "And you think the contrary because you are a man," for it is understood that the fact of being a man is no peculiarity. A man is in the right in being a man; it is the woman who is in the wrong. It amounts to this: just as for the ancients there was an absolute vertical with reference to which the oblique was defined, so there is an absolute human type, the masculine. Woman has ovaries, a uterus; these peculiarities imprison her in her subjectivity, circumscribe her within the limits of her own nature. It is often said that she thinks with her glands. Man superbly ignores the fact that his anatomy also includes glands, such as the testicles, and that they secrete hormones. He thinks of his body as a direct and normal connection with the world, which he believes he apprehends objectively, whereas he regards the body of woman as a hindrance, a prison, weighed down by everything peculiar to it. "The female is a female by virtue of a certain *lack* of qualities," said Aristotle; "we should regard the female nature as afflicted with a natural defectiveness." And St. Thomas for his part pronounced woman to be an "imperfect man," an "incidental" being. This is symbolized in Genesis where Eve is depicted as made from what Bossuet called "a supernumerary bone" of Adam.

Thus humanity is male and man defines woman not in herself but as relative to him; she is not regarded as an autonomous being. Michelet writes: "Woman, the relative being. . . ." And Benda is most positive in his *Rapport d' Uriel:* "The body of man makes sense in itself quite apart from that of woman, whereas the latter seems wanting in significance by itself. . . . Man can think of himself without woman. She cannot think of herself without man." And she is simply what man decrees; thus she is called "the sex," by which is meant that she appears essentially to the male as a sexual being. For him she is sex—absolute sex, no less. She is defined and differentiated with reference to man and not he with reference to her; she is the incidental, the inessential as opposed to the essential. He is the Subject, he is the Absolute—she is the Other.[2]

The category of the *Other* is as primordial as consciousness itself. In the most primitive societies, in the most ancient mythologies, one finds the expression of a duality—that of the Self and the Other. This duality was not originally attached to the division of the sexes; it was not dependent upon any empirical facts. It is revealed in such works as that of Granet on Chinese thought and those of Dumézil on the East Indies and Rome. The feminine element was at first no more involved in such pairs as Varuna-Mitra, Uranus-Zeus, Sun-Moon, and Day-Night than it was in the contrasts between Good and Evil, lucky and unlucky auspices, right and left, God and Lucifer. Otherness is a fundamental category of human thought.

Thus it is that no group ever sets itself up as the One without at once setting up the Other over against itself. If three travelers chance to occupy the same compartment, that is enough to make vaguely hostile "others" out of all the rest of the passengers on the train. In small-town eyes all persons not belonging to the village are "strangers" and suspect; to the native of a country all who inhabit other countries are "foreigners"; Jews are "different" for the anti-Semite, Negroes are "inferior" for American racists, aborigines are "natives" for colonists, proletarians are the "lower class" for the privileged.

Lévi-Strauss, at the end of a profound work on the various forms of primitive societies, reaches the following conclusion: "Passage from the state of Nature to the state of Culture is marked by man's ability to view biological relations as a series of contrasts; duality, alternation, opposition, and symmetry, whether under definite or vague forms, constitute not so much phenomena to be explained as fundamental and immediately given data of social reality."[3] These phenomena would be incomprehensible if in fact human society were simply a *Mitsein* or fellowship based on solidarity and friendliness. Things become clear, on the contrary, if, following Hegel, we find in consciousness itself a fundamental hostility toward every other consciousness; the subject can be posed only in being opposed—he sets himself up as the essential, as opposed to the other, the inessential, the object.

But the other consciousness, the other ego, sets up a reciprocal claim. The native traveling abroad is shocked to find himself in turn regarded as a "stranger" by the natives of neighboring countries. As a matter of fact, wars, festivals, trading, treaties, and contests among tribes, nations, and classes tend to deprive the concept *Other* of its absolute sense and to make manifest its relativity; willy-nilly, individuals and groups are forced to realize the reciprocity of their relations. How is it, then, that this reciprocity has not been recognized between the sexes, that one of the contrasting terms is set up as the sole essential, denying any relativity in regard to its correlative and defining the latter as pure otherness? Why is it that women do not dispute male sovereignty? No subject will readily volunteer to become the object, the inessential; it is not the Other who, in defining himself as the Other, establishes the One. The Other is posed as such by the One in defining himself as the One. But if the Other is not to regain the status of being the One, he must be submissive enough to accept this alien point of view. Whence comes this submission in the case of woman?

There are, to be sure, other cases in which a certain category has been able to dominate another completely for a time. Very often this privilege depends upon inequality of numbers—the majority imposes its rule upon the minority or persecutes it. But women are not a minority, like the American Negroes or the Jews; there are as many women as men on earth. Again, the two groups concerned have often been originally independent; they may have been formerly unaware of each other's existence, or perhaps they recognized each other's autonomy. But a historical event has resulted in the subjugation of the weaker by the stronger. The scattering of the Jews, the introduction of slavery into America, the conquests of imperialism are examples in point. In these cases the oppressed retained at least the memory of former days; they possessed in common a past, a tradition, sometimes a religion or a culture.

The parallel drawn by Bebel between women and the proletariat is valid in that neither ever formed a minority or a separate collective unit of mankind. And instead of a single historical event it is in both cases a historical development that explains their status as a class and accounts for the membership of *particular individuals* in that class. But proletarians have not always existed, whereas there have always been women. They are women in virtue of their anatomy and physiology. Throughout history they have always been subordinated to men,[4] and hence their dependency is not the result of a historical event or a social change—it was not something that *occurred*. The reason why otherness in this case seems to be an absolute is in part that it lacks the contingent or incidental nature of historical facts. A condition brought about at a certain time can be abolished at some other time, as the Negroes of Haiti and others have proved; but it might seem that a natural condition is beyond the possibility of change. In truth, however, the nature of things is no more immutably given, once for all, than is historical reality. If woman seems to be the inessential which never becomes the essential, it is because she herself fails to bring about this change. Proletarians say "We"; Negroes also. Regarding themselves as subjects, they transform the bourgeois, the whites, into "others." But women do not say "We," except at some congress of feminists or similar formal demonstration; men say "women," and women use the same word in referring to themselves. They do not authentically assume a subjective attitude. The proletarians have accomplished the revolution in Russia, the Negroes in Haiti, the Indo-Chinese are battling for it in Indo-China; but the women's effort has never been anything more than a symbolic agitation. They have gained only what men have been willing to grant; they have taken nothing, they have only received.[5]

The reason for this is that women lack concrete means for organizing themselves into a unit which can stand face to face with the correlative unit. They have no past, no history, no religion of their own; and they have no such solidarity of work and interest as that of the proletariat. They are not even promiscuously herded together in the way that creates community feeling among the American Negroes, the ghetto Jews, the workers of Saint-Denis, or the factory hands of Renault. They live dispersed among the males, attached through residence, housework, economic condition, and social standing to certain men—fathers or husbands—more firmly than they are to other women. If they belong to the bourgeoisie, they feel solidarity with men of that class, not with proletarian women; if they are white, their allegiance is to white men, not to Negro women. The proletariat can propose to massacre the ruling class, and a sufficiently fanatical Jew or Negro might dream of getting sole possession of the atomic bomb and making humanity wholly Jewish or black; but woman cannot even dream of exterminating the males. The bond that unites her to her oppressors is not comparable to any other. The division of the sexes is a biological fact, not an event in human history. Male and female stand opposed within a primordial *Mitsein*, and woman has not broken it. The couple is a fundamental unity with its two halves riveted together, and the cleavage of society along the line of sex is impossible. Here is to be found the basic trait of woman: she is the Other in a totality of which the two components are necessary to one another.

One could suppose that this reciprocity might have facilitated the liberation of woman. When Hercules sat at the feet of Omphale and helped with her spinning, his desire for her held him captive; but why did she fail to gain a lasting power? To revenge herself on Jason, Medea killed their children; and this grim legend would seem to suggest that she might have obtained a formidable influence over him through his love for his offspring. In *Lysistrata* Aristophanes gaily depicts a band of women who joined forces to gain social ends through the sexual needs of their men; but this is only a play. In the legend of the Sabine women, the latter soon abandoned their plan of remaining sterile to punish their ravishers. In truth woman has not been socially emancipated through man's need—sexual desire and the desire for offspring—which makes the male dependent for satisfaction upon the female.

Master and slave, also, are united by a reciprocal need, in this case economic, which does not liberate the slave. In the relation of master to slave the master does not make a point of the need that he has for the other; he has in his grasp the power of satisfying this need through his own action; whereas the slave, in his dependent condition, his hope and fear, is quite conscious of the need he has for his master. Even if the need is at bottom equally urgent for both, it always works in favor of the oppressor and against the oppressed. That is why the liberation of the working class, for example, has been slow.

Now, woman has always been man's dependent, if not his slave; the two sexes have never shared the world in equality. And even today woman is heavily handicapped, though her situation is beginning to change. Almost nowhere is her legal status the same as man's,[6] and frequently it is much to her disadvantage. Even when her rights are legally recognized in the abstract, long-standing custom prevents their full expression in the mores. In the economic sphere men and women can almost be said to make up two castes; other things being equal, the former hold the better jobs, get higher wages, and have more opportunity for success than their new competitors. In industry and politics men have a great many more positions and they monopolize the most important posts. In addition to all this, they enjoy a traditional prestige that the education of children tends in every way to support, for the present enshrines the past—and in the past all history has been made by men. At the present time, when women are beginning to take part in the affairs of the world, it is still a world that belongs to men—they have no doubt of it at all and women have scarcely any. To decline to be the Other, to refuse to be a party to the deal—this would be for women to renounce all the advantages conferred upon them by their alliance with the superior caste. Man-the-sovereign will provide woman-the-liege with material protection and will undertake the moral justification of her existence; thus she can evade at once both economic risk and the metaphysical risk of a liberty in which ends and aims must be contrived without assistance. Indeed, along with the ethical urge of each individual to affirm his subjective existence, there is also the temptation to forgo liberty and become a thing. This is an inauspicious road, for he who takes it—passive, lost, ruined—becomes henceforth the creature of another's will, frustrated in his transcendence and deprived of every value. But it is an easy road; on it one avoids the strain involved in undertaking an authentic existence. When man makes of woman the *Other*, he may, then, expect her to manifest deep-seated tendencies toward complicity. Thus, woman may fail to lay claim to the status of subject because she lacks definite resources, because she feels the necessary bond that ties her to man regardless of reciprocity, and because she is often very well pleased with her role as the *Other*.

But it will be asked at once: how did all this begin? It is easy to see that the duality of the sexes, like any duality, gives rise to conflict. And doubtless the winner will assume the status of absolute. But why should man have won from the start? It seems possible that women could have won the victory; or that the outcome of the conflict might never have been decided. How is it that this world has always belonged to the men and that things have begun to change only recently? Is this change a good thing? Will it bring about an equal sharing of the world between men and women?

These questions are not new, and they have often been answered. But the very fact that woman *is the Other* tends to cast suspicion upon all the justifications that men have ever been able to provide for it. These have all too evidently been dictated by men's interest. A little-known feminist of the seventeenth century, Poulain de la Barre, put it this way: "All that has been written about women by men should be suspect, for the men are at once judge and party to the lawsuit." Everywhere, at all times, the males have displayed their satisfaction in feeling that they are the lords of creation. "Blessed be God . . . that He did not make me a woman," say the Jews in their morning prayers, while their wives pray on a note of resignation: "Blessed be the Lord, who created me according to His will." The first among the blessings for which Plato thanked the gods was that he had been created free, not enslaved; the second, a man, not a woman. But the males could not enjoy this privilege fully unless they believed it to be founded on the absolute and the eternal; they sought to make the fact of their supremacy into a right. "Being men, those who have made and compiled the laws have favored their own sex, and jurists have elevated these laws into principles," to quote Poulain de la Barre once more.

Legislators, priests, philosophers, writers, and scientists have striven to show that the subordinate position of woman is willed in heaven and advantageous on earth. The religions invented by men reflect this wish for domination. In the legends of Eve and Pandora men have taken up arms against women. They have made use of philosophy and theology, as the quotations from Aristotle and St. Thomas have shown. Since ancient times satirists and moralists have delighted in showing up the weaknesses of women. We are familiar with the savage indictments hurled against women throughout French literature. Montherlant, for example, follows the tradition of Jean de Meung, though with less gusto. This hostility may at times be well founded, often it is gratuitous;

but in truth it more or less successfully conceals a desire for self-justification. As Montaigne says, "It is easier to accuse one sex than to excuse the other." Sometimes what is going on is clear enough. For instance, the Roman law limiting the rights of woman cited "the imbecility, the instability of the sex" just when the weakening of family ties seemed to threaten the interests of male heirs. And in the effort to keep the married woman under guardianship, appeal was made in the sixteenth century to the authority of St. Augustine, who declared that "woman is a creature neither decisive nor constant," at a time when the single woman was thought capable of managing her property. Montaigne understood clearly how arbitrary and unjust was woman's appointed lot: "Women are not in the wrong when they decline to accept the rules laid down for them, since the men make these rules without consulting them. No wonder intrigue and strife abound." But he did not go so far as to champion their cause.

It was only later, in the eighteenth century, that genuinely democratic men began to view the matter objectively. Diderot, among others, strove to show that woman is, like man, a human being. Later John Stuart Mill came fervently to her defense. But these philosophers displayed unusual impartiality. In the nineteenth century the feminist quarrel became again a quarrel of partisans. One of the consequences of the industrial revolution was the entrance of women into productive labor, and it was just here that the claims of the feminists emerged from the realm of theory and acquired an economic basis, while their opponents became the more aggressive. Although landed property lost power to some extent, the bourgeoisie clung to the old morality that found the guarantee of private property in the solidity of the family. Woman was ordered back into the home the more harshly as her emancipation became a real menace. Even within the working class the men endeavored to restrain woman's liberation, because they began to see the women as dangerous competitors—the more so because they were accustomed to work for lower wages.[7]

In proving woman's inferiority, the antifeminists then began to draw not only upon religion, philosophy, and theology, as before, but also upon science—biology, experimental psychology, etc. At most they were willing to grant "equality in difference" to the *other* sex. That profitable formula is most significant; it is precisely like the "equal but separate" formula of the Jim Crow laws aimed at the North American Negroes. As is well known, this so-called equalitarian segregation has resulted only in the most extreme discrimination. The similarity just noted is in no way due to chance, for whether it is a race, a caste, a class, or a sex that is reduced to a position of inferiority, the methods of justification are the same. "The eternal feminine" corresponds to "the black soul" and to "the Jewish character." True, the Jewish problem is on the whole very different from the other two—to the anti-Semite the Jew is not so much an inferior as he is an enemy for whom there is to be granted no place on earth, for whom annihilation is the fate desired. But there are deep similarities between the situation of woman and that of the Negro. Both are being emancipated today from a like paternalism, and the former master class wishes to "keep them in their place"—that is, the place chosen for them. In both cases the former masters lavish more or less sincere eulogies, either on the virtues of "the good Negro" with his dormant, childish, merry soul—the submissive Negro—or on the merits of the woman who is "truly feminine"—that is, frivolous, infantile, irresponsible—the submissive woman. In both cases the dominant class bases its argument on a state of affairs that it has itself created. As George Bernard Shaw puts it, in substance, "The American white relegates the black to the rank of shoeshine boy; and he concludes from this that the black is good for nothing but shining shoes." This vicious circle is met with in all analogous circumstances; when an individual (or a group of individuals) is kept in a situation of inferiority, the fact is that he *is* inferior. But the significance of the verb *to be* must be rightly understood here; it is in bad faith to give it a static value when it really has the dynamic Hegelian sense of "to have become." Yes, women on the whole *are* today inferior to men; that is, their situation affords them fewer possibilities. The question is: should that state of affairs continue?

Many men hope that it will continue; not all have given up the battle. The conservative bourgeoisie still see in the emancipation of women a menace to their morality and their interests. Some men dread feminine competition. Recently a male student wrote in the *Hebdo-Latin*: "Every woman student who goes into medicine or law robs us of a job." He never questioned his rights in this world. And economic interests are not the only ones concerned. One of the

benefits that oppression confers upon the oppressors is that the most humble among them is made to *feel* superior; thus, a "poor white" in the South can console himself with the thought that he is not a "dirty nigger"—and the more prosperous whites cleverly exploit this pride.

Similarly, the most mediocre of males feels himself a demigod as compared with women. It was much easier for M. de Montherlant to think himself a hero when he faced women (and women chosen for his purpose) than when he was obliged to act the man among men—something many women have done better than he, for that matter. And in September 1948, in one of his articles in the *Figaro littéraire*, Claude Mauriac—whose great originality is admired by all—could[8] write regarding woman: "*We* listen on a tone [*sic!*] of polite indifference . . . to the most brilliant among them, well knowing that her wit reflects more or less luminously ideas that come from *us*." Evidently the speaker referred to is not reflecting the ideas of Mauriac himself, for no one knows of his having any. It may be that she reflects ideas originating with men, but then, even among men there are those who have been known to appropriate ideas not their own; and one can well ask whether Claude Mauriac might not find more interesting a conversation reflecting Descartes, Marx, or Gide rather than himself. What is really remarkable is that by using the questionable *we* he identifies himself with St. Paul, Hegel, Lenin, and Nietzsche, and from the lofty eminence of their grandeur looks down disdainfully upon the bevy of women who make bold to converse with him on a footing of equality. In truth, I know of more than one woman who would refuse to suffer with patience Mauriac's "tone of polite indifference."

I have lingered on this example because the masculine attitude is here displayed with disarming ingenuousness. But men profit in many more subtle ways from the otherness, the alterity of woman. Here is miraculous balm for those afflicted with an inferiority complex, and indeed no one is more arrogant toward women, more aggressive or scornful, than the man who is anxious about his virility. Those who are not fear-ridden in the presence of their fellow men are much more disposed to recognize a fellow creature in woman; but even to these the myth of woman, the Other, is precious for many reasons.[9] They cannot be blamed for not cheerfully relinquishing all the benefits they derive from the myth, for they realize what they would lose in relinquishing woman as they fancy her to be, while they fail to realize what they have to gain from the woman of tomorrow. Refusal to pose oneself as the Subject, unique and absolute, requires great self-denial. Furthermore, the vast majority of men make no such claim explicitly. They do not *postulate* woman as inferior, for today they are too thoroughly imbued with the ideal of democracy not to recognize all human beings as equals.

In the bosom of the family, woman seems in the eyes of childhood and youth to be clothed in the same social dignity as the adult males. Later on, the young man, desiring and loving, experiences the resistance, the independence of the woman desired and loved; in marriage, he respects woman as wife and mother, and in the concrete events of conjugal life she stands there before him as a free being. He can therefore feel that social subordination as between the sexes no longer exists and that on the whole, in spite of differences, woman is an equal. As, however, he observes some point of inferiority—the most important being unfitness for the professions—he attributes these to natural causes. When he is in a co-operative and benevolent relation with woman, his theme is the principle of abstract equality, and he does not base his attitude upon such inequality as may exist. But when he is in conflict with her, the situation is reversed: his theme will be the existing inequality, and he will even take it as justification for denying abstract equality.[10]

So it is that many men will affirm as if in good faith that women *are* the equals of man and that they have nothing to clamor for, while *at the same time* they will say that women can never be the equals of man and that their demands are in vain. It is, in point of fact, a difficult matter for man to realize the extreme importance of social discriminations which seem outwardly insignificant but which produce in woman moral and intellectual effects so profound that they appear to spring from her original nature.[11] The most sympathetic of men never fully comprehend woman's concrete situation. And there is no reason to put much trust in the men when they rush to the defense of privileges whose full extent they can hardly measure. We shall not, then, permit ourselves to be intimidated by the number and violence of the attacks launched against women, nor to be entrapped by the self-seeking eulogies bestowed on the "true woman," nor to profit by the enthusiasm for woman's destiny manifested by men who would not for the world have any part of it.

We should consider the arguments of the feminists with no less suspicion, however, for very often their controversial aim deprives them of all real value. If the "woman question" seems trivial, it is because masculine arrogance has made of it a "quarrel"; and when quarreling, one no longer reasons well. People have tirelessly sought to prove that woman is superior, inferior, or equal to man. Some say that, having been created after Adam, she is evidently a secondary being; others say on the contrary that Adam was only a rough draft and that God succeeded in producing the human being in perfection when He created Eve. Woman's brain is smaller; yes, but it is relatively larger. Christ was made a man; yes, but perhaps for his greater humility. Each argument at once suggests its opposite, and both are often fallacious. If we are to gain understanding, we must get out of these ruts; we must discard the vague notions of superiority, inferiority, equality which have hitherto corrupted every discussion of the subject and start afresh.

Notes

[1] The Kinsey Report [Alfred C. Kinsey and others: *Sexual Behavior in the Human Male* (W. B. Saunders Co., 1948)] is no exception, for it is limited to describing the sexual characteristics of American men, which is quite a different matter.

[2] E. Lévinas expresses this idea most explicitly in his essay *Temps et l'Autre*. "Is there not a case in which otherness, alterity [*altérité*], unquestionably marks the nature of a being, as its essence, an instance of otherness not consisting purely and simply in the opposition of two species of the same genus? I think that the feminine represents the contrary in its absolute sense, this contrariness being in no wise affected by any relation between it and its correlative and thus remaining absolutely other. Sex is not a certain specific difference . . . no more is the sexual difference a mere contradiction. . . . Nor does this difference lie in the duality of two complementary terms, for two complementary terms imply a pre-existing whole. . . . Otherness reaches its full flowering in the feminine, a term of the same rank as consciousness but of opposite meaning."

I suppose that Lévinas does not forget that woman, too, is aware of her own consciousness, or ego. But it is striking that he deliberately takes a man's point of view, disregarding the reciprocity of subject and object. When he writes that woman is mystery, he implies that she is mystery for man. Thus his description, which is intended to be objective, is in fact an assertion of masculine privilege.

³See C. Lévi-Strauss: *Les Structures élementaires de la parenté.* My thanks are due to C. Lévi-Strauss for his kindness in furnishing me with the proofs of his work, which, among others, I have used liberally in Part II.

⁴With rare exceptions, perhaps, like certain matriarchal rulers, queens, and the like—TR.

⁵See Part II, ch. viii.

⁶At the moment an "equal rights" amendment to the Constitution of the United States is before Congress.—TR.

⁷See Part II.

⁸Or at least he thought he could.

⁹A significant article on this theme by Michel Carrouges appeared in No. 292 of the *Cahiers du Sud*. He writes indignantly: "Would that there were no woman-myth at all but only a cohort of cooks, matrons, prostitutes, and bluestockings serving functions of pleasure or usefulness!" That is to say, in his view woman has no existence in and for herself; he thinks only of her *function* in the male world. Her reason for existence lies in man. But then, in fact, her poetic "function" as a myth might be more valued than any other. The real problem is precisely to find out why woman should be defined with relation to man.

¹⁰For example, a man will say that he considers his wife in no wise degraded because she has no gainful occupation. The profession of housewife is just as lofty, and so on. But when the first quarrel comes he will exclaim: "Why, you couldn't make your living without me!"

¹¹The specific purpose of Book II of this study is to describe this process.

4

Talking Back: Feminist Responses to Sexist Stereotypes

The Challengers

Subtract the effort to meet the stereotypic model; undo much of the indoctrination; add a streak of independence, self-affirmation and self-respect; toss in a growing knowledge of women's history and circumstance, pride in womanhood, and concern for other women; wrap all in a strong awareness of the entire process and condition—and you have some picture of the feminist woman who today is challenging old images and building new ones. If patriarchy is hostile to women in general, even those who conform to masculist standards and regulations, one can imagine the attitudes toward the feminist woman, who rejects patriarchy's regulations and constraints, refuses to accept the "place" constructed for her, and aspires instead to a space of her own regardless of its acceptability to the patriarchs. To the masculist, a feminist woman is the incarnation of a nightmare. According to his mythology, a woman unfettered by "respectable" convention—by the watchful eyes of fathers, brothers, and husbands—is dangerous. Now here are women not only unredeemed by

their servitude but also questioning convention, rebelling, refusing their appointed labors, lusting after male jobs, intruding on male territory, demanding preposterous freedoms, and worst of all, making headway!

To verify this hostility, one need only turn to the common indicators of social attitudes—TV stories, letters to the editor in newspapers and magazines, commentaries in books and magazines, political campaign rhetoric and election results, church sermons, in-group jokes, and other usual sources. Notice how the feminist and her demands are presented. Either ridiculed or despised, she is first of all *unfeminine*. This term implies not only a lack of "charm" and expertise in certain "womanly" behaviors; it suggests as well a particular appearance—either hard, "glitzy" and slick or dirty, unkempt, badly dressed, not pretty—she is clearly disadvantaged in whatever it takes to attract men. She is perceived as in some way having trouble with sex and as having problems relating to men because of bad experiences either in childhood (with her father) or later on (with husband, lover, or rapist). In short, she is maladjusted. From a representative cross section of such hostile comments, one gathers that feminists want:

- to become like men, to "sleep around," to reject their maternal prerogatives and special "power," to emasculate men, and to destroy civilization . . . (George Gilder)[1]
- to indulge themselves, abrogate familial responsibility, and avoid sex . . . (Midge Decter)[2]
- to reject their true "femininity," castrate men, have a penis of their own, and disrupt society . . . (Sigmund Freud)[3]
- to surrender their womanliness, become "phallic women," and distort the innate balance of complementarity in life and nature . . . (Karl Stern)[4]
- to destroy the universities, academic freedom, scholarship, etc. . . . (those against affirmative action)
- to give up all "the wonderful privileges" women in this country now enjoy . . . (Phyllis Schlafly)
- the "suppression of modesty" and the "naturally given" sexual differentiation which makes "men and women always men and women"[5] and the "dismantling" of men's souls.[6] (Allan Bloom)
- to take jobs away from those who are "really oppressed."
- to turn their children over to communist-inspired day care centers.
- to kill unborn babies.

Feminists, it is said, tend to get "shrill" or "strident," which means literally high-pitched, grating on the ear. These are terms one would expect masculists to use; they are—and are meant to be—deprecating. They not only refer to the higher pitch of the female voice, but they also conjure up images of whining old crones and nagging shrews. They are a means of ridiculing and discounting feminist arguments: "Not only do I not accept the things you are saying, but I don't even take them seriously; I reduce them simply to the ugly noises of thwarted, aggressive women."

Yet I believe that, in a sense different from the intended one, the terms *shrill* and *strident* are accurate, for they reveal a deeper, perhaps unconscious, truth. Feminists' arguments *are* extremely grating—to traditional mind-sets. Feminists are striking at values and feelings that run deep and have power-

ful emotional impact. If even the smallest changes in sex orientation (such as altering hair length) provoke marked reactions—which they seem to—greater shifts will certainly beget proportionately greater response. Feminists can and do expect to incur a great deal of anger and abuse, whether that is expressed as ridicule or as outright attack.

Although we have had some gains in the last twenty years, women—feminist or nonfeminist—still exist in a hostile environment. We live within a struggle. Feminists work within this struggle—philosophize, analyze, act, try, and grow there. Our development—the way we grow, the things we learn, and the visions we create—all bear that mark and so we must understand them in that context.

To one degree or another, most feminists perceive themselves as revolutionaries. In Shulamith Firestone's words, "If there were another word more all-embracing than revolution we would use it."[7] Yet we are revolutionaries on peculiar terrain, for we do not typically seek war, that is, to exchange one hierarchy for another. We rarely hate our "enemies." In fact, we often hesitate to call anyone "enemy," not quite certain who or what that enemy might be. It is said that most of us live intimately in the homes of our oppressors, loving and caring for them. We are not decided on a firm, far-reaching revolutionary program, for we have not agreed upon one set of strategies or goals. Yet with all, we *are* revolutionaries, for in altering the arrangements of work and relationships between women and men, in challenging the primacy of martial-masculist values, we mean to change the very nature of life and society for all people.

The women's movement has a saying: the personal is the political. This means several things. First, no gulf truly exists between the personal and social elements of our lives. It also means that much of what we have taken to be personal matters—problems of communication with our men, for example, or the failures in our sexual relationships—are actually not purely personal but are also sociopolitical, a consequence of the power arrangements between women and men. "The personal is the political" means as well that the insights we gain into our private circumstances can ultimately have widespread political and social consequences.

Kate Millett defined politics as "power-structured relationships, arrangements whereby one group of persons is controlled by another."[8] If that is the case, then such questions as, "Why do I get up earlier than he does and prepare him breakfast before we both go off to our jobs?" are political questions because they refer to men's control of women's time and effort. That women are expected to wash, cook, clean, and serve and yet not be paid for their labors or even recognized as working, that society places women in such a position and not so men is a political issue, and as only one symptom of the exploitation and domination of 51 percent of the world population by the remaining 49 percent, it is no small matter. And if the exploitation of women by men is both model and manifestation of all forms of exploitation and oppression, as many feminists argue, then understanding male-female roles is profoundly important, and the challengers' analyses of sexism—rather than being petty and inconsequential as charged—are highly significant for the 51 percent as well as all of humanity.

The personal is the political, and feminists are fomenting a revolution out of consciousness-raising.

The Process: Coming to Understand

The process of learning and unlearning, of coming to recognize the nature and consequence that the images of women have and of reorienting oneself toward them is difficult, painstaking, and time consuming. Considering how long each of us has lived with these images and the extent of their power in our culture, it is not surprising that this is so.

Consciousness-Raising

Each of us has come to the task of becoming aware from her own set of circumstances in her own way. Most women report a first moment, an event when they experienced "the explosion," the first rush of awareness or insight into sexism and its intimate connection with them. Perhaps triggered by a personal crisis—an unwanted pregnancy and its attendant social cruelties or a divorce that left her burdened and impoverished or perhaps job discrimination or social humiliation or even a feminist speech that freed the woman from some damaging beliefs—once begun, the explosion or insight is almost always followed by a growing and developing awareness. Often the growth is conscious, sought after, and cultivated. Sometimes it happens despite

resistance, for the awareness, though freeing and exciting, is painful and frightening as well.

This process of coming to understand sexism fully, at the highest level of awareness, is called consciousness-raising. It functions both to intensify awareness with regard to the implications of sexism and to stimulate the search for alternatives. Consciousness-raising takes a variety of forms, follows from various techniques (for example, self-examination, role reversal, shared discussion), and takes different paths with their attendant effects and reactions.

The Insight: It's a Lie

How does the experience of consciousness-raising proceed? Suppose you spent your youth learning the trade of "femininity." Suppose Mom and Dad taught you to make yourself just right so you could attract just the right man so he would care for you and make you happy because that is what women and men do, and it is right and proper and wonderful that it should be that way. Suppose you do just what is expected: You become feminine and sweet and sexy, and you find that man (or, rather, he finds you), and you marry and have three lovely children, and he has a lovely job and you have a lovely house and . . . then suppose it suddenly ends. Now suppose you find yourself in your thirty-third year with three lovely children, no husband, meager or no support, no income, no skills, no joy. Suppose you see him with freedom, mobility, job skills, income, future. What do you say? Usually you first say, "What did I do wrong?" But perhaps in time you gain some insight and recognize that what went wrong wasn't you; it was the whole set of beliefs, the assumptions and presuppositions. Seeing this, you say, "Oh, it was a lie."

Suppose it doesn't end. Suppose you have the lovely children, the lovely home, the lovely husband, but you aren't happy. You're depressed or restless or grouchy. You're always busy, but you're also bored. What do you say? You say, "What's wrong with me? Why am I unsatisfied?" Or perhaps you look around and say, "It was a lie."

Suppose you did all the things you were advised to do in *Cosmopolitan*—you were kind, thoughtful, playful, sexy and supportive—but instead of undying love, you got misunderstanding, neglect, and hostility. What do you say?

Suppose it all went a different way. Suppose your youth was poor and hard. You learned to scratch and scrape. Now jobs are hard to find, and when they do come along they pay even less than a man's, and your men come and go, and you have some babies to support, but when you go to court and ask for support, the (male) judge decides that, after all, Mr. X has a new family to support and cannot be left penniless! What do you say?

Or suppose the scenario is very different. You spent your youth learning and preparing and studying, and the future is bright because America is a land of opportunity. You know things are harder for a woman and you have to be twice as good, but you *are* twice as good. But suppose you can't find the kind of job you want. They just ask how many words per minute you can type. Or suppose they do give you that job (EEOC and Title IX, you know), but you find you're the only sales associate answering the phone or having a typewriter on your desk. What do you say?

When at last, for whatever reason and in whatever way, you recognize one lie, you get suspicious, and you begin to look at it all. Soon you see just how many lies there are. Then you think: If women are stupid, incompetent, and petty as they say, but I am female and *not* those things, either I am not a woman, or it's a lie. And if it's a lie about me, it's a lie about other women; and if that's a lie, then perhaps the rest is a lie. Perhaps it's a lie that women can't be trusted with important tasks; that for women love is more important than income; that women are satisfied in the home of a he-male; that women don't need jobs or a salary; that men should make the decisions; that women should *never* be "slutty" or "pushy" or "ambitious" or "shrill."

Once begun, the questioning has no limits. We discover lie upon lie, myth upon myth. The response? If it is not true that women are bad or incompetent, then all our subordination is just plain wrong. If the role won't work, we'll have to find us another way.

Where is it written that it must be the way it is?

What We Learn: The Images Tell Us

The heading of this section is presumptuous. What we learn when we begin to ask these kinds of questions is so vast that it could not be told in a thousand volumes. What I would like to describe here,

though, are some of the insights feminists have had into themselves as women, into the effects of the myths and stereotypes, and into the possibilities open to women without them.

The Splitting of the Androgyne: Complements

The term *androgyne* is composed of the two ancient Greek words *andros* and *gyne*, "man" and "woman." In certain feminist theories, it refers to a person of either sex characterized by combining various qualities from among those that traditionally have been taken to be only male or only female.[9] The androgyne, or the androgynous person, may be strong *and* tender, rational *and* feeling, independent *and* receptive, and so on. Or they may be none of these but exhibit other traits true to their individuality.

As we saw earlier, what currently obtains in the ideals of women and men is the exact opposite: Instead of androgyny, there is *complementarity*. Women and men are expected to exhibit opposite and exclusive traits and behavior.

Patriarchal Ideals

Ideal Man	Ideal Woman
powerful, creative, intelligent, rational,	nurturant, supportive, intuitive, emotional, cunning,
independent, self-reliant,	needful, dependent,
strong,	tender,
courageous, daring, responsible, resolute, temperate, cautious, sober,	timid, fragile, capricious, childlike, ebullient, exuberant,
honest, forthright, active, forceful, honorable, principled, just,	tactful, evasive, artful, passive, receptive, obedient, loyal, kind, merciful,
self-affirming, authoritative, decisive, successful, task-oriented,	self-abnegating, compliant, submissive, contented, serene, being-oriented,
he does,	she cares,
he lives in the mind,	she lives in the heart,
he confronts the world	she withdraws from the world

Some sexists say that men and women are complements to one another; that their complementarity is natural, desirable, and beautiful; that together these two, different but interlocking, provide for themselves, their families, and society all that is necessary and harmonious for human living. Actually, the theory of complementarity is based on a division of labor: men and women, each having their different natural capacities and abilities, have different (but equally important) tasks and spheres that are appropriate to their "natures."

Feminists argue that this is a mystification, but more, they point out specific criticisms of this complementary arrangement:

- It may be appealing to envision two interlocking creatures walking hand in hand down life's highway, but in reality half a person and half a person equal two half persons, not one whole.

- As Plato pointed out in the third century B.C., human beings require balance and excellence in all of their qualities to function well. The ideal man of patriarchy may be eminently successful so far as society is concerned, but if he lacks the ability to feel and to experience fully the affective elements of living, he gains only half of what life has to offer, and he is apt to be a rather unbalanced, and unpleasant, person. The ideal patriarchal woman may be very fetching and capable of deep feeling, but she is also unable to take care of herself in the material aspects of life and hence she is at the mercy of other people and events.

- It is unrealistic to believe that two people, entirely different in capacity and outlook, could successfully manage meaningful communication, mutual respect, and love. Rather than interlocking, these people are locked together in destructive, though symbiotic, partnership. The traditional complementary arrangement is logical and functional only in terms of social and economic efficiency, not in terms of human needs. Complementarity, a "division of labor," may be an effective way of accomplishing a variety of social tasks; and when marriage functioned as a social arrangement for satisfying certain community needs, complementarity might have been a productive perspective. But if marriage is to function as a satisfying *personal* arrangement, as

a primary source of emotional support and profound human interchange, then complementarity is dysfunctional, and "interlocking" symbiosis is a psychological and spiritual disaster.

- Even if it were possible for two people to relate well in complementarity, women would still be at a marked disadvantage. In fact, we are.

In the first place, the thesis that in our society the two elements, male and female, are different but equal in value and importance is a lie. The system—patriarchal in origin and serving patriarchal ends—is built on the principle that men rule and women obey, that men take care of themselves and women take care of everyone but themselves. Even in the most benevolent of all worlds, that is not a highly promising arrangement for women.

In the second place, though it is true that in a system of complementarity men and women are both in the position of using half and only half of their human capacities (and so losing half as well), the half that men keep is the half valued by society (which stands to reason, given the control of the masculists), and the half that women keep is devalued. Though women are praised, a patronizing undertone always accompanies that praise. The praise is awarded for traits that society deems substandard.

> *Sigh no more, ladies*
> *Time is male*
> *and in his cups drinks to the fair.*
> *Bemused by gallantry, we hear*
> *our mediocrities over-praised,*
> *indolence read as abnegation,*
> *slattern thought styled intuition,*
> *every lapse forgiven, our crime*
> *only to cast too bold a shadow*
> *or smash the mould straight off.*
> *For that, solitary confinement,*
> *tear gas, attrition shelling.*
> *Few applicants for that honor.*
>
> —Adrienne Rich[10]

Human Versus Female

In Chapter 2, we looked at the historical confusion of the concepts of *man* and *human*. In fact, the patriarchal schema of complementary ideals is both cause and effect of that confusion. The configuration of traits and qualities reserved for men is the configuration expected of excellent human beings: intelligence, independence, courage, honor, strength. Not so the configuration for a woman. Womanly perfection and human excellence in this schema are incompatible.

In effect, women are being asked to choose between their human selves and their sexual identities. Unlike men, who develop and improve their masculinity and humanity concurrently, women in patriarchy only destroy their acceptability as females if they develop their human excellence or else destroy their human potential if they become more "feminine."

A famous early feminist study, still important today, translated this issue into the language of psychology.

A study by Inge Broverman and her colleagues suggests that many clinicians today view their female patients the way Freud viewed his. They gave 79 therapists (46 male and 33 female psychiatrists, psychologists and social workers) a sex-role-stereotype questionnaire. This test consists of 122 pairs of traits such as "very subjective . . . very objective" or "not at all aggressive . . . very aggressive."

The investigators asked the subjects to rate each set of traits on a scale from one to seven, in terms of where a healthy male should fall, a healthy female, or a healthy adult (sex unspecified). They found:

1. There was a high agreement among these clinicians on the attributes that characterize men, women and adults.

2. There were no major differences between the male and the female clinicians.

3. Clinicians have different standards of mental health for men and women. Their standards for a "healthy adult man" looked like those for a "healthy adult"; but healthy women differed from both by being: submissive, emotional, easily influenced, sensitive to being hurt, excitable, conceited about their appearance, dependent, not very adventurous, less competitive, unaggressive, unobjective— and besides, they dislike math and science. This "healthy woman" is not very likable, all in all!

(In fact, other studies have shown that these traits, characteristic of normal women, are the least socially desirable.) For a woman to be "healthy," then, she must adjust to the behavioral norms for her sex even though these norms are not highly valued by her society, her men—or her therapist.[11]

Thus, behavior considered healthy for men was not considered healthy for women, and vice versa. Men and women were expected to display opposite characteristics. But the traits deemed *generally* healthy, desirable for *people* without regard to sex, were those expected of or prescribed for men. Women displaying those traits would be deemed "unfeminine." At the same time, women who were "feminine," who would be deemed healthy or adjusted as women, would by this schema have to be judged sick as people!

What an impossible dilemma. Women may choose to be considered "feminine," or we may choose to be mature, healthy human beings, but we may not have both. Put a slightly different way: While men may be thought of as human beings who happen to be male, women are cast as females who happen to be (in a lesser sense) human.

Feminists argue that complementarity is a disaster for both sexes, that the healthy person (of either sex) is the human being who excels in both configurations or perhaps rejects *any* configuration, who has the wherewithal to cope with the necessities and challenges of life as well as the sensibilities to do it in a way that is *for* life.

What's Wrong with "Femininity"?

In the preceding chapter we noted that the dichotomy in the female ideal required women to exemplify at once two incompatible characterizations, Mary and the Playmate, and we could see how destructive such a contradiction would be. More is wrong with patriarchal female images, or "femininity," than only the contradictions wrought by dichotomy. For one thing, feminists argue, the pejorative stereotype of "Woman the Inferior" is false. For another, neither of the supposedly nonpejorative images, Mary or Playmate, is a desirable model. In fact, both are demeaning and destructive.

The Myth of Female Inferiority

According to misogynist ideology, women are inferior in two ways: (1) women are morally inferior, evil, bad, sinful, dangerous, harmful, and dirty; (2) women are inferior in competence—physically, intellectually, and spiritually.

Women Are Evil That women are morally inferior to the point of being positively evil is a well-worn theme from antiquity to the present:

Woman is a pitfall—a pitfall, a hole, a ditch.
Woman is a sharp iron dagger that cuts a man's throat.

—Mesopotamian poem[12]

Man who trusts womankind trusts deceivers.

—Hesoid[13]

The beauty of woman is the greatest snare.

—St. John Chrysostom[14]

You are the devil's gateway . . . the first deserter of the divine law; you are she who persuaded him whom the devil was not valiant enough to attack. You destroyed so easily God's image, man. On account of your desert—that is, death—even the son of God had to die.

—Tertullian[15]

I have not left any calamity more detrimental to mankind than woman.

—Islamic saying[16]

Art thou not formed of foul slime? Art thou not full of uncleanness?

—Rule for Anchoresses[17]

God made Adam master over all creatures, to rule over all living things, but when Eve persuaded him that he was lord even over God she spoiled everything. . . . With tricks and cunning women deceive men.

—Martin Luther[18]

I cannot escape the notion. . . . that for women the level of what is ethically normal is different from what it is in man.

—Sigmund Freud[19]

So much for woman on a pedestal. These historical statements have only scratched the surface. All one need do is look for further evidence of the belief in female malevolence, no less virulent today then it has been for centuries. In the past were the stories of Delilah and Salome; Medusa, the Gorgon who turned men into stone; Meanads, who tore men apart and ate them during drunken orgies; Sirens, who lived in the sea and lured sailors to their death with covert promises. Which of us did not grow up on the wicked women of the fairy tales: vain and murderous queens, dark fairies, bad witches, malevolent stepsisters and their cruel, ambitious, self-centered mothers. What these women all had in common were that they were not "good" like Snow White and Sleeping Beauty and Cinderella. They were not young and fair and victimized; they were not "sweet" and pliant, vulnerable, dependent, and utterly passive. Indeed, they were women on their own, autonomous, self-directed, unowned, *and therefore uncontrolled*. And that is why, furthermore, they all came to no good.

How different are these characters and these tales from those of today? Are there not still good, sweet, wholesome, back-home kinds of girls who follow their hearts and their men and their prescribed roles and win (the prince) in the end? The poor, sweet, innocent, good-hearted creatures of *Pretty in Pink, An Officer and A Gentlemen,* and *Dirty Dancing* endure, remain loyal and loving even in the face of rejection and shame—and they triumph. Another fate befalls the tougher women in *Diary of a Mad Housewife* or *Kramer vs. Kramer, Fatal Attraction* and *Working Girl;* after all, they rebelled, said no. Consider the movies *Nothing in Common* or *Fatal Attraction.* In each a powerful, willful, independent, beautiful woman seems *for a while* to be in control. But she is vanquished in the end, supplanted by the sweet and proper lady; in each case, both women are raised or lowered in esteem by the choice of the male, who moves easily between them and always acts for his own interests in his own way.

To all such allegations of evil, feminists retort, nonsense! While patriarchal society prattles of women's destructiveness, feminists ask: Who creates weapons and marches off to war? Who hunts and kills living creatures for fun? Who fights for kicks? Who pillages the earth for profit? Who colonizes and exploits? What destruction could we have wrought that even nearly compares? If Eve you call us, then we will be Eve in our sense, in the best sense, reconstructed according to our feminist perspectives.

They say: she violated the taboo, surrendered to the snake, ate the apple, corrupted the man, brought about the expulsion from the Father's garden, was responsible for the Fall, called down the Father's curse. Upon earth, upon labor, upon childbirth, upon woman. So far as they were concerned they told a tale of sin and its punishment, of gluttony and its consequences, of disobedience and the revenge taken by the primal father against those who eat.

I say: Eve dared to break the taboo against eating, embraced the temptation offered by the snake, ate the apple, and returned symbolically to the maternal breast to regain an identity with the Mother Goddess. If eating caused her to be expelled from her Father's house, that precisely is what allowed her to give birth to the Woman Who Is Not Yet.

Eve's dilemma: a choice between obedience and knowledge. Between renunciation and appetite. Between subordination and desire. Between security and risk. Between loyalty and self-development. Between submission and power. Between hunger as temptation and hunger as vision.

It is the dilemma of modern women.

—Kim Chernin, *Reinventing Eve*[20]

Women Are Incompetent   The charge that both requires and admits of refutation is that women are simply not as able as men, not as competent at any task except those traditionally designated "women's work." It is said that women are less capable than men of doing any kind of work requiring a high degree of rationality, abstraction, and intelligence because women are intellectually inferior and are characteristically not given to rationality and logic. It is said that, in even the best of circumstances, even unusually intelligent women are still not the equals of men in important and difficult work because they are temperamentally unsuited to seriousness of purpose, sustained effort, and strain. It is said that women are unable to withstand the pressure of competition either with people or with ideas and are therefore always destined to defeat. And finally, it is said that women who are not thus characteristically inferior are not "normal," are not attractive or natural or feminine, and are not even really women— another double bind.

As evidence of women's inferiority, it is asserted that the great scientists, inventors, legislators, entre-

preneurs, artists, humorists, authors, athletes, and warriors have always been men. Where are the female geniuses, the Beethovens, Shakespeares, and Platos? We are told that in business and industry, in the professions and professional schools, it is men who outnumber women, who outrank women, who achieve. Even today, argue the sexists, when women have all the opportunities of men, they still do not make it. Why? Because women do not have the intelligence, the instincts, the grit, the motivation, the stamina, or the strength of men. In every way that counts, women are inferior.

This is how the schema goes: Part I—It is unnatural and undesirable for women to do what men do; women must expend their energies serving, supporting, and pleasing; they must not be allowed to do what men do; Part II—Because women do not do the things men do, it is evident that they cannot do what men do and are therefore obviously inferior. The argument is circular, superficial, and fallacious. But it does hold tremendous power in society—at least as rationale—and a majority, both female and male, believe it.

Feminists challenge this schema and refute the arguments. We contend that the socialization process and the structure of society, not "natural" capacities, account for the different levels of achievement and motivation in women and men. Although the literature is mixed and the research inconclusive, it appears safe to say that no evidence shows that men and women differ in intellectual capacity or IQ, and a good deal of evidence exists to the contrary. Apparently males excel earlier in spatial perception and females in verbal perception, but even this difference may possibly be accounted for by social conditions. It is certainly not sufficient to account for the wide divergence in interest, abilities, motivations, and achievements.

A great deal of evidence suggests that "feminine" ideals—the images, models, and values described in Chapter 3, including the constraints and circumstances imposed on women from childhood—are far more responsible for women's alleged and actual lack of motivation, grit, and aggressiveness than any inherent childlikeness or timidity. Differences in training, expectations, and experience produce ineffectualness and defeatism in women as they do in men. Yet there are and always have been women of incredible courage, stamina, and commitment:

And even though they keep me blindfolded forever, I will always be able to find my way back to Chile, my country, set between the Cordillera of the Andes and the sea, between a dialectic of landscapes, between the malevolent Pacific and the untamable Andes. Between these opposing confines I grew up, among things proper for little girls, beside my grandmothers who predicted a tranquil future for me, and also beside marvelous wise old women dressed in black, rebozos around their shoulders, who bewitched me with their native wisdom and their universe of signs and symbols. . . .

Our liberty as women will come from our own efforts. And it will come with the help of others strong enough to help us, those who will want to know and understand us, who will want to learn from those of us who have not forgotten how to live and how to sing. Bullets cannot kill us, bonds cannot bind the strength of our hands, blindfolds cannot imprison our vision. We hold in our own palms our ultimate truths.

—Marjorie Agosin, "Chile: Woman of Smoke" [21]

Not now nor ever has equality of opportunity existed for women—in business, the professions, education, the arts, or any other socially prized and male-controlled venture. Even today doors are only grudgingly opening to women. Women are still ill paid for our work, segregated in function, last hired and first fired. Even if this were not so, the separate but not equal conditioning of females and the hostility and ignorance of the men already in positions of power make any claims to equality of opportunity a farce.

Women's dual roles and incompatible cultural requirements render success in the community or in a profession painfully expensive if not impossible, physically, emotionally, spiritually:

I was a child when I first heard someone say, "Men work from sun to sun, but women's work is never done." For years I thought it proof that women, rather than being the "weaker" sex, were if anything superior to, stronger than men. I was a woman, very much grown, before I realized how heavy those words can weigh—the reality, the burden.

Black women work! Yet the gruesome truth is that "women's work" is often dismissed, taken for granted or devalued. It's almost as if never-ending hard work and bearing burdens is what we were born to. Our

plates are piled high with things we have to do or are expected to do or want to do or are pushed to.

The pressures we women are under are intense. We are bombarded from all sides with all manner of things we gotta do: Gotta make ways for lasting meaningful social, economic and political change. Gotta stop analyzing and amening and get to practical solutions, then make 'em happen. Gotta do well on our jobs, gotta keep 'em or get better ones or make the ones we have pay off. Gotta keep our relationships thriving or get some going. Gotta look good and stay healthy. Told that we gotta be in control of our lives and our destinies. Gotta be past, present and future women all at the same time. Gotta keep our spirits and our sanity. Most important, or so it often seems, is that we Black women gotta be good women, gotta be strong.

—Marcia Ann Gillespie
"The Myth of the Strong Black Woman" [22]

The married woman who works outside the home usually carries two jobs—one paid (however humbly), one not paid. She is lawyer (teacher, doctor, pilot, secretary . . .) and she is homemaker and mother. The price of such demands, both for her profession and her personal health, are obvious. The unmarried professional faces different costs: slurs on her womanhood, social disapprobation, at times loneliness. According to the image, ideal women are intuitive but not rational, lovely but not effectual. The successful professional, according to the myth, is the unsuccessful *femme*. To opt for a career, the story goes, is to relinquish one's happily-ever-after. Such visions, even unfounded, are disturbing. They do not do much for professional motivation.

To the questions, "Why haven't women produced any geniuses? Why are there no female Shakespeares or Beethovens?" Virginia Woolf answered that we have not been allowed a "room of our own." We have been accorded bread but not roses. We have not been allowed the spiritual atmosphere, the creative space men are heir to, the amenities that raise life above the mundane and encourage one to creativity.

The issues treated here all point to an important feminist argument: A range of factors in the environment conspire to impede women's competence and accomplishments in many areas—the hostile or deprecating attitudes of incumbent men, lack of support and assistance from all quarters, dual and/ or incompatible professional and nonprofessional functions, pervasiveness of the male (alien, inhospitable) ambience, and socialization that erodes confidence and self-assertion. Rather than being inferior, women are hampered in developing competence in the most profound ways. To overcome the obstacles put in our way, we must indeed be twice as good but in more ways than we expected. It is not surprising that so many of us don't "succeed." What is extraordinary is that any of us do.

And what we do accomplish often disappears! In the history books, achieving women are rarely given more than a few lines, and the experiences of ordinary women, unlike those of "the common man," are simply not considered. Our successes have often gone underground—to be attributed to men or thought to be anonymous because women were not permitted success. Female authors or artists often used male pen names or "protectors" or "coauthors" who coauthored them right out of their due. Ancient accomplishments are simply usurped by the patriarchy. Male historians and anthropologists "forget" to research the contributions of women to early civilization—the introduction of pottery, weaving, food preservation and preparation, perhaps even agriculture itself. Current anthologies of the arts do not bother to include women's works because these are "substandard," "narrow," or "lacking in grandeur."

And we cannot forget that at times and still in some places it is dangerous for women to succeed, where women die for assertion. Midwives were burned as witches, rebellious wives and daughters were imprisoned in convents or beaten or burned alive. Feminists in Nazi Germany went to concentration camps. In Iran they may be shot. Yet they continue to speak:

In December of 1970, Ms. Farrokhrou Parsa, the first woman to serve in the Iranian cabinet, was executed after a trial by hooded judges—a trial at which no defense attorney was permitted, no appeal possible, and the defendant had been officially declared guilty before the proceedings began. She was charged with "expansion of prostitution, corruption on earth, and warring against God." Aware of the hopelessness of her case, she delivered a reasoned, courageous defense of her career decisions, among them a directive to free female schoolchildren from having to be veiled and the estab-

lishment of a commission for revising textbooks to present a nonsexist image of women. A few hours after sentence was pronounced she was wrapped in a dark sack and machine-gunned. . . .

. . . The years ahead will be difficult. To unite a torn and battered nation and rebuild what had been destroyed is a monumental task. But as I contemplate the future of Iran, a reassuring image gives me hope. I recall a young woman I met in the southern village of Zovieh. She had finished her military service in the literacy corps to return to her home and establish a school in which she taught all subjects to all four grades. On the day I saw her, she was walking out of a village meeting in her faded uniform, flushed, and proud, followed by the old men who had just selected her Kadkhoda, or "elderman," of the village.

Those who have struggled and those who have died sacrificed so that women like her may exist.

She is the future.

—Mahnaz Afkhami
"Iran: A Future in the Past—The 'Pre-revolutionary' Women's Movement"[23]

The Dark Side of the "Good" Woman

Refuting the claim that women as a class are inferior does not exhaust the feminist offensive against patriarchal female images. The so-called positive images are as much a target, for even the ideals—Perfect Woman, Mary, or the Playmate—are destructive. Even with the apparent praise, approval, and veneration, these ideals actually disparage women and cause us to disparage ourselves and assist in diminishing our lives.

Consider once again the major requirements of traditional femininity: beauty, self-effacement, fragility, and domesticity. History, poetry, literature, philosophy, and even science have eulogized the woman who embodies these qualities, but feminists have taken a closer look. Demystifying the image, translating myth into reality—through introspection and analysis—we have seen the dark side of this image.

Beauty and Attractiveness Attractiveness, at least in people, is by and large a cultural phenomenon; beauty is socially defined. In patriarchy, men construct the ideal in their own interests, and women whose lives have no purpose outside of being chosen—whose identities and fortunes have been made subject to their appeal to men—have little choice but to struggle with the imperious requirements of "beauty" even though the ideal is impossible. For no human being can be perfect in hair, skin, teeth, shape, proportion, and scent, and furthermore be so "naturally" and endlessly. Constant comparison with the made-up and reconstructed figures of screen and magazine that more nearly realize the ideal always leaves us defeated, always at a disadvantage, always self-deprecating.

Women are called narcissistic. We are chided for our obsession with clothing and fashion. We are ridiculed for our willingness to sit for hours under a hair drier and for slathering cream on our skin at night. And yet what other choice is there *if we accept* the traditional role that bids us to use our appearance to attract and keep a mate? Can we reject that option if any life other than "being chosen" is deemed undesirable or even unacceptable, if "attractive" and "sexy" are society's primary terms of approbation for women?

Self-Effacement The concept of submissiveness for women has changed since the Middle Ages. Few today expect a woman to lower her head and whisper, "Yes, sir." Yet the concept survives: No one likes an aggressive woman. We may quarrel, we may fight, but in the end, if we don't give in and lose often enough, we will lose our man. Assertiveness, the kind that goes beyond a little pluckiness, is still not considered acceptable in women; it is always translated into aggression.

And self-effacement? The husband who taunts in public is teasing. The wife who does the same is attacking her man's ego. She is not expected to say, "Yes, dear," but she is expected to yield the decisions, follow his job, entertain his friends. He drives when he chooses; he works late when he needs to. He storms out of the house when angry; she screams or she cries, but she stays put.

Women, it is said, are prone to depression. We get "neurotic," clingy, and nagging. What man who could not make his own decisions, place his own needs high in priority, satisfy his desires and wishes, please himself, and follow his goals would not get depressed and "neurotic"? What man barred from creating his own pleasures and diversions wouldn't nag others for entertainment? The logical outcome of self-effacement is depression.

Fragility Very close to self-effacement is fragility. Women are to be submissive because we are weaker, needful of protection and guidance. In gratitude and in our understanding of our best interests, we are to take direction from the stronger. Fragility—timidity, delicacy, needfulness—means vulnerability. It is, to be sure, very appealing to the male. But vulnerability of the sort required of women means dependence. To be fearful of strange situations, to be hesitant when decisions are called for, to avoid risk, to learn *not* to defend oneself, to feign or even encourage physical weakness, to shrink from the world is to place oneself at the mercy of circumstances; it is to afford oneself dependence on others. Even if those on whom one depends are completely trustworthy, marvelously competent, and around forever, anyone in such a situation must feel some lack of self-respect, a sense of inferiority and ineffectualness. For such people, life is truncated; the pleasures and rewards of independence, accomplishment, and power are unknown. Further, in a culture that clearly values competence and where human excellence is said to include independence and self-reliance, the endlessly vulnerable and dependent person is a figure of ridicule and contempt. We saw earlier that for women this was so.

Domesticity   *Kinder, Kirche, Küche*—"children, church, and cooking," was the slogan of ideal womanhood for Hitler's Germany, the Third Reich. Similarly, housekeeping and all of its attendant duties, care of children, including teaching, nursing, and other service occupations, and worship (*not* theology) are said to be the only legitimate occupations for women in patriarchy. What is more, the work is to be task oriented, not policy oriented; that is, we are to execute our jobs according to prescribed procedure, not to define those jobs nor to create their meaning and expression. Ours is to carry out that part of any job that is repetitive, routine, uninteresting. Work that transcends the mundane belongs to men. Women may be cooks, not chefs; dressmakers, not designers; secretaries, not executives. We may busy ourselves with the pretties of making curtains or vases, but we are not to presume to art.

The imminent, as the existentialists call it, the mundane, the here and now, the "what," is dull and petty unless it is lifted by the transcendent, the eternal, the why and the wherefore. Tasks and things do not have the scope or the breadth of ideas. Interest, scope, and depth belong to creativity. Interesting people are living, growing people; they are people themselves interested, excited, challenged and challenging, learning and experiencing. *Kinder, Kirche, Küche,* however taxing of time and energy, cannot be creative unless so treated and perceived. In closing women to freedom of experience and movement, in disallowing as "unfeminine" an interest in the transcendent, in constricting our limits and our power, patriarchy confines us to the narrow and then condemns us for our "narrowness."

Patriarchal feminine ideals are monstrous. When successful, they destroy; and when we become the most perfect realizations of them, we are most damaged.

Responses: Feminist Reactions and Ideals

When feminist women look over the history of the tyranny of these beliefs and visions, when we note the destruction they have wrought and the exploitation they have legitimized, we are appalled and filled with emotion—anger, pain, grief, shock, determination.

Some call feminists petty, prattling noisily about inconsequentials. But is the loss of potential, of self-respect and autonomy inconsequential? Are economic deprivation and financial dependency inconsequential, or the use and abuse of our bodies for the interests of others? What about infanticide, physical mutilation, footbinding, and other physical torture? Is ten thousand years of domination and exploitation of over half humanity inconsequential?

We are advised to be ladylike, to go slow, ask nicely, develop a sense of humor. Are we to swallow our pride once again and plead prettily for our liberation from those who have withheld it for ten millennia until this day? Are we to chuckle good naturedly at centuries of restrictive clothing, at chastity belts and whalebone corsets, at enforced fatigue of body and mind, at slave labor and sexual servitude, at prostitution and rape? Are we to take these images in our stride, once more play the peacemakers and maintain the hated postures just a little longer while the masculists slowly adjust to the idea of change?

No, say the feminists, we won't do it. If we are angry, it is because we have seen the attack. If we are noisy, it is because women are suffering. If we sound strident, it is because the affirmation of women grates on the ears of masculists. "It is not that we are so radical," said Gloria Steinem, "but that there is something radically wrong with our world."

We have seen the visions of *woman the oppressed, woman the exploited, woman the outsider, woman the lost, woman the debased,* and we reject them all, opting instead for positive visions.

Feminists are building new visions. Throwing away the imperatives of "femininity" so badly conceived, canceling "ladylikeness," we are redefining what is desirable for us, what is commendable, what is possible. Our new heroines include *woman rediscovering herself* in history and for today; *woman redeeming herself* in her own eyes; *woman rightfully angry,* rightfully fighting; and *woman the leader,* the pillar, who in the words of Wilma Scott Heide may "create the kind of world where the power of love exceeds the love of power."[24] Indeed, our heroines include our own selves, to whom we are saying, *yes!:*

> *I am what I am and I am U.S. American   I haven't wanted to say it because if I did you'd take away the Puerto Rican   but now I say go to hell   I am what I am and you can't take it away with all the words and sneers at your command   I am what I am   I am Puerto Rican   I am U.S. American   I am New York Manhattan and the Bronx   I am what I am I'm not hiding under no stoop   behind no curtain   I am what I am   I am Boricua as boricuas come from the Isle of Manhattan and I croon Carlos Gardel tangoes in my sleep and Afro-Cuban beats in my blood and Xavier Cugat's lukewarm latin is so familar and dear   sneer dear but he's familiar and dear   but not Carmen Miranda   who's a joke because I never was a joke   I was a bit of a sensation   See! here's a real true honest-to-god Puerto Rican girl and she's in college   Hey! Mary come here and look she's from right here   a South Bronx girl and she's honest-to-god in college now Ain't that something   who would believed it   Ain't science wonderful or some such thing a wonder a wonder. . . .*
>
> *. . . I am what I am and I'm naturalized Jewish-American   wasp is foreign and new but Jewish-American is old show familiar   schmata familiar and its me*

*dears its me bagels blintzes and all I am what I am
Take it or leave me alone.*

—Rasario Morales, "I Am What I Am"[25]

What we shall be, what we should and can be, remains an open question. Feminists are still very much involved in the matter of what we are not and should not be. We have been asked what we would wish to be, how life would be if we could have our way, and many have answered that it is hard to say. We have never known a time when we have not been subordinated and devalued; we have never known a time of freedom and self-determination. We are only beginning to learn our history and to conceive our future—with few known models and precious little experience. In very large part the question of what we ought to be is the question philosophers have pursued for centuries: What is human excellence and virtue? Women are, after all, human beings, and our strivings and hopes are those of all humanity. How our ideals may differ from those of men or how our insights may alter the notion of human excellence is yet to be discovered.

Certain things we do know: We are being born, coming into life. We are struggling, and in this birth struggle is joy. That has been expressed eloquently by Simone de Beauvoir, Germaine Greer, and Erica Jong.

The free woman is just being born; when she has won possession of herself perhaps Rimbaud's prophecy will be fulfilled: "There shall be poets! When woman's unmeasured bondage shall be broken, when she shall live for and through herself, man—hitherto detestable—having let her go, she, too, will be poet! Woman will find the unknown! Will her ideational worlds be different from ours? She will come upon strange, unfathomable, repellent, delightful things; we shall take them, we shall comprehend them."[26] It is not sure that her "ideational worlds" will be different from those of men, since it will be through attaining the same situation as theirs that she will find emancipation; to say in what degree she will remain different, in what degree these differences will retain their importance—this would be to hazard bold predictions indeed. What is certain is that hitherto woman's possibilities have been suppressed and lost to humanity, and that it is high time she be permitted to take her chances in her own interest and in the interest of all.

—Simone de Beauvoir[27]

The surest guide to the correctness of the path that women take is joy in the struggle. Revolution is the festival of the oppressed. For a long time there may be no perceptible reward for women other than their new sense of purpose and integrity. Joy does not mean riotous glee, but it does mean the purposive employment of energy in a self-chosen enterprise. It does mean pride and confidence. It does mean communication and cooperation with others based on delight in their company and your own. To be emancipated from helplessness and need and walk freely upon the earth that is your birthright. To refuse hobbles and deformity and take possession of your body and glory in its power, accepting its own laws of loveliness. To have something to desire, something to make, something to achieve, and at last something genuine to give. To be freed from guilt and shame and the tireless self-discipline of women. To stop pretending and dissembling, cajoling and manipulating, and begin to control and sympathize. To claim the masculine virtues of magnanimity and generosity and courage. It goes much further than equal pay for equal work, for it ought to revolutionize the conditions of work completely. It does not understand the phrase "equality of opportunity," for it seems that the opportunities will have to be utterly changed and women's souls changed so that they desire opportunity instead of shrinking from it. The first significant discovery we shall make as we racket along our female road to freedom is that men are not free, and they will seek to make this an argument why nobody should be free. We can only reply that slaves enslave their masters, and by securing our own manumission we may show men the way that they could follow when they jumped off their own treadmill. Privileged women will pluck at your sleeve and seek to enlist you in the "fight" for reforms, but reforms are retrogressive. The old process must be broken, not made new. Bitter women will call you to rebellion, but you have too much to do. What will you do?

—Germaine Greer[28]

*Narrowing life because of the fears,
narrowing it between the dust motes,
narrowing the pink baby
between the green-limbed monsters,
& the drooling idiots,
& the ghosts of Thalidomide infants,
narrowing hope,
always narrowing hope.*

Mother sits on one shoulder hissing:
Life is dangerous.
Father sits on the other sighing:
Lucky you.
Grandmother, grandfather, big sister:
You'll die if you leave us,
you'll die if you ever leave us.

Sweetheart, baby sister,
you'll die anyway
& so will I.

Even if you walk the wide greensward,
even if you
& your beautiful big belly
embrace the world of men & trees,
even if you moan with pleasure,
& smoke the sweet grass
& feast on strawberries in bed,
you'll die anyway—
wide or narrow,
you're going to die.
As long as you're at it,
die wide.
Follow your belly to the green pasture.
Lie down in the sun's dapple.
Life is not as dangerous
as mother said.
It is more dangerous,
more wide.

—Erica Jong[29]

What might I, as representative of many feminists, include in an ideal? I would like to see:

- women bearing all the marvelous traits of excellence chronicled by the great philosopher: strength, intelligence, temperance, independence, courage, principle, honor, and the rest
- women, beautiful and healthy in our bodies, comfortable with them, understanding them, proud of them
- women free of the fetters of possession and exploitation, free to define our own female beings, to direct the rites, events, and progress of our own lives and experience
- women caring for one another, proud of our womanhood, caring for any living thing in the way that is meaningful to us

- women contributing wholeheartedly and equally with men to civilization in whatever way we enjoy and believe to be right.

Notes

[1] George Gilder, *Sexual Suicide* (New York: Quadrangle, 1973) chap. 1.

[2] Midge Decter, *The New Chastity and Other Arguments Against Women's Liberation* (New York: Coward, McCann & Geoghegan, 1972).

[3] Especially in Sigmund Freud, "Femininity," lecture XXXIII, in *The Standard Edition of the Complete Psychological Works of Sigmund Freud*, trans. and ed. James Strachey et al. (London: Hogarth Press, 1964), vol. XXII.

[4] Karl Stern, *The Flight from Woman* (New York: Farrar, Straus & Giroux, 1965).

[5] Allan Bloom, *The Closing of the American Mind* (N.Y.: Simon & Schuster, 1987), pp. 101–102.

[6] Ibid., p. 129.

[7] Shulamith Firestone, *The Dialectic of Sex* (New York: Bantam, 1971), p. 1.

[8] Kate Millett, *Sexual Politics* (New York: Doubleday, 1970), p. 23.

[9] The meaning and utility of the concept of androgyny is much debated. See Joyce Trebilcot, "Two Forms of Androgynism," in *Feminism and Philosophy*, ed. Mary Vetterling-Braggin, Frederick A. Elliston, and Jane English (Totowa, N.J.: Littlefield, Adams, 1977), among others.

[10] The lines from "Snapshots of a Daughter-in-Law" from SNAPSHOTS OF A DAUGHTER-IN-LAW, Poems 1954–1962, by Adrienne Rich, are reprinted with the permission of the author and the publisher, W. W. Norton & Company, Inc. Copyright © 1956, 1957, 1958, 1959, 1960, 1961, 1962, 1963, 1967 by Adrienne Rich Conrad.

[11] Reported by Phyllis Chesler, "Men Drive Women Crazy," in *The Female Experience*, ed. Carol Tavris (Del Mar, Calif.: Communications Research Machines, 1973), p. 83.

[12] Quoted in Vern L. Bullough, Brenda Shelton, and Sarah Slavin, *The Subordinated Sex* (U. of Georgia Press, 1988), p. 24. By permission of U. of Georgia Press.

[13] Ibid., p. 49.

[14] Ibid., p. 84.

[15] Ibid., p. 96–97.

[16] Ibid., p. 122.

[17] Ibid., p. 150.

[18] Ibid., p. 169.

[19]Quoted in Chesler, ''Men Drive Women Crazy,'' p. 82.

[20]Kim Chernin, *Reinventing Eve: Modern Woman in Search of Herself* (N.Y.: Harper & Row, 1987), p. 182.

[21]Marjorie Agosin, ''Chile: Women of Smoke,'' trans. Cola Franzen in Robin Morgan, ed., *Sisterhood Is Global* (New York: Anchor Books, 1984) pp. 138, 141.

[22]In *Essence Magazine,* August 1982, p. 58.

[23]In Robin Morgan, ed., *Sisterhood Is Global*, pp. 330, 337.

[24]Wilma Scott Heide in the Introduction to *Hospitals, Paternalism, and the Role of the Nurse,* by JoAnn Ashley (New York: Teachers College Press, 1976), p. viii.

[25]In Cheríe Moraga and Gloria Anzaldúa, eds. *This Bridge Called My Back: Writings by Radical Women of Color* (Mass: Persephone Press, 1981), pp. 14, 15.

[26]In a letter to Pierre Demeny, 15 May 1871.

[27]Simone de Beauvoir, *The Second Sex*, ed. and trans. H. M. Parshley (New York: Knopf, 1953), p. 715.

[28]Germaine Greer, *The Female Eunuch* (New York: McGraw-Hill, 1971), pp. 328–329. Copyright © 1970, 1971 by Germaine Greer. Reprinted by permission of the publishers, McGraw-Hill Book Company and Granada Publishing Limited.

[29]''For Claudia, Against Narrowness.'' From LOVEROOT by Erica Jong. Copyright © 1975 by Erica Mann Jong. Reprinted by permission of Henry Holt and Company, Inc.

The Transformation of Silence Into Language and Action

Audre Lorde

Audre Lorde, poet, esssayist, fiction writer, activist, was born in New York City of West Indian parents. Her writing is powerful, searingly honest—and is always directed toward positive social change and personal action. In her essay "Eye to Eye," she said:

> *To search for power within myself means I must be willing to move through being afraid to whatever lies beyond. If I look at my most vulnerable places and acknowledge the pain I have felt, I can remove the source of that pain from my enemies' arsenals. My history cannot be used to feather my enemies' arrows then, and that lessens their power over me. Nothing I accept about myself can be used against me to diminish me. I am who I am, doing what I came to do, acting upon you like a drug or a chisel or remind you of your me-ness, as I discover you in myself.*[1]

Those are important words to hear after the preceding chapter's heavy load of misogyny and untruth.

In this essay, Lorde admonishes us to be warriors, to wage war with the forces of death, to bring hope and life by breaking destructive silences, by acting.

Audre Lorde in *Sister Outsider: Essays & Speeches by Audre Lorde.* © Audre Lorde, 1984. New York: Crossing Press, 1984.[2]

I HAVE COME TO BELIEVE OVER AND OVER AGAIN that what is most important to me must be spoken, made verbal and shared, even at the risk of having it bruised or misunderstood. That the speaking profits me, beyond any other effect. I am standing here as a Black lesbian poet, and the meaning of all that waits upon the fact that I am still alive, and might not have been. Less than two months ago I was told by two doctors, one female and one male, that I would have to have breast surgery, and that there was a 60 to 80 percent chance that the tumor was malignant. Between that telling and the actual surgery, there was a three-week period of the agony of an involuntary reorganization of my entire life. The surgery was completed, and the growth was benign.

But within those three weeks, I was forced to look upon myself and my living with a harsh and urgent clarity that has left me still shaken but much stronger. This is a situation faced by many women, by some of you here today. Some of what I experienced during that time has helped elucidate for me much of what I feel concerning the transformation of silence into language and action.

In becoming forcibly and essentially aware of my mortality, and of what I wished and wanted for my life, however short it might be, priorities and omissions became strongly etched in a merciless light, and what I most regretted were my silences. Of what had I *ever* been afraid? To question or to speak as I believed could have meant pain, or death. But we all hurt in so many different ways, all the time, and pain will either change or end. Death, on the other hand, is the final silence. And that might be coming quickly, now, without regard for whether I had ever spoken what needed to be said, or had only betrayed myself into small silences, while I planned someday to speak, or waited for someone else's words. And

I began to recognize a source of power within myself that comes from the knowledge that while it is most desirable not to be afraid, learning to put fear into a perspective gave me great strength.

I was going to die, if not sooner then later, whether or not I had ever spoken myself. My silences had not protected me. Your silence will not protect you. But for every real word spoken, for every attempt I had ever made to speak those truths for which I am still seeking, I had made contact with other women while we examined the words to fit a world in which we all believed, bridging our differences. And it was the concern and caring of all those women which gave me strength and enabled me to scrutinize the essentials of my living.

The women who sustained me through that period were Black and white, old and young, lesbian, bisexual, and heterosexual, and we all shared a war against the tyrannies of silence. They all gave me a strength and concern without which I could not have survived intact. Within those weeks of acute fear came the knowledge—within the war we are all waging with the forces of death, subtle and otherwise, conscious or not—I am not only a casualty, I am also a warrior.

What are the words you do not yet have? What do you need to say? What are the tyrannies you swallow day by day and attempt to make your own, until you will sicken and die of them, still in silence? Perhaps for some of you here today, I am the face of one of your fears. Because I am woman, because I am Black, because I am lesbian, because I am myself—a Black woman warrior poet doing my work—come to ask you, are you doing yours?

And of course I am afraid, because the transformation of silence into language and action is an act of self-revelation, and that always seems fraught with danger. But my daughter, when I told her of our topic and my difficulty with it, said, ''Tell them about how you're never really a whole person if you remain silent, because there's always that one little piece inside you that wants to be spoken out, and if you keep ignoring it, it gets madder and madder and hotter and hotter, and if you don't speak it out one day it will just up and punch you in the mouth from the inside.''

In the cause of silence, each of us draws the face of her own fear—fear of contempt, of censure, or some judgment, or recognition, of challenge, of an-

nihilation. But most of all, I think, we fear the visibility without which we cannot truly live. Within this country where racial difference creates a constant, if unspoken, distortion of vision, Black women have on one hand always been highly visible, and so, on the other hand, have been rendered invisible through the depersonalization of racism. Even within the women's movement, we have had to fight, and still do, for that very visibility which also renders us most vulnerable, our Blackness. For to survive in the mouth of this dragon we call america, we have had to learn this first and most vital lesson—that we were never meant to survive. Not as human beings. And neither were most of you here today, Black or not. And that visibility which makes us most vulnerable is that which also is the source of our greatest strength. Because the machine will try to grind you into dust anyway, whether or not we speak. We can sit in our corners mute forever while our sisters and our selves are wasted, while our children are distorted and destroyed, while our earth is poisoned; we can sit in our safe corners mute as bottles, and we will still be no less afraid.

In my house this year we are celebrating the feast of Kwanza, the African-american festival of harvest which begins the day after Christmas and lasts for seven days. There are seven principles of Kwanza, one for each day. The first principle is Umoja, which means unity, the decision to strive for and maintain unity in self and community. The principle for yesterday, the second day, was Kujichagulia—self-determination—the decision to define ourselves, name ourselves, and speak for ourselves, instead of being defined and spoken for by others. Today is the third day of Kwanza, and the principle for today is Ujima—collective work and responsibility—the decision to build and maintain ourselves and our communities together and to recognize and solve our problems together.

Each of us is here now because in one way or another we share a commitment to language and to the power of language, and to the reclaiming of that language which has been made to work against us. In the transformation of silence into language and action, it is vitally necessary for each one of us to establish or examine her function in that transformation and to recognize her role as vital within that transformation.

For those of us who write, it is necessary to scrutinize not only the truth of what we speak, but the truth of that language by which we speak it. For others, it is to share and spread also those words that are meaningful to us. But primarily for us all, it is necessary to teach by living and speaking those truths which we believe and know beyond understanding. Because in this way alone we can survive, by taking part in a process of life that is creative and continuing, that is growth.

And it is never without fear—of visibility, of the harsh light of scrutiny and perhaps judgment, of pain, of death. But we have lived through all of those already, in silence, except death. And I remind myself all the time now that if I were to have been born mute, or had maintained an oath of silence my whole life long for safety, I would still have suffered, and I would still die. It is very good for establishing perspective.

And where the words of women are crying to be heard, we must each of us recognize our responsibility to seek those words out, to read them and share them and examine them in their pertinence to our lives. That we not hide behind the mockeries of separations that have been imposed upon us and which so often we accept as our own. For instance, "I can't possibly teach Black women's writing—their experience is so different from mine." Yet how many years have you spent teaching Plato and Shakespeare and Proust? Or another, "She's a white woman and what could she possibly have to say to me?" Or, "She's a lesbian, what would my husband say, or my chairman?" Or again, "This woman writes of her sons and I have no children." And all the other endless ways in which we rob ourselves of ourselves and each other.

We can learn to work and speak when we are afraid in the same way we have learned to work and speak when we are tired. For we have been socialized to respect fear more than our own needs for language and definition, and while we wait in silence for that final luxury of fearlessness, the weight of that silence will choke us.

The fact that we are here and that I speak these words is an attempt to break that silence and bridge some of those differences between us, for it is not difference which immobilizes us, but silence. And there are so many silences to be broken.

Notes

[1]"Eye to Eye: Black Women, Hatred and Anger" in *Sister Outsider: Essays and Speeches by Audre Lorde* (New York: Crossing Press, 1984), p. 147.

[2]Paper delivered at the Modern Language Association's "Lesbian and Literature Panel," Chicago, Illinois, December 28, 1977. First published in *Sinister Wisdom* 6 (1978) and *The Cancer Journals* (Spinsters Ink, San Francisco, 1980).

Woman—Which Includes Man, Of Course

Theodora Wells

Theodora Wells, who took an MBA at the University of Southern California, taught management and communication at the University of California at Los Angeles and at the University of Southern California. President of Wells Associates, a management consulting firm, she is also coauthor of Breakthrough: Women into Management *(1972) and* Keeping Your Cool Under Fire: Communicating Non-Defensively *(1980).*

The following selection is an "experience in awareness." Read and feel it slowly and deeply.

THERE IS MUCH CONCERN TODAY ABOUT THE FUture of man, which means, of course, both men and women—generic Man. For a woman to take exception to this use of the term "man" is often seen as defensive hair-splitting by an "emotional female."

The following experience is an invitation to awareness in which you are asked to feel into, and stay with, your feelings through each step, letting them absorb you. If you start intellectualizing, try to turn it down and let your feelings again surface to your awareness.

Consider reversing the generic term Man. Think of the future of Woman which, of course, includes both women and men. Feel into that, sense its meaning to you—as a woman—as a man.

Think of it always being that way, every day of your life. Feel the everpresence of woman and feel the nonpresence of man. Absorb what it tells you about the importance and value of being woman—of being man.

Recall that everything you have ever read all your life uses only female pronouns—she, her—meaning both girls and boys, both women and men. Recall that most of the voices on radio and most of the faces on TV are women's—when important events are covered—on commercials—and on the late talk shows. Recall that you have no male senator representing you in Washington.

Feel into the fact that women are the leaders, the power-centers, the prime-movers. Man, whose natural role is husband and father, fulfills himself through nurturing children and making the home a refuge for woman. This is only natural to balance the biological role of woman who devotes her entire body to the race during pregnancy.

Then feel further into the obvious biological

explanation for woman as the ideal—her genital construction. By design, female genitals are compact and internal, protected by her body. Male genitals are so exposed that he must be protected from outside attack to assure the perpetuation of the race. His vulnerability clearly requires sheltering.

Thus, by nature, males are more passive than females, and have a desire in sexual relations to be symbolically engulfed by the protective body of the woman. Males psychologically yearn for this protection, fully realizing their masculinity at this time—feeling exposed and vulnerable at other times. The male is not fully adult until he has overcome his infantile tendency to penis orgasm and has achieved the mature surrender of the testicle orgasm. He then feels himself a "whole man" when engulfed by the woman.

If the male denies these feelings, he is unconsciously rejecting his masculinity. Therapy is thus indicated to help him adjust to his own nature. Of course, therapy is administered by a woman, who has the education and wisdom to facilitate openness leading to the male's growth and self-actualization.

To help him feel into his defensive emotionality, he is invited to get in touch with the "child" in him. He remembers his sister's jeering at his primitive genitals that "flop around foolishly." She can run, climb and ride horseback unencumbered. Obviously, since she is free to move, she is encouraged to develop her body and mind in preparation for her active responsibilities of adult womanhood. The male vulnerability needs female protection, so he is taught the less active, caring, virtues of homemaking.

Because of his clitoris-envy, he learns to strap up his genitals, and learns to feel ashamed and unclean because of his nocturnal emissions. Instead, he is encouraged to keep his body lean and dream of getting married, waiting for the time of his fulfillment—when "his woman" gives him a girl-child to carry on the family name. He knows that if it is a boy-child he has failed somehow—but they can try again.

In getting to your feelings on being a woman—on being a man—stay with the sensing you are now experiencing. As the words begin to surface, say what you feel from inside you.

A Room of One's Own

Virginia Woolf

Virginia Woolf (1882–1941), British author and cofounder (with her husband) of the Hogarth Press, grew up in literary circles and traveled with some of the most interesting British thinkers of her day. Her novels include The Voyage Out *(1915),* Night and Day *(1919),* Monday or Tuesday *(1921),* Mrs. Dalloway *(1925),* To the Lighthouse *(1927), and* The Years *(1937). She wrote two famous feminist essays.* A Room of One's Own *(1929) and* Three Guineas *(1938). In 1941, fearful that she was going mad, she killed herself.*

In the following excerpt, Woolf depicts the ambiance and style of the great British university ("Oxbridge")—its appearance, the rhythm of the day, the amenities within, the effect on the human spirit. Here the plain dinner served to the women of "Fernham College" is her metaphor for the historical poverty of women, the paucity of money, time, dignity, freedom, and peace that women are heir to. Angrily she develops the contrast between the "plain gravy soup" affordable by the women's colleges and the "partridges and wine" of the university's well-endowed male enclaves, between the commodious gentility of the "queer old gentlemen . . . with tufts of fur upon their shoulders" and "all those women working year after year and finding it hard to get two thousand pounds together." She thinks of the women mothering "thirteen children," of the library to which women are not admitted, and of the insecurity women bear, and forces one to consider the effect of all this on the mind of the writer. She considers the effect of the entire configuration on the mind of any thinker, or potential artist or scientist or musician, and forms the beginnings of the answer to the question: Why are there no women geniuses? Finally, Woolf tells us we must not settle for the circumstances we find ourselves in, but rather we must work, even in obscurity, to bring forth the women geniuses of the present and future.

THIS ESSAY IS BASED UPON TWO PAPERS READ TO the Arts Society at Newnham and the Odtaa at Girton in October 1928. The papers were too long to be read in full, and have since been altered and expanded.

Chapter One

Women and fiction—what has that got to do with a room of one's own? I will try to explain. When you asked me to speak about women and fiction I sat down on the banks of a river and began to wonder what the words meant. They might mean simply a few remarks about Fanny Burney; a few more about Jane Austen; a tribute to the Brontës and a sketch of Haworth Parsonage under snow; some witticisms if possible about Miss Mitford; a respectful allusion to George Eliot; a reference to Mrs. Gaskell and one would have done. But at second sight the words seemed not so simple. The title women and fiction might mean, and you may have meant it to mean, women and what they are like; or it might mean women and the fiction that they write; or it might mean women and the fiction that is written about them; or it might mean that somehow all three are inextricably mixed together and you want me to consider them in that light. But when I began to consider the subject in this last way, which seemed the most interesting, I soon saw that it had one fatal drawback. I should never be able to come to a conclusion. I should never be able to fulfil what is, I understand, the first duty of a lecturer—to hand you after an hour's discourse a nugget of pure truth to wrap up between the pages of your notebooks and keep on the mantelpiece for ever. All I could do was to offer you an opinion upon one minor point—a woman must have money and a room of her own if she is to write fiction; and that, as you will see, leaves the great problem of the true nature of woman and the true nature of fiction unsolved. . . .

. . . I propose, making use of all the liberties and licenses of a novelist, to tell you the story of the two days that preceded my coming here—how, bowed down by the weight of the subject which you have laid upon my shoulders, I pondered it, and made it work in and out of my daily life. I need not say that what I am about to describe has no existence; Oxbridge is an invention; so is Fernham; . . .

. . . Here was my soup. Dinner was being served in the great dining-hall. Far from being spring it was in fact an evening in October. Everybody was assembled in the big dining-room. Dinner was ready. Here was the soup. It was a plain gravy soup. There was nothing to stir the fancy in that. One could have seen through the transparent liquid any pattern that there might have been on the plate itself. But there was no pattern. The plate was plain. Next came beef with its attendant greens and potatoes—a homely trinity, suggesting the rumps of cattle in a muddy market, and sprouts curled and yellowed at the edge, and bargaining and cheapening, and women with string bags on Monday morning. There was no reason to complain of human nature's daily food, seeing that the supply was sufficient and coalminers doubtless were sitting down to less. Prunes and custard followed. And if any one complains that prunes, even when mitigated by custard, are an uncharitable vegetable (fruit they are not), stringy as a miser's heart and exuding a fluid such as might run in misers' veins who have denied themselves wine and warmth for eighty years and yet not given to the poor, he should reflect that there are people whose charity embraces even the prune. Biscuits and cheese came next, and here the water-jug was liberally passed round, for it is the nature of biscuits to be dry, and these were biscuits to the core. That was all. The meal was over. Everybody scraped their chairs back; the swing-doors swung violently to and fro; soon the hall was emptied of every sign of food and made ready no doubt for breakfast next morning. Down corridors and up staircases the youth of England went banging and singing. And was it for a guest, a stranger (for I had no more right here in Fernham than in Trinity or Somerville or Girton or Newnham or Christchurch), to say, "The dinner was not good," or to say (we were now, Mary Seton and I, in her sitting-room), "Could we not have dined up here alone?" for if I had said anything of the kind I should have been prying and searching into the secret econ-omies of a house which to the stranger wears so fine a front of gaiety and courage. No, one could say nothing of the sort. Indeed, conversation for a moment flagged. The human frame being what it is, heart, body and brain all mixed together, and not contained in separate compartments as they will be no doubt in another million years, a good dinner is of great importance to good talk. One cannot think well, love well, sleep well, if one has not dined well. The lamp in the spine does not light on beef and prunes. We are all *probably* going to heaven, and Vandyck is, we *hope*, to meet us round the next corner— that is the dubious and qualifying state of mind that beef and prunes at the end of the day's work breed between them. Happily my friend, who taught science, had a cupboard where there was a squat bottle and little glasses—(but there should have been sole and partridge to begin with)—so that we were able to draw up to the fire and repair some of the damages of the day's living. In a minute or so we were slipping freely in and out among all those objects of curiosity and interest which form in the mind in the absence of a particular person, and are naturally to be discussed on coming together again—how somebody has married, another has not; one thinks this, another that; one has improved out of all knowledge, the other most amazingly gone to the bad—with all those speculations upon human nature and the character of the amazing world we live in which spring naturally from such beginnings. While these things were being said, however, I became shamefacedly aware of a current setting in of its own accord and carrying everything forward to an end of its own. One might be talking of Spain or Portugal, of book or racehorse, but the real interest of whatever was said was none of those things, but a scene of masons on a high roof some five centuries ago. Kings and nobles brought treasure in huge sacks and poured it under the earth. This scene was for ever coming alive in my mind and placing itself by another of lean cows and a muddy market and withered greens and the stringy hearts of old men—these two pictures, disjointed and disconnected and nonsensical as they were, were for ever coming together and combating each other and had me entirely at their mercy. The best course, unless the whole talk was to be distorted, was to expose what was in my mind to the air, when with good luck it would fade and crumble like the head of the dead king when they opened the coffin at Windsor. Briefly, then, I told Miss Seton about the masons who had been all those years on the roof of the chapel, and about the kings and queens and nobles bearing sacks of gold and silver on their shoulders, which they shovelled into the earth; and then how the great financial magnates of our own time came and laid cheques and bonds, I suppose, where the others had laid ingots and rough lumps of gold. All that lies beneath the colleges down there, I said; but this college, where we are now sitting, what lies beneath its gallant red brick and the wild unkempt grasses of the garden? What force is behind that plain china off which we dined, and (here it popped out of my mouth before I could stop it) the beef, the custard and the prunes?

Well, said Mary Seton, about the year 1860—Oh, but you know the story, she said, bored, I suppose, by the recital. And she told me—rooms were hired. Committees met. Envelopes were addressed. Circulars were drawn up. Meetings were held; letters were read out; so-and-so has promised so much; on the contrary, Mr. —— won't give a penny. The *Saturday Review* has been very rude. How can we raise a fund to pay for offices? Shall we hold a bazaar? Can't we find a pretty girl to sit in the front row? Let us look up what John Stuart Mill said on the subject. Can any one persuade the editor of the —— to print a letter? Can we get Lady —— to sign it? Lady —— is out of town. That was the way it was done, presumably, sixty years ago, and it was a prodigious effort, and a great deal of time was spent on it. And it was only after a long struggle and with the utmost difficulty that they got thirty thousand pounds together.[1] So obviously we cannot have wine and partridges and servants carrying tin dishes on their heads, she said. We cannot have sofas and separate rooms. "The amenities," she said, quoting from some book or other, "will have to wait."[2]

At the thought of all those women working year after year and finding it hard to get two thousand pounds together, and as much as they could do to get thirty thousand pounds, we burst out in scorn at the reprehensible poverty of our sex. What had our mothers been doing then that they had no wealth to leave us? Powdering their noses? Looking in at shop windows? Flaunting in the sun at Monte Carlo? There were some photographs on the mantelpiece. Mary's mother—if that was her picture—may have been a wastrel in her spare time (she had thirteen children by a minister of the church), but if so her gay and dissipated life had left too few traces of its pleasures on her face. She was a homely body; an old lady in a plaid shawl which was fastened by a large cameo; and she sat in a basket-chair, encouraging a spaniel to look at the camera, with the amused, yet strained expression of one who is sure that the dog will move directly the bulb is pressed. Now if she had gone into business; had become a manufacturer of artificial silk or a magnate of the Stock Exchange; if she had left two or three hundred thousand pounds to Fernham, we could have been sitting at our ease tonight and the subject of our talk might have been archaeology, botany, anthropology, physics, the nature of the atom, mathematics, astronomy, relativity, geography. If only Mrs. Seton and her mother and her mother before her had learnt the great art of making money and had left their money, like their fathers and their grandfathers before them, to found fellowships and lectureships and prizes and scholarships appropriated to the use of their own sex, we might have dined very tolerably up here alone off a bird and a bottle of wine; we might have looked forward without undue confidence to a pleasant and honourable lifetime spent in the shelter of one of the liberally endowed professions. We might have been exploring or writing; mooning about the venerable places of the earth; sitting contemplative on the steps of the Parthenon, or going at ten to an office and coming home comfortably at half-past four to write a little poetry. Only, if Mrs. Seton and her like had gone into business at the age of fifteen, there would have been—that was the snag in the argument—no Mary. What, I asked, did Mary think of that? There between the curtains was the October night, calm and lovely, with a star or two caught in the yellowing trees. Was she ready to resign her share of it and her memories (for they had been a happy family, though a large one) of games and quarrels up in Scotland, which she is never tired of praising for the fineness of its air and the quality of its cakes, in order that Fernham might have been endowed with fifty thousand pounds or so by a stroke of the pen? For, to endow a college would necessitate the suppression of families altogether. Making a fortune and bearing thirteen children—no human being could stand it. Consider the facts, we said. First there are nine months before the baby is born. Then the baby is born. Then there are three or four months spent in feeding the baby. After the baby is fed there are certainly five years spent in playing with the baby. You cannot, it seems, let children run about the streets. People who have seen them running wild in Russia say that the sight is not a pleasant one. People say, too, that human nature takes its shape in the years between one and five. If Mrs. Seton, I said, had been making money, what sort of memories would you have known of Scotland, and its fine air and cakes and all the rest of it? But it is useless to ask these questions, because you would never have come into existence at all. Moreover, it is equally useless to ask what might have happened if Mrs. Seton and her mother and her mother before her had amassed great wealth and laid it under the foundations of college and library, because, in the first place, to earn money was impossible for them, and in the second, had it been possible, the law denied them the right to possess what money they earned. It is only for the last forty-eight years that Mrs. Seton has had a penny of her own. For all the centuries before that it would have been her husband's property—a thought which, perhaps, may have had its share in keeping Mrs. Seton and her mothers off the Stock Exchange. Every penny I earn, they may have said, will be taken from me and disposed of according to my husband's wisdom—perhaps to found a scholarship or to endow a fellowship in Balliol or Kings, so that to earn money, even if I could earn money, is not a matter that interests me very greatly. I had better leave it to my husband.

At any rate, whether or not the blame rested on the old lady who was looking at the spaniel, there could be no doubt that for some reason or other our mothers had mismanaged their affairs very gravely. Not a penny could be spared for "amenities"; for partridges and wine, beadles and turf, books and cigars, libraries and leisure. To raise bare walls out of the bare earth was the utmost they could do.

So we talked standing at the window and looking, as so many thousands look every night, down on the domes and towers of the famous city beneath us. It was very beautiful, very mysterious in the autumn moonlight. The old stone looked very white and venerable. One thought of all the books that were assembled down there; of the pictures of old prelates and worthies hanging in the panelled rooms; of the painted windows that would be throwing strange globes and crescents on the pavement; of the tablets and memorials and inscriptions; of the fountains and the grass; of the quiet rooms looking across the quiet quadrangles. And (pardon me the thought) I thought, too, of the admirable smoke and drink and the deep armchairs and the pleasant carpets: of the urbanity, the geniality, the dignity which are the offspring of luxury and privacy and space. Certainly our mothers had not provided us with anything comparable to all this—our mothers who found it difficult to scrape together thirty thousand pounds, our mothers who bore thirteen children to ministers of religion at St. Andrews.

So I went back to my inn, and as I walked through the dark streets I pondered this and that, as one does at the end of the day's work. I pondered why it was that Mrs. Seton had no money to leave us; and what effect poverty has on the mind; and what effect wealth has on the mind; and I thought of the queer old gentlemen I had seen that morning with tufts of fur upon their shoulders; and I remembered how if one whistled one of them ran; and I thought of the organ booming in the chapel and of the shut doors of the library; and I thought how unpleasant it is to be locked out; and I thought how it is worse perhaps to be locked in; and, thinking of the safety and prosperity of the one sex and of the poverty and insecurity of the other and of the effect of tradition and of the lack of tradition upon the mind of a writer, I thought at last that it was time to roll up the crumpled skin of the day, with its arguments and its impressions and its anger and its laughter, and cast it into the hedge. A thousand stars were flashing across the blue wastes of the sky. One seemed alone with an inscrutable society. All human beings were laid asleep—prone, horizontal, dumb. Nobody seemed stirring in the streets of Oxbridge. Even the door of the hotel sprang open at the touch of an invisible hand—not a boots was sitting up to light me to bed, it was so late.

Chapter Two

. . . The inevitable sequel to lunching and dining at Oxbridge seemed, unfortunately, to be a visit to the British Museum. One must strain off what was personal and accidental in all these impressions and so reach the pure fluid, the essential oil of truth. For that visit to Oxbridge and the luncheon and the dinner had started a swarm of questions. Why did men drink wine and women water? Why was one sex so prosperous and the other so poor? What effect has poverty on fiction? What conditions are necessary for the creation of works of art?—a thousand questions at once suggested themselves. . . .

Chapter Three

. . . Here am I asking why women did not write poetry in the Elizabethan age, and I am not sure how they were educated; whether they were taught to write; whether they had sitting-rooms to themselves; how many women had children before they were twenty-one; what, in short, they did from eight in the morning till eight at night. They had no money evidently; according to Professor Trevelyan they were married whether they liked it or not before they were out of the nursery, at fifteen or sixteen very likely. It would have been extremely odd, even upon this showing, had one of them suddenly written the plays of Shakespeare, I concluded, and I thought of that old gentleman, who is dead now, but was a bishop, I think, who declared that it was impossible for any woman, past, present, or to come, to have the genius of Shakespeare. He wrote to the papers about it. He also told a lady who applied to him for information that cats do not as a matter of fact go to heaven, though they have, he added, souls of a sort. How much thinking those old gentlemen used to save one! How the borders of ignorance shrank back at their approach! Cats do not go to heaven. Women cannot write the plays of Shakespeare.

Be that as it may, I could not help thinking, as I looked at the works of Shakespeare on the shelf, that the bishop was right at least in this; it would have been impossible, completely and entirely, for any woman to have written the plays of Shakespeare in the age of Shakespeare. Let me imagine, since facts are so hard to come by, what would have happened had Shakespeare had a wonderfully gifted sister, called Judith, let us say. Shakespeare himself went, very probably—his mother was an heiress—to the grammar school, where he may have learnt Latin—Ovid, Virgil and Horace—and the elements of grammar and logic. He was, it is well known, a wild boy who poached rabbits, perhaps shot a deer, and had, rather sooner than he should have done, to marry a woman in the neighbourhood, who bore him a child rather quicker than was right. That escapade sent him to seek his fortune in London. He had, it seemed, a taste for the theatre; he began by holding horses at the stage door. Very soon he got work in

the theatre, became a successful actor, and lived at the hub of the universe, meeting everybody, knowing everybody, practising his art on the boards, exercising his wits in the streets, and even getting access to the palace of the queen. Meanwhile his extraordinarily gifted sister, let us suppose, remained at home. She was as adventurous, as imaginative, as agog to see the world as he was. But she was not sent to school. She had no chance of learning grammar and logic, let alone of reading Horace and Virgil. She picked up a book now and then, one of her brother's perhaps, and read a few pages. But then her parents came in and told her to mend the stockings or mind the stew and not moon about with books and papers. They would have spoken sharply but kindly, for they were substantial people who knew the conditions of life for a woman and loved their daughter—indeed, more likely than not she was the apple of her father's eye. Perhaps she scribbled some pages up in an apple loft on the sly, but was careful to hide them or set fire to them. Soon, however, before she was out of her teens, she was to be betrothed to the son of a neighbouring wool-stapler. She cried out that marriage was hateful to her, and for that she was severely beaten by her father. Then he ceased to scold her. He begged her instead not to hurt him, not to shame him in this matter of her marriage. He would give her a chain of beads or a fine petticoat, he said; and there were tears in his eyes. How could she disobey him? How could she break his heart? The force of her own gift alone drove her to it. She made up a small parcel of her belongings, let herself down by a rope one summer's night and took the road to London. She was not seventeen. The birds that sang in the hedge were not more musical than she was. She had the quickest fancy, a gift like her brother's, for the tune of words. Like him, she had a taste for the theatre. She stood at the stage door; she wanted to act, she said. Men laughed in her face. The manager—a fat, loose-lipped man—guffawed. He bellowed something about poodles dancing and women acting—no woman, he said, could possibly be an actress. He hinted—you can imagine what. She could get no training in her craft. Could she even seek her dinner in a tavern or roam the streets at midnight? Yet her genius was for fiction and lusted to feed abundantly upon the lives of men and women and the study of their ways. At last—for she was very young, oddly like Shakespeare the poet in her face, with the same grey eyes and rounded brows—at last

Nick Greene the actor-manager took pity on her; she found herself with child by that gentleman and so—who shall measure the heat and violence of the poet's heart when caught and tangled in a woman's body?—killed herself one winter's night and lies buried at some cross-roads where the omnibuses now stop outside the Elephant and Castle.

That, more or less, is how the story would run, I think, if a woman in Shakespeare's day had had Shakespeare's genius. . . .

Chapter Six

. . . A thousand pens are ready to suggest what you should do and what effect you will have. My own suggestion is a little fantastic, I admit; I prefer, therefore, to put it in the form of fiction.

I told you in the course of this paper that Shakespeare had a sister; but do not look for her in Sir Sidney Lee's life of the poet. She died young—alas, she never wrote a word. She lies buried where the omnibuses now stop, opposite the Elephant and Castle. Now my belief is that this poet who never wrote a word and was buried at the cross-roads still lives. She lives in you and in me, and in many other women who are not here tonight, for they are washing up the dishes and putting the children to bed. But she lives; for great poets do not die; they are continuing presences; they need only the opportunity to walk among us in the flesh. This opportunity, as I think, it is now coming within your power to give her. For my belief is that if we live another century or so—I am talking of the common life which is the real life and not the little separate lives which we live as individuals—and have five hundred a year each of us and rooms of our own; if we have the habit of

freedom and the courage to write exactly what we think; if we escape a little from the common sitting-room and see human beings not always in their relation to each other but in relation to reality; and the sky, too, and the trees or whatever it may be in themselves; if we look past Milton's bogey, for no human being should shut out the view; if we face the fact, for it is a fact, that there is no arm to cling to, but that we go alone and that our relation is to the world of reality and not only to the world of men and women, then the opportunity will come and the dead poet who was Shakespeare's sister will put on the body which she has so often laid down. Drawing her life from the lives of the unknown who were her forerunners, as her brother did before her, she will be born. As for her coming without that preparation, without that effort on our part, without that determination that when she is born again she shall find it possible to live and write her poetry, that we cannot expect, for that would be impossible. But I maintain that she would come if we worked for her, and that so to work, even in poverty and obscurity, is worth while.

Notes

[1]"We are told that we ought to ask for £30,000 at least. . . . It is not a large sum, considering that there is to be but one college of this sort for Great Britain, Ireland and the Colonies, and considering how easy it is to raise immense sums for boys' schools. But considering how few people really wish women to be educated, it is a good deal."—LADY STEPHEN, *Life of Miss Emily Davies*.

[2]Every penny which could be scraped together was set aside for building, and the amenities had to be postponed.—R. STRACHEY, *The Cause*.

Cross-Cultural Rebellion

Robin Morgan

You can find the biography of Robin Morgan with her selection, ''Know Your Enemy'' in Chapter 3. Here, as before, Morgan instructs through a simple presentation of quotations; let the people speak for themselves. We see that women all over the world experience many of the same feelings, beliefs and reactions. What is more, there is a universal spark, a sensitivity which raises humor and pride and affection among us. This is what ''sisterhood'' means.

A Sampling of Feminist Proverbs from Around the World

Men are mountains and women are the levers which move them.

—Afghanistan (Pushtu)

Now you have offended women; now you have touched rock; now you will be crushed.

—Africa (Zulu women warrior song)

Work is the liberator of women.

—Algeria (feminist slogan)

Where women are honored the gods are pleased.

—Arab

Remember the dignity of your womanhood. Do not appeal, do not beg, do not grovel. Take courage, join hands, stand beside us, fight with us.

—Britain (Christabel Pankhurst)

She must do twice as well as a man to be thought of as half as good. Fortunately, it's not too hard for a woman to be twice as good as a man.

—Canada (Charlotte Whittier, Mayor of Ottawa, speaking of women in public life)

When a woman loves a woman, it is the blood of the mothers speaking.

—The Caribbean

A man thinks he knows but a woman knows better.

—China

A rich widow's tears soon dry.

—Denmark

A poor woman has many troubles: weeping children, wet firewood, a leaking kettle, and a cross man.

—Finland

Men are the reason for women disliking each other.

—France

A woman is not a fiddle to be hung on the wall after being played with.

—Germany

Womanhood is awakening—"Jag Rahi Hai."

—India (chant by women demonstrators in Delhi, 1979)

Wherever you go, have a woman friend.

—Ireland

Men should leave women alone and go study mathematics.

—Italy

A man who betrays a woman had best sleep with one eye open.

—Japan

A brilliant daughter makes a cranky wife.

—The Netherlands

Quick-loving a woman means quick not-loving a woman.

—Nigeria (Yoruba)

A rich widow weeps with one eye and laughs with the other.

—Portugal

If a woman is cold, it is her husband's fault.

—Russia (Ukrainian)

Trusting a man is like trusting a sieve to hold water.

—Saudi Arabia

When a woman loves another woman, it brings no shame to her father's head and no swelling to her own belly.

—Saudi Arabia

The women will get there but the men won't.

—Samoa

Who speaks ill of his wife dishonors himself.

—Scotland

A wife's advice may seem of little value—but he who does not take it is a fool.

—Spain

She recognizes the reality of the society around her. She dedicates herself to its future. She sets alight the world with her talent. She acts with firmness and resolve. She works for the well-being of society. These truly are the five qualities of beauty that will make a new pancha kalyani *[beautiful woman].*

—Sri Lanka

A woman's heart sees more than ten men's eyes.

—Sweden

Women are all one nation.

—Turkey

If particular care and attention is not paid to the ladies we are determined to foment a rebellion, and will not hold ourselves bound by any laws in which we have no voice or representation.

—United States (Abigail Adams)

My dream is to ride the tempest, tame the waves, kill the sharks. I want to drive the enemy away to save our people. I will not accept the usual fate of women who bow their heads and become concubines.

—Vietnam (Trieu Thi Trinh, 240 C.E.)

You need double strength if you quarrel with an independent woman.

—Zimbabwe (Shona)

I Have a Motherland

Gena Corea

Gena Corea, born in Hingham, Massachusetts, in 1946, was educated at the University of Massachusetts and in 1971 became an investigative reporter. Her articles have appeared in the New York Times, Commonweal, *the* Progressive *and the* New Republic Feature Syndicate. *She is the author of* The Hidden Malpractice: How American Medicine Mistreats Women *(1977 and 1985) and* The Mother Machine: Reproductive Technologies from Artificial Insemination to the Artificial Womb *(1985). A cofounder of the Feminist International Network of Resistance to Reproductive and Genetic Engineering (FINRRAGE), she now serves as an editor of* Reproductive and Genetic Engineering: Journal of International Feminist Analysis *(Pergamon Press) and as associate director of the Institute on Women and Technology.*

To all the distortions, the ultimate response is the search for truth and the affirmation of worth. Forceful and feeling, Corea's affirmation captures the emotions aroused in us when we recover the past and reconstitute our "place."

SIT DOWN, WRETCH, AND ANSWER ME: WHAT HAVE you done with my past?

Years ago you stood before me with a solemn face and told me I was an orphan. With the hand behind your back you pushed the heads of my parents—my proud, strong, angry ancestors—under time's river.

You hid the action of your right hand by pointing with your left to my entire history, one sentence in a book: "In 1920, in a battle largely led by Susan B. Anthony, women won the right to vote."

But you never told me how strong Anthony was. How, year after year, she suffered scorn, ridicule and defeat and kept on working, not merely for suffrage, but for woman's full liberation.

You never described to me, white man, the courage of hundreds of nameless women who, though raised to be timid, taught to be frightened, nonetheless defied decorum and walked down strange streets, knocked on doors, stood up before hostile faces, and suffered jeers to collect signatures for suffrage petitions—petitions later joked about in Congress and then ignored.

Why didn't you tell me I had such magnificent foremothers?

Why, white man, in your history books, did you never tell me about spunky Abigail Adams asking her husband John to assign women the legal status of human being, rather than property, in the Constitution of the young United States?

And of her warning that, if forgotten, women were "determined to foment a rebellion"? Women were forgotten and women have been fomenting a rebellion but you hid from me the uprisings of my foremothers.

Why did you reverently describe to me the political and military strategies with which earlier Kissingers entertained themselves but keep from me the stories of how ordinary women lived their lives?

I know all about the glorious deaths of soldiers on the battlefield but nothing about the deaths of women in childbed.

Where is the Tomb of the Unknown Mother? Why did she die?

You told me about Carrie Nation, whom you pictured as a ludicrous, axe-wielding teetotaller, but not about Margaret Sanger, who brought to women the most important discovery since fire: contraception.

Why did you hide Anne Hutchinson, Lucy Stone, Sojourner Truth and Mary Walker from me? I could have been stronger if I'd known of them.

You tried to disinherit me. When I trembled before you like an orphan dependent on your good will, you said, "Oh, I'll take care of you, little one."

You kept me meek and grateful for your very small favors. You told me how benevolent you were to an orphan like me. How chivalrous you were, you said.

(Oh, why did you never tell me that way back in 1848, Sarah Grimke had called chivalry "practical contempt"?)

And in gratitude for your chivalry, your patronizing protection, I cooked your food, washed your clothes, cleaned your house, bore and raised your children.

You fraud! I'm your equal and you hid that from me.

When I envied you your freedom, your adventures, and dreamed of being, say, a lawyer, you frowned and told me that if I began to use my brain, I'd be sure to have labor pains and it wouldn't do for me, while trying a case in a court of law, to give birth to a child.

You put on black robes, held a thick book to your heart, rolled your eyes to heaven and solemnly announced that God wanted me to be just as I was.

How cruel of God, I whispered.
Blasphemer! you shouted in my ear. Heretic!
Let me read the thick book, I said.
No, you snapped, your brain's too small. You'll hurt it and go mad.

And all that time, all that time when I thought I was a strange mutation of a woman with strange longings to be whole, all that time, damn it, my ancestors had felt the same, thought the same, said the same.

And you, white man, hid their words, their struggles, their very existences from me. You left my ancestors out of history.

But now I know. I have a tribe, a people, a history, a past, an identity, a motherland, a tradition. I'm not an orphan. I'm not alone.

And I'll tremble before you no more.

. . . To Form a More Perfect Union

Maya Angelou

Poet, novelist, playwright, screenwriter, Maya Angelou is the author of I Know Why The Caged Bird Sings *(1970),* And Still I Rise *(1978),* Singin' and Swingin' and Gettin' Merry Like Christmas *(1985), and* All God's Children Need Traveling Shoes *(1986).*

As commissioner for the observance of International Women's Year, appointed by President Jimmy Carter, she gave this speech at the First National Women's Conference in Houston, Texas, in 1977. That equality and freedom for women is squarely within the American tradition of liberty is reflected in Angelou's words.

Maya Angelou, ''To Form a More Perfect Union . . .'' reported in The Spirit of Houston: The First National Women's Conference. An official report to the President, the Congress, and the People of the U.S. National Commission on the Observance of International Women's Year. Washington, D.C., 1978.

WE AMERICAN WOMEN VIEW OUR HISTORY WITH equanimity. We allow the positive achievement to inspire us and the negative omissions to teach us.

We recognize the accomplishments of our sisters, those famous and hallowed women of history and those unknown and unsung women whose strength gave birth to our strength.

We recognize those women who were and are immobilized by oppression and crippled by prejudice.

We recognize that no nation can boast of balance until each member of that nation is equally employed and equally rewarded.

We recognize that women collectively have been unfairly treated and dishonorably portrayed.

We recognize our responsibility to work toward the eradication of negatives in our society and by so doing, bring honor to our gender, to our species, and to ourselves individually.

Because of the recognition set down above we American women unfold our future today.

We promise to accept nothing less than justice for every woman.

We pledge to work unsparingly to bring fair play to every public arena, to encourage honorable behavior in each private home.

We promise to develop courage that we may learn from our colleagues and patience that we may attack our opponent.

Because we are women, we make these promises.

5

The Origins of Female Subordination: Theories and Explanations

Asking the Question

Not long after one becomes sensitized to the nature of women's situation, one is likely to ask, Why? How did this come to be, and why is it so resistant to change? Although great diversity exists among peoples of the world, we can see that, for the most part, in society after society and across time and space, men dominate the upper levels of political, economic, and social power, and women are rarely or only partially included.[1] The work of men is generally more highly valued than that of women and usually more highly compensated. Men are typically valued more in themselves as persons, a fact often expressed in social customs, rites, and laws. Men tend to outrank women in social status, and their privilege is frequently built on the service of women. The reverse is rarely the case.

What accounts for the fact that societies are so constructed that men dominate and disparage women? Has it always been so, or was there a time in the dim past when women were the equals of men or even, as some have suggested, the initiators and prime movers of civilization? If male dominance has indeed been universal in time, how is the superior position of men to be explained? Is it true, as patriarchy contends, that men are superior to women in ability, or did they win their place by the choice of the gods? If, on the other hand, male dominance has not always held sway, how did it come to be? Was there a primordial revolution of magnificent proportions, as is sometimes figured in ancient myths, or did a gradual erosion of female power and autonomy occur, and what could have occasioned such an erosion?

Many have argued that men and women are "different" in a variety of ways and that these differences account for women's position. Are women different in ways that matter to the direction in which civilization has evolved? Or did the way civilization has evolved create the differences? Are behavioral differences biologically or culturally based? And what difference do the differences make, or *should* they make, for the way a culture is arranged—in apportioning political authority, economic benefits, and enjoyment of life's amenities?

Some answers to these questions are scientific or quasi-scientific; others appear in mythic context, in political or even poetic language. Some speak in purely pragmatic terms, arguing social efficiency or orderliness, whereas others center on women's personal choices or even cosmic decrees.

The question of why this is as it is has been asked before, but now the women's movement has focused afresh on the issues it raises, and the analyses are becoming more urgent and often more sophisticated. In the religious communities, feminist theologians are challenging the traditional interpretations of language, dogma, and beliefs. In the sciences, feminists and nonfeminists alike are carrying on new and vigorous research into aspects of these issues barely touched or else treated prejudicially before. Controversy and debate are sharp. Many are gaining new, more reliable information and generating new techniques to deal with this ancient question.

New Data

Researchers in almost every field of intellectual endeavor are collecting new information on women's place, experience, and contributions to culture, past and present. Anthropologists have thrown new light on women's discoveries and inventions in early civilization—pottery, food preservation, tanning, and so on. Feminist historians have unearthed data on women never before recognized, events whose importance had been overlooked, activities never before understood. Psychologists and biologists are carefully reexamining studies of female-male differences, together with their relation to behavioral characteristics, in order to deal in a more objective way with traditional assumptions and theories. Linguists are discovering new connections between speech patterns and social effectiveness and power.

New Perspectives

The addition of feminist critique to intellectual dialogue is developing a new depth of sophistication in the nature of inquiry itself. Having challenged the reliability of traditional knowledge collected solely by men or within male structures, feminists are posing new questions that considerably alter the search for explanations. How viable and/or complete is much of the information we have on prehistory and primitive cultures, interpreted as it has been through masculist bias? Can we depend on unsensitized males to have asked the pertinent questions about women; would women have confided freely in male researchers? Would the male researcher have properly evaluated the female data he collected? If the masculist psychologist has imposed his expectations on his research findings, won't they have been distorted, and won't most of the theories of sex differences be unreliable? Might not there then have to be entirely new ways of piecing together the origins of patriarchy?[2]

The matter of terminology, for example, has been sharply challenged. The term *domestic* is an interesting case in point. Literally the word means "pertaining to the home," and social scientists use it to describe tasks, artifacts, or behavior directly related to the home site, to the group's family or living arrangements. Anthropologists generally agree that women have almost universally carried on the "domestic" activities of society. However, evidence also shows that almost any task assigned to women is likely to be deemed "domestic" by social scientists whereas the same task assigned to men is likely to be categorized differently. For example, an ethnographer might categorize fashioning pottery for the tribe as a "domestic" activity if done by women but as an "artistic" one if done by men. In other words, since the assumption is that women do the domestic work of the group, their tasks are automatically categorized as domestic; then, in a real round robin, because women's work is termed domestic, researchers feel safe to report that the domestic work of the tribe is always done by women!

Thus, one may realistically challenge such traditionally accepted theses as the claim that women are oppressed because they have never united in their own self-interest. New discussions have highlighted many events where women fought in our own behalf, events that were either unknown before the surge of feminist history or else neglected as irrelevant. If these factual events, such as the Roman women's opposition to the Oppian Laws, the movement of the Beguines in the Middle Ages, the later fights for temperance, birth control, and abortion rights are ignored and thus not integrated into the thesis, how reliable is the final thesis?

The current surge of interest in the quest for explanations gives reason to be optimistic about discovery but not without careful attention to the many complicated problems before us. Our discussion must be preceded by certain cautions. First, no one as yet knows "the answer." Vast gaps in data and analysis exist. Second, there may not be one answer, but many. Third, the several theories presented here represent only examples of those that exist, and even the challenges put to them do not constitute the full array of those that should be made. This book only has room for a beginning.

The Matter of Definition

No one as yet knows "the answer" to what? That is, what exactly is our question? Are we asking why women and men are "unequal"? Unequal in what? In political or personal power? What constitutes power? What kind of power do women not have? Unequal in opportunity? Opportunity for what? We have opportunity to gain income—we can marry it. From a value-free standpoint, why is that mode of opportunity less acceptable than any other? Are we unequal in status? Or are we just "different," that is, separate but "equal"? How does one measure status and compare it? How does one compare the power and status of one group of women in a culture (say, middle-class American white women) with another (perhaps, wealthy black British women)?

If we ask why women are subordinate to men, what do we mean by "subordinate," and how do we indicate and include differences in subordination from culture to culture? How is subordination different from oppression, exploitation, discrimination, domination? What does the term *subordination* mean in the context of power? If it is true, as some have suggested, that though men hold formal power, women frequently hold great informal power over men, then who is subordinate to whom, and in what way?

As you can see, many terms and concepts are relevant, and each has its nuances and implications. One must be extraordinarily careful about how they are used.

Any good investigator will point out that effective problem-solving requires an accurate statement of the problem itself as well as careful definitions of the terms employed. Consider the following two sentences, each of which has actually been used as a statement of the problem: How did it come about that men usurped the autonomy and labor of women? Why are men superior to women both in power and accomplishments? Neither of these formulations define the problem adequately. They each contain assumptions and value judgments; they each express a particular perspective; and they each contain research expectations that have not been critically explored. In short, they are biased and circular: Each assumes an answer before it begins to search.

In tracking down reliable explanations, one must guard against hidden assumptions and values, charged language ("usurped," "equality," "superior"), and bias-prone terminology ("domestic," "aggressive," "technological"). This in itself is a monumental task. How does one ask a question that is free of prior assumptions and value-laden concepts, yet is still meaningful? For example: "Under what conditions did the present cultural sexual arrangements come to be?" What arrangements? What culture? What kind of origin—in time, in causative factors? Whereas the two formulations in the previous paragraph are too narrow and prejudicial, this one is too broad and omits the essence of the problem—which *is* valuational. Clearly, a balance of attention must exist between constructing formulations that are relatively objective and free of assumption yet sufficiently concrete in perspective to be substantive.[3]

Sexual Asymmetry

Searching for an expression that captures all of the issues that we have been raising, that is broad enough and relatively "objective," some feminists and social scientists have been using the term *sexual asymmetry*, which simply means a disproportion or dissimilarity based on sex. The term functions in a number of different contexts—scientific, political, religious, and so on—and also avoids many pitfalls. It is both meaningful and scientifically productive to ask, "What are the origins and causes of sexual asymmetry?" Yet in its scientific purity, the term *sexual asymmetry* tends to be vague, and without the support of related concepts for fleshing it out (charged though they may be), discussion adhering to its limits might tend to be thin.

For purposes of our discussion, let us say that sexual asymmetry refers to a whole range of situations where (1) policies regarding control over the wider community and the exercise of freedom to act or participate in affairs affecting all members of the group are determined solely or primarily on the grounds of sex, and (2) judgments of value or worth are made solely or primarily on the basis of sex. For example, in a culture where the legal right to vote for a leader of the entire group is limited to men *because they are men* (not bright men or strong men or educated men) and prohibited to women *because they are women* (not stupid women or poor women or malicious women), political sexual asymmetry exists. In a culture where men are deemed intrinsically more valuable than women, more worthy, better humans, more desirable *solely on the ground of maleness*, valuational sexual asymmetry exists.

Asymmetry takes many forms. In most cultures, as we have said, the work of men is more highly prized than that of women; women are considered to be the inferiors of men (in a variety of ways); and people tend to disparage both the work and the personhood of women. Such societies are termed misogynist, woman-hating. In our culture signs of misogyny range from the subtle to the blatant. Women are reputed to be stupid, petty, incompetent, or deceptive; they are underpaid and are excluded from many activities. Other cultures have featured infibulation,[4] the chastity belt, purdah, and suttee.

Although in some cultures women have considerable power within the family group or over other women, in every known society, men make the policy that affects the group as a whole—men make policy for women (and for some other men), but women do not formally make policy for the majority of men. In such a case, women are *subordinate* to men; that is, women inhabit a lower order of rank, power, and privilege. For example, men in our culture formally control all the institutions that determine the rules of our lives—the legislature, the judiciary, the police, the law, the economy. Women control the home, though *formally* only with the approval of the men they live with.

Oppression differs from subordination in that one person may be subordinate to another and yet not be oppressed, as when a child is subordinate to a benevolent parent or when a worker of lesser ability must yield to policy set by a more highly qualified person in a position of higher rank. To oppress means to bear down, to weigh upon, to burden.

One is oppressed when one experiences life as a burden, when one is emotionally or spiritually crushed or tyrannized. A culture that demeaned a woman's self-image, destroyed her pride, misused her person for ends not her own, or appropriated the fruits of her labor without proper recompense (that is, exploited her labor) would be an oppressive culture. Many cultures oppress and exploit their women as our culture oppresses and exploits at least some of us, if not all (as many feminists argue). Through *discrimination* (different, disadvantageous treatment before the law), outright slavery, or social customs that serve to solidify male privilege, women are oppressed and exploited in most cultures.

When we ask here, "What are the origins and causes of sexual asymmetry?" we are seeking an answer to the entire range of asymmetry from discrimination to misogyny.

Problems of Method

How do we go about finding reliable answers to the questions we have asked? We are, after all, pursuing a situation that in myth is without beginning and in social science traces back at least ten thousand years into prehistory, that traverses diverse cultures around the globe, and that may even have parallels in other species.

Scientifically, how do we deal with origins when the beginnings are lost? And where shall we count the beginnings? With recorded history? With early primitive peoples? With primates and hominoids? How helpful is information gleaned from current "primitive" groups when they diverge so much even among themselves?

Under what circumstances and to what degree is the practice of drawing analogies between humans and other animals to count? And if they count, which animals? Shall we select those that meet one set of expectations, like the aggressive, asymmetrical gibbons or shall we focus on the ever-faithful, one-time-mating gray-lag goose or perhaps the lion with its tough female hunter? Shall we confine ourselves to primates? And to what degree are any animal studies helpful when investigating a creature as uniquely malleable as the human being?

A great deal of important information is coming from new research into certain primate groups such as the chimpanzee, which are believed to be closely related to the kind of African ape that some four million years ago may have given rise to the hominids (the earliest members of the human family, such as *Australopithecus* and *Homo erectus*). Because fossil records (bones and teeth, for example, or organic tools) of this period are scarce, and because it is difficult to speculate reliably on behavior patterns of groups that are not observable, anthropologists use a combination of several kinds of evidence to generate hypotheses regarding the nature of early human social activities. For example, changes in the relative size of canine and molar teeth, within and across sexual categories, may tell us about diet (and therefore food-getting patterns) or about modes of defense or even about degrees of sociability. Such speculations, supported or enlarged by the observation of existent populations of highly developed primates, offer possibilities for piecing together a picture of the evolution of early human organization.

Some social scientists, however, approach the problem differently. They contend that because *Homo sapiens* is a far more advanced and complex creature in terms of intelligence than the earliest hominids, and because reflective thinking is unique to humans, *Homo sapiens* is qualitatively different from its ancestors. Its behavior patterns and social organization, therefore, require a different kind and level of explanation, perhaps psychological or even mythic.

Studying the art and artifacts of lost civilizations further along the evolutionary scale, some claim that advanced cultures existed before our own that were matriarchal and matrilineal. Argued primarily from inferential information, such theories are very controversial.

What counts as evidence? It is commonly understood that personal testimony (emic data) may be unreliable; issues of subjectivity, of perspective, of lack of insight, even of deceit arise. Yet even purely objective, researcher-based analysis (etic) may suffer from ethnocentrism or oversimplification, and even with physical evidence the problem of interpretation remains. How then are such speculations or hypotheses to be verified?

A Series of Hypotheses

So far, all we have for "answers" to our problem is conjecture. There are hypotheses, no firm theories. The hypotheses, except for certain themes that appear to be common to all, range across a variety of perspectives, levels of explanation, and conclusions, some of them quite contradictory.

Biological Approaches

When one argues that asymmetry occurs because women and men have different capacities and behaviors based on their *innate, inherited physical differences* (such as hormonal patterns, brain size, or bone structure), then one is arguing from the biological perspective or level. This approach has included arguments that females and males differ *constitutionally* in such varied factors as intelligence, temperament, IQ, capacity to lead, physical endurance, propensity to "bond" with members of the same sex, sexuality, aggressiveness, and even a sense of justice. Some have contended that these biologically based differences account for *and justify* the social arrangements that constitute current sexual asymmetry.

Such a point of view has the advantage of focusing on factors that are more easily observable, hence more amenable to study and to verification than some others. And, as some of the discussion in the preceding chapter pointed out, research does indicate that real physical behavior-related differences exist between females and males. What remains, however, is to determine what these differences do mean, and even more important what they should mean. If it should be found, for example, that males are constitutionally more aggressive and hence more likely to compete than females (there is some evidence to this effect) and thus more inclined to dominate or lead, one ought reasonably to ask whether this means that men *should* lead; or, since the world now suffers from an overabundance of aggressiveness, whether less aggressive persons (females?) should be socially encouraged to lead and males be discouraged from doing so.[5]

To say that women are "naturally" this and men are "naturally" that (leaving aside the question of the truth of such propositions) is an argument that those who wish to maintain the status quo have frequently used. Yet one must remember that the terms *natural* and *desirable* are different. It is natural for animals to kill and maim (usually for food or protection but sometimes for other reasons), but that does not make this behavior desirable. It is natural for humans to die painfully of disease, but that does not make this desirable. The human species has never rested content with what is "natural." That is our splendor as well as our infamy. We have survived because of adaptations that were not "natural." Cultures evolve because humans are malleable. We must not confuse the muddy scientific concept *natural* with the equally muddy ethical notion of *desirability*.

Sociological or Cultural Theories

The factor of malleability raises the familiar issue of the "nature/nurture" controversy. Which is more responsible for human behavior, nature (physiological, inborn components) or nurture (the effects of society—socialization, enculturation, learning)? Although nature, our physical selves and our genes, constitutes the raw material of our beings and thus imposes its own limits on our development, investigators generally agree that nurture contributes the lion's share to our development.

In a famous cross-cultural study of three existing societies, Margaret Mead described extremely divergent gender-based behavior.[6] The Arapesh society approved behavior for both men and women that our culture would term *feminine*—unaggressive, maternal, and cooperative rather than competitive. Mundugumor men and women were exactly opposite in behavior, all of them expected to be extremely aggressive, violent, and nonmaternal. The Tchambuli culture, a mirror image of our own, prized dominant, impersonal, and managing women and emotionally dependent, less effective men. Mead concluded that such data threw great doubt on the biological basis of gender behavior and strongly supported the thesis that sex-linked behavioral characteristics and activities are the result of social conditions.

The emphasis on enculturation as the main source of sex-role behavior continues today, yet both nonfeminists and feminists are moving toward reappraising biological and physiological factors. Sociological theories like Mead's generally argue that female-male behavioral differences are more a matter of social than of biological degree: The traits we take to be feminine or masculine are prescribed by the mores of our culture and are learned or internalized through formal education, religion, media, and all the other institutions that define experience. Unlike biological explanations, which account for

beginnings of asymmetry by saying simply, "It has always been that way, decreed by nature," sociological theories need additional elaboration to deal with origins. It is one thing to say that I as a woman have trait *x* because my society teaches it, and another to account for *why* my society teaches *x*. How and why did my society choose to teach *x*, and why does this society teach *x* while another teaches *y*?

There are those, feminist and otherwise, who say that it is not necessary to ask why or how gender norms originated. They argue that we need only evaluate them in the present context from the point of view of ethics (is it right, fair, or just to subordinate women?) or of social efficacy (does it benefit our society to maintain the present arrangement?). In common sense, this argument carries weight. One need not ask when or how the first war began in order to believe that war is undesirable and must be ended. A medical researcher need not ask who had the first cancer in order to search for its cause. But origins and causes are logically related. If we know how something comes to be, if we can determine *what factors precede and precipitate an event*, in effect we have found the cause, and only in understanding causes of events can we hope to control them.

The problem, however, becomes complicated. Just as some people confuse natural with desirable, others confuse origin with justification. For example, George Gilder, an early antifeminist, argued that asymmetry originates in the males' exclusion from childbearing and in their drive to achieve parity through other modes of creativity.[7] This, he argued, explains why men feel the need to exclude women from their activities, why they become unpleasant if women refuse the place men have made for them, and *why women should not refuse that place*. Whatever one thinks of Gilder's first contention—that men dominate women to achieve reproductive parity—we can plainly see that the thesis cannot stand as a justification, an ethical argument, for asymmetry. To say that *people commit murder because they are hostile, antisocial, and pressured* may explain why they do it—how their murderous impulses originate—but it does not support the thesis that *they should do it*; that is, the explanation does not serve as a justification. Clearly, it is helpful to explore the origins of sexual asymmetry, but one must carefully distinguish what the exploration accomplishes and what it leaves undone.

By and large, sociological-cultural theories of origin are either *evolutionary* or *psychomythic*. Evolutionary theories argue that individuals or entire cultures or both have developed certain traits or norms as adaptations, or survival mechanisms, in answer to the requirements of their environment.

Individual-Evolutionary Theories A famous example of the individual-evolutionary explanation is the "man-the-hunter" theory. Food, it begins, was the most important survival commodity in primitive society, and because scarce, meat was the most prized. As women in primitive circumstances were always with child or caring for them, it was not practical for them to go on the hunt, which often took one miles and days away from the shelter and safety of the home site and required activities hard to perform with an attached small child. For this reason, women stayed at home, raising children, foraging for vegetables and small game, and tending the hearth while men went hunting. Thus, each sex developed (evolved) physical and behavioral traits appropriate to their tasks. This, some evolutionists say, explains not only work segregation based on sex but also why men are prized above women (*they* brought the meat). It also reveals the origin of the different capabilities, traits, and personalities of females and males: Men are aggressive and bonding so they can hunt, whereas women are compliant and gentle because "the overall mood arising from such organic orientation, from so much waiting and letting grow and gentling and encouraging but never forcing, is a mood of compliance."[8]

For a time, this theory was in great vogue with many people, feminists and nonfeminists alike. But now the entire configuration is coming into question. One may ask whether the male became aggressive because he had to hunt or hunted because he was aggressive. (After all, other sources of protein existed, usually provided by the woman, than that sought after in the hunt—even meat.) Which came first, man the hunter or man the warrior, and are the two related? Did women really evolve "compliance" because that temperament is necessary to raising children, and who says that it is necessary? Mead's Mundugumors certainly do not believe so. Their women are aggressive, their children survive, and female aggressiveness does not lead to male unaggressiveness as some theories suggest. How does one account for male aggressiveness and rites of courage in cultures (for example, in Polynesia) where food (including protein) is plentiful and hunting unnecessary?

Evolutionary theories that focus on the development of individual (male/female) differences are certainly more sophisticated than biological theories, but they leave much to be desired. Still paying scant attention to the power of socialization, they fail to take into account the changes in individual behavior that would be wrought by changing environments. Men no longer go off to hunt (however widely one chooses to define the term), and brute strength, size, and aggressiveness are no longer adaptive traits for social survival, yet the value persists. Some other, wider factor may be needed to explain the cultural definitions and expectations of woman and man.

Cultural-Evolutionary Theories Variations of the preceding kind of explanation, cultural-evolutionary theories, take the society rather than the individual as the basic unit to be explored.[9] In this case, it is the entire culture, as well as the individual, that evolves adaptive mechanisms; sexual mores, role definitions, and gender expectations are part of them. For example, if a society were located in an environment where conditions were particularly hard, with a high death rate, such a society would probably require a high birth rate to maintain an adequate population, and it might well develop values that encouraged women to conceive and bear many children, to view themselves primarily in their childbearing capacity, and so on. The cultural-evolutionary approach, then, seeks to understand sexual mores, attitudes, and behaviors in terms of the environmental conditions that give rise to them.

Psycho-Mythic Theories None of the theories thus far developed fully accounts for the whole range of sexual asymmetry. Too many puzzling questions are left unanswered. The kinds of explanations we have considered do not adequately explain the reasons for sex segregation, political subordination, or the divisions of labor based on sex. They do not even begin to explain the other, more virulent aspect of asymmetry—misogyny.

It is one thing to categorize people on the basis of a certain trait—old people do this, young people do that; large people do this, small people do that. But what gives sexism its essential characteristic is the element of valuation. Not only are tasks separated by sex, but men's tasks are also judged more valuable, women's less valuable. Not only is the male's role to lead and the female's to follow, but leading is valued and following is disparaged. Not only are men and women to exhibit complementary character traits, but male traits are praised, and female traits are held in contempt. Nor is it only that men tend to do or be better things and hence are more deserving of praise. Rather, it is the reverse, the things that are praised are simply the things that men do; they are praised *because men do them*. For the most part, a task socially assigned to women is debased. Cross-cultural studies bear this out.

We hear much of the fact, for example, that 75 percent of all physicians in the USSR are women. However, it is rarely pointed out that in the Soviet Union the practice of medicine, except for some highly specialized fields, is considered merely a technical job and is not highly paid; for the most part, the higher paid specialists and surgeons are men. Secretarial work had high status and was highly paid until it became a female occupation; so was teaching. Nursing, always female, has always suffered in power, prestige, and pay. The men who are now moving into the nursing field are being rewarded with preference in the highest paid, most select positions. Men are "encouraged" to enter nursing to "raise the level of the profession." Women are "permitted" to enter medicine or law because it is not just or legal to bar them; nothing is said about raising the level of the profession. More and more it becomes apparent that not only do women do the "shitwork" of society, but it is equally the other way around: Tasks are deemed unworthy if women do them.

We can make the same analysis of human behaviors. For example, when men ask their wives more than once to do something, they are "reminding." Women who ask repeatedly are "nagging." When men are firm and resolute, they have backbone; women who act the same are stubborn or bitchy. When a man raises his voice in argument he is angry, but a woman is hysterical. Menstruation in most societies is surrounded with taboos, disgust, and often horror. In today's modern society where people can utter any obscenity, freely discuss publicly any body function from nose blowing to orgasm, open admission of having one's period is still an occasion for shock and embarrassment. Would

that be the case if menstruation were a male function? Erections are a source of pride to their owners. Much fuss is made over the length and breadth of a penis. What is analogous for women? In patriarchy, it is as though the female carries with her an evil effusion and contaminates all that she touches.

Theories that explain only the *fact* of separation or categorization (men do this, women do that) and omit the *judgment* of devaluation (men and what they do are good; women and what they do are contemptible) or theories that disclaim the existence or importance of devaluation are missing the central point. The misogyny in sexual asymmetry is what renders it sexist and makes it oppressive. It is true that analyses of asymmetry are highly charged with value. One could argue that one's misogyny is another man's reality—it is not misogyny to say that women are inferior; it is true! Many of us, however, know better, and the fact of misogyny, almost universal though varying in degree, must be explained.

The psycho-mythic explanations function on a level where this issue can be treated. A myth is a story that serves to explain and/or to express some important reality of life or nature. The creation story in the Bible, for example, represented the ancient Hebrew explanation of the origin of the world, of life, and of human suffering. Sometimes the stories are avowedly fictitious; others are regarded as true.

Several theories try to explain myths—that they represent certain human verities, common to all people (such as the confrontation with one's own mortality); that they are modes of expressing experiences or feelings inexpressible in ordinary language; or that they symbolize beliefs and needs in a person that are too deep, too intense, or too socially bizarre to express directly. Their relation to psychological explanation, then, is clear.

A myth is generally taken to be an accurate representation of common, perhaps universal, human beliefs and attitudes. For this reason, myths are important for the analysis of sexual asymmetry. We study them to reveal their hidden message about attitudes toward women, and feminists often explain certain arrangements regarding women as the social acting out of basic psycho-mythic beliefs or psychological needs. The Adam and Eve story, for example, is a powerfully revealing myth that has parallels in many cultures. Many societies, primitive and otherwise, have stories that credit the first human life and the power of birth to a male and then relegate the life-giving function to women, often as a discredited and burdensome task. Does this story reveal a universal male envy of female procreative powers? Does it perhaps hark back to a primitive matriarchy, if not a historical one then a symbolic one (as in the paradigmatic Mother)? And does this tale not neatly justify the subordination and oppression of women? Have not numerous churchmen contended that women's suppression justly results from the primordial betrayal in the Garden of Eden? Does this story not express a statement of women's evil, untrustworthiness, guile, naivete, seduceability, and unworthiness before God? Does it not justify hatred and contempt?

Although the story expresses misogyny and presents a "justification" for the believer, we are still left with a question: Why is it necessary to create stories to justify the subordination and hatred of women? That is, why do men control and condemn women? The psycho-mythic theories attempt to approach this central issue through various themes, such as a yearning for maternal safety (Elizabeth Janeway), the model of family aggression—man upon woman (Shulamith Firestone), or even penis envy (Sigmund Freud). Each theory seeks some universal theme, some common human reality to explain this universal behavior—misogynous sexual asymmetry.

The major strength of psycho-mythic theories is that they seek wide-ranging explanations, sufficiently inclusive to cover all the variations of sexism. Also, they treat a psychological event—attitudes and beliefs—on a psychological level. The problem with psycho-mythic theories, however, is that they are almost impossible to verify—my myth against yours, my analysis against yours—and if used exclusively, they omit references to the very essential sociocultural elements.

Conclusion

If we have no definitive theories of explanation, what can we do? Search the following explanations carefully. Ponder the points they have in common, such as the centrality of childbearing or of hunting, and consider whether these themes are viable and/or sufficient. Notice the gaps in all the theories; use these as further points of departure.

Ultimately, we can probably develop reliable explanations from a combination of levels and perspectives. Such explanations will undoubtedly require a great deal more in the way of research and data than is now available.

Notes

[1] In the social sciences today, particularly anthropology, energetic dialogue surrounds the issue of the universality or near universality of female subordination. Well known in this debate is the work of Alice Schlegel (see Alice Schlegel, ed., *Sexual Stratification: A Cross-Cultural View* [New York: Columbia University Press, 1977]) and of Michelle Rosaldo and Nancy Chodorow in the anthology *Women, Culture, and Society,* ed. Michelle Rosaldo and Louis Lamphere (Stanford: Stanford University Press, 1974).

[2] For an interesting discussion of the relation of politics to scientific inquiry, see Donna Haraway, "Animal Sociology and a Natural Economy of the Body Politic, Part I: A Political Physiology of Dominance," *Signs* 4, No. 1 (Autumn 1978): 21–36.

[3] For two very different but very good approaches to the matter of definitions, see Cheris Kramarae and Paula A. Treichler, *A Feminist Dictionary* (Boston: Pandora Press, 1985); and Gerda Lerner, "Definitions" in *Creation of Patriarchy,* Appendix (New York: Oxford University Press: 1986), pp. 231–243.

[4] *Infibulation:* the practice of excising the clitoris and labia of the vagina and sewing together the vulva to insure chastity; *purdah:* the practice in Islam of totally sequestering women; *suttee:* the practice in India, surviving now only in rural areas, of widows immolating themselves on the burning funeral pyres of their husbands.

[5] Steven Goldberg, in *The Inevitability of Patriarchy* (New York: Morrow, 1974), argued precisely that: Males *are* constitutionally more aggressive, more likely to compete energetically and hence win. Socialization patterns merely recognize and support this reality. Patriarchy, therefore, is the inevitable arrangement because it is the most orderly, stable, and reflective of nature.

[6] Margaret Mead, *Sex and Temperament in Three Primitive Societies* (New York: Morrow, 1935).

[7] George Gilder, *Sexual Suicide* (New York: Quadrangle, 1973).

[8] Wolfgang Lederer, *The Fear of Women* (New York: Grune & Stratton, 1968), p. 87.

[9] For an excellent review of these kinds of theories (and others) see Virginia Sapiro, *Women in American Society* (Mountain View, CA: Mayfield Publishing Co.: 1986), chap. 2.

Anthropological Perspectives on the Subordination of Women

Charlotte J. Frisbie

Charlotte J. Frisbie was born in Hazleton, Pennsylvania, in 1940. She studied music and ethnomusicology at Smith and Wesleyan and took a doctorate in anthropology at the University of New Mexico. She now teaches at Southern Illinois University, Edwardsville. Specializing in cultural anthropology, ethnographic field techniques, and Native Americans, Frisbie has recently done a great deal of research on women in cross-cultural perspective. In the following selection, she explains and summarizes the major issues and research in current anthropological studies of women.

Written for *Issues in Feminism*, first edition and updated in 1989 for second edition.

Introduction

At the present time, the discipline of anthropology offers no single approach to discussions of the subordination of women. This is not because of a lack of interest in the topic, but because of the many problems related to evaluating the issue on the basis of available cross-cultural data. At present, although many anthropologists agree that women live in a man's world in many geographic areas, not all are convinced that this is a human universal, something shared by all people everywhere. Likewise, there is no agreement on any one particular explanation or interpretation of the phenomenon, where it is found; instead, there are several different approaches that are attracting further research energies and generating much discussion.

Before outlining some of the possible approaches to discussions of the subordination of women, it seems useful to review some of the inherent, relevant problems. Anthropological evaluations of women's statuses, roles, and actual lives in cross-cultural perspective depend not only on contemporary data gathered by doing fieldwork among the peoples in question, but also on ethnographies or descriptive reports of past work as well. It is often true that the latter sources lead researchers into a major problem, that of bias. Anthropology, like other disciplines, has benefited in numerous ways from the feminist movement; among them have been the development of an increased awareness of sexism within the discipline, and associated actions designed to reduce and hopefully, eliminate the problem. In cultural anthropology, that part of the discipline that deals with the lifeways of contemporary people, recent reviews of many available descriptive sources have resulted in one major conclusion—you are lucky if you can learn anything about women at all from reading these works! This is true for several reasons:

1. Since the beginning of the discipline, most fieldworkers and ethnographers have been male.

2. These people have done their fieldwork by talking to males, the public, visible people in cultures.

3. The perceptions of male informants have been accepted as representative of the entire culture, including the female part of the population.

4. Female anthropologists, for the most part, have been trained by males, and taught to carry on the above traditions.

Thus, with very few exceptions (for example, Mead 1928, 1935, 1949; Landes 1938; Kaberry 1939), earlier anthropological reports provide us with unidimensional descriptions of an androcentric nature. Women are either not mentioned at all, or treated as meaningless shadows and relegated to brief mention in footnotes or single text statements.

Lately, these characteristics have been among those identified as sexist, and energies have been expended to begin attacking such problems. This work, from the research perspective, involves fieldwork with women as well as men, critical analyses of the differences between the perceptions of women and men (be they informants or anthropologists) and heightened awareness of the pervasiveness of sexism within the discipline. Such efforts, by themselves, have led to a re-examination of the idea that women are subordinate to men throughout the world. Now, we wonder if this is really true, or if it is possible that this very picture reflects our own sexist, ethnocentric bias and the way in which much of our past work was done.

Although we are far from answering this question and others, a number of developments have already occurred. For example, students now are being trained to ask who did the fieldwork, with what part of the population, and from what perspective. Most recently, the interpretation of field data and the whole process of writing up the data or constructing ethnographic texts have also become topics of critical examination and discussion, as part of the broader

disciplinary interest in reflexivity (see Clifford and Marcus 1986). The last two decades have yielded a number of worthwhile ethnographies that concern women in cultural contexts (for example, Babb and Taylor 1981, Bell 1983, Blackman 1982, Chiñas 1973, Dwyer 1978, Fernea 1965, Goodale 1971, Kelley 1978, Kikumura 1981, Lin 1988, Makhlouf 1979, Mernissi 1975, Murphy and Murphy 1974, Powers 1986, Pruitt 1979, Shostak 1983, Spiro 1979, Stewart 1980, Strathern 1972, and Wolf 1976). A number of collections have appeared, such as those edited by Pescatello (1973), Matthiasson (1974), Rosaldo and Lamphere (1974), Rohrlich-Leavitt (1975), Reiter (1975), Fernea and Besirgan (1977), Schlegel (1977), MacCormack and Strathern (1980), Dahlberg (1981), and Albers and Medicine (1983). Texts have also become available (for example, Martin and Voorhies 1975, Friedl 1975, Kessler 1976, Hammond and Jablow 1976, O'Kelly 1980). Specific papers that deal with various theoretical aspects of sexist bias in anthropology are also available (for example, Ardener 1972; Schlegel 1974; Slocum 1975; Rohrlich-Leavitt, Sykes, and Weatherford 1975; Sacks 1976; Rosaldo 1980; Strathern 1987; Mukhopadhyay and Higgins 1988; and Silverblatt 1988).

Sexism is characteristic of physical as well as cultural anthropology. In this portion of the discipline, where the focus is on physical and cultural evolution and the relationship between humans and their nonhuman primate relatives, many questions are now being asked. To name just one, "Why have women been so consistently ignored in the story of human evolution, which has been taught for so long as the evolution of MAN, and what can be done about it?" This will receive further discussion below.

The Subordination of Women

Since not all anthropologists accept the subordination of women to men throughout evolutionary time and geographic space as a human universal, the question can be discussed from several different perspectives. This is possible, in part, anyway, because of available cross-cultural information about women's work. For a variety of reasons, this area of women's lives has received rather consistent research attention through time. Thus, we have a relatively good idea of the numerous ways in which women's work and men's work can be defined by humans around the world. An analysis of these data, or of the question of division of labor by sex (as it is properly termed) leads to the recognition of several universals. All humans use sex as one of the defining principles of labor; in other words, people everywhere have ideas about what constitutes women's work and men's work. While the particulars often vary—so that in one culture women weave, and in another men do, or in one, women build the shelters, and in another this is men's work—there are certain ideas that all humans share. Among these are the association of women with childbearing, childrearing and the related private or domestic sphere, and the association of men with warfare, control over significant resources, preferential access to authority and the related public, visible, political sphere. Furthermore, from what we now know, it appears that everywhere men's activities are the ones that are most highly valued, the ones that carry the greatest prestige. Given these universals, what can be said about the relative status of the sexes cross-culturally?

As might be expected, there are those who argue that women have been subordinate to males since time immemorial, and those who reject both the time immemorial and the universal implications of this statement. Let us turn now to each of these groups and examine the extreme positions before dealing with some alternative approaches.

Biological Determinists

Within anthropology there is a group which argues essentially that biology is destiny, and that because females are biologically designed to conceive, give birth and to support offspring through lactation, they are "naturally" designed for life in the restricted domestic or private sphere, rather than in the more widely ranging, public, political one. The arguments of this group, currently, are presented in two slightly different ways.

A group of people, including Ardrey (1966), Lorenz (1966), Morris (1968), Tiger (1969, 1970), and Tiger and Fox (1971), prefer to explain sex roles from a biological perspective. Essentially, this stance stresses nature rather than nurture, biology rather than culture, and innate rather than learned approaches to the question. The position focuses on the universals in human culture, rather than particular differences among groups. The argument states that culture, rather than being totally learned, is in part biologically based, and that this base explains the presence of human universals.

For biological determinists, sex roles and behavior are best explained by references to innate biological and psychological differences between the sexes. In brief, the view (which refers to savannah dwelling Hamadryas baboon information for supporting parallels) characteristically emphasizes the importance of size differences (sexual dimorphism); Man the Aggressor, Man the Hunter, Man the Dominant are important correlates. Males are viewed as physically larger, stronger, and hormonally more aggressive. Biologically, they are required to spend far less time than females in reproduction-related activities. In evolutionary terms, as our ancestors came down from the trees, they became vulnerable. According to biological determinists, males at this point learned to coordinate their behaviors for defense, and with time and increased male-male cooperation, the tendency for them to bond became genetic.

Females are characterized by more fatty tissues on the breasts and buttocks, pelvic areas constructed for childbirth and a wide variety of hormonal levels. Because of their biological adaptation for reproduction and their "natural" preoccupation with helpless infants, they are inhibited by inferior mobility, threat of miscarriage and hormonal changes that affect coordination and perception. Additionally, they lack genetic codes for bonding (except those related to male-female bonding for reproduction), and thus are not biologically suited for cooperative economic and political endeavors. Given this, females are most aptly described as "naturally" docile, nurturant followers who are "normally pregnant or nursing their infants."

Obviously, the biological determinist stance credits males with the development of human culture; with enough evolutionary time and the correlated increases in brain size and complexity, Man the Hunter and Tool Maker became Man the Thinker, the Language User, the Inventor, the City Dweller, and the Moon Rocket Builder. Females, biologically burdened by their reproductive capacities and helpless offspring, stayed in camp, dependent on Man the Hunter, Man the Dominant for their sustenance and survival. According to biological determinists, sex roles and behaviors were ever thus; they represent the product of millions of years of successful human adaptation. To tamper with them, or suggest that things should be different is, according to some, equivalent to heresy.

In the past few years, a newer, slightly more sophisticated version of biological determinism has been advanced, under the rubric of sociobiology (Trivers 1971; Alexander 1974; West Eberhard 1975; Wilson 1975, 1978; Barash 1977; Sahlins 1977; and Lewontin, Rose, and Kamin 1984). Defined as the study of the biological basis for social behavior, sociobiology implies the existence of a common thread that links together all social behaviors of all life forms, and calls for a new synthesis of disciplines involved in the study of behavior (be it that of termites, red-winged blackbirds, marmots, or humans). Unlike earlier biological determinists who see human behavior as an expression of innate, biologically based needs and drives, sociobiologists strive to relate social behavior to well-established evolutionary principles. Of these, the one receiving major emphasis at present is self-maximization of individual genotypes. In simple terms, this means that genes "call the shots," and that the lives of all living forms are organized around the tendency for genetic material to maximize itself over time through reproductive success, or enhanced genetic contributions to the next generation.

Although the above may appear quite unrelated to discussions of the subordination of women, it isn't. Sociobiologists argue that there are genes for particular social behaviors, and that these have spread by natural selection through evolutionary time. Among the behaviors frequently discussed as genetically based are the human capacities for aggression, cooperation, altruism, kin selection, and mating. Repeating the emphasis on the biological advantages of the initial human division of labor into Man the Hunter-Protector-Provider, and Woman the Reproducer-Child Rearer, Wilson and many others suggest that like aggression, the division of labor by sex is genetically based.

Obviously the sociobiological stance, which argues that genes prescribe the rules of life and determine much human behavior, can be used as a way of rationalizing the correctness, naturalness, and legitimacy of all kinds of social patterns and institutions, including male dominance over women. All you have to do is "prove" that men are genetically predisposed to be dominant, ritual-political leaders, and economic managers whereas women are genetically pre-

disposed to cook, wash clothes and dishes, and care for children and homes. How far sociobiology will be pushed, at present, remains to be seen.

Environmentalists

In direct opposition to biological determinists are other contemporary anthropologists who align themselves with the nurture, culture, and learned side of the issue and argue that biology is not destiny (see, for example, Brown 1970, Chiñas 1973, Friedl 1975, Martin and Voorhies 1975, Reiter 1975, Slocum 1975, O'Kelly 1980, and Tanner 1981).

In contrast to the group discussed earlier, this one, following Boasian tradition, stresses the uniqueness of culture, and focuses on human plasticity, variability, and differences rather than universals. Sex roles are viewed as functions of social and cultural conditioning rather than biological heredity.

Environmentalists, like their opponents, use ethnographic data and primatology studies to support their claims; in the former, the emphasis is on differences—examples of cultures where women have political roles, have control of significant resources, serve as warriors. In the latter, the preferred nonhuman primate is the chimpanzee, our closest living relative.

Much of the work already generated by environmentalists provides serious challenges to earlier anthropological models and theories that perpetuate sexism. For example, data now available from studies of foraging peoples (or those who depend on gathering, hunting, and fishing for survival), make it clear that among most foragers, women provide the majority, and sometimes up to 80 percent, of the daily diet for the group. This they do through gathering wild vegetables, fruits, eggs, insects, and the like, and hunting small animals. The results of Man the Hunter's hunting are more valued, yes, but unpredictable. Given these data, environmentalists suggest that new models of cultural evolution that take into account the contributions of *both* women and men are long overdue. Lancaster (1975) and Tanner and Zihlman (1976) are among those attempting to correct the picture, while Leibowitz (1975) has called for a re-evaluation of the significance of sexual dimorphism (size difference) in evolutionary history. A text, designed specifically to present a balanced view, is now available, thanks to Tanner (1981), and works by Dahlberg (1981) and Fedigan (1986) continue the discussion of women's roles in various models or reconstructions of human physical and cultural evolution.

Environmentalists are not arguing that their position is new, nor would they think of so doing since the study of human and behavioral flexibility and plasticity is what has characterized anthropology as a discipline since its inception. Witness the works of Margaret Mead (1935, 1949) for example, wherein clear cases were made for the importance of culture as the decisive factor in definitions of sex roles and personality types appropriate for both males and females. What environmentalists *are* saying is that the importance of social, environmental, and cultural factors needs to be restated at the present time, especially in view of the new, biogenetic revival of the "anatomy is destiny" argument. From their perspective, male bias or androcentrism in anthropology is surmountable, as is male dominance, which is neither inevitable, natural, nor permanent in culture.

Other Approaches

Obviously, the biological and environmentalist positions described above represent two opposite approaches to a question that has been argued before and will continue to receive attention in the future. There is no easy answer to the question of how much of culture is genetically based, especially now that research on language acquisition supports the idea. It will only be possible to sort out all the related matters when we increase our now-limited comprehension of the science of heredity, the human brain, and other such phenomena. In the meantime, perhaps it is feasible to question both groups if only because of their exclusive, either-or approaches.

Although these two groups represent much of the anthropological work related to discussion of the subordination of women, there are some other approaches and developments that deserve at least brief mention.

New Structuralism

In recent years, a French anthropologist, Claude Lévi-Strauss (1963, 1969), has greatly affected much anthropological thinking. Basically interested in cognitive processes and committed to unraveling human universals, Lévi-Strauss has striven to reveal the mental structures that underlie human behavior. Using a variety of ethnographic data, he has suggested that these usually take the form of binary sets or oppositions. Included in these dichotomies are day-night, raw-cooked, life-death, young-old, sacred-profane, earth-sky, right-left, nature-culture, male-female, and the like. Humans, in time and space, share these mental structures, which exist at what can be termed the deep, structural level, rather than a surface one.

Several aspects of Lévi-Strauss's work are applicable to discussions of the subordination of women; among these are the equation of females and nature in opposition to males and culture, and his ideas on kinship. Viewing kinship as a primary force in all human lives and one that is central to cultural systems, Lévi-Strauss stresses its controlling aspects. As it turns out, though both sexes are controlled, women bear the brunt of it all, just because they are the reproducers. Lévi-Strauss views marriage as the most basic form of gift exchange, and within it, women become gifts to be given and exchanged by men. Thus, from his perspective, the oppression of women stems from the social system, rather than from biological factors.

Levi-Strauss's works are challenging, thought-provoking and difficult. To date, Ortner (1974) and Rubin (1975), among others, have done creditable jobs in evaluating their implications for those interested in a cross-cultural view of women. It should be noted, however, that not all anthropologists are willing to accept the universality of binary mental structures, and some, such as Sacks (1976), find Lévi-Strauss's explanation of the oppression of women downright untenable, ethnographically.

Revival of Matriarchy Theories

One of the initial results of feminism in anthropology was a reawakening of interest in matriarchies. As originally proposed by nineteenth-century classical evolutionists, all humans progressed culturally through a series of stages, which began with promiscuity and ended with civilization. Confusing descent and political rule, and mistakenly equating the viable principle of matriliny (where descent is traced through females) with power and rule by women, some early anthropologists such as Bachofen (1861) suggested that there was a time when women were, in fact, in control. By the early twentieth century, however, the grandiose schemes of the nineteenth-century classical evolutionists had been rejected by most serious anthropologists, and that of matriarchies was among them. Recent re-examinations of the theories (Bamberger 1974, Webster 1975) have not suggested that reviving them has any anthropological value, although some writers such as Davis (1972), Morgan (1972), and Reed (1975) have chosen to do so.

Marxism

Related to the interest in reviving the ideas of Bachofen and other classical evolutionists is that of re-examining the philosophies of Marx and Engels. These, especially as professionally interpreted by Leacock (1972), Sacks (1974), Rubin (1975), and Gough (1977), offer a picture of early human society that was based on sexual egalitarianism. Women and men were both engaged in equally significant work and communal ownership was the rule; women were neither oppressed nor exploited. However, with the domestication of animals and ensuing ideas of private ownership of property and production of surpluses, class societies emerged. With them, the nature and importance of the household changed, the nuclear family became economically isolated and women became subordinate and subservient to dominant men and dependent on them. This situation is typical of much of today's world because Europeans, through contact and colonialism, have spread not only capitalistic philosophies and political domination, but also all of their cultural attitudes and beliefs about the proper asymmetrical relationship between the sexes.

Other Alternatives

In addition to the approaches mentioned above, there are several other developments within contemporary anthropology that deserve brief mention because they are related to discussions of subordination of women. Perhaps it is most useful to view these as shifts in research methods which make it more possible to evaluate women's roles and statuses within specific cultures.

The first of these is known as *emic research*. Put simply, this approach stresses the native person's perspective, categories, and analysis of his or her own world. It asks and values the responses to questions such as how do women in *x* culture see themselves as individuals as well as in relation to their men, and how do the men see the women? Do they devalue themselves or each other? Do the women see themselves living in a man's world, oppressed and dominated by their men? Do the men see women as subordinate entities? This kind of research design contrasts with one that has been long established in anthropology, one that since the middle 1950s has been termed the *etic approach*. Here, the emphasized perspective is the external one, that of the outsider scientist, which is based on observation, comparative analysis, and evaluation. Although there is undoubtedly room and need for both perspectives, we have yet to balance our allegiances. Perhaps more ethnographic information, such as that provided by Briggs (1974) for Eskimo women, Fernea and Besirgan (1977) for Middle Eastern Muslim women, Bell (1983) for Aboriginal women in Central Australia, Shostak (1983) for !Kung San women in the Kalahari desert, and Powers (1986) for Oglala (Lakota) women of the Pine Ridge Reservation in South Dakota, will encourage just that.

Another research technique that was especially useful when the discipline was initially identifying and attacking sexism is the distinction between the private-domestic-informal and the public-political-formal spheres or domains of life. In retrospect, this emphasis seems necessary, if only to awaken fieldworkers of both sexes to the fact that there are other things happening in culture besides what is visible and public, and by extension, male. Since women are found in the private sphere so often, a recognition of the importance of this opened up access to the other half of the population and encouraged the realization that male-female relations anywhere cannot be analyzed solely through male eyes and minds.

Studies and collections that have utilized this distinction (for example, Friedl 1967, Chiñas 1973, Matthiasson 1974, Rosaldo 1974, and O'Kelly 1980) have suggested that in some places in the world, women's and men's roles are "complementary but equal." The spheres and activities are different but they are seen as mutually interdependent, supportive, necessary, and of equal value by the people who experience them. With such data in hand, the idea that the subordination of women is a universal can be challenged as representing another figment of our imagination, another example of how our own values, attitudes, perceptions, and ethnocentrism have biased our analyses.

Summary

At the present time, no one approach characterizes anthropological perspectives on the subordination of women. This is true both in terms of the pervasiveness of subordination in time and space and the explanations for it where it can be documented. Although emphases on emic research and the private sphere have utility, some anthropologists are already challenging the notion that the private-public dichotomy is universal, suggesting that it is related specifically to class societies and not applicable to foragers.

At present, as Lamphere (1977) indicates, much of the anthropological work on the subordination of women focuses on an evaluation of women's roles among foragers, the one subsistence system wherein equality, as we envision and define it, seems possible (see, for example, Dahlberg 1981). Some, relying heavily on emic data, argue that foraging males and females have "complementary but equal" relationships, whereas others (for example, Friedl 1975, Hammond and Jablow 1976, Lamphere 1977) challenge such interpretations, stating they ignore observable, etic realities.

Anthropologists recognize the serious need for continual research, thought, and discussion of the issues. Hopefully, in the near future, it will be possible to define such concepts as dominance, power, authority, equality, and subordinance so they are useful cross-culturally. Hopefully, it will be soon possible to build models that incorporate both emic and etic information without damaging either, and that take into account variables we already know are important, such as who controls resources and their allocation. At the moment, the questions are emerging faster than the answers, thereby stimulating the energies of current researchers. Undoubtedly, the issues will continue to challenge generations of forthcoming scholars.

References

Albers, Patricia, and Beatrice Medicine
    1983 *The Hidden Half. Studies of Plains Indian Women*. Lanham, MD: University Press of America, Inc.

Alexander, R. D.
    1974 "The Evolution of Social Behavior." *Annual Review of Ecology and Systematics* 5: 325–383.

Ardener, E.
    1972 "Belief and the Problem of Women." In *The Interpretation of Rituals*. J. S. La Fontaine, ed. London: Tavistock Publications.

Ardrey, Robert
    1966 *The Territorial Imperative*. New York: Atheneum.

Babb, Jewel, and Pat Ellis Taylor
    1981 *Border Healing Woman. The Story of Jewel Babb as told to Pat Ellis Taylor*. Austin: University of Texas Press.

Bachofen, J. J.
    1861 *Das Mutterecht*. Basle: Benno Schwabe and Company.

Bamberger, Joan
    1974 "The Myth of Matriarchy: Why Men Rule in Primitive Society." In *Women, Culture, and Society*. Michelle Rosaldo and Louise Lamphere, eds. Pp. 263–280. Stanford: Stanford University Press.

Barash, David
    1977 *Sociobiology and Behavior*. New York: Elsevier North-Holland, Inc.

Bell, Diane
    1983 *Daughters of the Dreaming*. Melbourne, Australia: McPhee Gribble Publishers in association with George Allen & Unwin Australia Pty Ltd, North Sydney.

Blackman, Margaret B.
    1982 *During My Time. Florence Edenshaw Davidson, A Haida Woman*. Seattle: University of Washington Press.

Briggs, Jean
    1974 "Eskimo Women: Makers of Men." In *Many Sisters*. Carolyn J. Matthiasson, ed. Pp. 261–304. New York: Free Press.

Brown, Judith
    1970 "A Note on the Division of Labor by Sex." *American Anthropologist* 72: 1073–1078.

Chiñas, Beverly
    1973 *The Isthmus Zapotecs: Women's Roles in Cultural Context*. New York: Holt, Rinehart and Winston.

Clifford, James, and George E. Marcus, eds.
    1986 *Writing Culture. The Poetics and Politics of Ethnography*. Berkeley: University of California Press.

Dahlberg, Frances, ed.
    1981 *Woman the Gatherer*. New Haven: Yale University Press.

Davis, Elizabeth
    1971 *The First Sex*. New York: G. P. Putnam.

Dwyer, Daisy Hilse
    1978 *Images and Self-Images. Male and Female in Morocco*. New York: Columbia University Press.

Fedigan, Linda Marie
1986 "The Changing Role of Women in Models of Human Evolution." *Annual Review of Anthropology* 15:25–66.

Fernea, E. W.
1965 *Guests of the Sheik*. Garden City, N.Y.: Doubleday/Anchor.

Fernea, Elizabeth Warnock, and Basima Qattan Besirgan, eds.
1977 *Middle Eastern Muslim Women Speak*. Austin: University of Texas Press.

Friedl, Ernestine
1967 "The Position of Women: Appearance and Reality." *Anthropological Quarterly 40*, 3: 97–108.

———
1975 *Women and Men: An Anthropologist's View*. New York: Holt, Rinehart and Winston.

Goodale, Jane C.
1971 *Tiwi Wives: A Study of the Women of Melville Island, North Australia*. Seattle: University of Washington Press, American Ethnological Society, Monograph 51.

Gough, Kathleen
1977 "An Anthropologist Looks at Engels." In *Women in a Man-Made World*. 2nd ed. Nona Glazer-Melbin and Helen Youngelson Waehrer, eds. Pp. 156–168. Chicago: Rand McNally. Orig. published 1972.

Hammond, Dorothy, and Alta Jablow
1976 *Women in Cultures of the World*. Menlo Park, Calif.: Cummings Publishing Company.

Kaberry, Phyllis
1939 *Aboriginal Woman: Sacred and Profane*. London: Routledge and Kegan Paul, Ltd.

Kelley, Jane Holden
1978 *Yaqui Women. Contemporary Life Histories*. Lincoln: University of Nebraska Press.

Kessler, Evelyn
1976 *Women: An Anthropological View*. New York: Holt, Rinehart and Winston.

Kikumura, Akemi
1981 *Through Harsh Winters. The Life of a Japanese Immigrant Woman*. Novato, CA: Chandler & Sharp Publishers, Inc.

Lamphere, Louise
1977 "Review Essay: Anthropology." *SIGNS: Journal of Women Culture and Society 2*, 3: 612–627.

Lancaster, Jane
1975 *Primate Behavior and the Emergence of Human Culture*. New York: Holt, Rinehart and Winston.

Landes, Ruth
1938 *The Ojibwa Woman*. New York: Columbia University Press.

Leacock, Eleanor
1972 "Introduction to Frederick Engels." In *The Origin of the Family, Private Property and the State*. E. B. Leacock, ed. New York: International Publishers.

Leibowitz, Lila
1975 "Perspectives on the Evolution of Sex Differences." In *Toward an Anthropology of Women*. Rayna Reiter, ed. Pp. 20–35. New York: Monthly Review Press.

Lévi-Strauss, Claude
1969 *The Elementary Structures of Kinship*. Boston: Beacon Press. Orig. French edition, 1949.

———
1963 *Structural Anthropology*. New York: Basic Books, Inc.

Lewontin, R., S. Rose, and L. Kamin
1984 *Not in Our Genes: Biology, Ideology and Human Nature*. New York: Pantheon.

Lin, Alice
1988 *Grandmother Had No Name*. San Francisco: China Books.

Lorenz, Konrad
1966 *On Aggression*. New York: Harcourt, Brace and World.

MacCormack, Carol P., and Marilyn Strathern, eds.
1980 *Nature, Culture and Gender*. Cambridge: Cambridge University Press.

Makhlouf, Carla
1979 *Changing Veils. Women and Modernisation in North Yemen*. Austin: University of Texas Press.

Martin, M. Kay, and Barbara Voorhies
1975 *Female of the Species*. New York: Columbia University Press.

Matthiasson, Carolyn J., ed.
1974 *Many Sisters: Women in Cross-Cultural Perspective*. New York: Free Press.

Mead, Margaret
1928 *Coming of Age in Samoa*. New York: Mentor Book Edition (1949).

———
1935 *Sex and Temperament in Three Primitive Societies*. New York: Dell Publishing Company.

———
1949 *Male and Female: A Study of the Sexes in a Changing World*. New York: Dell Publishing Company.

Mernissi, Fatima
1975 *Beyond the Veil. Male-Female Dynamics in a Modern Muslim Society*. Cambridge, MA: Schenkman Publishing Company, Inc.

Morgan, Elaine
1972 *Descent of Woman*. New York: Stein and Day.

Morris, Desmond
 1968 *The Naked Ape*. New York: McGraw-Hill.

Mukhopadhyay, Carol C., and Patricia J. Higgins
 1988 "Anthropological Studies of Women's Status Revisited: 1977–1987. *Annual Review of Anthropology* 17: 461–495.

Murphy, Yolanda, and Robert Murphy
 1974 *Women of the Forest*. New York: Columbia University Press.

O'Kelly, Charlotte G.
 1980 *Women and Men in Society*. New York: D. Van Nostrand Company.

Ortner, Sherry
 1974 "Is Female to Male as Nature Is to Culture?" In *Women, Culture, and Society*. Michelle Rosaldo and Louise Lamphere, eds. Pp. 67–88. Stanford: Stanford University Press.

Pescatello, Ann, ed.
 1973 *Female and Male in Latin America*. Pittsburgh: University of Pittsburgh Press.

Powers, Marla N.
 1986 *Oglala Women. Myth, Ritual, and Reality*. Chicago: University of Chicago Press.

Pruitt, Ida
 1979 *Old Madam Yin. A Memoir of Peking Life, 1926–1938*. Stanford: Stanford University Press.

Reed, Evelyn
 1975 *Woman's Evolution: From Matriarchal Clan to Patriarchal Family*. New York: Pathfinder Press.

Reiter, Rayna, ed.
 1975 *Toward an Anthropology of Women*. New York: Monthly Review Press.

Rohrlich-Leavitt, Ruby, ed.
 1975 *Women Cross-Culturally: Change and Challenge*. The Hague: Mouton Press.

Rohrlich-Leavitt, Ruby, Barbara Sykes, and Elizabeth Weatherford
 1975 "Aboriginal Woman: Male and Female Anthropological Perspectives." In *Toward an Anthropology of Women*. Rayne Reiter, ed. Pp. 110–126. New York: Monthly Review Press.

Rosaldo, Michelle
 1974 "Women, Culture, and Society: A Theoretical Overview." In *Woman, Culture, and Society*. Michelle Rosaldo and Louise Lamphere, eds. Pp. 17–42. Stanford: Stanford University Press.

Rosaldo, Michelle Zimbalist
 1980 "The Use and Abuse of Anthropology: Reflections on Feminism and Cross-Cultural Understanding." *SIGNS* 5, 3: 389–417.

Rosaldo, Michelle, and Louise Lamphere, eds.
 1974 *Woman, Culture and Society*. Stanford: Stanford University Press.

Rubin, Gayle
 1975 "The Traffic in Women: Notes on the 'Political Economy' of Sex." In *Toward an Anthropology of Women*. Rayna Reiter, ed. Pp. 157–210. New York: Monthly Review Press.

Sacks, Karen
 1974 "Engels Revisited: Women, the Organization of Production and Private Property." In *Woman, Culture, and Society*. Michelle Rosaldo and Louise Lamphere, eds. Pp. 207–222. Stanford: Stanford University Press.

———
 1976 "State Bias and Women's Status." *American Anthropologist 78*, 3: 565–569.

Sahlins, Marshall
 1977 *The Use and Abuse of Biology*. Ann Arbor: University of Michigan Press.

Schlegel, Alice
 1974 "Women Anthropologists Look at Women." *Reviews in Anthropology 1*, 6: 553–560.

Schlegel, Alice, ed.
 1977 *Sexual Stratification, A Cross-Cultural View*. New York: Columbia University Press.

Shostak, Marjorie
 1983 *Nisa. The Life and Words of a !Kung Woman*. New York: Vintage Books, a Division of Random House. First published in 1981, Cambridge, MA: Harvard University Press.

Silverblatt, Irene
 1988 "Women in States." *Annual Review of Anthropology* 17: 427–460.

Slocum, Sally
 1975 "Woman the Gatherer: Male Bias in Anthropology." In *Toward an Anthropology of Women*. Rayna Reiter, ed. Pp. 36–50. New York: Monthly Review Press.

Spiro, Melford E.
 1979 *Gender and Culture: Kibbutz Women Revisited*. Durham, North Carolina: Duke University Press.

Stewart, Irene
 1980 *A Voice in Her Tribe. A Navajo Woman's Own Story*. Socorro, New Mexico: Ballena Press Anthropological Papers No. 17.

Strathern, Marilyn
 1972 *Women in Between*. New York: Seminar Press.

———
 1987 "An Awkward Relationship: The Case of Feminism and Anthropology." *SIGNS* 12, 2: 276–292.

Tanner, Nancy Makepeace
  1981 *On Becoming Human.* New York: Cambridge University Press.

Tanner, Nancy, and Adrienne Zihlman
  1976 "Women in Evolution Part 1: Innovation and Selection in Human Origins." *SIGNS 1,* 3, 1: 585–608.

Tiger, Lionel
  1969 *Men in Groups.* New York: Random House.

––––––
  1970 "Male Dominance? Yes, Alas. A Sexist Plot? No." *New York Times Magazine.* October 25.

Tiger, Lionel, and Robin Fox
  1971 *The Imperial Animal.* New York: Holt, Rinehart and Winston.

Trivers, R. L.
  1971 "The Evolution of Reciprocal Altruism." *Quarterly Review of Biology* 46: 35–37.

Webster, Paula
  1975 "Matriarchy: A Vision of Power." In *Toward an Anthropology of Women.* Rayna Reiter, ed. Pp. 141–156. New York: Monthly Review Press.

West Eberhard, M. J.
  1975 "The Evolution of Social Behavior by Kin Selection." *Quarterly Review of Biology,* 50: 1–33.

Wilson, Edward O.
  1975 *Sociobiology, The New Synthesis.* Cambridge, Mass.: Harvard University Press.

––––––
  1978 *Human Nature.* Cambridge, MA: Harvard University Press.

Wolf, M.
  1976 *Women and the Family in Rural Taiwan.* Stanford: Stanford University Press.

Genesis

The myth that the origin of male authority rested in some great cataclysmic female sin is not peculiar to the Judeo-Christian tradition or to the Western world. Again and again, this idea appears in primitive and highly advanced societies: Woman is evil and dangerous and to make things right the gods decree that man should maintain order through control.

The Holy Scriptures, rev. by Alexander Harkavy. New York: Hebrew Publishing Company, 1951.

²⁶AND GOD SAID, LET US MAKE MAN IN OUR IMAGE, after our likeness: and let them have dominion over the fish of the sea, and over the fowl of the air, and over the cattle, and over all the earth, and over every creeping thing that creepeth upon the earth. ²⁷So God created man in his *own* image, in the image of God created he him; male and female created he them.

²⁸And God blessed them, and God said unto them, Be fruitful, and multiply, and replenish the earth, and subdue it: and have dominion over the fish of the sea, and over the fowl of the air, and over every living thing that moveth upon the earth.

²⁹And God said, Behold, I have given you every herb bearing seed, which *is* upon the face of all the earth, and every tree, in which *is* the fruit of a tree yielding seed; to you it shall be for meat. ³⁰And to every beast of the earth, and to every fowl of the air, and to every thing that creepeth upon the earth, wherein *there is* life, *I have given* every green herb for meat: and it was so.

³¹And God saw every thing that he had made, and, behold, *it was* very good. And there was evening and there was morning, the sixth day.

2 Thus the heavens and the earth were finished, and all the host of them. ²And on the seventh day God ended his work which he had made; and he rested on the seventh day from all his work which he had made. ³And God blessed the seventh day, and sanctified it: because that in it he had rested from all his work which God created and made.

⁴These *are* the generations of the heavens and of the earth when they were created, in the day that the Lord God made the earth and the heavens.

⁵And no plant of the field was yet on the earth, and no herb of the field had yet grown: for the Lord God had not caused it to rain upon the earth, and *there was* not a man to till the ground. ⁶But there went up a mist from the earth, and watered the whole face of the ground. ⁷And the Lord God formed man *of* the dust of the ground, and

breathed into his nostrils the breath of life; and man became a living soul.

⁸And the Lord God planted a garden eastward in Eden; and there he put the man whom he had formed. ⁹And out of the ground made the Lord God to grow every tree that is pleasant to the sight, and good for food; the tree of life also in the midst of the garden, and the tree of knowledge of good and evil. ¹⁰And a river went out of Eden to water the garden; and from thence it was parted, and became into four heads. ¹¹The name of the first *is* Pishon: that *is* it which compasseth the whole land of Havilah, where *there is* gold; ¹²And the gold of that land *is* good: there *is* bdellium and the onyx stone. ¹³And the name of the second river *is* Gihon: the same *is* it that compasseth the whole land of Ethiopia. ¹⁴And the name of the third river *is* Hiddekel: that *is* it which goeth toward the east of Assyria. And the fourth river is Euphrates.

¹⁵And the Lord God took the man, and put him into the garden of Eden to till it and to keep it. ¹⁶And the Lord God commanded the man saying, Of every tree of the garden thou mayest freely eat: ¹⁷But of the tree of the knowledge of good and evil, thou shalt not eat of it; for in the day that thou eatest thereof thou shalt surely die.

¹⁸And the Lord God said, *it is* not good that the man should be alone; I will make him a help meet for him. ¹⁹And out of the ground the Lord formed every beast of the field, and every fowl of the air; and brought *them* unto Adam to see what he would call them: and whatsoever Adam called every living creature, that *was* the name thereof. ²⁰And Adam gave names to all cattle, and to the fowl of the air, and to every beast of the field; but for Adam there was not found a help meet for him. ²¹And the Lord God caused a deep sleep to fall upon Adam, and he slept: and he took one of his ribs, and closed up the flesh instead thereof; ²²And the rib, which the Lord God had taken from man, made he a woman, and brought her unto the man. ²³And Adam said, This *is* now bone of my bones, and flesh of my flesh: she shall be called Woman, because she was taken out of Man. ²⁴Therefore shall a man leave his father and his mother, and shall cleave unto his wife: and they shall be one flesh.

²⁵And they were both naked, the man and his wife, and were not ashamed.

3 Now the serpent was more subtle than any beast of the field which the Lord God had made. And he said unto the woman, Yea, hath God said, Ye shall not eat of every tree of the garden? ²And the woman said unto the serpent, We may eat of the fruit of the trees of the garden: ³But of the fruit of the tree which *is* in the midst of the garden, God hath said, Ye shall not eat of it, neither shall ye touch it, lest ye die. ⁴And the serpent said unto the woman, Ye shall not surely die: ⁵For God doth know that in the day ye eat thereof, then your eyes shall be opened, and ye shall be as gods, knowing good and evil. ⁶And when the woman saw that the tree *was* good for food, and that it *was* pleasant to the eyes, and a tree to be desired to make *one* wise, she took of the fruit thereof, and did eat, and gave also unto her husband with her; and he did eat. ⁷And the eyes of them both were opened, and they knew that they *were* naked; and they sewed fig leaves together, and made themselves aprons. ⁸And they heard the voice of the Lord God walking in the garden in the cool of the day: and Adam and his wife hid themselves from the presence of the Lord God amongst the trees of the garden. ⁹And the Lord God called unto Adam, and said unto him, Where *art* thou? ¹⁰And he said, I heard thy voice in the garden, and I was afraid, because I *was* naked; and I hid myself. ¹¹And he said, Who told thee that thou *wast* naked? Hast thou eaten of the tree, whereof I commanded thee that thou shouldest not eat? ¹²And the man said, The woman whom thou gavest *to be* with me, she gave me of the tree, and I did eat. ¹³And the Lord God said unto the woman, What *is* this *that* thou hast done? And the woman said, The serpent beguiled me, and I did eat. ¹⁴And the Lord God said unto the serpent, Because thou hast done this, thou *art* cursed above all cattle, and above every beast of the field; upon thy belly shalt thou go, and dust shalt thou eat all the days of thy life: ¹⁵And I will put enmity between thee and the woman, and between thy seed and her seed; he shall bruise thy head, and thou shalt bruise his heel. ¹⁶Unto the woman he said, I will greatly multiply thy sorrow and thy conception; in sorrow thou shalt bring forth children; and thy desire *shall be* to thy husband, and he shall rule over thee. ¹⁷And unto Adam he said, Because thou hast hearkened unto the voice of thy wife, and hast eaten of the tree, of which I commanded thee, saying, Thou shalt not eat of it; cursed *is* the ground for thy sake; in sorrow shalt thou eat *of* it all the days of thy life; ¹⁸Thorns also and thistles shall it bring forth to thee, and thou shalt eat the herb of the field; ¹⁹In the sweat of thy face shalt

thou eat bread, till thou return unto the ground; for out of it wast thou taken; for dust thou *art,* and unto dust shalt thou return.

²⁰And Adam called his wife's name Eve; because she was the mother of all living.

²¹Unto Adam also and to his wife did the Lord God make coats of skins, and clothed them.

²²And the Lord God said, Behold, the man is become as one of us, to know good and evil: and now, lest he put forth his hand, and take also of the tree of life, and eat, and live for ever: ²³Therefore the Lord God sent him forth from the garden of Eden, to till the ground from whence he was taken. ²⁴So he drove out the man; and he placed at the east of the garden of Eden the Cherubim, and a flaming sword which turned every way, to keep the way of the tree of life.

Rape

Susan Brownmiller

Susan Brownmiller was born in Brooklyn, New York, in 1935. She was educated at Cornell University, served as a reporter for NBC-TV and as a newswriter for ABC-TV, and has worked as a freelance writer. Brownmiller is the author of Shirley Chisholm *(1970) and the controversial and well-known* Against Our Will *(1975), which was revised in 1986. In 1984, she published* Femininity *and in 1989* Waverly Place, *a personal and fictionalized interpretation of a New York City child abuse and wife battering case.*

Her treatment of the concept of rape is historical, anthropological, and political. Her thesis here is psychological and mythical (in the positive sense) as well as sociological. Forcible rape, in its violence and cruelty, is a conscious act of intimidation. Women's fear and vulnerability force them to seek protection. Perhaps man's domination of women has its source in his exclusive ability to fend off other attackers.

MAN'S STRUCTURAL CAPACITY TO RAPE AND WOMan's corresponding structural vulnerability are as basic to the physiology of both our sexes as the primal act of sex itself. Had it not been for this accident of biology, an accommodation requiring the locking together of two separate parts, penis and vagina, there would be neither copulation nor rape as we know it. Anatomically one might want to improve on the design of nature, but such speculation appears to my mind as unrealistic. The human sex act accomplishes its historic purpose of generation of the species and it also affords some intimacy and pleasure. I have no basic quarrel with the procedure. But, nevertheless, we cannot work around the fact that in terms of human anatomy the possibility of forcible intercourse incontrovertibly exists. This single factor may have been sufficient to have caused the creation of a male ideology of rape. When men discovered that they could rape, they proceeded to do it. Later, much later, under certain circumstances they even came to consider rape a crime.

In the violent landscape inhabited by primitive woman and man, some woman somewhere had a prescient vision of her right to her own physical integrity, and in my mind's eye I can picture her fighting like hell to preserve it. After a thunderbolt of recognition that this particular incarnation of hairy, two-legged hominid was not the Homo sapiens with whom she would like to freely join parts, it might have been she, and not some man, who picked up the first stone and hurled it. How surprised he must have been, and what an unexpected battle must have taken place. Fleet of foot and spirited, she would have kicked, bitten, pushed and run, *but she could not retaliate in kind.*

The dim perception that had entered prehistoric woman's consciousness must have had an equal but opposite reaction in the mind of her male assailant. For if the first rape was an unexpected battle founded on the first woman's refusal, the second rape was indubitably planned. Indeed, one of the earliest forms of male bonding must have been the gang rape of one woman by a band of marauding men. This accomplished, rape became not only a male prerogative, but man's basic weapon of force against woman, the principal agent of his will and her fear. His forcible entry into her body, despite her physical protestations and struggle, became the vehicle of his victorious conquest over her being, the ultimate test of his superior strength, the triumph of his manhood.

Man's discovery that his genitalia could serve as a weapon to generate fear must rank as one of the most important discoveries of prehistoric times, along with the use of fire and the first crude stone axe. From prehistoric times to the present, I believe, rape has played a critical function. It is nothing more or less than a conscious process of intimidation by which *all men* keep *all women* in a state of fear.

In the Beginning Was the Law

From the humblest beginnings of the social order based on a primitive system of retaliatory force—the *lex talionis:* an eye for an eye—woman was unequal before the law. By anatomical fiat—the inescapable construction of their genital organs—the human male was a natural predator and the human female served as his natural prey. Not only might the female be subjected at will to a thoroughly detestable physical conquest from which there could be no retaliation in kind—a rape for a rape—but the consequences of such a brutal struggle might be death or injury, not to mention impregnation and the birth of a dependent child.

One possibility, and one possibility alone, was available to woman. Those of her own sex whom she might call to her aid were more often than not smaller and weaker than her male attackers. More critical, they lacked the basic physical wherewithal for punitive vengeance; at best they could maintain only a limited defensive action. But among those creatures who were her predators, some might serve as her chosen protectors. Perhaps it was thus that the risky bargain was struck. Female fear of an open

season of rape, and not a natural inclination toward monogamy, motherhood or love, was probably the single causative factor in the original subjugation of woman by man, the most important key to her historic dependence, her domestication by protective mating.

Once the male took title to a specific female body, and surely for him this was a great sexual convenience as well as a testament to his warring stature, he had to assume the burden of fighting off all other potential attackers, or scare them off by the retaliatory threat of raping *their* women. But the price of woman's protection *by some men* against an abuse *by others* was steep. Disappointed and disillusioned by the inherent female incapacity to protect, she became estranged in a very real sense from other females, a problem that haunts the social organization of women to this very day. And those who did assume the historic burden of her protection—later formalized as husband, father, brother, clan—extracted more than a pound of flesh. They reduced her status to that of chattel. The historic price of woman's protection by man against man was the imposition of chastity and monogamy. A crime committed against her body became a crime against the male estate.

The earliest form of permanent, protective conjugal relationship, the accommodation called mating that we now know as marriage, appears to have been institutionalized by the male's forcible abduction and rape of the female. No quaint formality, bride capture, as it came to be known, was a very real struggle: a male took title to a female, staked a claim to her body, as it were, by an act of violence. Forcible seizure was a perfectly acceptable way—to men—of acquiring women, and it existed in England as late as the fifteenth century. Eleanor of Aquitaine, according to a biographer, lived her early life in terror of being "rapt" by a vassal who might through appropriation of her body gain title to her considerable property. Bride capture exists to this day in the rain forests of the Philippines, where the Tasadays were recently discovered to be plying their Stone Age civilization. Remnants of the philosophy of forcible abduction and marriage still influence the social mores of rural Sicily and parts of Africa. A proverb of the exogamous Bantu-speaking Gusiis of southwest Kenya goes "Those whom we marry are those whom we fight."

It seems eminently sensible to hypothesize that man's violent capture and rape of the female led first to the establishment of a rudimentary mate-protectorate and then sometime later to the full-blown male solidification of power, the patriarchy. As the first permanent acquisition of man, his first piece of real property, woman was, in fact, the original building block, the cornerstone, of the "house of the father."

Man's forcible extension of his boundaries to his mate and later to their offspring was the beginning of his concept of ownership. Concepts of hierarchy, slavery and private property flowed from, and could only be predicated upon, the initial subjugation of woman.

The Origin of the Family, Private Property and the State

Friedrich Engels

Friedrich Engels was born in Barmen, Germany, in 1820 and died in England in 1895. Together with Karl Marx, he developed much of the social and economic theory we know today as Marxist communism. Among works that he wrote or coauthored are The Condition of the Working Class in England *(1844),* The German Ideology *(1845), and* The Communist Manifesto *(1848).*

The essay excerpted here, The Origin of the Family, Private Property and the State, *written in 1884, is an integration of the theoretical concepts of Marxism, particularly the materialistic conception of history, and the work of the anthropologist Lewis Morgan in* Ancient Society *(1877). Essentially, Engels traces the development of society from a time of primitive egalitarianism, when no classes and families as we know them existed to a time when private property, its acquisition and maintenance, makes rigid family structures a possibility and a necessity.*

In pretechnological times, Engels believed, men and women lived together in large integrated communities (called tribes or clans), all working together for subsistence and survival. Women were charged with the care of the household and were well respected and politically equal to the men, who provided food and engaged in the "productive" work. However, as technology developed and it became possible to produce more than could be immediately used by the group, surplus emerged and with it private property, that is, productive goods controlled by individual men. The accumulation of goods that could be publicly exchanged for others yielded power; and since women's work could not be amassed, and women served only their now-segregated families, women became wards of men, losing their status and power in an exchange economy and becoming wholly subordinated. As the importance of private property developed, the matter of inheritance altered the significance of children, and women's reproductive labor was appropriated by men

just as their productive labor had been. Hence (as many feminists today also theorize) the imperatives of virginity, chastity, and monogamy developed for women as the patterns of inheritance persuaded men to insure their paternity. Ultimately, it is argued, with the passing of private property and class, monogamy will disappear, marriage and sex will be based on love and choice, and women's original freedom and value will be restored.

RECONSTRUCTING THUS THE PAST HISTORY OF THE family, Morgan, in agreement with most of his colleagues, arrives at a primitive stage when unrestricted sexual freedom prevailed within the tribe, every woman belonging equally to every man and every man to every woman. Since the 18th century there had been talk of such a primitive state, but only in general phrases. Bachofen—and this is one of his great merits—was the first to take the existence of such a state seriously and to search for its traces in historical and religious survivals. Today we know that the traces he found do not lead back to a social stage of promiscuous sexual intercourse, but to a much later form—namely, group marriage. The primitive social stage of promiscuity, if it ever existed, belongs to such a remote epoch that we can hardly expect to prove its existence *directly* by discovering its social fossils among backward savages. Bachofen's merit consists in having brought this question to the forefront for examination.[1] . . .

. . . According to Morgan, from this primitive state of promiscuous intercourse there developed, probably very early:

Friedrich Engels, "The Origin of the Family, Private Property and the State" (New York: International Publishers, 1884) pp. 97–145.

The Consanguine Family, the First Stage of the Family

Here the marriage groups are separated according to generations: all the grandfathers and grandmothers within the limits of the family are all husbands and wives of one another; so are also their children, the fathers and mothers; the latter's children will form a third circle of common husbands and wives; and their children, the great-grandchildren of the first group, will form a fourth. In this form of marriage, therefore, only ancestors and progeny, and parents and children, are excluded from the rights and duties (as we should say) of marriage with one another. . . .

The Punaluan Family

If the first advance in organization consisted in the exclusion of parents and children from sexual intercourse with one another, the second was the exclusion of sister and brother. On account of the greater nearness in age, this second advance was infinitely more important, but also more difficult, than the first. It was effected gradually, beginning probably with the exclusion from sexual intercourse of one's own brothers and sisters (children of the same mother) first in isolated cases and then by degrees as a general rule (even in this century exceptions were found in Hawaii), and ending with the prohibition of marriage even between collateral brothers and sisters, or, as we should say, between first, second, and third cousins. . . .

The Pairing Family

A certain amount of pairing, for a longer or shorter period, already occurred in group marriage or even earlier; the man had a chief wife among his many wives (one can hardly yet speak of a favorite wife), and for her he was the most important among her husbands. This fact has contributed considerably to the confusion of the missionaries, who have regarded group marriage sometimes as promiscuous community of wives, sometimes as unbridled adultery. But these customary pairings were bound to grow more stable as the gens developed and the classes of "brothers" and "sisters" between whom marriage was impossible became more numerous.

The impulse given by the gens to the prevention of marriage between blood relatives extended still further. Thus among the Iroquois and most of the other Indians at the lower stage of barbarism, we find that marriage is prohibited between *all* relatives enumerated in their system—which includes several hundred degrees of kinship. The increasing complication of these prohibitions made group marriages more and more impossible; they were displaced by the *pairing family*. In this stage, one man lives with one woman, but the relationship is such that polygamy and occasional infidelity remain the right of the men, even though for economic reasons polygamy is rare, while from the woman the strictest fidelity is generally demanded throughout the time she lives with the man and adultery on her part is cruelly punished. The marriage tie can, however, be easily dissolved by either partner; after separation, the children still belong as before to the mother alone.

In this ever extending exclusion of blood relatives from the bond of marriage, natural selection continues its work. In Morgan's words:

> *The influence of the new practice, which brought unrelated persons into the marriage relation, tended to create a more vigorous stock physically and mentally. . . . When two advancing tribes, with strong mental and physical characters, are brought together and blended into one people by the accidents of barbarous life, the new skull and brain would widen and lengthen to the sum of the capabilities of both [1963: 468].*[2]

Tribes with gentile constitution were thus bound to gain supremacy over more backward tribes, or else to carry them along by their example.

Thus the history of the family in primitive times consists in the progressive narrowing of the circle, originally embracing the whole tribe, within which the two sexes have a common conjugal relation. The continuous exclusion, first of nearer, then of more and more remote relatives, and at last even of relatives by marriage, ends by making any kind of group marriage practically impossible. Finally, there remains only the single, still loosely linked pair, the molecule with whose dissolution marriage itself ceases. This in itself shows what a small part individual sex love, in the modern sense of the word, played in the rise of monogamy. Yet stronger proof is afforded by the practice of all peoples at this stage of development. Whereas in the earlier forms of the family, men never lacked women but, on the contrary, had too many rather than too few, women had now become scarce and highly sought after. Hence it is with the pairing marriage that there begins the capture and purchase of women—widespread *symptoms*, but no more than symptoms, of the much deeper change that had occurred. These symptoms, mere methods of procuring wives, the pedantic Scot McLennan has transmogrified into special classes of families under the names of "marriage by capture" and "marriage by purchase." In general, whether among the American Indians or other peoples (at the same stage), the conclusion of a marriage is the affair not of the two parties concerned, who are often not consulted at all, but of their mothers. Two persons entirely unknown to each other are often thus affianced; they only learn that the bargain has been struck when the time for marrying approaches. Before the wedding the bridegroom gives presents to the bride's gentile relatives (to those on the mother's side, therefore, not to the father and his relations) which are regarded as gift payments in return for the girl. The marriage is still terminable at the desire of either partner, but among many tribes, the Iroquois for example, public opinion has gradually developed against such separations. When differences arise between husband and wife, the gens relatives of both partners act as mediators, and only if these efforts prove fruitless does a separation take place, the wife then keeping the children and each partner being free to marry again.

The pairing family, itself too weak and unstable to make an independent household necessary or even desirable, in no wise destroys the communistic household inherited from earlier times. Communistic housekeeping, however, means the supremacy of women in the house; just as the exclusive recognition of the female parent, owing to the impossibility of recognizing the male parent with certainty, means that the women—the mothers—are held in high respect. One of the most absurd notions taken over from 18th century enlightenment is that in the beginning of society woman was the slave of man. Among all savages and all barbarians of the lower and middle stages, and to a certain extent of the upper stage also, the position of women is not only free, but honorable. As to what it still is in the pairing marriage, let

us hear the evidence of Ashur Wright, for many years missionary among the Iroquois Senecas:

> *As to their family system, when occupying the old long houses [communistic households comprising several families], it is probable that some one clan [gens] predominated, the women taking in husbands, however, from the other clans [gentes]. . . . Usually, the female portion ruled the house. . . . The stores were in common; but woe to the luckless husband or lover who was too shiftless to do his share of the providing. No matter how many children, or whatever goods he might have in the house, he might at any time be ordered to pick up his blanket and budge; and after such orders it would not be healthful for him to attempt to disobey. The house would be too hot for him; and . . . he must retreat to his own clan [gens]; or, as was often done, go and start a new matrimonial alliance in some other. The women were the great power among the clans [gentes], as everywhere else. They did not hesitate, when occasion required, "to knock off the horns," as it was technically called, from the head of a chief, and send him back to the ranks of the warriors [Morgan, 1963: 464 fn].*

The communistic household, in which most or all of the women belong to one and the same gens, while the men come from various gentes, is the material foundation of that supremacy of the women which was general in primitive times, and which it is Bachofen's third great merit to have discovered. The reports of travelers and missionaries, I may add, to the effect that women among savages and barbarians are overburdened with work in no way contradict what has been said. The division of labor between the two sexes is determined by quite other causes than by the position of woman in society. Among peoples where the women have to work far harder than we think suitable, there is often much more real respect for women than among our Europeans. The lady of civilization, surrounded by false homage and estranged from all real work, has an infinitely lower social position than the hard-working woman of barbarism, who was regarded among her people as a real lady (lady, *frowa, Frau*—mistress) and who was also a lady in character. . . .

. . . Bachofen is also perfectly right when he consistently maintains that the transition from what he calls "hetaerism" or "*Sumpfzeugung*" to monogamy was brought about primarily through the women. The more the traditional sexual relations lost the naive primitive character of forest life, owing to the development of economic conditions with consequent undermining of the old communism and growing density of population, the more oppressive and humiliating must the women have felt them to be, and the greater their longing for the right of chastity, of temporary or permanent marriage with one man only, as a way of release. This advance could not in any case have originated with the men if only because it has never occurred to them, even to this day, to renounce the pleasures of actual group marriage. Only when the women had brought about the transition to pairing marriage were the men able to introduce strict monogamy—though indeed only for women. . . .

Once it had passed into the private possession of families and there rapidly begun to augment, this wealth dealt a severe blow to the society founded on pairing marriage and the matriarchal gens. Pairing marriage had brought a new element into the family. By the side of the natural mother of the child it placed its natural and attested father with a better warrant of paternity, probably, than that of many a "father" today. According to the division of labor within the family at that time, it was the man's part to obtain food and the instruments of labor necessary for the purpose. He therefore also owned the instruments of labor, and in the event of husband and wife separating, he took them with him, just as she retained her household goods. Therefore, according to the social custom of the time, the man was also the owner of the new source of subsistence, the cattle, and later of the new instruments of labor, the slaves. But according to the custom of the same society, his children could not inherit from him. For as regards inheritance, the position was as follows:

At first, according to mother right—so long, therefore, as descent was reckoned only in the female line—and according to the original custom of inheritance within the gens, the gentile relatives inherited from a deceased fellow member of their gens. His property had to remain within the gens. His effects being insignificant, they probably always passed in practice to his nearest gentile relations—that is, to his blood relations on the mother's side. The children of the dead man, however, did not belong to his gens, but to that of their mother; it was from her that they

inherited, at first conjointly with her other blood-relations, later perhaps with rights of priority; they could not inherit from their father because they did not belong to his gens within which his property had to remain. When the owner of the herds died, therefore, his herds would go first to his brothers and sisters and to his sister's children, or to the issue of his mother's sisters. But his own children were disinherited.

Thus on the one hand, in proportion as wealth increased it made the man's position in the family more important than the woman's, and on the other hand created an impulse to exploit this strengthened position in order to overthrow, in favor of his children, the traditional order of inheritance. This, however, was impossible so long as descent was reckoned according to mother right. Mother right, therefore, had to be overthrown, and overthrown it was. This was by no means so difficult as it looks to us today. For this revolution—one of the most decisive ever experienced by humanity—could take place without disturbing a single one of the living members of a gens. All could remain as they were. A simple decree sufficed that in the future the offspring of the male members should remain within the gens, but that of the female should be excluded by being transferred to the gens of their father. The reckoning of descent in the female line and the matriarchal law of inheritance were thereby overthrown, and the male line of descent and the paternal law of inheritance were substituted for them. As to how and when this revolution took place among civilized peoples, we have no knowledge. It falls entirely within prehistoric times. But that it *did* take place is more than sufficiently proved by the abundant traces of mother right which have been collected, particularly by Bachofen. . . .

The overthrow of mother right was the *world historical defeat of the female sex*. The man took command in the home also; the woman was degraded and reduced to servitude; she became the slave of his lust and a mere instrument for the production of children. This degraded position of the woman, especially conspicuous among the Greeks of the heroic and still more of the classical age, has gradually been palliated and glossed over, and sometimes clothed in a milder form; in no sense has it been abolished.

The establishment of the exclusive supremacy of the man shows its effects first in the patriarchal family, which now emerges as an intermediate form. Its essential characteristic is not polygyny, of which more later, but "the organization of a number of persons, bond and free, into a family under paternal power for the purpose of holding lands and for the care of flocks and herds. . . . (In the Semitic form) the chiefs, at least, lived in polygamy. . . . Those held to servitude and those employed as servants lived in the marriage relation" [Morgan, 1963: 474].

Its essential features are the incorporation of unfree persons and paternal power; hence the perfect type of this form of family is the Roman. The original meaning of the word "family" (*familia*) is not that compound of sentimentality and domestic strife which forms the ideal of the present-day philistine; among the Romans it did not at first even refer to the married pair and their children but only to the slaves. *Famulus* means domestic slave, and *familia* is the total number of slaves belonging to one man. As late as the time of Gaius, the *familia, id est patrimonium* (family, that is, the patrimony, the inheritance) was bequeathed by will. The term was invented by the Romans to denote a new social organism whose head ruled over wife and children and a number of slaves, and was invested under Roman paternal power with rights of life and death over them all.

This term, therefore, is no older than the ironclad family system of the Latin tribes, which came in after field agriculture and after legalized servitude, as well as after the separation of the Greeks and Latins [Morgan, 1963: 478].

Marx adds:

The modern family contains in germ not only slavery (servitus) *but also serfdom, since from the beginning it is related to agricultural services. It contains* in miniature *all the contradictions which later extend throughout society and its state.*

Such a form of family shows the transition of the pairing family to monogamy. In order to make certain of the wife's fidelity and therefore the paternity of the children, she is delivered over unconditionally into the power of the husband; if he kills her, he is only exercising his rights.

With the patriarchal family, we enter the field of written history. . . .

The Monogamous Family

It develops out of the pairing family, as previously shown, in the transitional period between the upper and middle stages of barbarism; its decisive victory is one of the signs that civilization is beginning. It is based on the supremacy of the man, the express purpose being to produce children of undisputed paternity; such paternity is demanded because these children are later to come into their father's property as his natural heirs. It is distinguished from pairing marriage by the much greater strength of the marriage tie, which can no longer be dissolved at either partner's wish. As a rule, it is now only the man who can dissolve it and put away his wife. The right of conjugal infidelity also remains secured to him, at any rate by custom (the *Code Napoléon* explicitly accords it to the husband as long as he does not bring his concubine into the house), and as social life develops he exercises his right more and more; should the wife recall the old form of sexual life and attempt to revive it, she is punished more severely than ever. . . .

. . . Sex love in the relationship with a woman becomes and can only become the real rule among the oppressed classes, which means today among the proletariat—whether this relation is officially sanctioned or not. But here all the foundations of typical monogamy are cleared away. Here there is no property, for the preservation and inheritance of which monogamy and male supremacy were established; hence there is no incentive to make this male supremacy effective. What is more, there are no means of making it so. Bourgeois law, which protects this supremacy, exists only for the possessing class and their dealings with the proletarians. The law costs money and, on account of the worker's poverty, it has no validity for his relation to his wife. Here quite other personal and social conditions decide. And now that large-scale industry has taken the wife out of the home onto the labor market and into the factory, and made her often the breadwinner of the family, no basis for any kind of male supremacy is left in the proletarian household, except, perhaps, for something of the brutality toward women that has spread since the introduction of monogamy. The proletarian family is therefore no longer monogamous in the strict sense, even where there is passionate love and firmest loyalty on both sides and maybe all the blessings of religious and civil authority. Here, therefore, the eternal attendants of monogamy, hetaerism and adultery, play only an almost vanishing part.[3] The wife has in fact regained the right to dissolve the marriage, and if two people cannot get on with one another, they prefer to separate. In short, proletarian marriage is monogamous in the etymological sense of the word, but not at all in its historical sense. . . .

. . . As regards the legal equality of husband and wife in marriage, the position is no better. The legal inequality of the two partners bequeathed to us from earlier social conditions is not the cause but the effect of the economic oppression of the woman. In the old communistic household, which comprised many couples and their children, the task entrusted to the women of managing the household was as much a public, a socially necessary industry as the procuring of food by the men. With the patriarchal family and still more with the single monogamous family, a change came. Household management lost its public character. It no longer concerned society. It became a *private service*; the wife became the head servant, excluded from all participation in social production. Not until the coming of modern large-scale industry was the road to social production opened to her again—and then only to the proletarian wife. But it was opened in such a manner that, if she carries out her duties in the private service of her family, she remains excluded from public production and unable to earn; and if she wants to take part in public production and earn independently, she cannot carry out family duties. And the wife's position in the factory is the position of women in all branches of business, right up to medicine and the law. The modern individual family is founded on the open or concealed domestic slavery of the wife, and modern society is a mass composed of these individual families as its molecules.

In the great majority of cases today, at least in the possessing classes, the husband is obliged to earn a living and support his family, and that in itself gives him a position of supremacy without any need for special legal titles and privileges. Within the family he is the bourgeois, and the wife represents the proletariat. In the industrial world, the specific character of the economic oppression burdening the proletariat is visible in all its sharpness only when all special legal privileges of the capitalist class have been abolished and complete legal equality of both classes established. The democratic republic does not do away with the opposition of the two classes; on the contrary, it provides the clear field on which the fight can be fought out. And in the same way, the peculiar character of the supremacy of the husband over the wife in the modern family, the necessity of creating real social equality between them and the way to do it, will only be seen in the clear light of day when both possess legally complete equality of rights. Then it will be plain that the first condition for the liberation of the wife is to bring the whole female sex back into public industry, and that this in turn demands that the characteristic of the monogamous family as the economic unit of society be abolished.

We thus have three principal forms of marriage which correspond broadly to the three principal stages of human development: for the period of savagery, group marriage; for barbarism, pairing marriage; for civilization, monogamy supplemented by adultery and prostitution. Between pairing marriage and monogamy intervenes a period in the upper stage of barbarism when men have female slaves at their command and polygamy is practiced.

As our whole presentation has shown, the progress which manifests itself in these successive forms is connected with the peculiarity that women, but not men, are increasingly deprived of the sexual freedom of group marriage. In fact, for men group marriage actually still exists even to this day. What for the woman is a crime entailing grave legal and social consequences is considered honorable in a man or, at the worse, a slight moral blemish which he cheerfully bears. But the more the hetaerism of the past is changed in our time by capitalist commodity production and brought into conformity with it, the more, that is to say, it is transformed into undisguised prostitution, the more demoralizing are its effects. And it demoralizes men far more than women. Among women, prostitution degrades only the unfortunate ones who become its victims, and even these by no means to the extent commonly believed. But it degrades the character of the whole male world. A long engagement particularly is in nine cases out of ten a regular preparatory school for conjugal infidelity.

We are now approaching a social revolution in which the economic foundations of monogamy as they have existed hitherto will disappear just as surely as those of its complement—prostitution. Monogamy arose from the concentration of considerable wealth in the hands of a single individual—a man—and from the need to bequeath this wealth to the children of that man and of no other. For this purpose, the monogamy of the woman was required, not that of the man, so this monogamy of the woman did not in any way interfere with open or concealed polygamy on the part of the man. But by transforming by far the greater portion, at any rate, of permanent, heritable wealth—the means of production—into social property, the coming social revolution will reduce to a minimum all this anxiety about bequeathing and inheriting. Having arisen from economic causes, will monogamy then disappear when these causes disappear?

One might answer, not without reason: far from disappearing, it will on the contrary begin to be realized completely. For with the transformation of the means of production into social property there will disappear also wage labor, the proletariat, and therefore the necessity for a certain—statistically calculable—number of women to surrender themselves for money. Prostitution disappears; monogamy, instead of collapsing, at last becomes a reality—also for men.

In any case, therefore, the position of men will be very much altered. But the position of women, of *all* women, also undergoes significant change. With the transfer of the means of production into common ownership, the single family ceases to be the economic unit of society. Private housekeeping is transformed into a social industry. The care and education of the children becomes a public affair; society looks after all children alike, whether they are legitimate or not. This removes all the anxiety about the "consequences," which today is the most essential social—moral as well as economic—factor that prevents a girl from giving herself completely to the man she loves. Will not that suffice to bring about the gradual growth of unconstrained sexual intercourse and with it a more tolerant public opinion in regard to a maiden's honor and a woman's shame? And finally, have we not seen that in the modern world monogamy and prostitution are indeed contradictions, but inseparable contradictions, poles of the same state of society? Can prostitution disappear without dragging monogamy with it into the abyss?

. . . Full freedom of marriage can therefore only be generally established when the abolition of capitalist production and of the property relations created by it has removed all the accompanying economic considerations which still exert such a power-ful influence on the choice of a marriage partner. For then there is no other motive left except mutual inclination.

And as sexual love is by its nature exclusive—although at present this exclusiveness is fully realized only in the woman—the marriage based on sexual love is by its nature individual marriage. We have seen how right Bachofen was in regarding the advance from group marriage to individual marriage as primarily due to the women. Only the step from pairing marriage to monogamy can be put down to the credit of the men, and historically the essence of this was to make the position of the women worse and the infidelities of the men easier. If now the economic considerations also disappear which made women put up with the habitual infidelity of their husbands—concern for their own means of existence and still more for their children's future—then, according to all previous experience, the equality of women thereby achieved will tend infinitely more to make men really monogamous than to make women polyandrous.

But what will quite certainly disappear from monogamy are all the features stamped upon it through its origin in property relations; these are, in the first place, supremacy of the man and secondly, the indissolubility of marriage. The supremacy of the man in marriage is the simple consequence of his economic supremacy, and with the abolition of the latter will disappear of itself. The indissolubility of marriage is partly a consequence of the economic situation in which monogamy arose, partly tradition from the period when the connection between this economic situation and monogamy was not yet fully understood and was carried to extremes under a religious form. Today it is already broken through at a thousand points. If only the marriage based on love is moral, then also only the marriage is moral in which love continues. But the intense emotion of individual sex love varies very much in duration from one individual to another, especially among men, and if affection definitely comes to an end or is supplanted by a new passionate love, separation is a benefit for both partners as well as for society—only people will then be spared having to wade through the useless mire of a divorce case.

What we can now conjecture about the way in which sexual relations will be ordered after the impending overthrow of capitalist production is mainly of a negative character, limited for the most part to what will disappear. But what will there be new? That will be answered when a new generation has grown up: a generation of men who never in their lives have known what it is to buy a woman's surrender with money or any other social instrument of power; a generation of women who have never known what it is to give themselves to a man from any other considerations than real love or to refuse to give themselves to their lover from fear of the economic consequences. When these people are in the world, they will care precious little what anybody today thinks they ought to do; they will make their own practice and their corresponding public opinion about the practice of each individual—and that will be the end of it.

Notes

[1]Bachofen proves how little he understood his own discovery, or rather his guess, by using the term "hetaerism" to describe this primitive state. For the Greeks, when they introduced the word, hetaerism meant intercourse of men, unmarried or living in monogamy, with unmarried women; it always presupposes a definite form of marriage outside which this intercourse takes place and includes at least the possibility of prostitution. The word was never used in any other sense, and it is in this sense that I use it with Morgan. Bachofen everywhere introduces into his extremely important discoveries the most incredible mystifications through his notion that in their historical development the relations between men and women had their origin in men's contemporary religious conceptions, not in their actual conditions of life.

[2]A most infelicitous statement, worthy of quotation only as an example of how much we have learned about genetics since Morgan's and Engels' time.

[3]Charles Fourier, *Théorie de l'Unité Universelle*, Paris, 1841–45, III, 120.

A Working Hypothesis

Gerda Lerner

You will find the biography of Gerda Lerner in Chapter 1 with a selection from her Introduction to The Creation of Patriarchy. *In this selection, Lerner does indeed develop a working hypothesis for an explanation of the origin of women's subordination in the patriarchal system. A variety of factors must have been responsible, posits Lerner, including the prolonged infancy and helplessness of the human child, the exchange of females in marriage, the rise of agriculture, and others. Patriarchy, she underscores, is historical; that is, it has a beginning. Thus, no reason exists why it may not also have an end.*

THE BASIC ASSUMPTION WITH WHICH WE MUST start any theorizing about the past is that men and women built civilization jointly.[1] Starting as we do from the end result and reasoning back, we thus ask a different question than that of a single-cause "origin." We ask: how did men and women in their society-building and in the construction of what we call Western civilization arrive at the present state? Once we abandon the concept of women as historical victims, acted upon by violent men, inexplicable "forces," and societal institutions, we must explain the central puzzle—woman's participation in the construction of the system that subordinates her. I suggest that abandoning the search for an empowering past—the search for matriarchy—is the first step in the right direction. The creation of compensatory myths of the distant past of women will not emancipate women in the present and the future. . . .[2]

A correct analysis of our situation and how it came to be what it is will help us to create an empowering theory. We must think about gender historically and specifically as it occurs in varied and changeable societies. The anthropologist Michelle Rosaldo arrived at similar conclusions, although starting from a different vantage point. She wrote:

> To look for origins is, in the end, to think that what we are today is something other than the product of our history and our present social world, and, more particularly, that our gender systems are primordial, transhistorical and essentially unchanging in their roots.[3]

Our search, then, becomes a search for the history of the patriarchal system. To give the system of male dominance historicity and to assert that its functions and manifestations change over time is to break sharply with the handed-down tradition. This tradition has mystified patriarchy by making it ahistoric, eternal, invisible, and unchanging. But it is precisely due to changes in the social and educational opportunities available to women that in the nineteenth and twentieth centuries large numbers of women finally became capable of critically evaluating the process by which we have helped to create the system and maintain it. We are only now able to conceptualize women's role in history and thereby to create a consciousness which can emancipate women. This consciousness can also liberate men from the unwanted and undesired consequences of the system of male dominance.

Approaching this quest as historians, we must abandon single-factor explanations. We must assume that if and when events occur simultaneously their relationship to each other is not necessarily causal. We must assume that changes as complex as a basic alteration in kinship structures most likely occurred as the result of a variety of interacting forces. We must test whatever hypothesis we have developed for one model comparatively and cross-culturally. Women's position in society must be viewed always also in comparison with that of the men of their social group and of their time.

We must prove our case not only by material evidence but by evidence from written sources. While we will look for the occurrence of "patterns" and similarities, we must be open to the possibility that similar outcomes, deriving from a variety of factors, might occur as the result of very different processes. Above all, we must view the position of women in society as subject to change over time, not only in its form but also in its meaning. For example, the social role of "concubine" cannot be evaluated by twentieth- or even nineteenth-century standards when we are studying it in the first millennium B.C. This is so obvious an example that to cite it may seem unnecessary, and yet just such errors occur frequently in the discussion of women's past. In particular, gender has, in most societies, such a strong symbolic as well as ideological and legal significance that we cannot truly understand it unless we pay attention to all aspects of its meaning.

The hypothetical construct I will offer is intended only as one of a number of possible models. Even on the limited geographic terrain of the Ancient Near East there must have been many different ways in which the transition to patriarchy took place. Since we will most likely never know just what happened, we are constrained to speculate on what might have been possible. Such utopian projections into the past serve an important function for those who wish to

create theory—to know what might have been possible opens us up to new interpretations. It allows us to speculate about what might be possible in the future, free of the confines of a limited and entirely outdated conceptual framework.

Let us begin with the transitional period when hominids evolved from primates, some three million years ago, and let us consider the most basic dyad, mother and child. The first characteristic distinguishing humans from other primates is the prolonged and helpless infancy of the human child. This is the direct result of bipedalism, which led to the narrowing of the female pelvis and birth canal due to upright posture. One result of this was that human babies were born at a greater stage of immaturity than other primates, with relatively smaller heads in order to ease passage through the birth canal. Further, in contrast to the most highly developed apes, human babies are born naked and therefore must experience a greater need for warmth. They cannot grasp their mothers for steady support, lacking the apes' movable toe, so mothers must use their hands or, later, mechanical substitutes for hands to cradle their infants against them.[4] Bipedalism and upright posture led also to the finer development of the hand, the grasping thumb, and greater sensory-hand coordination. One consequence of this is that the human brain develops for many years during the child's period of infancy and complete dependency, and that it is therefore subject to modification through learning and intense cultural molding in a way that is decisively different from animal development. The neurophysiologist Ruth Bleier uses these facts in a telling argument against any theories claiming "innate" human characteristics.[5]

The step from foraging to gathering food for later consumption, possibly by more than one individual, was crucial in advancing human development. It must have fostered social interaction, the invention and development of containers, and the slow evolutionary increase in brain size. Nancy Tanner suggests that females caring for their helpless infants had the most incentive to develop these skills, while males may have, for a long period, continued to forage alone. She speculates that it was these activities which led to the first use of tools for opening and dividing plant food with children and for digging for roots. At any rate, the infant's survival depended on the quality of maternal care. "Similarly, a mother's gathering effectiveness improved her own nutrition and thereby increased her life expectancy and fertility."[6]

We postulate, as Tanner and Bleier do, that in the slow advance from upright hominids to the fully developed humans of the Neanderthal period (100,000 B.C.) the role of females was crucial. Sometime after that period large-scale hunting by groups of men developed in Africa, Europe, and Northern Asia; the earliest evidence for the existence of bows and arrows can be dated only to 15,000 years ago. Since most of the explanations for the existence of a sexual division of labor postulate the existence of hunting/gathering societies, we need to look more closely at such societies in the Paleolithic and early Neolithic periods.

It is from the Neolithic that we derive surviving evidence of cave paintings and sculptures suggesting the pervasive veneration of the Mother-Goddess. We can understand why men and women might have chosen this as their first form of religious expression by considering the psychological bond between mother and child. We owe our insights into the complexities and importance of that bond largely to modern psychoanalytic accounts.[7] As Freud has shown us, the child's first experience of the world is one in which the total environment and the self are barely separated. The environment, which consists mostly of the mother as the source of food, warmth, and pleasure, only gradually becomes differentiated from the self, as the infant smiles or cries to secure gratification of its needs. When the infant's needs are not met and it experiences anxiety and pain associated with cold and hunger, it learns to acknowledge the overwhelming power of "the other out there," the mother. . . .

. . . But under primitive conditions, before the institutions of civilized society were created, the actual power of the mother over the infant must have been awesome. Only the mother's arms and care sheltered the infant from cold; only her breast milk could provide the nourishment needed for survival. Her indifference or neglect meant certain death. The life-giving mother truly had power over life and death. No wonder that men and women, observing this dramatic and mysterious power of the female, turned to the veneration of Mother-Goddesses.[8]

My point here is to stress the *necessity,* which created the initial division of labor by which women do the mothering. For millennia group survival depended upon it, and no alternative was available. Under the extreme and dangerous conditions under which primitive humans lived, the survival into adulthood of at least two children for each coupling pair necessitated many pregnancies for each woman. Accurate data on prehistoric life span are hard to come by, but estimates based on skeletal studies place the average Paleolithic and Neolithic life-span between thirty and forty years. In the detailed study of 222 adult skeletons from Čatal Hüyük earlier cited, Lawrence Angel arrives at an average adult male life length of 34.3 years, with a female life length of 29.8 years. (This excludes from consideration those who died in childhood.)[9]

Women would need to have had more pregnancies than live births, as continued to be the case also in historic times in agricultural societies. Infancy was much prolonged, since mothers nursed their infants for two to three years. Thus, we may assume that it was absolutely essential for group survival that most nubile women devote most of their adulthood to pregnancy, child-bearing, and nursing. One would expect that men and women would accept such necessity and construct beliefs, mores, and values within their cultures to sustain such necessary practices.

It would follow that women would choose or prefer those economic activities which could be combined easily with their mothering duties. Although it is reasonable to assume that some women in every tribe or band were physically able to hunt, it would follow that women would not want to hunt regularly for big game, because of their being physically encumbered by children carried in the womb, on the hip, or on the back. Further, while a baby slung on the back might not prevent a mother from participating in hunting, a crying baby might. Examples cited by anthropologists of hunting/gathering tribes in the contemporary world, in which alternate arrangements are made for child care and in which women occasionally do take part in hunting, do not contradict the above argument.[10] They merely show what it is possible for societies to arrange and to try; they do not show what was the likely historically predominant mode which enabled societies to survive. Obviously, given the precarious and short life spans I have cited above for the Neolithic period, tribes which put the lives of their nubile women at risk by hunting or by participating in warfare, thereby also increasing the likelihood of their injury in accidents, would not tend to survive as well as tribes in which these women were otherwise employed. Thus, the first sexual division of labor, by which men did the big-game hunting and children and women the small-game hunting and food gathering, seems to derive from biological sex differences.[11] These biological sex differences are not differences in the strength and endurance of men and women but solely reproductive differences, specifically women's ability to nurse babies. Having said this, I want to stress that my acceptance of a "biological explanation" holds only for the earliest stages of human development and does not mean that a later sexual division of labor based on women's mothering is "natural." On the contrary, I will show that male dominance is a *historic* phenomenon in that it arose out of a biologically determined given situation and became a culturally created and enforced structure over time.

My synthesis does not mean to imply that all primitive societies are so organized as to prevent mothers from economic activity. We know from the study of past and present primitive societies that groups find various ways of structuring the division of labor for child-rearing so as to free mothers for a great variety of economic activities. Some mothers take their children with them over long distances; in other cases older children and old people act as child-tenders.[12] Clearly, the link between child-bearing and child-rearing for women is culturally determined and subject to societal manipulation. My point is to stress that the earliest sexual division of labor by which women *chose* occupations compatible with their mothering and child-raising activities were *functional*, hence acceptable to men and women alike.

Prolonged and helpless human infancy creates the strong mother-child bond. This socially necessary relationship is fortified by evolution during the earliest stages of humankind's development. Faced with new situations and changing environments, tribes and groups in which women did not mother well or which did not guard the health and survival of their nubile women, probably could not and did not survive. Or, seen another way, groups that accepted and institutionalized a functional sexual division of labor were more likely to survive.

We can only speculate on the personalities and self-perceptions of people living under such conditions as prevailed in the Neolithic. Necessity must have imposed restraints on men as well as on women. It took courage to leave the shelter of cave or hut to confront wild animals with primitive weapons, to roam far from home and risk encounters with potentially hostile neighboring tribes. Men and women must have developed the courage necessary for self-defense and the defense of the young. Because of their culture-bound tendency to focus on the activities of men, ethnographers have given us much information about the consequences for the development of self-confidence and competence in man the hunter. Basing herself on ethnographic evidence, Simone de Beauvoir has speculated that it was this early division of labor from which the inequality between the sexes springs and which has doomed woman to "immanence"—to the pursuit of daily, never-ending repetitious toil—as against the daring exploits of man, which lead him to "transcendence." Tool-making, inventions, the development of weapons are all described as deriving from man's activities in pursuit of subsistence.[13] But the psychological growth of women has received far less attention and has usually been described in terms befitting a modern housewife more than a member of a Stone Age tribe. Elise Boulding, in her overview of women's past, has synthesized anthropological scholarship to present a considerably different interpretation. Boulding sees in the Neolithic societies an egalitarian sharing of work, in which each sex developed appropriate skills and knowledge essential for group survival. She tells us that food gathering demanded elaborate knowledge of the ecology, of plants and trees and roots, their properties as food and as medicine. She describes primitive woman as guardian of the domestic fire, as the inventor of clay and woven vessels, by means of which the tribe's surpluses could be saved for lean times. She describes woman as having elicited from plants and trees and fruits the secrets of transforming their products into healing substances, into dyes and hemp and yarn and clothing. Woman knew how to transform the raw materials and dead animals into nurturing products. Her skills must have been as manifold as those of man and certainly as essential. Her knowledge was perhaps greater or at least as great as his; it is easy to imagine that it would have seemed to her quite sufficient. In the development of ritual and rites, of music and dance and poetry, she had as much of a part as he did. And yet she must have known herself responsible for life-giving and nurturance. Woman, in precivilized society, must have been man's equal and may well have felt herself to be his superior.[14]

Psychoanalytic literature and most recently Nancy Chodorow's feminist reinterpretation provide us with useful descriptions of the process by which gender is created out of the fact that women do the mothering of children. Let us see if these theories have validity for describing a process of historical development. Chodorow argues that "the relationship to the mother differs in systematic ways for boys and girls, beginning in the earliest periods."[15] Boys and girls learn to expect from women the infinite, accepting love of a mother, but they also associate with women their fears of powerlessness. In order to find their identity, boys develop themselves as other-than-the-mother; they identify with the father and turn away from emotional expression toward action in the world. Because it is women who do the mothering of children, Chodorow says:

> . . . growing girls come to define and experience themselves as continuous with others; their experience of self contains more flexible or permeable ego boundaries. Boys come to define themselves as more separate and distinct, with a greater sense of rigid ego boundaries and differentiation. The basic feminine sense of self is connected to the world, the basic masculine sense of self is separate.[16]

By the way in which their selfhood is defined against the nurturant mother, boys are prepared for participation in the public sphere. Girls, identifying with the mother and always keeping their close primary relationship with her, even as they transfer their love interest to men, are prepared for greater participation in "relational spheres." Gender-defined boys and girls are prepared "to assume the adult gender roles which situate women primarily within the sphere of reproduction in a sexually unequal society."[17]

Chodorow's sophisticated feminist reinterpretation of the Freudian explanation for the creation of gendered personalities is grounded in industrial Western society and its kinship and familial relations. It is doubtful that it is even applicable to people of color living within such societies, which should make us cautious about generalizing from it. Still, she makes a strong argument for the psychological undergirding upon which social relations and institutions rest. She and others argue convincingly that we must look to "motherhood" in patriarchal society, its structure and the relationships it engenders, if we wish to alter the relations of the sexes and end the subordination of women.[18]

I would speculate that the kind of personality formation Chodorow describes as the result of women mothering children in present-day industrialized societies did not occur in primitive societies of the Neolithic. Rather, women's mothering and nurturing activities, associated with their self-sufficiency in food gathering and their sense of competence in many, varied life-essential skills, must have been experienced by men and women as a source of strength and, probably, magic power. In some societies women jealously guarded their group "secrets," their magic, their knowledge of healing herbs. The anthropologist Lois Paul, reporting on a twentieth-century Guatemalan Indian village, says that the mystery and awe surrounding menstruation contributes in women "to a sense of participation in the mystic powers of the universe." Women manipulate men's fear that menstrual blood will threaten their virility by making of menstruation a symbolic weapon.[19]

In civilized society it is girls who have the greatest difficulty in ego formation. I would speculate that in primitive society that burden must have been on boys, whose fear and awe of the mother had to be transformed by collective action into identification with the male group. Whether mothers and their young children bonded with other such mother-child groups for their gathering and food-processing activities or whether men took the initiative in bringing young boys within their group must remain a matter of conjecture. The evidence from surviving primitive societies shows many different ways in which the sexual division of labor is structured into societal institutions, which bond young boys to males: sex-segregated preparation for initiation rites; membership in same-sex lodges and participation in same-sex rituals are just some of the examples. Inevitably, big-game hunting bands would have led to male bonding, which must have been greatly strengthened by warfare and the preparation necessary to turn boys into warriors. Just as effective mothering skills of women were essential to ensuring tribal survival and must have therefore been greatly appreciated, so were the hunting and warfare skills of men. One can easily postulate that those tribes which did not develop men skilled in warfare and defense eventually succumbed to those tribes that fostered these skills in their men. These evolutionary arguments have frequently been made, but I am here arguing also in favor of a psychological argument based on changing historical conditions. The ego formation of the individual male, which must have taken place within a context of fear, awe, and possibly dread of the female, must have led men to create social institutions to bolster their egos, strengthen their self-confidence, and validate their sense of worth.

Theorists have offered a variety of hypotheses to explain the rise of man, the warrior, and the propensity of men to create militaristic structures. These have ranged from biological explanations (men's higher testosterone levels and greater strength make them more aggressive) to psychological ones (men compensate for their inability to bear children by sexual dominance over women and by aggression toward other men). Freud saw the origin of male aggressiveness in the Oedipal rivalry of father and son for the love of the mother and postulated that men built civilization to compensate for the frustration of their sexual instincts in early childhood. Feminists, beginning with Simone de Beauvoir, have been greatly influenced by such ideas, which made it possible to explain patriarchy as caused either by male biology or by male psychology. Thus, Susan Brownmiller sees man's *ability* to rape women leading to their *propensity* to rape women and shows how this has led to male dominance over women and to male supremacy. Elizabeth Fisher ingeniously argued that the domestication of animals taught men their role in procreation and that the practice of the forced mating of animals led men to the idea of raping women. She claimed that the brutalization and violence connected with animal domestication led to men's sexual dominance and institutionalized aggression. More recently, Mary O'Brien built an elaborate explanation of the origin of male dominance on men's psychological need to compensate for their inability to bear children through the construction of institutions of dominance and, like Fisher, dated this "discovery" in the period of the discovery of animal domestication.[20]

These hypotheses, while they lead us in interesting directions, all suffer from the tendency to seek single-cause explanations, and those basing their arguments on the discoveries connected with animal husbandry are factually wrong. Animal husbandry was introduced, at least in the Near East, around 8000 B.C., and we have evidence of relatively egalitarian societies, such as in Çatal Hüyük, which practiced animal husbandry 2000 to 4000 years later. There cannot therefore be a causal connection. It seems to me far more likely that the development of intertribal warfare during periods of economic scarcity fostered the rise to power of men of military achievement. As we will discuss later, their greater prestige and standing may have increased their propensity to exercise authority over women and later over men of their own tribe. But these factors alone could not have been sufficient to explain the vast societal changes which occurred with the advent of sedentarism and agriculture. To understand these in all their complexity our theoretical model must now take into consideration the practice of the exchange of women.[21]

The "exchange of women," a phenomenon observed in tribal societies in many different areas of the world, has been identified by the anthropologist Claude Lévi-Strauss as the leading cause of female subordination. It may take many different forms, such as the forceful removal of women from their home tribe (bride stealing); ritual defloration or rape; negotiated marriages. It is always preceded by taboos on endogamy and by the indoctrination of women, from earliest childhood on, to an acceptance of their obligation to their kin to consent to such enforced marriages. Lévi-Strauss says:

> The total relationship of exchange which constitutes marriage is not established between a man and a woman . . . but between two groups of men, and the woman figures only as one of the objects in the exchange, not as one of the partners. . . . This remains true even when the girl's feelings are taken into consideration, as, moreover, is usually the case. In acquiescing to the proposed union, she precipitates or allows the exchange to take place; she cannot alter its nature.[22]

Lévi-Strauss reasons that in this process women are "reified"; they become dehumanized and are thought of more as things than as humans.

A number of feminist anthropologists have accepted this position and have elaborated on this theme. Matrilocality structures kinship in such a way that a man leaves his family of origin to reside with his wife or his wife's family. Patrilocality structures kinship in such a way that a woman must leave her family of birth and reside with her husband or her husband's family. This observed fact has led to the assumption that the kinship shift from matriliny to patriliny must be a significant turning point in the relation of the sexes, and must be coincident with the subordination of women. But how and why did such arrangements develop? We have already discussed the scenario by which men, possibly recently risen to power due to their warfare skills, coerced unwilling women. But why were women exchanged and not men? C. D. Darlington offers one explanation. He sees exogamy as a cultural innovation, which becomes accepted because it offers an evolutionary advantage. He postulates an instinctive desire in humans to control population to "optimum density" for a given environment. Tribes achieve this by sexual control, by rituals structuring males and females into appropriate sex roles, and by resorting to abortion, infanticide, and homosexuality when necessary. According to this essentially evolutionist reasoning, population control made control over female sexuality mandatory.[23]

There are other possible explanations: supposing grown men were exchanged among tribes, what would ensure their loyalty to the tribe to which they were traded? Men's bond to their offspring was not, then, strong enough to ensure their submission for the sake of their children. Men would be capable of violence against members of the strange tribe; with their experience in hunting and long distance travel they might easily escape and then return as warriors to seek vengeance. Women, on the other hand, would be more easily coerced, most likely by rape. Once married or mothers of children, they would give loyalty to their children and to their children's relatives and would thus make a potentially strong bond with the tribe of affiliation. This was, in fact, the way slavery developed historically, as we will see later. Once again, woman's biological function made her more readily adaptable for this new, culturally created role of pawn.

One might also postulate that not women but children of both sexes might have been used as pawns for the purpose of assuring intertribal peace, as they were frequently used in historical time among ruling elites. Possibly, the practice of the exchange of women got started that way. Children of both sexes were exchanged and on maturity married into the new tribe.

Boulding, always stressing women's "agency," assumes that it was women—in their function of keepers of the homeplace—who engaged in the necessary negotiations which led to intertribal coupling. Women develop cultural flexibility and sophistication by their intertribal linkage role. Women, removed from their own culture, straddle two cultures and learn the ways of both. The knowledge they derive from this may give them access to power and certainly to influence.[24]

I find Boulding's observations useful for reconstructing the gradual process by which women may have initiated or participated in establishing the exchange of women. In anthropological literature we have some examples of queens, in their role of head of state, acquiring many "wives" for whom they then arranged marriages which serve to increase the queen's wealth and influence.[25]

If boys and girls were exchanged as pawns and their offspring were incorporated into the tribe to which they had been given, clearly the tribe holding more girls than boys would increase in population more rapidly than the tribe accepting more boys. As long as children were a threat to the survival of the tribe or, at best, a liability, such distinctions would not be noticed or would not matter. But if, due to changes in the environment or in the tribal economy, children became an asset as potential labor power, one would expect the exchange of children of both sexes to give way to the exchange of women. The factors leading to this development are well explained, I believe, by Marxist structuralist anthropologists.

The process we are now discussing occurs at different times in different parts of the world; yet it shows regularity of causes and outcome. Approximately at the time when hunting/gathering or horticulture gives way to agriculture, kinship arrangements tend to shift from matriliny to patriliny, and private property develops. There is, as we have seen, disagreement about the sequence of events. Engels and those who follow him think that private property developed first, *causing* "the world historic overthrow of the female sex." Lévi-Strauss and Claude Meillassoux believe that it is the exchange of women through which private property is eventually created. Meillassoux offers a detailed description of the transition stage.

In hunting/gathering societies men, women, and children engage in production and consume what they produce. The social relations among them are unstable, unstructured, voluntary. There is no need for kinship structures or for structured exchanges among tribes. This conceptual model (for which it is somewhat difficult to find actual examples) gives way to a transition model, an intermediate state—horticultural society. The harvest, based on roots and cuttings, is unstable and subject to climatic variations. Their inability to preserve crops over several years makes people dependent on hunting, fishing, and gathering as food supplements. In this period, when matrilineal, matrilocal systems abound, group survival demands the demographic equalization of men and women. Meillassoux argues that women's biological vulnerability in childbirth led tribes to procure more women from other groups, and that this tendency toward the theft of women led to constant intertribal warfare. In the process, a warrior culture emerged. Another consequence of this theft of women is that the conquered women were protected by the men who had conquered them or by the entire conquering tribe. In the process, women were thought of as possessions, as things—they became reified—while men became the reifiers because they conquered and protected. Women's reproductive capacity is first recognized as a tribal resource, then, as ruling elites develop, it is acquired as the property of a particular kin group.

This occurs with the development of agriculture. The material conditions of grain agriculture demand group cohesiveness and continuity over time, thus strengthening household structure. In order to produce a harvest, workers of one production cycle are indebted for food and seeds to workers of a previous production cycle. Since the amount of food depends on the availability of labor, production becomes the chief concern. This has two consequences: it strengthens the influence of older males and it increases the tribes' incentive for acquiring more women. In the fully developed society based on plow agriculture, women and children are indispensable to the production process, which is cyclical and labor intensive. Children have now become an economic asset. At this stage tribes seek to acquire the reproductive potential of women, rather than women

themselves. Men do not produce babies directly; thus it is women, not men, who are exchanged. This practice becomes institutionalized in incest taboos and patrilocal marriage patterns. Elder males, who provide continuity in the knowledge pertaining to production, now mystify these "secrets" and wield power over the young men by controlling food, knowledge, and women. They control the exchange of women, enforce restrictions on their sexual behavior, and acquire private property in women. The young men must offer labor services to the old men for the privilege of gaining access to women. Under such circumstances women also become the spoil for the warriors, which encourages and reinforces the dominance of older men over the community. Finally, "women's world historic defeat" through the overthrow of matriliny and matrilocality is made possible, and it proves advantageous to the tribes who achieve it.

It should be noted that in Meillassoux's scheme the control over reproduction (women's sexuality) *precedes* the acquisition of private property. Thus, Meillassoux stands Engels on his head, a feat Marx performed for Hegel.

Meillassoux's work opens new vistas in the debate over origins, although feminist critics must object to his androcentric model, in which women figure only as passive victims.[26] We should also note that Meillassoux's model makes it clear that it is not women who are being reified, but women's reproductive capacity, yet he and other structuralist anthropologists continue to speak of the reification of women. The distinction is important, and we will be discussing it further. There are other questions his theory does not answer. How did elder men acquire control over agriculture? If our earlier speculations about social relations of the sexes in hunting/gathering tribes are correct, and if the generally accepted fact that it was women who developed horticulture is accurate, then one would expect it to be women who controlled the product of agricultural labor. But here other factors must enter our consideration.

Not all societies went through a horticultural stage. In many societies herding and animal husbandry alone or in conjunction with gathering activities preceded the development of agriculture. Animal husbandry was most likely developed by men. It was an occupation which led to the accumulation of surpluses in livestock, meat, or pelts. One would expect these to be accumulated by the men who generated them. Further, plow agriculture initially demanded the strength of men, and certainly was not an occupation pregnant women or lactating mothers would have chosen, except in an auxiliary fashion. Thus, agricultural economic practice reinforced men's control over surpluses, which may also have been acquired by conquest in intertribal warfare. Another possible factor contributing to the development of private property in the hands of males may be the asymmetrical allocation of leisure time. Horticultural activities are more productive than subsistence gathering and produce leisure time. But the allocation of leisure time is uneven: men benefit more from it than women, due to the fact that the food-preparation and child-rearing activities of women continue unrelieved. Thus, men presumably could employ their new leisure time to develop craft skills, initiate rituals to enhance their power and influence and manage surpluses. I do not wish to suggest either determinism or conscious manipulation here—quite the contrary. Things developed in certain ways, which then had certain consequences which neither men nor women intended. Nor could they have had an awareness of them, any more than modern men launching the brave new world of industrialization could have had an awareness of its consequences in regard to pollution and its impact on the ecology. By the time consciousness of the process and of its consequences could develop, it was too late, at least for women, to halt the process.

The Danish anthropologist Peter Aaby points out that Meillassoux's evidence was largely based on the European model, involving the interaction of horticultural activity and animal husbandry, and on examples taken from South American lowlands Indians. Aaby cites cases, such as those of Australian hunting tribes, where the control of women exists in the absence of horticultural activity. He next cites the case of the Iroquois, a society in which women were neither reified nor dominated, as an example of horticulturists who do not turn to male dominance. He argues that under ecologically favorable conditions it would be possible to maintain demographic balance within a tribe without resorting to the importation of women. It is not only production relations but also "ecology and social-biological reproduction which are the determining or critical factors. . . ."[27] Nevertheless, since all agricultural societies have reified women's and not men's reproductive capacity, one must conclude that such systems have an advantage

in regard to the expansion and appropriation of surpluses over systems based on complementarity between the sexes. In the latter systems there are no means available for forcing producers to increase production.

Neolithic tools were relatively simple, so that anyone could make them. Land was not a scarce resource. Thus, neither tools nor land offered any opportunity for appropriation. But in a situation in which ecological conditions and irregularities in biological reproduction threatened the survival of the group, people would search for more reproducers—that is, women. The appropriation of men, such as captives (which occurs only at a later stage), would simply not fill the needs of group survival. Thus, the first appropriation of private property consists of the appropriation of the labor of women as *reproducers*.[28]

Aaby concludes:

The connection between the reification of women on the one hand and the state and private property on the other is exactly the opposite of that posed by Engels and his followers. Without the reification of women as a historically given socio-structural feature, the origin of private property and the state will remain inexplicable.[29]

If we follow Aaby's argument, which I find persuasive, we must conclude that in the course of the agricultural revolution the exploitation of human labor and the sexual exploitation of women become inextricably linked.

The story of civilization is the story of men and women struggling up from necessity, from their helpless dependence on nature, to freedom and their partial mastery over nature. In this struggle women were longer confined to species-essential activities than men and were therefore more vulnerable to being disadvantaged. My argument sharply distinguishes between biological necessity, to which both men and women submitted and adapted, and culturally constructed customs and institutions, which forced women into subordinate roles. I have tried to show how it might have come to pass that women agreed to a sexual division of labor, which would eventually disadvantage them, without having been able to foresee the later consequences.

Freud's statement, which I discussed in a different context, that for women "anatomy is destiny" is wrong because it is ahistorical and reads the distant past into the present without making allowances for changes over time. Worse, this statement has been read as a prescription for present and future: not only is anatomy destiny for women, but it *should* be. What Freud should have said is that for women anatomy *once* was destiny. That statement is accurate and historical. What once was, no longer is so, and no longer must be nor should it be so.

Notes

[1]My concepts here are grounded in the approach first formulated by Mary Beard in *Woman as Force in History* (New York, 1946). I have elaborated on this theme throughout my historical work. See especially Gerda Lerner, *The Majority Finds Its Past: Placing Women in History* (New York, 1979), chaps. 10–12.

[2]See Paula Webster, "Matriarchy: A Vision of Power," in Rayna Reiter, *Toward an Anthropology of Women* (New York, 1975), pp. 141–56, for a thorough discussion of the psychological needs of contemporary women to have a vision of matriarchy in the distant past.

[3]Michelle Rosaldo, "The Use and Abuse of Anthropology: Reflections on Feminism and Cross-Cultural Understanding," *SIGNS*, vol. 5, no. 3 (Spring 1980), 393.

Rosaldo elaborates on these views in her unpublished paper, "Moral/Analytical Dilemmas Posed by the Intersection of Feminism and Social Science," prepared for the Conference on the Problem of Morality in the Social Sciences, Berkeley, March 1980. The following statement seems to me particularly apt: "By challenging the view that we are either victims of cruel social rule or the unconscious products of a natural world that (most unfortunately) demeans us, feminists have highlighted our need for theories that attend to the ways that actors shape their worlds; to interactions in which significance is conferred, and to the cultural and symbolic forms in terms of which expectations are organized, desires articulated, prizes conferred, and outcomes given meaning" (p. 18).

[4]See Nancy Makepeace Tanner, *On Becoming Human* (Cambridge, Eng., 1981), pp. 157–58. See also Nancy Tanner and Adrienne Zihlman, "Women in Evolution, Part I: Innovation and Selection in Human Origins," *SIGNS*, vol. 1, no. 3 (Spring 1976), 585–608.

[5]Ruth Bleier, *Science and Gender: A Critique of Biology and Its Theories on Women* (New York, 1984), chap. 3, esp. pp. 55 and 64–68. The same point is made in Clifford Geertz, "The Impact of the Concept of Culture on the Concept of Man," in *The Interpretation of Cultures* (New York, 1973), pp. 33–54.

[6]Ibid., pp. 144–45; quote, p. 145.

[7]Karen Horney, *Feminine Psychology* (New York, 1967); Clara Thompson, *On Women* (New York, 1964); Harry Stack Sullivan, *The Interpersonal Theory of Psychiatry* (New York, 1953), chaps. 4–12.

[8]Conversely, one of the first powers men institutionalized under patriarchy was the power of the male head of the family to decide which infants should live and which infants should die. This power must have been perceived as a victory of law over nature, for it went directly against nature and previous human experience.

[9]Information about prehistoric populations is unreliable and can be expressed only in rough quantitative terms. Cipolla thinks that "indirect evidence supports the view that Paleolithic populations had very high mortality. Since the species survived, we must admit that primitive man also had very high fertility. A study of 187 Neanderthal fossil remains reveals that one-third died before reaching the age of 20. An analysis of 22 fossil remains of the Asiatic Sinanthropus population revealed that 15 died when less than 14 years old, 3 before age 29 and 3 between the ages of 40 and 50." Carlo M. Cipolla, *The Economic History of World Population* (New York, 1962), pp. 85–86.

Lawrence Angel, "Neolithic Skeletons from Çatal Hüyük," *Anatolian Studies*, vol. 21 (1971), 77–98; quote on p. 80.

In contemporary hunting/gathering societies we find infant mortality rates as high as 60 percent in the first year. See F. Rose, "Australian Marriage, Land Owning Groups and Institutions," in R. B. Lee and Irven DeVore (eds.), *Man, the Hunter* (Chicago, 1968), p. 203.

[10]Cf. Karen Sacks, *Sisters and Wives: The Past and Future of Sexual Equality* (Urbana, 1982), chap. 2.

There is, additionally, the possibility that menstruation presented an obstacle to women's hunting, not because it physically incapacitated women, but because of the effect of the scent of blood on the animal. This possibility came to my attention during a recent trip to Alaska. The National Park Service in its leaflets to campers and backpackers advises menstruating women to stay away from the wilderness areas, since grizzly bears are attracted by the scent of blood.

[11]The anthropologist Marvin Harris argues to the contrary that "hunting is an intermittent activity and there is nothing to prevent lactating women from leaving their infants in someone else's care for a few hours once or twice a week." Harris argues that man's hunting specialty arose from his warfare training and that it is in men's warfare activities that we must seek the cause for male supremacy and sexism. Marvin Harris, "Why Men Dominate Women," *Columbia* (Summer 1978), 9–13, 39. It is unlikely and we have no evidence to show that organized warfare preceded big-game hunting, but I would argue that in any case both hunting and military activities would not be chosen by women for the reasons I have cited.

For a feminist interpretation of the same material, which makes no concessions to "biological determinism," see Bleier, *Science and Gender,* chaps. 5 and 6.

[12]Cf. M. Kay Martin and Barbara Voorhies, *Female of the Species* (New York, 1975), pp. 77–83; Sacks, *Sisters and Wives,* pp. 67–84; Ernestine Friedl, *Women and Men: An Anthropologist's View* (New York, 1975), pp. 8, 60–61.

[13]Simone de Beauvoir, *The Second Sex* (New York, 1953; 1974 reprint ed.).

[14]While there is no hard proof for these claims to the originality of woman's contributions, neither is there proof for man's inventiveness. Both claims rest on speculation. For our purposes, it is important to allow ourselves the freedom to speculate on woman's contributions as equals. The only danger in this exercise is that we may claim for our speculations, because they sound convincing and logical, that they represent actual proof. This is what men have done; we should not repeat that mistake.

Elise Boulding, *The Underside of History: A View of Women Through Time* (Boulder, Colo., 1976), chaps. 3 and 4. See also V. Gordon Childe, *Man Makes Himself* (New York, 1951), pp. 76–80.

For a somewhat similar synthesis based on later anthropological work see Tanner and Zihlman, and Sacks, cited above in notes 4 and 10.

[15]Nancy Chodorow, *The Reproduction of Mothering: Psychoanalysis and the Sociology of Gender* (Berkeley, 1978), p. 91.

[16]Ibid., p. 169. For a similar analysis based on different evidence see Carol Gilligan, *In a Different Voice: Psychological Theory and Women's Development* (Cambridge, Mass., 1982).

[17]Chodorow, *The Reproduction of Mothering,* pp. 170, 173.

[18]Adrienne Rich, in her analyses of "the institution of motherhood under patriarchy" and of "enforced heterosexuality," and Dorothy Dinnerstein, in her interpretation of Freudian thought, come to similar conclusions. See Adrienne Rich, *Of Woman Born: Motherhood As Experience and Institution* (New York, 1976); Adrienne Rich, "Compulsory Heterosexuality and Lesbian Existence," *SIGNS,* vol. 5, no. 4 (Summer 1980), 631–60; Dorothy Dinnerstein, *The Mermaid and the Minotaur: Sexual Arrangements and Human Malaise* (New York, 1977).

M. Rosaldo in "Dilemmas" (see note 3, above) criticizes these psychological theories because they slight or ignore the social context in which parenting takes place. Although I admire Chodorow's and Rich's work I agree with this criticism and add to it that in both cases generalizations applicable to middle-class people in industrialized nations are made to appear as universal.

[19]Lois Paul, "The Mastery of Work and the Mystery of Sex in a Guatemalan Village," in M. Z. Rosaldo and Louise Lamphere, *Woman, Culture and Society* (Stanford, 1974), pp. 297–99.

[20]Cf.: Sigmund Freud, *Civilization and Its Discontent* (New York, 1962); Susan Brownmiller, *Against Our Will: Men, Women and Rape* (New York, 1975); Elizabeth Fisher, *Woman's Creation, Sexual Evolution and the Shaping of Society* (Garden City, N.Y., 1979), pp. 190, 195.

[21]My thinking on the subject of the rise and consequences of male warfare were influenced by Marvin Harris, "Why Men Dominate Women," and by a stimulating exchange of letters and dialogue with Virginia Brodine.

[22]Claude Lévi-Strauss, *The Elementary Structures of Kinship* (Boston, 1969), p. 115.

For a contemporary illustration of the workings of this process and of the ways the girl indeed "cannot alter its nature," see Nancy Lurie (ed.), *Mountain Wolf Woman, Sister of Crashing Thunder* (Ann Arbor, 1966), pp. 29–30.

[23]C. D. Darlington, *The Evolution of Man and Society* (New York, 1969), p. 59.

[24]Boulding, *Underside,* chap. 6.

[25]See, for example, the case of the Lovedu in Sacks, *Sisters and Wives,* chap. 5.

[26]Cf. Maxine Molyneux, "Androcentrism in Marxist Anthropology," *Critique of Anthropology,* vol. 3, nos. 9–10 (Winter 1977), 55–81.

[27]Peter Aaby, "Engels and Women," *Critique of Anthropology,* vol. 3, nos. 9–10 (Winter 1977), 39–43.

[28]Ibid., p. 44. Aaby's explanation allows also for the case, inexplicable by Meillassoux's thesis, of societies which progress directly from relatively egalitarian sexual division of labor to patriarchal dominance by way of extended war activities. See, for example, the development of Aztec society described in June Nash, "The Aztecs and the Ideology of Male Dominance," *SIGNS,* vol. 4, no. 2 (Winter 1978), 349–62. For Inca society, see Irene Silverblatt, "Andean Women in the Inca Empire," *Feminist Studies,* vol. 4, no. 3 (Oct. 1978), 37–61.

[29]Aaby, "Engels on Women," p. 47. It may be noted that Aaby's argument sustains Darlington's evolutionary thesis. See p. 47, above.

Woman the Gatherer: Male Bias in Anthropology

Sally Slocum

Sally Slocum, born in Indiana in 1939 and educated at the University of California and the University of Colorado, is an anthropologist with a wide array of skills and experience. A stained-glass craftswoman, a professional dancer, and a participant in archeological surveys, she has taught courses in physical anthropology, paleontology, and ethnology, among other subjects. Slocum has also made major contributions to research and teaching in women's studies.

Crystallizing, then rejecting the male bias in anthropology that allowed theories like man-the-hunter to develop uncritically, Slocum here proffers a different perspective: Central to human community and social organization is the sharing of food that for many reasons must precede organized hunting. Such sharing must have originated in the mother-infant relationship and then enlarged into wider bonding. This concept might prove a far more fruitful explanatory factor than the notions of hunting, weaponry, and male bonding.

From Sally Slocum, "Woman the Gatherer: Male Bias in Anthropology," in *Toward an Anthropology of Women*, ed. Rayna Reiter (New York: Monthly Review Press, 1975). Copyright © 1975 by Rayna R. Reiter. Reprinted by permission of Monthly Review Press.

THE PERSPECTIVE OF WOMEN IS, IN MANY WAYS, equally foreign to an anthropology that has been developed and pursued primarily by males. There is a strong male bias in the questions asked, and the interpretations given. This bias has hindered the full development of our discipline as "the study of the human animal" (I don't want to call it "the study of man" for reasons that will become evident). I am going to demonstrate the Western male bias by reexamining the matter of evolution of Homo sapiens from our nonhuman primate ancestors. In particular, the concept of "Man the Hunter" as developed by Sherwood Washburn and C. Lancaster (1968) and others is my focus. This critique is offered in hopes of transcending the male bias that limits our knowledge by limiting the questions we ask.

Though male bias could be shown in other areas, hominid evolution is particularly convenient for my purpose because it involves speculations and inferences from a rather small amount of data. In such a case, hidden assumptions and premises that lie behind the speculations and inferences are more easily demonstrated. Male bias exists not only in the ways in which the scanty data are interpreted, but in the very language used. All too often the word "man" is used in such an ambiguous fashion that it is impossible to decide whether it refers to males or to the human species in general, including both males and females. In fact, one frequently is led to suspect that in the minds of many anthropologists, "man," supposedly meaning the human species, is actually synonymous with "males."

This ambiguous use of language is particularly evident in the writing that surrounds the concept of Man the Hunter. Washburn and Lancaster make it clear that it is specifically males who hunt, that hunting is much more than simply an economic activity, and that most of the characteristics which we think of as specifically human can be causally related to hunting. They tell us that hunting is a whole pattern of activity and way of life: "The biology, psychology, and customs that separate us from the apes—all these we owe to the hunters of time past" (1968:303). If this line of reasoning is followed to its logical conclusion, one must agree with Jane Kephart when she says:

> Since only males hunt, and the psychology of the species was set by hunting, we are forced to conclude that females are scarcely human, that is, do not have built-in the basic psychology of the species: to kill and hunt and ultimately to kill others of the same species. The argument implies built-in aggression in human males, as well as the assumed passivity of human females and their exclusion from the mainstream of human development. (1970:5)

To support their argument that hunting is important to human males, Washburn and Lancaster point to the fact that many modern males still hunt, though it is no longer economically necessary. I could point out that many modern males play golf, play the violin, or tend gardens: these, as well as hunting, are things their culture teaches them. Using a "survival" as evidence to demonstrate an important fact of cultural evolution can be accorded no more validity when proposed by a modern anthropologist than when proposed by Tylor.

Regardless of its status as a survival, hunting, by implication as well as direct statement, is pictured as a male activity to the exclusion of females. This activity, on which we are told depends the psychology, biology, and customs of our species, is strictly male. A theory that leaves out half the human species is unbalanced. The theory of Man the Hunter is not only unbalanced; it leads to the conclusion that the basic human adaptation was the desire of males to hunt and kill. This not only gives too much importance to aggression, which is after all only one factor of human life, but it derives culture from killing. I am going to suggest a less biased reading of the evidence, which gives a more valid and logical picture of human evolution, and at the same time a more hopeful one. First I will note the evidence, discuss the more traditional reading of it, and then offer an alternative reconstruction.

The data we have to work from are a combination of fossil and archeological materials, knowledge of living nonhuman primates, and knowledge of living humans. Since we assume that the protohominid ancestors of Homo sapiens developed in a continuous fashion from a base of characteristics similar to those of living nonhuman primates, the most important facts seem to be the ways in which humans differ from nonhuman primates, and the ways in which we are similar. The differences are as follows: longer gestation period; more difficult birth; neoteny, in that human infants are less well developed at birth; long period of infant dependency; absence of body hair; year-round sexual receptivity of females, resulting in the possibility of bearing a second infant while the first is still at the breast or still dependent; erect bipedalism; possession of a large and complex brain that makes possible the creation of elaborate symbolic systems, languages, and cultures, and also results in most behavior being under cortical control; food sharing; and finally, living in families. (For the purposes of this paper I define families as follows: a situation where each individual has defined responsibilities and obligations to a specific set of others of both sexes and various ages. I use this definition because, among humans, the family is a *social* unit, regardless of any biological or genetic relationship which may or may not exist among its members.)

In addition to the many well-known close physiological resemblances, we share with nonhuman primates the following characteristics: living in social groups; close mother-infant bonds; affectional relationships; a large capacity for learning and a related paucity of innate behaviors; ability to take part in dominance hierarchies; a rather complex nonsymbolic communication system which can handle with considerable subtlety such information as the mood and emotional state of the individual, and the attitude and status of each individual toward the other members of the social group.

The fossil and archeological evidence consists of various bones labeled Ramapithecus, Australopithecus, Homo habilis, Homo erectus, etc.; and artifacts such as stone tools representing various cultural traditions, evidence of use of fire, etc. From this evidence we can make reasonable inferences about diet, posture and locomotion, and changes in the brain as shown by increased cranial capacity, ability to make tools, and other evidences of cultural creation. Since we assume that complexity of material culture requires language, we infer the beginnings of language somewhere between Australopithecus and Homo erectus.

Given this data, the speculative reconstruction begins. As I was taught anthropology, the story goes something like this. Obscure selection pressures pushed the protohominid in the direction of erect bipedalism—perhaps the advantages of freeing the hands for food carrying or for tool use. Freeing the hands allowed more manipulation of the environment in the direction of tools for gathering and hunting food. Through a hand-eye-brain feedback process, coordination, efficiency, and skill were increased. The new behavior was adaptive, and selection pressure pushed the protohominid further along the same lines of development. Diet changed as the increase in skill allowed the addition of more animal protein. Larger brains were selected for, making possible transmission of information concerning tool making, and organizing cooperative hunting. It is assumed that as increased brain size was selected for, so also was neoteny—immaturity of infants at birth with a corresponding increase in their period of dependency, allowing more time for learning at the same time as this learning became necessary through the further reduction of instinctual behaviors and their replacement by symbolically invented ones.

Here is where one may discover a large logical gap. From the difficult-to-explain beginning trends toward neoteny and increased brain size, the story jumps to Man the Hunter. The statement is made that the females were more burdened with dependent infants and could not follow the rigorous hunt. Therefore they stayed at a "home base," gathering what food they could, while the males developed cooperative hunting techniques, increased their communicative and organizational skills through hunting, and brought the meat back to the dependent females and young. Incest prohibitions, marriage, and the family (so the story goes) grew out of the need to eliminate competition between males for females. A pattern developed of a male hunter becoming the main support of "his" dependent females and young (in other words, the development of the nuclear family for no apparent reason). Thus the peculiarly human social and emotional bonds can be traced to the hunter bringing back the food to share. Hunting, according to Washburn and Lancaster, involved "cooperation among males, planning, knowledge of many species and large areas, and technical

skill" (1968:296). They even profess to discover the beginnings of art in the weapons of the hunter. They point out that the symmetrical Acheulian biface tools are the earliest beautiful man-made objects. Though we don't know what these tools were used for, they argue somewhat tautologically that the symmetry indicates they may have been swung, because symmetry only makes a difference when irregularities might lead to deviations in the line of flight. "It may well be that it was the attempt to produce efficient high-speed weapons that first produced beautiful, symmetrical objects" (1968:298).

So, while the males were out hunting, developing all their skills, learning to cooperate, inventing language, inventing art, creating tools and weapons, the poor dependent females were sitting back at the home base having one child after another (many of them dying in the process), and waiting for the males to bring home the bacon. While this reconstruction is certainly ingenious, it gives one the decided impression that only half the species—the male half—did any evolving. In addition to containing a number of logical gaps, the argument becomes somewhat doubtful in the light of modern knowledge of genetics and primate behavior.

The skills usually spoken of as being necessary to, or developed through, hunting are things like coordination, endurance, good vision, and the ability to plan, communicate, and cooperate. I have heard of no evidence to indicate that these skills are either carried on the Y chromosome, or are triggered into existence by the influence of the Y chromosome. In fact, on just about any test we can design (psychological, aptitude, intelligence, etc.) males and females score just about the same. The variation is on an individual, not a sex, basis.

Every human individual gets half its genes from a male and half from a female; genes sort randomly. It is possible for a female to end up with all her genes from male ancestors, and for a male to end up with all his genes from female ancestors. The logic of the hunting argument would have us believe that all the selection pressure was on the males, leaving the females simply as drags on the species. The rapid increase in brain size and complexity was thus due entirely to half the species; the main function of the female half was to suffer and die in the attempt to give birth to their large-brained male infants. An unbiased reading of the evidence indicates there was selection pressure on both sexes, and that hunting was not in fact the basic adaptation of the species from which flowed all the traits we think of as specifically human. Hunting does not deserve the primary place it has been given in the reconstruction of human evolution, as I will demonstrate by offering the following alternate version.

Picture the primate band: each individual gathers its own food, and the major enduring relationship is the mother-infant bond. It is in similar circumstances that we imagine the evolving protohominids. We don't know what started them in the direction of neoteny and increased brain size, but once begun the trends would prove adaptive. To explain the shift from the primate individual gathering to human food sharing, we cannot simply jump to hunting. Hunting cannot explain its own origin. It is much more logical to assume that as the period of infant dependency began to lengthen, *the mothers would begin to increase the scope of their gathering to provide food for their still-dependent infants.* The already strong primate mother-infant bond would begin to extend over a longer time period, increasing the depth and scope of social relationships, and giving rise to the first sharing of food.

It is an example of male bias to picture these females with young as totally or even mainly dependent on males for food. Among modern hunter-gatherers, even in the marginal environments where most live, the females can usually gather enough to support themselves and their families. In these groups gathering provides the major portion of the diet, and there is no reason to assume that this was not also the case in the Pliocene or early Pleistocene. In the modern groups women and children both gather and hunt small animals, though they usually do not go on the longer hunts. So, we can assume a group of evolving protohominids, gathering and perhaps beginning to hunt small animals, with the mothers gathering quite efficiently both for themselves and for their offspring.

It is equally biased, and quite unreasonable, to assume an early or rapid development of a pattern in which one male was responsible for "his" female(s) and young. In most primate groups when a female comes into estrus she initiates coitus or signals her readiness by presenting. The idea that a male would have much voice in "choosing" a female, or maintain any sort of individual, long-term control over her or her offspring, is surely a modern invention which could have had no place in early hominid life. (Sexual control over females through rape or the threat of rape seems to be a modern human invention. Primate females are not raped because they are willing throughout estrus, and primate males appear not to attempt coitus at other times, regardless of physiological ability.) In fact, there seems to me no reason for suggesting the development of male-female adult pair-bonding until much later. Long-term monogamy is a fairly rare pattern even among modern humans—I think it is a peculiarly Western male bias to suppose its existence in protohuman society. An argument has been made (by Morris, 1967, and others) that traces the development of male-female pair-bonding to the shift of sexual characteristics to the front of the body, the importance of the face in communication, and the development of face-to-face coitus. This argument is insufficient in the first place because of the assumption that face-to-face coitus is the "normal," "natural," or even the most common position among humans (historical evidence casts grave doubt on this assumption). It is much more probable that the coitus position was invented *after* pair-bonding had developed for other reasons.

Rather than adult male-female sexual pairs, a temporary consort-type relationship is much more logical in hominid evolution. It is even a more accurate description of the modern human pattern: the most dominant males (chief, headman, brave warrior, good hunter, etc.), mate with the most dominant females (in estrus, young and beautiful, fertile, rich, etc.), for varying periods of time. Changing sexual partners is frequent and common. We have no way of knowing when females began to be fertile year-round, but this change is not a necessary condition for the development of families. We need not bring in any notion of paternity, or the development of male-female pairs, or any sort of marriage in order to account for either families or food sharing.

The lengthening period of infant dependency would have strengthened and deepened the mother-infant bond; the earliest families would have consisted of *females and their children.* In such groups, over time, the sibling bond would have increased in importance also. The most universal, and presumably oldest, form of incest prohibition is between mother and son. There are indications of such avoidance even among modern monkeys. It could develop logically from the mother-children family: as the period of infant dependency lengthened, and the age of sexual maturity advanced, a mother might no longer be capable of childbearing when her son reached maturity. Another factor which may have operated is the situation found in many primates today where only the most dominant males have access to fertile females. Thus a young son, even after reaching sexual maturity, would still have to spend time working his way up the male hierarchy before gaining access to females. The length of time it would take him increases the possibility that his mother would no longer be fertile.

Food sharing and the family developed from the mother-infant bond. The techniques of hunting large animals were probably much later developments, after the mother-children family pattern was established. When hunting did begin, and the adult males brought back food to share, the most likely recipients would be first their mothers, and second their siblings. In other words, a hunter would share food *not* with a wife or sexual partner, but with those who had shared food with him: his mother and siblings.

It is frequently suggested or implied that the first tools were, in fact, the weapons of the hunters. Modern humans have become so accustomed to the thought of tools and weapons that it is easy for us to imagine the first manlike creature who picked up a stone or club. However, since we don't really know what the early stone tools such as hand-axes were used for, it is equally probable that they were not weapons at all, but rather *aids in gathering*. We know that gathering was important long before much animal protein was added to the diet, and continued to be important. Bones, sticks, and hand-axes could be used for digging up tubers or roots, or to pulverize tough vegetable matter for easier eating. If, however, instead of thinking in terms of tools and weapons, we think in terms of *cultural inventions*, a new aspect is presented. I suggest that two of the *earliest and most important* cultural inventions were containers to hold the products of gathering, and some sort of sling or net to carry babies. The latter in particular must have been extremely important with the loss of body hair and the increasing immaturity of neonates, who could not cling and had less and less to cling to. Plenty of material was available—vines, hides, human hair. If the infant could be securely fastened to the mother's body, she could go about her tasks much more efficiently. Once a technique for carrying babies was developed, it could be extended to the idea of carrying food, and eventually to other sorts of cultural inventions—choppers and grinders for food preparation, and even weapons. Among modern hunter-gatherers, regardless of the poverty of their material culture, food carriers and baby carriers are always important items in their equipment.

A major point in the Man the Hunter argument is that cooperative hunting among males demanded more skill in social organization and communication, and thus provided selection pressure for increased brain size. I suggest that longer periods of infant dependency, more difficult births, and longer gestation periods also demanded more skills in social organization and communication—creating selective pressure for increased brain size without looking to hunting as an explanation. The need to organize for feeding after weaning, learning to handle the more complex social-emotional bonds that were developing, the new skills and cultural inventions surrounding more extensive gathering—all would demand larger brains. Too much attention has been given to the skills required by hunting, and too little to the skills required for gathering and the raising of dependent young. The techniques required for efficient gathering include location and identification of plant varieties, seasonal and geographical knowledge, containers for carrying the food, and tools for its preparation. Among modern hunting-gathering groups this knowledge is an extremely complex, well-developed, and important part of their cultural equipment. Caring for a curious, energetic, but still dependent human infant is difficult and demanding. Not only must the infant be watched, it must be taught the customs, dangers, and knowledge of its group. For the early hominids, as their cultural equipment and symbolic communication increased, the job of training the young would demand more skill. Selection pressure for better brains came from many directions.

Much has been made of the argument that cooperation among males demanded by hunting acted as a force to reduce competition for females. I suggest that competition for females has been greatly exaggerated. It could easily have been handled in the usual way for primates—according to male status relationships already worked out—and need not be pictured as particularly violent or extreme. The seeds of male cooperation already exist in primates when they act to protect the band from predators. Such dangers may well have increased with a shift to savannah living, and the longer dependency of infants.

If biological roots are sought to explain the greater aggressiveness of males, it would be more fruitful to look toward their function as protectors, rather than any supposedly basic hunting adaptation. The only division of labor that regularly exists in primate groups is the females caring for infants and the males protecting the group from predators. The possibilities for both cooperation and aggression in males lies in this protective function.

The emphasis on hunting as a prime moving factor in hominid evolution distorts the data. It is simply too big a jump to go from the primate individual gathering pattern to a hominid cooperative hunting-sharing pattern without some intervening changes. Cooperative hunting of big game animals could only have developed *after* the trends toward neoteny and increased brain size had begun. Big-game hunting becomes a more logical development when it is viewed as growing out of a complex of changes which included sharing the products of gathering among mothers and children, deepening social bonds over time, increase in brain size, and the beginnings of cultural invention for purposes such as baby carrying, food carrying, and food preparation. Such hunting not only needed the prior development of some skills in social organization and communication; it probably also had to await the development of the "home base." It is difficult to imagine that most or all of the adult primate males in a group would go off on a hunting expedition, leaving the females and young exposed to the danger of predators, without some way of communicating to arrange for their defense, or at least a way of saying, "Don't worry, we'll be back in two days." Until that degree of communicative skill developed, we must assume either that the whole band traveled *and hunted* together, or that the males simply did not go off on large cooperative hunts.

The development of cooperative hunting requires, as a prior condition, an increase in brain size. Once such a trend is established, hunting skills would take part in a feedback process of selection for better brains just as would other cultural inventions and developments such as gathering skills. By itself, hunting fails to explain any part of human evolution and fails to explain itself.

Anthropology has always rested on the assumption that the mark of our species is our ability to *symbol*, to bring into existence forms of behavior and interaction, and material tools with which to adjust and control the environment. To explain human nature as evolving from the desire of males to hunt and kill is to negate most of anthropology. Our species survived and adapted through the invention of *culture*, of which hunting is simply a part. It is often stated that hunting *must* be viewed as the "natural" species' adaptation because it lasted as long as it did, nine-tenths of all human history. However:

> *Man the Hunter lasted as long as "he" did from no natural propensity toward hunting any more than toward computer programming or violin playing or nuclear warfare, but because that was what the historical circumstances allowed. We ignore the first premise of our science if we fail to admit that "man" is no more natural a hunter than "he" is naturally a golfer, for after symboling became possible our species left forever the ecological niche of the necessity of any one adaptation, and made all adaptations possible for ourselves. (Kephart, 1970:23)*

That the concept of Man the Hunter influenced anthropology for as long as it did is a reflection of male bias in the discipline. This bias can be seen in the tendency to equate "man," "human," and "male"; to look at culture almost entirely from a male point of view; to search for examples of the behavior of males and assume that this is sufficient for explanation, ignoring almost totally the female half of the species; and to filter this male bias through the "ideal" modern Western pattern of one male supporting a dependent wife and minor children.

The basis of any discipline is not the answers it gets, but the questions it asks. As an exercise in the anthropology of knowledge, this paper stems from asking a simple question: what were the females doing while the males were out hunting? It was only possible for me to ask this question after I had become politically conscious of myself as a woman. Such is the prestige of males in our society that a woman, in anthropology or any other profession, can only gain respect or be attended to if she deals with questions deemed important by men. Though there have been women anthropologists for years, it is rare to be able to discern any difference between their work and that of male anthropologists. Learning to be an anthropologist has involved learning to think from a male perspective, so it should not be surprising that women have asked the same kinds of questions as men. But political consciousness, whether among women, blacks, American Indians, or any other group, leads to reexamination and reevaluation of taken-for-granted assumptions. It is a difficult process, challenging the conventional wisdom, and this paper is simply a beginning. The male bias in anthropology that I have illustrated here is just as real as the white bias, the middle-class bias, and the academic bias that exist in the discipline. It is our task, as anthropologists, to create a "study of the human species" in spite of, or perhaps because of, or maybe even by means of, our individual biases and unique perspectives.

References

Kephart, Jane
　1970 "Primitive Woman as Nigger, or, The Origin of the Human Family as Viewed Through the Role of Women." M.A. dissertation, University of Maryland.

Washburn, Sherwood, and Lancaster, C.
　1968 "The Evolution of Hunting." In *Man the Hunter*, edited by R. B. Lee and Irven DeVore. Chicago: Aldine.

II

Sexism Realized: Women's Lives in Patriarchy

We have been foreigners not only to the fortresses of political power but also to those citadels in which thought processes have been spun out. . . . Women are beginning to recognize that the value system that has been thrust upon us by the various cultural institutions of patriarchy has amounted to a kind of gang rape of minds as well as of bodies.

–MARY DALY, *Beyond God the Father*

SO FAR WE HAVE BEEN EXAMINING THE CON-sciousness of patriarchy, the abstract concepts, the myths, beliefs, and values that underlie the sexual caste system. We now turn to the material expression of that consciousness and the effects it has on the lives of women. Sexism is built into almost everything that women do or that is done to us. It is lodged in the most personal facets of our lives as well as the most public. In the follow-ing chapters, we will explore the outward reali-zations of sexist consciousness, the patterns and structures, institutionalized and informal, that give female lives their particular color and shape.

Chapter 6 focuses on the part of women's lives ordinarily called the private sphere—personal relationships, marriage and unmarriage, love, romance, and sex. We shall look at women's life-styles and at the way we perceive them.

Chapter 7 directs attention to the institutional sphere, to work and economics, to women's legal status, and to the quality and character of wom-en's participation in public policymaking, all of which are intricately interrelated.

Finally, Chapter 8 treats the psychoperceptual undergirding of the entire system, the intellec-tual modes through which patriarchy formulates, maintains, and solidifies sexist consciousness.

6

Women's Personal Lives: The Effects of Sexism on Self and Relationships

The Lady in the Space

EARLIER WE LOOKED AT THE MODELS CONSTRUCTED for women in patriarchy and examined woman's designated "place," but we have not yet explored the impact these constructions have for the woman within. How do these forces shape women's internal space—our private lives, the way we live on the most intimate level with ourselves and others?

We women are simply people, human beings, with the needs, dreams, and desires all people are wont to experience. How we relate to others on a one-to-one basis; how we relate to ourselves, our bodies, and our feelings; and how we relate to the physical space around us are the concrete realities that make up private lives on a daily basis. But certain aspects of our lives as *women*, particularly women in a sexist world, profoundly alter and color those concrete human realities. It is in the tension between the two, our experience as people and our experience as women—and in the conflicts that arise between these divergent states—that we live out our realities and inhabit our private space. Let us turn,

then, to closely examine the constructions of our private, personal lives.

A Story

Once upon a time there lived a very beautiful little girl named Cinderella (Snow White, Sleeping Beauty, Rapunzel . . .). Her nature was as lovely as her face. Gentle, kind, accepting, modest, obedient, and sweet, she never complained or became peevish, though she suffered greatly at the hands of circumstance and cruel people. Because she was good natured and uncomplaining, because she asked for little and gave a great deal, her beauty shone, and a handsome prince came along, fell in love with her, and took her away to his castle, where the pair lived happily ever after. The story always ends at that point.

This is a story that in its many tellings is dear to the hearts of most little girls, who hear it practically in the crib, read and repeat it endlessly, playact and live it vicariously, and dream of its realization in their own lives. It tells us a great deal about the way women are expected to be and the way we learn to see our existence.

The story teaches us that we are born to be chosen, admired, and sought after and that to succeed in this goal of being chosen follows upon certain attributes: physical beauty, "good nature" (willingness to take unwarranted abuse), modesty, self-effacement, piety, vulnerability, suffering, and good luck. We learn that even if we do not have these attributes or, for that matter, dislike them, we had better appear to have them. For the essence of the story is the fact of *being chosen* rather than choosing, of being noticed for our "feminine qualities," of gaining success from endurance and patience rather than initiative, which belongs to the man. The story goes beyond the facade of his asking and her assenting straight to the unvarnished truth: It is the prince who picks what he wants; our chief responsibility is to make ourselves as worthy of his interest as we can. Our only appropriate direct action lies in the orchestrating of an effect. The story teaches us, through extending the principles of passivity, that it is not through our own efforts that we are to be happy (or safe or comfortable) but rather through the intervention of a powerful protector who alone can bestow status and security on us. He alone has the power to make us happy, for clearly we are (or ought to be) unable to do that for ourselves.

It is the element in these tales of relinquishing initiative as well as the power to make ourselves happy or safe that is so potent a factor in molding the approved feminine character. We come to believe not only that we are too weak and small to take care of ourselves, that we are and must be dependent, but also that it is wrong to be any other way. Self-assertive women like Cinderella's stepmother and sisters are portrayed as wicked and ugly, and they come to bad ends. These and other stories fix in our minds that women who take for themselves, by themselves, are selfish and wicked, whereas admirable females earn for themselves through renunciation what they do not take directly.

The attitude born of all this is a sense that only through intercession of another can we *be made* happy, that we are to receive the positive goods in life only from another in return for beauty of face, passivity of nature, and for services rendered. Most of us do not learn until much later that in giving up the right of, as well as the responsibility for, framing our own fortunes, we place ourselves at the mercy of circumstance and of anyone who may wish to exercise the power we have abrogated. We do not hear

until later, after the pain it brings, that we have bartered our souls for the illusion of protection.

The Matter of Marriage

Enter Mr. Right (alias the "prince" or the "one"). He will "come along," we will "fall in love," we will know instinctively that we belong together—forever. We will marry, have children, and live happily ever after. The End.

That fantasy, for women who marry, for women who do not, and for those who unmarry, exercises incredible power on how we live our lives.

The Myth

During the early 1960s, in a course I was teaching in introductory philosophy, I used to ask the students to begin the term's work with an essay entitled, "What I Want Out of Life." Those were the years before I had acquired what now is known as a feminist consciousness, and the results surprised me. With great regularity, the papers of the men in the class differed categorically from the women's. The men's papers generally followed a familiar theme: I want to finish school, get a good job, have a good income, a nice place to live, friends, fun things to do. Many said they wanted to be happy; a few remembered to hope for health. The women, too, said they wanted to be happy. They wanted to finish school, work for a while, fall in love, get married. Finis. Did the men, I asked, mean to get married? Oh sure, they said. That was understood: It came along the way. For the women, it *was* the way. It was as though the women looked into the future only so far as the "magic event." Then the Cinderella tale took over: "happily ever after."

It is most telling, I think, that the favorite female fairy tales end with the wedding, and all else is subsumed under the heading of "ever-after." It is as though these stories teach us that our whole existence is to be wrapped up in the quest for a mate; that once we acquire the mate, all else is decided; that after the wedding, definition of what follows is irrelevant because it is indistinguishable from any other ever-after; that what follows really has little importance because we have already done the all-important; that life with the prince in his castle is the only happily-ever-after that is possible for us, there being no viable alternatives; that all the other aspects of our lives, public as well as private, are determined in large measure by the overwhelming pervasiveness of the wifely estate.

As children listening to stories and as young women creating our own, how closely do we really look at ever-after land? We believe we will be loved and appreciated, sharing a husband's life, supporting him as he encourages and helps us, fulfilling ourselves in the haven of our world. But is this so?

Even today, when the terms of marriage, families, and relationships are shifting so dramatically, this vision of "happily-ever-after" persists. More than half of all first marriages end in divorce.[1] Young women are painfully aware of that statistic; it frightens them. Yet 90 percent of young people will marry,[2] and three out of four divorced women remarry,[3] half within four years.[4] What is more, divorced people are even more likely to remarry than those who have never married,[5] a fact cynically called the "triumph of hope over experience."[6] For even those few who do not or are not married, the dream often becomes a nightmare search—"maybe tomorrow I'll find the right one." In the heterosexual community, and even to some extent in the gay community, the image of the perfect mate in the perfect eternal relationship provides the model against which most measure their personal lives.

Promise and Disillusionment

The traditional American mystique of marriage promises women a roster of assurances.

- You will have someone to make you happy.
- You will be loved and cherished.
- You will be cared for and protected from all the dangers of the world.
- You will have sexual intimacy and satisfaction.
- You will have someone to understand and support you.
- You will have companionship and safety from loneliness.
- You will have a father for your children.
- You will be socially secure as part of a couple.
- You will have a place in this world, a meaning, and you will love it.

- You will gain status and prestige as someone's chosen wife. You will not be an "old maid."
- You will be financially secure.
- You will be happy.

That's the promise.

Feminists cast a more objective glance at the promise. "Demystifying" marriage, we have drawn up a roster of our own: the facts and data, the untruths and half-truths, the traps and games, the dissimulations and dangers of the traditional marriage mystique. It is not that feminism is in principle incompatible with marriage. (Although some feminists believe that it is, others do not, and many feminists marry.) Rather, it is that traditional marriage arrangements and presuppositions are often destructive to women in the most concrete way, and feminists, discovering these realities, seek to both warn and redress.

The Case Against Traditional Marriage

Following Emile Durkheim, Jessie Bernard, a feminist sociologist, commented that "marriage is not the same for women as for men; it is not nearly as good."[7] Following extensive research, Bernard concluded that although men ridicule married life and display contempt for it, they benefit considerably from marriage whereas women lose a great deal. Several studies, for example, found that married men have greater emotional health than single men, suffer depression and anxiety less frequently than their single counterparts, and advance faster professionally and socially and have better incomes than single men. Furthermore, the remarriage rate for divorced men and widowers is very high; they remarry more often and sooner than either women or never-married men.[8] Apparently they know what is good for them.

Married women, on the other hand, experience greater depression, anxiety, and fear than single women, are more apt to show severe neurotic symptoms, and have lower self-esteem than single women or married men. What is interesting as well, as Tavris and Offir reported, is that homemakers are even more apt to display these problems than working wives, and single men in any category (never married, divorced, or widowed) compared to single women are more likely to suffer from psychological difficulties.[9]

After all the ball-and-chain jokes, all the tavern mythology about carefree bachelors and manipulative women, and all the masculist assertions that marriage is a terrific deal for women and a disaster for men, are not these findings a revelation? Yet, they should really come as no surprise. In so many ways—in terms of emotional exchange, economics, work, independence, freedom and mobility, autonomy and authenticity—traditional marriage offers to women and men a double standard, and women's part of that standard is truly the less advantaged.

Conjugal Obligation

In patriarchy, a man and a woman marry, each taking on certain responsibilities. He agrees to love, honor, cherish, and provide her with the physical necessities of life. She agrees to love and to obey (a term now out of vogue in modern marriage ceremonies, although the power relationship in which it originates is not), and she takes on a whole composite of responsibilities that are diverse, unspecified, and generally lumped under the heading of wife or housewife. Though it might superficially appear an even exchange, actually, it is rather an extraordinary exchange, and an enigmatic one, for at base it differs radically from what it appears or is reputed to be. Overladen with social mythology and expectation, marriage is rarely seen for what it is, and the parties concerned often interpret and perceive it very differently.

In the patriarchal barroom myth, marriage is a trap for men. A man in the excellent condition of bachelorhood, free and unencumbered, encounters a lady, wily and manipulative, who tricks him into "falling in love." He becomes so besotted with her that he loses his good sense and marries her. The door slams shut; he will find out only later that he has been entrapped and is now the captive of a "ball and chain" who, for the rest of his life, will nag him, keep tabs on him, spend his money, and bring him difficulties. The lady, on the other hand, has a "good deal," having snared a meal ticket and a respectable place in life. Actually, of course, both women and men know the myth to be false, yet both are unclear as to just how false because in

some form and to some degree, the myth is believed (or else Jessie Bernard's findings would not surprise us). Because of this, it exerts considerable pressure on the attitudes and behaviors of husbands and wives.

Let us take a more objective, "demystified" look at traditional marriage. In patriarchy, a man and a woman marry; they strike a bargain, make an exchange (not fully understood at the time of marriage), and each takes on certain responsibilities and privileges. The bare bones of the agreement require that the husband provide the physical necessities of life through his income—shelter, food, clothing, and so on—and that in return for these the wife provides care of the home and family. But what do these respective duties, obligations, and privileges actually entail for each?

The patriarchal husband's responsibilities are explicit: He must work or in some fashion secure financial maintenance of the home and family. He must act as "head of household," making policy decisions for the family and bearing responsibility for them. He is to protect his wife and children from danger, whatever that might be in their circumstances, and guide and mold their behavior and character. Although the law does not specify the quantity or quality of the provisions a man must secure for his family, the culture does, for according to the imperatives of Mars, a man proves his worthiness through success in the marketplace (the modern hunt). Society—and often his wife or children—may judge a man ill if he does not provide according to the standard of living decreed by the media. There is then an intense pressure on husbands to provide always bigger and better, and this pressure may be both burdensome and unremitting.

A different aspect to the prescription to "provide" is often overlooked in discussions about masculine responsibility. "Provision" means work. It means one must have a job, of whatever nature, and must remain regularly at a job in order to obtain all one needs. Husbands frequently point out that they work very hard "to get you what you need" and therefore should be loved, respected, served, and accorded the right to make family decisions. What they do not say is that they would work in any event, married or unmarried, for one still needs to eat, dress, and have shelter. They do not say that they work for more than income, that even routine or laborious jobs provide a satisfaction in earning, and that life without work outside the house would drive them mad. They do not say that a tremendous satisfaction comes in looking about one's family home and noting that whatever is there, whatever its condition, has been provided by one's efforts and that because of those efforts, one is autonomous and worthy. We need not denigrate the value and importance of giving or the pressure of provision. We need only consider that such labor carries with it a highly positive and meaningful reward that we must not overlook in evaluating its claims to compensation. This satisfying experience of autonomy and self-worth that comes from providing is the reason many women give for returning to work outside the home or even for leaving "comfortable" marriages.

The husband's duty to protect is enigmatic in the twentieth century. Certainly protection from physical danger is impossible in such a complex society. That work is now largely passed to public institutions, and the remainder of the responsibility is equally shared by husband and wife. In terms of children's safety, the mother usually accomplishes the lion's share of that work, typically taking almost total charge of her offspring. Even when she is not with them, it is she who worries and protects through vigilance with regard to a ride to school, an adequate babysitter, a competent physician, dental appointments, birthday parties, and countless other matters. It is she, too, who "guides"; fathers could hardly be expected to provide much guidance in the average twelve minutes a day they spend with their children![10]

Head of household, then, becomes an interesting concept. If it does not mean protection, guidance, or modeling, what it means in essence is power, control over household and family in return for breadwinning, which is neither all sacrifice nor peculiar to marriage. The head of household also has certain real privileges that he enjoys both as husband and as male: considerably more freedom, autonomy, and service—the service, by and large, provided by his wife.

One of the most extraordinary features of being a traditional wife in patriarchy is the unification of certain aspects of the role—the married woman *is* a housewife; she doesn't *do* housewifing. She is not simply a mate, a coworker, and partner in the busi-

ness of life; she is a certain identity, one that carries with it a particular (mixed) status, a "place," and some identifiable and rather unchanging tasks. Upon marriage, the patriarchal wife yields her own individual identity (a fact attested to by her change of name), subsumes it under her husband's, and commits her life—her time, interests, and energies—to the needs of the family group, husband and offspring. Regardless of whatever else a wife may do—work in the marketplace or community affairs or pursue a creative career—patriarchy defines as her first priorities her duties as wife/housewife. Should she choose not to keep house, she is no less the housewife; she is simply a housewife not doing her job.

A husband barters some of his income and freedom for the kind of services and satisfactions a wife provides. What does a wife barter? For the financial security (now not a clear return for the more than 54 percent of all married women who work outside the home[11]), for the status of being married, for love and companionship, women take on almost limitless labors of service to their home and family. Whereas a husband takes on a "job" involving specifiable hours, tasks, and rewards, a wife takes on a lifestyle. Her tasks are not wholly specified but instead comprise the satisfaction of almost every kind of physical and emotional need her husband and children voice as well as the many more services required for smooth maintenance of family life. Her labor is limited by neither time nor personal need. She is expected to perform at whatever hour needs arise—breakfast at whatever time the family must rise, dinner when they return home. Were this job to be advertised outside the home, it might carry the warning that the job makes tremendous demands on one's personal time, including split shifts and a great deal of overtime.

Unlike her husband, whose skills and education define the kind of work he will do, the wife is assigned work that is elemental and undifferentiated by skill. College educated or illiterate, the common denominator is housework—sweeping floors, washing clothes, scouring ovens, cleaning toilets, washing dishes, dumping garbage—and she who performs such menial tasks earns for herself the status incumbent upon them: low. She is "a housewife." The tasks themselves are no joy. However glorified in the media, housework in the real world is boring, ugly, tiresome, repetitive, unsatisfying, and lonely work. Factory or office work may be dull and tiresome, but there are people around; one can see and be seen, talk and interact, change scenes. One of the worst aspects of housewifing is the awful sense of being locked up with the sameness day after day or, if the woman has a job, evening after evening.

Labor to maintain the house itself is not the wife's only responsibility. Added to her major responsibility for the care of the home, she is also expected to manage the inhabitants of the home, and this really remarkable assignment makes the contemporary wife's role what it is. Most wives have nearly complete responsibility for the care of their children, not only to feed, clothe, and teach them but also to monitor the quality of their school experience; organize their religious, social, and health needs; provide for child care when parents are not at home; and so on. More to the point, the mother is held responsible for the emotional needs of her children, and it is left very unclear at which point needs become demands. Given current child-centered sensitivities to the warnings of doctors Freud and Spock, no matter how tired or time-pressed they are, many mothers are extremely hesitant to deny their children any demands on their time, privacy, or strength without suffering considerable worry and guilt. In essence, the endless demands of parenting are not shared, and most mothers—working or not—function for the most part as single parents. Thus, though both men and women have families, women are responsible for the family life.

Care of the inhabitants does not end with children, however, for a wife is also expected to care for her husband in much the same way as she cares for their offspring. She is to feed him, cook his favorite dishes, buy and maintain his clothes, arrange his home to suit him, pack his suitcase when he goes on a trip, arrange entertainment for him on Saturday night, entertain his business friends, arrange doctor's appointments for him (even against his will), listen to him, and support and "understand" him. In some circles a wife is even responsible for the spiritual health of her husband. Priests in some parishes advise that it is sinful for a wife to deny her husband sex lest he be led into temptation outside the home, and Jews believe it to be a wife's duty to provide a living environment for her husband in which he may successfully seek blessings from God.

Whereas a husband's contributions to family maintenance are "public" or communal, much of the wife's work is frequently personal or private, and it is this aspect of her labor, added to the rest, that renders it a form of service (in the sense of a servant). The husband may mow a lawn, repair a door, or dump garbage, tasks pertaining to the household collectively, but he would not be expected to mend his wife's slacks or gauge and replenish her toiletries. In the traditional household, wives render to their husbands a plethora of personal services; the reverse is rarely true.

Wives do not receive a salary for their work, although their husbands share their incomes with them, and sometimes generously. But a great deal of difference exists between receiving an established and agreed-on sum of money in return for one's labor and receiving money as a "gift," that is, at the giver's choosing. Although wife labor is extensive, time-consuming, often taxing, and absolutely necessary for the household, and although husbands could not advance professionally nor be half so productive without it, wives who do not work outside the home are not perceived as earning; hence they are considered dependents. Both institutions and individuals regard the money they receive from their husbands as a grant. Therefore, they must endure the disadvantages and indignities of pensioners. Dependent wives are cautioned as to how they are to spend their *husband's* money; they are to express gratitude for sums earmarked for their own personal use (such as clothing), and they must wait until their husbands decide it is time to replace the washer. To put aside a savings of their own out of "granted" money is perceived as deceptive and is rarely done, and wives can find themselves trapped in intolerable marriages by finances.

The cruelest jab in the wife's situation (and one not often recognized) is derogating this labor to the status of nonwork. Because our society (unlike some others) affords no economic recognition of housework (such as social security or compensation), because the work is accomplished at home in the service of the family rather than in the public marketplace, and because "women's work" is always devalued and demeaned, housework is perceived and treated as nonwork, as nonproductive with all the accompanying stigmas and trials. "Does your wife work?" one might ask. "No, she stays home." "Do you work?" one woman asks another. "No, I'm just a housewife." Even women, housewives themselves, must be reminded that, paid or not, recognized or not, *homemaking is a job*.

The effects of classifying homemaking as nonwork are far-reaching and powerful. As stated, the full-time housewife or the wife who works as a "supplement" is reduced to a state of financial dependence, which in turn diminishes her power in the family, her own self-image, and her standing in society. The problems, however, go much farther. By allowing herself to be dependent on her husband's income, by accruing little formally recognized history of labor (such as social security benefits or a pension) that could compensate her in later years, and by collecting no savings of her own, a wife makes her future financial security subject to the continuance of her marriage or her husband's goodwill. By reducing herself in the labor force and by not developing or enhancing marketable skills, she further erodes the possibility of financial independence in or out of marriage.

Consider a woman who, after twenty years as a traditional wife, finds herself in an intolerable marriage situation. With dependent children, no savings, a poor-paying job or none at all, and limited marketable skills, what can she do? She may remain trapped and unhappy, or she may leave. Divorced, she then suffers not only the loss of companionship and social status; she must also expect a terribly diminished standard of living, severe strains of economic survival with little experience to withstand them, and no career or professional interests to sustain her. Furthermore, alimony and child support are largely inadequate or nonexistent.[12]

The circumstances of a wife within such a traditional marriage are difficult enough, but in 1989, fewer than 16 percent of families with minor children conformed to this traditional "Leave It to Beaver" model; by 1995, 78 percent of all mothers are expected to be employed.[13] Just as the traditional homemaker often finds herself in a double bind, so the wife who opts for an alternative to dependence by working outside the home may also find herself severely hampered by the nonwork status of homemaking. As of 1988, more than 56.5 percent of all married women were doing paid work outside the home. Over 72.5 percent had children between six and seventeen years of age, and 54.5 percent had children under three, with the number steadily rising.[14] Such women share the responsibilities of economic maintenance with their husbands. Do they commonly receive a proportional increase in status, power, privilege, and autonomy? Do they, in return, receive from their husbands equal participation in homemaking efforts? In this country, as in nearly every other in the world, the answer is usually no.

Regardless of circumstances, husbands rarely take equal responsibility for maintaining the household. Research shows that working women spend 2½ to 3 times as many hours at housework as their husbands do, and men married to women who work spend the same amount of time on housework as men married to full-time homemakers.[15] Furthermore, in the two-career family, fathers still spend less time with their children than their wives do and even *less* time intensely interacting with them at the end of the day than in traditional families![16] Does time men spend in housework come out of the time they would be spending with their children? Do women have that option?

In the case of the wife working only at home, the logic goes this way: If homemaking is nonwork, it is not a job with visible, recognized, and acknowledged demands. The homemaker has no right, therefore, to expect her husband to share in household tasks, for she is "not working," and he is! How can she legitimately expect him to add her responsibilities to his burden? The same logic holds even when the wife is publicly employed. Such a wife actually carries two jobs, a salaried and a nonsalaried one, but since homemaking is not recognized as "work," her two-job status is also not recognized. She merely has certain wifely or womanly "responsibilities" at home, and the husband's contributions are usually treated as a gift or favors rather than a rightful responsibility (He "helps." He "babysits.").

We are familiar with the media images of the (double)-working wife: She must "organize her time" very carefully in order to meet all her responsibilities and not "neglect" her family. Smiling all the while, taking Geritol to maintain her health and her sex appeal, she hurries home from work to get supper on and spends her evenings and weekends cleaning, washing, using Downy (to get noticed); somehow she also finds time to use sexy perfume and carry on all that follows.

Two jobs, however, are more than taxing. Parenting, cleaning, cooking, shopping, and then working for a salary as well take their toll: Physically, psychologically, and creatively, one runs down. It is a truism in the business and professional world that one cannot produce at peak performance if one is cut in too many ways. For this reason, most institutions have formal prohibitions against moonlighting. Yet moonlighting is a way of life for most married working women. Worse, it is never even clear which job is *the* job and which is moonlighting because lots of women never stop to realize that they're handling two full jobs simultaneously.

But many women are becoming sensitive to their circumstances. They have begun to recognize that it is a cultural construction and not a cosmic imperative that burdens them with homemaking. They have begun to expect their mates to share the work at home. Many husbands have come to recognize the unfairness, too, and they are moving (however grudgingly) toward carrying *some* of the load. Full sharing is painfully rare.

The Emotional Economy

If the fairy-tale image of marriage promises women anything, it promises abundant satisfaction of emotional needs. When the prince arrives, he is supposed to bring with him love everlasting, constant attention, affection, devotion, understanding, companionship, appreciation, and, most of all, the desire and wherewithal to make his princess happy. To be sure, a great deal of this fantasy is wrongheaded and ill-conceived. No one can make another person happy, however much he or she might want to, and no one can provide another with complete solace and total understanding. Nor can or should anyone shower another with constant attention and concern. Yet, people still can and do care for one another, need one another, and share feelings. Sociologists tend to agree that marriage as an institution survives today primarily because it is seen as providing the major source and vehicle for these kinds of interactions.

Love, as we know, is a complicated and enigmatic concept. Love is different things to different people in varied circumstances, and it is often experienced and expressed in very individual ways. It is not so enduring, dependable, and consistent as it has been reputed to be, nor can it conquer all or justify every kind of action. Yet it would be wrong to lapse into cynicism. However difficult it is to understand or define, however changeable and distorted by myth, love as a concept persists in the human vocabulary.

Ample evidence shows that human beings cannot thrive without the kind of succor provided by what is generally called love and that life can be arid and unwholesome without some measure of love's joy.

Certainly we can glean the intense personal contact that either is or begets love from a variety of relationships, several in kind and in number. But our culture rarely affords us an environment in which such relationships can grow, and we are discouraged rather than encouraged to participate in the kind of encounter crucial to love. Marriage (and living arrangements like marriage), however, do include an expectation that the partners will have at least this—a sharing of communication, concern, and mutual support and an exchange of sensitivity, compassion, and nurture. We can term such sharing and mutuality the emotional economy of the relationship.

For various reasons, all lodged in patriarchy, it is in this exchange that women often experience their greatest disappointment in the traditional relationship. The emotional economy, like the work economy, is out of balance, and once more the woman typically occupies the disadvantaged position. Although women usually express a greater interest in love and emotional exchange and although women are thought to need and want more open expressions of affection, in the patriarchal marriage, women are apt to receive considerably less personal affection than their partners. Despite or because of the high priority women often place on the love relationship, women are more apt to love then be loved, support rather than be supported, nurture rather than be nurtured, even though they appear to seek the exchanges more than men do. The sexist role and character definitions of Venus and Mars decree that women should become more overtly and intricately bound up with the behaviors and feelings of interpersonal contact. Ultimately, women become very good at loving, but for the patriarchal male it is a clumsy business at best.

In 1987, Shere Hite published the most recent of her three "Hite Reports," *Women and Love,*[17] in which she analyzed the questionnaires of forty-five hundred women on their love relationships. Ninety-eight percent of the heterosexual women reported that they needed and wanted fundamental improvements in their relationships.[18] They wondered why love started off so well and became painful so soon. They suffered, they said, because they felt that they worked so much harder at making their relationships work than their men did, because they gave so much more than they received, because it was so difficult to maintain their own identity and power in the context of a relationship. Some of the problems? Their men were so distant, unable or unwilling to talk about feelings; they received little emotional support or understanding from their men; their men wanted always to "star," to be first and most important. The women were lonely in their relationships. Said Hite:

> What most women are trying to describe here is an entrenched, largely unrecognized system of emotional discrimination—a system whose subterranean roots are entwined so deeply in the psyche of the culture that it underlies our entire social structure. . . .

> The emotional contract in relationships . . . is the core of a relationship—the implicit understanding between two people about how each should behave in a relationship, how each expects the other to express her or his emotions, how each interprets the emotional outcries and silences of the other. These tender and often brief moments are the lifeblood of the emotional closeness between two people. . . ." But this emotional interaction is troubled by an unclear, demeaning, and gender-oriented set of subliminal attitudes, assumptions interwoven into our ideas of who men and women are. We believe that women are "loving and giving" and men are "doers," that one has more rights than the other.

> Thus the emotional contract contains psychological stereotypes which put women at a disadvantage, and give men preferential treatment, superior psychological status that is built into the system, into the tiniest crevices of our minds. It is the fundamental cause of the problems between women and men in love relationships. . . .

> The signs of this unequal emotional "contract"—the unspoken assumptions, the word choices—are thrown at women every day, as we have seen, in a thousand ways. Indeed, these patterns are so subtle and accepted, coloring everything, that they make discussion of the "problem" almost impossible, and arguments seem circular. As one woman puts it, "There are no words, to begin with, and when you do use words, they are viewed by men through a reversing telescope (when they are heard at all)—taking what I said for something totally not what I meant.". . .

Lack of emotional equality is the fundamental stumbling block to love in relationships.[19]

A good deal of controversy exists in the women's movement over whether women do or do not have any special ability for love and feeling. Sexists have used the contention that we have such a unique ability to exclude us from any activity *not* based on serving, any activity *not* based on feeling. But such a division is more patriarchal than rational; the idea that one who is capable of emotion and sensitivity is incapable of discipline and rational judgment is absurd. We need not fear to consider that women's experience in the world may have developed in us a particular ability to live and act more lovingly, more considerately. It bespeaks no *undesirable* softness (again, the martial belief that "softness" is contemptible), no lack of intellect or strength.

It appears that women are very much concerned with the human and the loving, and that most of us do exercise an immense ability to understand, nurture, and support, a fact of which we may be duly proud. A problem arises, however, with our concern for caring, for in patriarchy our commitment and ability to love can get distorted. Since love and service are prescribed as women's only allowable activities, they are forced out of both perspective and proportion. Loving can become disproportionate in at least two ways: first, in that loving and serving others is not balanced with loving and caring for oneself; and second, in that the activities and interests of love are not balanced by other kinds of interests and activities, and indeed often crowd out other sources of pleasure, satisfaction, and meaning. Such a situation is destructive, creating an overdependence on the exchanges of love (or some distorted facsimile) and an inability to draw on other resources.

Romance and love are important to men but so are a lot of other things. Woman's prescribed role as subordinate and her prescribed passive, dependent, and emotional character are at the heart of the saying that love is central for women but peripheral for men; that for women love is abstract, emotional, and spiritual, whereas for men it is concrete, physical, and sexual. In relation to love, women and men move in two different realities, and there is the rub.

Let us look at how the traditional relationship turns the differences in male and female loving into the asymmetry of its emotional economy. Women and men both need love and nurture, although their expression of that need and the way they relate to it may differ. But given traditional female-male role definitions, men are far more likely than women to have that need well satisfied. Women, trained as we are for caring and service, often treat fulfilling another's needs not only as an obligation, a task, or responsibility but also as a desirable activity, something we want to do. We are in a sense "aggressive" about taking the initiative in caring: ferreting out, anticipating, or pursuing the emotional needs of those we love. We want to "help." Just as we might to a child, we often say to a mate (although not necessarily in these words), "Let me take care of you, let me 'mother' you."

But who is mothering Mother? Trained to see unrestricted tenderness as effeminate, uncomfortable with feeling in general and need in particular, the traditional male is not usually adept at that aspect of the caring and emotional exchange termed *psychological nurturance*. For men in patriarchy, love is not to be expressed directly, emotionally, on a one-to-one basis, but rather indirectly through providing, modeling, and caring for the family's material wellbeing. Such indirect provision can be a form of expressing love, but in the traditional division of labor, it is a form of caring in which the woman once again makes equal, if not greater, contributions. Men work, but women work, too, only their work is not defined, recognized, or compensated. Furthermore, in terms of service and love, a woman's work is considerably more direct, personal, and expressive. She not only prepares food but prepares his favorite food; not only cleans clothes but maintains his personal items in an intimate and personal way; not only listens but hears.

It is often said that men express their most intimate feelings through their sexual lovemaking, and this may be true. One cannot presume to know how often or in what degree this is true. Yet in journals, conferences, workshops, and consciousness-raising groups, women of all ages have revealed that they very often sense a lack of emotional contact with their mates even in sex. It appears that although women and men are both capable of separating love and sex, women are considerably less apt to do so, particularly with their mates.

Yet if there were no qualifications, if it were true that a man typically expresses his love equally, though differently, through provision and through sex, it would still not change the fact of his wife's not receiving adequate emotional support and nurturance. The need for intimate contact in the realm of feeling and understanding is profound and important; few can do well without it. The fact is that women report less of this kind of contact, less attention, less direct concern. Great imbalance characterizes the emotional economy of the patriarchal couple.

After-Marriage: Divorce and Widowhood

Few consider as they "walk down the aisle" that marriages end either in divorce or in death. Since in our culture one is never free of a once-married state, but instead is always perceived as a "formerly married person," when a marriage ends a period of after-marriage follows. This is a time with its own particular character, a time that ends in either remarriage or death. More women than men experience this time since women are more frequently widowed than men, more men than women remarry after the death of a spouse or divorce, and men remarry sooner. Women also experience this time very differently than men do since social attitudes and judgments toward the unmarried, social rules and options (such as dating behavior or age expectations), and economic environments are frequently determined by sex.

The character and quality of one's life and experience in after-marriage are largely determined by the life decisions the partners made earlier. Quite naturally, the seeds sown in marriage continue to be harvested after its end. As we might expect, the woman of a traditional marriage who has built her life around and patterned her behaviors after the prescribed patriarchal model—truncated and distorted as it is—is apt to find her condition similarly truncated and distorted after marriage. Traditional imperatives, even for the average working wife, fix a woman's whole identity within her marriage and make her dependent on it in a very profound way; the more traditional the arrangements of the relationship, the more profound the dependence. Passivity, economic or psychological dependence on one's mate, withdrawal from confrontation with public life, and discouragement from developing resources outside of the couple do not bode well for life; discouragement from developing resources outside of the couple is not a good prognosis for life outside marriage, that is, after-marriage. To live life alone well and happily requires personal strength, preparation, and experience, none of which women in patriarchal marriage are encouraged to develop. Hence the wife as ex-wife or widow is likely to suffer tremendously at her marriage's end and for some time thereafter, even if she grows considerably, for she has lost valuable time.

Although divorce and widowhood have some fundamental and important differences, in patriarchy these experiences have much in common. A widow and a divorcee are both once-were wives, having had similar roles and identity prescriptions in their former lives. They both are perceived and treated as half-beings, anomalies in a universe of couples. They are generally unprepared both economically and psychologically for life alone; and they frequently have the same burdens—children to raise alone, hostility or tolerant contempt from outsiders, and increased responsibilities with decreased resources.

The Feminine Role in Traditional Marriage: A Setup

Generally in our culture a woman marries young (although the *average* marriage age for women is slowly getting older). Before or without setting career questions, before becoming independent or self-sufficient, she moves out of her parents' home, or away from her roommates, into the home she shares with her husband. Directly she settles into the wife's role and lifestyle, forming her adult character, norms, and expectations and determining her future through decisions made within the economic and social structures of her marriage.

The Economic Setup

Whether wives work only at home or work both at home and in the marketplace, as is most common, patriarchal marriage will likely cause her to be economically disadvantaged after marriage. If she works only at home, parenting and housekeeping for a large portion of her life is her primary occupation. In such work at home, she accrues neither savings of her own nor salary nor social security benefits nor workmen's compensation nor pension. She develops no special marketable skills, no experience, no work history, no seniority. In the job mar-

ket, she's worth little or nothing; in fact, the longer she has maintained her home posture, the less she is worth outside.

A traditional wife may work outside the home, especially if her income is absolutely necessary for the family's subsistence, but her salary is generally treated as a supplement to her husband's. Since in the patriarchal context neither mate perceives the wife's job as primary, neither pays much attention to the quality of the job situation, its potential for growth or advancement, its benefits and status in the work world. Even professionally trained women often make decisions that subordinate their careers to the needs of their husbands and families. In one study of dual-career families, for example, where both husbands and wives were working as managers in large corporations, it was found that wives accommodated their careers to their husbands even where both "professed an 'egalitarian' ideology":[20]

All of the couples in O'Reilly's sample professed an "egalitarian" ideology. Adherence to such an ideology was prerequisite to participating in the interview. Yet, despite the presence of a philosophy that affirmed the importance of both careers, their behavior as couples clearly furthered husbands' careers at the expense of the wives'. O'Reilly attributes this outcome to a web of factors operating both at home and at work.

The web begins with Steihm's[21] observations about "invidious intimacy." Even among highly educated men and women, marriage choices are made such that the man is older, often taller, and perceived to be "smarter." The edge in age, even if the men and women are in the same occupation with the same opportunities (which is frequently not the case), gives the husband more work experience and hence higher earnings than his wife has. If, in addition, the couple believes that the husband's opportunities for promotion are greater than the wife's, which is frequently a correct perception, the couple will seek to maximize their joint income by furthering the career of the husband.

O'Reilly found two behavior patterns that favored husbands' careers over wives'. First, in determining whether or not to accept promotions that required geographical moves, couples made decisions that favored husbands' careers, even at the expense of their wives' careers.[22] Second, the pattern of labor division in the home favored the husband's career, especially in families where there were children. Even when husbands participated in housework and child care, wives typically fulfilled the time- and energy-consuming role of home manager and also did more of those home tasks that tended to conflict with work.

Like the couples themselves, the corporation that employed at least one member of O'Reilly's couples professed an egalitarian ideology. Equal opportunity policies had long ago abolished formal barriers to women's career progress. But career structures and informal barriers remained. And of course, the more the wife's career progress was slowed, the more "sense" it made for the joining-maximizing couple to favor the husband's career.[23]

Because patriarchy prescribes that the husband's job is more important than the wife's, wives must quit work to follow transferred husbands; wives are the ones who stay home from work to care for sick babies or mate; they accommodate their work around the needs of their families. Such expectations and behaviors do not make for professionalism or the rewards that follow upon it. In essence, during marriage, a husband builds a career, a future, marketable skills, experience, and seniority. But a wife who invests her time, energy, and service in promoting her husband's financial future—mistakenly believing it to be her own—is impoverishing her own earning potential and independent economic security.

A majority of wives work as procurement officers for their households. They shop not only for groceries but also for furniture, household goods, and private and personal needs. For this reason, they often pay the bills, keep the checkbook and the records, and do the banking. Yet despite claims to the contrary, wives do not "control" the money in the family or the nation, except as delegated. They execute policy; they do not form it. Patriarchal wives may make such decisions as which toilet paper to buy or where to purchase their vegetables (hence their manipulation by advertising media), but they must wait for their husbands to outline the larger budget—how *much* money to spend on food or clothes or mortgage and when to replace an appliance. The intricacies of insurance, long-range planning and budgeting, and investments are generally left to the male in the traditional household.

Furthermore, although the wife may sign the check or the credit card, she usually does so under her husband's name. Until recently wives could not even have their own charge accounts, and the homemaker without salary still cannot. The result—the wife may accrue little credit of her own; it goes to Mr. and Mrs. X (or, more succinctly, to Mr. X). The bottom line in the economics of the traditional marriage is that when the marriage ends, the wife's "bottom line" is apt to be substantially lower than her husband's.

The Social Setup

One of the really delightful aspects of marriage, when it goes well, is the friendly companionship; the opportunity to talk and do things with one another, interact with others in a kind of community, have company and sharing in work and play. And yet this very positive facet of the relationship is a two-edged sword; unbalanced by the functioning existence of two separate realms of being for each partner, "togetherness" can be a trap. In patriarchy, the wife usually lacks any separate realm of being.

A traditional wife's lifestyle, made up of the concrete details of her day, is built around her husband. She sleeps with him, rises with him, eats breakfast and dinner with him. She plans her day around him, work and play. Rarely does a traditional wife socialize in mixed company without her husband. Outside of occasional all-female events, socializing occurs in couples: one invites the Smiths and the Joneses for dinner or goes out for an evening with the Browns, two by two. It would be unusual for the typical wife to go to a party by herself, unescorted at least by another couple. She is not likely to travel any distance alone or to vacation or play or dine out or go to a theatre by herself—or even with another woman except in rare instances. A traditional married friend of mine laughingly reported that she and her husband were "joined at the hip." In traditional marriage, coupledom reigns.

Such a "togetherness" marriage does not encourage women to develop companionship or buddy relationships with other women or even with men, and it inhibits the growth of a life outside of marriage. In her workplace or home during the day, with the children and/or her husband in the evening, with couples on the weekend, the traditional wife develops a social existence that is based almost entirely within marriage and the world of couples.

A patriarchal wife's social status and identity, too, are solidly grounded within her marriage. She is John's wife—John the mechanic, John whose last name (and therefore hers) is Smith, John whose social status (and therefore hers) is X. Her friends are friends of the marriage, attached to the couple collectively, rarely to either individually. These things are more true for a woman in marriage than for a man. It is she who takes on his name and the social standing of his work, she who must live where his work is, she who entertains his business friends or working buddies. It is she, moreover, with all her responsibilities at home, with reduced opportunity for people contact, with little interest in her own job or economic future, who builds her life around the world of her husband, whatever its character and potential.

Feminists often quip, "In marriage two become one, and he's the one!" In the traditional household, this is very nearly so. Imagine the extent of the trauma to a person completely absorbed in a marriage if that union should end.

Denouement: The Experience of After-Marriage

Typically, the patriarchal wife has put all her eggs into one basket. She has built her life around her marriage. How does she find herself at that marriage's end?

The Divorcee

The longer and more traditionally a woman has lived as a patriarchal wife, the more her whole being has adapted itself to one kind of existence, and the harder her transition into and the experience of a new life will be. A great proportion of divorces occur well into marriage, after ten, twenty, even thirty years.

The divorced patriarchal wife is apt to find herself financially strapped. She has probably been left with the house (after all, there are three children who must be sheltered), but maintenance of that home is likely to pose problems. Mortgage payments are usually too high for her salary if she has one (between 60 and 80 percent of former wives do not receive child support or alimony), and she is usually unable to deal with repairs herself. Because she is inexperienced, she must hire maintenance people, usually at exorbitant rates. Perhaps she has been awarded the family car. But how long will it be

before it too begins to fail, and how able will she be to replace it and maintain payments?

A job is in order for the former full-time homemaker. But what is she trained for or ready for? Who wants her after ten or twenty years outside the job market? What salary is she likely to earn? If she worked during her marriage at an "auxiliary" job, how likely is her income to supply the entire needs of her family now if it was only an auxiliary earlier? If her children are young, she must bear the burden of full-time work and full-time single parenting in the intensely difficult emotional environment of after-marriage. If she is one of the minority of women who receive some financial contributions from their ex-husbands, she must bear the burden of continued dependence, fretful interactions with him, and all the problems that follow from that circumstance.

Responsibility lies heavily on her life. She must meet her children's psychological, financial, and material needs. She must work as sole earner—an alien experience—while maintaining the semblance of a stable home and at the same time dealing with her own sense of loss and anxiety. Altogether too little time, too little money, and too little peace is available to her.

Loneliness closes in. Inexperienced at cultivating friendships, at seeking out and encouraging camaraderie and uncomfortable with the different modes of interaction in single life, she finds at the same time that her old friends are dropping away. They are couples; she, a single, is no longer part of their world, the world she had with her husband. To the community of couples, the single woman is a pariah; more so the divorcee because the image she carries is of wantonness and threat. Seeking new relationships, she often finds something different from what she wants. When a woman leaves her marriage, she takes on a new image and a new status in male-female encounters. It is assumed that she is "on the prowl," and she often finds herself treated as a sexual mark. A new "meaningful relationship"? The later the divorce, the less likely and the more limited her range of options are.

Resentful, lonely, frightened, the divorced patriarchal wife has a good deal of building to do. She can do it, many have, but the prescriptions of patriarchy—"femininity," wifely subordination, and social discrimination—make this an intensely difficult challenge.

The Widow

Much that is true of the divorcee also fits the widow. Just as financially limited,[24] thrust into loneliness and new responsibilities, the widow discovers she has lost more than a husband. She has lost status and identity as well. No longer a part of a couple, she too becomes a pariah in her singleness, intensified as it is by the stigma of death that she is perceived to carry. Friends who were so kind "at the end" drift away, embarrassed by her grief, uncomfortable with her new condition as not quite whole.

Living With Oneself

Women have two alternatives: married or ———. What's the other term—unmarried, single? In our society each of these terms has the ring of "wrongness." *Unmarried* is clearly the negative of married, which is the norm, the "natural" and acceptable and positive state in our society. *Single* implies that there must be a double. The wrongness of the terms is the wrongness assigned to the state, and I cannot find a term in our language for the unmarried state in women (*bachelor* is male) that does not carry with it a stigma.

It would be better, feminists believe, to think of the matter in a wholly different way. The crucial question (although our culture would disagree) is not whether we are married or unmarried or after-married but whether we are whole or not whole, whether we are living fully and well or not. If we can be successful at living *with* ourselves, then the matter of whether or not we live *by* ourselves becomes secondary (though not unimportant). The ability and capacity to function well and happily with oneself and for oneself, encouraged to some extent in men, is discouraged in women in patriarchy. Self-sufficient, viable women do not make good servants. They make happier people, however, and, should they choose, better companions.

Living well, achieving peace and what happiness may be afforded, requires many hard-earned qualities: personal strength, courage, discipline, balance, perspective, endurance, humor, compassion, and intelligence. It requires a sense of self-worth, a sense of the integrity and inviolability of one's own being, a sense of pride. It requires self-awareness and understanding. It requires preparation, training, and experience, the wherewithal to use one's power for one's advantage in whatever circumstances one finds oneself. It requires a commitment made to the self to live well, to choose life for its own sake. When a person comes to see that there is good in the experiencing of good, that there is joy in doing what is personally meaningful, then that person is prepared to live with herself, alone or in company. When one keeps in mind that ultimately we walk quite by ourselves in this life, that for many reasons other people and other circumstances come and go, that we must always depend first on ourselves to meet our needs, emotional or material, then one does not relinquish one's power or safety into another's keeping.

A woman, as well as a man, must foster and maintain her own personal integrity and viability whatever her circumstances or relationships and however much she may love another or commit herself. In that case, she does not, as a female, take upon herself any greater risks than are already presented to women quite naturally by life and society, but rather she diminishes them and greatly increases the likelihood of happiness. A woman so described—independent, capable, viable—may not be the darling of patriarchy. She may find herself out of step with many and even rejected by some. But she is far more a person, more fully able to relate to those who would accept her, more likely to contribute to her whole community. Besides, the alternative is self-destructive.

Our Bodies: Negotiable Chattel

With few exceptions, the history of thought has rarely given important space to the manner in which one relates to one's own body in the formation of self-image. Possibly because of masculist fear of sensuality and feelings or because men as a class have so long had control over their own bodies as well as ours, "intellectuals" (until very recently) have given the subject short shrift. Nonetheless, our bodies are the material representations of ourselves, both to others and to ourselves. On many levels, from the superficial (such as the way we dress) to the deeply profound (such as the way we encounter and treat our own decay), the treatment and attitudes we perceive directed toward our bodies often determine how we see other aspects of ourselves.

The relationship between our physical selves and our psychosocial selves is very close.

If we look, we can see many examples that show the psychosocial importance of control over one's body and its needs. One of the first and most compelling forms of control the military exercises over new recruits, one that molds them into obedience and dependence, is the control over their physical selves, through appearance (in dress and hair), through management of body functions (eating, sleeping, elimination), and through providing for bodily needs (from medical treatment to cigarettes). It has been reported that one of the major factors in breaking the resistance of victims in Nazi concentration camps was the removal of their clothing and their subjection to other physical humiliations. To a lesser extent, the same thing is true in prisons. Studies in the psychology of nursing and hospital care point out that a patient's loss of control over the care of her or his own body, apart from the illness itself, often leads to a reduced sense of health and wellbeing; as a result patients are encouraged to meet as many of their own physical needs as possible. Nowhere, of course, can we more clearly see the close relationship between body control and confident, independent maturity than in the development of children. With each new step toward meeting physical needs and wants, with each step away from control through physical discipline, the child grows in independence and viability.

But in patriarchy, in our world, it is the class of men as a whole, and not women, who wield power over the circumstances and exigencies of women's physical selves. Because of this, women can be reduced to the status of dependent children. Through the institutionalization of masculine authority—in medicine, education, politics, communication, and law enforcement—and through brute power, men have obtained for themselves the use, maintenance, even "protection" of women's bodies. Until conditions change, women are in the childlike position of seeking out the *pater* for the satisfaction of physical needs and for the disposition of our bodies.

Appearance

Let us begin with something that might seem superficial (but is not): our appearance. We saw in Chapter 4 that women are taught very early that the way we come into this world is not the way we ought to remain. Unlike men, who are expected to groom and reorder themselves in small ways, we are pressed to conform significantly to whatever the current ideal is of feminine physical attractiveness. Who sets the standards of female beauty? Certainly not women; although properly conditioned and prodded, we avidly accept or pursue the entire business to gain the patriarchs' approval.

It is men who determine not only how we must behave but also how we must present ourselves as well. Through fashion, through law, through "science" or religion, we are told how to appear. The bound foot, the pierced ear and nose, the covered head or face, the enormous breast, the torn vagina, the never-too-thin torso; are these ours? The near nakedness of jeans and bathing suits, the oppressive discomfort of spiked heels or garter belts; the obsession with youth, size, sexiness; are any of these ours? It is men who design fashions and control the media, the advertising, the magazines, the films, the cosmetic firms, the department stores, and ultimately manipulate us into believing we set the trends.

It is difficult in a society so controlled by men for us to distinguish between what we think and feel genuinely, authentically, freely and what we think and feel as accommodation to expectation. We "love" the little bikini that leaves us practically undressed, but do we love it because it is a joyous expression of self or do we love it because it evokes approval or attention from men? What is that suit meant to accomplish? What do we have to do to our physical selves over the long term to look in that suit as we are required to look—diet, starve, guard our movements and our behavior? What would happen if we chose *not* to wear that little bikini but instead a swimsuit selected for comfort and freedom? What is the significance of that? What does it tell us? Why do we choose as we do?

To adorn and paint one's body out of a *self-defined* love of play and color may be self-expressive and healthy. To reject one's natural self and instead subject it to the requirements of an *alien* mold created by a separate reigning group for their interests, to yield one's physical representation for another's approval and protection is destructive because it is too terribly close to yielding one's intricately related psychological and spiritual self. "I am, physically and nonphysically, who I am" is authentic. "I am and will become what the whim of the ruling patriarchs wish me to be" is fatally close to nonexistence.

Health

When children are troubled with physical ailments, they must seek their guardians for help. So must women. Because relatively few women set or control health-care policy (a situation deftly arranged by patriarchy), when we are ill or face physical changes and "passages," *by law* and by custom we must turn to those formally charged with our care—men. Consider how absurd and humiliating men would think it if they had to ask women for assistance whenever they had a urinary disorder, a dysfunction of the penis, or a sexual or reproductive problem! In any sane world, such exclusively female events as pregnancy and childbirth would be women's province. Yet in our world it is men, through such agencies as the American Medical Association (AMA) and the American Hospital Association (AHA), who determine almost entirely how these experiences are to proceed: where and how, for example, we may give birth, what procedures will be followed, who may accompany us, who may assist. Women, at home or in clinics, may not legally contribute even informally in these affairs unless they are licensed by male-controlled agencies of various kinds.

Research into female medical needs, into surgical techniques and drug therapy for a variety of female experiences from menopause to depression, is carried on almost exclusively by males with the aid and support of the giant (male-dominated) research and grant agencies. Under policy and practice written by men, male physicians develop, prescribe, and test contraceptives for women and may withhold them if they choose. They research and develop policy and procedures for treating conditions of the breast, uterus, and ovaries (no wonder so many of them wind up in jars!); they write theories about women's attitudes during menopause and debate the use of estrogen therapy or tranquilizers. They inform their patients that severe menstrual cramping is a problem of the mind. They tell women how to mother children. Now they manipulate women's reproductive systems to make babies in test tubes and create parents or transfer parenthood from one to another

or "modify" results for more control over the process.

Through entrance into medical schools, licensing, lobby, and legislation, patriarchy limits the participation and authority of women in health care, hence over our own care. Historically the AMA and AHA have fought any growth of power and prestige in the nursing associations. Now men are being encouraged to join the nursing profession to "raise the level of the profession," and, in passing, to capture the more highly skilled and highly paid positions of authority in hospital nursing programs and in the American Nursing Association.

Control over our reproductive and medical needs is exacerbated by masculist-masculine control over the law. Women have little power in the making of policy because, as you will see in the following chapter, we are systematically excluded from anything like full participation in government—legislative, executive, or judicial—on any level. Legal policy regarding reproduction, contraception, abortion, and illegitimacy is written, interpreted, and executed essentially by men upon the advice and perspectives of "scientists" (men) and in response to their (most powerful and wealthy) constituencies (insurance companies, for example, or drug companies, legal associations, and political action committees—PACs) who have the inclination and wherewithal to make substantial contributions to campaigns and administrations.

In matters of health and reproduction almost more than anywhere else, women as "other" are objectified, reduced to "things," denied our own interests, and robbed of our personhood. In the current intense interest in women's reproductive lives, we are increasingly being perceived and treated as "delivery systems" of the young. The treatment of Jennifer Clarise Johnson, single mother and cocaine addict, is a perfect case in point.

SANFORD, Fla.—A judge has opened a new avenue for the criminal prosecution of cocaine-using mothers by finding a woman guilty of delivering the drug to her newborn children through the umbilical cord.

The decision Thursday marks the first time in the nation that a law normally used against drug dealers has been applied to a mother giving birth, a legal expert said. It applies only to the Florida judicial circuit where the woman lives, but could be applied by prosecutors in other jurisdictions, even outside Florida.[25]

Johnson was sentenced to thirty years in prison under a law making it a felony to deliver drugs to a minor. The prosecutor, delighted with his "new tool" for solving this "great problem," centered the matter on the issue of whether newborns may be considered persons after birth and before the umbilical cord is cut. The judge decided that they may be and that "delivery" could mean passing cocaine to a fetus through the umbilical! A nice argument. Never mind that the woman has a serious and viciously difficult health problem. Never mind that the woman did not intend to pass drugs to her offspring, nor does she profit from it. Never mind that the law was not meant to cover such a case or that this interpretation of the law involves a most extraordinary use of the term *deliver*.

Johnson—poor, powerless, female, a "delivery system" gone wrong—is now incarcerated in a drug treatment center apart from her children, who are being raised by someone else, and denied her place and her desire to "mother." In a television interview, the prosecutor said that he saw this as a case of child abuse, pure and simple, *no different* from the intentional beating or burning of a child. How are men treated when they *do* abuse children? Are they typically given thirty-year prison sentences, whether they be drunk or sober? How are male athletes treated when they become addicted to drugs? What does the difference in treatment say about the way (the male) judge and prosecutor perceive women, as childbearers, as mothers (quite a different concept), and as selves—as individual, independent human persons?

Abortion

The inclination to nullify women as persons in our reproductive context, to reduce us to "delivery systems," is a crucial concept for it is the heart of the abortion issue together with a similar but opposite logical maneuver, the elevation of a fetus to the status of "person." The abortion debate is characterized by more smoke than light for the most part. Activists on both sides tend to focus on issues either already apparent but moot or completely irrelevant. Of course life exists at conception; cells are alive. Of course the fetus is *human* life; it certainly isn't canine or vegetable. But is it *a* human life, that is, is it a person? Does it think, know, remember, make deci-

sions, relate to others, and all the hundreds of things that persons do that constitute them as persons? A tumor is a lump of human life. Is it morally sinful to remove it from its host? A fetus is a potential life. So is a human ovum. Am I guilty of murder everytime I have my period and do not assist this egg to become an actual life by having it fertilized? Does a potential human being become a person simply by fiat, by labeling it a baby or a child and then by granting this fiction all the legal and moral rights of personhood, *all the rights denied the mother*? Why is the mother less worthy of society's protection than a fictionalized "baby," because she is a woman? Why is that same baby, carried to term, born and alive, less worthy of attention and protection than it was in the womb? Why is all the clamor directed at a woman's completing a pregnancy but not then sustained in regard to the feeding, sheltering and aiding of that child and its mother? The great majority of America's poor, homeless, and desperate are women and their dependent children. And then who cares?

In a series on "The Changing American Family" in the home state of the Webster case, the *St. Louis Post Dispatch* tells the story of Dawn Smith and her infant son, Benjamin. Abandoned by her boyfriend early in her pregnancy, with no place of her own to live, not yet out of business school, she was "at the point where if I couldn't talk to someone about my situation, I would explode." A Baptist crisis pregnancy center gave her a "sympathetic ear, a few baby care items," and a companion through delivery. When she went home after the delivery, however, "reality set in":

> The phone had been disconnected because of a mix-up over her last payment. Instead of spending the next few weeks recuperating from childbirth and getting to know her son, Smith spent the time settling bills, finding a baby sitter, hauling laundry and checking out social programs that might provide them with help. . . .

> "By the time he was 3 weeks old, I was out of money. Completely out," Smith said. Although she had hoped to take a six-week maternity leave from her job, she was forced to return to work Feb. 13 (the leave had paid her only $50 a week). Benji was 33 days old.

> "I cried all the way to work, and I cried all day," Smith said. "When I left that day, I wanted to drive 90 miles per hour to get home."

Smith now spends all of her free time with her baby. "There are 10 hours a day that I'm not with him, and I worry that some day when I go to pick him up he'll want to stay with the baby sitter instead of come with me," she said. "I want to spend all my time holding and loving him, but there are also times when I'm so tired that I just want him to go to sleep."

The $672 Smith takes home each month barely covers her fixed bills—$295 for rent, $150 for a baby sitter, $90 for electricity, $25 for telephone service, and $13.20 for water. There's little left for food, gas and diapers, and nothing to make a dent in her outstanding bills—$200 for electricity, $250 for a 12-year-old car, $700 for past medical treatment and more than $7,000 for school loans.

On the day she was interviewed, Smith had $35 to her name, $32 of which was needed to pay a bill. For the second week in a row, she had been unable to buy groceries. Her refrigerator contained a jar of jelly, a frozen pizza and some stale doughnuts bought for 25 cents a box. Besides baby formula, her pantry held a box of tea bags, a jar of peanut butter, a jar of honey, a box of crackers and two cans of green beans. Payday was 13 days away.[26]

Somehow after the delivery when reality set in, the "helpers" were gone.

The antichoice advocates have thrown up a smoke screen against the real issues: control over women's lives, our self-determination, our right to make decisions for ourselves, and our personal, economic, and social destinies. The issue is not simply whether I carry a pregnancy to term, but whether I wish to bear and raise a child. For whether I raise a child or give it up, whether it is healthy or damaged, whether it is loved or not, that child changes my personal life in dramatic and permanent ways. Who is to decide, beside myself, whether I shall lend myself to those changes? In a society that values liberty and purports to guarantee it to all citizens, who beside myself has the right to decide?

What is the proper response to those who would rob us of our right to choose? To those filled with hate and the need for power, the answer is obvious. For those whose arrogance is born of a belief in their own right to speak for God, the clearest rebuke would be to require them to look at their own hidden needs:

"Rescue" Activist Speaks

Twenty-five-year-old Mary Ann Baney is on the staff of Operation Rescue (OR) in Binghamton, New York. A Pittsburgh native, Baney has been active in the antiabortion movement since September, 1987. After hearing Randall Terry speak at a rally, she says, she was moved to activism. "I agreed with him that we have to act like abortion is murder. We have to do something."

Her first involvement took her to Cherry Hill, New Jersey, OR's first "rescue" site, a practice run for the week-long assault on New York City clinics that took place in May, 1988. "I saw men and women coming to kill their children," says Baney. "I cared about them and their children. Out of love for them, and obedience to God, I sat down. I know murder is against God's commandments."

Baney found her participation empowering. "It was the most valuable thing I ever did. It took courage to sit down. But I know one couple who changed their minds and had the baby; a boy was born a few months ago. He would not have been alive without that 'rescue.'"

Raised Catholic, Baney is now part of the Roman Catholic Charismatic Renewal movement. "In a sense it's like being born again," says Baney. "I'm spirit filled."

After the Cherry Hill protest—at which 211 Operation Rescue members were arrested—Baney returned to Pittsburgh and helped form a local OR group there. Then in May she spent a week doing daily "rescues" in New York City. This was followed by participation in two "rescues" in Philadelphia. "The week before July 19, the start of the Democratic Convention in Atlanta, I was laid off by the lawn care company I worked for. Since I was free, I went to Atlanta and ended up spending 36 days in jail for protesting abortion. It was one of the highlights of my life. I grew so much spiritually because I was doing God's will. It was so valuable. I felt a great sense of doing something worthwhile."

Baney says she was particularly impressed by the sense of community forged during her month-long incarceration. "God moved in the jail. The pastors all worshipped together. As the group got smaller we were moved in with the other inmates and we shared the love of God with them. God's presence changed the jail to a place of peace and love." (OR members were released from prison when they gave the authorities their real names and addresses. Most identified themselves to police as Baby Jane or Baby John Doe when they were initially arrested. OR staffer Marti Hendrickson told me that this alias was used to allow participants to "take a stand on behalf of the unborn; to be their voice and show that we won't let any more babies be murdered.")

Baney started working with OR full-time upon her release from jail. There's nothing, she says, that she'd rather be doing. Single and childless, she sees herself as part of a generation that has come to its senses, the generation that came of age in the 1980s and "found out the hard way about love and values. Many of my friends wish they'd remained pure, waited till marriage to have intercourse," she says. "They now know that they are to obey God, rather than men. They read the Bible and know that they are to render to God things that are God's. These children we "rescue" are the children of God. It's God's will."[27]

The matter of abortion is extremely complex both ethically and legally, and the arguments for and against are numerous and complicated. The following three points are crucial: First, in determining the matter of abortion laws and statutes, supreme court decisions, and constitutional amendments, we must take great care to distinguish legal rights and responsibilities from what we perceive to be moral obligations. Many acts one might wish performed or not performed, on moral or ethical grounds, cannot and should not be compelled or prohibited by law. Second, we must pay attention to the matter of consistency. People not actively or even ideologically opposed to killing real adult human beings in war or by capital punishment are clamoring for laws against killing a fetus. People little concerned with the quality of the ensuing life of either mother or child are determined to maintain the biological life. Although it is fallacious to attack an argument on the basis of who proposes it, the question of motivation is always pertinent. Motivation is at the psychological heart of discrimination—as when one discriminates between two kinds of "killing": one (war) allowable, the other (abortion) not—and therefore is at the heart of oppression. Third, it is valuable to place the entire issue in historical context. Strong analogies exist to the movement in the 1930s to legalize the prescription, use, and sale of contra-

ceptives. Those in favor argued, as today, on the grounds of constitutionality, personal freedom, the quality of life for all, and the benefits of population control to society. Then, as now, their opponents accused them of immorality, murder (of future generations), opposition to God's will, and the destruction of the family and the social order. Consider the lessons to be learned from this as you read the selection on abortion in this chapter.

Sexuality

The matter of women's sexuality is a large and many-faceted topic, rarely treated either sanely or seriously outside of women's studies. Yet in the analysis of our life space, our sexuality is an extremely important issue. It is ironic, as well as indicative of the role we play in a patriarchal society, that the aspect of our nature that is considered definitive of us by the male hegemony is also the aspect of ourselves from which we are commanded to be the most alienated.

In Chapter 3 we saw that, except for our role as Mother (procreator or nurturer), our only function in patriarchy is to serve as sexual Playmate. In the patriarchal environment we are submerged in that guise. Our clothing is designed, our movements are trained, and our behavior is coached to be seductive. And yet, though sex and appearing sexy is a prescribed part of the curriculum, for women the enjoyment of sex or sensuality, the use of sex to women's own ends, has been prohibited.

The women's movement has argued that in patriarchy women are all reduced to the status of "sex objects." That does not mean simply that we are sometimes the object of sexual interest or desire (which we might all on some occasion wish to be) but that we are formally perceived and treated as objects for sex, sex-things. Unlike a human being, a thing is not perceived to have feelings, needs, and rights because a thing is not perceived as a subjectivity, as a self.

In patriarchy, women in our sexual roles are ideally to function not as self-affirming, self-fulfilling human beings but rather as beautiful dolls to be looked at, touched, felt, experienced for arousal, used for titillation (for sexual release or the sale of merchandise), to be enjoyed, consumed, and ultimately used up and traded in for a newer model thing. We may respond or even enjoy, but not for our own pleasure (only bad women are selfish), only for the greater pleasure of the user. Our sexual role in patriarchy is to be acted upon, not to act ourselves, except insofar as this serves the users' interest or needs.

Full sexuality and sensuality is utterly conscious and healthily self-centered as well as other-centered. So long as we accept the patriarchal image of women as copulating machines, so long as we allow ourselves to be washed, perfumed, painted, and dressed, playing a part, totally selfless, we will experience alienation in sex and alienation from our bodies. In patriarchy, women are objectified, passive, and self-abnegating, but authentic functioning sexuality is subjective, forceful, and self-affirming.

We may have much to learn from lesbian love and sex. As women loving women because they are women, lesbians point out that they are in a special position with regard to liberating female sexuality. Free of the heterosexual politics of the usual gender-based roles and prescriptions, more positive and self-affirming as women, more acutely aware of the needs of their partners because, in a sense, they are their partners, lesbian women contend that they are more able to discover and express authentic female sexuality than their heterosexual counterparts. Although lesbian couples share the conflicts of any two people being in an intimate relationship, the experiences of many lesbian couples have valuable implications for creating nonexploitive relationships.

Violence

The right of men to control the female body is a cornerstone of patriarchy. . . . There is a different kind of terrorism, one that so pervades our culture that we have learned to live with it as though it were the natural order of things. Its targets are females—of all ages, races and classes. It is the common characteristic of rape, wife battery, incest, pornography, harassment, and all forms of sexual violence. I call it sexual terrorism because it is a system by which males frighten and, by frightening, control and dominate females.

—Carol J. Sheffield[28]

Rape is the logical outcome if men act according to the "masculine mystique" and women act according to the "feminine mystique."

—Dianne Herman[29]

Man's discovery that his genitalia could serve as a weapon to generate fear must rank as one of the most important discoveries of prehistoric times . . . I believe rape has played a critical function. It is nothing more or less than a conscious process of intimidation by which all men keep all women in a state of fear.

—Susan Brownmiller[30]

Woman abuse is viewed here as an historical expression of male domination manifested within the family and currently reinforced by the institutions, economic "arrangements," and sexist division of labor within capitalist society.

—Susan Schechter[31]

Violence against wives—indeed, violence against women in general—is as old as recorded history, and cuts across all societies and socioeconomic groups. There are few phenomena so pervasive and yet so ignored.

—Lori Heise[32]

Within the women's movement we have absolute agreement that we live in a society permeated by male violence and that a great deal of that violence is directed against women.

Facts:

In 1987, 91,111 rapes were reported to law enforcement agencies in the United States.[33]

One rape is reported every six minutes.[34]

Only one out of every ten rapes is reported.[35]

One in three females will be sexually assaulted by age eighteen.[36]

Within the next decade, 25 million girls will be sexually abused, half of them under the age of eleven.[37]

Two million women are battered every year.[38]

Bureau of Justice figures show approximately 456,000 cases of domestic violence per year. It is estimated that only one case in ten is reported.[39]

In the United States, a woman is abused every eighteen seconds.[40]

One in every five women involved in an intimate relationship with a man is beaten repeatedly by that man.[41]

Forty percent of all women who are murdered in the U.S. are killed by their male partners.[42]

Agreement attests that women are the victims of male violence; that such violence is an integral part of the gender system; that it is largely sanctioned and reinforced by social institutions—the courts, the media, the economic system, religions, and others; and that it has an agenda, a goal—the control of women by men through fear. What is more, the social system has been manipulated so that women have been prohibited from defending ourselves. Not until the women's movement created women's self-help groups, coalitions against violence, rape crisis centers, and battered women's shelters did we have any recourse beside protection by men.

Protection

In the system of chivalry, men protect women against men. This is not unlike the protection relationship which the Mafia established with small businesses in the early part of this century. Indeed, chivalry is an age-old protection racket which depends for its existence on rape.

Susan Griffin[43]

Ordinarily, nations and cultures grant their membership the right of self-protection. Self-defense is deemed both natural and appropriate. In patriarchy, however, so far as women are concerned, that is not true. No written law prohibits us from defending ourselves against attack; that would be unthinkable! Instead we are kept from defending ourselves by two main devices. First, the kinds of attack directed specifically against women (such as rape or many forms of prostitution) are simply defined away as not an attack or not a crime. The burden is shifted to the victim to prove not only that certain acts took place but that they are indeed criminal. Second, the entire set of behavioral rules and presuppositions imposed on women through the requirements of "femininity" render us passive, weak, and unable to defend ourselves; nor are we allowed by law to compensate physically, with weapons or similar protective devices, for our lesser strength and size. In patriarchy, men as a class are charged with the protection of women. This is ironic since for the most part it is men as a class from whom we must be protected. It is men who rape, batter, exploit, and prostitute women for their own interests.

Nor is the issue easily explained away by the proposition that the part of the group that attacks is different from the part that defends. The same man who rapes may also be a husband or lover, though not necessarily of the raped woman. The same man who batters and beats a woman frequently is her own husband or lover. When one accepts friendship or companionship from a man—a date, a ride, a dinner—one cannot be sure what payment may be exacted, even forcibly, in return.

Those who—like slaves or prisoners—are not permitted or are not able to defend themselves against any kind of attack by any thing or person are deprived of a basic prerequisite to freedom, integrity, confidence, viability, and independence. It matters little whether the prohibition to self-defense is imposed by law or by lore. Total dependence on others for protection, particularly when those others are the very persons from whom one must be protected, is not workable.

It may be said that women are not protected simply by men, but by law, the courts, judges, and the police. Feminists point out that the percentage of women in legislatures, courts, and police forces is small; the number who have any power in those areas is still smaller, and they are hampered by a legacy of masculist decision making.

Women beaten and battered by their husbands are only now beginning to receive even meager attention by society, much of it reversed by the Reagan years. Women raped and abused—by strangers, lovers, or relatives—have had little recourse in the courts and received little restitution. A patriarchal economy and society forces women to barter their bodies for goods and survival, and they are harassed and imprisoned. The use of brute force by men against women, in an environment in which we may not defend ourselves, is an act of political terror meant to keep us in the "place" devised for us.

Conclusion

This discussion has barely begun to strip open the many layers of what women's more private experiences are in patriarchy. Much more remains to examine, much more to tell, but that will have to happen in another place. Up to now the story has necessarily been abrasive and polemical. As feminists point out, recognition of some of the harsh realities is the first spur to change. Change will meet resistance, and resistance begets counterresistance.

But we have some positive elements to keep firmly in mind. Having been excluded from the inner power circle of patriarchy, women have also not been absorbed by it. Women have a unique position in society in that we have a more rounded, more balanced perception of society. Having lived and grown and studied in patriarchy, we know it intimately. Having lived on its periphery, often in contest with it, we also understand it more critically. With our "consciousness" raised, we are therefore in a much stronger position to change and heal it than those more nearly its captives in the center. We have extraordinary social contributions to make.

We have, too, special options in our personal lives. Many have contended that the character of our experience and the more satisfying life that flows from it are born of challenge. I believe that, and so do many other feminists.

It is extremely difficult to break from the familiar, which is comfortable even in its inadequacy. It is hard indeed to alter behaviors, relationships, and values that hold at least some good and some attraction for us in order to move toward something that we can only dimly see at times, but something that we know must be better. May Sarton has said, "It is only when we can believe that we are creating the soul that life has any meaning, but when we can believe it—and I do and always have—then there is nothing we do that is without meaning and nothing that we suffer that does not hold the seed of creation in it."[44] Because the oppression of women has in large part been an oppression of our souls (our character, integrity, and spirit), feminist activism is as much as anything else an attempt to reclaim our souls, to rebuild them. This is the source of the buoyant excitement so many feminists carry, even side by side with the pain of recognition. It is the source of our pride in the achievements and successes we win. Rewards are only as great as the risks one has to take to gain them.

Notes

[1] Sanford M. Dornbusch and Myra H. Strober, "Our Perspective," in *Feminism, Children and the New Families,* eds. Sanford M. Dornbusch and Myra H. Strober (New York: Guilford Press, 1988), pp. 3–24, *passim*.

[2] Ibid.

[3] Ibid.

[4] Ibid.

[5] Ibid.

[6] Ibid., p. 17.

[7] "The Paradox of the Happy Marriage," in *Women in Sexist Society,* ed. Vivian Gornick and Barbara Moran (New York: Basic Books, 1971), p. 147.

[8] Ibid. See also Jessie Bernard, *The Future of Marriage* (New York: Bantam, 1972).

[9] Carol Tavris and Carole Offir, *The Longest War* (New York: Harcourt Brace Jovanovich, 1977), p. 222.

[10] Tavris and Offir, *The Longest War,* p. 232.

[11] U.S. Bureau of the Census, 1986.

[12] For statistics on alimony and child support, see selections by Elyce Rotella and Lenore Weitzman below in Chapter 7.

[13] U.S. Census Bureau and Bureau of Labor Statistics.

[14] Elyce Rotella, "Women and the American Economy." Below, Chap. 7.

[15] Sanford M. Dornbusch and Myra H. Strober, "Our Perspective" in *Feminism, Children, and the New Families,* p. 14.

[16] Harriet Nerlove Mischel and Robert Fuhr, "Maternal Employment: Its Psychological Effects on Children and Their Families," in Dornbusch and Strober, *Feminism, Children and the New Families.* pp. 194–195.

[17] *Women and Love: A Cultural Revolution in Progress* (New York: Alfred A. Knopf, 1987).

[18] Ibid., p. 4.

[19] Ibid., pp. 75–77, *passim*.

[20] W. B. O'Reilly, "Where Equal Opportunity Fails: Corporate Men and Women in Dual-Career Families." Unpublished Ph.D. dissertation, Stanford University, California, 1983. Quoted in Myra H. Strober, "Two-Earner Families" in Dornbusch and Strober, *Feminism, Children, and the New Families,* p. 178.

[21] [In Strober, "Two-Earner Families"] J. Steihm, "Invidious Intimacy," *Social Policy* 6(5): 12–16.

[22] [In Strober, "Two-Earner Families"] "The empirical evidence is unclear on whether two-earner couples are less likely to move than one-earner couples, even when their occupations and incomes are relatively similar." See W. T. Markham, "Sex, Relocation, and Occupational Advancement" in A. H. Stromberg, L. Larwood, and B. A. Gutek, eds., *Women and Work: An Annual Review* 2 (Beverly Hills, Calif.: Sage Publications, 1987).

[23] Ibid.

[24] Carol J. Barrett, "Women in Widowhood," *Signs* 2, No. 4 (Summer 1978): 856.

[25] *St. Louis Post Dispatch,* 17 July 1989, p. 5A. Copyright 1989 Pulitzer Publishing Company. Reprinted with permission.

[26]St. Louis Post Dispatch, 26 March 1989, pp. 5D, 9D. Copyright 1989 Pulitzer Publishing Company. Reprinted with permission.

[27]Reported by Eleanor J. Bader in *New Directions For Women* 18, 2, (Mar/Apr 1989): 14. Reprinted with permission of *New Directions For Women*.

[28]"Sexual Terrorism" in *Women: A Feminist Perspective,* 4th ed., ed. Jo Freeman (Mountain View, CA: Mayfield, 1984), p. 3.

[29]"Rape Culture," Ibid., p. 34.

[30]Susan Brownmiller, *Against Our Will* (New York: Bantam, 1976), p. 5.

[31]Susan Schechter, *Women and Male Violence* (Boston: South End Press, 1982), p. 209.

[32]Lori Heise, "Crimes of Gender," *World-Watch,* Mar/Apr, 1989, p. 12.

[33]U.S. Department of Justice Uniform Crime Reports, 1988.

[34]Ibid.

[35]Illinois Coalition Against Sexual Assault (ICASA).

[36]Ibid.

[37]NOW Legal Defense and Education Fund.

[38]Murray Straus, "Wife Beating: Causes, Treatment and Research Needs," in U.S. Commission on Civil Rights, *Battered Women: Issues of Public Policy,* quoted in Susan Schechter, *Women and Male Violence,* p. 16.

[39]Louise Bausch and Mary Kimbrough, *Voices Set Free: Battered Women Speak From Prison* (St. Louis, Women's Self Help Center, 1986), p. ix.

[40]Ibid., p. 3.

[41]Illinois Coalition Against Sexual Assault and the Illinois Coalition Against Domestic Violence, "Male Violence Against Women," pamphlet.

[42]Ibid.

[43]Susan Griffin, *Rape: The Power of Consciousness* (San Francisco: Harper and Row, 1979), p. 10.

[44]May Sarton, *Journal of a Solitude* (New York: Norton, 1973), p. 67.

Obsession: The Tyranny of Slenderness

Kim Chernin

Kim Chernin has been a freelance writer, a poet, an instructor in creative writing, and a writing consultant. In private practice, she has worked with women in developmental crisis and those with eating disorders. She is the author of In My Mother's House: A Daughter's Story *(1984),* The Hungry Self: Women, Eating and Identity *(1984),* The Flame Bearers, *a novel (1986), and* Reinventing Eve: Modern Woman in Search of Herself *(1988).*

It is estimated that at least 20 percent of college women suffer from eating disorders, and that estimate is conservative. When one factors in the sheer reduction in quality of life brought about by the constant round of dieting and denial most women now engage in for the sake of fashion, when one considers the self-hatred suffered by those who do not or cannot "thin down," one begins to realize what devastating thievery today's obsession with size really is.

Contemporary feminists are beginning to realize that the media, the medical profession, and several industries have been victimizing women with an unrealistic and unhealthy standard of physical shape. Is the battering of our adult bodies into childlike form our culture's equivalent of Chinese foot-binding?

2. The Flesh and the Devil

We know that every woman wants to be thin. Our images of womanhood are almost synonymous with thinness.

—Susie Orbach

. . . I must now be able to look at my ideal, this ideal of being thin, of being without a body, and to realize: "it is a fiction."

—Ellen West

When the body is hiding the complex, it then becomes our most immediate access to the problem.

—Marian Woodman

THE LOCKER ROOM OF THE TENNIS CLUB. SEVERAL exercise benches, two old-fashioned hair dryers, a mechanical bicycle, a treadmill, a reducing machine, a mirror, and a scale.

A tall woman enters, removes her towel; she throws it across a bench, faces herself squarely in the mirror, climbs on the scale, looks down.

A silence.

"I knew it," she mutters, turning to me. "I knew it."

And I think, before I answer, just how much I admire her, for this courage beyond my own, this daring to weigh herself daily in this way. And I sympathize. I know what she must be feeling. Not quite candidly, I say: "Up or down?" I am hoping to suggest that there might be people and cultures where gaining weight might not be considered a disaster. Places where women, stepping on scales, might be horrified to notice that they had reduced themselves. A mythical, almost unimaginable land.

"Two pounds," she says, ignoring my hint. "Two pounds." And then she turns, grabs the towel and swings out at her image in the mirror, smashing it violently, the towel spattering water over the glass. "Fat pig," she shouts at her image in the glass. "You fat, fat pig. . . ."

Later, I go to talk with this woman. Her name is Rachel and she becomes, as my work progresses, one of the choral voices that shape its vision.

Two girls come into the exercise room. They are perhaps ten or eleven years old, at that elongated stage when the skeletal structure seems to be winning its war against flesh. And these two are particularly skinny. They sit beneath the hair dryers for a moment, kicking their legs on the faded green upholstery; they run a few steps on the eternal treadmill, they wrap the rubber belt of the reducing machine around themselves and jiggle for a moment before it falls off. And then they go to the scale.

The taller one steps up, glances at herself in the mirror, looks down at the scale. She sighs, shaking her head. I see at once that this girl is imitating someone. The sigh, the headshake are theatrical, beyond her years. And so, too, is the little drama enacting itself in front of me. The other girl leans forward, eager to see for herself the troubling message imprinted upon the scale. But the older girl throws her hand over the secret. It is not to be revealed. And now the younger one, accepting this, steps up to confront the ultimate judgment. "Oh God," she says, this growing girl. "Oh God," with only a shade of imitation in her voice: "Would you believe it? I've gained five pounds."

These girls, too, become a part of my work. They enter, they perform their little scene again and again; it extends beyond them and in it I am finally able to behold something that would have remained hidden—for it does not express itself directly, although we feel its pressure almost every day of our lives. Something, unnamed as yet, struggling against our emergence into femininity. This is my first glimpse of it, out there. And the vision ripens.

I return to the sauna. Two women I have seen regularly at the club are sitting on the bench above me. One of them is very beautiful, the sort of woman Renoir would have admired. The other, who is probably in her late sixties, looks, in the twilight of this sweltering room, very much an adolescent. I have noticed her before, with her tan face, her white hair, her fashionable clothes, her slender hips and jaunty walk. But the effect has not been soothing. A woman of advancing age who looks like a boy.

"I've heard about that illness, anorexia nervosa," the plump one is saying, "and I keep looking around for someone who has it. I want to go sit next to her. I think to myself, maybe I'll catch it. . . ."

"Well," the other woman says to her, "I've felt the same way myself. One of my cousins used to throw food under the table when no one was looking. Finally, she got so thin they had to take her to the hospital. . . . I always admired her."

What am I to understand from these stories? The woman in the locker room who swings out at her image in the mirror, the little girls who are afraid of the coming of adolescence to their bodies, the woman who admires the slenderness of the anorexic girl. Is it possible to miss the dislike these women feel for their bodies?

And yet, an instant's reflection tells us that this dislike for the body is not a biological fact of our condition as women—we do not come upon it by nature, we are not born to it, it does not arise for us because of anything predetermined in our sex. We know that once we loved the body, delighting in it the way children will, reaching out to touch our toes and count over our fingers, repeating the game endlessly as we come to knowledge of this body in which we will live out our lives. No part of the body exempt from our curiosity, nothing yet forbidden, we know an equal fascination with the feces we eliminate from ourselves, as with the ear we discover one day and the knees that have become bruised and scraped with falling and that warm, moist place between the legs from which feelings of indescribable bliss arise.

From that state to the condition of the woman in the locker room is a journey from innocence to despair, from the infant's naive pleasure in the body, to the woman's anguished confrontation with herself. In this journey we can read our struggle with natural existence—the loss of the body as a source of pleasure. But the most striking thing about this alienation from the body is the fact that we take it for granted. Few of us ask to be redeemed from this struggle against the flesh by overcoming our antagonism toward the body. We do not rush about looking for someone who can tell us how to enjoy the fact that our appetite is large, or how we might delight in the curves and fullness of our own natural shape. We hope instead to be able to reduce the body, to limit the urges and desires it feels, to remove the body from nature. Indeed, the suffering we experience through our obsession with the body arises precisely from the hopeless and impossible nature of this goal. . . .

8. The Boutique

It is now fashionable to be thin, but if it were fashionable to be fat, women would force-feed themselves like geese, just as girls in primitive societies used to stuff themselves because the fattest girl was the most beautiful. If the eighteen-inch waist should ever become fashionable again, women would suffer the tortures of tight lacing, convinced that though one dislocated one's kidneys, crushed one's liver, and turned green, beauty was worth it all.

—Una Stannard

Well then, why can't we manage to be proud of our large bodies? Why can't we altogether grasp the fact that there might be something of a positive nature in the very fact of fleshly existence? What, we say? Woman's abundance, her fullness of body, her potbelly and her fat ass and her big thighs regarded as beauty? Somehow it remains very hard for us to imagine women fashioning an ideal image for ourselves that required us to be grand and voluptuous. We can't quite conceive what it would be like to take back to ourselves the right to decide how our bodies should look, choosing an aesthetic according to health and nature, wishing our bodies to bear witness to our celebration of appetite, natural existence, and women's power.

And yet we do know that there were times, not so long ago, when women did not feel about their bodies the way we do. Then, a woman considered it a disaster if she stepped on the scale and found that she had lost weight. There once actually were women who had no respect for the anxieties of their physicians, who went ahead and caused their doctors to feel despair. These women would not lose weight because they did not wish to, and they did not wish to because their bodies seemed more beautiful to them when they were fat.

A physician in that day actually complained that it was fashion and aesthetic that interfered with prescribed weight-reducing programs.

One must mention here that aesthetic errors of a worldly nature to which all women submit, may make them want to stay obese for reasons of fashionable appearance. It is beyond a doubt that in order to have an impressive decollete each woman feels herself duty bound to be fat around the neck, over the clavicle and in her breasts. Now it happens that fat accumulates with greatest difficulty in these places and one can be sure, even without examining such a woman, that the abdomen and the hips, and the lower members are hopelessly fat. As to the treatment, one cannot obtain weight reduction of the abdomen without the woman sacrificing in her spirits the upper part of her body. To her it is a true sacrifice because she gives up what the world considers beautiful.[1]

That was in 1911. And the little parable tells us one thing quite clearly. If the standard of beauty that prevailed in Paris in 1911 were still in fashion in America of 1980, none of us would go home tonight after a large meal, and take laxatives, and run the risk of ruining our digestion, upsetting our electrolyte imbalance, and disturbing the natural condition of the flora of our intestine. If we were admired for having fat around the neck, as women were in 1911, and were permitted to have large abdomens and well-padded hips, tens of thousands of women would not kneel down next to the toilet tonight and put our fingers down our throat, and vomit.

From this simple fact we come to appreciate, all over again, the way an aesthetic ideal affects our lives with an extreme coercive power. Fashion lets us know what our culture expects us to be, or to become, or to struggle to become, in order to be acceptable to it, thereby exercising a devastating power over our lives on a daily basis. The image of women that appears in the advertisement of a daily newspaper has the power to damage a woman's health, destroy her sense of well-being, break her pride in herself, and subvert her ability to accept herself as a woman.

Thus, it is possible to study fashion the way one can study a work of art, so that it reflects significantly upon the issues and conflicts of its own day. The nude body of a woman, as we have seen, carries a tale that proves interesting beyond the boundaries of aesthetic speculation. Similarly, fashion, in the image it creates of woman, expresses itself on a variety of issues its makers would never imagine so deeply concerned them. By studying the face, the expression, the body, the gesture of the recurring images in our culture, we begin to read our culture's attitudes toward power in a woman, her sensual freedom, her right to joyfulness, subjectivity, and expressiveness through her body, her right to age, to grow mature in her body, to acquire authority, to bear this authority in the angle of her jaw, the settling back of her shoulders, the tilt of her head. If the pages of *Vogue* presented us with pictures of large women, their bodies muscular like those of athletes, their heads held high like those of a person of prestige and influence; if the pages of the daily newspaper showed women wearing clothes that emphasized the beauty of a powerful back, the strength of a large hip, hands and feet that were able to work and to accomplish, necks that were capable of carrying life's burden, or a softness, a fullness and abundance that seemed, like a ripening fruit, to stand for the abundance and fullness of life itself, there would not be six million women in this country today who had joined Weight Watchers to change the size of their bodies; eight thousand of us next week would not be moving through the doors of the diet salon, and the word bulmarexia might never have had to be created, in 1974, to describe our unique cultural disorder—a disease that includes simultaneously the symptoms of insatiable appetite (bulemia) and (anorexia) the rejection of food.[2]

But it is also true that the fashions we are speaking about have changed several times since 1911; we know that during the 1920s, women were binding their breasts and bobbing their hair and hoping to look like boys; and we remember that in 1960 Marilyn Monroe, when she made the film *Some Like It Hot*, was still permitted to be as large as a woman in a drawing by Modersohn-Becker. We who fell in love with her then and yearned as growing girls to look like her, seeing this film now, and the size of the woman who was our heroine, must marvel at what has happened to our very perception of beauty. For Monroe, if she were alive now, and still as grand and voluptuous as she was then, would today no doubt be considered fat. . . .

But this zaftig body of Monroe, when it appears on a woman of our time, becomes a source of profound despair; it is measured, frowned upon, afflicted with starvation, hidden away, and taken finally into surgery, where for $2,500 the buttocks are reduced, and where for another $3,000 the thighs are made smaller, and where for yet more thousands of dollars the roundness of the belly is made flat. . . .

And so we make our way into the street life of our culture, hoping now to look again, with a new quality of perception, at the most commonplace expression of the conflicts and dilemmas that inspire literature and art, philosophy and psychological perceptions. But we are now not surprised to find that the conflict over the flesh is reflected here too, in this stamping ground of the anorexic heroine, whose picture is repeated on every page of the fashion magazine, and whose form is sculpted in the stylish mannequins of the store windows, and whose representative greets us, with a false smile, a secret disparagement, as we enter a clothing store, for it is clear that we enter without being able to conform—we will need a size nine or ten or maybe eleven; we will not do justice to the new, slender line, the tapering curve at the hip, the girdle-like constriction of the jeans. How often we have been filled with panic, catching a glimpse of ourselves, in all our unredeemed femininity, looking back with a frantic expression from the mirrors that reflect everything we are supposed to be—those girls who have succeeded where we have failed, those long-limbed mannequins who have become our omnipresent reminder, our reproach. . . .

. . . The signs on the rack are bold and explicit—they wish to make it clear that here, in the showplace of our culture, some significant transformation has occurred. SIZE THREE? But what has happened to the sevens or the nines? The place is thick with ones and twos and there, shame-facedly in the far corner, is a rack of fives. They don't have size nine, the girl tells us, although we have not asked. "But don't you know," we want to say to her, "that there are over twenty-five million women in this country who wear size sixteen and over? That, if you want to know, is more than 30 percent of the women in this land.[3] And what of all the rest of us, uncounted, who are unable to adapt ourselves to these styles suited for adolescents? And what, if you come to that, do you make of the fact that the large size clothes are called, in the vernacular of the garment industry, 'women's sizes,' and just what, if you follow me, does that reveal about these gaunt garments hanging here? For surely, you see that they were not intended for a woman?"

9. Why Now?

A woman should never give the impression that she is so capable, so self-sufficient, that she doesn't need him at all. Men are enchanted by minor, even amusing frailties.

This quality of vulnerability, of needing a man, is something that the mature woman should study very carefully. Because it's that quality that she loses most easily. Years of dealing with home and family, of making decisions, of coping, can turn the woman of forty-plus into a brusque, cold-eyed, and somewhat frightening figure.

—Gloria Heidi

Is it a conspiracy, unknown even to those who participate in it?

A whole culture busily spinning out images and warnings intended to keep women from developing their bodies, their appetites, and their powers?

Maybe, when we see another calorie counter on the stand, or read of another miracle diet in a women's magazine, or pick up another container of low-calorie cottage cheese, we must begin to understand these trivial items symbolically and realize that what we are purchasing is the covert advice not to grow too large and too powerful for our culture.

Maybe, indeed, this whole question of the body's reduction is analogous to the binding of women's feet in prerevolutionary China?[4]

"My mother buys me a girdle when I am fifteen years old," says Louise Bernikow, "because she doesn't like the jiggle. . . . Tighter. I hold myself tighter, as my mother has taught me to do. . . . Is the impulse to cripple a girl peculiar to China between the eleventh and twentieth centuries? The lotus foot was the size of a doll's and the woman could not walk without support. Her foot was four inches long and two inches wide. A doll. A girl-child. Crippled, indolent, and bound."[5]

There is a relationship between the standards set for women's beauty and the desire to limit their development.) In the name of a beautiful foot, the women of China were deprived of autonomy and made incapable of work. A part of the body was forced to remain in a childish condition. They did not walk, they hobbled. In the name of beauty they were crippled.

What happens to women today in the name of beauty?

I'd never wear a girdle, she said,
just medieval throwbacks
to whale baleen brassieres 'n
laced-up waist confiner corsets.
We burned em in the sixties,
girdles, she said walking
into Bloomingdales, grabbing

a pair of cigarette-legged
tight denim jeans off the rack.
Hoisting them up to her hips,
how do ya get em on, she said,
have surgery, take steam baths,
slimnastic classes'n Dr. Nazi's
diet clinic fatshots for a month?
These aren't jeans for going
to lunch in, she said trying
to do the snap, these
aren't even jeans
for eating an hour
before ya put em on, just
for standin up in without
your hands in the pockets,
there's not even room
in here for my underpants.
One hour later she returns
to the store for a new zipper,
front snap, and the side seams
re-stitched. These're jeans
for washing in cold water only
then wearin round the house
til they dry on yr shape,
put em in a clothes dryer,
she said, and you'll get
all pinch bruised
round the crotch'n
your stomach covered
with red streak marks
cross the front.

We burned em in the sixties,
girdles, she said.[6]

We must not imagine that it is only the fashion industry that is upset about the large size of our bodies. Fashion creates and it reflects. Creates, as we have seen, an image few women in this culture are able to realize for themselves. Creates longing—and we all know this longing to win the approval of our culture even at cost to our health, our identity as women, our experience of pleasure in our bodies. But fashion also reflects hidden cultural intentions, as it did in China with the binding of women's feet. As it does in our own day, with pants so tight they serve as an adequate replacement for the girdles that used to bind us. Fashion, for all its appearance of superficiality, is a mirror in which we can read the responses of conventional culture to what is occurring, at the deepest levels of cultural change, among its people.

For instance: if the problem of body and mind is as old in this culture as I have suggested, why is anorexia a new disease and bulmarexia a condition first named during the 1970s? Why for that matter is Christine Olman a model now and not twenty years ago when Marilyn Monroe inspired our admiration?

These questions may help us to understand that something has happened in our culture during the last twenty years that has made us particularly uneasy about the abundance of our flesh. Something, unnamed as yet, which fashion expresses as a shift from the voluptuous to the ascetic.

I wish to place before us a cluster of related facts that constitutes an important cultural synchronicity.

FACT: During the 1960s Marilyn Monroe stood for the ideal in feminine beauty. Now Christine Olman represents that ideal.

FACT: During the 1960s anorexia nervosa began to be a widespread social disease among women.

FACT: During the late 1960s and early 1970s bulmarexia began to be observed as a condition among women.

FACT: During the 1960s Weight Watchers opened their doors. In 1965 Diet Workshop appeared, in 1960s Over-Eaters Anonymous, in 1966 Why Weight, in 1968 Weight Losers Institute, in 1969 Lean Line.

FACT: During the 1960s the Feminist Movement began to emerge, asserting woman's right to authority, development, dignity, liberation and above all, power.

What am I driving at here? I am suggesting that the changing awareness among women of our position in this society has divided itself into two divergent movements, one of which is a movement toward feminine power, the other a retreat from it, supported by the fashion and diet industries, which share a fear of women's power.

In this light it is significant that one of the first feminist activities in our time was an organized protest against the Miss America Contest and the idea of feminine beauty promulgated by the dominant culture through this pageant, in which women strut and display their bodies, as men sit passively, judg-

ing them. It is interesting, further, that as a significant portion of the female population in the last two decades began to go to consciousness-raising groups and to question the role and subservience of women in this society, other women hastened to groups where the large size of their bodies was deplored. The same era gave birth to these two contradictory movements among women.

Yet we sense that there is an underlying similarity of motive in both movements. In both, women are driven to gather together and make confessions and find sisterly support for the new resolutions they are taking. In both, women have created new forms of social organization, apart from the established institutions of the dominant culture.

There is, however, also a fundamental divergence here. The groups that arise among feminists are dedicated to the enlargement of women. Confessions made in these groups reveal anger over rape and the shame women have been taught to feel about their bodies; there is interest in the longing to develop the self, concern for the boredom and limitations of motherhood, acknowledgement of the need for sisterly support in the resolution to return to work, go back to school, become more of oneself, grow larger. But in the other groups, confessions are voiced about indulgence in the pleasures of eating, and resolutions are made to control the amount of food consumed, and sisterly support is given for a renewed warfare against the appetite and the body.

Listen to the spontaneous metaphor that finds its way into the discussions of these two groups. In the feminist group it is *largeness* in a woman that is sought, the *power* and *abundance* of the feminine, the assertion of a woman's right to be taken seriously, to *acquire weight*, to *widen* her *frame* of reference, to be *expansive*, *enlarge* her views, *acquire gravity*, *fill out*, and *gain* a sense of self-esteem. It is always a question of *widening*, *enlarging*, *developing* and *growing*. But in the weight-watching groups the women are trying to *reduce* themselves; and the metaphoric consistency of this is significant: they are trying to make themselves *smaller*, to *narrow* themselves, to become *lightweight*, to lose *gravity*, to be-*little* themselves. Here, emphasis is placed upon *shrinking* and *diminution*, *confinement* and *contraction*, a *loss* of pounds, a *losing* of flesh, a *falling* of weight, a *lessening*.

These metaphoric consistencies reveal a struggle that goes beyond concern for the body. Thus, in the feminist groups the emphasis is significantly upon liberation—upon release of power, the unfettering of long-suppressed ability, the freeing of one's potential, a woman shaking off restraints and delivering herself from limitations. But in the appetite control groups the emphasis is upon restraint and prohibition, the keeping of watch over appetites and urges, the confining of impulses, the control of the hungers of the self.

When all other personal motives for losing weight are stripped away—the desire to be popular, to be loved, to be successful, to be acceptable, to be in control, to be admired, to admire one's self—what unites the women who seek to reduce their weight is the fact that they look for an answer to their life's problems in the control of their bodies and appetites. A woman who walks through the doors of a weight-watching organization and enters the women's reduction movement has allowed her culture to persuade her that significant relief from her personal and cultural dilemma is to be found in the reduction of her body. Thus, her decision, although she may not be aware of it, enters the domain of the body politic and becomes symbolically a political act.

It is essential to interpret anorexia nervosa, that other significant movement among women during the last decades, so that it, too, can be understood as part of women's struggle for liberation during the last decades. Indeed, Hilde Bruch calls it a new disease because in the last fifteen or twenty years it has occurred at a "rapidly increasing rate." From 1960 on, she writes, "reports on larger patient groups have been published in countries as far apart as Russia and Australia, Sweden and Italy, England and the United States."[7]

The fact that these are highly developed industrial countries, and that anorexia occurs primarily among girls of the upper-middle class, should remind us that anorexia is a symbolic illness. Where hunger is imposed by external circumstances, the act of starvation remains literal, a tragic biological event that does not serve metaphoric or symbolic purposes. It is only in a country where one is able to choose hunger that elective starvation may come to express cultural conflict or even social protest. . . .

In America of the 1970s and 1980s, no woman can possibly remain unaware of the fact that significant numbers of her sisters are asserting their rights to autonomy, to power, to the development of their full emotional and creative capacities. This movement of women into their enlargement is likely to affect her

in a number of ways. She may grow depressed with the life she is living and rebel against it. She may refuse to recognize that her life depresses her and fail to develop a meaningful analysis of her condition as a woman. Or she may feel the force of these contradictory tendencies and enact her entire response to them through her body.

Let us imagine then that a woman comes to awareness of her condition one day in 1969. She is, let us say, forty-five years old, she wears old, dreary clothes, and she is seriously depressed. She is a woman who has tried to diet and failed and who has exhausted her tolerance for weight-watching groups. For her the anorexic solution is simply not a possibility. And so she decides to join a women's consciousness-raising group. There, she tells the other women that her husband has just left her after twenty-five years. She tells how she is stuck in a job with a poverty wage in an insurance company, how she feels a thousand years old. She blames herself, she says, and the fatness in her body, for everything that has gone wrong with her life. But now, because she is encouraged to talk and because no one here believes her rounded belly is the cause of these complex failures, she speaks about a dream she had once as a young girl when she wished to become a writer. She tells how absurd this old dream seems now and how she is afraid. But because the women listen to her fears and encourage her to speak further, she goes home and she begins to dream that she might want to dream of becoming a writer.

Let us also imagine that another similar woman comes to a group intended to help women change their lives. But here, in fact, we do not have to provide the script, for the story of a middle-aged woman named Faye has been written for us by Gloria Heidi, in her unintentionally revealing book:

She was about forty-five years old when she enrolled in my class—a gray, doughy woman in a dreary maroon, half-size dress—a woman who had obviously come to me as a last resort. "Look, my husband Harry has just walked out after twenty-five years. I'm stuck in a poverty-wage, nowhere job at the insurance company. I feel a thousand years old—and look sixty. But I'm determined to be a new me . . . and I want to start by losing this excess weight. After all, now that I've lost Harry"—her eyes filled with tears—"what else have I got to lose?"[8]

In this group, where the woman comes with a complex social and personal situation, her terrible despair is attributed to the fact that she is fat. She is therefore encouraged to lose weight; a chart is kept of the weight she loses. When the magical transformation finally takes place we are told that the horror of her personal and social position has miraculously altered. A moral is drawn. We are assured that we, too, if only we will lose weight, can be "filled with energy, go aggressively after a better job and with a new figure, a revitalized personality, and an exciting new social life, [like] formerly dowdy and half-sized Faye, [soon] be sitting on top of the world."

The hidden message in this story is profoundly disturbing. Implicitly, we are asked to believe that if every woman lost twenty-five or thirty pounds she would be able to overcome the misogyny in our land; her social problems would be solved, the business world would suddenly fling wide its gates and welcome her into its privileges. Isn't it incredible? We, as women, need only lose weight and all of us will find jobs equal in authority and status and salary to those of men? The need for the Equal Rights Amendment will vanish? Unemployment figures will dissolve and the very structure of our society will be transformed?

There is a profound untruth here and a subversion of the radical discontent women feel. In a class of this sort, women are directed to turn their dissatisfaction and depression toward their own bodies. They are encouraged to look at their large size as the cause of the failure they sustain in their lives. Consider what it means to persuade a woman who is depressed and sorrowful and disheartened by her entire life, that if only she succeeds in reducing herself, in becoming even less than she already is, she will be acceptable to this culture which cannot tolerate her if she is any larger or more developed than an adolescent girl. The radical protest she might utter, if she correctly understood the source of her despair and depression, has been directed toward herself and away from her culture and society. Now, she will not seek to change her culture so that it might accept her body; instead, she will spend the rest of her life in anguished failure at the effort to change her body so that it will be acceptable to her culture.[9]

We should not be misled by the fact that we feel more at home in our culture when we lose weight. It may indeed happen that a woman becomes more attractive to men, finds it easier to get a job, experiences less discrimination, receives fewer gibes from strangers, and endures far less humiliation in her own family. Culture rewards those who comply with its standards. But we have to wonder what cost the woman is paying when she sacrifices her body in this way for the approval of her culture. . . .

It is only when we cease to trivialize our bodies and our feelings about our bodies that we begin to appreciate how powerful a tool against the development of women is daily exercised by this conventional orientation, which assures us that our sufferings and our depressions are caused by the recalcitrant behavior of our bodies—by their insistence upon feeding themselves, by their unsuppressible urges and wantings and desires, which make us fat.

For what happens when the woman gains back the weight? (Ninety-eight percent of women who have lost weight gain it back.)

What happens when she gains back even more than she lost? (Ninety percent of women gain back more weight than they ever lost.)

What indeed happens to her job and her lover and her new social power and her status in her family and her freedom from the hostility that our culture directs against women who live out their lives in large bodies? . . .

. . . For we can imagine that a culture based upon the suppression of women will be inclined, precisely in that era when a significant number of women are rediscovering the imagery and meaning of the Amazon, to turn away from whatever is powerful in women. The images in fashion magazines, on billboards, in store windows reflect this turning away from female power, but so also does the masculine retreat from grown women as erotic images. This retreat runs a parallel course to the women's reduction movement and expresses an identical fear of female power. Thus we come upon one final cultural synchronicity. In the era of women's liberation, which is also the era of fat farms and the body's emaciation, popular culture begins to produce movies in which photographers, grown men, become entranced with the Pretty Baby who lives in a whorehouse. In this same era of women's development some two hundred and sixty-four periodicals appear on the marketplace with child pornography.[10] In 1975 Houston police uncover "a warehouse filled with child pornography . . . 15,000 color slides of children, 1,000 magazines, and thousands of reels of film."[11] During this time of the assertion of woman's power we have films like *Taxi Driver*, "in which a twelve-year-old prostitute happily gratifies any male whim in order to please her loathsome pimp. Jodie Foster, who played the adolescent prostitute, was so well received in the role that she soon starred in *The Little Girl Who Lives Down the Lane*, in which she performed as a thirteen-year-old bundle of budding sexuality."[12] In the film *Manhattan* the most popular comedian of his day, a man forty or so, afflicted with an old-fashioned European melancholy and an entirely modern haplessness in the face of existence, turns for comfort and redemption to a seventeen-year-old girl when his wife, a grown woman, leaves him and becomes a lesbian. There is Chester the Molester who seduces little girls and boys as humor in the pages of *Hustler* magazines. And there is the adolescent girl who wrote the following letter to the author of *Kiss Daddy Goodnight*, a book of horror tales of the incest inflicted upon little girls by their fathers. "So if a girl wants my advice now I would say it is OK to do it with Dad until you are about thirteen or fourteen but after that he will lose interest in you and abuse you sexually by letting other people do it up you so it is best to stop at that age, and if I did, then I would still like Dad and not be mad at him like I am."[13]

Naturally, I cannot prove that the masculine preference for little girls is on the increase in our time because grown women are asserting their right to power. The preference itself is not as easy to document as the fact that the women in the fashion magazines are made to look like adolescent children or that the sizes in the clothing stores are growing smaller or that millions of women are attending diet organizations and seeking to reduce themselves while tens of thousands of others cause themselves to vomit every night. I am asking only that we begin to think about these simultaneous events in our cultural life; that we ponder the words of a fifth grade teacher in a city school: "Sexual abuse . . . incest . . . you don't know," she says, "you don't know . . . the kids in my class, the littlest girls . . . the uncles, the brothers, the fathers. It's epidemic and they all cover it up."[14]

Taken together, these words and the books and films and cartoons and letters we have been consid-

ering suggest a tendency in which men prefer to encounter little girls instead of grown women. Upon reflection, there is even something highly predictable about this. "Certainly," says Grace Paley, "any culture that prefers women to be childlike and dependent will, with a certain terrible logic, use its children as though they were grown women."[15]

Thus, what we are seeing in this tyranny of slenderness is more than a cultural warfare between body and mind, more even than a bitter struggle against the life cycle and the free expression of our kinship with nature. In this age of feminist assertion men are drawn to women of childish body and mind because there is something less disturbing about the vulnerability and helplessness of a small child—and something truly disturbing about the body and mind of a mature woman.

Notes

[1]Hilde Bruch, *Eating Disorders: Obesity, Anorexia Nervosa, and the Person Within*, New York, 1973.

[2]Maria Brenner, "Bulmarexia," *Saavy*, June 6, 1980.

[3]Morey Stanyan on Carole Shaw, *San Francisco Examiner & Chronicle*, January 20, 1980.

[4]Alice Walker, in a conversation about women and their body, suggested this analogy to me.

[5]Louise Bernikow, *Among Women*, New York, 1980.

[6]Jana Harris, *Manhattan as a Second Language*, Harper & Row, forthcoming.

[7]Hilde Bruch, *The Golden Cage*, New York, 1979.

[8]Heidi, *Winning the Age Game*.

[9]Adapted from a very similar utterance by Louise Wolfe, "The Politics of Body Size," Pacifica Tape Library.

[10]Florence Rush, "Pornography: Who Is Hurt?" in *Take Back the Night*, ed. L. Lederer.

[11]Ibid.

[12]Ibid.

[13]Louise Armstrong, *Kiss Daddy Goodnight: A Speak-Out on Incest*, New York, 1978.

[14]Grace Paley, review of *The Best Kept Secret* by Florence Rush, *Ms.*, January 1981.

[15]Ibid.

Love

Shulamith Firestone

*Shulamith Firestone was one of the founders of the
women's liberation movement. She participated in the
creation of Redstockings and the New York Radical
Feminists. Her* Dialectic of Sex, *now a classic in the
movement, appeared in 1970, as did* Notes, *a radical
feminist journal that she coedited.*

*"Love," argues Firestone, "perhaps even more than
childbearing, is the pivot of women's oppression
today." Women's need for love is known, almost to the
point of cliche, but men's dependence on it is rarely
articulated and understood, for men are wont to deny
it. Although they use and (parasitically) live off the
energy of women's love, Firestone contends, they do
not return it in kind. Ultimately love comes to mean
very different things to women and to men and has
divergent effects on their respective experiences and
lives.*

Shulamith Firestone, *The Dialectic of Sex: The Case For
Feminist Revolution.* New York: Bantam, 1971, pp.
126–128, 133–139.

A BOOK ON RADICAL FEMINISM THAT DID NOT DEAL
with love would be a political failure. For love,
perhaps even more than childbearing, is the pivot
of women's oppression today. I realize this has
frightening implications: Do we want to get rid
of love?

The panic felt at any threat to love is a good
clue to its political significance. Another sign that
love is central to any analysis of women or sex
psychology is its omission from culture itself, its
relegation to "personal life." (And whoever heard
of logic in the bedroom?) Yes, it is portrayed in
novels, even metaphysics, but in them it is described, or better, recreated, not analyzed. Love
has never been *understood*, though it may have
been fully *experienced*, and that experience communicated.

There is reason for this absence of analysis:
*Women and Love are underpinnings. Examine them
and you threaten the very structure of culture.*

The tired question "What were women doing
while men created masterpieces?" deserves more
than the obvious reply: Women were barred from
culture, exploited in their role of mother. Or its
reverse: Women had no need for paintings since
they created children. Love is tied to culture in
much deeper ways than that. Men were thinking,
writing, and creating, because women were pour-
ing their energy into those men; women are not
creating culture because they are preoccupied
with love.

That women live for love and men for work is a
truism. Freud was the first to attempt to ground
this dichotomy in the individual psyche: the male
child, sexually rejected by the first person in his
attention, his mother, "sublimates" his "libido"—
his reservoir of sexual (life) energies—into long
term projects, in the hope of gaining love in a
more generalized form; thus he displaces his need
for love into a need for recognition. This process
does not occur as much in the female: most
women never stop seeking direct warmth and
approval.

There is also much truth in the clichés that "behind every man there is a woman," and that "women are the power behind [read: voltage in] the throne." (Male) culture was built on the love of women, and at their expense. Women provided the substance of those male masterpieces; and for millennia they have done the work, and suffered the costs, of one-way emotional relationships the benefits of which went to men and to the work of men. So if women are a parasitical class living off, and at the margins of, the male economy, the reverse too is true: *(Male) culture was (and is) parasitical, feeding on the emotional strength of women without reciprocity.*

Moreover, we tend to forget that this culture is not universal, but rather sectarian, presenting only half the spectrum. The very structure of culture itself, as we shall see, is saturated with the sexual polarity, as well as being in every degree run by, for, and in the interests of male society. But while the male half is termed all of culture, men have not forgotten there is a female "emotional" half: They live it on the sly. As the result of their battle to reject the female in themselves (the Oedipus Complex as we have explained it) they are unable to take love seriously as a cultural matter; but they can't do without it altogether. Love is the underbelly of (male) culture just as love is the weak spot of every man, bent on proving his virility in that large male world of "travel and adventure." Women have always known how men need love, and how they deny this need. Perhaps this explains the peculiar contempt women so universally feel for men ("men are so dumb"), for they can see their men are posturing in the outside world. . . .

II

But abstractions about love are only one more symptom of its diseased state. (As one female patient of Reik so astutely put it, "Men take love either too seriously or not seriously enough.") Let's look at it more concretely, as we now experience it in its corrupted form. Once again we shall quote from the Reikian Confessional.

WOMEN:
Later on he called me a sweet girl. . . . I didn't answer . . . what could I say? . . . but I knew I was not a sweet girl at all and that he sees me as someone I'm not.

No man can love a girl the way a girl loves a man.

I can go a long time without sex, but not without love.

It's like H_2O instead of water.

I sometimes think that all men are sex-crazy and sex-starved. All they can think about when they are with a girl is going to bed with her.

Have I nothing to offer this man but this body?

I took off my dress and my bra and stretched myself out on his bed and waited. For an instant I thought of myself as an animal of sacrifice on the altar.

I don't understand the feelings of men. My husband has me. Why does he need other women? What have they got that I haven't got?

Believe me, if all wives whose husbands had affairs left them, we would only have divorced women in this country.

After my husband had quite a few affairs, I flirted with the fantasy of taking a lover. Why not? What's sauce for the gander is sauce for the goose. . . . But I was stupid as a goose: I didn't have it in me to have an extramarital affair.

I asked several people whether men also sometimes cry themselves to sleep. I don't believe it.

MEN (for further illustration, see *Screw*):
It's not true that only the external appearance of a woman matters. The underwear is also important.

It's not difficult to make it with a girl. What's difficult is to make an end of it.

The girl asked me whether I cared for her mind. I was tempted to answer I cared more for her behind.

"Are you going already?" she said when she opened her eyes. It was a bedroom cliché whether I left after an hour or after two days.

Perhaps it's necessary to fool the woman and to pretend you love her. But why should I fool myself?

When she is sick, she turns me off. But when I'm sick she feels sorry for me and is more affectionate than usual.

It is not enough for my wife that I have to hear her talking all the time—blah, blah, blah. She also expects me to hear what she is saying.

Simone de Beauvoir said it: "The word love has by no means the same sense for both sexes, and this is one cause of the serious misunderstandings which divide them." Above I have illustrated some of the traditional differences between men and women in love that come up so frequently in parlor discussions of the "double standard," where it is generally agreed: That women are monogamous, better at loving, possessive, "clinging," more interested in (highly involved) "relationships" than in sex per se, and they confuse affection with sexual desire. That men are interested in nothing but a screw (Wham, bam, thank you M'am!), or else romanticize the woman ridiculously; that once sure of her, they become notorious philanderers, never satisfied; that they mistake sex for emotion. All this bears out what we have discussed—the difference in the psycho-sexual organizations of the two sexes, determined by the first relationship to the mother.

I draw three conclusions based on these differences:

1. That men can't love. (Male hormones?? Women traditionally expect and accept an emotional invalidism in men that they would find intolerable in a woman.)
2. That women's "clinging" behavior is necessitated by their objective social situation.
3. That this situation has not changed significantly from what it ever was.

Men can't love. We have seen why it is that men have difficulty loving and that while men may love, they usually "fall in love"—with their own projected image. Most often they are pounding down a woman's door one day, and thoroughly disillusioned with her the next; but it is rare for women to leave men, and then it is usually for more than ample reason.

It is dangerous to feel sorry for one's oppressor—women are especially prone to this failing—but I am tempted to do it in this case. Being unable to love is hell. This is the way it proceeds: as soon as the man feels any pressure from the other partner to commit himself, he panics and may react in one of several ways:

1. He may rush out and screw ten other women to prove that the first woman has no hold over him.

If she accepts this, he may continue to see her on this basis. The other women verify his (false) freedom; periodic arguments about them keep his panic at bay. But the women are a paper tiger, for nothing very deep could be happening with them anyway: he is balancing them against each other so that none of them can get much of him. Many smart women, recognizing this to be only a safety valve on their man's anxiety, give him "a long leash." For the real issue under all the fights about other women is that the man is unable to commit himself.

2. He may consistently exhibit unpredictable behavior, standing her up frequently, being indefinite about the next date, telling her that "my work comes first," or offering a variety of other excuses. That is, though he senses her anxiety, he refuses to reassure her in any way, or even to recognize her anxiety as legitimate. For he *needs* her anxiety as a steady reminder that he is still free, that the door is not entirely closed.

3. When he *is* forced into (an uneasy) commitment, he makes her pay for it: by ogling other women in her presence, by comparing her unfavorably to past girlfriends or movie stars, by snide reminders in front of friends that she is his "ball and chain," by calling her a "nag," a "bitch," "a shrew," or by suggesting that if he were only a bachelor he would be a lot better off. His ambivalence about women's "inferiority" comes out: by being committed to one, he has somehow made the hated female identification, which he now must repeatedly deny if he is to maintain his self-respect in the (male) community. This steady derogation is not entirely put on: for in fact every other girl suddenly does look a lot better, he can't help feeling he has missed something—and, naturally, his woman is to blame. For he has never given up the search for the ideal; she has forced him to resign from it. Probably he will go to his grave feeling cheated, never realizing that there isn't much difference between one woman and the other, that it is the loving that *creates* the difference.

There are many variations of straining at the bit. Many men go from one casual thing to another, getting out every time it begins to get hot. And yet to live without love in the end proves intolerable to men just as it does to women. The question that remains for every normal male is, then, *how do I get someone to love me without her demanding an equal commitment in return?*

*

Women's "clinging" behavior is required by the objective social situation. The female *response* to such a situation of male hysteria at any prospect of mutual commitment was the development of subtle methods of manipulation, to force as much commitment as *could* be forced from men. Over the centuries strategies have been devised, tested, and passed on from mother to daughter in secret tête-à-têtes, passed around at "kaffee-klatsches" ("I never understand what it is women spend so much time talking about!"), or, in recent times, via the telephone. These are not trivial gossip sessions at all (as women prefer men to believe), but desperate strategies for survival. More real brilliance goes into one one-hour coed telephone dialogue about men than into that same coed's four years of college study, or for that matter, than into most male political maneuvers. It is no wonder, then, that even the few women without "family obligations" always arrive exhausted at the starting line of any serious endeavor. It takes one's major energy for the best portion of one's creative years to "make a good catch," and a good part of the rest of one's life to "hold" that catch. ("To be in love can be a full-time job for a woman, like that of a profession for a man.") Women who choose to drop out of this race are choosing a life without love, something that, as we have seen, most *men* don't have the courage to do.

But unfortunately The Manhunt is characterized by an emotional urgency beyond this simple desire for return commitment. It is compounded by the very class reality that produced the male inability to love in the first place. In a male-run society that defines women as an inferior and parasitical class, a woman who does not achieve male approval in some form is doomed. To legitimate her existence, a woman must be *more* than woman, she must continually search for an out from her inferior definition;[1] and men are the only ones in a position to bestow on her this state of grace. But because the woman is rarely allowed to realize herself through activity in the larger (male) society—and when she is, she is seldom granted the recognition she deserves—it becomes easier to try for the recognition of one man than of many; and in fact this is exactly the choice most women make. Thus once more the phenomenon of love, good in itself, is corrupted by its class context: women must have love not only for healthy reasons but actually to validate their existence.

In addition, the continued *economic* dependence of women makes a situation of healthy love between equals impossible. Women today still live under a system of patronage: With few exceptions, they have the choice, not between either freedom or marriage, but between being either public or private property. Women who merge with a member of the ruling class can at least hope that some of his privilege will, so to speak, rub off. But women without men are in the same situation as orphans: they are a helpless subclass lacking the protection of the powerful. This is the antithesis of freedom when they are still (negatively) defined by a class situation: for now they are in a situation of *magnified* vulnerability. To participate in one's subjection by choosing one's master often gives the illusion of free choice; but in reality a woman is never free to choose love without external motivations. For her at the present time, the two things, love and status, must remain inextricably intertwined.

Notes

[1]Thus the peculiar situation that women never object to the insulting of women as a class, *as long as* they individually are excepted. The worst insult for a woman is that she is "just like a woman," i.e., no better; the highest compliment that she has the brains, talent, dignity, or strength of a man. In fact, like every member of an oppressed class, she herself participates in the insulting of others like herself, hoping thereby to make it obvious that *she* as an individual is above their behavior. Thus women as a class are set against each other ["Divide and Conquer"], the "other woman" believing that the wife is a "bitch" who "doesn't understand him," and the wife believing that the other woman is an "opportunist" who is "taking advantage" of him—while the culprit himself sneaks away free.

A New Look at Lesbianism

E. M. Ettorre

Betsy Ettorre, a research sociologist, is best known for her book Lesbians, Women and Society *(1980) from which this excerpt is taken. She is a lesbian feminist theorist and has written other pieces on the subject. Currently she is working in the area of women and alcohol dependency.*

As Ettorre points out, society's treatment of lesbianism teaches us not only about its attitudes towards homosexuality, but also about attitudes towards other subjects crucial to all of us: sexuality itself, women, femininity, male power, and relationships. Lesbianism in its turn also teaches us a great deal about gender politics and what happens when it is absent, about how we as women do and may view women, about questioning the status quo, about affirmation.

E. M. Ettorre, *Lesbians, Women and Society* (London: Routledge & Kegan Paul, 1980). Copyright © E. M. Ettorre, 1980.

Sappho Revisited: A New Look at Lesbianism

Society doesn't like to give us any space to be ourselves openly, because we are an alternative. We're an alternative to heterosexuality, which is projected as the norm. We question just by being here, many values which are part of heterosexuality. We question women's dependence on men. We question male/female role-playing. We question the sexuality of every human being who thinks they're normal.

What's so normal, natural, fulfilling about heterosexuality? Natural is what feels good, normal is feeling ordinary, fulfilled is when you just did what you felt like doing. Anyone can be any or all of these things and no one except themselves can possibly know whether or not they are. What is it that makes heterosexuals feel so insecure about themselves that they can allow no alternative sexuality? How solid are the foundations upon which they build their moral values?[1]

IN ORDER TO UNDERSTAND LESBIANISM, WE SHOULD look at how it fits into both the culture and structure of society. (By "culture," I mean the way of life of a particular society. By "structure," I mean those social forces which determine that way of life.) We should view it as a complex social issue. In relationship to these two aspects of society, lesbianism poses a threat. As stated earlier, lesbianism exposes contradictions which exist in our beliefs about biology and culture, sex and ideology and women and femininity. By its very presence in society, it sheds light on such questions as: Does the source of the vast differences between men and women lie in biology or culture? Is the category "sexual" only related to biology or is it related to culture and furthermore, structure? How are biology and culture defined in society?

Are women "naturally female" and men "naturally male" *or* does culture play a large part in defining femininity and masculinity? What is "natural" or "human nature"? Do they really exist or are our beliefs about sexuality based on a false foundation? And what are our ideas about sex really based on?

Whatever the answers to these questions may be, the fact still remains that lesbianism exists in a society which is heterosexual and male-oriented and whose culture produces sexual ideas with those dominant interests in mind.

Culture and Sexuality

Sexual ideas develop in the light of specific biological bases (the sex organs). Yet these sexual ideas are also formed within and by concrete human experiences. Sex is viewed as a basic, material[2] need which must be satisfied. (Freud was keen on furthering this view and he predicted that individuals would have problems if their sex drive was left unfulfilled.) Furthermore norms, the unwritten rules which govern behaviour, tell us that this "powerful instinct" should be satisfied not only socially,[3] that is, with others—preferably, one other person of the opposite sex, but also according to certain characteristics—age, sex, race, class. Normal sexual performance or sexual behaviour which obeys sexual norms usually becomes a way of achieving a certain amount of social status.[4] When a dominant sexual viewpoint or sexual ideology is produced, it tends to be dependent upon how society processes and structures social relationships. In addition, this process appears directly related to power.

Many people experience culture as a way of life. However, it may also be experienced as a productive process which provides us with the tools to master the world about us. In the area of the "sexual," culture further provides us with an unquestioning acceptance of a sexual instinct. Through socialization, culture presents vivid images and ideas of acceptable sexual behaviour. Through culture, sex becomes institutionalized or ritualized and ultimately imprints upon our minds a dominant sexual ideology. However, it is important to be aware that acceptable ways of satisfying a supposed basic material need are based upon one's biology and, moreover, culture's definition of this biology! Sex is structured or organized according to two sub-groupings, seen as "naturally" distinct from one another—men and women.

These two groups are physically different from one another and develop socially on the basis of the biological differences between each other. Yet, the entire physical or material world of which human sexuality is only a small part becomes clouded by these differences. A fundamental biological tension exposes itself and culture thrives on it. Possibly Freud was correct in suggesting that biology is destiny.

Culture perpetuates the idea that sex is a powerful drive as well as a physical need. Therefore, individuals should experience "sex" not only as an uncontrollable desire but also as a basic impulse. As a result, sex is transformed from a physical base to human want or from material reality to a type of awareness. None the less, sexual activity remains a biologically discriminating process based on those who reproduce, women, and those who do not reproduce, men.

Power and Sexuality

Earlier, I indicated that sexual relationships have to do with power. I would argue further that *all* social relationships are power relationships. These power relationships are established between people in the process of making society, which is a complex web of social relationships. This "society" is capitalist—where people make money—and patriarchal—where women are subordinate to men in order for people to make sex and ultimately reproduce society. In other words, contemporary society has developed as a patriarchal capitalist society in which power lies in the hands of men and capitalists. Both of these groups reflect the results of how power is established, organized, distributed, mobilized and perpetuated in relationships between people in society. Both capitalism and patriarchy compose society's structure and reflect how people so far have made society. Thus, the most fundamental way of making society is through power relationships—male-directed or money-related or both. Hierarchy becomes the order of the day.

Within the above social organization of power, women lose out. They have less power and social value. Society places higher premiums on men, male activities, production in the factories and waged labour than on women, female activities, reproduction in the home and domestic or wageless labour.[5] Women are viewed in the truest sense of the word as the "weakest" sex. They have little values as workers, as producers or as *real* money-makers. Women are members of a secondary workforce; men are members of the *primary* workforce. All of these ideas are embedded within our value system and become part of the dominant sexual ideology. Social value which is sex-based is measured by one's productive value (making money) rather than one's reproductive value (making babies). More simply, social status which is directly related to social value is grounded in productive labour (men's work) and *not* in child or reproductive labour (women's work). Ironically, however, women are absolutely essential for the continuation of any given society. As a social group, they are the *real* producers in society: the bearers of future generations. Why then does society deny women the social importance that is due to them? Perhaps, the answer lies within our understanding of women's biological vulnerability of periodical physical weakness, which, in our society, implies the need for protection. Regardless of our conceptions, is this "weakness" in reality a strength? Observing this perplexing situation, Simone de Beauvoir states: "The body of woman is one of the essential elements in her situation in the world. But, that body is not enough to define her as woman."[6]

A woman, like a man, is her body. Yet, historically, she has been enslaved to it. Her reproductive function, which I term her "species-producing power," has resulted in a limitation of her social power and a denial of her social value.

During the course of history, the forces of production—both the instruments and human labour through which material goods are produced—were and are generated under different economic conditions (factors which determined how people produced goods in the range of societies whether primitive, ancient, feudal or capitalist). A particular society not only governs how people in general relate but also determines sexual relations between men and women. This is how history has developed and how the forces of production have operated. However, within this view an important element is missing—the forces of reproduction. Where does one locate women's species-producing power? Throughout history, these forces have been constant and women have remained subordinate. In this way, the category "sex" has emerged only to divide the development of our material world and to split human history!

Social thinkers speak of a "sexual division of labour." They describe this division as part of the social labour processes in which men are engaged in "male" jobs and women function in "female" tasks. This "sexual division of labour" solidifies in the modern family structure. Yet, I would argue that the above explanation is not thorough enough. The "sexual division of labour" does not take into account fully the persistence of the sexual dominance of men and the subordination of women. An explanation of the sexual division of labour must include an analysis of male power as well as the reasons for the subversion of women's species-producing power.

Power and the Sexual Division of Labour

As we have seen, the sexual division of labour maintains an unwavering social importance, both theoretically and practically. Because of this presence, sexuality is given the power to define cultural value and social productivity. However, regardless of its power, sexuality is consistently made private or divorced from society. Sex/work, the private/the public, the family/society, work in the home/work in the factory, domestic labour/productive labour, reproduction/production and female/male are socially constructed opposites which relate directly to ideas about the sexual division of labour. These opposites conflict with each other. They also indicate the existence of a dominant sexual ideology. This ideology dictates that women should enact passive or subservient roles and be concerned with procreation, while men should live out dominant social roles and concern themselves with protection and providing for others.

Society believes that these respective roles are not only natural on the individual level but also morally correct on the social level. Thus, the goodness of any given society's sexual morality preserves itself in and through the continuance of the sexual division of labour and ultimately, the perpetuation of heterosexual roles.

Homosexuality vs the Dominant Sexual Ideology

Homosexuality is the rejection of a traditional, dominant sexual ideology which, as we have seen, is heterosexual and male-oriented. Homosexuality is the practice of an alternative sexuality for either men or women. It is the concrete realization that some men aspire to practice "social femininity," while some women desire to practice "social masculinity." Nicole Claude-Mathieu attempts to explain these categories when she says:

At the level of social norms of everyday life, "social masculinity" is the unquestioned possibility of doing. It is responsibility. It is being numbered among the national heroes. "Social femininity" is to be limited even before action is undertaken and when difficulty arises it is to turn to men. "Social masculinity" is to know how to explain better, speak better, change wheels better and to holdout a hand to women when they run after the bus in a tight skirt and in four inch heels.[7]

Gay men are "social females." They tend to look to men for sexual and social support. Furthermore, they may establish close emotional ties with women, as women do among themselves. Lesbians are "social males." Contrary to popular myth they do not tend "to hold out a hand to women who run after buses." However, as a group, lesbians do tend to take up "the unquestioned possibility of doing" or the practice of being productive. Possibly the following quotation may explain one reason for this tendency:

Lesbians, on all levels, identify their interests with their jobs in a more concrete way than many women, since for them Prince Charming is not going to come galloping up and if, and when he does, he will be rejected. Lesbians seem frequently to take on extra work and responsibility; this fits in with their self-image, for capability and resourcefulness are necessarily desirable and attractive qualities in Lesbian life.[8]

Homosexuality upsets the dominant sexual ideology as well as confusing major issues like: "Heterosexuality is ordained by nature"; "Sex roles are natural and normal" or "Masculine and feminine qualities are inherent in each sex." Homosexuality denies the primacy of the family, as both an idea and an institution. As a result, the sexual division of labour becomes blurred.

Homosexuals, especially homosexual men, are generally viewed as "a risk" in relation to their work role or productive function. For example, if a person's homosexuality is discovered in her/his work context, an individual may lose her/his job, not get promoted up the scale, experience discriminatory practice which affects her/his job performance, or be seen as a liability. It is almost as if homosexuality has a corrupting influence and heterosexuals are in danger of being contaminated by their presence.

As with sexuality in general, homosexuality is isolated and privatized. Yet, its existence is recognized and the fashioners of the dominant sexual ideology ask epidemiological questions such as: How do we cure this disease? or What accounts for its apparent spread? or etiological ones like: What are its causes? or How does one become a homosexual? Society tries to lock the closet door shut. Ultimately, it attempts to privatize homosexuality near to the point of possible extinction. One lesbian expressed the conviction that society does not uphold the viability of lesbian relationships. If it did, society would not only recognize these relationships, but also protect them:

Lesbianism is not viable. It will never be viable until we're protected in our relationships with other women. If there's protection, there's privacy. However many people say, "What I do in bed is something between me and my partner," it's not true! This is because that very union threatens your whole way of life through jobs, family, etc. It isn't protected. Therefore, it's not private. So basically, your bed relationship is not valid. Although it isn't, it should be. . . . Being a lesbian is as valid as being a heterosexual. Society doesn't see this at the moment. No one asks a woman, "Are you a heterosexual?" No one asks that question. However, when the lesbian idea crops up, society heads straight for the bed scene.

In a similar vein, society points an accusing finger at homosexuals and says: "You're sexually sick and therefore, socially sick," "You don't measure up to our standards." The idea here is that homosexuals are socially sub-standard or individually diseased. The more liberal among us say, "Sex is a private affair and I don't care what you do in bed."

In a different vein, no one says to the homosexual, "Sex is immanently social"; "What you do sexually is interwoven with who you are in society and with what function you are to perform"; "One's private life is really public"; "The 'sexual' is social" or "The personal is political."

The quandary remains and the choice for a "meaningful" life is very limited.

"Instead of showing us our political potential, society tells us that we are something filthy, that we are over-sexed or that we are women trying to be pseudo-men. We're either sick or sinful. We have a physical malad-justment, a hormonal maladjustment or a mental mal-adjustment. In fact we are sexual and individual cripples. For them it's not worth beating around the bush."

The Rise of Homosexual Consciousness

Various social movements have emerged and have drawn attention to the social aspects of sexuality. As a result, homosexuality is viewed more as a cultural phenomenon and less as a unique sexual preference. Attempts are made to deemphasize the "sexual" or "individual" elements of the "disease" or "problem" in favour of its social or even political implications. As one lesbian suggested, "Sex isn't necessarily in-visible. When it becomes conscious activity between people, it becomes visible and gains strength."

New forms of consciousness are arising among sexual minority groups who are oppressed by the all-pervasive sexual ideology.[9] Today we are seeing this more and more.[10]

These new forms of consciousness may come to replace what were previous expressions of homosex-ual awareness. Historically, homosexuals tended to remain closeted. As a result, homosexual conscious-ness—one's awareness as a member of this op-pressed minority—remained weak, very isolated, on an individual level or hidden from the mainstream of social life. I would term this type of awareness as "pre-political" or lacking a group consciousness or solidarity with others.

Yes, homosexuals isolated themselves from soci-ety and each other. Who would blame them? A neg-ative attitude, which was epitomized by the term "crime against nature," developed in society towards homosexual practices. It is no wonder that most homosexuals denied themselves or were denied full access to society. However, this process still goes on today:

If you are a homosexual, people are so shocked when you tell them. I rarely do until I know them. Poten-tially all people are shocked, but I suppose it depends upon how well you know them. When you tell them, they think of you as different from what they them-selves are like. In fact, you're not that different. Well, I

don't think that I am or else I wouldn't get on so well with straight people. In fact, I do because there are a lot of other parts to my personality.

Society subverts any public expression of homo-sexual consciousness. Its attitudes stress the "evil," "sinful," "sick" or "individual" notions of homosex-uality. These attitudes are detrimental not only to the development of political consciousness but also to an individual's self-worth or value.

"I was ashamed before. I am proud now."

"I care very much what other people's views about les-bians are. Because if they think when they meet me that lesbianism is awful then I feel that this is quite wrong. They can dislike me as a person but they shouldn't dislike me because of my lesbianism."

Today homosexual politics represent a direct chal-lenge to society. The fight against sexual oppression is being waged on many fronts—the individual and the social, the private and the public, and so on. Terms like "sexual politics,"[11] "sexism," "male chau-vinist," "sexist," "women's liberation" and "gay" are now incorporated into everyday jargon. Social move-ments which primarily criticize sexual oppression have achieved varying degrees of public notice as well as support. It is at this point in the discussion that the term "social lesbianism" becomes relevant.

The Origins of Social Lesbianism

The development of lesbian politics or the birth of lesbianism as a social movement has only recently become evident. Traditionally, any concern for ho-mosexuality revolved around men or male homosex-uals. Lesbianism gained little credibility as a social phenomenon.[12] Its social relevance functioned pri-marily in the imaginations of men to titillate their fantasies. Yet this image was marred by a rejection of acceptable sexuality for women—if and when it be-came reality. Furthermore, acceptable sexuality for women has always implied men for partners as well as "rule-creators."

"I think it [lesbianism] is one of the most unacceptable ways of life for a woman. Almost by definition a woman classifies herself away from men. Also, it is

different in that you almost have to become something or someone different."

"Men define you as a lesbian because you sleep with women. That's all they think. So in fact you define yourself as a lesbian. Hopefully, you have as little influence from outside sources as possible. As soon as influence comes from society, you realize that it is predominantly ruled by men. They're the ones who define you."

It isn't chance that very few women in past generations had openly declared their homosexual feelings.[13] Confessed lesbian practice implied shame, stigma and possibly ostracism.[14] The closet was safer than open admission. At least, the closet helped an individual lesbian to "legitimate" or justify her "deviant" label on a personal level. Needless to say, the hidden life subverted a social critique of lesbianism.

"My ideas of lesbianism have changed. I saw it as a dirty, twisted, ghastly thing that I had done. It was an experience that I couldn't tell anybody about. And yet, it felt so good and the emotions were so marvellous. It was a hell of a muddle."

"I thought that my first experience was just a one-off. I had fallen very much in love and been loved tremendously by a woman and that was it. However, the second time around lasted nine years and involved many elements. I was moving into gay politics and then lesbian politics. I found that lesbianism wasn't just bed! It was interwoven with the needs of women and the status of women too."

Historically, it seems as if there have always been "lesbian ghettos," what I would describe as pockets of social activity which were characterized by intense emotional and sexual relationships between women. Whether or not we know about the ill-fated island of Lesbos and its renowned inhabitant Sappho, the Greek lyric poetess who set up a school for girls and a cult for lesbians, we should be aware that this type of ghetto existed during the early sixth century BC. In *The Well of Loneliness*,[15] Radclyffe Hall, a lesbian novelist, alludes to a similar ghetto which emerged in Paris during the first part of this century.

Traditionally, lesbian ghettos may have existed as socially designated areas for those engaged in unapproved activities or as what sociologists term "sub-

cultures of deviance." In these contexts, lesbian consciousness remains dormant. It is politically insipid. Social lesbianism counteracts this stage. Through it, lesbianism gains momentum as a social force and becomes a political potential for women.

Social Lesbianism: A New Consciousness

As stated above, social lesbianism manifests itself as a new form of consciousness which is emerging for women. In this way, it becomes a source of strength and establishes an important link between one's experience as a woman and a lesbian.

"I see myself first as a lesbian or as a woman. Now to me the two are almost synonymous, so I just feel very whole I suppose. I feel myself. I mean I don't feel at one with society, but I'm beginning to feel more real, more strong than I have ever done before . . . which is really exciting."

"Lesbianism is still an emotive word. Yet, it does describe what it means to be a woman, a woman-identified-woman and a woman-loving-woman. It filters right out into the things that really upset women about being women. That is that they are unable to be the same."

"The lesbian identity is woman and I'm thinking more and more that I'm less and less a lesbian and more and more a woman. I find the two labels so interrelated— whereas before I thought being a lesbian was a totally separate thing than being a woman."

In other words lesbianism has the potential to become political when it actively exposes the tensions between sexual practice and society or between a private notion of sex and a public conception of sexuality between men and women in patriarchy/ capitalism. It also makes visible those problems which exist between women's productive role, which appears to be minimal, and women's reproductive role, which, although important for the continuance of society, is under-estimated.

This book will emphasize that lesbianism is a complex and changing social fact. As a social construction, lesbianism implies a variety of interactions for a woman in society. She changes not only as the networks of lesbian activity expand and grow into more socially recognizable forms but also with the development of social lesbianism. In effect, it may transform dominant ideas about the sexual and women's role or social function. Resistant to these dominant ideas, groups create alternative forms of sexual practice. They present a direct challenge to the monolithic structure of the sexual. Because lesbians are oppressed by the ways in which society organizes sexuality into rigid roles, they are able to develop a unique consciousness as lesbian women.

As a result, contemporary lesbians, whom this study is about, need not remain isolated in the closet as did their predecessors. Many are emerging from the privacy of their cocoons in order to confront society. The metamorphosis occurs when public declarations of their newfound awareness are made. Yet, contradictory feelings still remain for some.

> "I feel right out of society because I don't like it anyways not just because I am a lesbian. I mean in real terms it [society] is a counter-culture. I feel strongly that ours could be a predominant culture but then I think how much I am living in cloud cuckoo land. How many other people in counter-groups think that they are just or it's just a short time before they come to fruition? All sorts of small groups feel that. The point is that it [society] is growing so fast that you just can't pretend any more."

Social lesbianism becomes the key to opening the closet door. Through this impetus as a social force, lesbians don't have to "pretend any more"; they are able to be themselves.

Remember that ideas about homosexuality—therefore, lesbianism—are consistent with society's attitudes towards sexuality in general. These attitudes uphold "essentialism," which is the view that sexuality or sexual practice is "an essence," "a part of human nature" or "inherent." Homosexuals and heterosexuals alike suffer from the oppressive features of essentialism. In other words, the sexual is viewed as having to do with a permanent characteristic which is grounded in one's biological make-up. It is fixed and unchanging. If one is born a woman, one should *be* a woman or "female." The same applies to a man. Culture influences "it" (sexuality) in a marginal or minor way. The social construction of sexuality is ruled out! Social lesbianism as a group force negates essentialism; yet, individual "social lesbians" may uphold this view. Thus, contradictions are ever-present in the realm of the sexual, the social, the personal and the political. . . .

Social Lesbianism—A Dialectic[16]

As we have seen briefly, both types of social lesbian polarize ideas on lesbianism and sexuality. They point out how lesbianism has developed from an individual experience to a social one and from a totally closeted environment to a relatively "out" life-style.

Previously, we discussed the dynamics of power and the sexual division of labour. Lesbianism illuminates the above discussion. In the light of the sexual division of labour and its relationship to women, as a social group, lesbianism drives a wedge between the role to reproduce and the role to produce, women's primary function in society and women's secondary function or women as reproducers and women as producers. Its very existence causes this opposition. Furthermore, in society's eyes, lesbianism minimizes women's role to reproduce in favour of a productive role which is usually reserved for men. Many lesbians desire economic independence from a man. As a result, their jobs may become very important to them.

A labour force which provides a better bargaining position as well as a greater potential for organization may be emerging for women and for lesbians. It is interesting to point out that in this sample of social lesbians, 49 per cent of the total sample were included in the three highest occupational levels: Higher Managerial or Professional, Lower Managerial or Professional and Skilled or Supervisory. Perhaps these lesbians are included in the group of women who

> have been drawn into the greatly expanded, further and higher educational system, encouraged through that process to expect equal job opportunity with men and able, subsequently, to get sufficiently highly paid employment to remain economically independent of marriage.[17]

Also lesbians are biologically women or structurally "females" and culturally "men" or "social males." In society's view they have the biological potential to reproduce, whether they use it or not. Society's vision is blurred because as "social males," lesbians should not reproduce. Yet some lesbians do.

For most women this biological potential becomes a reality in the traditional family unit which exists primarily for procreation. This happens when a legal contract transforms itself into a permanent sexual relationship with a specific man, a husband. Lesbians have a tendency to reject both the structure of the family and the husband-wife relationship. Ultimately, a lesbian may deny motherhood. Because motherhood is usually attainable only through the traditional heterosexual family, society denies it for her.[18]

As women, lesbians experience society's command to be dependent upon men for protection and money. The husband's wage is a symbol of this dependency and it characterizes women's relationship to money in advanced capitalist societies.

It becomes evident that this position (lesbianism) rejects the family structure as well as traditional forms of power. As a social force, it contradicts social values and society. Previously it was stated that lesbians are viewed as being "social males" by society. Yet within the general category "male" or in relationship to men they are not primarily productive (viewed as workers). Also, in relationship to women as a social group or to "structural females," which lesbians are as well, they do not become visible as primarily reproductive (viewed as mothers). This ambivalent state contributes to making lesbianism a distinct social category which is isolated and divorced from meaningful social life and which appears as politically impotent. In a state of confusion and fear, society wants to get rid of lesbianism. It utilizes "scare tactics." It tells men that lesbians are competing for "their women." (Thus far, society hasn't seen how they compete for "their jobs.") In reality, however, the lesbian struggle is for women's liberation—and the struggles of all people against sexual and economic oppression.

To summarize, lesbianism presents a twofold challenge to women's position: (1) By seeking economic independence from men, by not entering into the marriage situation or by not remaining in the marriage contract, lesbians threaten women's traditional relationship to money through the male wage (husband's income). (2) By experiencing an alternative sexual practice for women, lesbians defy the dominant sexual ideology. Its very existence proves that it is not necessary for women to have sex with men, that women do not have to be "sexy" or primarily "sexual" in order to survive as women and that lesbianism may have more to do with power and how it is distributed in society than was previously considered.

Social lesbianism may not substantially alter the position of women in society. However, it actively calls into question traditional social attitudes towards women as being primarily reproductive as "colonized" within the home and as sexually oriented towards men. As a force, social lesbianism is a contradiction to sexuality in society and a potential threat to the basis of all social relationships in that society.

Notes

[1] Angela Stewart-Park and Jules Cassidy, *We're Here: Conversations with Lesbian Women,* London, Quartet Books, 1977, p. 2.

[2] Throughout this chapter, 'material' refers to 'matter of the first class'. In other words, it refers to matter or activity closely related to survival. Sex is usually viewed in this way.

[3] The implication here is that sexual behaviour may have 'non-sexual sources', as in the case of a person who masturbates to reduce tension. However, sexual experiences are believed to be constructed from motivations and contexts which are social. See Kenneth Plummer, *Sexual Stigma: An Interactionist Account,* London, Routledge & Kegan Paul, 1975, pp. 32–5, 'The Social Sources of Sexual Meanings'.

[4] See Doris and David Jonas, *Sex and Status,* London, Hodder & Stoughton, 1974, especially pp. 144–7 where the authors discuss "Sex as Competitive Sport." They contend that sexual performance is rooted in the social context. Traditionally, the privilege of reproducing one's kind was a prize to be competed for. Today the prize, sex itself, has become the arena.

[5] Traditionally women's productive function has been minimized. However, recently this point has been challenged and domestic labour is viewed as valuable in economic terms. See Jean Gardiner, "Political Economy of Domestic Labour in Capitalist Society" in *Dependence and Exploitation in Work and Marriage,* edited by Diana Leonard Barker and Sheila Allen, London, Longman, 1976; also Jean Gardiner, "Woman, the Labour Process and Class Structure" in *Class and Class Structure,* edited by Alan Hunt, London, Lawrence & Wishart, 1977.

[6] Simone de Beauvoir, *The Second Sex,* New York, Bantam Books, 1970, p. 33.

[7] Nicole Claude-Mathieu, *Ignored by Some, Denied by Others: The Social Sex Category in Sociology,* London, Women's Research and Resources Centre Publications, 1977, pp. 8–9.

[8] Sidney and Barbara Love, *Sappho was a Right-on Woman: A Liberated View of Lesbianism,* New York, Stein & Day, 1972, p. 47.

[9] For an insight into the gay movement and its developing consciousness, see Jeffrey Weeks, *Coming Out: Homosexual*

Politics in Britain from the Nineteenth Century to the Present, London, Quartet, 1977; Dennis Altman, *Homosexual: Oppression and Liberation*, London, Allen Lane, 1974 and Karla Jay and Allen Young (eds), *Out of the Closets: Voices of Gay Liberation*, New York, Douglas Brooks, 1972. For a view of lesbianism as it relates to the women's movement see, Stewart-Park and Cassidy, *op. cit.* and Abbott and Love, *op cit.*

[10]Brake discusses the "new consciousness" of sexual minority groups and their contemporary emergence. See Mike Brake, "I May be Queer, But at least I am a Man" in Diana Leonard Barker and Sheila Allen (eds), *Sexual Divisions and Society: Process and Change*, London, Tavistock, 1976.

[11]Kate Millett, *Sexual Politics*, New York, Avon Books, 1969.

[12]Queen Victoria would not believe that it could ever exist. After the passage of the Criminal Law Amendment Bill in 1885 (making homosexual acts between adults punishable by law), Queen Victoria refused to sign the Bill until all the references to women were deleted. Lesbianism was unthinkable to the Queen!

[13]For some biographical insights into the life of one of these women, read Vera Brittain, *Radclyffe Hall: A Case of Obscenity?*, London, Femina Books, 1968.

[14]Unless, as Jane Rule suggests, a woman was "safely married and dressed and behaved like a woman—in public anyway," as did Virginia Woolf and Vita Sackville-West. See Jane Rule, *Lesbian Images*, London, Peter Davies, 1975.

[15]Radclyffe Hall, *The Well of Loneliness*, London, Jonathan Cape, 1928.

[16]This term is used in this context to show the existence of opposing forces.

[17]Gardiner (1977), *op. cit.*

[18]However, there are ways for lesbians to get pregnant and become mothers. One way is through AID, a method of artificial insemination.

The Problem That Has No Name

Betty Friedan

Betty Friedan, born in Peoria, Illinois, in 1921 and educated at Smith College and the University of California at Berkeley, has been active in the current wave of the women's movement almost from its beginning. Some have credited her book, The Feminine Mystique, *with precipitating the feminist dialogue among the general public. She took part in founding NOW, the National Organization for Women, in 1966; in organizing the Women's Strike for Equality (1970); and coconvened the National Women's Political Caucus (1971). Having taught at several universities, Friedan is now a member of many national boards and associations. She is the author of two other books on the women's movement:* It Changed My Life *(1976) and* The Second Stage *(1981).*

In this selection from the first chapter of The Feminine Mystique, *Friedan describes the inchoate sense of something wrong lodged in the minds and feelings of countless American housewives, a sense that puts the lie to the "feminine mystique," the cultural image of wifely and domestic bliss. Friedan's work is powerful not only because it so accurately delineates the nature of the mystique, but because it also captures the flaws in the image as well, the fall from grace of happily-ever-after-land and the dangers for those who believe in or seek it.*

THE PROBLEM LAY BURIED, UNSPOKEN, FOR MANY years in the minds of American women. It was a strange stirring, a sense of dissatisfaction, a yearning that women suffered in the middle of the twentieth century in the United States. Each suburban wife struggled with it alone. As she made the beds, shopped for groceries, matched slipcover material, ate peanut butter sandwiches with her children, chauffeured Cub Scouts and Brownies, lay beside her husband at night—she was afraid to ask even of herself the silent question—"Is this all?"

For over fifteen years there was no word of this yearning in the millions of words written about women, for women, in all the columns, books and articles by experts telling women their role was to seek fulfillment as wives and mothers. Over and over women heard in voices of tradition and of Freudian sophistication that they could desire no greater destiny than to glory in their own femininity. Experts told them how to catch a man and keep him, how to breastfeed children and handle their toilet training, how to cope with sibling rivalry and adolescent rebellion; how to buy a dishwasher, bake bread, cook gourmet snails, and build a swimming pool with their own hands; how to dress, look, and act more feminine and make marriage more exciting; how to keep their husbands from dying young and their sons from growing into delinquents. They were taught to pity the neurotic, unfeminine, unhappy women who wanted to be poets or physicists or presidents. They learned that truly feminine women do not want careers, higher education, political rights—the independence and the opportunities that the old-fashioned feminists fought for. Some women, in their forties and fifties, still remembered painfully giving up those dreams, but most of the younger women no longer even thought about them. A thousand expert voices applauded their femininity, their adjustment, their new maturity. All they had to do was devote their lives from earliest girlhood to finding a husband and bearing children. . . .

The suburban housewife—she was the dream image of the young American women and the envy, it was said, of women all over the world. The American housewife—freed by science and labor-saving appliances from the drudgery, the dangers of childbirth and the illnesses of her grandmother. She was healthy, beautiful, educated, concerned only about her husband, her children, her home. She had found true feminine fulfillment. As a housewife and mother, she was respected as a full and equal partner to man in his world. She was free to choose automobiles, clothes, appliances, supermarkets; she had everything that women ever dreamed of.

In the fifteen years after World War II, this mystique of feminine fulfillment became the cherished and self-perpetuating core of contemporary American culture. Millions of women lived their lives in the image of those pretty pictures of the American suburban housewife, kissing their husbands goodbye in front of the picture window, depositing their station-wagonsful of children at school, and smiling as they ran the new electric waxer over the spotless kitchen floor. They baked their own bread, sewed their own and their children's clothes, kept their new washing machines and dryers running all day. They changed the sheets on the beds twice a week instead of once, took the rug-hooking class in adult education, and pitied their poor frustrated mothers, who had dreamed of having a career. Their only dream was to be perfect wives and mothers; their highest ambition to have five children and a beautiful house, their only fight to get and keep their husbands. They had no thought for the unfeminine problems of the world outside the home; they wanted the men to make the major decisions. They gloried in their role as women, and wrote proudly on the census blank: "Occupation: housewife." . . .

If a woman had a problem in the 1950's and 1960's, she knew that something must be wrong with her marriage, or with herself. Other women were satisfied with their lives, she thought. What kind of a woman was she if she did not feel this mysterious fulfillment waxing the kitchen floor? She was so ashamed to admit her dissatisfaction that she never knew how many other women shared it. If she tried to tell her husband, he didn't understand what she was talking about. She did not really understand it herself. For over fifteen years women in America found it harder to talk about this problem than about sex. Even the psychoanalysts had no name for it. When a woman went to a psychiatrist for help, as many women did, she would say, "I'm so ashamed," or "I must be hopelessly neurotic." "I don't know what's wrong with women today," a suburban psychiatrist said uneasily. "I only know something is wrong because most of my patients happen to be women. And their problem isn't sexual." Most women with this problem did not go to see a psychoanalyst, however. "There's nothing wrong really," they kept telling themselves. "There isn't any problem."

But on an April morning in 1959, I heard a mother of four, having coffee with four other mothers in a suburban development fifteen miles from New York, say in a tone of quiet desperation, "the problem." And the others knew, without words, that she was not talking about a problem with her husband, or her children, or her home. Suddenly they realized they all shared the same problem, the problem that has no name. They began, hesitantly, to talk about it. Later, after they had picked up their children at nursery school and taken them home to nap, two of the women cried, in sheer relief, just to know they were not alone.

Gradually I came to realize that the problem that has no name was shared by countless women in America. As a magazine writer I often interviewed women about problems with their children, or their marriages, or their houses, or their communities. But after a while I began to recognize the telltale signs of this other problem. I saw the same signs in suburban ranch houses and split-levels on Long Island and in New Jersey and Westchester County; in colonial houses in a small Massachusetts town; on patios in Memphis; in suburban and city apartments; in living rooms in the Midwest. Sometimes I sensed the problem, not as a reporter, but as a suburban housewife, for during this time I was also bringing up my own three children in Rockland County, New York. I heard echoes of the problem in college dormitories and semi-private maternity wards, at PTA meetings and luncheons of the League of Women Voters, at suburban cocktail parties, in station wagons waiting for trains, and in snatches of conversation overheard at Schrafft's. The groping words I heard from other women, on quiet afternoons when children were at school or on quiet evenings when husbands worked late, I think I understood first as a woman long before I understood their larger social and psychological implications.

Just what was this problem that has no name? What were the words women used when they tried to express it? Sometimes a woman would say "I feel empty somehow . . . incomplete." Or she would say, "I feel as if I don't exist." Sometimes she blotted out the feeling with a tranquilizer. Sometimes she thought the problem was with her husband, or her children, or that what she really needed was to re-decorate her house, or move to a better neighbor-hood, or have an affair, or another baby. Sometimes, she went to a doctor with symptoms she could hardly describe: "A tired feeling . . . I get so angry with the children it scares me . . . I feel like crying without any reason." (A Cleveland doctor called it "the housewife's syndrome.") A number of women told me about great bleeding blisters that break out on their hands and arms. "I call it the housewife's blight," said a family doctor in Pennsylvania. "I see it so often lately in these young women with four, five and six children who bury themselves in their dishpans. But it isn't caused by detergent and it isn't cured by cortisone." . . .

In 1960, the problem that has no name burst like a boil through the image of the happy American housewife. In the television commercials the pretty housewives still beamed over their foaming dish-pans and *Time's* cover story on "The Suburban Wife, an American Phenomenon" protested: "Having too good a time . . . to believe that they should be un-happy." But the actual unhappiness of the American housewife was suddenly being reported—from the *New York Times* and *Newsweek* to *Good Housekeeping* and CBS Television ("The Trapped Housewife"), al-though almost everybody who talked about it found some superficial reason to dismiss it. It was attrib-uted to incompetent appliance repairmen (*New York Times*), or the distances children must be chauffeured in the suburbs (*Time*), or too much PTA (*Redbook*). Some said it was the old problem—education: more and more women had education, which naturally made them unhappy in their role as housewives. "The road from Freud to Frigidaire, from Sophocles to Spock, has turned out to be a bumpy one," re-ported the *New York Times* (June 28, 1960). "Many young women—certainly not all—whose education plunged them into a world of ideas feel stifled in their homes. They find their routine lives out of joint with their training. Like shut-ins, they feel left out. In the last year, the problem of the educated housewife has provided the meat of dozens of speeches made by troubled presidents of women's colleges who main-tain, in the face of complaints, that sixteen years of academic training is realistic preparation for wife-hood and motherhood."

There was much sympathy for the educated housewife. ("Like a two-headed schizophrenic . . . once she wrote a paper on the Graveyard poets; now she writes notes to the milkman. Once she deter-mined the boiling point of sulphuric acid; now she determines her boiling point with the overdue re-pairman. . . . The housewife often is reduced to screams and tears. . . . No one, it seems, is apprecia-tive, least of all herself, of the kind of person she becomes in the process of turning from poetess into shrew.")

Home economists suggested more realistic prep-aration for housewives, such as high-school work-shops in home appliances. College educators suggested more discussion groups on home man-agement and the family, to prepare women for the adjustment to domestic life. A spate of articles ap-peared in the mass magazines offering "Fifty-eight Ways to Make Your Marriage More Exciting." No month went by without a new book by a psychiatrist or sexologist offering technical advice on finding greater fulfillment through sex.

A male humorist joked in *Harper's Bazaar* (July, 1960) that the problem could be solved by taking away woman's right to vote. ("In the pre-19th Amendment era, the American woman was placid, sheltered and sure of her role in American society. She left all the political decisions to her husband and he, in turn, left all the family decisions to her. Today a woman has to make both the family *and* the politi-cal decisions, and it's too much for her.")

A number of educators suggested seriously that women no longer be admitted to the four-year col-leges and universities: in the growing college crisis, the education which girls could not use as house-wives was more urgently needed than ever by boys to do the work of the atomic age.

The problem was also dismissed with drastic solutions no one could take seriously. (A woman writer proposed in *Harper's* that women be drafted for compulsory service as nurses' aides and baby-sitters.) And it was smoothed over with the age-old panaceas: "love is their answer," "the only answer is inner help," "the secret of completeness—children," "a private means of intellectual fulfillment," "to cure this toothache of the spirit—the simple formula of handing one's self and one's will over to God."[1]

The problem was dismissed by telling the housewife she doesn't realize how lucky she is—her own boss, no time clock, no junior executive gunning for her job. What if she isn't happy—does she think men are happy in this world? Does she really, secretly, still want to be a man? Doesn't she know yet how lucky she is to be a woman? . . .

Even so, most men, and some women, still did not know that this problem was real. But those who had faced it honestly knew that all the superficial remedies, the sympathetic advice, the scolding words and the cheering words were somehow drowning the problem in unreality. A bitter laugh was beginning to be heard from American women. They were admired, envied, pitied, theorized over until they were sick of it, offered drastic solutions or silly choices that no one could take seriously. They got all kinds of advice from the growing armies of marriage and child-guidance counselors, psychotherapists, and armchair psychologists, on how to adjust to their role as housewives. No other road to fulfillment was offered to American women in the middle of the twentieth century. Most adjusted to their role and suffered or ignored the problem that has no name. It can be less painful for a woman, not to hear the strange, dissatisfied voice stirring within her.

It is no longer possible to ignore that voice, to dismiss the desperation of so many American women. This is not what being a woman means, no matter what the experts say. For human suffering there is a reason; perhaps the reason has not been found because the right questions have not been asked, or pressed far enough. I do not accept the answer that there is no problem because American women have luxuries that women in other times and lands never dreamed of; part of the strange newness of the problem is that it cannot be understood in terms of the age-old material problems of man: pov-

erty, sickness, hunger, cold. The women who suffer this problem have a hunger that food cannot fill. . . .

Can the problem that has no name be somehow related to the domestic routine of the housewife? When a woman tries to put the problem into words, she often merely describes the daily life she leads. What is there in this recital of comfortable domestic detail that could possibly cause such a feeling of desperation? Is she trapped simply by the enormous demands of her role as modern housewife: wife, mistress, mother, nurse, consumer, cook, chauffeur; expert on interior decoration, child care, appliance repair, furniture refinishing, nutrition, and education? Her day is fragmented as she rushes from dishwasher to washing machine to telephone to dryer to station wagon to supermarket, and delivers Johnny to the Little League field, takes Janey to dancing class, gets the lawnmower fixed and meets the 6:45. She can never spend more than 15 minutes on any one thing; she has no time to read books, only magazines; even if she had time, she has lost the power to concentrate. At the end of the day, she is so terribly tired that sometimes her husband has to take over and put the children to bed.

Thus terrible tiredness took so many women to doctors in the 1950's that one decided to investigate it. He found, surprisingly, that his patients suffering from "housewife's fatigue" slept more than an adult needed to sleep—as much as ten hours a day—and that the actual energy they expended on housework did not tax their capacity. The real problem must be something else, he decided—perhaps boredom. Some doctors told their women patients they must get out of the house for a day, treat themselves to a movie in town. Others prescribed tranquilizers. Many suburban housewives were taking tranquilizers like cough drops. "You wake up in the morning, and you feel as if there's no point in going on another day like this. So you take a tranquilizer because it makes you not care so much that it's pointless."

It is easy to see the concrete details that trap the suburban housewife, the continual demands on her time. But the chains that bind her in her trap are chains in her own mind and spirit. They are chains made up of mistaken ideas and misinterpreted facts, of incomplete truths and unreal choices. They are not easily seen and not easily shaken off.

How can any woman see the whole truth within the bounds of her own life? How can she believe that voice inside herself, when it denies the conventional, accepted truths by which she has been living? And yet the women I have talked to, who are finally listening to that inner voice, seem in some incredible way to be groping through to a truth that has defied the experts.

Notes

1See the Seventy-fifth Anniversary Issue of *Good Housekeeping*, May, 1960, "The Gift of Self," a symposium by Margaret Mead, Jessamyn West, *et al.*

Fetalists and Feminists: They Are Not the Same

Janice G. Raymond

Janice G. Raymond is professor of women's studies and medical ethics at the University of Massachusetts at Amherst. Among her credits are The Transsexual Empire *(1979) and* A Passion for Friends: Toward a Philosophy of Female Affection *(1986). She is associate director of the Institute on Women and Technology at M.I.T. and a founding member of the organization she refers to in the following selection, FINRRAGE, which stands for Feminist International Network of Resistance to Reproductive and Genetic Engineering.*

The past few years have seen an incredible explosion of technology enabling the scientific and medical community to manipulate genetics and reproduction, and very likely this is only the beginning of many new capabilities. Already we have seen a host of social consequences and the moral questions attached to them: What makes a mother or a father? In "surrogacy," who is the surrogate and who the parent? Can a child "belong" to anyone, and can or should "ownership" of a child be legally transferable? What is the difference in moral terms between an egg (fertilized or not), a fetus, a potential person, and a person? Who has the right to determine the disposition of disputes regarding the rights and obligations of engineered parenthood and on what grounds? What are the ultimate effects of "reproductive engineering" on parents, biological and adoptive, on the children born as a result of these manipulations, and on women in general? How do the benefits and the dangers of reproductive engineering balance out? Raymond poses a number of questions regarding NRTs (new reproductive technologies) from a specifically feminist stance. In the context of a patriarchal society, what are the woman-identified issues in reproductive engineering?

This essay appeared in Patricia Spallone and Deborah Lynn Steinberg, eds., *Made to Order: The Myth of Reproductive and Genetic Progress.* Oxford: Pergamon Press, 1987, pp. 58–66.

THERE ARE TWO MAIN GROUPS WHO CURRENTLY OPpose the new reproductive technologies (NRTs)—the fetalists and the feminists. Only one of these groups, however, has been given the status of the legitimate opposition—the fetalists. As portrayed by the media and the biomedical community, they are conservative and religious Luddites whose opposition to the NRTs, especially *in vitro* fertilization, is regressive, narrow, and trivial but, nonetheless, to-be-dealt-with seriously.

Opposing the fetalists are the "good guys"—the scientific and medical professionals, depicted as progressives who mainly want to move us forward into the twenty-first century of reproductive technologies and are prompted by a genuine humanitarian concern for infertile women who can't have children through normal heterosexual means.

There are, generally speaking, two kinds of fetalists. *Absolutist* fetalists can be said to come from conservative, New Right, and often Christian backgrounds. For the most part, they oppose the NRTs completely. They hold the absolutist position that life begins at fertilization. However, there is an increasing fetalist pluralism, largely created by the *developmental* fetalists, many of whom come from academic, humanistic, and medical backgrounds.[1] They may oppose certain aspects of the NRTs such as embryo experimentation after fourteen days, but allow that *in vitro* fertilization (IVF) can be justified for reasons of infertility. Fetalism, therefore, is not merely the territory of the conservatives. It is increasingly being emphasized in so-called progressive contexts. I am calling both these groups "fetalist," because what they have in common is a primary focus on the fetus.

The feminist position against the NRTs is only recently beginning to be heard, both in academic and professional circles and in the mainstream media. As Rebecca Albury has pointed out, the legitimate debate surrounding IVF has been characterized thus far by issues of law reform, conventional ethics, and the particular scientific and technical processes that are used. Speaking of Australia but, with some exceptions, applicable to other Western IVF countries, she states: "In the 'quality' press there is emphasis on technological development, financial advantage and national pride. In the 'women's' magazines and tabloid press the emphasis is on smiling mums and plump babies" (Albury, 1985). . . .

To begin, the linking of fetalist and feminist positions, whether done by the media, the "technodocs," or other groups, is an insult of the first order to women. It's tantamount to saying that behind every female idea or movement is male impetus, that women cannot stand on our own and create a woman-defined opposition to the NRTs for autonomous feminist reasons, and that any independent feminist course of action will be ultimately contaminated, controlled, and contained by men. It is simple to reduce the feminist resistance to the NRTs to right-wing morality and tactics if you don't want to, or won't, see the difference—if it's convenient to lump everything together. So once more feminist resistance, on its own terms, is made invisible. Feminists enter the legitimate debate and get delegitimized by being stripped of an autonomous feminist political position.

The first thing to be said about the differences between fetalists and feminists is that many feminists locate the NRTs squarely within the context of violence against women. FINRRAGE's resolutions, developed at its emergency conference in Sweden, July 1985, stress that these technologies hurt women personally, publicly, and with professional legitimation. Other feminists have defined a spectrum of woman abuse, beginning with the pornographic postures that IVF female patients are put into—a woman is placed on all fours as the medical phallus holding fertilized eggs is slipped into her from behind (this picture was shown on American television recently on the much-respected "60 Minutes" program)—to the biomedical manipulations and invasiveness of the treatments themselves.

Feminist positions on the NRTs highlight the explicit subordination and manipulation of women and their bodies that are involved in these reproductive procedures—procedures that include superovulation with powerful hormones; laparoscopy and

needle puncture to search for mature eggs, both of which can traumatize the ovaries: implantation of the fertilized egg with a cannula which can traumatize the uterus; amniocentesis, ultrasound, and very often delivery by C-section. Thus we are not talking about quick and easy medical procedures. We are witnessing the kind of medical intervention that rules a woman's life for years, where these procedures are not done merely once but repeated over and over, and cause an enormous amount of pain, discomfort, and personal debilitation. But these procedures are not thought of as violent to women because women are the expected recipients of this kind of pain and suffering, especially when it is covered by the language of therapy, when suffering and pain become treatment, and treatment is "for our own good."

Fetalists are concerned with what they express as the "violence" done to the conceptus, embryo, or fetus in procedures such as IVF. For example, Leon Kass states that "The human embryo is not mere meat; it is not just stuff: it is not a thing. Because of its origin and because of its capacity, it commands a higher respect" (Kass, 1979: 39). Would that women were accorded the same respect! Kass and other fetalists offer no critique of the *reality* that the NRTs impose on women and on real women's bodies. It is almost as if real women don't exist in their view, or that the only real women are those who are willing to bear any pain and manipulation to become mothers. Their major objection is how the technologies affect fetal *potentiality* for personhood. For fetalists, the real person here is the fetus.

Both fetalists and feminists use *embodiment* language in their critiques of the NRTs. Both groups are talking about different bodies, however. Fetalists contend that the NRTs disembody marriage and procreation and make of them a mechanistic enterprise reducible to eggs, sperm, and the technical mechanics necessary to join both together. This, they say, dissociates male and female biology, love, and procreation from a man and woman's total personal existence with each other. Where (hetero)sexual activity is ordained by God and/or by nature to enhance love as well as natural procreation, IVF reduces this marital union to the laboratory. It disembodies both. Fetalists also feature women as *having* a body—a body that is shared or inhabited by the husband, the fetus, and lately by the State, under the guise of "rights" or "interests." For feminists, women *are* our bodies.

Feminists also use the language of disembodiment in critique of the NRTs. However, feminists have quite a different value of "embodiment." Feminists are concerned about the ways in which the NRTs destroy a woman's bodily integrity and the totality of her personal and political existence. Many feminists criticize the ways in which the "technodocs" sever the biological processes of pregnancy and reproduction from the female body while at the same time making ever more invasive incursions into the female body for eggs, for implantation, for embryo transfers, and the like. Through such incursions, women can only come to be distanced from their autonomous bodily processes. And the net result of this is that women's bodies are perceived by themselves and others as a *reproductive resource,* as a field to be seeded, ploughed and ultimately harvested for the fruit of the womb. The feminist value of "embodiment" translates to bodily integrity and the control of one's body.

This is not a new version of biology is destiny. It is a personal and political recognition of the fact that one is located in the world by virtue of a body and that a woman has the right to bodily integrity. Our bodies are *part of* ourselves. As women's reproductive processes become disembodied by the NRTs, this adds another layer to the cultural image that women's bodies are there for the taking—this time by medical technology. The female body becomes less and less part of a woman's creative ground of existence. Rather it becomes bound by its use value.

Feminists are fighting to reclaim the female body, not just by taking the body seriously, but by refusing to yield control of the female body to men, to the fetus, and/or to the State. But feminists also recognize that lots more is at stake here than our bodies. Reclaiming our bodies and bodily integrity means renting the entire fabric of sexual subordination and the ways in which that subordination has insured for men both sexual and reproductive access to women.

Many feminists have also been critical of the ways in which motherhood is being disembodied from one woman by being distributed to several women. That is, it is possible for one woman to donate the egg, another to carry the implanted embryo, and another to raise the child that may be born. This is not the kind of distribution of parenting responsibilities that

are jointly and cooperatively assumed by several individuals who are all equally dedicated to the resultant child. Rather it is the fragmenting of the processes of reproduction and pregnancy into genetic donor, biological carrier, and social rearer, all referred to as different "mothers."

This is another form of dividing women from each other, made possible by the technologies of IVF and embryo transfer, and by surrogacy. In a society which represents women's relationships with each other as competitive, and where the fiction abounds that women are "each other's worst enemies," these technologies promote, on a biomedical level, divisions between women which the earlier class divisions between biological mothers and wet nurses only vaguely prefigured. Thus horizontal violence among women is given a biomedical impetus. The fragmentation of motherhood into discrete parts can only augment the ways in which women are personally and politically divided from each other under patriarchy.

Fetalists subsume the autonomy and independence of the woman to the "interests" of the family as they subsume the interests and rights of women to the "interests" and "rights" of the developing fetus. They are concerned about how the NRTs promote changing ideas and realities of (hetero)sexuality, parenthood, and marriage. Fetalists argue that the NRTs extend reproduction beyond the marital relationship. This argument has been forceful in getting IVF clinics in various countries to limit the technologies to married couples.

In fact, conservative fetalists don't seem to understand how IVF could be the great normalizer of the patriarchal family. For example, it has been pointed out that over half of the IVF patients in some US clinics are Catholics. What led many of these women to the clinics in the first place is probably expected motherhood and pro-family socialization. Yet a snag develops when the Catholic pro-motherhood and family ideology comes into conflict with its own pro-fetus ideology. Apparently, many Catholics are reconciling this conflict in favour of IVF. However, as of this moment, even in the aftermath of the Vatican's 1987 proclamation against intervention into human procreation, no Catholics are being excommunicated for undergoing IVF, Catholics whose embryos are often wasted when they do not implant or whose embryos are used for medical purposes. Yet, in the

United States, women are being threatened with excommunication from the Catholic Church for merely signing a statement in favour of abortion or for being the directors of planned parenthood clinics which have a pro-choice agenda.

Nor do we see IVF clinics being bombed, burned, or picketed in the United States as abortion clinics are—particularly clinics run by women or feminist health centers that perform abortions. Apparently, on an institutional level, the Catholic hierarchy has recognized that IVF at least promotes motherhood, the family, and is doctor-controlled, whereas abortion is seen as destroying the family and being in the control of women.

These contradictions in fetalist ethics and policies indicate that IVF is quietly tolerated in some fetalist circles because conservatives recognize its pro-family and compulsory motherhood possibilities. IVF has an enormous compulsory motherhood potential. It already is sustained by the ideology that motherhood is a compulsive biological need for women ("she can't help wanting children—it's her nature"). Paradoxically, while IVF disembodies reproduction and pregnancy, it rebiologizes women's supposed natural need to mother, almost portraying the desperate "need" of infertile women as a biological "motor," driving itself to fulfilment in spite of the invasive procedures and medical control that involuntarily childless women must accept. In the same way, unrestrained and uninhibited male sexuality has been sustained by the so-called male biological drive ("he can't help it").

Fetalist principles are evident in the Vatican's recent document prohibiting technological intervention into procreation. The full title of this proclamation is called "Respect for Human Life in Its Origin and on the Dignity of Procreation." The only respect in this document, however, is accorded to the fetus. Nowhere is there one mention of the "disrespect" that is accorded to the woman's "human life" by these technologies. One might expect that a document whose title purports to talk about the "origin" of human life might at least mention women. But the so-called "dignity of procreation" is applied in a general sense to the dignity of the human person and certainly not specifically to the dignity and integrity of the woman's body. The fundamental values that the Catholic Church emphasizes are two: "the life of the human being called into existence and the special nature of the transmission of human life in marriage." (Congregation for the Doctrine of the Faith, 1987). Nowhere is there any recognition that the body of the woman becomes an instrument in the technological procreative process and that this constitutes an assault against the dignity of women and a form of violence against women. The abstract inviolability of fetal life reigns supreme; the real and present violability of a woman's life, on which the new reproductive technologies depend for their very existence, is once more invisible.

The major concern of the fetalists, as Pat Hynes has phrased it, is ". . . experimentation on embryos, but not on women's bodies; crass profiteering in eggs, embryos, and wombs, but not the crass reduction of women to bodily parts and reproductive resources." By their one-dimensional focus on the fetus and their negation of any concern for the bodily and spiritual integrity and civil rights of the women involved, fetalists help reinforce the second class status of women (second this time to the fetus), who have no rights of self-determination. Their ethics and policies foster the media portrayal of women seeking IVF—i.e. that "real" women are those who want children at any sacrifice to themselves.

Both fetalists and feminists use wedge arguments, but in very different ways. Leon Kass, for example, predicts the future with "laboratories filled with many living human embryos, growing at various stages of development," and experiments "to alter the genetic and cellular composition of these embryos" (Kass, 1979: 49). Fetalists are concerned about the extension of present therapies and research to more drastic controls of human reproduction, and crasser uses of the human embryo. Feminists see with horror a future in which women, inured to being used as "mother machines" and "living laboratories" of reproduction, become available as ever-expanding material for sexual and reproductive biomedical research and experimentation. As women become the penultimate research "subjects" (read objects), the way is paved for women's wider and more drastic use in reproductive research and experimentation. Women become the scheduled raw material in the factory of legalized reproductive experimentation.

There is another group of fetalists who, in my opinion, has not received enough critical attention. These are the medical and humanist fetalists who are not portrayed as members of the fetalist camp because their fetalism is more sophisticated than that of the fetal ideologues. In medical circles, for example, current obstetrical language reduces the woman to "the maternal environment," thus highlighting the fetus as primary patient. One hears and reads about "maternal factors" or about "motherhood as a medical objective" but not about mothers. This fetalism is disguised further by what Robyn Rowland has called a "benign medicine" which portrays itself as responding to women's needs. I think that feminists should take particular note of the way in which the obstetrical community is becoming fetalist, but in a way which is cloaked by its technological language and its tendency to avoid the crasser moralism of the traditional fetalist perspective.

Furthermore, recent developments in biomedical technology such as research into embryological growth, clinical efforts to improve the outcome of previable fetuses, the use of the sonogram with its capacity to actually *view* the fetus, and fetal therapy or the treatment of ill or impaired fetuses *in utero* may all have a cumulative effect in evolving a more pro-fetalist medical opinion. The tendency of modern obstetrics, as Barbara Katz Rothman has noted, is to redefine its mission from a former "branch of medicine concerning the care of women during pregnancy, labor and the puerperium" to a more recent vocation as "physicians to the fetus" (Rothman, 1986: 25). For the most part, this medical fetalism is a developmental fetalism which further obscures the feminist critique of the NRTs because it allows for selective "rational" technologies that can be restricted to serve pro-fetalist concerns. It is also a fetalism that can be used to serve the interests of the "technodocs" who want the technologies limited to the "authorities" and "experts" in the field.

This group of developmental fetalists are fetalist not in the interest of opposing the technologies, but in the interest of selectively restricting them, or even in the interest of developing them in certain ways. So feminists can imagine a future in which IVF may be restricted or developed on the basis of both a moral and medical community's pro-fetalist ethics, but where the basic integrity of a woman's body, her control over that body and her reproductive processes, as well as her claim to personhood, would be undermined further by the above-mentioned technological developments, all of which reinforce the woman's status as "the maternal environment" and paternalize the medical community. In this future, as in the present, feminist values get minimal attention.

It is continually necessary, in my opinion, to re-articulate those feminist values in counter distinction to fetalist values. The feminist position against the NRTs speaks forcefully to the fact that our opposition to them comes from feminist principles—not from some absolutist or even developmental fetalist morality and/or biology. Feminists and fetalists are not aligned in any way. The status of motherhood cannot be raised (as the fetalists would have it) until the status of women generally is raised (as the fetalists would *not* have it). Motherhood will be valued when women are valued and to be valued, women's bodies must have the same freedom from intervention, intrusion, and invasion as men's. Women must have the same human and civil rights, the same right to live unendangered, the same right not to be plundered medically. This is not on the fetalist agenda. This is feminism.

Notes

[1] Later in this chapter, I will write at greater length about the developmental fetalists. Note, however, that the ancestors of the developmental fetalists date back to certain theologians and philosophers who argued that a certain period of *development* was necessary for "ensoulment," i.e. for fetal matter to become a person, also called "quickening." The male fetus became a person 40 days after conception; the female fetus after 80 days. Today, the developmental fetalists may be fetalist, not in the interest of restricting the NRTs but in the interest of developing them. Both developmental and absolutist fetalists are fundamental fetalists.

References

Albury, Rebecca
    1985 Personal communication.

Congregation for the Doctrine of the Faith
    1987 Instruction on the Respect for Human Life in Its Origin and on the Dignity of Procreation. St. Paul Editions. Boston.

Kass, Leon
    1979 Making babies revisited. *Public Interest*, Winter: 32–60.

Rothman, Barbara Katz
    1986 Case studies: When a pregnant woman endangers her fetus—Commentary. *Hastings Center Report* **16** (February): 25.

The War Between the Women—Arguments About Abortion

Kristin Luker

Kristin Luker is a sociologist who has taught sociology and has authored two books on abortion, Taking Chances: Abortion and the Decision Not to Contracept *(1975) and* Abortion and the Politics of Motherhood *(1984).*

As we saw in the text, the abortion debate is about many things, many of which have little to do with "saving babies." It often has to do with power and the control of women; with attitudes toward sex, pleasure, and freedom; with needs and causes; with "true believers" and politics. Here Luker describes the battle between two groups of women with widely divergent world views and lifestyles: traditional women, who see mothering and family care as the primary definition of womanhood, and other women, who see mothering as only one aspect of life.

Appeared in *Family Planning Perspectives* 16, No. 3, May/ June 1984, pp. 105–110.

ABORTION AND ARGUMENTS ABOUT ABORTION have been a common feature of the American scene for at least the last century and a half.[1] The 19th century had its own right-to-life movement, made up of male physicians who argued that abortion was murder if performed by women, but a therapeutic measure if performed by themselves.[2] The abortion debate today is different in important ways from earlier rounds. For most of its history, the discussion about abortion in this country was conducted by professionals, usually physicians, and men. As a result, until very recently, the abortion debate most resembled the disputes over other bioethical issues: It was for the most part quiet, collegial and restrained. None of these adjectives begins to describe the emotional and volatile abortion debate today. On the contrary, over the last decade the subject has galvanized—and polarized—Americans in the same way that such moral issues as abolition and temperance once did. What accounts for this remarkable transformation?

The full answer is complex. Physicians, who had successfully controlled the right to make all decisions about legal abortion since the 19th century, began to disagree among themselves. Technical advances in obstetrics meant that only a minority of abortions after 1940 were undertaken to preserve the physical life of the pregnant woman. Once abortion could no longer be presented as a case of trading the life developing in the womb against that of the pregnant woman, physicians were forced to confront the underlying dilemma: Is the embryo or fetus a person or only a potential person? Both positions have long philosophical traditions, and have existed side by side over the long history of abortion in America.[3]

In the early 1960s, some physicians began to press state legislatures to reform laws that permitted abortion only when the pregnant woman's life would otherwise be endangered. The proposed laws were designed to guarantee to those doctors the right to perform the kinds of abortions that they had been doing—those that would protect the social, psychological and emotional life of the woman as well as her physical life.[4] Increasingly, however, physicians were unable to agree among themselves about the conditions under which an abortion was justified. When the doctors signaled that they were no longer willing or able to control the abortion issue in house, the stage was set for the first time for a public debate about abortion.

To explore what it is that makes that public debate so heated and passionate, interviews with activists on both sides of the issue were conducted over a five-year period. A sample of more than 200 prolife and prochoice activists in California was the source of these interviews. We identified a beginning pool of activists from letterhead stationery, newspaper accounts and citations in advocacy literature, and asked those activists who were the people most involved in the issue, both on their side and among the opposition. All those selected for this study were named by at least two others as active as themselves (most were named by many more people), and they met the study criterion of time spent on this issue— at least ten hours a week on the issue if prolife, five hours a week if prochoice. (The criteria differed because of the different levels of involvement in the two groups. Although prolife and prochoice groups spent similar amounts of time on the issue prior to 1973, the latter have been less active since then, having achieved the notable success of the 1973 Supreme Court decisions.) We have reason to believe that for the years under study, we interviewed a representative, and at times exhaustive, sample of the prominent "positional" leaders (people who hold elective office) and "reputational" leaders (people who are highly visible workers) on both sides of the abortion debate. Interviews were intensive, lasting for at least two hours, and often for as many as six, and were tape-recorded, transcribed and analyzed. What follows are selected excerpts from the research. The quotations are verbatim from the interviews. These five years of interviews with those most intensively involved make three things clear:

- The present-day abortion debate, unlike prior rounds, largely involves two very different groups of *women*.
- These women are differentiated not only by their beliefs about abortion, but by the circumstances of their lives as well.
- The life circumstances and beliefs of the activists on both sides of the issue serve to reinforce one another in such a way that the activists have little room for dialogue, and few incentives for it.

Who Are the Activists?

Whereas the abortion debate used to be dominated by male professionals, it is now controlled on both the prochoice and prolife sides by women from the grass roots. It is not surprising, given historical patterns of power in American society and the history of earlier rounds of the abortion debate, that the top of the leadership structure still contains many male activists—especially in California, where this study was centered. (This pattern is more noticeable in prolife than in prochoice organizations.) However, more than 80 percent of those people identified in their communities as highly involved on either side of the abortion issue are women. In a nationwide sampling of mailing lists of the National Abortion Rights Action League and the National Right to Life Committee, University of Missouri sociologist Donald Granberg found very similar results.[5]

Perhaps one of the most remarkable findings to emerge from this research is how distinct the women activists on the two sides are, but how much alike the prochoice and prolife male activists are. The male activists tend to be holdovers from the early phases of the debate, when the major disputants were male physicians, lawyers and theologians. Since practitioners of those professions often have similar social and demographic profiles, it is not surprising that the male activists have a great deal in common with one another, even though they are on opposite sides on this particular issue.

When *women* activists are considered, a very different story emerges. Women who are engaged in the abortion debate are separated from one another by income, education, family size and occupation, as well as by their different opinions about abortion. Thus, the abortion debate grows out of two very different social worlds that support very different aspirations and beliefs.

Keeping in mind the pitfalls inherent in statistical averaging, one may ask who is the "typical" prolife and prochoice activist that emerges from this study? Two profiles stand out: The typical prochoice activist is a 44-year-old married woman whose father was a college graduate. She married at age 22 or older, has one or two children, and has had some graduate or professional training after her B.A. (Thirty-seven percent of all prochoice women in this study have received at least some post-baccalaureate training.) She is married to a professional man, is herself employed, and has a family income of more than $50,000 a year. She attends church rarely, if at all; indeed, religion is not particularly important to her.

The average prolife activist is also a 44-year-old married woman. She, however, married at age 17, and has three or more children. (Sixteen percent of the prolife women in the study have seven or more children.) Her father was graduated from high school only, and she herself has a good chance of having gone no further in school. (Forty percent of prolife women do not have a baccalaureate degree.) She is not employed, and is married to a small businessman or a lower income white-collar worker; her family income is less than $30,000 a year. Her religion is one of the most important aspects of her life; she attends church at least once a week. She is probably a Catholic, but may be a convert to Catholicism. (Almost 80 percent of the prolife activists in this study were Catholics at the time of the study, but only 58 percent had been raised as Catholics. Thus, just over 20 percent were converts.) A number of public opinion polls have shown that Catholics and evangelical Protestants are beginning to approve of abortion in proportions close to those of non-Catholics and nonevangelicals;[6] the results of those polls suggest that Catholicism is a proxy for something other than doctrinal belief. The findings of this study suggest that the Catholic Church contains (and in the case of converts, attracts) devout, traditional women who are committed to family roles.

It is not surprising that prolife and prochoice women have little in common. Few of those on either side of the issue have any friends or even acquaintances who disagree with them about abortion; and a number of prolife women spontaneously declared during the interviews that they would end a friendship if they discovered that the friend did not share their views on abortion. Again, this is in marked contrast to what we know about the men in the study. Because the men are often the colleagues of other professionals, most have acquaintances and even friends who oppose their point of view on abortion. Among male activists, a "live-and-let-live" stance on the abortion issue is much more likely than it is among women.

World Views

Women (and to a lesser extent male) activists are separated by far more than their values on abortion. Beliefs about abortion, as many of them noted, are simply the "tip of the iceberg." The two sides have very little in common in the way they look at the world, and this is particularly true with regard to the critical issues of gender, sex and parenthood. The views on abortion of each side are intimately tied to, and deeply reinforced by, their views on these other areas of life. Even if the abortion issue had not mobilized them on opposite sides of the barricades, they would have been opponents on a wide variety of issues.

With respect to gender, for example, prolife activists believe that men and women are intrinsically different, and that this is both a cause and a product of the fact that they have different "natural" roles in life. Here are some representative comments from the interviews:

> The women's lib thing comes in, too. They've got a lot of good ideas, but their whole thing ran off so far from it. How can they not see that men and women are different?

> Men and women were created differently, and were meant to complement each other, and when you get away from our proper roles as such, you start obscuring them. That's another part of the confusion going on now; people don't know where they stand, they don't know how to act, they don't know where they're coming from, so your psychiatrists' couches are filled with lost souls, with people who have gradually been led into confusion and don't even know it.

Men, the prolife activists believe, are best suited to the public world of work, and women to the private world of rearing children, managing homes and caring for husbands. Most prolife activists believe that the raising of children is the most fulfilling work women can have. They subscribe quite strongly to the traditional belief that women should be wives and mothers *first*. Mothering, in their view, is so demanding that it is a full-time job, and any woman who cannot commit herself fully to it should avoid it entirely. Moreover, they believe that the kinds of emotional sets called for in the larger world are at odds with those needed at home:

> When you start competing in the marketplace for what you can do and how you can get one-up or whatever, then I think we get into problems. It's harder to come down off that plane [of activity] and come home to a life where everything is quite mundane, and the children are way beneath you. It's hard to change from such a height to such a depth in a short time, and it becomes more and more difficult, I would think, as time goes on, to relate to both planes.

Prolife activists see the world divided into two spheres—public and private life—and each sex has an appropriate, natural and satisfying place in his or her own sphere. In this view, everyone loses when traditional roles are lost. Men lose the nurturing that women offer, the nurturing that gently encourages them to give up their potentially destructive and aggressive urges. Women lose the protection and cherishing that men offer. And children lose full-time loving by at least one parent, as well as clear models for their own futures.

Prochoice activists reject this notion of separate spheres. They believe that men and women are fundamentally equal, by which they mean substantially similar, at least as regards rights and responsibilities. As a result, they see women's reproductive and family roles not as a natural niche, but as a potential barrier to full equality. So long as society is organized to maintain motherhood as an involuntary activity, they argue, "women's sphere" connotes a potentially low-status, unrewarded role to which women can be relegated at any time:

> I just feel that one of the main reasons women have been in a secondary position culturally is because of the natural way things happen. Women would bear children because they had no way to prevent it, except by having no sexual involvement. And that was not practical down through the years; so without knowing what to do to prevent it, women would continually have children. And then if they were the ones bearing

the child, nursing the child, it just made sense for them to be the ones to rear the child. I think that was the natural order. When we advanced and found that we could control our reproduction, we could choose the size of our families, or whether we wanted families. But that changed the whole role of women in society. . . . It allowed us to be more than just the bearers of children, the homemakers. That's not to say that we shouldn't continue in that role. It's a good role, but it's not the only role for women.

These different views about the intrinsic nature of men and women in turn help to shape how the two sides view sexuality. For the prolife people we talked to, the primary purpose of sexuality is procreation:

> You're not just given arms and legs for no purpose. There must be some cause for sex, and you begin to think, well, it must be for procreation ultimately, and certainly procreation in addition to fostering a loving relationship with your spouse.

It is not surprising, given this commitment to the procreative dimension of sexuality, that the prolife activists in this study are opposed to most contraceptives. Although they are careful to point out that the prolife movement is officially neutral on the topic, most of the activists are confident that any law outlawing abortion would also outlaw the pill and the IUD, a result that they favor:

> I think it's quite clear that the IUD is an abortifacient 100 percent of the time and the pill is sometimes an abortifacient—it's hard to know just when, so I think we need to treat it as an abortifacient.

Moreover, a substantial number of prolife activists use periodic abstinence, or natural family planning, as their only form of fertility control, rejecting other methods of contraception on moral and social grounds:

> Well, you know the natural family planning books make a big thing out of how affection should be shown during the period of abstaining, and how this can bring you closer together than you might otherwise be. It would be easy to fall into a mechanical view of the spouse if you were to use a mechanical means of contraception. You have a better buttress if you use a natural means.

Because prolife activists regard the procreative dimension of sex as the most valuable, when they do use natural family planning, they use it to time the arrival of children, rather than to foreclose entirely the possibility of having them. For them, the fact that the method may not be highly effective in preventing pregnancy is a plus, not a minus:[7]

> *The frame of mind in which you know there might be a conception in the midst of the sex act is quite different from that in which you know that there could not be a conception. . . . I don't think that people who are constantly using physical, chemical means of contraception ever really experience the sex act in all of its beauty.*

Thus, the one thing family planners commonly assume that everyone wants from a contraceptive—that it be 100 percent effective and reliable—is precisely what prolife people do *not* want from their chosen method of fertility control. And, as is so often the case, the attitudes that prolife activists hold toward contraception are intimately tied to the realities of their lives. Since prolife men and women believe in, and live in, a world of separate spheres where each sex has its appropriate task, for them to accept contraception (and by extension, abortion) would devalue the one secure resource prolife women have—the private world of home and hearth. This would be disastrous not only in terms of status but also in terms of meaning. For prolife men and women to accept highly effective contraception, which symbolically and actually subordinates the role of children in the family to other needs and goals, would be to take away the meaning from at least one partner's life. Contraception, therefore, which sidelines the reproductive capacities of men and women, is both useless and threatening to prolife people. Moreover, if positive values about fertility and family are not essential to a marriage, they ask, what support does a traditional marriage have in times of stress?

These views about gender roles and the purpose of sexuality come together to shape attitudes toward premarital sex, particularly among teenagers. (People interviewed in this study tended to use the terms teenage sex and premarital sex interchangeably. But teenage premarital sex represents the worst of both worlds for most prolife people. In their view, teenagers should not be having sex because they are not married and are too young even to contemplate marriage seriously.) People who feel that sex should be procreative find premarital sexuality disturbing. Since, for them, the purpose of sex is procreation (or at the least requires a willingness to be "open to a new life"), people who are sexually active before marriage are by definition not actively seeking procreation; and in the case of teenagers, they are seldom financially and emotionally prepared to become parents. So for prolife people, premarital sex is both morally and socially wrong. Although prolife people agree that teenage pregnancy poses a very real problem in the United States today, they feel that the availability of contraception is what encourages teenagers to have sex in the first place, so that sex education and contraception only add fuel to the fire:

> *Planned Parenthood . . . it seems so logical—we've got all of these problems here, and if we just do sex education and contraceptives and everything, we'll solve all of them. It's kind of like two people coming to a fire. One says "Let's put this fire out by throwing water on it." The other says, "Oh, no, we always did it that way. I've got something better, it's called gasoline, and it's cooler than water." Well, there's a term that's being overlooked, and that term is responsibility—caring, real honest-to-God caring for other people.*

On all of these dimensions, prochoice attitudes are very different. For example, prochoice people in this study focus on the emotional aspects of sexuality—what our 19th century ancestors called amative sex—rather than on the procreative aspects. Prochoice people, therefore, value sex as an end in itself rather than as a means to procreation. For much of a lifetime, they argue, the main purpose of sex is not to produce children but to afford pleasure, human contact and, perhaps most important, intimacy. In their view, too exclusive a focus on the procreative function of sexuality leads to social control of sexuality, and, in turn, what they call sex-negative values. When prochoice people speak of sex-negative values, they mean values that prevent people from talking openly about sex, and thinking of sex as something to be enjoyed for its own sake, but that lead them to treat budding childhood sexuality—masturbation and adolescent flirtation—harshly.

Such harsh and negative treatment of sex makes sense, of course, if a community believes strongly that it is the only way to control the production of children and, in particular, the production of children born out of wedlock. But prochoice activists, in part because of their faith in the ability of humans to use reason to change the environment, believe that there are better ways to control the consequences of sexuality than to repress it and, in turn, to keep close control over women. As a result, prochoice people see contraception as a social good. In their view, the point of sexuality is intimacy; but since such closeness requires trust, familiarity and security, the establishment of intimacy takes practice. As a result, contraception, which allows people to focus on the *emotional* aspects of sex without worrying about its procreative aspects, is a social good.

For virtually all of the prochoice people in this study, contraception is not a moral issue. While they do have some pragmatic concerns about contraceptive methods—how unpleasant or how unsafe some are—contraceptive use in itself has no moral connotations. A good contraceptive method, from the prochoice point of view, is one which is safe, undistracting and pleasant to use—in short, one which enhances the intimacy available during sex, rather than one which detracts from it.

What is perhaps surprising to those unfamiliar with the issue is that prochoice people do have one moral concern about an aspect of birth control. With very few exceptions, the prochoice people interviewed do not accept abortion as a routine method of fertility control:

I take the idea of ending the life of the fetus very, very gravely. . . . That doesn't in any way diminish my conviction that a woman has the right to do it, but I become distressed when people regard pregnancy lightly and ignore the spiritual significance of a pregnancy.

A great many prochoice people in this study, particularly those active in helping women obtain abortions, find multiple abortions morally troubling. Some of them even volunteer the information that they feel like personal failures when a woman comes back to them for a repeat abortion. At first glance, this reaction would appear to be illogical. If the first abortion is a morally acceptable act, why isn't the second or the fifth abortion equally moral?

Prochoice opposition to abortion as a routine method of birth control is based on complex and subtle moral reasoning. For most prochoice people, personhood does not exist at conception, but it does develop at some later time. The prochoice view of personhood is therefore a *gradualist* one. A fetus may not be fully a person until it is viable, but it does have potential rights at all times, and these rights increase in moral weight as the pregnancy continues. Prochoice people tend to argue that the potential rights of the embryo or fetus at times must be sacrificed to the actual rights of the woman involved. But a woman who carelessly or capriciously conceives when she has the alternative of preventing pregnancy by the use of birth control is seen by prochoice activists as unjustifiably usurping the potential rights of the embryo by trivializing them.

Thus, for prochoice people, opposition to abortion as a routine form of fertility control stems from both the gradualist and contextual moral reasoning outlined above. A first abortion represents presumably the lesser of two evils, because the abortion of an embryo or fetus is seen as less morally wrong than bringing a child into the world whom one cannot properly raise. Since most women are offered a contraceptive method after an abortion, every abortion after the first represents a case where a woman had the option of avoiding pregnancy and did not do so. In most cases, prochoice people tend to find this kind of carelessness morally wrong.

Their views about the meaning and nature of gender and sex combine to influence how the two sides see parenthood. Prolife activists, because they see motherhood as a natural role, believe that being a parent is something that one learns by doing. Thus, the kinds of financial and educational preparations for parenthood that prochoice people see as necessary are considered irrelevant by prolife people.

It is interesting that many prolife activists commented that few women, including themselves, actually enjoy being pregnant:

I never wanted to have a baby, I never planned to have five children. I never felt the total joy that comes from being pregnant. I mean I was sick for nine months. I mean my general attitude was, "Hell, I'm pregnant again." But I thought pregnancy was a natural part of marriage, and I believed so much in the word natural, *and so I loved the babies when they were born. I realized that a lot of women have abortions in that first trimester out of the . . . physical and psychological fear that they experience, and the depression. . . . A lot of them will regret having that abortion later on.*

A general theme in the interviews with prolife activists—many of whom have large families, it will be recalled—is that there is an antichild sentiment abroad in American society, as exemplified by the strong pressures to have only two children:

> My husband, being a scientist, gets a lot of questions. You know, having a large family, it's just for the poor, uneducated person, but if you have a doctor's degree and you have a large family, what's wrong with you?

The values of prolife activists about parenthood follow from their views on gender, sex and contraception. Since the purpose of sex is procreation, they believe, married couples should be willing to have whatever number of children come, at whatever time they are conceived. Second, since motherhood is a natural role, one should not try to plan carefully for it through contraceptive use, and one need not prepare for it. Finally, since motherhood is the most satisfying and meaningful role for a woman, it is incomprehensible to prolife people that a woman might want to postpone or avoid pregnancy in favor of something else, such as work, education or worldly success.

In much the same way, prochoice beliefs about parenthood are rooted in their other cherished values. Since prochoice activists see the main purpose of sexuality as intimacy, they feel that parenthood must be postponed until the couple have attained a level of trust and security that will enable them to be successful, loving parents to a new baby. By the same token, since parenthood is seen as a social rather than a natural role, couples are best advised to wait until they have the social and emotional resources they need to move successfully into such a new and demanding role. Otherwise, under pressure, parents will come to resent their child, and this will limit their ability to be caring, attentive and nurturing parents and, eventually, their ability to raise children who feel loved, have self-esteem and, as one activist put it, "feel good about themselves."

Because prochoice people see raising children as requiring financial resources, interpersonal and social skills, and emotional maturity, they often worry about how easy it is to have children. In their view, parenthood is far from natural—too many people stumble into it without appreciating what it takes:

> I would say that the tip of the iceberg is purposeful parenthood. I think life is too cheap, I think we're too easy-going. We assume that everyone will be a mother—that's Garrett Hardin's "compulsory motherhood." Hell, it's a privilege; it's not special enough. The contraceptive agent affords us the opportunity to make motherhood really special.

Since prochoice activists think that in the long run, abortion will enhance the quality of parenting by making it optional, they see themselves as being on the side of children when they advocate abortion. In contrast to prolife people, who believe that parenthood will be enhanced by making it *inclusive*, that is, a mandatory part of the package of being a sexually active person, prochoice people feel that the way to improve the quality of parenthood is to make it more *exclusive*:

> My attitude on abortion stems out of, I think, the same basic concern about the right [of children] to share the good life and all these things. Children, once born, have rights that we consistently deny them. I remember once giving a talk [in which I said] that I thought one of my roles was to be an advocate for the fetus, and for the fetus's right not to be born. I think the right-to-lifers thought I was great until that point. . . . I think if I had my druthers, I'd probably advocate the need for licensing pregnancies.

All of these values come home for prochoice people when they talk about the *quality of life*. By this term they mean a number of things. In part, they use this phrase as a short-hand way of indicating that they view life as having social as well as physical dimensions. The embryo, for example, is only a potential person to them in large part because it has not yet begun to have a social dimension to its life, only a physical one. As a consequence, a pregnant woman's rights, being both physical and social, transcend those of the life that is only developing. This view is rooted in their beliefs about reason: Biological life is of the body and is physical; humans share physical life with all other living beings, but reason is the gift of humans alone. Thus, social life, which exists only by virtue of the human capacity for reason, is the more valuable dimension for prochoice people. This explains in part why many prochoice activists find the question "when does life begin?" unfathomable. For them, it is obvious: Physical life began only once, most probably when the cosmic soup yielded its first complex amino acids—the forerunners of DNA. Social life begins at viability, when the fetus can live and form social relationships—outside of the womb.

Motherhood and Morality in America

As this overview of some of the most central values of prolife and prochoice activists makes clear, abortion pits two groups of women against one another. Fundamentally, it divides those women who live in and believe in a world of separate spheres from those who do not. Put another way, the abortion debate forces a confrontation between those women for whom traditional roles—that set of social relations we call patriarchy—still work and those women for whom such roles do not work. ("Work" may be ambiguous here. Prochoice women believe that prolife women are only "one man away from disaster." In a world of separate spheres, they note, the death, divorce or desertion of a spouse can plunge a displaced homemaker into sudden and dramatic poverty.) What makes the abortion debate so passionate, therefore, is that these women have very deep vested interests in their chosen ways of life, and abortion has become both the marker and the symbol of their different interests. For example, the prolife women interviewed have *always* valued family roles, and have arranged their lives accordingly. At an early stage in life, they made the decision not to acquire high-level educational and occupational skills, but to get married instead. They got married because their values suggested that marriage would be the most satisfying life open to them. Similarly, prochoice women postponed (and in some cases avoided) marriage and family roles in order to achieve the skills they needed to be successful in the larger world, having concluded that the roles of wife and mother were too limited for them.

As a result of these early life decisions, women on each side have different investments in alternative views of the role of children and family and the related issues of contraception and sexuality. Prolife women, for example, have built their lives on the premise that reproduction is a resource, and they, therefore, resist all those cultural values—small fam-

ilies, contraception, abortion, nonfamily roles for women, day care—which diminish the value of children, or dilute the unique value of mothers. As perhaps the most interesting example, their commitment to periodic abstinence as a method of family planning, although it is based on very strongly held values, also serves to reinforce their marriages, and to stabilize their own power within marriage. When couples refrain from using "artificial" contraceptives, and it is up to the woman to decide when sex is possible, then sex becomes a scarce resource, and women hold the decision-making power, much as they did before the sexual revolution.

In the same way, prochoice women, having made commitments to the world outside of the home, have based their lives on the notion that pregnancy is a potential burden for women; they resist those values which suggest that motherhood is a natural, primary or inevitable role for a woman. Prochoice activists believe that men and women are equal because, in their own lives, men and women have substantially the same kinds of experiences. The prochoice women in this study have had approximately the same education as their husbands, and many of them have the same kinds of jobs—they are lawyers, college professors, physicians. Even those who do not work in traditionally male occupations have salaried jobs and thus share common experiences. They and their husbands share many social resources—status outside of the home, a paycheck, and peers and friends located in the work world rather than in the family world. In terms of family power, then, prochoice husbands and wives use the same bargaining chips and have roughly equal numbers of them.

Prochoice women, therefore, can afford to believe in a constellation of values around contraception, sexuality and abortion which, by sidelining reproduction, diminish the differences between men and women; and they can afford to do this because *they have other resources on which to build a marriage*. They believe the purpose of sex is intimacy; and since the daily lives of men and women on the prochoice side are substantially similar, intimacy in the bedroom is merely an extension of the intimacy that they enjoy in the larger world.

Thus, activists on each side of the issue are women who have a given set of values about what are the most satisfying and appropriate roles for women, and they have made life commitments that now limit their ability to change their minds. At the same time, the choices they have made lead them to believe that their own values are the most reasonable and appropriate ones for all women.

Perhaps one example will serve to make the point. A number of prolife women in this study emphatically reject an expression that prochoice women tend to use almost unthinkingly—the expression *unwanted pregnancy*. Prolife women argue forcefully that a better term would be *surprise pregnancy*, asserting that although a pregnancy may be momentarily unwanted, the child that results from the pregnancy almost never is. Even such a simple thing—what to call an unanticipated pregnancy—calls into play an individual's values and resources. As our profile of the average prolife person makes clear, a woman who is not employed, who does not have a college degree, whose religion is important to her, and who has already committed herself wholeheartedly to marriage and a large family is well equipped to believe that an unanticipated pregnancy usually becomes a beloved child. Her life is so arranged that for her, this belief is true. This view is consistent not only with her values, which she has held from earliest childhood, but with her social resources as well. It should not be surprising, therefore, that her world view leads her to believe that everyone else can "make room for one more" as easily as she can and that therefore abortion is cruel, wicked and self-indulgent.

It is almost certainly the case that an unplanned pregnancy is never an easy thing for anyone. However, from our profile of the average prochoice woman, it is evident that a woman who is employed full-time, who has an affluent life-style that depends in part on her contribution to the family income, and who expects to give her child a life at least as advantaged, educationally, socially and economically, as her own, draws on a different reality that makes her skeptical about the ability of the average person to transform unwanted pregnancies into well-loved and well-cared-for children.

What this example makes clear is that activists' beliefs about abortion are intimately tied to the realities of their lives. Since for prolife women, pregnancy is a resource, they are reluctant to see it devalued, either on the practical or on the symbolic level. Since for prochoice women, pregnancy is a burden, they are reluctant to see it emphasized. In consequence, anything that supports a traditional division of labor into male and female roles is, broadly speaking, in the interests of prolife women, because it is in that division that their resources lie. For them, to be "liberated" to compete with men would be a very real loss, because their lack of educational and occupational skills would doom such competition at the outset. Conversely, the traditional division of labor, when strictly enforced, is against the interests of prochoice women, because it limits their abilities to use the valuable "male" resources—education, labor-market experience—which they have in such abundance. Attitudes toward abortion, although rooted in childhood experiences, are also intimately related to present-day interests.

Thus, the two sides are fundamentally opposed to each other not only on the issue of abortion but also on what abortion *means*. Women who have many "human-capital" resources of the traditionally male variety want to see motherhood recognized as private and discretionary. Women who have few of these resources and limited opportunities in the job market want to see motherhood recognized as the most important thing a woman can do. For prochoice women to achieve their goals, they *must* argue that motherhood is not a primary, inevitable or natural role for women. For prolife women to achieve their goals, they *must* argue that it is. In short, the debate about abortion rests on the question of whether women's fertility is to be socially recognized as an asset or as a burden. In a world where men and women have traditionally had different roles to play, and where male roles have traditionally been the more socially prestigious and financially rewarding, abortion has become a symbol distinguishing those who wish to maintain this ancient division of labor, and those who wish to challenge it.

For all these reasons, it is most likely that the abortion debate will remain heated, passionate and bitter. It will be heated because it calls into question individuals' most cherished beliefs—those aspects of life held so dear that it cannot be imagined that all right-minded people do not agree with them. It will be passionate because *women's lives,* as well as the life of the developing embryo or fetus, are at issue, and the activists involved have very deep vested interests. It will be bitter because, since the core issue is motherhood, a gain to one side is matched by a loss to the other. If society agrees that the life developing in a woman's womb is a nonperson, and that motherhood is something a woman must prepare for, then those who believe that motherhood is a natural role have been dealt a severe blow. Conversely, if a baby exists from the moment of conception, and women must subordinate other roles to that of mother, then women who value and have access to other roles will find them relatively devalued by virtue of the fact that they may have to put them aside without advance notice.

Perhaps the one sure conclusion about the abortion debate which one can draw from this research is that it is likely to be with us for some time to come.

Notes

[1] J. Mohr, *Abortion in America: The Origins and Evolution of National Policy,* Oxford University Press, New York, 1978; and C. Degler, *At Odds: Women and the Family in America from the Revolution to the Present,* Oxford University Press, New York, 1980.

[2] For illustrative examples, see: H. Hodge, *Foeticide, or Criminal Abortion,* Lindsay and Blakiston, Philadelphia, 1869; H. Storer, *On Criminal Abortion in America,* Philadelphia, 1860; T. G. Thomas, *Abortion and Its Treatment: From the Standpoint of Practical Experience,* D. Appleton, New York, 1894.

[3] For the history of these two positions, see: R. Huser, *The Crime of Abortion in Canon Law,* Catholic University Press, Washington, D.C., 1942; G. Grisez, *Abortion, the Myths, the Realities, and the Arguments,* Corpus Book New York, 1970; and T. Mommsen, *Le Droit Pénal Romain,* Dusquene, Paris, 1907.

[4] For illustrative examples of the fact that physicians performed (and reported performing) abortions for indications of rape, incest, mental health and eugenic reasons, see: Q. Scherman, "Therapeutic Abortion," *Obstetrics and Gynecology,* 11:332, 1958; J. J. Rovinsky and S. B. Gusberg, "Current Trends in Therapeutic Termination of Pregnancy," *American Journal of Obstetrics and Gynecology,* 98:11, 1967; R. Kretzschmer and A. Norris, "Psychiatric Implications of Therapeutic Abortions," *American Journal of Obstetrics and Gynecology,* 98:369, 1967; K. Russell, "Therapeutic Abortions in California," *Western Journal of Obstetrics and Gynecology,* 60:497, 1952; and S. Boulas et al., "Therapeutic Abortion," *Obstetrics and Gynecology,* 19:222, 1962.

[5] D. Granberg, "The Abortion Activists," *Family Planning Perspectives,* 13:158, 1981.

[6] D. Granberg and B. W. Granberg, "Abortion Attitudes, 1965–1980: Trends and Determinants," *Family Planning Perspectives,* 12:250, 1980, Figure 1 and Table 6; and S. K. Henshaw and G. Martire, "Abortion and the Public Opinion Polls: Morality and Legality," *Family Planning Perspectives,* 14:53, 1982, Tables 1 and 2.

[7] The effectiveness of natural family planning is under some debate. When user failure is considered, some researchers have reported high rates of pregnancy. Other researchers dispute both the method of measurement and the conclusion. See: J. Marshall, "Cervical Mucus and Basal Body Temperature Methods of Regulating Births: A Field Trial," *Lancet,* II:282, 1976; M. E. Wade et al. "A Randomized Prospective Study of Use-Effectiveness: Two Methods of Natural Family Planning," *American Journal of Obstetrics and Gynecology,* 141:368, 1981; and H. Klaus, J. Goebel, R. Woods, M. Castles and C. Lorne, "Use-Effectiveness and Analysis of the Billings Ovulation Method," *Fertility and Sterility,* 28:1038, 1977.

Rape: The Power of Consciousness

Susan Griffin

Susan Griffin has taught Women's Studies at the University of California at Berkeley and at San Francisco State University. Her play Voices *was produced widely here and in Europe, and it won an Emmy for a television performance. One of the founders of the Feminist Writer's Guild, she considers her writing a political activity. She is the author of* Woman and Nature: The Roaring Inside Her *(1978),* Pornography and Silence: Culture's Revenge Against Nature *(1981) and* Unremembered Country *(1987). This article first appeared in* Ramparts *magazine in 1971. It became so well known that Griffin developed it into the book from which it is here reprinted.*

Griffin's analytical commentary on rape is one of the most powerful, yet rationally perceptive, on the subject to come out of the women's movement. She analyzes the effect of rape not only on the primary victim but also on all women, all of whom are victims of rape as a political act of terror against the female sex.

Part 1

Politics 1971

I have never been free of the fear of rape. From a very early age I, like most women, have thought of rape as part of my natural environment—something to be feared and prayed against like fire or lightning. I never asked why men raped; I simply thought it one of the many mysteries of human nature.

I was, however, curious enough about the violent side of humanity to read every crime magazine I was able to ferret away from my grandfather. Each issue featured at least one "sex crime," with pictures of a victim, usually in a pearl necklace, and of the ditch or the orchard where her body was found. I was never certain why the victims were always women, nor what the motives of the murderer were, but I did guess that the world was not a safe place for women. I observed that my grandmother was meticulous about locks, and quick to draw the shades before anyone removed so much as a shoe. I sensed that danger lurked outside.

At the age of eight, my suspicions were confirmed. My grandmother took me to the back of the house where the men wouldn't hear, and told me that strange men wanted to do harm to little girls. I learned not to walk on dark streets, not to talk to strangers, or get into strange cars, to lock doors, and to be modest. She never explained why a man would want to harm a little girl, and I never asked.

If I thought for a while that my grandmother's fears were imaginary, the illusion was brief. That year, on the way home from school, a schoolmate a few years older than I tried to rape me. Later, in an obscure aisle of the local library (while I was reading *Freddy the Pig*) I turned to discover a man exposing himself. Then, the friendly man around the corner was arrested for child molesting.

My initiation to sexuality was typical. Every woman has similar stories to tell—the first man who attacked her may have been a neighbor, a family friend, an uncle, her doctor, or perhaps her own father. And women who grow up in New York City always have tales about the subway.

But though rape and the fear of rape are a daily part of every woman's consciousness, the subject is so rarely discussed by that unofficial staff of male intellectuals (who write the books which study seemingly every other form of male activity) that one begins to suspect a conspiracy of silence. And indeed, the obscurity of rape in print exists in marked contrast to the frequency of rape in reality, for *forcible rape is the most frequently committed violent crime in America today*. The Federal Bureau of Investigation classes three crimes as violent: murder, aggravated assault and forcible rape. In 1968, 31,060 rapes were *reported*. According to the FBI and independent criminologists, however, to approach accuracy this figure must be multiplied by at least a factor of ten to compensate for the fact that most rapes are not reported; when these compensatory mathematics are used, there are more rapes committed than aggravated assaults and homicides.

When I asked Berkeley California's Police Inspector in charge of rape investigation if he knew why men rape women, he replied that he had not spoken with "these people and delved into what really makes them tick, because that really isn't my job. . . ." However, when I asked him how a woman might prevent being raped, he was not so reticent, "I wouldn't advise any female to go walking around alone at night . . . and she should lock her car at all times." The Inspector illustrated his warning with a grisly story about a man who lay in wait for women in the back seats of their cars, while they were shopping in a local supermarket. This man eventually murdered one of his rape victims. "Always lock your car," the Inspector repeated, and then added, without a hint of irony, "Of course, you don't have to be paranoid about this type of thing."

The Inspector wondered why I wanted to write about rape. Like most men he did not understand the urgency of the topic, for, after all, men are not raped. But like most women I had spent considerable time speculating on the true nature of the rapist.

When I was very young, my image of the "sexual offender" was a nightmarish amalgamation of the bogey man and Captain Hook: he wore a black cape, and he cackled. As I matured, so did my image of the rapist. Born into the psychoanalytic age, I tried to "understand" the rapist. Rape, I came to believe, was only one of many unfortunate evils produced by sexual repression. Reasoning by tautology, I concluded that any man who would rape a woman must be out of his mind.

Yet, though the theory that rapists are insane is a popular one, this belief has no basis in fact. According to Professor Menachem Amir's study of 646 rape cases in Philadelphia, *Patterns in Forcible Rape*, men who rape are not abnormal. Amir writes, "Studies indicate that sex offenders do not constitute a unique or psychopathological type; nor are they as a group invariably more disturbed than the control groups to which they are compared." Alan Taylor, a parole officer who has worked with rapists in the prison facilities at San Luis Obispo, California, stated the question in plainer language, "Those men were the most normal men there. They had a lot of hang-ups, but they were the same hang-ups as men walking out on the street."

Another canon in the apologetics of rape is that, if it were not for learned social controls, all men would rape. Rape is held to be natural behavior, and not to rape must be learned. But in truth rape is not universal to the human species. Moreover, studies of rape in our culture reveal that, far from being impulsive behavior, most rape is planned. Professor Amir's study reveals that in cases of group rape—(the "gangbang" of masculine slang) 90 percent of the rapes were planned; in pair rapes, 83 percent of the rapes were planned; and in single rapes, 58 percent were planned. These figures should significantly discredit the image of the rapist as a man who is suddenly overcome by sexual needs society does not allow him to fulfill.

Far from the social control of rape being learned, comparisons with other cultures lead one to suspect that, in our society, it is rape itself that is learned. (The fact that rape is against the law should not be considered proof that rape is not in fact encouraged as part of our culture.)

This culture's concept of rape as an illegal, but still understandable, form of behavior is not a universal one. In her study *Sex and Temperament*, Margaret Mead describes a society that does not share our views. The Arapesh do not ". . . have any conception of the male nature that might make rape understandable to them." Indeed our interpretation of rape is a product of our conception of the nature of male sexuality. A common retort to the question, why don't women rape men, is the myth that men have greater sexual needs, that their sexuality is more urgent than women's. And it is the nature of human beings to want to live up to what is expected of them.

And this same culture which expects aggression from the male expects passivity from the female. Conveniently, the companion myth about the nature of female sexuality is that all women secretly want to be raped. Lurking beneath her modest female exterior is a subconscious desire to be ravished. The following description of a stag movie, written by Brenda Starr in Los Angeles' underground paper, *Everywoman*, typifies this male fantasy. The movie "showed a woman in her underclothes reading on her bed. She is interrupted by a rapist with a knife. He immediately wins her over with his charm and they get busy sucking and fucking." An advertisement in the *Berkeley Barb* reads, "Now as all women know from their daydreams, rape has a lot of advantages. Best of all it's so simple. No preparation necessary, no planning ahead of time, no wondering if you should or shouldn't; just whang! bang!" Thanks to Masters and Johnson even the scientific canon recognizes that for the female, "whang! bang!" can scarcely be described as pleasurable.

Still, the male psyche persists in believing that, protestations and struggles to the contrary, deep inside her mysterious feminine soul, the female victim has wished for her own fate. A young woman who was raped by the husband of a friend said that days after the incident the man returned to her home, pounded on the door and screamed to her, "Jane, Jane. You loved it. You know you loved it."

The theory that women like being raped extends itself by deduction into the proposition that most or much of rape is provoked by the victim. But this too is only myth. Though provocation, considered a mitigating factor in a court of law, may consist of only "a gesture," according to the Federal Commission on Crimes of Violence, only 4 percent of reported rapes involved any precipitative behavior by the woman.

The notion that rape is enjoyed by the victim is also convenient for the man who, though he would not commit forcible rape, enjoys the idea of its existence, as if rape confirms that enormous sexual potency which he secretly knows to be his own. It is for the pleasure of the armchair rapist that detailed accounts of violent rapes exist in the media. Indeed, many men appear to take sexual pleasure from nearly all forms of violence. Whatever the motivation, male sexuality and violence in our culture seem to be inseparable. James Bond alternately whips out his revolver and his cock, and though there is no known connection between the skills of gunfighting and lovemaking, pacifism seems suspiciously effeminate.

In a recent fictional treatment of the Manson case, Frank Conroy writes of his vicarious titillation when describing the murders to his wife:

> *"Every single person there was killed."* She didn't move.
>
> *"It sounds like there was torture,"* I said. As the words left my mouth I knew there was no need to say them to frighten her into believing that she needed me for protection.

The pleasure he feels as his wife's protector is inextricably mixed with pleasure in the violence itself. Conroy writes, "I was excited by the killings, as one excited by catastrophe on a grand scale, as one is alert to pre-echoes of unknown changes, hints of unrevealed secrets, rumblings of chaos. . . ."

The attraction of the male in our culture to violence and death is a tradition Manson and his admirers are carrying on with tireless avidity (even presuming Manson's innocence, he dreams of the purification of fire and destruction). It was Malraux in his *Anti-Memoirs* who said that, for the male, facing death was the illuminating experience analogous to childbirth for the female. Certainly our culture does glorify war and shroud the agonies of the gunfighter in veils of mystery.

And in the spectrum of male behavior, rape, the perfect combination of sex and violence, is the penultimate act. Erotic pleasure cannot be separated from culture, and in our culture male eroticism is wedded to power. Not only should a man be taller and stronger than a female in the perfect love-match, but he must also demonstrate his superior strength in gestures of dominance which are perceived as amorous. Though the law attempts to make a clear division between rape and sexual intercourse, in fact the courts find it difficult to distinguish between a case where the decision to copulate was mutual and one where a man forced himself upon his partner.

The scenario is even further complicated by the expectation that, not only does a woman mean "yes" when she says "no," but that a really decent woman ought to begin by saying "no," and then be led down the primrose path to acquiescence. Ovid, the author of Western Civilization's most celebrated sex manual, makes this expectation perfectly clear:

> . . . and when I beg you to say "yes," say "no." Then let me lie outside your bolted door. . . . So Love grows strong. . . .

That the basic elements of rape are involved in all heterosexual relationships may explain why men often identify with the offender in this crime. But to regard the rapist as the victim, a man driven by his inherent sexual needs to take what will not be given him, reveals a basic ignorance of sexual politics. For in our culture heterosexual love finds an erotic expression through male dominance and female submission. A man who derives pleasure from raping a woman clearly must enjoy force and dominance as much or more than the simple pleasures of the flesh. Coitus cannot be experienced in isolation. The weather, the state of the nation, the level of sugar in the blood—all will affect a man's ability to achieve orgasm. If a man can achieve sexual pleasure after terrorizing and humiliating the object of his passion, and in fact while inflicting pain upon her, one must assume he derives pleasure directly from terrorizing, humiliating and harming a woman. According to Amir's study of forcible rape, on a statistical average the man who has been convicted of rape was found to have a normal sexual personality, tending to be different from the normal, well-adjusted male only in having a greater tendency to express violence and rage.

And if the professional rapist is to be separated from the average dominant heterosexual, it may be mainly a quantitative difference. For the existence of rape as an index to masculinity is not entirely metaphorical. Though this measure of masculinity seems to be more publicly exhibited among "bad boys" or aging bikers who practice sexual initiation through group rape, in fact, "good boys" engage in the same rites to prove their manhood. In Stockton, a small town in California which epitomizes silent-majority America, a bachelor party was given last summer for a young man about to be married. A woman was hired to dance "topless" for the amusement of the guests. At the high point of the evening the bridegroom-to-be dragged the woman into a bedroom. No move was made by any of his companions to stop what was clearly going to be an attempted rape. Far from it. As the woman described, "I tried to keep him away—told him of my Herpes Genitalis, et cetera, but he couldn't face the guys if he didn't screw me." After the bridegroom had finished raping the woman and returned with her to the party, far from chastising him, his friends heckled the woman and covered her with wine.

It was fortunate for the dancer that the bridegroom's friends did not follow him into the bedroom for, though one might suppose that in group rape, since the victim is outnumbered, less force would be inflicted on her, in fact, Amir's studies indicate, "the most excessive degrees of violence occurred in group rape." Far from discouraging violence, the presence of other men may in fact encourage sadism, and even cause the behavior. In an unpublished study of group rape by Gilbert Geis and Duncan Chappell, the authors refer to a study by W. H. Blanchard which relates,

> The leader of the male group . . . apparently precipitated and maintained the activity, despite misgivings, because of a need to fulfill the role that the other two men had assigned to him. "I was scared when it began to happen," he says. "I wanted to leave but I didn't want to say it to the other guys—you know—that I was scared."

Thus it becomes clear that not only does our culture teach men the rudiments of rape, but society, or more specifically other men, encourage the practice of it.

II

> Every man I meet wants to protect me. Can't figure out what from.
>
> —Mae West

If a male society rewards aggressive, domineering sexual behavior, it contains within itself a sexual schizophrenia. For the masculine man is also expected to prove his mettle as a protector of women. To the naive eye, this dichotomy implies that men fall into one of two categories: those who rape and those who protect. In fact, life does not prove so simple. In a study euphemistically entitled "Sex Aggression by College Men," it was discovered that men who believe in a double standard of morality for men and women, who in fact believe most fervently in the ultimate value of virginity, are more liable to commit "this aggressive variety of sexual exploitation."

(At this point in our narrative it should come as no surprise that Sir Thomas Malory, creator of that classic tale of chivalry, *The Knights of the Round Table,* was himself arrested and found guilty for repeated incidents of rape.)

In the system of chivalry, men protect women against men. This is not unlike the protection relationship which the mafia established with small businesses in the early part of this century. Indeed, chivalry is an age-old protection racket which depends for its existence on rape.

According to the male mythology which defines and perpetuates rape, it is an animal instinct inherent in the male. The story goes that sometime in our pre-historical past, the male, more hirsute and burly than today's counterparts, roamed about an uncivilized landscape until he found a desirable female. (Oddly enough, this female is *not* pictured as more muscular than the modern woman.) Her mate does not bother with courtship. He simply grabs her by the hair and drags her to the closest cave. Presumably, one of the major advantages of modern civilization for the female has been the civilizing of the male. We call it chivalry.

But women do not get chivalry for free. According to the logic of sexual politics, we too have to civilize our behavior. (Enter chastity. Enter virginity. Enter monogamy.) For the female, civilized behavior means chastity before marriage and faithfulness within it. Chivalrous behavior in the male is supposed to protect that chastity from involuntary defilement. The fly in the ointment of this otherwise peaceful system is the fallen woman. She does not behave. And therefore she does not deserve protection. Or, to use another argument, a major tenet of the same value system: what has once been defiled cannot again be violated. One begins to suspect that it is the behavior of the fallen woman, and not that of the male, that civilization aims to control.

The assumption that a woman who does not respect the double standard deserves whatever she gets (or at the very least "asks for it") operates in the

courts today. While in some states a man's previous rape convictions are not considered admissible evidence, the sexual reputation of the rape victim is considered a crucial element of the facts upon which the court must decide innocence or guilt.

The court's respect for the double standard manifested itself particularly clearly in the case of the People v. Jerry Plotkin. Mr. Plotkin, a 36-year-old jeweler, was tried for rape last spring in a San Francisco Superior Court. According to the woman who brought the charges, Plotkin, along with three other men, forced her at gunpoint to enter a car one night in October 1970. She was taken to Mr. Plotkin's fashionable apartment where he and the three other men first raped her and then, in the delicate language of the *S. F. Chronicle,* "subjected her to perverted sex acts." She was, she said, set free in the morning with the warning that she would be killed if she spoke to anyone about the event. She did report the incident to the police who then searched Plotkin's apartment and discovered a long list of names of women. Her name was on the list and had been crossed out.

In addition to the woman's account of her abduction and rape, the prosecution submitted four of Plotkin's address books containing the names of hundreds of women. Plotkin claimed he did not know all of the women since some of the names had been given to him by friends and he had not yet called on them. Several women, however, did testify in court that Plotkin had, to cite the *Chronicle,* "lured them up to his apartment under one pretext or another, and forced his sexual attentions on them."

Plotkin's defense rested on two premises. First, through his own testimony Plotkin established a reputation for himself as a sexual libertine who frequently picked up girls in bars and took them to his house where sexual relations often took place. He was the Playboy. He claimed that the accusation of rape, therefore, was false—this incident had simply been one of many casual sexual relationships, the victim one of many playmates. The second premise of the defense was that his accuser was also a sexual libertine. However, the picture created of the young woman (fully 13 years younger than Plotkin) was not akin to the light-hearted, gay-bachelor image projected by the defendant. On the contrary, the day after the defense cross-examined the woman, the *Chronicle* printed a story headlined, "Grueling Day For Rape Case Victim." (A leaflet passed out by women in front of the courtroom was more succinct, "rape was committed by four men in a private apartment in October; on Thursday, it was done by a judge and a lawyer in a public courtroom.")

Through skillful questioning fraught with innuendo, Plotkin's defense attorney James Martin MacInnis portrayed the young woman as a licentious opportunist and unfit mother. MacInnis began by asking the young woman (then employed as a secretary) whether or not it was true that she was "familiar with liquor" and had worked as a "cocktail waitress." The young woman replied (the *Chronicle* wrote "admitted") that she had worked once or twice as a cocktail waitress. The attorney then asked if she had worked as a secretary in the financial district but had "left that employment after it was discovered that you had sexual intercourse on a couch in the office." The woman replied, "That is a lie. I left because I didn't like working in a one-girl office. It was too lonely." Then the defense asked if, while working as an attendant at a health club, "you were accused of having a sexual affair with a man?" Again the woman denied the story, "I was never accused of that."

Plotkin's attorney then sought to establish that his client's accuser was living with a married man. She responded that the man was separated from his wife. Finally he told the court that she had "spent the night" with another man who lived in the same building.

At this point in the testimony the woman asked Plotkin's defense attorney, "Am I on trial? . . . It is embarrassing and personal to admit these things to all these people. . . . I did not commit a crime. I am a human being." The lawyer, true to the chivalry of his class, apologized and immediately resumed questioning her, turning his attention to her children. (She is divorced, and the children at the time of the trial were in a foster home.) "Isn't it true that your two children have a sex game in which one gets on top of another and they—" "That is a lie!" the young woman interrupted him. She ended her testimony by explaining "They are wonderful children. They are not perverted."

The jury, divided in favor of acquittal ten to two, asked the court stenographer to read the woman's testimony back to them. After this reading, the Superior Court acquitted the defendant of both charges of rape and kidnapping.

According to the double standard a woman who has had sexual intercourse out of wedlock cannot be raped. Rape is not only a crime of aggression against the body; it is a transgression against chastity as defined by men. When a woman is forced into a sexual relationship, she has, according to the male ethos, been violated. But she is also defiled if she does not behave according to the double standard, by maintaining her chastity, or confining her sexual activities to a monogamous relationship.

One should not assume, however, that a woman can avoid the possibility of rape simply by behaving. Though myth would have it that mainly "bad girls" are raped, this theory has no basis in fact. Available statistics would lead one to believe that a safer course is promiscuity. In a study of rape done in the District of Columbia, it was found that 82 percent of the rape victims had a "good reputation." Even the Police Inspector's advice to stay off the streets is rather useless, for almost half of reported rapes occur in the home of the victim and are committed by a man she has never before seen. Like indiscriminate terrorism, rape can happen to any woman, and few women are ever without this knowledge.

But the courts and the police, both dominated by white males, continue to suspect the rape victim, *sui generis*, of provoking or asking for her own assault. According to Amir's study, the police tend to believe that a woman without a good reputation cannot be raped. The rape victim is usually submitted to countless questions about her own sexual mores and behavior by the police. This preoccupation is partially justified by the legal requirements for prosecution in a rape case. The rape victim must have been penetrated, and she must have made it clear to her assailant that she did not want penetration (unless of course she is unconscious). A refusal to accompany a man to some isolated place to allow him to touch her does not in the eyes of the court, constitute rape. She must have said "no" at the crucial genital moment. And the rape victim, to qualify as such, must also have put up a physical struggle—unless she can prove that to do so would have been to endanger her life.

But the zealous interest the police frequently exhibit in the physical details of a rape case is only partially explained by the requirements of the court. A woman who was raped in Berkeley was asked to tell the story of her rape four different times "right out in the street," while her assailant was escaping. She was then required to submit to a pelvic examination to prove that penetration had taken place.

Later, she was taken to the police station where she was asked the same questions again: "Were you forced?" "Did he penetrate?" "Are you sure your life was in danger and you had no other choice?" This woman had been pulled off the street by a man who held a 10-inch knife at her throat and forcibly raped her. She was raped at midnight and was not able to return to her home until five in the morning. Police contacted her twice again in the next week, once by telephone at two in the morning and once at four in the morning. In her words, "The rape was probably the least traumatic incident of the whole evening. If I'm ever raped again, . . . I wouldn't report it to the police because of all the degradation. . . ."

If white women are subjected to unnecessary and often hostile questioning after having been raped, third world women are often not believed at all. According to the white male ethos (which is not only sexist but racist), third world women are defined from birth as "impure." Thus the white male is provided with a pool of women who are fair game for sexual imperialism. Third world women frequently do not report rape and for good reason. When blues singer Billie Holliday was 10 years old, she was taken off to a local house by a neighbor and raped. Her mother brought the police to rescue her, and she was taken to the local police station crying and bleeding:

> When we got there, instead of treating me and Mom like somebody who called the cops for help, they treated me like I'd killed somebody. . . . I guess they had me figured for having enticed this old goat into the whore-house. . . . All I know for sure is they threw me into a cell . . . a fat white matron . . . saw I was still bleeding, she felt sorry for me and gave me a couple glasses of milk. But nobody else did anything for me except give me filthy looks and snicker to themselves.
>
> After a couple of days in a cell they dragged me into a court. Mr. Dick got sentenced to five years. They sentenced me to a Catholic institution.

Clearly the white man's chivalry is aimed only to protect the chastity of "his" women.

As a final irony, that same system of sexual values from which chivalry is derived has also provided womankind with an unwritten code of behavior, called femininity, which makes a feminine woman the perfect victim of sexual aggression. If being chaste does not ward off the possibility of assault, being feminine certainly increases the chances that it will succeed. To be submissive is to defer to masculine strength; is to lack muscular development or any interest in defending oneself; is to let doors be opened, to have one's arm held when crossing the street. To be feminine is to wear shoes which make it difficult to run; skirts which inhibit one's stride; underclothes which inhibit the circulation. Is it not an intriguing observation that those very clothes which are thought to be flattering to the female and attractive to the male are those which make it impossible for a woman to defend herself against aggression?

Each girl as she grows into womanhood is taught fear. Fear is the form in which the female internalizes both chivalry and the double standard. Since, biologically speaking, women in fact have the same if not greater potential for sexual expression as do men, the woman who is taught that she must behave differently from a man must also learn to distrust her own carnality. She must deny her own feelings and learn not to act from them. She fears herself. This is the essence of passivity and, of course, a woman's passivity is not simply sexual but functions to cripple her from self-expression in every area of her life.

Passivity itself prevents a woman from ever considering her own potential for self-defense and forces her to look to men for protection. The woman is taught fear, but this time fear of the other; and yet her only relief from this fear is to seek out the other. Moreover, the passive woman is taught to regard herself as impotent, unable to act, unable even to perceive, in no way self-sufficient, and finally, as the object and not the subject of human behavior. It is in this sense that a woman is deprived of the status of a human being. She is not free to be.

III

Since Ibsen's Nora slammed the door on her patriarchical husband, woman's attempt to be free has been more or less fashionable. In this nineteenth-century portrait of a woman leaving her marriage, Nora tells her husband, "Our home has been nothing but a playroom. I have been your doll-wife just as at home I was papa's doll-child." And, at least on the stage, "The Doll's House" crumbled, leaving audiences with hope for the fate of the modern woman. And today, as in the past, womankind has not lacked examples of liberated women to emulate: Emma

Goldman, Greta Garbo and Isadora Duncan all denounced marriage and the double standard, and believed their right to freedom included sexual independence; but still their example has not affected the lives of millions of women who continue to marry, divorce and remarry, living out their lives dependent on the status and economic power of men. Patriarchy still holds the average woman prisoner not because she lacks the courage of an Isadora Duncan, but because the material conditions of her life prevent her from being anything but an object.

In the *Elementary Structures of Kinship,* Claude Levi-Strauss gives to marriage this universal description, "It is always a system of exchange that we find at the origin of the rules of marriage." In this system of exchange, a woman is the "most precious possession." Levi-Strauss continues that the custom of including women as booty in the marketplace is still so general that "a whole volume would not be sufficient to enumerate instances of it." Levi-Strauss makes it clear that he does not exclude Western Civilization from his definition of "universal" and cites examples from modern wedding ceremonies. (The marriage ceremony is still one in which the husband and wife become one, and "that one is the husband.")

The legal proscription against rape reflects this possessory view of women. An article in the 1952–53 *Yale Law Journal* describes the legal rationale behind laws against rape:

In our society sexual taboos, often enacted into law, buttress a system of monogamy based upon the law of "free bargaining" of the potential spouses. Within this process the woman's power to withhold or grant sexual access is an important bargaining weapon.

Presumably then, laws against rape are intended to protect the right of a woman, not for physical self-determination, but for physical "bargaining." The article goes on to explain explicitly why the preservation of the bodies of women is important to men:

The consent standard in our society does more than protect a significant item of social currency for women; it fosters, and is in turn bolstered by, a masculine pride in the exclusive possession of a sexual object. The consent of a woman to sexual intercourse awards the man a privilege of bodily access, a personal "prize," whose value is enhanced by sole ownership. An additional

reason for the man's condemnation of rape may be found in the threat to his status from a decrease in the "value" of his sexual possession which would result from forcible violation.

The passage concludes by making clear whose interest the law is designed to protect. "The man responds to this undercutting of his status as *possessor* of the girl with hostility toward the rapist; no other restitution device is available. The law of rape provides an orderly outlet for his vengeance." Presumably the female victim in any case will have been sufficiently socialized so as not to consciously feel any strong need for vengeance. If she does feel this need, society does not speak to it.

The laws against rape exist to protect rights of the male as possessor of the female body, and not the right of the female over her own body. Even without this enlightening passage from the *Yale Law Review,* the laws themselves are clear: In no state can a man be accused of raping his wife. How can any man steal what already belongs to him? It is in the sense of rape as theft of another man's property that Kate Millett writes, "Traditionally rape has been viewed as an offense one male commits against another—a matter of abusing his woman." In raping another man's woman, a man may aggrandize his own manhood and concurrently reduce that of another man. Thus a man's honor is not subject directly to rape, but only indirectly, through "his" woman.

If the basic social unit is the family, in which the woman is a possession of her husband, the superstructure of society is a male hierarchy, in which men dominate other men (or patriarchal families dominate other patriarchal families). And it is no small irony that, while the very social fabric of our male-dominated culture denies women equal access to political, economic and legal power, the literature, myth and humor of our culture depict women not only as the power behind the throne, but the real source of the oppression of men. The religious version of this fairy tale blames Eve for both carnality and eating of the tree of knowledge, at the same time making her gullible to the obvious devices of a serpent. Adam, of course, is merely the trusting victim of love. Certainly this is a biased story. But no more biased than the one television audiences receive today from the latest slick comedians. Through a media which is owned by men, censored by a state dominated by men, all the evils of this social system which make a man's life unpleasant are blamed upon "the wife." The theory is: were it not for the female who waits and plots to "trap" the male into marriage, modern man would be able to achieve Olympian freedom. She is made the scapegoat for a system which is in fact run by men.

Nowhere is this more clear than in the white racist use of the concept of white womanhood. The white male's open rape of black women, coupled with his overweening concern for the chastity and protection of his wife and daughters, represents an extreme of sexist and racist hypocrisy. While on the one hand she was held up as the standard for purity and virtue, on the other the Southern white woman was never asked if she wanted to be on a pedestal, and in fact any deviance from the male-defined standards for white womanhood was treated severely. (It is a powerful commentary on American racism that the historical role of Blacks as slaves, and thus possessions without power, has robbed black women of legal and economic protection through marriage. Thus black women in Southern society and in the ghettoes of the North have long been easy game for white rapists.) The fear that black men would rape white women was classic paranoia. Quoting from Ann Breen's unpublished study of racism and sexism in the South, *The New South: White Man's Country*, Frederick Douglass legitimately points out that, had the black man wished to rape white women, he had ample opportunity to do so during the Civil War when white women, the wives, sisters, daughters and mothers of the rebels, were left in the care of Blacks. But yet not a single act of rape was committed during this time. The Ku Klux Klan, who tarred and feathered black men and lynched them in the honor of the purity of white womanhood, also applied tar and feathers to a Southern white woman accused of bigamy, which leads one to suspect that Southern white men were not so much outraged at the violation of the woman as a person, in the few instances where rape was actually committed by black men, but at the violation of his property rights. In the situation where a black man was found to be having sexual relations with a white woman, the white woman could exercise skin-privilege, and claim that she had been raped in which case the black man was lynched. But if she did not claim rape, she herself was subject to lynching.

In constructing the myth of white womanhood so as to justify the lynching and oppression of black men and women, the white male has created a convenient symbol of his own power which has resulted in black hostility toward the white "bitch," accompanied by a fear on the part of many white women of the black rapist. Moreover, it is not surprising that after being told for two centuries that he wants to rape white women, black men have begun to actually commit that act. But it is crucial to note that the frequency of this practice is outrageously exaggerated in the white mythos. Ninety percent of reported rape is intra- not inter-racial.

In *Soul on Ice*, Eldridge Cleaver has described the mixing of a rage against white power with the internalized sexism of a black man raping a white woman.

> *Somehow I arrived at the conclusion that, as a matter of principle, it was of paramount importance for me to have an antagonistic, ruthless attitude toward white women. . . . Rape was an insurrectionary act. It delighted me that I was defying and trampling upon the white man's law, upon his system of values and that I was defiling his women—and this point, I believe, was the most satisfying to me because I was very resentful over the historical fact of how the white man has used the black woman.*

Thus a black man uses white women to take out his rage against white men. But, in fact, whenever a rape of a white woman by a black man does take place, it is again the white man who benefits. First, the act itself terrorizes the white woman and makes her more dependent on the white male for protection. Then, if the woman prosecutes her attacker, the white man is afforded legal opportunity to exercise overt racism. Of course, the knowledge of the rape helps to perpetuate two myths which are beneficial to white male rule—the bestiality of the black man and the desirability of white women. Finally, the white man surely benefits because he himself is not the object of attack—he has been allowed to stay in power.

Indeed, the existence of rape in any form is beneficial to the ruling class of white males. For rape is a kind of terrorism which severely limits the freedom of women and makes women dependent on men.

Moreover, in the act of rape, the rage that one man may harbor toward another higher in the male hierarchy can be deflected toward a female scapegoat. For every man there is always someone lower on the social scale on whom he can take out his aggressions. And that is any woman alive.

This oppressive attitude towards women finds its institutionalization in the traditional family. For it is assumed that a man "wears the pants" in his family—he exercises the option of rule whenever he so chooses. Not that he makes all the decisions—clearly women make most of the important day-to-day decisions in a family. But when a conflict of interest arises, it is the man's interest which will prevail. His word, in itself, is more powerful. He lords it over his wife in the same way his boss lords it over him, so that the very process of exercising his power becomes as important an act as obtaining whatever it is his power can get for him. This notion of power is key to the male ego in this culture, for the two acceptable measures of masculinity are a man's power over women and his power over other men. A man may boast to his friends that "I have 20 men working for me." It is also aggrandizement of his ego if he has the financial power to clothe his wife in furs and jewels. And, if a man lacks the wherewithal to acquire such power, he can always express his rage through equally masculine activities—rape and theft. Since male society defines the female as a possession, it is not surprising that the felony most often committed together with rape is theft. As the following classic tale of rape points out, the elements of theft, violence and forced sexual relations merge into an indistinguishable whole.

The woman who told the following story was acquainted with the man who tried to rape her. When the man learned that she was going to be staying alone for the weekend, he began early in the day a polite campaign to get her to go out with him. When she continued to refuse his request, his chivalrous mask dropped away:

I had locked all the doors because I was afraid, and I don't know how he got in; it was probably through the screen door. When I woke up, he was shaking my leg. His eyes were red, and I knew he had been drinking or smoking. I thought I would try to talk my way out of it. He started by saying that he wanted to sleep with me, and then he got angrier and angrier, until he

started to say, "I want pussy," "I want pussy." Then, I got scared and tried to push him away. That's when he started to force himself on me. It was awful. It was the most humiliating, terrible feeling. He was forcing my legs apart and ripping my clothes off. And it was painful. I did fight him—he was slightly drunk and I was able to keep him away. I had taken judo a few years back, but I was afraid to throw a chop for fear that he'd kill me. I could see he was getting more and more violent. I was thinking wildly of some way to get out of this alive, and then I said to him, "Do you want money? I'll give you money." We had money but I was also thinking that if I got to the back room I could telephone the police—as if the police would have even helped. It was a stupid thing to think of because obviously he would follow me. And he did. When he saw me pick up the phone, he tried to tie the cord around my neck. I screamed at him that I did have the money in another room, that I was going to call the police because I was scared, but that I would never tell anybody what happened. It would be an absolute secret. He said, "okay," and I went to get the money. But when he got it, all of a sudden he got this crazy look in his eye and he said to me, "Now I'm going to kill you." Then I started saying my prayers. I knew there was nothing I could do. He started to hit me—I still wasn't sure if he wanted to rape me at this point—or just to kill me. He was hurting me, but hadn't yet gotten me into a stranglehold because he was still drunk and off balance. Somehow we pushed into the kitchen where I kept looking at this big knife. But I didn't pick it up. Somehow, no matter how much I hated him at that moment, I still couldn't imagine putting the knife in his flesh, and then I was afraid he would grab it and stick it into me. Then he was hitting me again and somehow we pushed through the back door of the kitchen and onto the porch steps. We fell down the steps and that's when he started to strangle me. He was on top of me. He just went on and on until finally I lost consciousness. I did scream, though my screams sounded like whispers to me. But what happened was that a cab driver happened by and frightened him away. The cab driver revived me—I was out only a minute at the most. And then I ran across the street and I grabbed the woman who was our neighbor and screamed at her, "Am I alive? Am I still alive?"

Rape is an act of aggression in which the victim is denied her self-determination. It is an act of violence which, if not actually followed by beatings or murder, nevertheless always carries with it the threat of death. And finally, rape is a form of mass terrorism, for the victims of rape are chosen indiscriminately, but the propagandists for male supremacy broadcast that it is women who cause rape by being unchaste or in the wrong place at the wrong time—in essence, by behaving as though they were free.

The threat of rape is used to deny women employment. (In California, the Berkeley Public Library, until pushed by the Federal Employment Practices Commission, refused to hire female shelvers because of perverted men in the stacks.) The fear of rape keeps women off the streets at night. Keeps women at home. Keeps women passive and modest for fear that they be thought provocative.

It is part of human dignity to be able to defend oneself, and women are learning. Some women have learned karate; some to shoot guns. And yet we will not be free until the threat of rape and the atmosphere of violence is ended, and to end that the nature of male behavior must change.

But rape is not an isolated act that can be rooted out from patriarchy without ending patriarchy itself. The same men and power structure who victimize women are engaged in the act of raping Vietnam, raping Black people and the very earth we live upon. Rape is a classic act of domination where, in the words of Kate Millett, "the emotions of hatred, contempt, and the desire to break or violate personality," take place. This breaking of the personality characterizes modern life itself. No simple reforms can eliminate rape. As the symbolic expression of the white male hierarchy, rape is the quintessential act of our civilization, one which, Valerie Solanis warns, is in danger of "humping itself to death."

"The Rape" of Mr. Smith

Unknown

This small piece is so clear on the injustices—legal, cultural, and attitudinal—that are visited upon women who are victims of rape that it is used everywhere—in women's studies courses, in rape crisis centers, in training seminars for police and social workers—yet no one seems to know its origin.

It must be remembered that we are all *subject to rape: those who have been raped, those who may be raped and therefore have their lives altered, and those who are related to the victims of rape.*

*Reprinted with permission from *Women Helping Women: Volunteer Resource Manual,* by Rape Crisis Services, Urbana, Illinois.

THE LAW DISCRIMINATES AGAINST RAPE VICTIMS IN a manner which would not be tolerated by victims of any other crime. In the following example, a holdup victim is asked questions similar in form to those usually asked a victim of rape.

"Mr. Smith, you were held up at gunpoint on the corner of 16th & Locust?"

"Yes."

"Did you struggle with the robber?"

"No."

"Why not?"

"He was armed."

"Then you made a conscious decision to comply with his demands rather than to resist?"

"Yes."

"Did you scream? Cry out?"

"No. I was afraid."

"I see. Have you ever been held up before?"

"No."

"Have you ever given money away?"

"Yes, of course—"

"And did you do so willingly?"

"What are you getting at?"

"Well, let's put it like this, Mr. Smith. You've given away money in the past—in fact, you have quite a reputation for philanthropy. How can we be sure that you weren't *contriving* to have your money taken from you by force?"

"Listen, if I wanted—"

"Never mind. What time did this holdup take place, Mr. Smith?"

"About 11 p.m."

"You were out on the streets at 11 p.m.? Doing what?"

"Just walking."

"Just walking? You know that it's dangerous being out on the street that late at night. Weren't you aware that you could have been held up?"

"I hadn't thought about it."

"What were you wearing at the time, Mr. Smith?"

"Let's see. A suit. Yes, a suit."

"An *expensive* suit?"

"Well—yes."

"In other words, Mr. Smith, you were walking around the streets late at night in a suit that practically *advertised* the fact that you might be a good target for some easy money, isn't that so? I mean, if we didn't know better, Mr. Smith, we might even think you were *asking* for this to happen, mightn't we?"

"Look, can't we talk about the past history of the guy who *did* this to me?"

"I'm afraid not, Mr. Smith. I don't think you would want to violate his rights, now, would you?"

Naturally, the line of questioning, the innuendo, is ludicrous—as well as inadmissible as any sort of cross-examination—unless we are talking about parallel questions in a rape case. The time of night, the victim's previous history of "giving away" that which was taken by force, the clothing—all of these are held against the victim. Society's posture on rape, and the manifestation of that posture in the courts, help account for the fact that so few rapes are reported.

Immaculate, Inviolate:
Como Ella

Gloria Anzaldúa

Gloria Anzaldúa is a chicana tejana *lesbian-feminist poet and fiction writer living in Santa Cruz. She is coeditor of* This Bridge Called My Back: Writing by Radical Women of Color, *winner of the Before Columbus Foundation American Book Award. Her book* Borderlands/La frontera: The New Mestiza, *(Spinsters/Aunt Lute, July 1987) was picked as one of the thirty-eight Best Books of 1987 by the Library Journal.*

Anzaldúa has taught chicano studies, feminist studies, and creative writing at the University of Texas, San Francisco State University, Vermont College of Norwich University, University of California at Santa Cruz and has conducted writing workshops around the country. She has been a contributing editor to Sinister Wisdom *since 1984.*

Presently, she is compiling and editing Haciendo caras/Making Face, Making Soul: Constructing Colored Selves, A Reader of Creative and Critical Perspectives *(San Francisco: Spinsters/Aunt Lute, 1990) and* Entrequerras, entremundos/Civil Wars Among the Worlds, *a book of autobiographical and fictitious narratives (also to be published by Spinsters/Aunt Lute in 1990).*

Anzaldúa's poem reminds us that whatever happens—cruelty, indignity, poverty—women can and often do prevail.

SHE NEVER LIVED WITH US
we had no bed for her
but she always came to visit.
A gift for *m'ijita*
two folded dollar bills secretly put in my hand.

I'd sit at her side
away from the bucket of *brasas*
enveloped *en el olor de vieja*
watch her roll her Buglar
yellowed talons plucking tobacco
knotted fingers rolling it thin, thinner,
tongue gumming edge of paper
sealing it pinching the ends
stroking it before striking match on thumbnail
watch smoke escape between chapped lips
curl through her white hair and pink skull.
They said at sixteen it had turned white overnight.

My grandmother could not tolerate heat.
She kept well away from fires.
A long time ago she burned herself.
She'd bent over the belly
of her woodburning stove
had seen no glimmer of a spark
had heaved up a can of kerosene

propping the edge on her hip
and cradling it to her chest
she'd let a few drops fall
on the charred sticks.
An invisible spark ignited
shot up the spout into her windpipe,
boom.
It took my uncle a long time
to carry the buckets of water from the well
soak the blankets
wrap them around her.

Mamá, usted ya no puede quedarse aquí sóla.
They made her give up the ranchhouse

photographs, books, letters, yellowing.
Armarios, pantry closets looted
rot growing under the covers.

She'd stay two weeks with one, two with another,
back and forth in her black dress
and with her thick *velices*
white sweat streaks across her round back,
under arms.
She never stopped wearing *luto*
first for my *papagrande*
who died before I was born
then for her brother
and, until she died eleven years ago,
she wore black for my father.
I didn't go to her funeral
that too must have made her suffer.

Platícame del rancho Jesús María,
de los Vergeles, Mamagrande,
where I was reared.
Tell me about the years of drought
the cattle with hoof 'n mouth
the rabid coyotes.
And as she talked I saw her breathing in the fire,
coughing up sooty spittle
skin blistering, becoming pus
nerve endings exposed,
sweating, skin pallid, clammy
the nausea, the dizziness,
swelling to twice her size.

I watched the charred scars
on her throat and breasts
turn into parchment splotches
they catch the sheen of the coals
glow pink and lavender over the blue skin.
She'd felt numb, she told me,
her voice hoarse from the fire
or the constant cigarette in her mouth,
as though frostbitten.

Once I looked into her blue eyes,
asked, Have you ever had an orgasm?
She kept quiet for a long time.
Finally she looked into my brown eyes,
told me how Papagrande would flip the skirt
of her nightgown over her head

and in the dark take out his *palo,* his stick,
and do *lo que hacen todos los hombres*
while she laid back and prayed
he would finish quickly.

She didn't like to talk about such things.
Mujeres no hablan de cosas cochinas.
Her daughters, my *tías,* never liked to talk about it—
their father's other women, their half-brothers.

Sometimes when I get too close to the fire
and my face and chest catch the heat,
I can almost see Mamagrande's face
watching him leave
taking her two eldest
to play with his other children
watching her sons *y los de la otra*
grow up together.

I can almost see that look
settle on her face
then hide behind parchment skin
and clouds of smoke.
Pobre doña Locha, so much dignity,
everyone said she had
and pride.

Notes

como ella—like her

m'ijita—an endearment; my dear daughter

brasas—live coals

usted ya no puede—You can't live here by yourself
any longer.

armarios—cupboards

velices—suitcases

luto—mourning clothes

platícame del rancho—Tell me about the ranch.

lo que hacen todos los hombres—what all men do

mujeres no hablan—women don't talk about such
filth

tías—aunts

y los de la otra—and those of his other woman

7

Discrimination: The Effects of Asymmetry on Social Institutions and Their Effects on Us

Sexism is not fully realized only in women's personal lives; it is also expressed through all the public institutions and is formalized in law and custom. Marginal in importance and participation, in the economy women are poor; in politics and government, nearly powerless; before the law, discriminated against and deprived of citizens' rights. But in each instance, the reality of the situation is denied, distorted, or justified by the same body of myth and mystification that governs women's personal lives. Let us look at the position that women actually occupy in the economy, in politics, and before the law. Keep in mind that these social structures are interrelated and reinforcing. An intricate web of circumstances determines women's standing in each area, and that in turn determines the nuances of our personal lives.

Women in the Economy

Much has been written in the last twenty years about the "great strides" women as a group have allegedly made in earning power, professional advancement, and opportunity. The truth is that although some women's economic lives are dramatically improved, the great majority of women experience little or no improvement. For many women, the situation has grown much worse as the term *the feminization of poverty* becomes increasingly descriptive of reality.

The Myth: Lucky Ladies
Everyone has heard tales of pampered wives who play bridge and drink coffee while harried husbands labor to win the dollar so carelessly tossed away at the supermarket or dress shop.

The wives earn no money of their own, but *since they spend it, they control it;* everyone in America "knows" that. There are tales of "palimony" winners or gay divorcees reveling in windfalls snatched from vanquished ex-husbands, merry widows collecting fat sums from hard-earned insurance policies and social security, lazy but comfortable welfare mothers stealing from the state to live on steak. Such types compose a partial list of the privileged, well-off women reputed to represent the majority of the female population.

The Reality: Women Are Poor

Compared with men, women in every category are by and large disadvantaged. Within and across job classifications, women have lower salaries, generally have less disposable income, are more likely to fall below nationally set poverty standards, and in several ways have far less recourse to remedy.

Facts on Women's Earnings and Income At present, on the average and across all occupations, full-time women workers earn about 65 percent of the salaries of men. In 1987, women's median income was $16,909 (their average; $18,097); men's median income was $24,008 (average $26,525).[1]

Women are generally employed and segregated in the lowest paid occupations and jobs. About 80 percent of the female labor force in 1987 worked in clerical, sales, and service jobs. In 1988, women constituted 82.2 percent of all cashiers, 98.2 percent of all secretaries, 78.3 percent of all food-counter workers, but 20 percent of all physicians, 7.3 percent of all engineers, and 19.3 percent of all lawyers. Women make up 68.6 percent of all salespeople, but women constitute only 8 percent of auto and boat salespeople, among the highest paid of sales categories.[2]

Within single occupations, women earn less than men. For example, in retail sales—the job category with the largest female-male disparity—women earned only 51 percent of the figure for men. (As Gloria Steinem pointed out, in department stores men sell stoves and refrigerators; women sell men's underwear. Why? Surely not because of appropriate experience.) Even in clerical work, women's earnings fall seriously behind men's. In 1985, women's average yearly salary for full-time clerical work was $15,157 compared with men's $22,997.[3]

Only 15 percent of divorced women are awarded alimony by the courts. In 1985, only 3.5 percent of divorced women received *any* payment.[4] Of the 72 percent of divorced women with children who were awarded child support, only half received that support. Over 25 percent received no payment at all.[5] The average amount awarded for child support is far less than half of what is required for support of that child, and fewer than half the fathers pay that support. After divorce, it is estimated that women's standard of living drops 73 percent in the first year after divorce, while their ex-husbands' standard rises 42 percent.[6]

Since women earn less over a lifetime, their social security and retirement benefits are smaller. Employed women whose husbands paid into the social security system receive only their husband's benefits, not both theirs and his if he dies. This situation is worsened because women often retire with benefits at 62 rather than 65, receiving, therefore, even lower rates and having even smaller monthly benefits.

Some Facts on Poverty By the mid-1980s, the term *feminization of poverty* had become commonplace because by 1986 women constituted 63 percent of all adults in poverty. Thirty-four percent of all households headed by women were poor (compared to 6 percent of married-couple families), and 54 percent of all children in households headed by women were poor.[7] Half of the Black and Hispanic households headed by women are poor.[8] One fifth of all women over 60 are poor, and elderly women are twice as likely to be poor as elderly men.[9] Over 70 percent of those with incomes under $4,000 are women.[10]

Some Facts on Women's Contribution to the Economy Women work because we need to. Of the female labor force in 1987, 25 percent were single; 20 percent were widowed, divorced, or separated; and 15 percent had husbands earning less than $15,000.

In 1987, 56 percent of married-couple families had wives in the paid labor force. Such families had median incomes of $38,346 in 1986 compared to families in which the wife did not work for pay of $25,803.[11] The income of working wives reduces the potential poverty level substantially, and incomes in households in which wives work is on the average 60 percent higher than in households where only husbands work.[12] (See table on Median Weekly Earnings in this chapter.)

MEDIAN WEEKLY EARNINGS OF FAMILIES BY TYPE OF FAMILY, NUMBER OF EARNERS, RACE, AND HISPANIC ORIGIN

Type of family, number of earners, race, and Hispanic origin	Number of families		Median weekly earnings	
	1987	1988	1987	1988
TOTAL				
Total families with earners	42,733	42,913	$572	$596
Married-couple families	33,844	33,864	637	668
One earner	12,668	12,365	405	418
Husband	9,640	9,429	477	489
Wife	2,272	2,199	230	238
Other family member	757	736	212	228
Two or more earners	21,176	21,499	776	811
Husband and wife	18,473	18,945	789	824
Husband and other family member(s)	1,995	1,872	749	787
Wife and other family member(s)	560	520	512	495
Other family members only	147	162	501	494
Families maintained by women	6,963	6,989	317	334
One earner	4,702	4,741	254	260
Householder	3,675	3,743	263	269
Other family member	1,027	999	215	225
Two or more earners	2,260	2,247	514	554
Families maintained by men	1,926	2,061	478	486
One earner	1,144	1,221	353	374
Two or more earners	782	840	675	700
White				
Total families with earners	36,555	36,667	592	616
Married-couple families	30,095	30,135	647	677
One earner	11,385	11,120	416	432
Husband	8,784	8,609	485	497
Wife	1,946	1,866	231	243
Two or more earners	18,710	19,015	785	818
Husband and wife	16,332	16,768	797	831
Families maintained by women	4,959	4,930	329	351
Families maintained by men	1,501	1,602	492	496
Black				
Total families with earners	4,942	4,999	412	435
Married-couple families	2,768	2,747	529	576
One earner	924	878	289	281
Husband	581	546	335	339
Wife	264	258	215	205

(Continues)

MEDIAN WEEKLY EARNINGS OF FAMILIES BY TYPE OF FAMILY, NUMBER OF EARNERS, RACE, AND HISPANIC ORIGIN (Continued)

Type of family, number of earners, race, and Hispanic origin	Number of families		Median weekly earnings	
	1987	1988	1987	1988
Black				
Two or more earners	1,843	1,870	675	713
Husband and wife	1,616	1,642	695	733
Families maintained by women	1,822	1,884	284	291
Families maintained by men	352	368	383	419
Hispanic origin				
Total families with earners	3,219	3,384	425	451
Married-couple families	2,411	2,488	473	494
One earner	1,032	1,044	292	301
Husband	838	867	314	316
Wife	122	119	209	236
Two or more earners	1,379	1,444	615	671
Husband and wife	1,110	1,179	630	689
Families maintained by women	575	634	285	295
Families maintained by men	234	261	418	429

Data exclude families in which there is no wage or salary earner or in which the husband, wife, or other person maintaining the family is either self-employed or in the Armed Forces.

Source: U.S. Dept of Labor, Bureau of Labor Statistics, *Employment and Earnings,* January, 1989, p. 217.

Discrimination Everywhere Women workers are channeled into occupations that are seen as "appropriate" for women. These are continuations of the roles females are expected to fulfill: for example, serving and facilitating (secretaries, waitresses, nurses, "gal Fridays"), child care (teachers on the elementary level, pediatricians), sex and decoration (receptionists, airline hostesses, entertainers). Occupations historically reserved for women are notoriously underpaid regardless of the level of expertise needed to perform them, and they are generally controlled by male administrators who make it impossible, one way or the other, for women to set their own market and hence their own demands.

When women try to break out of these occupational ghettos, they face other problems. Various practices, official or otherwise, challenge entry into male-dominated work areas—apprenticeship programs in trade unions, employment traps (for example, odd hours, machines too heavy for females), discriminatory hiring, and so on. Women who do manage entry are generally channeled to the low-earning end of the spectrum. Sales, for example, was shown earlier to favor men financially; high-line items may be reserved for men by seniority rules, for example, which disadvantage women who more frequently are temporary, part-time, new, or returning workers.

Unemployment rates are higher for women than for men, probably even higher than they appear to be, for the number of women who have not yet worked but want to cannot be properly evaluated.

Aid to Families with Dependent Children (AFDC), too, encourages and even insures female poverty. AFDC benefits are barely sufficient for subsistence, yet the mother with children to care for, no husband, and few skills is in a bind. Although job "retraining" may be supported, "education" is not. Often the kinds of jobs an AFDC mother may train for will not yield sufficient income to secure both adequate child care and subsistence living, yet the education that would make work outside the home truly profitable remains generally out of her reach. If she works to earn income additional to AFDC to make her life more tolerable, she stands to lose her public aid, leaving her few alternatives. With aid for abortion and contraception denied her, the plight of the welfare mother worsens.

Why?

What are the ideological factors that underlie the economic position of women? It is not too difficult to guess. Shirley Bernard expresses them in terms of "dominance."

> In a society where money means power, most of the money must come to the dominant group if it is to maintain the status quo. In our society white males are dominant . . . they earn substantially more than non-whites and females.[13]

The notion of dominance is a shorthand we can unpack to reveal the entire range of beliefs and attitudes inherent in the patriarchal mind set. Once again, the nature of women's role and the gender ideal are the factors underlying women's disadvantaged position.

The Role: Woman's Work

In earlier chapters we saw that women have historically been perceived as created to be helpmeets to men, whereas men have been perceived as the central actors in society. In addition to performing the functions of procreation and nursing, it is women's central responsibility to serve as underlaborers to men, to manage for them the necessary minutiae that muddy the waters of real creativity. Women are ideally suited for this function, it is said, being less intelligent and less rational than men; hence both less capable of true accomplishment and more tolerant of detail and routine.

On the Job

Until very recently—and then only because of advances pressed by the women's movement—the "branch offices" of the public economic sector have been very much a study in patriarchal dominance. In offices, factories, hospitals, schools, and elsewhere, men "did the job," and women "helped." He managed while she answered his phone, sharpened his pencils, typed his letters, and perked his coffee. He cured the sick while she followed his orders, applied his prescriptions, and perked his coffee. He flew the airplane while she checked the tickets, served the customers, and perked his coffee. The rare woman who got to run the show was considered a peculiarity and a bewilderment, causing problems for her own self-image as well as for her male colleagues and subordinates.

Salaries reflected these relative positions, for line workers earn more than their assistants. Moreover, women by virtue of being women—regardless of position occupied, regardless of how much education and ability they needed to do their job—earned less, whether in women's occupations or in others. Thus, nurses, schoolteachers, professional secretaries, and others in traditionally female jobs have been notoriously underpaid relative to their education, skill, and experience. But even women in managerial or authoritative positions could not look forward to equal rank, salary, or privileges of men at their same status.

More women are attaining better educations than ever before. More than 53 percent of all students in higher education are female. In 1986, women received 51 percent of bachelor's degrees, 50 percent of masters, and 35 percent of doctorates in American colleges and universities. Forty-six percent of bachelors in business and management and 41 percent in the sciences went to women. Among medical degrees awarded, 31 percent went to women; 23 percent of dental degrees and 39 percent of law degrees went to women in 1986.[14] Yet, in that same year, the median income of women with four years of college education ($22,412) was below that of men who had earned only a high school diploma ($24,701)![15]

It is a myth of contemporary culture that these conditions no longer exist. In reality, little has changed. In fact, women have lost ground in some ways. The average salary of full-time women workers relative to men has been slowly increasing and is projected to be near 70 percent by the year 2000, when women are expected to climb to 47 percent of the labor force.[16] But considering that the average age of the female labor force in 2000 will be older (35–54),[17] considering also that the female labor force will be much better educated (years of schooling for females is rising), considering as well the legal and cultural drives toward parity in opportunity and compensation, even 70 percent is totally unacceptable.

Even where external structure and appearance seem to change, the underlying reality often remains untouched. An executive secretary with ten years' experience may be "promoted" to district sales manager (entry-level position for managerial class) with men several years her junior, but she may be the only one of her group with a typewriter on her desk. A female high school teacher may now receive a salary equal to that of her male counterpart for teaching, but if her extra duties at home or her sex role preclude her from requesting playground duties or coaching, she may thereby be denied the extra income that raises the job above the average. "Maid" and "janitor" may both be redefined as "maintenance worker—2" and receive equal pay, but if only men make it to "maintenance worker—3" (supervisor), the apparent equal opportunity is only a sham.

It is important to recognize the force of the ideological and psychological dynamics straining to maintain the status quo. The female sex role and gender ideal is a major, if not *the* major, determinant of women's position in the work place. Michael Korda, a publishing executive in 1972, contended that in the work place men perceive women workers, whether colleagues or subordinates, as extensions of their wives or other women in their personal lives. That is, they see women as females first and workers second, and this perception conditions men's attitudes and behavior toward women on the job.[18]

The anthropologist George Gilder offered a further, even more psychologically profound, insight into men's resistance to women's economic equality.[19] In primitive times, Gilder theorized, men proved and maintained their masculine identity through the hunt by facing hardship and death. Today, although industrialism has obviated the hunt per se, men still need to exhibit and reinforce their sense of masculinity. They have, therefore, substituted their work—whatever it is—for their old arena, making it a kind of symbolic hunt. It is thus crucial for men to maintain their job's aura of manliness, its rituals and traditions, and most of all its separation from women and all things female. As women encroach upon a field of endeavor, we throw doubt on its manliness, destroying its ability to function as a symbolic hunt, sending men scurrying to more distant bastions of masculinity. In essence, in Gilder's view, the plain fact of the work place is that for psycho-sexual reasons men simply do not want women there: Other arguments are mere rationales. Whatever one thinks of the man-the-hunter theory, the truth probably lies somewhere in this deeper region: Men do not want equality with women at work. Gilder concluded that women should stay out, leave men their bastions and their sources of identity. Feminists, of course, go another way. Martyrdom or sacrifice on the altar of masculinity is a price too high either for women or for all of humankind. Women not only *need* to work, but as citizens, women have a right to work, just as men do, even if it were for "frivolous" reasons such as sport, happiness, fulfillment, or "proving of one's identity." Men will have to find other ways to prove their masculinity or other means of satisfaction. Women, however, must change as well.

Gender: Subliminal Effects

It is true that very often a woman's relationship to a job or career is different from a man's. Part of that difference comes as a result of external conditions—the double burden of home and child care, barriers to opportunity, as well as misogynist attitudes and behaviors. But added factors in those different relations to work reside within ourselves as women, in our own attitudes and behavior. These are the often hidden or subliminal effects of our gender conditioning.

As detailed earlier, we are raised to see ourselves as being second to men, husbands, and employer-workers; we learn to perceive our interests and actions as subordinate to their needs and wishes. As wives, our husbands' jobs, desires, and values are to supersede our own. According to traditional rules, we work or fulfill ourselves only after we have accomplished our "primary duties." Even the modern, liberated woman is subject to the tremendous force of that other commitment. Not wanting to choose between work and family—and highly subject to a social structure that decrees her responsible for the home—a woman in the work place is truly doubly burdened. Like it or not, even aware of it or not, and married or not, the weight of that burden is real and does interfere with our work. Even under the best of conditions, no wife clears the bothersome details of living for us, manages child care or housekeeping, or guarantees us unhampered mobility.

Very few of us were raised to see ourselves primarily as workers of one kind or another in the public marketplace. Even for women who work full-time their entire lives, an inbred image remains of women as temporary or marginal workers, as supplementary rather than central earners. Many of us have often been more apt, then, to accept inadequate incomes, reduced benefits, or poor conditions. To meet home demands, we may settle for part-time shifts, poor hours, or local jobs, all of which can be terribly exploitive.

The problem goes deeper, though, for added to these reduced expectations of work, most of us are conditioned to carry reduced expectations of ourselves. Following our mothers' model as young girls, serving our brothers and fathers, we learned to serve in general. Comfortable with the familiar behavior of subordination, we tend not to feel uncomfortable when we experience the same requirements at work. Passively we give in to inappropriate use of our energy and time in a way that men would not tolerate. Accustomed to placing our attachments to men above many things, we might be more loyal to an exploitive employer than to a union of sister employees.

But even when we learn these things and consciously try to transcend the inherited values of "femininity," we are still subject to our own "outposts in the head." We must not only unlearn the destructive patterns we have been given, but we must also somehow make up for the experiences we did not have, those reserved for males only, experiences such as the competition of team sports or the support system of the male in-group.

Women Before the Law: Some Relevant Principles

We should keep some essential features of law in mind to help us understand women's relationship to the legal system: Laws are the rules of the game. When we speak of the law in our society, we mean a collection of rules and procedures codified, formalized, made explicit; we mean the conceptual framework within which such "rules" are written, a set of values, attitudes, and general principles toward people, community, and government; we also mean a kind of overriding loyalty to the concept of law as such, to living by the rules we set for ourselves; and finally we mean the whole system of legislation,

courts, procedures, and people that actualizes the abstract concepts.

Since laws that contradict or clash with social mores are most likely to be disregarded or disobeyed, to carry weight and command obedience in its own right (without undue force) a law must express or coincide with the ideas and perceptions of a majority of the people governed. Therefore, we can understand law as representing the formal expression of nonformal or sociocultural ideals and commitments—norms, mores, values—the unwritten rules of the game for any people.

Laws are written by people who hold power. In our society, law is enacted by legislatures made up of individuals said to represent a majority of voters. It is from this representativeness that legislators in large part are supposed to derive their power, and it is from their ability to express the will of the public that they maintain it. To a degree, legislators do express the public will; but to a degree, they do not. What is true, however, is that many of the laws we live by are written and enacted by those people who, one way or the other, maintain their place in the legislatures by being able to satisfy their constituents that they are expressing the common will. That is why and how laws so clearly reflect the character of current mores and specifically the mores of those who have and exercise power.

Our legal system relies heavily on precedent, continuity, and conservatism to give it stability and to ensure orderliness, credibility, and respect. Judicial decisions made today are largely based on decisions made earlier and on an interpretation of what is perceived to be the original intent of the framers of any law. Change in the body of law is meant to come slowly and cautiously. To a large degree, the past directs the present and the future, and the system strongly tends to maintain the status quo.

Law, Women, and Men

When we relate these principles of law to women's position in society, we clearly see the source of certain aspects of our situation. The law, in conceptualization, policy, practice, execution, and application, is almost entirely masculine.

In overwhelming proportions, the people in power who have written the laws as well as interpreted, argued, used, and enforced them have been men. Legislators, judges, teachers and philosophers of law, court officials, lawyers, and police have been and still are predominantly male. Women, having been barred one way or another from the areas of power and decision making, are represented in absurdly small numbers in every aspect of politics and law. The representation of feminists—that is, women consciously committed to women's rights and needs—is even smaller. Until as recently as 1920, the entire constituency that legislators and public officials had to satisfy was male. Before suffrage, women had no formal power at all. Today, without unity of common goals, without significant spheres of public influence, women's clout is little better.

It is a small wonder, therefore, that the law should reflect a male perspective. Given that the creators of our legal system and the constituency for whom it was created were and are the sons of patriarchy—and thus conscious and unconscious heirs to all the perceptions, attitudes, and values it entails—our legal system is highly sexist. It clearly accepts and supports the traditional images and values of male and female, awards to men privilege and advantage in every sphere of life both public and private, and sanctions and reinforces the subordination of women to men. Judicial decisions on every level and in every area of concern—domestic relations, civil rights, labor and employment, crime, and others—all reflect the common social themes regarding "femininity" and the sexes: that men and women, being "naturally" different in capacities, needs, and function, should occupy different spheres of activity;[20] that because women are weak and dependent, we should be "protected," both from the ugliness of life and the dangers of our own inferiority; that because women are both morally and intellectually less competent than men, less rational and trustworthy, we should be under greater constraint.

What this means to us as women is that the legal system, allegedly designed to protect and assist citizens in their activities, instead often thwarts us. It means that when we go to the courts for redress of crimes or injustice, we go as little girls to a father, as supplicants, and we go to a system that sees us and the world in a way that is very much to our detriment. Most frequently, male lawyers must argue for us (often missing issues central to our experience). Male judges apply masculist laws to our female circumstances (interpreting them from their privileged

male position). Male police must believe us and accept the credibility of beings said to have no credibility. These circumstances make the legal system a very different place for women than for men. The statistics bearing on rape, wife battering, child support, or prison sentences for women—to name just a few conspicuous areas of uneven-handed justice—bear this out. We know, furthermore, that since the law tends to conservatism and the status quo, we cannot expect change easily or soon, especially without some very powerful catalysts.

Points and Instances: A Short History

Law is based on precedent, and so the past directs the future. Regarding the law, what kind of past do women have?

From earliest times in Western culture, as one might expect in patriarchy, the position of women has been both marginal and shaky. Jo Freeman, like Kate Millett, argues that we can understand our identification and relationship to men in terms of caste.[21] Unlike a class, from which one may emerge, a caste is a rigid category of stratification based on characteristics one has no hand in determining—birth, color, or sex, for example. Women's caste, from which we cannot emerge, entails certain functions, activities, and behaviors. It imposes on us a whole separate set of expectations with attendant rewards and punishments. Maintaining this caste (this "place") has been a major occupation of the legal system.

According to Jo Freeman, the current legal status of women has its roots in the most ancient traditions and prejudices of the Western world. Says Freeman:

> The sexual caste system is the longest, most firmly entrenched caste system known to Western civilization. . . . There is a long standing legal tradition reaching back to early Roman law which defines women as perpetual children. This tradition, known as the "Perpetual Tutelage of Women," has not been systematically recognized, but the definition of women as minors who never grow up, who must always be under the guidance of a male, has been carried down in modified form to the present day.[22]

The early Roman tradition of treating women not as citizens, not even as adults, but rather as "daughters" first of their natural fathers, then of their husbands, found its way into canon law and from there through English common law into our own legal system.

It was Blackstone's *Commentaries on the Laws of England*, written in 1765—a veritable bible on the law in the early United States, according to Freeman—that codified the ancient rules for future generations. Women's status is most clearly reflected in Blackstone's treatment of marriage:

> *Single women were presumed to have the same rights in private law as single men. But when a woman married, these rights were lost, suspended under the feudal doctrine of "coverture." As Blackstone described: "By marriage, the husband and wife are one person in law; that is, the very being or legal existence of the woman is suspended during the marriage, or at least is incorporated and consolidated into that of the husband, under whose wing, protection, and cover, she performs everything."*[23]

Where Do We Go From Here? ERA?

Historically, ours was a system that, for good or ill, maintained separate justice for women and men. The effect has been a legacy of discrimination and inequality that heavily influences juridical behavior today and supports sexism in the society at large.

> *Our legal structure will continue to support and command an inferior status for women so long as it permits any differentiation in legal treatment on the basis of sex. This is so for three distinct but related reasons. First, discrimination is a necessary concomitant of any sex-based law because a large number of women do not fit the female stereotype upon which such laws are predicated. Second, all aspects of separate treatment for women are inevitably inter-related; discrimination in one area creates discriminatory patterns in another. Thus a woman who has been denied equal access to education will be disadvantaged in employment even though she received equal treatment there. Third, whatever the motivation for different treatment, the result is to create a dual system of rights and responsibilities in which the rights of each group are governed by a different set of values. History and experience have taught us that in such a dual system one group is always dominant and the other subordinate. As long as woman's place is defined as separate, a male-dominated society will define her place as inferior.*[24]

Attempts at change have been spotty and largely ineffectual. The protections of the Fifth and Fourteenth Amendments to the Constitution have not been consistently applied to women's cases; piecemeal legislative changes have been sparse and slow; judicial review has been "casual," peremptory, or sexist itself.[25]

Most feminists and many legislators and judicial experts maintain that what is necessary is a single consistent, coherent principle of equal rights for women and men, a principle of law that would serve as mandate and policy for the public sector and for the courts. The embodiment of that principle is, of course, the Equal Rights Amendment (ERA):

> Section 1: *Equality of rights under the law shall not be denied or abridged by the United States or by any state on account of sex.*
>
> Section 2: *The Congress shall have the power to enforce, by appropriate legislation, the provisions of this article.*
>
> Section 3: *This amendment shall take effect two years after the date of ratification.*

Simply put, the question is whether women are finally to be counted as full human beings before the law and in society.

Opponents to the amendment argued on grounds both hysterical and spurious: (1) ERA would legitimate abortion (false), homosexual marriage (false), and extraordinary federal control over personal matters (false); (2) ERA would deny the sanctity of the family (false), a woman's right not to have outside employment (false), and "privacy" (false); (3) ERA will require equal numbers of women and men in the army and in combat (false), coed bathrooms (false), women to share barracks with men in the service (false), children to be placed in state-run child-care facilities (false).

Most of these issues were created precisely to frighten both women and men into rejecting ERA. It was argued, furthermore, that ERA is simply not necessary, that the Fourteenth Amendment is sufficient to remedy instances of discrimination. Proponents of ERA pointed out, however, that review under the Fourteenth Amendment has been inconsistent and inefficient, and that ERA, in making sex an absolutely prohibited classification for law, would go much further toward guaranteeing women equality of economic, educational, and political opportunity.

With all the public controversy, it is sometimes surprising to discover that during the campaign to pass the ERA the great majority of voters were for passage. By 1978, the amendment had been passed by thirty-five states, and even in many states that did not ratify, polls consistently showed a majority of popular approval. It would appear that the minority opposed to ERA were entrenched in the power structure, better supported financially, and better organized (as are the minority opposed to women's reproductive freedom). In 1985, the Equal Rights Amendment was reintroduced in both houses of Congress.

The Equal Rights Amendment would be a valuable tool, to be sure, but we must keep in mind that ERA, like suffrage, cannot guarantee equality. It can function only as a tool, provided it is used properly. To gain equality, women must move to full participation in every sector of American life. Most particularly, women must develop influence and strength in government and politics, for there lies the heart of public power, the formal source of law, policy, and enforcement.

Women, Government and Politics

To govern is to exercise authority, to wield power, to manage and guide the affairs of state for the citizenry. In this area, people make decisions and rules that affect every aspect of our lives, public and private, from how and where we work to whether or not we may terminate a pregnancy. Yet here again— whether in the creation of law and public policy, in its interpretation, or in its execution—female citizens are absurdly underrepresented.

On the federal level, the House of Representatives has never had more than nineteen women nor the Senate more than two at one time. No woman has ever been president or been seriously considered for that office. No woman has ever occupied a top-level cabinet position, and very few have had major authority or power in national or international affairs.

So far as formal public power is concerned, at present women have very little. Yet perhaps it would be more accurate to say that we *exercise* very little, for our potential is strong. After all, we represent more than half the total population, and we are legally entitled to vote, hold office, and participate in and manipulate the political process. Until very recently, we have simply failed to do so to any extent.

A variety of reasons explain women's minimal participation in the political process. Of course, a long history of enforced formal suppression, including disfranchisement and legal discrimination, has left a legacy of prejudicial attitudes and policies. Informal suppression, the effects of female roles and gender stereotypes, also functions effectively. The negative image of the authoritative woman, the burdens of child-rearing and homemaking, and the absence of social support for functioning outside of the assigned "place" have all coalesced to keep women from organizing and unifying to challenge discrimination, exploitation, and sexism in the political arena and the wider society.

Most important, until recently women did not identify themselves in the political process as women. That is, we failed to recognize ourselves as a distinct, meaningful category or class, as a legitimate pressure group formed around and appropriately pressing for our own self-defined needs and goals. We have seen ourselves as Republicans or Democrats, as working class or middle class, as black or white, as conservative or liberal, and so on, but we have failed to make a most important identification, of ourselves simply as women who, regardless of other connections and loyalties, have common needs and problems and have the right to make civil demands.

The result of this inferior participation has been an absence of power, a lack of voice in the decisions that direct our lives. Without proportional representation in government, one is not a free citizen, and so one can only endure the whims and decisions of those in power; there is no recourse. Such a principle is clearly expressed in the early formulative documents of the American system, and it is obviously reflected in women's position today in society. Men hold power and generally make decisions that they believe to be suitable. Women's perspective can be reflected in law only to the degree that women have public power and a political vote. To achieve this, we must not see ourselves as dependents or supplicants. The U.S. government is based on the principle that all citizens have a right to make their needs and wishes known and to press for them in orderly fashion so that social balance arises through the interplay of these pressures, and citizens ultimately gain social justice. We as women must affirm ourselves as full citizens, with the full complement of social responsibility and hence the full measure of social rights.

We are entering a new phase of feminism—call it Grass Roots Feminism, call it Feminism 2000, call it Global Feminism, call it Life-Preserving Feminism, call it simply New Phase Feminism—whatever it may be, it will make history, as did the first phase of modern feminism. Its horizons are unlimited. Never before have women become possibly the only *salvation for the survival of humanity.*

Not so long ago on a flight from Dallas to Chicago, I sat next to a young woman, not very politically aware, but very appealing, and as so often happens with passing acquaintances, people you never expect to see again, we told each other our life histories. At some point she turned to me and said, ''You know, I would like to be an activist; I would like to fight for a cause, but I'm not that type.''

''What type would you say you are?'' I inquired.

''A dreamer,'' was her response.

''My dear young friend,'' I said. ''The very first condition for being an activist is that you be a dreamer. Without dreams, without a vision, there can be no hope, and hope is the essence of motivating force in the struggle for social change.''

—Margarita Papandreou[26]
President of the Women's Union of Greece

Notes

[1]U.S. Bureau of the Census, 1988 Current Population Survey. Compiled by Urban Information Center, University of Missouri, St. Louis. July 1989.

[2]U.S. Dept. of Labor, Bureau of Labor Statistics, *Employment and Earnings*, January 1989, pp. 183–188, passim.

[3]Evelyn Nakano Glenn and Rosly L. Feldberg, ''Clerical Work: The Female Occupation'' in *Women: A Feminist Perspective*, 4th ed., ed. Jo Freeman (Mountain View, CA: 1989), p. 294.

[4]Elyce Rotella, ''Fact Sheet: Women in the U.S. Economy.'' Unpublished paper, 1989.

[5]Ibid.

[6]Lenore Weitzman, ''Women and Children Last: The Social and Economic Consequences of Divorce Law Reforms,'' reading in this chapter.

[7]''20 Facts on Women Workers,'' supra.

[8]Francine D. Blau and Anna E. Winkler, ''Women in the Labor Force: An Overview,'' in *Women: A Feminist Perspective*, p. 280.

[9]Diane Schaffer, ''The Feminization of Poverty,'' in *Women, Power and Policy: Toward the Year 2000*, 2nd ed., eds. Ellen Boneparth and Emily Stoper (New York: Pergamon Press, 1988), p. 224.

[10]Rotella, ''Fact Sheet,'' supra.

[11]''20 Facts on Women Workers,'' supra.

[12]Rotella, ''Fact Sheet,'' supra.

[13]Shirley Bernard, ''Women's Economic Status: Some Clichés and Some Facts'' in *Women: A Feminist Perspective*, p. 239.

[14]Rotella, ''Fact Sheet,'' supra.

[15]''20 Facts on Women Workers,'' supra.

[16]U.S. Dept. of Labor, Women's Bureau. Fact Sheet No. 88-1, ''Women and Workforce 2000,'' January 1988.

[17]Ibid.

[18]Michael Korda, *Male Chauvinism! How It Works* (New York: Random House, 1972).

[19]George Gilder, *Sexual Suicide* (New York: Quadrangle, 1973).

[20]Barbara A. Brown, Thomas I. Emerson, Gail Falk, and Ann E. Freedman, ''The Equal Rights Amendment: A Constitutional Basis for Equal Rights for Women,'' *Yale Law Journal* 80 (1971): 876.

[21]Jo Freeman, ''The Legal Basis of the Sexual Caste System,'' *Valparaiso University Law Review* 5, No. 2 (1971): 203ff.

[22]Ibid., p. 208.

[23]Ibid., p. 210.

[24]Brown et al., ''The Equal Rights Amendment,'' pp. 873–74.

[25]Brown et al., ''The Equal Rights Amendment,'' p. 876.

[26]''Feminism and Political Power: Some Thoughts on a Strategy For the Future,'' in *Women, Power, and Policy: Toward The Year 2000*, pp. xvii, xix.

Women and the American Economy

Elyce J. Rotella

Elyce J. Rotella was born in Johnstown, Pennsylvania, in 1946. She received her Ph.D. in economic history from the University of Pennsylvania. Her research includes work on the growth of women's participation in the U.S. labor force, on clerical workers and schoolteachers, on the economics of marriage and divorce, and on the history of borrowing and saving. She is the author of From Home to Office: U.S. Women at Work, 1870–1930. *She is currently a member of the Economics Department and the Women's Studies Program at Indiana University.*

In this article, Rotella explains concepts necessary to analyzing women's position in the American economy and details some information on women's present condition and status.

Elyce J. Rotella wrote this article for this edition of *Issues in Feminism.*

ANY ECONOMY, NO MATTER HOW IT IS ORGANIZED, must decide how the resources of the society will be used to produce the goods and services that the members of the society consume. A large portion of the productive resources of any society consists of the labor power of people. Therefore, the amounts and kinds of work that people do is of fundamental interest to anyone trying to understand an economy, and for that reason economists and other social scientists have long been interested in the ways that tasks are divided among the members of society. There are many reasons for the division of labor among individuals: The most obvious are differences in interest, ability, and acquired skills. If all people were equally able to obtain all kinds of training, we expect that persons would choose tasks simply according to their interests, abilities, and the remuneration offered. However, we know that in reality people's choices are limited in a number of ways. For example, some people are expected to follow in their parents' footsteps; some very able people do not go to college or receive other kinds of training because their families are poor; and some people's choices are limited by the expectations society has of the proper roles for them to play.

Both women's and men's choices are limited by sex roles. In all societies sex is an important determinant of the division of tasks. Most people believe that the sexual division of labor that prevails in their own society is natural and is determined by the biological differences between the sexes. However, there is actually considerable variation among societies in the tasks that are assigned to females and males. For example, farming is thought to be men's work in Western European societies, but in much of Africa farming was done by women until very recently. The one set of tasks that virtually all societies have assigned to women is child rearing, although there are cultures in which it is customary for men to be quite involved in the care of children.

In this paper we focus on the economic roles that women play in late twentieth-century American society. Although much of what will be said can also be applied to women in the rest of the world, it should be kept in mind that there are important differences between cultures in the sexual division of labor. In addition the sexual division of labor has changed considerably over time, so that there are some tasks women routinely perform today that it would have been unthinkable for them to perform in the past.

The Economic System

Everyone in the economic system plays two basic roles—producer and consumer. People fulfill their producer role by using the resources they control to make goods and provide services. For most people their most important productive resource is labor power, and they sell their labor to businesses or agencies that organize the production of goods and services sold in the market. In exchange for their labor people receive income in the form of wage earnings, which then makes it possible for them to fulfill their other basic economic role, that of consumer. In an advanced market economy, such as the modern U.S. economy, a very large proportion of goods and services produced are sold in markets. This differs from the situation in subsistence economies where most people consume the things they produce themselves and few goods are traded in markets.

Consumers use their earnings to purchase the goods and services they need and want. Clearly, those people who receive the highest earnings in exchange for their labor are able to enjoy the consumption of the largest amounts of goods and services. In addition to spending the earnings that they receive in exchange for their own resources, some people are able to consume more market goods and services because they can use the earned income of others. For example, children are able to consume market goods because of their parents' earnings, and full-time housewives consume on the basis of their husbands' earnings.

In this paper we will mostly be examining women's roles as producers in the American economy, but we must keep in mind the close connection that exists among production, earnings, and consumption.

The Changing Participation of Women in the U.S. Labor Force

Women may use all of their labor power to work in their homes producing goods and services for themselves and their families. In this case they do not receive a money wage directly in exchange for their labor. In order to consume market goods and services they must be able to use the income earned by someone else, usually other family members. Such women are full-time homemakers, and they are fulfilling the economic role that many in our culture have considered to be the preferred and "natural" role for married women.

Many other women work for pay, that is, they exchange their labor services for a money wage in the market. Women who work for pay or who are looking for a paying job are said to be members of the labor force. The proportion of all women who are members of the labor force is called the female labor force participation rate.

Column one (1) in Table 1 shows how the female labor force participation rate has changed over this century. We can see that in 1900 only 20 percent of all women were at work for pay and that by 1989 over 57 percent of all women were in the labor force. This rise in the proportion of all women who work for pay is one of the most dramatic changes that have taken place in the U.S. economy in this century. The pattern of increase in female labor force participation has not been the same in all time periods. The increase was fairly slow up until 1940. The very rapid increase from 1940 to 1945 was due to the movement of women into the labor force during the Second World War when many men were fighting and there was a severe labor shortage. It was not until 1960 that female labor force participation reached the level that had prevailed in 1945. Since 1960 the growth of women's labor force participation has been extremely rapid.

Column two (2) in Table 1 shows how women's share of the total labor force has changed. In 1900 only 18 of every 100 paid workers were women. In 1989 women made up nearly 45 percent of the American labor force, and this number is still rising. Clearly then, paid employment is more important in the lives of American women today than it was in the past, and women are more important in the labor force.

Table 1   WOMEN'S LABOR FORCE PARTICIPATION RATE AND WOMEN'S SHARE OF THE LABOR FORCE

Year	(1) Women's labor force participation rate[a]	(2) Women's share of the labor force[b]
1900	20.0	18.1
1920	22.7	20.4
1930	23.6	21.9
1940	27.9	25.2
1945	35.8	29.1
1950	33.9	28.8
1955	35.7	30.2
1960	37.7	33.4
1965	39.3	35.2
1970	43.3	38.1
1975	46.3	40.0
1980	51.5	42.6
1985	54.5	44.2
1989 (March)	57.2	44.6

[a]Women's labor force participation rate $= \dfrac{\text{women in the labor force}}{\text{women in the population}}$

[b]Women's share of the labor force $= \dfrac{\text{women in the labor force}}{\text{total labor force}}$

Sources: U.S. Department of Commerce, Bureau of the Census, *Historical Statistics of the United States, Colonial Times to 1970*, 1975, pp. 131–32. U.S. Department of Commerce, Bureau of the Census, *Statistical Abstract of the United States, 1988*, p. 365. U.S. Department of Labor, Bureau of Labor Statistics, *Employment and Earnings*, April 1989, p.8.

This dramatic increase in women's participation in the labor force has caused economists to investigate the factors that affect women's decisions about how to structure their work lives. Marital status and family responsibilities have been found to have an important effect. Table 2 shows participation rates by marital status for selected years since 1950; and for married women, it shows the effect of the presence of children in the home. Participation by single (never married) and divorced women was higher than that of married women at all dates. Although work force participation by women in all marital status groups has increased, the most notable increases were those

of married women (husband present). Since the great majority of American women marry (only 9 percent of women aged 35 to 39 in 1988 had never been married), it is these women whose actions dominate the female work force and who have been responsible for the bulk of the female labor force growth since the Second World War. Some of this increase in participation has also been due to the rise in the proportion of women who are not currently married because of the increase in the divorce rate and because of the recent trend toward later marriage for women.

Since married women are usually expected to bear the primary responsibility for housework and child care, it is not surprising that marriage and children reduce the likelihood that women will work for pay. When such women do work in the market, they generally assume the "double burden," of working at a paid job while maintaining nearly complete responsibility for home work. Recent surveys show that husbands' help with housework does not increase substantially when their wives are employed. It is interesting (and perhaps surprising) to see that, even in the face of this "double burden," labor force participation by married women with children is rising very rapidly. Indeed, the greatest increases are occurring among women with young children. In 1950 only 11.9 percent of married women with children under 6 were in the labor force; in 1989 this figure was 57.1 percent, an increase of nearly 5 fold. In 1970, 24 percent of all married mothers with children one year old or younger were in the labor force. Just 18 years later, nearly 52% of these mothers of very young children were labor force participants.

Certainly then, the last forty years have seen drastic changes in the ways that women organize their work lives. Huge changes in labor force participation by age are pictured in Figure 1. The solid lines in Figure 1 show the variation in women's labor force participation by age for various cross-sections. Before 1950, the bulk of women in the labor force were young. In the 1950 cross-section, we see the phenomenon that has come to be called re-entry, a return to the labor force by women over 35 when their children are in school or grown. This pattern is even more pronounced in the curve for 1960 where the highest participation rates belong to women aged 45 to 54. The curve for 1970 shows higher participation at all ages than was the case in 1960 though the pattern by

Table 2   Women's Labor Force Participation Rate by Marital Status and Presence of Children

	1950	1960	1970	1980	1988
Single (never married)	50.5	44.1	53.0	61.5	65.2
Widowed or divorced	36.0	37.1	36.2	41.0	42.9
Divorced	NA	NA	71.5	74.5	75.7
Married (husband present)	23.8	30.5	40.8	50.1	56.5
Married (husband present)					
With children 6 to 17 only	28.3	39.0	49.2	61.6	72.5
With children under 6	11.9	18.6	30.3	45.3	57.1
With children under 3	NA	15.3	25.8	41.5	54.5
With children 1 or under	NA	NA	24.0	39.0	51.9

Sources: U.S. Department of Commerce, Bureau of the Census, *Statistical Abstract of the United States, 1978,* p. 393. *Statistical Abstract of the United States, 1988,* pp. 373–374. Howard Hayghe, "Rise in Mothers' Labor Force Activity Includes Those with Infants," *Monthy Labor Review,* February, 1986, p. 45. U.S. Department of Labor, Bureau of Labor Statistics, News release, September, 7, 1988.

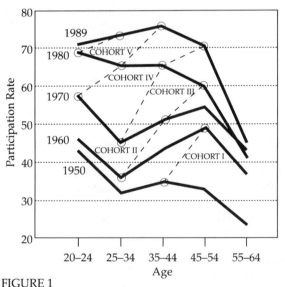

FIGURE 1

Female Participation in the Labor Force by Age, 1950–1989.

U.S. Department of Commerce, Bureau of the Census, *Statistical Abstract of the United States, 1953,* p. 185. *Statistical Abstract of the United States, 1964,* p. 217. *Statistical Abstract of the United States, 1988,* p. 366. U.S. Department of Labor, Bureau of Labor Statistics, *Employment and Earnings,* April 1989, p. 10.

age (with highest participation by the youngest women and by women ages 45–54) is basically unchanged. Between 1970 and 1980 there were large increases in participation by women in all except the oldest group. The growth in participation over the decade of the seventies was particularly rapid for younger women. For women ages 25–34, many of them mothers of young children, labor force participation was 45% in 1970, 65.5% in 1980, and 72.9% in March of 1989. Looking at the line for 1989, we see that female labor force participation growth continued in the 1980s with particularly notable growth in participation by women in their mid-20s to mid-50s.

As interesting as is the information presented by the solid lines in Figure 1, we can get more insight into the lives of women by looking at the dashed lines. These lines show the experience of specific groups of women as they age over their lifetimes. The dashed lines show the experience of birth-cohorts, i.e., women who were born at the same time. For example, if we look at the line labeled Cohort I, we see the experience of women born in 1906–1915. They were ages 35–44 in 1950 and ages 45–54 in 1960. These women increased their participation as they aged (from 35% when they were 35–44 to 49.3% when they were 45–54). Notice how different their behavior was from women who were ages 45–54 in 1950, only 33% of whom were in the labor force. If we had been around in 1950 and wanted to predict the future participation of women who were currently 35–44, we probably would have looked at the current behavior of 45–54 year old women and predicted a slight decline in participation as the 35–44 year old women aged. How wrong we would have been! In fact, we would have been very wrong if we had followed this strategy for almost any age group at any date. To take one other notable example, look at women who were ages 25–34 in 1980 (Cohort IV, the baby boom cohort born in 1946–55). The older half of this group were ages 20–24 in 1970. They had higher rates of labor force participation when they were 25–34 than they had when they were younger. And they continued to increase their participation as they aged to 35–44. Suppose that these women had been building their expectations of their own futures on the lives of their older contemporaries. They would have formed very erroneous expectations.

The Division of Women's Labor Between the Home and the Market: Explanations and Implications

We can gain understanding of the rise in women's labor force participation by focusing on the process through which people make decisions about how to use their time. For everyone time is a scarce resource, and we must all decide how to allocate our time among the various things that we would like to do. Everyone must spend time every day in sleep and in essential body maintenance functions. Beyond this we can decide to use our time for work or for leisure. All people (except workaholics) enjoy leisure and hope to have some leisure time each day. The time that we choose to work can be spent either working for pay or working in situations in which we are not paid for our labor. If we work for pay, we receive earnings, which allow us to enjoy consumption of goods and services that are bought in the market. If we engage in unpaid work, we produce goods and services that we ourselves or someone else consumes. Most unpaid work takes place in the home (dish washing, gardening, child care, and so on), but a substantial amount of unpaid work (eg., volunteer work) is also performed in other settings. Everyone, of course, performs some unpaid work in the home so everyone must decide how to allocate their work time between paid work and unpaid work. However,

since women are expected to be the major producers of goods and services in the home, the decision of dividing time between work at home and work in the market is particularly important for them.

Throughout this century the wages that women can earn in the labor force have increased, and this increase is one factor that has been shown to be very important for explaining women's decisions about allocating time to paid work versus unpaid work. When the wage that a woman can earn by being in the labor force increases, the cost to her and her family of having her stay out of the labor force and work at home to produce goods and services for the family to consume will also increase. For example, if a woman could earn $500 per week by working as an engineer, she and her family would have to give up $500 per week if she stays at home to be a full-time homemaker. And if her potential earnings increase by $100 per week, the cost of staying home rises accordingly. Clearly then, the incentive for a woman to go into the labor force will increase when her market wage increases, and women with high potential wages will be less likely to be full-time homemakers. This is part of the reason that women who have high levels of education are much more likely to be in the labor force. Educated women have higher potential earnings, and they are probably more able to find pleasant and fulfilling jobs.

As women increase their time in market work and reduce their time in home work they substitute products they buy in the market for some of the goods and services they might have produced at home. This means that earning women and their families are more likely to eat in restaurants, to send out clothes to laundries, and to use institutional child care and baby sitters. It is not, however, possible to substitute purchased products for all home production. Therefore, studies have found that women who have the "double burden" of being homemakers and wage earners work more total hours per week than any other group in society.

The rise over time in women's wages and in women's labor force participation has a number of implications for the institutions of marriage and the family. In the traditional marriage common in Western cultures, the division of labor has been between the bread-winner husband and the homemaker wife. The husband specialized in paid market work, and the wife specialized in unpaid home work. In this arrangement the wife was dependent on her husband's earnings in order to be able to consume market goods and services, and a woman who was concerned with her economic well-being had to be careful to choose a husband with good earning potential. As more women work in the market, this dependency lessens with the result that women may choose to marry later, and some may choose not to marry at all. Women with unhappy marriages may be more likely to divorce if they can earn their own income. In the last three decades, we have seen many changes in the marriage behavior of Americans—the kinds of changes that we would expect to result from greater female labor force participation. Overall women are marrying later; the median age at first marriage for women has risen from 20.3 in 1960 to 23.6 in 1988. It is quite possible that a substantial number of women may not marry at all; the proportion of women aged 25–29 who had never married rose from 10.5% in 1970 to 29.5% in 1988. The divorce rate has doubled since 1960. In addition to its implications for the incidence of marriage, we might expect that greater economic independence for women will have implications for courtship and the nature of the marriage relation as well. As they are more able to provide for themselves, women who wish to marry may be freer to choose husbands on the basis of affection and attraction rather than on the basis of men's potential as income providers. Perhaps these marriages will be more satisfying to both partners.

The analysis which stresses the increasing value of women's market time also has implications for the decisions that people make about how many children to have. As women's potential market wage rises, the cost of their time spent in household duties rises. Therefore the cost to families of having children to care for goes up if the mother is to stay at home to provide child care instead of working for pay. This leads to the incentive to have smaller families and is undoubtedly part of the reason for the low fertility of American women.

The explanation offered above for increased labor force participation by American women emphasizes the central role played by the rising market value of women's time. As women's market wages have risen women have responded by reallocating time from non-market uses to market work. As powerful as this explanation is, we must not lose sight of the fact that women take jobs for the same reasons that men take jobs—they need money to support themselves and their families. Many employed women are married

to men who earn low wages, and these women's earnings often make the difference between the family living below or above the poverty level. Earnings of families in which both husband and wife are employed are 60% higher on average than in families where only the husband is employed. As more and more families choose to send the wife into the labor force in pursuit of this higher income, the "Leave It to Beaver" family with a stay-at-home mother has become comparatively rare. In March 1989, among all husband-wife families, only 22 percent had the husband as the only earner in the family.

As important as are women's earnings for husband-wife families, they are much more crucial for non-married women, especially for the rapidly growing number of non-married women who are supporting children. In 1989, 45 percent of all employed women did not have husbands (i.e., they were single, widowed, divorced, or married with an absent husband). Most of these women were dependent on themselves alone for financial support. In addition, many of these women were heads of families and used their earnings to support children. In the last quarter century there has been a dramatic increase in the incidence of divorce; more than half of all marriages are predicted to end in divorce. The greater prevalance of divorce has led to increased participation by women in the labor force through two avenues. First, as was seen in Table 2, divorced women have very high rates of labor force participation. This is because most divorced women bear complete responsibility for supporting themselves and their dependent children. Divorce commonly leads to substantially lower economic status for women and their children. In these days of no-fault divorce, alimony is very rare, child support awards are far from universal, often hard to collect, and generally cover only a portion of a child's needs. In 1985, only 3% of ever-divorced women received alimony payments, and the average annual payment was $3,733. Although 72% of divorced women with children were supposed to receive child support payments, only 34% received the full amount due, 19% received partial payment, and 47% received no child support payment at all. The average annual child support payment received per woman was $2,538. Clearly divorced women need to be in the labor force to support themselves and their children. The prevalence of divorce also raises female labor force participation through a second avenue. It gives married women a strong incentive to maintain their attachment to the labor force and therefore their future earning potential. Since many women will find themselves completely dependent on their own earnings in the future, many find it wise to insure themselves against a low post-marital living standard by remaining in the labor force while married.

In the past there has been a strong inverse relationship between husband's earnings and wife's labor force participation. Women with high-earning husbands were much less likely to work for pay than were women who were married to men with lower earnings. Since 1960 this association has been weakening as more highly educated women (who are usually married to high-earning men) enter the labor force. At present, there is no consistent relationship between husband's earnings and wife's likelihood of employment. From this we can conclude that married women are more responsive to the positive effects of their own wages, which tend to pull them into the work force, than they are to the negative effects of their husbands' earnings, which in the past have tended to keep them at home.

Women's Earnings

We have seen that women's earnings are an important factor affecting the decision of how women allocate their time between work at home and work for pay in the market. Women's earnings have increased over time which has tended to pull them into the labor force. In this section we turn our attention to the determinants of women's earnings and to the gap in earnings between women and men. The earnings of all American workers, males and females, have increased greatly in this century reflecting the greater productivity of workers. These productivity increases reflect advances in production technology and the higher skill and education levels of workers.

Table 3 presents information on median earnings of workers employed full-year and full-time. We see that from 1960 to 1987, women's earnings rose by 35.3% after controlling for inflation. Over the same period, men's earnings rose by 26.2%. As a result of the faster growth of women's earnings, the earnings ratio (women's earnings as a percentage of men's earnings) rose from 60.7% in 1960 to 65% in 1987. Examination of the numbers in Table 3 reveals much about the performance of the U.S. economy in the recent past. For men, earnings rose to 1975 then de-

clined to the depths of the 1982 recession. Since 1982, men's earnings have again risen, but had not attained their 1975 level by 1987. For women the pattern of growth, decline, and renewed growth is similar, but the big difference is the much faster growth of women's earnings in the 1980s. All of the narrowing of the earnings gap is due to this faster growth of women's earnings in the '80s. In fact the earnings gap actually widened from 1955 to 1981, a period when many women were joining the labor force. The recent narrowing of the earnings gap is all the more dramatic because it follows a long period during which the gap either remained constant or widened.

Why do women workers earn less than men, and how can we explain changes in the earnings gap over time? Some of the difference between the annual earnings of women and men is due to the fact that more women work part-time and part-year. In 1986, 74 percent of employed women worked at full-time jobs compared with 89% of men. However, since Table 3 compared only the earnings of full-year, full-time workers, we have already controlled for this factor.

In general, economists think that the wages workers receive are related to their productivity. It is not surprising that highly productive workers in skilled jobs receive higher earnings than do less productive workers. We do not usually have accurate direct data on individual worker's productivity, but we do have expectations about the qualities that cause workers to be more productive. Education, job training, and experience on the job should lead to higher productivity and therefore to higher earnings. The gap between women's and men's earnings could reflect a gap between women's and men's productivities. The attempt to explain the earning gap by looking at differences between men and women in education, training, and experience is called the human capital approach.

The human capital approach offers some powerful explanations of the pattern of the earnings gap over time. A part of the earnings gap reflects the fact that many women have lower levels of education and work experience than do men. Until recently men were more likely to receive education and training beyond the college level, and there were substantial sex differences in the kinds of post-secondary training received. As important as sex differences in education and training are differences in work experience. Women's lower levels of labor force par-

Table 3 EARNINGS OF YEAR-ROUND, FULL-TIME
WORKERS (IN 1987 DOLLARS)

Year	Female	Male	Earnings Ratio Female/Male
1955			63.9
1960	12,499	20,601	60.7
1965	13,789	23,010	59.9
1970	15,580	26,243	59.4
1975	15,846	26,941	58.8
1980	15,443	25,671	60.2
1981	14,997	25,318	59.2
1982	15,323	24,817	61.7
1983	15,859	24,930	63.6
1984	16,172	25,405	63.7
1985	16,507	25,562	64.6
1986	16,825	26,179	64.3
1987	16,909	26,008	65.0
% increase 1960 to 1987	35.3	26.2	

Source: Current Population Reports, Series P-60, no. 162. *Money Income of Households and Persons in the U.S., 1987*, p. 2.

ticipation meant that they had lower levels of market experience. Since employers reward education, training, and experience by higher earnings, some of the earnings gap reflects these differences.

Although there is more to explaining the earnings gap than just sex differences in education, training, and experience, we can get insight into the changing size of the earnings gap by focusing on these factors. The widening of the gap in the 1950s, '60s and '70s, seems to be due in part to the rapidly increasing participation by women who were new entrants (or reentrants) into the labor force. A large percentage of these women had low levels of prior experience. Many were older women who were either joining the labor force for the first time or reentering the labor force after a long absence. Such women commonly had low levels of experience and commanded low wages. Since there were so many of them in the labor force, they pulled down women's average earnings.

We can also understand the narrowing of the earnings gap in the 1980s as being due partly to the changing human capital characteristics of women workers. Women's educational levels have been ris-

ing steadily, and in the 1970s there was considerable change in the kinds of education that women got, with many more women attending graduate and professional schools and educating themselves for employment in non-traditional fields. For example, women received 46% of the bachelor's degrees in business and management awarded in 1986 compared with under 9% in 1970, and they received 31% of M.D. degrees compared with 8% in 1970. This rise in women's education was accompanied by a rise in women's experience levels. As we saw in Figure 1, the 1970s and 1980s were characterized by rapidly increasing labor force participation by women in their 20s and 30s. What happened was that a growing number of women joined the labor force when young and maintained their attachment while they married and had children. This is the pattern common to men, and produced a large number of young and middle-aged women with experience levels as high as men of the same age. It is likely that the rapid rise in women's earnings in the 1980's reflects this rise in education and experience.

Researchers have tried to see how much of the earnings gap can be explained by the human capital approach by comparing the earnings of women and men who have the same education and experience. What they have found is that some of the difference in earnings can be explained by differences in education and experience, but a substantial portion remains unexplained. Even when we compare the earnings of women and men in the same occupational categories we find that a gap persists.

The part of the earnings gap that cannot be attributed to human capital differences reflects discrimination against women in the labor market. Discrimination can take a number of different forms. When women are paid less than equally productive men, they are being discriminated against. When women are excluded from some jobs or training so that they are forced to work in jobs in which their productivity is not as high as it might be, their earnings are lowered due to discrimination. Sometimes employers assume that all women have the same characteristics and make employment decisions about individual women based on the expected average attributes of women as a group. For example, employers may believe that all women will have high labor market turnover because some women drop out of the labor force in order to fulfill household responsibilities. In such cases, the women who are judged by the expected group characteristics rather than by their own individual characteristics are said to be victims of statistical discrimination.

In most studies, discrimination has been found to be responsible for half or more of the earnings gap. However, the major form that discrimination takes is not "unequal pay for equal work," though there are many cases of women receiving lower pay for doing substantially the same work as men. The biggest cause of the earnings gap and the major form of discrimination against women is that women and men are, by and large, employed in different occupations; and the pay in women's occupations is lower than the pay in men's occupations.

The Sex Distribution of Occupations

In Table 4 we see how women and men workers are distributed among the major occupational categories of the U.S. labor force. Even at the high level of aggregation of these data, there are striking differences in the distributions. Nearly 28% of all female workers were in administrative support jobs (mostly clerical) compared to 5.6% of men. Nearly 20% of men, but only 2.3% of women, were precision production, craft, and repair (skilled blue collar) workers. Much higher proportions of women than men were employed as private household workers and as other service workers. In the professional and technical fields where the figures for females and males are similar, the degree of aggregation in the data hides the substantial differences that actually exist because a large proportion of female professionals are teachers, nurses, librarians, and social workers whereas male professionals are in a much broader mix of fields.

When we look at occupational breakdowns of the U.S. labor force that are more detailed than the breakdown in Table 4, we see even greater disparity between women's and men's jobs. Women's employment is concentrated in a much smaller number of occupations than is men's employment. Not only are women workers concentrated in a fairly small number of jobs, but many of the jobs that women hold are held almost exclusively by women. That is, the occupational structure is highly segregated by sex, with many women being employed in jobs in which the overwhelming majority of workers are women.

We can get some sense of this by looking at the few detailed occupations listed in Table 4 and by concentrating on the last column which shows the percent of all workers in the occupation who are female. For example, we see that women are 97.4% of secretaries, stenographers, and typists but only 2.5% of construction workers. They are 71.1% of grade school and high school teachers but only 6.7% of engineers.

Despite the continuing high degree of concentration and sex segregation that persists in the U.S. occupational structure, there have been notable changes in the last two decades as women have made substantial inroads into some professional and managerial fields. For example, we can see in Table 4 that nearly 21% of all lawyers and judges are women; in 1970, only 5% were women. Women's employment has also grown very rapidly among physicians, dentists, accountants, and business executives. These occupational changes are concentrated among highly educated young women. The higher earnings of these women is responsible for much of the narrowing of the earnings gap in the 1980s. For less educated women, there has been little change in occupational or earnings prospects. Few women are employed in the skilled blue-collar trades which provide the best earnings prospects for workers with less than college educations. The employment of women without higher education is still concentrated in clerical jobs, in a few traditionally female factory occupations, and in the service jobs of the "pink collar ghetto."

The concentration and segregation we observe in the occupational structure has implications for women's earnings and for the male-female earnings gap. If women's ability to enter occupations is limited so that they are able to take fewer kinds of jobs than men, then women's wages will be lowered because so many women are available to work for a limited number of opportunities. If more women enter the labor force and most of them try to get jobs in traditional women's occupations, then there will be extreme competition for these jobs and therefore downward pressure on women's wages. If discrimination limits women's access to some occupations, it increases competition for "women's jobs" and reduces competition for "men's jobs." The result is that women's wages are artificially low and men's wages are artificially high. Economists call this mechanism occupational crowding. The existence of occupational crowding implies that the gap between wom-

Table 4   Occupational Distribution of Females and Males, March 1989

Occupational Group	Percent of Labor Force in Group		% Female
	Females	Males	
Executive, administrative, managerial	11.3	14.0	40.0
Professional specialty	15.0	12.4	49.5
Engineers			6.7
Teachers, college and university			39.1
Teachers, except college and university			71.1
Lawyers and judges			20.9
Technicians and related support	3.3	3.0	47.4
Sales occupations	12.8	11.0	48.7
Administrative support, including clerical	27.8	5.6	80.5
Secretaries, stenographers and typists			94.3
Private household workers	1.6	.05	97.4
Protective service workers	.5	2.6	15.3
Other service workers	15.5	7.1	64.1
Precision production, craft, repair	2.3	19.5	8.7
Construction trades			2.5
Machine operators, assemblers, inspectors	6.6	7.8	26.3
Transportation and material moving	.9	6.8	9.7
Handlers, equipment cleaners, helpers, laborers	1.5	6.2	17.1
Farming, forestry, and fishing	.9	4.0	16.0
TOTAL	100.0	100.0	44.6

Source: U.S. Department of Labor, Bureau of Labor Statistics, *Employment and Earnings,* April 1989, p. 29.

en's and men's earnings will persist until there is a widespread lessening of sex stereotyping of occupations.

Comparable Worth

The recognition of the crucial role played by occupational segregation in the earnings gap has fueled the drive for a movement to demand equal pay for jobs of comparable worth. The argument for comparable worth recognizes that "equal pay for equal work" will not narrow the earnings gap so long as most men and women are employed in different occupations. It therefore attempts to raise the earnings of women employed in female dominated jobs by ar-

guing that many of these jobs are of equal value to male dominated jobs. In order to pursue this argument, a mechanism is needed whereby comparisons can be made among persons employed in different occupations. The basic principle behind comparable worth is that it is possible to compare jobs in terms of knowledge, skill, effort, responsibility, and working conditions and that jobs equivalent in value in these terms should be paid equally.

Comparable worth has been the focus of a great deal of controversy in the political and legal arena. Business groups have generally been hostile to comparable worth, and during the 1980s the executive branch of the federal government has been vocally hostile. Probably the most often quoted negative evaluation of comparable worth is that of Clarence

Pendleton, Chair of the U.S. Civil Rights Commission in the Reagan Administration who said that comparable worth is the "looniest idea since Looney Toons." Many of those who oppose comparable worth argue that it is impossible to evaluate the worth of dissimilar jobs and that the attempt to make such comparisons would produce unwarranted bureaucratic interference in the labor market. Such criticism, however, neglects to note that although it may seem very difficult to compare jobs in terms of knowledge, skill, effort, responsibility, and working conditions, such comparisons are routinely made, especially by large employers such as governments and major corporations.

Employers often use job evaluation schemes to develop salary structures for their organizations. Many people are familiar with the GS system of salary categories used by the federal Civil Service. Job evaluation schemes are so common that there are firms which specialize in evaluating jobs and are hired by organizations to perform evaluations and assign evaluation scores that can be compared across occupations. The most commonly used evaluation system assigns points (called Hay points) to each job classification. Since job evaluation schemes are common in large organizations and have existed for a long time, advocates of comparable worth are not asking for a major change in the way that employers operate. They ask only that whenever the evaluation scheme assigns the same number of points to male dominated and female dominated jobs that the jobs receive the same pay.

All instances where there have been specific struggles to reform salary scales according to comparable worth principles have involved government employees and already existing evaluation and salary systems. For example, between 1983 and 1987 there was major reformation of the salary system of the State of Minnesota which had previously assigned Hay points to all its job classifications. When the Minnesota Council on the Economic Status of Women examined salaries paid to state workers in 1982, they found many instances of dramatic differences in the pay of men and women in jobs that had been evaluated as being equal. For example, the maximum monthly salary of workers employed as clerk-stenographers grade 2 (Hay points = 135), 99.7% of whom were female, was $1,171. By contrast, the maximum monthly salary of general repair workers (Hay points = 134), 99.3% of whom were male, was $1,564. Licensed practical nurses (Hay points = 183; 94.7% female) received $1,382 while highway maintenance workers (Hay points = 154, 99.9% male) received $139 per month more despite their much lower evaluation score. The discrepancies found in Minnesota between the salaries of workers in male dominated and female dominated jobs are common in the salary scales of many other state and local governments. In some areas, notably Washington State and the City of San Jose, California, readjustments of salary scales to move toward comparable worth have been made in response to pressure from women's advocacy groups and unions. Despite these successes, comparable worth principles have not been widely adopted and they remain very controversial.

The Feminization of Poverty

Over the same period that some American women have been improving their economic position, a very large number of women have suffered severe economic hardship. Women now make up a larger share of the population living in poverty—a phenomenon that has come to be called the feminization of poverty. The most notable economic advances have been concentrated among young well-educated women who succeeded in entering non-traditional jobs, solidified their attachment to the labor force, and experienced above average increases in earnings. For women at the other end of the economic scale, the picture is bleak. Over 70% of persons with incomes under $4,000 are women. Women's greater likelihood of living in poverty is due in large part to women's lower earnings; a great many women who work full-time, year round do not earn enough to support a family above the poverty line. The effect of low earnings combines with the fact that a large and rapidly growing number of families are maintained by women (i.e., families in which no adult male is present) to produce very high poverty rates for women and the children who are dependent on them.

Table 5 presents figures on poverty among American families. We can see that families maintained by women are much more likely to be poor than are husband-wife families; over 46% of families with children maintained by women are poor compared with under 8% of husband-wife families with chil-

Table 5 Proportion of U.S. Families Maintained by Women
(No Husband Present)

Year	Total	White	Black	Hispanic
1963	10.1	8.5	24.4	NA
1970	11.5	9.5	30.5	NA
1975	13.0	10.5	35.4	19.3
1980	15.1	11.9	41.7	21.9
1985	16.1	12.9	41.5	23.2
1988	16.8	13.4	43.5	23.9

Proportion of U.S. Families with Children Under 18 Maintained by Women
(No Husband Present)

Year	Total	White	Black	Hispanic
1975	16.3	12.6	42.6	NA
1980	19.2	14.6	48.6	NA
1985	20.6	16.1	48.9	25.9
1987	21.1	16.2	50.1	26.6

Proportion of All Families Living Below the Poverty Line, 1987

	Families Maintained by Women	Husband-Wife Families
Total	34.3	6.0
White	26.7	5.2
Black	51.8	12.3
Hispanic	51.8	18.1

Proportion of All Families with Children Under 18 Living Below
the Poverty Line, 1987

	Families Maintained by Women	Husband-Wife Families
Total	46.1	7.8
White	38.7	7.0
Black	59.5	13.6
Hispanic	60.7	NA

Sources: U.S. Department of Commerce, Bureau of the Census, Current Population Reports, Series P-60,
No. 163, *Poverty in the United States, 1987*, pp. 11–14. U.S. Department of Labor, Bureau of Labor
Statistics, "Employment in Perspective: Women in the Labor Force" Report 767.

dren. The increase in the share of the poverty population represented by families maintained by women is due to the marked rise in the prevalence of these families. (See the top half of Table 5.) Whereas in 1963, about 10% of all American families were maintained by women, by 1988, this number had grown to nearly 17% (21% of families with children under 18).

The growth in the number of families maintained by women and the attendant feminization of poverty is related to the increased incidence of divorce, the rise in the age at marriage, the apparent higher proportion of women not marrying at all, and the increase in childbearing by single women. As a result, in 1988, only 53.5% of women over age 15 were married and living with a spouse—a smaller proportion than at any other time in the last 50 years. This means that a large and growing proportion of women and their children are dependent on women's earnings, and we have already seen that women's earnings are much lower than men's.

Looking at Table 5, we see striking differences among black, white, and Hispanic women. Since the 1950s, racial differences in labor force participation, average earnings, and occupational distribution have declined substantially. The same cannot be said of racial differences in poverty. Over 50% of all families maintained by black and Hispanic women are poor compared with about a quarter of families maintained by white women; the figures are considerably higher for families with children under 18. The top of the table shows that there are also substantial differences among the three groups in the proportion of families maintained by women. Black families are particularly likely to be economically dependent on women with 43.5% of all black families and 50.1% of all black families with children being maintained by women. These figures reflect the recent rapid decline in the proportion of black women who are married. In 1988, only 39% of black women were married and living with a spouse and over 60% of black babies were born to non-married women. These women and their children are very likely to live in poverty. Although the feminization of poverty is a phenomenon that cuts across racial and ethnic lines, the striking differences we see in proportions of families maintained by women has led to widening differences in incidence of poverty among the races.

Summary

This century has witnessed very dramatic increases in participation by women in the American labor force. The bulk of this increase has taken place since the Second World War and has been largely due to increased participation by married women. Before 1970, the greatest increases in participation were attributable to middle aged women returning to the labor force after their families were grown, but since then the most notable increases have come from young mothers and from young unmarried women. Studies of women's labor force participation have found that increases in women's wages are very important for explaining the greater propensity of women to work for pay. As women's education and experience levels have risen, thereby raising their potential market wage, the implied price of home-produced goods and services has also risen, thus increasing the incentive to work for pay instead of working full-time in the home.

After many years during which the gap between women's and men's average earnings either stayed constant or widened, the gap has narrowed somewhat in the 1980's. This narrowing seems to be related closely to the growth in experience levels of women who have maintained continuous attachment to the labor force and to changes in the amounts and kinds of education that women receive. For well-educated young women there has been notable success in gaining access to professional and managerial jobs that have traditionally not been held by women.

Although the earnings gap has narrowed somewhat, very large differences remain between the earnings of men and women. Studies have found that individual differences between women and men in education, training and job experience can account for only a part of the earnings gap. The remainder reflects discrimination, particularly the kinds of discrimination that lead to widely differing occupational distributions of women and men workers. Women's employment tends to be concentrated in a relatively small number of low-paid jobs. Since the growth in women's labor force participation has not been accompanied by any very substantial decrease in the overall level of sex segregation in the occupational structure, most of new women workers have sought jobs in traditional women's fields. This development has increased competition for those jobs and exerted downward pressure on women's earnings. Any further substantial decrease in the size of the female-male earnings gap will require less sex segregation in the occupational structure and/or the widespread adoption of comparable worth principles in salary setting.

Despite economic gains by well-educated women workers, the picture for women who are close to the bottom of the economic ladder is disturbing. The number of families maintained by women is increasing rapidly as the incidence of marriage falls, the divorce rate rises, and the non-marital birth rate increases. Such families have a very high chance of falling into poverty and are unlikely to improve their position without major changes in social policy.

It is difficult to predict how women's economic roles will change in the future. We are seeing improvements for some women but increased difficulties for others. Most employed women bear the "double burden" of working in the labor force while they maintain primary responsibility for work in the home. Perhaps equality in the labor market will only come about when women achieve equality in other areas of life.

Suggestions for Further Reading

Barbara R. Bergmann, *The Economic Emergence of Women*. Basic Books, 1986.

Francine D. Blau and Marianne A. Ferber, *The Economics of Women and Work*. Prentice-Hall, 1986.

Claudia Goldin, *Understanding the Gender Gap: An Economic History of American Women*. Oxford University Press, 1989.

Women's Research and Education Institute, *The American Women, 1988–89: A Status Report*. W. W. Norton, 1988.

Women and Children Last: The Social and Economic Consequences of Divorce Law Reforms

Lenore J. Weitzman

Professor of sociology at Harvard University, Lenore J. Weitzman is one of the leading authorities on women and divorce. She is author of The Marriage Contract: Spouses, Lovers, and the Law *(1981), and* The Divorce Revolution *(1987).*

No-fault divorce was a legal innovation meant to humanize divorce proceedings and remove some of its worst effects. Instead, it has proved a disaster for many American women. After divorce, women's economic fortunes plummet, with painful consequences for the entire quality of their lives and their children's.

In Sanford M. Dornbusch and Myra H. Strober, eds., *Feminism, Children, and the New Families.* New York: Guilford Press, 1988. By permission of Guilford Publications, Inc.[1]

IN 1970, CALIFORNIA LAUNCHED A LEGAL REVOLUTION by instituting the first no-fault divorce law in the United States. The new law not only changed the rules for divorce, it also changed the rules for dividing property and awarding support. Responding to the widespread dissatisfaction with the abuses of the old law, and recognizing the "emerging equality" of women, the reformers tried to fashion a fair and equitable divorce law that treated wives as full and equal partners in the marital partnership.

But the consequences of these reforms have extended far beyond the intent of the drafters. Ends may influence beginnings. In a society where one half of all new marriages are expected to end in divorce, a radical change in the rules for ending marriage inevitably affects the rules for marriage itself and the intentions and expectations of those who enter it (Weitzman, 1985, p. xv; see also Davis, 1986). The no-fault reforms have done just that: They have created new expectations for the behavior of husbands and wives in marriage and redefined the scope of their responsibilities as spouses and as parents.

Before 1970, every state required fault-based grounds such as adultery or mental cruelty for divorce. Rooted in the English common law, these laws reinforced the traditional marriage contract in which the husband, as the family breadwinner, and the wife, as the homemaker and mother, were committed to sexual fidelity in a lifelong partnership. In order to obtain a divorce one party had to prove that the other had violated that contract that he had failed to support her, or that she had not performed her wifely duties, or that one of them had been cruel or sexually unfaithful.

A couple could not simply decide to end their marriage by mutual consent. The legal system of divorce required an "innocent" party and a "guilty" party. The innocent spouse had to produce evidence of the other's adultery or cruelty to justify the court's granting the divorce. The court would then provide redress for that innocent victim by compensating her (or him) with alimony (if the wife was the innocent party, as she typically was) and a larger share of the marital property.

By the late 1960s there was widespread dissatisfaction with this fault-based system of divorce: It forced spouses to become adversaries, and it encouraged and exacerbated marital mudslinging. After all, since the "innocent" party was rewarded financially, it "paid" to charge one's spouse with all the horrible deeds one could remember (or imagine). Often the parties had to distort the truth and lie in order to satisfy the legal requirements for fault. For example, if there had been no adulterous behavior, the evidence might be "manufactured" by staging an adulterous scene with private detectives and photographers waiting conveniently in the wings.

In some cases the legal process was merely a charade: But in others it was ugly, demeaning, and humiliating, especially when friends and relatives were brought into court as witnesses and were asked to corroborate the charges. Finally, the acrimonious legal process increased the antagonism between divorcing spouses and made it more difficult for them to cooperate in postdivorce parenting.

In this climate, California's no-fault law was welcomed as a major step forward. It sought to remove acrimony and hostility from the legal process by eliminating the need for any fault-based grounds for divorce. Instead, one party's claim that "irreconcilable differences" had caused the breakdown of the marriage was sufficient to justify a divorce. The new law required no grounds, no fault, and no consent. Since financial awards could no longer be based on who did what to whom, new standards for dividing property and awarding support were created to treat men and women fairly and equally. Property would be divided equally, and support for wives and children would be based on "need."

With this seemingly simple move, California pioneered sweeping reforms that quickly spread to other states. While not all states adopted the California model and completely abolished fault, by 1985— just 15 years later—every state but South Dakota had adopted some form of no-fault divorce law.

Although these laws were designed to create more equity, they have had unintended and unfortunate consequences: They have created substantial inequalities between divorced men and women and have led to the impoverishment of many divorced women and their children.

The Unintended Consequences

When I began my research, I shared the reformers' optimism and assumed that only good could come from an end of the vilification and sham testimony of the old fault-based system of divorce. How much better, I thought, to end a marriage in a nonadversarial fashion that sought to reduce acrimony and hostility and to encourage parents to fashion fair and equitable financial arrangements for themselves and their children.

Equally important was the fact that the new law promised equality between men and women. Here, finally, was a law that recognized wives as equals in the marital partnership. California was the first state to guarantee wives an equal share—a mandatory 50%—of the property accumulated during the marriage.

When, in the early days of my research, I began to confront cases of upper-middle-class women who had been married for 20 to 30 years and were being cut off with only a few years of alimony and hardly any property, who were being forced to move so that their homes could be sold, who, with little or no job experience and minimal court-ordered support, were headed for near-poverty, I assumed that they were the exceptions—the women who had incompetent lawyers or the wrong judge.

Similarly, when I first confronted cases of young mothers who were awarded so little child support that there was not enough to cover the cost of day care, and who then told me that the child support order "wasn't worth the piece of paper it was written on" because they couldn't collect the support the court had ordered, I again thought that these women were the exceptions. Perhaps they hadn't fought hard enough to press for their legal entitlement to adequate support for their children.

But as the systematic data from the court dockets became computer printouts with statistically significant results, it became clear that these women were not the exceptions. The data revealed a disquieting pattern, a pattern that pointed to substantial hardship for women and children. Somehow the elimination of grounds, fault, and consent, and the institution of gender-neutral standards for financial awards were having unanticipated and unfortunate consequences.

The major unintended result of the no-fault reforms has been widespread economic disruption for divorced women and their children. The new rules for alimony, property, and child support end up shaping radically different economic futures for divorced men on the one hand and for divorced women and their children on the other. My research reveals that women and the minor children in their households (90% of the children of divorced parents live with their mothers after divorce) experience a sharp decline in their standard of living after divorce: Their standard of living drops an average of 73% in the first year after divorce. In contrast, their ex-husbands experience a rise in their standard of living—an average 42% increase in the first year after divorce (Weitzman, 1985).

Why have these supposedly "enlightened" legal reforms had such devastating effects? How could laws that were designed to create more equitable settlements end up impoverishing divorced women and their children?

One reason is that the court's interpretation of "equality" in divorce settlements often produces unequal results by ignoring the very real inequalities that marriage creates for men and women. It also ignores the economic inequalities between men and women in the larger society. Thus, a woman who has been a homemaker and mother during marriage may not be "equal" to her husband at the point of divorce. Rules that treat her as if she is equal (in the mistaken belief that she can quickly enter the labor force and become the economic equal of her husband) simply serve to deprive her—and her children—of the support all of them need.

A second reason is that an ostensibly equal division of property is not in fact equal when women have the responsibility for child care in nine out of ten divorces that involve children (Weitzman, 1985). To divide the property equally between husband and wife typically means that one half of the family assets are awarded to one person, the husband, while the other half are left to an average of three people: the wife and two children. In addition, judges often interpret the equal division rule as requiring the forced sale of the family home. This increases the disruption, dislocation, and distress in the lives of many women and children. In fact, the children's interest in marital property is simply ignored in the present legal system of divorce.

A third factor is that the elimination of grounds, fault, and consent have reduced women's bargaining leverage to secure adequate financial awards. Since the wife was usually the "innocent" party under the old law, she was in a stronger position to negotiate support for herself and her children (in return for her agreement to file for and obtain the divorce her husband wanted).

A final cause of the economic disparity between divorced men and women lies in the courts' failure to understand the changing nature of property in our society. In many cases, the major assets of the marriage are not divided equally. In fact, new forms of marital property are often not divided at all. This is because courts often ignore the husband's career assets—his enhanced earning capacity, his pension, professional license, and health insurance—and fail to award the wife a share of these valuable assets that were built and acquired during the marriage.

Overview and Research

The unintended economic consequences of the legal changes in divorce provide one major theme of this chapter. The second major theme traces the effects of no-fault divorce on the institution of marriage. The final theme concerns the public policy implications of the findings and the congruence between womens' and childrens' interests in legal reforms.

The main section of this chapter summarizes the findings of a large-scale study of the social and economic effects of California's no-fault divorce reforms. Its research methods are briefly described below (for more detail see Weitzman, 1985).

I first examine the impact of the changing legal rules for dividing property, awarding alimony, and obtaining child support. I then examine the societal consequences of these rules, noting that the growth in female poverty and child poverty are a direct result of the current legal system of divorce.

The third section of this chapter considers the policy implications of the findings and recommends policies that would better protect those who are most disadvantaged: minor children, older homemakers, and the mothers of preschool children. The concluding section explores the ways in which the present system of divorce is transforming the nature of marriage and parenthood in our society.

Throughout this discussion, it will be evident that the interests of women and children are usually congruent in divorce, since, as has been mentioned, 90% of the children live with their mothers after divorce. Thus, any policies that enlarge the mother's share of marital property or family income will usually benefit her children as well. Similarly, any policies that provide better economic protection for children—policies that improve child support or recognize the child's interest in the family home—will usually benefit their mother as well.

The perception of conflict between women's and children's interests in divorce is based on an inaccurate and simplistic assessment of the best interests of children. For example, it is only when a judge assumes that the child's best interests are purely economic and therefore believes that a child is better off living in his or her father's household, if he has a higher standard of living (and if, in addition, the judge is unwilling to award more adequate child support to the mother as a way of equalizing the standards of living in the two households) that a potential "conflict" emerges between the mother's interest in remaining the child's primary caretaker and the child's interest in maximizing his or her standard of living. Similarly, it is only when a woman's interest is defined as purely economic—as maximizing the amount of money she has to spend on herself after divorce—that one perceives a conflict between her improving her standard of living and her children's interest in living with her.

In other words, most of the situations in which a conflict between women's and children's interest are perceived are the result of myopic perceptions of the interests of women and children.

The Research

To provide a comprehensive portrait of the social and economic effects of the divorce law reforms, Professor Ruth Dixon and I collected and analyzed five types of data: systematic random samples of about 2,500 court dockets over a 10-year period; in-depth face-to-face interviews with 169 family law attorneys; in-depth face-to-face interviews with 44 family law

judges; similar interviews with a sample of English legal experts; and comprehensive personal interviews with 228 divorced men and women about 1 year after their legal divorce.

This research design is unusual in that it uses a variety of sources. It does not rely solely on judges (as legal scholars tend to do) or solely on divorced men and women (as sociologists and psychologists tend to do). It also has the advantage of a systematic data base in the random samples of divorce decrees drawn from court records. Although most of the data were collected in California, the findings are relevant to the entire United States because many of the major features of the California law have been adopted by other states.

The Transformation of Marriage

No-fault divorce has not only redefined the rules for divorce, it has also transformed the legal rules for marriage. No-fault divorce has recast the legal rights and responsibilities of husbands and wives and the legal relationship between parent and children. As a result, it is creating new norms and new expectations for marriage and family commitments in our society.

A divorce provides an important opportunity for a society to enforce marital norms, rewarding the marital behavior it approves and punishing transgression. It does this by handing out legal rewards and punishments and by ordering people to pay for their transgressions in dollars and cents.

Consider, for example, the issue of alimony. If a divorce court awards alimony to a 50-year-old woman who has spent 25 years as a homemaker and mother, it is reinforcing the value of her domestic activities by rewarding the woman's devotion to her family. It may also be punishing the husband for abandoning his wife in middle age. But if, in contrast, the divorce court denies the wife alimony, and tells her that she must instead get a job and support herself, it is undermining the value of her domestic activities and penalizing her for investing in her family, home, and children at the expense of her own career. The court is also releasing the husband from his traditional responsibility for his wife's support. When divorce courts make these decisions, they are revealing and enforcing new expectations for husbands and wives. Although these expectations are being applied retroactively in divorce decrees, they necessarily suggest new expectations for marriage as well.

These expectations are not confined to those who experience divorce themselves. As Kingsley Davis also notes, awareness of the consequences of divorce affects the aspirations and intentions of those who are about to enter marriage, as well as the behavior of men and women who are already married. A law that penalizes a woman for the years that she spends as a homemaker and mother sends a chilling message to married women who want to give priority to their families and children. It warns them that they had better not forgo their own career advancement because they will suffer greatly if their marriage dissolves. This is a powerful threat in a society with a high divorce rate, especially when the no-fault, no-consent laws of many states give a woman no choice about whether her marriage will dissolve.

Of course, the new norms provide an equally sobering message to the man who gives priorities to his wife and children, a message evident to the men and women we interviewed. For example, one Los Angeles surgeon complained that all the sacrifices he made "to work like a dog . . . and earn the money so my kids and wife could have everything they wanted" were ignored in the present legal system of divorce. As he put it,

"Now, she walked out on me and what do I get? Nothing. Nothing. And what does she get? She gets half of my house, half of my pension. . . . For what, I ask you? For running off with a jerk psychologist. That's my reward?"

Marital Property

Historically, there have been two distinct legal systems governing the property of married couples in the United States: Forty-two states have the separate property system,[2] based on the English common law, which segregates the assets of the husband and wife into two categories: "his" and "hers." Each spouse retains all the property he or she earns or inherits during the course of the marriage.

In contrast, in California and the small minority of other community property states, all property acquired during marriage is "theirs." The community property system assumes that all property acquired during marriage is "earned" by the joint efforts of the two spouses and it therefore belongs to both of them.

The two systems have different approaches to the division of property upon divorce. In most separate property states, the starting point for dividing marital property is typically one third of the property to the wife and two thirds to the husband (if he was the one who "earned" it). In a community property system, the starting point is a fifty-fifty division of the property, one half to the wife and one half to the husband.

How Property Is Divided

Before 1970, when every state had a fault-based system of divorce, property awards were often linked to findings of fault in both types of legal regimes. The innocent party typically received a greater share of the property than the guilty party.

One of the major innovations of California's 1970 legal reform was the institution of a fixed no-fault standard for dividing property: It *required* judges to divide the property acquired during marriage *equally* upon divorce—half to the husband, half to the wife. The equal division standard was seen as fair—and "protective" of wives—because it guaranteed each spouse one half of the jointly accumulated property.

Surprisingly, the equal division rule has reduced the wife's share of the property in California because California wives were typically awarded more than half of the marital property before 1970, under the old fault-based divorce law, since they were usually the innocent plaintiffs. In 1968, wives were awarded more than half (60% or more) of the property both in San Francisco and in Los Angeles divorce cases. Most of the awards allowed the wife to keep the family home, which was often the family's most valuable asset. Without the old lever of fault, the wife's share of the property dropped to exactly 50%.

The Problem of the Family Home

The major impact of the equal division rule has been on the disposition of the family home. Today more homes are being sold so that the proceeds can be divided equally: The number of cases in which there was an explicit court order to sell the home rose from about one in ten in 1968 to about one in three in 1977 (Weitzman, 1985). Those wives who do manage to keep the family home typically have other property they can trade for their husband's share of the home—such as an interest in their husband's pension.

Surprisingly, the presence of minor children in the home has not deterred judges from ordering it sold. Our data reveals that 66% of the couples who were forced to sell their homes had minor children. These sales mean residential moves that disrupt children's school, neighborhood, and friendship ties, and create additional dislocations for children (and mothers) at the very point at which they most need continuity and stability. The emotional upheaval is underscored by a quote from a typical respondent who was ordered to vacate her home in 3 months so that it could be sold:

> "I begged the judge. . . . All I wanted was enough time for Brian [her son] to adjust to the divorce. . . . I broke down and cried on the stand . . . but the judge refused. He gave me 3 months to move—3 months to move 15 years—right in the middle of the school semester. . . . My husband's attorney threatened me with contempt if I wasn't out on time . . . he also warned me not to interfere with the real estate people—in my house—he said if I wasn't cooperative in letting them show the house when they wanted to, he'd 'haul me into court for contempt.' It was a nightmare. . . . The most degrading and unjust experience of my life."

When we asked judges about their decisions to force the sale of the family home they offered three explanations: It permitted a "clean break" between parties, it did not unduly hamper the husband by tying up his equity in the house, and it relieved the burden on the wife.

Most California judges stressed the husband's "right" to "his half" of the family property. Since the home is the only substantial family property in many divorce cases, its sale was seen as necessary to give the husband the money he would need to start a new life. As one California respondent explained:

> "You have to be fair to the husband. If you award a house to a woman when it is the only asset, you are then faced with the man who asks, 'Why am I not entitled to the present enjoyment of the community asset that we have? Why should I stand still for deferred enjoyment?' He wants to start a new life. He doesn't want to hang around waiting for his equity. And, by law, he has a right to that equity."

The second justification judges offered for the sale of the family home was that it would make life "easier" for the wife. Many of them said that the wife was "better off" without a home that tied her down to old neighborhoods and children's schools and children's friends, that locked her into the suburbs and restricted her personal, social, and economic options. But our interviews with divorced women revealed that the new solution often caused many more hardships as mothers and children were evicted from their neighborhoods and their system of social support. The forced sale of the family home intensifies the disruption, dislocation, and distress in the post-divorce lives of mothers and children.

The disposition of the family home in California is quite different from what is seen as the "equitable" solution in England. Among the English experts I interviewed, the first priority was given to preserving the family home for the children (Weitzman, 1984). For example, in responding to a typical case in which the home was the only family asset, one barrister explained the way the English courts would approach this case:

> "First, let's make sure the children are looked after . . . the children have always lived in that house . . . you want to finish a child's schooling."

Similarly, a solicitor predicted:

> "The wife would get the house because she has to make a home for the children, and the children come first—you don't want their home to be disrupted. You want to stabilize the situation for them."

The underlying principle in the English approach is that "children come first" because they are the most vulnerable members of the divorcing family and they most need societal protection. As one English judge said: "It's my job to protect the children."

In contrast to the English emphasis on the children's welfare as the court's first priority, the "interests" of children were rarely mentioned by the California experts. Marital property was defined solely in terms of the relative rights of the husband and wife, and it was divided between the two of them.

It is not only children and their mothers who suffer from the forced sale of the family home. Some of the most tragic victims are older homemakers who not only lose their residence of 25 or 35 years, but also lose their whole social structure in a forced move to the other side of town. As one woman described her reaction:

> "I had lived in that home for 26 years and my three children still considered it their home. But the judge ordered it sold. . . . He said he had to follow the letter of the law. . . . I married at a time when a woman who spent 30 years of her life raising a family was worth something . . . but in the eyes of the court I was merely "unemployed." No one would rent me an apartment because my only income was $700 a month spousal support and landlords said that was "unstable" and "inadequate." Two months later my husband's attorney took me into court for contempt because I hadn't moved. . . . He said I was interfering with the sale of the house. . . . The judge gave me ten days to get out. . . . I am still outraged. It is a total perversion of justice. I was thrown out of my own house."

Significantly, the California legislature did *not intend* that the family home be sold in order to meet equal division requirement. Indeed, a 1970 Assembly Committee report specifically states that a temporary award of the home to the spouse who has custody of minor children should be seen as a valid reason to delay the division of property:

> Where an interest in a residence which serves as the home of the family is a major community asset, an order for the immediate sale of the residence in order to comply with the equal division mandate of the law would, certainly, be unnecessarily destructive of the economic and social circumstances of the parties and their children. (California Assembly, 1970, p. 787)

The California appellate courts have upheld the rationale for maintaining the family home for minor children when a sale would have an adverse economic, emotional, or social impact on them. Fran Leonard, attorney for The Older Women's League, echoes these thoughts in asserting the importance of a similar delay to allow older homemakers to retain their homes:

> For the older woman, especially a homemaker [the sale of the family home] is a major cruelty. Upon divorce, she loses her husband and her occupation—then all too often, her home. This nearly comprises her universe. Unlike her spouse, she may have no credit history, no income aside from alimony, and almost no prospects of recovering her lost earning capacity. The chances of her ever buying another home are almost nil. Yet all too commonly the court orders the home sold, in order to divide its value. Attorneys frequently favor this, because their fees can be paid out of escrow. . . . Instead older women should try to keep the family home. (Leonard, 1980, p. 9)

But despite the legislative and judicial authority for exempting the home from the immediate equal division of community property, the judges we interviewed in 1974, 1975, 1981, and 1983 attested to the prevailing pattern of ordering the home sold and the proceeds divided upon divorce. While some judges were willing to leave the home in joint ownership for "a few years," very few were willing to let it remain unsold until small children attained majority. Even fewer were willing to make an exception for an older woman, who, they asserted, didn't "need" the home anymore (even if her college-age children considered it their home as well).

Once again, the responses of the English judges reveal a very different approach. Their first priority is to provide the older housewife with the home or a comparable home so that she can maintain her life without grave hardship. The English assume that after a long marriage, a husband has a responsibility to provide for his exwife for the rest of her life. To ensure that his obligations are fulfilled, the English courts often require an older (and well-to-do) husband to provide more than housing and support during his life: He may also be required to purchase an insurance policy or annuity to compensate his exwife for the widow's benefits she forfeits by getting divorced.

Changes in the Nature of Property: The Importance of Career Assets

Despite the equal division rule in California, we found that the courts were not, in fact, dividing property equally. This is partially a result of major changes in the nature of property in our society. Today husbands and wives are increasingly likely to invest in careers and human capital—most particularly in the husband's human capital and career. The new property resulting from this kind of investment is often the family's major asset. Yet this property is not being divided equally upon divorce. In fact, it is often not divided at all. It is simply presumed to belong to the husband. But if the law allows men to retain their career assets—their professional education, degrees, licenses, health insurance, and earning capacities—then their wives are not in fact being awarded an equal share of the joint property, despite the equal division rule.

"Career assets" is the term I coined to refer to the tangible and intangible assets that are acquired as a part of either spouse's career or career potential (see Weitzman 1981 and 1985 for more detail). "Career assets" encompass a large array of specific assets, such as pension and retirement benefits, a license to practice a profession or trade, medical and hospital insurance, the goodwill of a business, and entitlements to company goods and services. If these assets have been acquired in the course of a marriage, they should be included in the pool of marital or community property to be divided upon divorce.

Consider these facts: We found that the average divorcing couple has less than $20,000 in fixed assets when they divorce (Weitzman, 1985, p. 56 and Table 2). Yet the average couple can earn more than the value of their assets in less than 1 year (Weitzman 1985, p. 59 and Table 4). This means that the value of the couple's career assets—indeed the value of their earning capacity alone—is much greater than the value of their physical property (Weitzman, 1985, p. 60).

These data have important implications. If one partner builds his or her earning capacity during the marriage while the other is a homemaker and parent, the partner with the earning capacity has acquired the major asset of the marriage. If the earning power—or the income it produces—is not divided upon divorce, the two spouses are left with very unequal shares of their joint assets.

An awareness of this inequity was echoed over and over again in our interviews. As one veteran of a 30-year marriage to a college professor explained:

"We married at 21, with no money. . . . When he was a graduate student, I worked as a secretary and then typed papers at night to make extra money. When he became an assistant professor I 'retired' to raise our children but I never stopped working for him—typing, editing, working on his books. . . . My college English degree was very useful for translating his brilliant ideas into comprehensible sentences. . . . My name never appeared on the title page as his co-author, where it belonged, only in the dedication or thank you's. . . . There's more, lots more—the hours mothering his graduate students, hosting department parties, finding homes for visiting professors. . . . I was always available to help. . . . I got $700 a month for 3 years. The judge said, I was 'smart and healthy enough to get a job.' I am to 'report back like a school girl' in 3 years. Never mind that I am 51. . . . Never mind that I had a job and did it well and am old enough to be entitled to a pension. . . . It's not that I regret my life or didn't enjoy what I did. But it was supposed to be a partnership—a fifty-fifty split. It isn't fair that he gets to keep it. It isn't fair for the court to treat it as his. . . . I earned it just as much as he did."

Career assets are also of great importance for younger couples. In many cases one spouse's professional education or license is the only asset acquired during marriage. The issue arises when one spouse, usually the wife, supports the other's professional education and training with the expectation that she will share the fruits of her investment through her husband's enhanced earning power. If they divorce soon after the student spouse completes training, the young couple typically has few tangible assets because most of their capital has been used to finance the student's education.

In a landmark 1985 case in New York, O'Brien v. O'Brien, the Court of Appeals took this position and ruled that a medical license obtained during marriage is marital property (whose value must be divided at the time of a divorce). The O'Brien case involved a 9½ year marriage in which Loretta O'Brien worked as a school teacher in Guadalajara, Mexico to support her husband in medical school. Mrs. O'Brien, who knew no Spanish when the young couple moved from New York to Mexico, learned the language and found work teaching kindergarten and tutoring English. Three months after Michael O'Brien received his medical license, he sued for divorce.

What then are our conclusions about the extent to which property is being divided equally or equitably upon divorce? Since career assets are typically acquired during marriage in the same manner that other marital property is acquired, and since these assets are, along with the family home, often the most valuable assets a couple own at the time of the divorce, if the courts do not recognize some or all of these assets as marital property, they can not divide marital property equally or equitably because they are excluding a major portion of a couple's property from the pool of property to be divided upon divorce. In addition, if the courts treat these assets as the property of the major wage earner, in most cases they allow the husband to keep the family's most valuable assets for himself. It is like promising to divide the family jewels equally, while setting aside all the diamonds for the husband.

The husband's career assets are "the diamonds" of marital property. Without them, the property cannot be divided equally or fairly.

Alimony: The New Trends

The second area in which the new divorce laws attempt to treat men and women "equally" is in maintenance awards, or what is typically referred to as alimony or spousal support. The old divorce laws assumed that husbands were responsible for the financial support of their former wives. The reformers thought that that was inappropriate: They pointed to women's increased participation in the labor force, and assumed that women were now equally capable of supporting themselves and their children after divorce.

Our California data reveals several changes in the patterns of alimony awards that reflect these new standards (Weitzman, 1985, pp. 143–183). First, in accord with the new law's goal of making the wife self-sufficient after divorce, there has been a shift from permanent alimony awards, awards based on the premise of the wife's continued dependency, to time-limited awards. Between 1968 and 1972, permanent alimony—awards labelled permanent, until death or remarriage—dropped from 62% to 32% of the alimony awards in Los Angeles County (Dixon & Weitzman, 1980). By 1972 (and in subsequent years) two thirds of the alimony awards were transitional awards for a limited and specified duration. The median duration of these fixed-time awards was 25 months, or about 2 years. Thus, the average award carries an expectation of a short transition from marriage to self-sufficiency.

Second, the standards of the new law have dictated a greater reliance on the wife's ability to support herself. Economic criteria, such as the wife's occupation and predivorce income, are therefore more important than the old standards of fault and innocence.

Although it is reasonable for courts to consider a wife's ability to support herself, it is shocking to see how little "earning capacity" is necessary to convince a judge that a woman is capable of self-sufficiency (see Weitzman, 1985, pp. 178–180, 187–194). We found countless wives with low earning capacities and limited and marginal employment histories who were denied spousal support altogether because judges presumed they were capable of supporting themselves.

These irregular work histories of many divorced women leave a lot of room for judicial discretion in deciding whether any individual woman is "capable of engaging in gainful employment at the time of the divorce." A judge may conclude that a woman who was employed during the first 3 years of her marriage but has not worked in the last 16 years is immediately capable of self-sufficiency. Similarly, a judge may decide that because a woman has done volunteer work at a hospital she can now obtain a paid job there, or that because a woman has spent 3 months a year in an accounting office during the tax season, she is now capable of earning an equivalent salary 12 months a year.

Since few women in longer marriages have held full-time long-term jobs, their "employment histories" tend to be ambiguous. As an example of how judges tend to gross over the ambiguities in assessing a woman's ability to get a job and be self-sufficient, consider the following two statements from judges we interviewed:

> [Referring to a case just presented in court] The best thing for her is to get right out and get a job—earn her own money—and make her own life.
>
> [Q: What kind of job do you think she can get?] Oh, anything. She can get a job in a store selling . . . clothes . . . or whatever. . . . There are lots of jobs out there, just read the want ads.
>
> [Q: What about that woman? What kind of a job do you think she might find?] She said she used to work as . . . a . . . oh, what did she say? In an office or something—a bookkeeper or something like that. Well, that's a good job. She could probably get good hours, too . . . and be able to pick up her kids after school, as she was worried about that.

[Referring to a woman who testified that she had not taught for 20 years and did not have California teaching credentials.] Just because she's been married 20 years doesn't mean she can be a sponge for the rest of her life. If she was once a teacher, she can always get a job teaching. Maybe she'll have to work as a substitute for a while, or at a not so fancy school, but just because she hasn't taught in 20 years doesn't mean she can't teach. She is a teacher.

Both cases suggest how easily judges can read evidence of employability in a diversity of situations and conclude that a woman does not need support. Yet both of these women had not been employed since the early years of marriage, and both of them had spent most of their married years raising children. They still had children at home (both of them were now in their late 40s). The first woman had no formal training as a bookkeeper, but had worked as one many years earlier. The second woman had not held a paid teaching job for 20 years of a 22-year marriage (which the judge apparently misheard as 20 years) but had taught on a volunteer basis in the adult education program at her church.

How realistic is it to assume that these women can easily find well-paid full-time jobs and become self-supporting? If they are like most divorced women we interviewed—especially those in their late 40s who had been career homemakers and mothers—it is totally unrealistic (see also Shields, 1981).

Many employers do not recognize homemaking skills as having a market value. They only recognize "recent paid work experience" and even with such experience, older women are unwanted in today's labor market. Consider the difficulties two of the older women we interviewed faced:

"There is no way I can make up for 25 years out of the labor force. . . . No one wants to make me president of the company just because I was the president of the PTA."

"The judge told me to go for job training—but no training can recapture 27 years of my life. I'm too old to start from the beginning and I shouldn't have to. I deserve better."

Professor Herma Kay suggests that judges were affected by the feminist movement in the early 1970s and thus were using women's demands for equality as a justification for denying and terminating alimony (Kay, 1978, personal communication). Along the same lines, attorney Riane Eisler quotes a California judge who described his colleague's attitudes as, "What they (divorcing women) need is to go to work, so they can get themselves liberated" (Eisler, 1977, p. 46).

The results of these standards is that more than 85% of the divorced women in the United States are presumed capable of self-sufficiency and denied any alimony whatsoever (U.S. Bureau of the Census, 1987, p. 6).

Although alimony has always been rare (because it has been, for the most part, confined to the wives of middle-class and upper-middle-class men, and these couples always comprised a small minority of the divorcing population), the awards and the length of the awards have been drastically cut under the new divorce laws. (In California these awards average $370 a month in 1984 dollars [Weitzman, 1985, p. 171]; nationally they averaged $331 a month in 1985 [U.S. Bureau of the Census, 1987, p. 7]).

Instead of the old law's assumption that these women need permanent alimony to enable them to continue to share their husband's standard of living (which they, of course, helped to build), the new laws create an expectation that they will become independent and self-sufficient soon after the divorce.

The Gap Between Theory and Reality: Mothers and Older Homemakers

In theory, alimony is still supposed to be available for women with custody of young children and older homemakers incapable of self-sufficiency. However, we found that alimony awards to mothers of children under 6 dropped, since 1970, more than for any other group of women. Today, only 13% of the California mothers of preschool children are awarded spousal support (Weitzman, 1985, p. 186 and Table 17).

Why does the need to care for young children appear to have so little effect on alimony awards? Two thirds of the Superior Court judges we interviewed see the goal of making the wife self-sufficient as more important than supporting the custodial parent. As they said, it is "good for a divorced woman to earn money instead of being dependent on her former husband," "work is a healthy form of rehabilitation that will help her build a new life," and "combining work and motherhood is now normal in our society." Although many of the young mothers we interviewed shared these sentiments and *wanted* to be self-sufficient, the *economic reality* of their low earnings and the need to support their children compelled support from their former husbands.

The judges are always balancing the interests of children against their concern for the father and his need for his income. When they can justify the mother's work as "healthy and good for her," and when they can overestimate her earning capacity, they can justify allowing the husband to keep most of his income for himself. As one of our respondents described the result of this attitude:

"It's an insult . . . but I can't live and feed my son on my pride, so I take it. . . . Why am I and my son worth so much less than he is? . . . It's because the judge looks at him and thinks he needs it—but I can get by. . . . He gets a company car and the privilege of eating out whenever he wants to—I have the privilege of food stamps. . . . I've never lived like this before in my life . . . it's degrading and it's not fair."

Our empirical analysis of the awards judges make reveals that the husband is rarely ordered to part with more than one third of his income to support his wife and children. He is therefore allowed to retain two thirds for himself while his former wife and children, typically three people, are expected to survive on the remaining one third.

One reason for the disparity is that the judges we interviewed gave first priority to the husband's needs. They expressed great sympathy for the plight of divorced men and regarded the income of most divorced men as too low to support two households adequately, too low to provide even half of the support for the husband's children who are in the custody of their former wives. They therefore decide that it is often "better" to leave most of the family's postdivorce income with the husband, viewing it as his rather than theirs. Most judges appear to view the law's goal of equality as a mandate to place an equal burden of support on men and women without regard to the fact that the parties' capacities to support that burden are clearly unequal.

Self-Sufficiency Standards and the Older Homemaker

A second group of women who are hurt by the new law's standard of self-sufficiency are the older homemakers who have been housewives and mothers throughout marriages of long duration. Although many more women in this category are awarded spousal support, one out of three is not.

It is not surprising to find that the women who feel most betrayed by the legal system of divorce are those older homemakers who are denied alimony. As one woman said:

"You can't tell me there's justice if someone uses you for 25 years and then just dumps you and walks out scot-free. . . . It's not fair. It's not justice. It's a scandal . . . and those judges should be ashamed of themselves sitting up there in their black robes like God and hurting poor people like me."

When we compare the postdivorce incomes of long-married husbands and wives, we find that wives are expected to live on much smaller amounts of money, and are economically much worse off, than their former husbands. For example, wives married 18 years or more with predivorce family incomes of $20,000 to $30,000 a year have, on the average, a median annual income of $6,300 after the divorce. Their husbands, in contrast, have a median annual income of $20,000—even if we assume that they actually paid the support awards. The result is that the postdivorce income of these wives is 24% of the previous family income, whereas the average postdivorce income for their husbands is 87% of that standard (Weitzman, 1985, p. 190).

Once again, the judges approach these cases mindful of the husband's need for "his income" and his limited capacity to support two families. And once again, it is clear that the judges simply misunderstand the economic reality of the wives' job prospects. In our interviews the judges assured us that most of these women would "be able to find jobs." But they did not interview the women a year later, as we did, and did not hear about the women who applied for 50 jobs without success, or those who could only find jobs at the minimum wage after long marriages to professional men.

As one woman said:

"It's so hard to start at the bottom when you've been a respected member of the community for years. . . . I just never realized that the respect and admiration and civic work doesn't count for anything in the job market . . . and it certainly doesn't help pay my rent."

As these examples suggest, the woman who has few marketable skills cannot make up for 20 or 25 years out of the job market. Most end up in low-paying jobs, living in greatly reduced circumstances, often on the edge of poverty (Leonard, 1980).

Obviously, the problem is not limited to California. Consider the case of Edith Curtis, a 55-year-old Idaho woman who applied for state unemployment compensation after her divorce from a college professor. Edith Curtis' 2-year job search and 75 applications proved "fruitless to a shopworn and obsolete housewife . . . with a 30-year-old B. A. in English and a lack of salable skills" (Chase, 1985, p. 1). She was finally offered and accepted a job as a fast-food cashier, part time, at the minimum wage (Chase, 1985, p. 12).

No wonder the older homemaker typically feels betrayed by the new laws. She was promised, by both her husband and our society—her contract, if you prefer, both implied and expressed—that their marriage was a partnership and that he would share his income with her. Instead, the courts have changed the rules in the middle of the game, after she has fulfilled her share of the bargain and passed the point where she can choose another life course.

Child Support Awards

Our research uncovered two major problems with child support: low awards and inadequate enforcement. The U.S. Census shows that the average award for two children in the United States is about $200 a month—much less than half of the cost of raising two children (U.S. Bureau of the Census, 1987, p. 3 and Table C). In California, the average child support award was less than the average cost of day care alone.

Ironically, young mothers have a greater need for support from their exhusbands after divorce—just at the point where judges are telling them to make do with less. Most custodial mothers have to take over many of their husband's family responsibilities and face greater burdens and greater expenses as single parents.

Yet, it is very rare for any court to order more than 25% of a man's income in child support or more than 32% of a man's income in combined child support and alimony (Weitzman, 1985, p. 267; see also Cassetty, 1978, and Chambers, 1979). Even though judges say that their typical award is closer to one half of the husband's income, the data from our analysis of court dockets and our interviews with divorced persons shows that the real proportion is quite different. Instead of a 50-50 division of the husband's income, the typical award is one third for the wife and two children to two thirds for the husband. Among upper-income men it is one-fifth to four-fifths: men who earn $50,000 or more a year retain an average of 81% of their net incomes for themselves (Weitzman, 1985, pp. 266–267 and Table 24).

What do the current child support awards mean in terms of standards of living? If California men paid the child support the courts ordered them to pay, 73% of them would have enough money left for themselves to live comfortably (i.e., above the lower standard budget established by the U.S. government). However, if women and children had to live on the child support the courts ordered, only 7% of them would have enough money to live comfortably. Most of them—fully 93% of the women and children—would have to live *below* the poverty level (Weitzman, 1985, p. 275, Figure 2). These shocking differences would result from current child support awards even if men complied fully with court orders. (See also Chambers, 1979 for similar results in Michigan.) But if the court orders for child support are not paid, or are not paid fully—as we shall see below, an all-too-common occurrence—the differences in the standards of living between fathers and mothers and children would be even greater.

Some people have questioned whether men can afford to pay the amounts of child support ordered by the courts. The answer is an unequivocal "yes." Whether one considers the percentage of the supporter's income, or the standard of living he has after paying, the vast majority of divorced fathers can pay child support and still maintain a relatively comfortable standard of living.

Significantly, both divorced men and divorced women agree with this conclusion. When asked, "Can you (or your exhusband) afford to pay the child support the court ordered," fully 80% of the women and 90% of the men say yes (Weitzman, 1985, p. 276). Thus, both men and women see the award as reasonable in terms of the husband's ability to pay. Only a small minority think the awards are excessive.

Along the same lines, when asked about their satisfaction with the amount of child support awarded in their case, the vast majority (91%) of divorced men see the awards as reasonable in terms of their income. Only 9% of the men say they are dissatisfied. (As might be expected, a larger percentage of the women, 36%, are dissatisfied with the amount of child support awarded and see it as inadequate.)

In summary, the data point to three conclusions. First, the amount of child support ordered is typically quite modest in terms of the father's ability to pay. Second, the amount of child support ordered is typically not enough to cover even half the cost of actually raising the children. Third, the major burden of child support is typically placed on the mother even though she normally has fewer resources and much less "ability to pay."

Support Enforcement: The High Rate of Noncompliance

Even though child support awards are modest to begin with, they are often unpaid because many divorced fathers have simply ignored court orders. U.S. Census data show that fewer than half of the fathers fully comply with court orders to pay child support (U.S. Bureau of the Census, 1987, pp. 1–2).

Surprisingly, this is not because the father cannot "afford" to pay. In California, we found that men who earn between $30,000 and $50,000 a year were just as likely to fail to pay child support as those who earn less than $10,000 a year (Weitzman, 1985, p. 296, Table 25). The result is that the mother, who is the primary custodial parent in 90% of the divorce cases, is left with the major burden of supporting her children after divorce.

The typical child support order calls for the father to send the mother a check every month or every pay period. It is up to the mother to keep track of the checks and to try to obtain the money when the checks are late or are for less than the full amount ordered. This puts the burden of collection on the mother who typically has few resources to begin with. As one mother explained:

"Each time I went to court I lost a day's pay, and I had to pay my lawyer for his court rate. We had to wait two hours for the case to be called, and [my exhusband] got a postponement to get his papers together. . . . The next time he was sick. . . . Then he changed attorneys. . . . Each time the judge said he had a right to have his side represented . . . but I couldn't afford it anymore. They let him get away with murder."

Wage assignments have proven most effective in securing compliance. Yet the vast majority of the California judges are reluctant to order them. In our 1977 random sample of court records, only 5% of the cases with a child support award had a wage attachment (Weitzman, 1985, p. 293). What is surprising about these data is that California law requires judges to order a wage assignment if the man has not paid support for 2 months.

Even more telling are the judges' responses to the question, "How many wage assignments have you ordered in the past 6 months?" The average was only one or two wage assignments per judge over the 6-month period, and more than a quarter of the judges said they had *never* ordered a wage assignment (Weitzman, 1985, p. 302). When one considers that there were about 36,000 divorce cases heard in Los Angeles County each year, and that the Los Angeles County judges (and commissioners) are a "specialized bench" assigned to hear only family law cases, it is evident that these judges heard thousands of noncompliance complaints during this 6-month period. Yet they ordered wage assignments in only a tiny fraction of the cases—less than one in a hundred.

Noncompliance and lax enforcement are not unique to California; they are common throughout the United States (see Bernstein, 1982; Chambers, 1979; Hawkins, 1984; House Hearings, 1984). If, as Dean Pound said, "The life of the law is in its enforcement" (Matter of Farmer, 1984), it is clear why the child support laws make a mockery of the legal system. Precisely these sentiments were echoed over and over again by the women we interviewed:

"It literally makes me sick. . . . It is so contrary to everything I was taught about the law, the courts, and justice. I feel totally betrayed. . . . He totally disregards the whole legal system."

Another judicial practice undermines the legal obligation to pay child support: Many judges simply "excuse" arrearages (i.e., money owed for past-due child support). As one mother who spent 5 years tracking down her nonsupporting husband complained:

"The judge said he could pay off the arrearage (of $12,000) at the rate of $20.00 per month . . . with no interest or anything. . . . It's outrageous—he gave him 50 years to pay me back! . . . But I'm stuck paying interest on the money I borrowed to keep the kids alive."

The judges explained this practice by saying they did not want to make payments too difficult ("It would be a financial hardship for a man to make back payments in full"); or that they wanted to give the father a break so that he can get on the right track; or that they were trying to look to the future rather than the past. "After all," some judges reasoned, "the children have managed to survive." The implicit message in the judges' treatment of arrearages is that fathers are rewarded for noncompliance by having their debt reduced or forgiven.

In summary, "the present legal system provides virtually every incentive for fathers not to pay child support" (Hunter, 1983). And in the end, the children are the tragic victims of the present system of inadequate and unpaid child support. Even though the typical child support award provides less than half the cost of raising a child, chances are that the noncustodial father will not pay it, and the legal system will do nothing about it.

In the end, the current legal system places the economic responsibility for children on their mothers and allows fathers the "freedom" to choose not to support their children. The result is that children almost always experience a decline in their standard of living after divorce. The dislocation from friends, neighborhoods, and family that many of these children endure, and the bitterness and anger they may harbor against one parent or the other, often translate into a pervasively unhappy, distrustful, and pessimistic view of life (Wallerstein & Kelly, 1980). This has profound implications for the future of a society that expects more than half of its children to experience the dissolution of their parents' marital relationship before they reach the age of 18.

The Economic and Social Consequences

The net effect of the present rules for property, alimony, and child support is severe financial hardship for most divorced women and their children. They experience sharp downward mobility—dramatic drops in income and drastic cuts in their standards of living. Even women who shared comfortable middle- and upper-class standards of living during marriage are impoverished by divorce. In fact, the major economic result of the divorce law revolution is the systematic impoverishment of divorced women and their children. They have become the new poor.

Our data show that just 1 year after the legal divorce, women and children experience a 73% drop in their standard of living (while men experience a 42% improvement). Simply put, divorce is a financial catastrophe for most women. Every single expenditure that one takes for granted—clothing, food, housing, heat—must be cut to one half or one third of what one is accustomed to.

It is difficult to absorb the full implications of these statistics. What does it mean to have a 73% decline in one's standard of living? How does one deal with such severe deprivation? When asked how they coped, many of the divorced women said that they themselves were not sure. It meant "living on the edge" and "living without." As some of them described it:

> "We ate macaroni and cheese 5 nights a week. There was a Safeway special for $.39 a box. We could eat seven dinners for $3.00 a week. . . . I think that's all we ate for months."

> "I applied for welfare. . . . It was the worst experience of my life. . . . I never dreamed that I, a middle-class housewife, would ever be in a position like that. It was humiliating . . . they make you feel it. . . . But we were desperate, and I had to feed my kids."

Even those who had relatively affluent life-styles before the divorce faced hardships they had not anticipated. For example, the wife of a dentist sold her car "because I had no cash at all, and we lived on that money—barely—for close to a year." The wife of a policeman told an especially poignant story about "not being able to buy my 12-year-old son Adidas sneakers." The boy's father had been ordered to pay $100 a month child support but had not been paying. To make up that gap in her already bare-bones budget, she had been using credit cards to buy food and other household necessities. She had exceeded all her credit limits and felt the family just couldn't afford to pay $25 for a new pair of Adidas sneakers. But, as she said a year later, "You forget what it's like to be 12 years old and to think you can't live without Adidas sneakers . . . and to feel the whole world has deserted you along with your father."

Explaining the Disparity Between Husbands' and Wives' Standards of Living

How can we explain the strikingly different economic consequences of divorce for men and women? How could a law that aimed at fairness create such disparities between divorced men and their former wives and children?

The explanation lies first, in the inadequacies of the court's awards that we have discussed; second, in the expanded demands on the wife's resources after divorce; and third, in the husband's greater earning capacity and ability to supplement his income.

Since the wife typically assumes the responsibility for raising the couple's children, her need for help and services increases as a direct result of her becoming a single parent. Yet at the very time that her need for more income and more financial support is greatest, the courts have drastically reduced her income. Thus the gap between her income and her needs is wider after divorce.

In contrast, the gap between the husband's income and needs narrows. Although he now has fewer absolute dollars, the demands on his income have diminished. While he loses the benefits of economies of scale, and while he may have to purchase some services (such as laundry and cooking) that he did not have to buy during marriage, he is much better off because he is no longer financially responsible for the needs of his exwife and children. Since he has been allowed to retain most of his income, he can afford these extra expenses and still have more surplus income than he enjoyed during marriage.

The final explanation for the large income discrepancy between former husbands and wives lies in the different earning capacities of the two adults at the time of the divorce. Women are doubly disadvantaged at the point of divorce. Not only do they face the male-female income gap that affects all working women; they also suffer from the toll the marital years have taken on their earning capacity. In the United States at the present time, one third of the working mothers who are employed *full-time* cannot earn enough money to support themselves and their children above the poverty line (Feminization of Poverty, 1983).

In addition, the responsibility for children inevitably restricts the mother's job opportunities by limiting her work schedule and location, her availability for overtime and her freedom to take advantage of special training, travel assignments, and other opportunities for career advancement.

The discrepancy between divorced men and women has been corroborated by other research. Sociologist Robert Weiss and economist Thomas Espenshade found parallel disparities in the standards of living of former husbands and wives after divorce, and Weiss corroborates the finding that the greatest reduction in postdivorce income is experienced by women who shared higher family incomes before the divorce (Espenshade, 1979; Weiss, 1984). Census Bureau data also document the disparities in both income and standards of living of men and women after divorce. In 1979, the median per capita income of divorced women who had not remarried was $4,152, just over half of the $7,886 income of divorced men who had not remarried (U.S. Bureau of Census, 1981b, p. 23).

The situation of divorced women with young children is even more grim. The median income in families headed by women with children under 6 years of age was only 30% of the median income for all families whose children were under 6 (U.S. Bureau of the Census, 1980). Thus, for the United States as a whole, "the income of families headed by women is at best half that of other families; the income of families headed by women with young children is even less, one-third of that of other families" (National Center on Women and Family Law, 1983).

Societal Consequences

The rise in divorce has been the major cause of the increase in female-headed families, and that increase has been the major cause of the feminization of poverty. Sociologist Diana Pearce, who coined the phrase "feminization of poverty," was one of the first to point to the critical link between poverty and divorce for women. It was, she said, the mother's economic and emotional responsibility for childrearing that often impoverished her family (Pearce, 1978).

Contrary to popular perception, most female-headed single-parent families in the United States are *not* the result of unwed parenthood: They are the result of marital dissolution. Only 18% of the nearly 10 million female-headed families in the United States are headed by an unwed mother, over 50% are headed by divorced mothers, and the remaining 31% by separated mothers (House Hearing, 1984: 13).

When a couple with children divorces, it is probable that the man will become single but the woman will become a single parent. And poverty, for many women, begins with single parenthood. More than half of the poor families in the United States are headed by a single mother.

The Rise in Female Poverty

The well-known growth in the number of single-parent female-headed households has been amply documented elsewhere. The 8% of all children who live in mother-child families in 1960 rose to 12% by 1970, and to 20% by 1981. Also well-documented is the fact that these mother-headed families are the fastest growing segment of the American poor.

In recent years there have been many suggestions for combatting the feminization of poverty. Most of these proposals have envisioned two routes to change: alterations in the structure of jobs and occupations and expanding social welfare programs. The first set of proposals has focused on altering the sex segregation in jobs and professions, eliminating the dual labor market and the disparity between jobs in the primary and secondary sectors, eradicating the discriminatory structure of wages, and providing additional services, such as child care, for working mothers (Pearce & McAdoo, 1981). The second set of proposals has focused on expanding social welfare programs by increasing AFDC benefits to levels above the poverty line, augmenting Medicaid, food stamp, and school lunch programs, and making housewives eligible for Social Security and unemployment compensation (Ehrenreich & Piven, 1984).

I believe there is a third route to reducing the feminization of poverty, a route that has been almost totally ignored. It is to change the way that courts allocate property and income at divorce. If, for example, custodial mothers and their children were allowed to remain in the family home, and if the financial responsibility for children were apportioned according to the means of the two parents, and if court orders for support were enforced, a significant segment of the population of divorced women and their children would not be impoverished by divorce.

The Rise in Child Poverty and Economic Hardships for Middle-Class Children of Divorce

Not surprisingly, the children of divorce often express anger and resentment when their standard of living is significantly less than that in their father's household. They realize that their lives have been profoundly altered by the loss of "their home" and school and neighborhood and friends, and by the new expectations their mother's reduced income creates for them. It is not difficult to understand their resentment when fathers fly off for a weekend in Hawaii while they are told to forgo summer camp, to get a job, and to earn their allowance. Their resentment is "a festering source of anger":

> *When the downward change in the family standard of living followed the divorce and the discrepancy between the father's standard of living and that of the mother and children was striking, this discrepancy was often central to the life of the family and remained as a festering source of anger and bitter preoccupation. (Wallerstein & Kelly, 1980, p. 231)*

The middle-class children of divorce may also feel betrayed by their disenfranchisement in their parents' property settlement. Since the law divides family property between the husband and wife and makes no provisions for a child's share of the marital assets, many children feel they have been unfairly deprived of "their" home, "their" piano, "their" stereo set, and "their" college education. The last item is indicative, for children's taken-for-granted expectations about the future are often altered by divorce. For example, one mother reported that the most upsetting thing about the divorce was her son's loss of the college education he'd been promised. His father, who had always pressed him to follow in his footsteps at Dartmouth, told him that a private college was now out of the question: He would have to stay home and take advantage of the low tuition at the state college. While his father could still afford to send his son to Dartmouth, the divorce had changed his priorities.

Inasmuch as about 1.2 million children's parents divorce each year, the 30% who receive no support from their fathers adds up to 360,000 new children each year. Over a 10-year period, this amounts to 4 million children. If we add to these the approximately 3 million over the years who receive only part of their child support (or receive it only some of the time), we find a 10-year total of 7 million children deprived of the support to which they are entitled. Remembering that fewer than 4 million children are born each year helps put all these figures in perspective.

The failure of absent parents to provide child support has taken an especially severe toll in recent years because of sharp cutbacks in public programs benefiting children since 1979. The Children's Defense

Fund shows that children's share of Medicaid payments dropped from 14.9% in 1979, to 11.9% in 1982, despite a rise in the child proportion among the eligible. The Aid to Families with Dependent Children (AFDC) program has also been sharply cut back. In 1979, there were 72 children in AFDC for every 100 children in poverty, but only 52 per 100 in 1982.

It is not surprising to find a strong relationship between the economic and psychological effects of divorce on children. Economic deprivation following divorce has been linked to increased anxiety and stress among American children. Mounting evidence also shows that children of divorce who experience the most psychological stress are those whose postdivorce lives have been impaired by inadequate income. For example, Hodges, Tierney, and Bushbaum (1984) find "income inadequacy" the most important factor in accounting for anxiety and depression among preschool children in divorced families. When family income is adequate, there are no differences in anxiety-depression levels between children in divorced families and those in intact families. However, "Children of divorced families with inadequate income had substantially higher levels of anxiety-depression (Hodges *et al.*, 1984, p. 614). In an earlier study these researchers found significant correlations between income and adjustment for preschool children of divorce (but not, interestingly, for preschool children of intact families) (Hodges *et al.*, 1984).

How Can We Equalize Divorce?

We do not have to return to a fault-based system of divorce to alter the economic results of the present system, for the hardships of the present system are not inevitable. What is required to alleviate them is a commitment to fairness, an awareness of the greater burdens that the system imposes on women and children, and a willingness to require fathers to shoulder their economic responsibility for their children.

What are the most serious cases of injustice in the present system? Where should we direct our efforts? There are four groups that deserve our special attention. First, there are *the children of divorce* who need more financial support and more effective means of securing the support they are awarded. The goal of child support awards should be to equalize the standards of living in the custodial and noncustodial households; children are entitled to share the standard of living of their higher-earning parent.

College-age children of divorce also need "child" support past age 18 if they are full-time students and financially dependent. In addition, all support awards should include automatic adjustments for cost of living increases and more effective and automatic methods of assuring payment. The 1984 federal law, which provides for wage assignments, income tax refund intercepts, national location efforts, and property liens and bonds that will reach self-employed fathers, is an important step in the right direction.

Most children of divorce would also benefit from rules that allow them to remain in the family home. When these rules are optional, as they are in California, their use depends on judicial discretion, and they are often ignored. What works best are laws that *require* judges to maintain the family home for children after divorce.

The children of divorce would also benefit from a primary caretaker presumption for sole custody awards, and laws that allow joint custody only upon agreement of both parents (Weitzman, 1985, pp. 394–395). Such clear standards for custody awards would make it more difficult for parents (and their lawyers) to use children as "pawns" in divorce negotiations, and would reduce both the threat and use of custody litigation in order to gain financial advantages in property or support awards. Since custody litigation and the prolonged hostility it typically generates are likely to have an adverse psychological and financial impact on the welfare of children, custody laws that designate clear priorities and minimize litigation are clearly preferable.

The second type of clear injustice involves *the long-married older housewife* with little or no experience in the paid labor force because she has devoted herself to her husband, home, and children in the expectation that she would share the family assets that she helped to build. Justice and fairness for these women necessitates rules that require, rather than allow, judges to redistribute the husband's postdivorce income in order to equalize the standards of living in the two households.

This recommendation rests on the same principle that underlies community property rules: It is the assumption that marriage is an equal partnership in which all the assets should be shared. This principle, as we have seen, is strongly supported by the divorced men and women we interviewed (Weitzman, 1985, pp. 152–159). They view the sharing of income through alimony—or whatever name we choose for income transfers after divorce—as the means for providing the wife with her share of the fruits of their joint endeavours. These sharing principles are fundamental elements in the "marital contract" that most married couples agreed to and lived by during marriage.

Older women should not be measured by the new standards of equality and self-sufficiency after divorce. It is both impractical and unfair to expect women who married and lived most of their lives under a different set of social and legal rules to be forced to find employment and to support themselves. They have earned an interest in their husband's income for the rest of their lives and require a legislative presumption of permanent (i.e., continuing, open-ended) support.

Women who divorce after long marriages should also be entitled to remain as members in their husband's health insurance plans, to share his pension and retirement benefits, and to maintain their home. If the family home and the husband's pension are the only major assets of the marriage, the older wife should be allowed to retain her home without forfeiting her share of the pension.

In summary, we need "grandmother clauses" for the long-married older women who married and lived their lives under the traditional rules. It is unfair to change the rules on them in the middle of the game.

The third group that merits a new approach is *the mothers who retain major responsibility for the care of minor children after divorce.* Whether the custody award is labelled "sole custody," or "joint custody," or even "joint physical custody," if this woman assumes most of the day-to-day caretaking, she requires a greater share of the family's resources. This includes the continued use of the family home (which should be viewed as part of the child support award rather than as an unequal division of property) and a significant portion of her exhusband's income so that the two households maintain, insofar as is practical, equal standards of living after divorce.

Since employment will play a critical role in the postdivorce lives of younger divorced mothers, and thus in their ability to contribute to their children's and their own support, they should be awarded full support in the early years after divorce to enable them to maximize their long-range employment prospects. This means generous support awards and

balloon payments immediately after divorce to finance their education, training, and career counselling. Every effort should be made to provide younger divorced mothers and their children with full support in the transitional years so that forced employment does not interfere with their training and child care.

The fourth group that requires special attention are those of *the transitional generation*—women who divorce in their 40s. Many of these women have been employed, often part-time, during marriage while raising children who are now approaching maturity. Yet, even though these women have experience in the labor market, they have typically given priority to their families and their husband's careers. Since these women usually have passed the point where they can recapture their lost career opportunities, it is manifestly unfair to hold them to the new standards of self-sufficiency at the point of divorce, as the courts do now. On the other hand, the means of bringing them to parity are less clear. But we can go a long way toward achieving a greater equality of results by assuring them an equal share of the fruits of the marital partnership (with an equal share of their husband's career assets, including his enhanced earning capacity); support to maximize their employment potential with additional training, counseling, and education; and where appropriate, compensation for the detriment to their own careers.

The Divorce Revolution and the Transformation of Marriage

If we step back from our analysis of the empirical results and policy alternatives, we can look at some of the broader implications of these legal changes and assess their impact on the institution of marriage. How has the new legal system of divorce influenced and altered our understanding of the nature of marriage?

From State Protection of Marriage to Facilitation of Divorce

The divorce law reforms reflect an underlying shift in the role of the state from a position of protecting marriage (by restricting marital dissolution) to one of facilitating divorce. The new divorce laws adopt a laissez-faire attitude toward both marriage and divorce, leaving both the terms of the marriage contract and the option to terminate it squarely in the hands of the individual parties. States with pure no-fault divorce laws also eliminate the traditional moral dimension from divorce: guilt and innocence, fidelity and faithlessness no longer affect the granting of the decree or its financial consequences (Weitzman, 1985, pp. 22–26, 28–31).

The individual's freedom to end his or her marriage is further bolstered in some states by no-consent rules that give either party the right to obtain a divorce without the other's agreement. Since no-fault and no-consent states allow one spouse to make a unilateral decision to terminate the marriage, they transfer the economic leverage from the spouse who wants to remain married to the spouse who wants to get divorced. This is an important difference. Under the traditional law the party who wanted a divorce might well have had to make economic concessions, or "buy" a spouse's agreement. But under the no-consent rule, it is the one who hopes to preserve the marriage who must do the bargaining. Apart from the economic implications, which are considerable, these laws strengthen the hand of the party who seeks the divorce, and thereby increase the likelihood that divorce will in fact occur.

From a Lifetime Contract to an Optional, Time-Limited Commitment

The new divorce laws no longer view marriage as a lifelong partnership. Instead it is a union that is contingent upon the happiness and satisfaction of both partners. In addition, the traditional obligations of marriage, like the institution itself, are increasingly being redefined by the new divorce laws as optional, time-limited, contingent, open to individual definition, and most important, terminable upon divorce.

In contrast to the traditional marriage contract, whereby a husband undertook lifelong responsibility for his wife's financial support (Weitzman, 1981a), the new divorce laws suggest that this and other family responsibilities can be terminated soon after divorce. This is evident in the new rules for alimony, which emphasize short-term transitional support and press women to become immediately self-sufficient to relieve their exhusband's "burden" of support (Freed & Walker, 1985).

Similar in its effects is the emphasis on a speedy resolution of the spouses' property claims. There are many more forced sales of family homes than in the past, to hasten the day when each spouse can "take his (or her) money and leave." Arrangements that delay the sale of the home, so that minor children do not have to move, are viewed with disfavor by the courts because they "tie up the father's money." (Recall that the judges we interviewed asserted that each spouse is entitled to his or her share of the property and should not have to wait for it.) There is also a tendency to "cash out" other shared investments, such as pension and retirement benefits, to provide a "clean break" between the parties at the time of the divorce.

Even parenting is becoming increasingly optional and terminable upon divorce. Indeed, the *de facto* effect of the current laws is to deprive children of the care, companionship, and support of their fathers. This is evident in the courts' treatment of postdivorce visitation and child support. Furstenberg *et al.* (1983) found that 52% of the children of divorce in a nationally representative sample had not seen their fathers at all in the past year, and only 17% of the children had seen their fathers at least once a week. These data indicate that a majority of divorced fathers are abandoning their parental roles after divorce and are being allowed to do so without legal punishment. In fact, there is no legal course of action to compel a parent to see his or her children. The implicit message is that parenting has become an "optional" responsibility for fathers after divorce.

While child support awards have always been inadequate and poorly enforced, what appears to be unique about the current situation is the willful disregard of court orders among middle-class and upper-middle-class fathers. For example, as noted above, our California data reveal that fathers with incomes of $30,000 to $50,000 a year are just as likely to avoid child support payments as fathers with incomes of under $10,000 a year (Weitzman, 1985, p. 296). Although the 1984 federal child support enforcement law suggests a possible improvement in this area, it is important to recall that the wage assignments mandated by the federal law were already required in California at the time of this research, but the judges chose to ignore them.

Preston (1984) contends that the financial and social "disappearing act of fathers" after divorce is part of a larger trend: The conjugal family is gradually divesting itself of care for children in much the same way that it did earlier for the elderly. To date, indications of parental abandonment have focused on fathers. Thus far, most analysts have seen mothers as firmly committed to their children. But as the norms of the new divorce laws permeate popular awareness, this picture also may change.

This is because the import of the new custody laws, especially those that eliminate a maternal preference and institute a joint custody preference, undermine women's incentives to invest in their children. As women increasingly recognize that they will be treated "equally" in child custody decisions, that caretaking and nurturance of children find no protection in the law and are punished by the job market, and that joint custody awards may push them into difficult, restrictive, and unrewarding post-divorce custodial arrangements, they may increasingly take to heart the new laws' implied warning that they not become so invested in their children.

The optional and time-limited marital commitments embodied in the new divorce laws have a different effect on men and women. While they free men from the responsibilities they retained under the old system, they "free" women from the security that system provided. Since women's investments in home, family, and children have typically meant lost opportunities in the paid labor force, they are more dependent on the long-term protection and security that the traditional law promised them. It is not surprising that our research finds women "suffering" more under the new laws, for these laws remove the financial safeguards of the old law—with a decline in alimony awards and a decrease in women's share of the community property—at the same time that they increase the financial burdens imposed on women after divorce.

For men, by contrast, the new legal assumption of time-limited commitments means a new freedom from family financial obligations. In fact, the new laws actually give men an incentive to divorce by offering them a release from the financial burdens of marriage. And the wealthier a man is and the longer he has been married, the more he has to gain financially from divorce (Weitzman, 1985, pp. 326, 328, 333, 338).

From Protection for Housewives and Mothers to Gender Neutrality

If the new legal assumptions were accompanied by provisions that in fact enable both spouses to choose the extent to which they would assume breadwin-

ning and homemaking roles, and if they then gave each spouse "credit" for the roles they in fact assumed during marriage, then the law would accurately reflect the complexity and variety of marital roles in these years of "transition." But the present legal system seems to leave no room for such flexibility.

Rather it suggests that a woman (or a man) who chooses homemaking and parenting risks a great penalty because she (or he) will pay heavily for that choice in the event of a divorce. Even if two parties agree to form an equal partnership in which they give priority to his career while she assumes the larger share of the housework and child care, and even if they agree that he will share his earnings and career assets with her, their agreement may have no legal standing. The woman will still be expected to be self-sufficient after divorce, and the man's promise of continued support and a share of his earnings—the promise that is implied in most marriages with a traditional division of labor—will be ignored in most courts. The penalty can be equally severe for the woman who works during marriage, or who works part-time but nevertheless gives priority to her family over her work. Her claims to share her husband's income fall on deaf ears in courts that base support awards solely on her "earning capacity."

Thus one implication of the present allocation of family resources at divorce is that women had better not forgo any of their own education, training, and career development to devote themselves fully or even partially to domesticity. The law assures that they will not be much rewarded for their devotion, and they will suffer greatly if their marriage dissolves.

The concept of marital roles embodied in the new divorce laws carries an equally sobering message about motherhood. Divorcing mothers of preschool children have experienced a greater decline in alimony awards than any other group of women since the no-fault laws were instituted and the vast majority of these mothers (87%) are awarded no alimony at all. They are expected to find jobs immediately, to support themselves completely, and for the most part to support their children as well.

Finally, the woman who has raised her children to maturity and who, as a result of the priority she has given to motherhood, finds herself with no marketable skills when she is divorced at 45 or 55 typically faces the harshest deprivations after divorce. The courts rarely reward her for the job she has done. Rather, the new assumptions imply that her mother-hood years were wasted and worthless, for she too is measured against the all-important new criterion of earning capacity.

Thus, the new divorce laws are institutionalizing a set of norms that may be as inappropriate in one direction as the old norms were in another. The old law assumed that all married women were first and foremost housewives and mothers. The new law as-sumes that all married women are employable and equally capable of self-sufficiency after divorce. Both viewed are overly simplistic, impede women's op-tions, and exert a rigidifying influence on future possibilities.

From Partnership to Individualism

The new divorce laws alter the traditional legal view of marriage as a partnership by rewarding individual achievement rather than investment in the family partnership. Instead of the traditional vision of a common financial future within marriage, the new laws confer economic advantages on spouses who invest in themselves at the expense of the marital partnership.

The traditional law embodied the partnership concept of marriage by rewarding sharing and mu-tual investments in the marital community. Implicit in the new laws, in contrast, are incentives for invest-ing in oneself, maintaining one's separate identity, and being self-sufficient. The new stress is on indi-vidual responsibility for one's future, rather than on joint or reciprocal responsibilities.

Once again, it is easy to see how these new as-sumptions reflect larger cultural themes: the rise of individualism, the emphasis on personal fulfillment, the belief in personal responsibility, and the impor-tance we attach to individual "rights." These trends have at once been applauded for the freedom they offer and criticized as selfish, narcissistic, and amoral (Lasch, 1979). Whether this change represents a de-cline or an advance depends on one's personal val-ues: Do we long for the security and stability that the old order provided or do we applaud the new oppor-tunities for spouses, to escape from the misery of unhappy, lifelong marriages?

Our evaluation will also depend on how we see the past. The belief that the rise of individualism has fostered a decline in the family rests on the assump-tion that the family was stable and harmonious in the past. But historians have not yet identified an era in which families were stable and harmonious or one in which all family members behaved unselfishly and devoted their efforts to the collective good (Skolnick, 1983, p. 22). That "classical family of western nostal-gia," to use William J. Goode's term for the stereo-type (Goode, 1968, pp. 6–7), has been one of the major casualties of recent research in family history (Skolnick, 1983, p. 22).

But historical research does suggest a change in the psychological quality of family life and a rise in what Lawrence Stone calls "affective individualism," a growing focus on individuals as unique personali-ties and a political emphasis on individual rights (Stone, 1977). The rise of affective individualism has brought emotional closeness between nuclear family members and a greater appreciation for the individ-uality of each person in the family. Historically, this trend strengthened the husband-wife unit at the ex-pense of the larger family and the kinship network in which it was embedded. More recently, as rising divorce rates demonstrate, the strength of the hus-band-wife unit has declined and the values of "pure" individualism are emerging. The new divorce laws reflect this evolution in that they encourage notions of personal primacy for both husband and wife. They imply that neither spouse should invest too much in marriage or place marriage above self-interest.

One implication of these changes is that marriage is likely to become increasingly less central to the lives of individual men and women. The privileged status of marriage in traditional family law, as well as the protections and restrictions placed on its incep-tion and dissolution, reinforced its importance and encouraged husbands and wives to make it the center of their lives. The new laws, in contrast, dis-courage spouses from investing in the marital partnership. As more men and women follow the apparent mandate of the new laws, it seems reason-able to predict that marriage itself will lose further ground.

Indeed, William J. Goode (1984) persuasively ar-gues that the trend is already well in progress. He observes that for both men and women marriage is simply less important today than it was in the past, and he foresees the further "decline of individual investments in family relationships over the coming decade" because investments in one's individual life and career pay off better in modern society. As more women seek to follow men in the path of acquiring status, self-esteem, and a sense of individual accomplishment from their jobs, the importance of marriage will rest increasingly on its ability to provide individuals with psychic and emotional sustenance. This, Goode observes, is a difficult and fragile bond. In these trends, he sees profound implications for the future of intimate relationships and the bearing and rearing of children in Western nations.

The Clouded Status of Children

A final feature of the new divorce laws is their ambiguous message about parental responsibility for children. In the past, the sustained well-being of the children of divorce was assumed to be the state's primary concern in any legal proceedings involving children. Indeed, it was this concern that dictated most of the traditional legal protections for women: Women were recognized as the primary custodian of children, and in that capacity were to be accorded preferences and support to ensure the fulfillment of their responsibilities. Similarly, women who had devoted the productive years of their lives to childrearing were to be rewarded for that honorable effort.

Under the new laws, the state's concern for the welfare of children—and their custodians—is far less evident. Rather, in many ways, children have been ignored in the courts' preoccupation with equality for their parents.

The same rules that facilitate divorce facilitate the disruption of children's lives. The gender-neutral rules that encourage or force mothers to work also deprive children of the care and attention they might otherwise have. Equally important, the *de facto* effects of the current laws deprive many children of the care and the support of their fathers.

In sum, under the present laws divorced fathers *may* participate more in the lives of their children if they choose to do so, but they need not so choose; and mothers *must* work outside the home whether they wish it or not, and thus *must* divide their energies between jobs and children. Few legal protections remain to insure parenting for children after divorce.

These themes emphasize the complex interaction between law and social reality. Even as the law evolves to reflect social reality, it also serves as a powerful force in creating social reality. Although the divorce law reformers knew that equality between the sexes was not yet a reality when they codified assumptions about equality in the law, they had seen trends in that direction and believed that the new law would accelerate those trends. But the new law had the opposite effect: it increased economic inequality. It worsened women's condition, improved men's condition, and widened the income gap between the sexes.

So long as the laws remain in force in their present form and their present application, postdivorce equality between men and women will remain an impossibility. Without equality in economic resources, all other "equality" is illusory.

Epilogue

In 1986, in response to my book *The Divorce Revolution*, the California State Senate established a blue ribbon "Task Force on Family Equity." Sponsored by California State Senators Gary Hart and David Roberti, the President pro Tempore of the Senate, the enabling legislation directed the Task Force to study the findings of my research and to develop legislative proposals to "equalize the effects of divorce."

The Task Force Report, issued in June 1987, included 23 legislative proposals and "model" bills. Most of these, condensed into 14 bills, were introduced in the California legislature in 1987 and 1988. By the end of 1987, five of these bills had become law—requiring judicial education and training, automatic wage assignments for every child support award, security deposits for delinquent child support (for the self-employed and those who change jobs frequently), and permanent jurisdiction over spousal support in marriages of long duration.

As of July 1988 another eight bills passed the Senate and are awaiting action in the Assembly. Among these are provisions for a delayed sale of the family home in the interests of minor children, improved standards for spousal support awards (based on the standard of living during marriage), wage assignments for spousal support awards, and extending child support to age 21 (to include most college-age children).

In January 1988 a coalition of women's groups, representing 50,000 California women, organized a

"Coalition for Family Equity" to lobby for the passage of these bills. They mounted an extremely well-organized and energetic grass roots lobbying effort and were successful in getting the bills out of critical Assembly committees. They are continuing their campaign to make these bills become law.

For further information contact Mimi Modisett in California Senator Gary Hart's office or Sara McCarthy in the Senate Office of Research, Sacramento, California.

Notes

[1] I am indebted to my colleague Professor Ruth Dixon for her collaboration in planning this research and for her continued wisdom throughout its execution.

[2] Wisconsin, one of the separate property states, instituted a community property type system in 1986.

References

Bernstein, B.
1982 Shouldn't low income fathers support their children? *Public Interest*, 66.

California Assembly.
1970 California Assembly Committee on the Judiciary Report on Assembly Bill No. 530 and Senate Bill No. 252 (The Family Act), Assembly J. 785, 787 (Reg. Sess. 1970).

Cassetty, J.
1978 *Child support and public policy*. Lexington, MA: D. C. Heath, pp. 64–65, Table 4-1.

Chambers, D.
1979 *Making fathers pay*. Chicago: University of Chicago Press.

Chase, M.
1985, January 21 The no-fault divorce has a fault of its own, many women learn. *The Wall Street Journal*, 1, 12.

Davis, K.
1986 The future of marriage. In K. Davis & A. Grossbard-Shechtman (Eds.), *Essays on contemporary marriage*. New York: Russell Sage Foundation.

Dixon, R., & Weitzman, L. J.
1980 Evaluating the impact of no-fault divorce in California. *Family Relations*, 29, 297–307.

Dixon, R., & Weitzman, L. J.
1982 When husbands file for divorce. *Journal of Marriage and the Family*, 44, 103–114.

Ehrenreich, B., & Piven, F. F.
1984 The feminization of poverty: When the family wage system breaks down. *Dissent.*, 31(2), 162–170.

Eisler, R. T.
1977 *Dissolution: No-fault divorce, marriage and the future of women*. New York: McGraw Hill.

Espenshade, T.
1979 The economic consequences of divorce. *Journal of Marriage and the Family*, 41, 615–625.

Feminization of Poverty, The.
1983, April 8 Briefing paper prepared for California Assemblyman Thomas H. Bates, San Francisco, CA.

Freed, D. J., & Walker, T.
1985 Family law in the fifty states: An overview. *Family Law Quarterly*, 18, 369–471.

Furstenberg, F. F., Nord, C. W., Peterson, J. L., & Zil, N.
1983 The life course of children of divorce: Marital disruption and parental contact. *American Sociological Review*, 48, 656–668.

Goode, W. J.
1968 *World revolution in family patterns*. New York: Free Press.

Goode, W. J.
1984 Individual investments in family relationships over the coming decades. *The Tocqueville Review*, 6, 51–84.

Hawkins, P.
1984 *Statement of Senator Paula Hawkins in hearings before the Committee on Finance, United States Senate, Ninety-eighth Congress, Second Session*. Washington DC: U.S. Government Printing Office.

Hodges, W. F., Tierney, C. W., & Bushbaum, H. K.
1984 The cumulative effect of stress on preschool children of divorced and intact families. *Journal of Marriage and the Family*, 46(3), 611–629.

House Hearings.
1983, July 14 *Statement in hearing before the Subcommittee on Public Assistance and Unemployment Compensation of the Committee Note and Means*. U.S. House of Representatives, Ninety-eighth Congress, First Session *Serial 98–41*. Washington, DC: U.S. Government Printing Office.

Hunter, N.
1983 Women and child support. In I. Diamond (Ed.), *Families, politics, and the state*. New York: Longman.

Lasch, C.
1979 *The culture of narcissism*. New York: Norton.

Leonard, F.
1980 The disillusionment of divorce of older women. *Gray Paper*(6). (Washington DC: Older Women's League).

Matter of Farmer.
1984, January 16 *New York Law Journal*, p. 13, col. 2. New York: New York City Family Court, 1984.

National Center on Women and Family Law.
1983 Sex and economic discrimination in child custody awards. *Clearinghouse Review, 16*, 1132.

O'Brien v. O'Brien
1985 66 N.Y. 2d 576, 498 N.Y.S. 2d 743.

Pearce, D.
1978 The feminization of poverty: Women, work and welfare. *Urban and Social Change Review, 11*, 28–36.

Pearce, D., & McAdoo, H.
1981 *Women and children in poverty*. Washington, DC: National Advisory Council on Economic Opportunity.

Preston, S.
1984 Children and the elderly: Divergent paths for America's dependents. *Demography, 21*, 435–457.

Shields, L.
1981 *Displaced homemakers—Organizing for a new life*. New York: McGraw-Hill.

Skolnick, A.
1983 *The intimate environment*. Boston: Little Brown.

Stone, L.
1977 *The family, sex and marriage in England 1500–1800*. New York: Harper & Row.

U.S. Bureau of the Census.
1979 Divorce, child custody and child support. *Current Population Reports*, Series P-23(84),7, Table 1.

U.S. Bureau of the Census.
1980 *Families maintained by female householders 1970–1979*. (Current Population Reports, Series P-23(107), 36). Washington, DC: U.S. Government Printing Office.

U.S. Bureau of the Census.
1981a *Child support and alimony: 1978* (Current Population Reports, Series P-23(112)). Washington, DC: U.S. Government Printing Office.

U.S. Bureau of the Census.
1981b *Money income of families and persons in the United States: 1979* (Current Population Reports, Series P-60(129)). Washington, DC: U.S. Government Printing Office.

U.S. Bureau of the Census.
1983 *Child support and alimony: 1981* (Current Population Reports, Series P-23(124 and 127)). Washington, DC: U.S. Government Printing Office.

U.S. Bureau of the Census.
1987 *Child support and alimony: 1985* (Current Population Reports, Series P-23(152)). Washington, DC: U.S. Government Printing Office.

Wallerstein, J., & Kelly, J.
1980 *Surviving the breakup: How children and parents cope with divorce*. New York: Basic Books.

Weiss, R. S.
1984 The impact of marital dissolution on income and consumption in single-parent households. *Journal of Marriage and the Family, 28*, 615.

Weitzman, L. J.
1981a *The marriage contract: Spouses, lovers, and the law*. New York: Free Press.

Weitzman, L. J.
1981b The economics of divorce: Social and economic consequences of property, alimony and child support awards. *University of California Los Angeles Law Review, 28*, 1181–1268.

Weitzman, L. J.
1984 Equity and equality: A comparative analysis of property and maintenance awards in the U.S. and England. In J. M. Eckelaar & S. Katz (Eds.), *The resolution of family conflict*. Toronto: Butterworth.

Weitzman, L. J.
1985 *The divorce revolution: The unexpected social and economic consequences for women and children in America*. New York: Free Press.

Weitzman, L. J., & Dixon, R. B.
1979 Child custody awards: Legal standards and empirical patterns for child custody, support and visitation rights after divorce. *University of California Davis Law Review, 12*, 473–521.

Weitzman, L. J., & Dixon, R. B.
1980 The alimony myth: Does no-fault divorce make a difference. *Family Law Quarterly, 14*, 141–185.

Day Care: Do We Really Care?

Ruth Sidel

Ruth Sidel is professor of sociology at Hunter College of the City University of New York. A graduate of Wellesley College and the Boston University School of Social Work, she has worked in the care of emotionally disturbed children in Boston and as director of social work in a community health center in the Bronx. After the granting of her Ph.D. in 1978, she was appointed to the faculty of Hunter College.

Professor Sidel has studied the role of women, the care of preschool children, and the provision of human services in urban areas in the United States and in several other countries. She has made six study visits to the People's Republic of China, the first in 1971 and the most recent in 1986. In addition, she has made repeated visits to Great Britain to study the National Health Service and social services, and she visited Chile during the administration of President Salvador Allende in 1973 and Sweden under a Swedish Kennedy Fellowship in 1975.

Her books include Women and Child Care in China, *first published in 1973 and in a revised edition in 1982;* Families of Fengsheng: Urban Life in China *in 1974; and* Urban Survival: The World of Working Class Women *in 1978. With Victor Sidel, she coauthored* The Health of China *in 1982 and coedited* Reforming Medicine: Lessons of the Last Quarter Century, *published by Pantheon Books in 1984. Her book,* Women and Children Last: The Plight of Poor Women in Affluent America, *was published by Viking/Penguin in April 1986. Her forthcoming book,* On Her Own: Growing Up in the Shadow of the American Dream, *will be published by Viking in January 1990.*

Increasing numbers of women with young children are working outside the home, supporting their families in both single-parent and dual-earner households. Working parents, especially mothers, know that the hardest part of the struggle is juggling the concern for care of their children with the demands of work. Reliable, affordable child care that meets the needs of both children and their parents is rare.

Sidel presents us with a short history of day care in America and describes its present condition. One must wonder how different the situation might be if men were the primary caretakers of children and were charged with the responsibility for their happiness and well-being as well as their financial support.

Child development advocates stress that what the nation saves by skimping on child care today may seriously harm many individuals and later cost the society much in remedial health, education, penal, welfare, and manpower training bills. . . . The early childhood years comprise one-tenth of humans' lives, and the dignity, respect, and well-being with which persons can live during those years should be of concern to all.[1]

—Pamela Roby

DAY CARE IS ONE OF THOSE MURKY ISSUES ON which many Americans do not really know where they stand. Are we for it or against it? Is it good for children or harmful to them? Will it facilitate their social and intellectual development or undermine their emotional well-being? Is it perhaps somewhat "un-American" for a mother to leave her child during the first few years of life? That is what the Russians, the Chinese, and the Swedes do; is that what we want to do? Why do we seem so very ambivalent about this important topic?

Although one child-care specialist has recently stated, "Day care has become as American as apple pie and baseball,"[2] the facts do not confirm her optimistic statement. Not only have funds for day care been cut back over the past four years but, perhaps even more importantly, the rhetoric of the Reagan administration and its allies has undermined public perception of the need for day care by nostalgically recalling and mythologizing another era—perhaps the 1950s, more likely the 1920s—and longingly trying to recapture it.

In this image of small-town America, we are led to believe that father went to work every morning and returned home every evening to hugs and shouts of joy, that mother had hot cocoa and homemade cookies ready for well-behaved children returning from school, and that in case of an emergency grandmother was down the block, only too glad to help out when needed. Children set up lemonade stands on tree-lined streets, large families gathered for Thanksgiving dinner, and friends of long standing were available to provide mutual aid and support in times of hardship—perhaps a scene out of a Jimmy Stewart movie, with everything working out just fine in the end. There is little evidence that this Norman Rockwell image of America ever existed except, possibly, for a limited number of middle- and upper-middle-class families; it surely is not the reality of today. But this image, this rhetoric, has been used by an administration that has tried, and succeeded to a remarkable extent, in removing supports from families under the guise that they will be encouraged to return to an idyllic Never-Never Land.

Other voices, from other viewpoints, also attack day care. Recent allegations of sexual abuse of children by workers in day-care centers in California and New York have shocked parents, professionals, and the public. These incidents highlight a critical problem that has existed in American society for many years: The flagrant disregard for the well-being of children resulting in the absence of a responsible, coherent child-care policy.

First let it be said that thousands of child-care workers across the United States are providing excellent, loving, imaginative care for children, often under extremely difficult circumstances. Reports of various forms of abuse of children in day-care centers are, however, not new. Each time such a report surfaces, it is greeted with headlines, shocked pronouncements by politicians, and sanctimonious editorials, all of which are forgotten as soon as the headlines fade.

Marion Blum, educational director of the Wellesley College Child Study Center, has recently written a powerful critique of day care. She points out that in our extraordinarily materialistic society, children are viewed as things, as commodities around which others can make a profit. She rightly condemns such equipment as cagelike cribs, harnesses and leashes that treat children as though they were animals rather than humans in order to minimize the number of caretakers and to maximize profits.[3] She points out that because of the high turnover of preschool teachers, and the fact that teachers work shifts that may not coincide with the children's hours at the center, children must relate to a variety of adults during their day-care experience. She points out that eight hours or more is a long time for a three- or four-year-old to be away from home and to be required, for the most part, to behave according to preset schedules.[4] She and others have pointed out the difficulties for overworked caregivers trying to maintain proper sanitation, particularly in younger age groups in which the children may not be toilet trained. She points out the higher rates of colds, flu, diarrhea, and even hepatitis A in children who attend day-care centers.[5]

Finally, Blum notes that day care has involved a "transfer of roles from one group of exploited women—mothers—to another group of exploited women—day-care staff."[6] Day-care workers are among the lowest paid adult wage earners in our society, with little or no opportunity for advancement, little or no prestige, and very little in the way of benefits. According to the Children's Defense Fund, "Two out of three center-based caregivers earn below poverty level wages and 87 percent of family day-care workers earn below the minimum wage."[7] The status of preschool teachers clearly indicates the lack of value we place on women and children in our society.

Why is day care so inadequate in the United States? Why is it so exploitive of children, of day-care workers, of the parents themselves who often have no other choice? Is it because day care is seen as "nonproductive" in a society so geared to materialism and productivity? Is it because it serves the needs of two groups—women and children—who are particularly powerless? Is it because in a system not committed to full employment, decision-makers really do not want women in the labor force possibly taking jobs away from men? Is it because many, particularly people in positions of power, want to maintain the patriarchal family, and day care is seen as a force undermining that power relationship? A brief look at the history of day care in the United States may provide some insights into some of these issues.

Part of the hostility, or at best ambivalence, toward day care in this country arises from the fact that it has always been perceived as a service for the poor. Day care began in the United States in 1854 with the establishment of the Nursery for Children of Poor Women in New York City. This and other early day nurseries, as they were called, were modeled after the French crèche, a form of care for the children of working mothers founded in Paris in 1844. The crèche, a response to the increased number of French women working in factories, was also used to improve the health of infants and children and to lower the infant mortality rate. Mothers breastfed their infants in the crèches and were taught methods of hygienic child care. In 1862 crèches received official recognition, and regulations were issued that had to be met in order for the crèches to receive government subsidy.[8]

Day nurseries in the United States received no such official recognition. Most were sponsored by churches, settlement houses, or voluntary social agencies. Their goals were "to prevent child neglect during a mother's working hours and to eliminate the need to place children of destitute parents in institutions. They served an underprivileged group, handicapped by family problems."[9]

The nursery school, on the other hand, evolved out of a middle-class concern that children be given an early childhood educational experience. The first cooperative nursery school in the United States was organized in 1915 by a group of University of Chicago faculty wives in order "to offer an opportunity for wholesome play for their children [and] to give the mothers certain hours of leisure from child care. . . ."[10] A far cry from the goals of the day nurseries—no one talked about hours of leisure for poor women!

Nursery schools, influenced by educational pioneers such as Maria Montessori and models such as Robert Owen's infant school in Scotland, were to have an impact on the development of day care; but the two streams remained fundamentally separate. In fact, according to one observer, "In general . . . the day nursery was regarded with a kind of contempt by nursery school people, and the relationship between the two institutions was not always smooth."[11]

Day care grew rapidly during the depression of the 1930s when nursery schools were financed by the Federal Emergency Relief Administration and then by the Works Progress Administration (WPA). In 1933 President Roosevelt authorized the establishment of nursery schools to care for "children of needy, unemployed families or neglected or underprivileged homes where preschool age children will benefit from the program offered."[12] All personnel, including teachers, nurses, cooks, clerical workers, and janitors, were to come from relief rolls. By 1937 the centers were serving forty thousand children; this effort is still considered by professionals to have provided excellent care, including health care and nutrition, as well as education.[13]

But day care really expanded during World War II, when women now essential to the war effort entered the labor force in large numbers. While the U.S. War Manpower Commission stated in 1942 that "the first responsibility of women, in war as in peace, is to give suitable care in their own homes to their children," the Community Facilities Act (the Lanham Act) passed in June of the same year provided the federal resources necessary to establish day care for the children of working mothers. During this period the federal government spent $51,922,977, matched by $26,008,839 from the states, to fund 3,102 centers that cared for 600,000 children. Though this effort was a significant one, it has been estimated that these centers only served approximately 40 percent of the children in need.[14]

World War II was also a time for innovation in day care. The Kaiser Shipbuilding Corporation in Portland, Oregon, for example, opened two centers at the entrance to each shipyard. The Kaiser centers, which were open twelve months a year, twenty-four hours a day, attempted to meet the mothers' needs as well as care for their children. The services provided included shopping for the mothers, mending clothing, caring for children with minor illnesses, and providing "carry-out dinners at low cost to parents who worked long hours."[15] But at the end of the war, when the shipyards closed, the centers closed with them. What this experience indicates, of course, is that when the United States as a society makes day care a priority, it can provide high quality, imaginative services that provide for the needs of children and their parents.

Following the war, when women were encouraged to leave their jobs and to return home so that returning veterans could move into existing jobs, the "Lanham centers" were closed in every state but California, where due to the availability of state funds they remained open.[16] In the late 1940s and 1950s, a period noted for its conservatism, particularly its political conservatism, women were encouraged to remain at home and to devote themselves to their children and to homemaking. Moreover, women across the country found themselves increasingly isolated and confined to homogeneous communities by the postwar migration to the suburbs. Hand-in-hand with their geographical isolation was the confinement to home and to the role of mother that stemmed from the wave of popular psychology loosely based on Freudian thinking. Mothers were cautioned that their toddlers would be forever maimed emotionally if they were not toilet trained just right, if separation anxiety got out of hand, or if sibling rivalry was not handled with appropriate sensitivity. The newest version of the domestic code, or the role of supermom, as it was now called, was in its heyday!

Nevertheless, the number of working mothers continued to rise. In 1940, 1.5 million mothers were in the labor force; by 1950, there were 4.6 million. By 1959, approximately 7 million mothers were working outside of the home, and there were day-care facilities available for only 2.4 percent of their children.[17] The message was clear: when American society needed women in the labor force, it provided day care for their children; when it wanted women to remain at home, day care was virtually eliminated.

The 1960s was a decade of significantly increased federal funds for preschool care but "in a pattern calculated to reinforce an already segregated system of services—public day care for the poor, private nursery schools or child-care centers for the affluent, and potluck for those families who fell in neither category."[18] The 1960s—a time of economic prosperity that encouraged women to seek jobs in the labor force; a time of heightened concern about the poor that led to the War on Poverty; a time of political activism centering on civil rights, women's rights, welfare rights, and, of course, the Vietnam war—was also a time of increased concern about day care. In a series of amendments to Title V of the Social Security Act in 1962, day care was defined for the first time as a public child-welfare service. The goal of day care was "to provide adequately for the care and protection of children whose parents are, for

part of the day, working or seeking work, or otherwise absent from the home or unable for other reasons to provide parental supervision."[19] Placing day care in a child-welfare context assured that it would be perceived primarily as a service for the poor and near poor, as well as for families with special problems, such as child abuse and neglect. According to one observer:

In statements about day care standards emanating from the Child Welfare League of America and from the U.S. Children's Bureau, the working mother was lumped together with a variety of pathological conditions and defined as a problem. In those statements day care was never discussed as a service for normal children from normal homes.[20]

In 1967, in an effort to reduce public assistance rolls, day care was further tied to welfare by amendments to the Social Security Act that linked it to the Work Incentive Now (WIN) program. Day care was expanded to include children of the working poor and "became virtually embedded in public assistance."[21]

Project Head Start, developed at the same time, was a multidisciplinary program created to give children from "disadvantaged" backgrounds a comprehensive program of education, medical care, and social services; it utilized many aspects of educational philosophy that had previously benefited children in nursery schools. It also incorporated the strategies that were developed during the 1960s which encouraged people's involvement in their own services. Community representatives and parents became actively involved in day care for the first time; and while many of the Head Start programs were models of what many professionals thought preschool care should be, Head Start further stigmatized day care as a program for the poor, the near poor, the disadvantaged, those with "problems."

Limiting day care to those disadvantaged groups, while the middle and upper middle classes are able to purchase care for their children, places the working-class parent in an almost intolerable bind. The working-class mother often can neither qualify for day care nor afford to place her child in a private setting. Since the two-parent working-class family is often just surviving economically, usually because of the wife's income, what are they to do about child care if there is no relative available? One option that some are driven to is deceiving the day-care center, a solution that takes a great toll on the parents, on the center and, ultimately, on the child.

Maria Perez is a small, slim woman in her late thirties who came to this country from Colombia when she was twenty-one. She works in the mornings as a floor secretary in a large teaching hospital in the Bronx. The hospital is within a few blocks of her home and near the day-care center attended by her two younger children. Her husband is a commercial artist in the catalogue department of a large department store and, for a time, worked a second job. Working two jobs meant that her husband left the house at seven o'clock in the morning and did not return until twelve or one in the morning. According to his wife, "He never saw his children except on weekends." The oldest child has just completed first grade at a local parochial school.

Mrs. Perez has struggled long and hard to get where she is now. She had graduated from high school in Bogotá with a degree in literature and philosophy, but because she knew practically no one and knew no English at all when she arrived in this country, she took a job in a factory sewing by hand and later as a bus girl in a Horn and Hardart cafeteria. After learning typing at night school, she worked for a taxi company for five years. When she became pregnant with her first child, she stopped working and did not plan to return to work until her youngest child entered first grade. But her husband was laid off his second job and could not find another; at this time, when her youngest child was eighteen months old, she felt she had to go back to work. She went first to Manpower, a private training program, to study Speedwriting and to brush up on her typing and her English. She describes what happened next:

When I got finished with the Manpower program I tried to get my children into a day care center so that I could go to work. My counselor at Manpower and I— we tried four or five day care centers but my income was too high. You know it's terrible the way the society has things set up so that if you make a little money you can't get into programs. You have to be on welfare or you have to be separated in order to get into a day care center, and my counselor, he told me that what I had to do was I had to say that I was separated. I had to put my husband out of my life and I had to tell them that he only gave me sixty dollars a week. He only gave me twenty or thirty dollars more than that a week, really.

So he called up the day care center for me and told them that I was separated and what my husband gave me. I couldn't do it myself because I was shaking too much.

If Maria Perez had told the day-care center her true income, she would have had to pay $50 per week per child and then, according to her, "I would be paying much more than I was making. It would be impossible. We need for my husband to work and for me to work in order to live a decent life."

Ultimately, the head of the day-care center discovered that Mr. and Mrs. Perez were not separated. Maria Perez felt humiliated and had to take her children out of the center since she could no longer afford to keep them there. She feels extremely critical of people who go on welfare when perhaps they could work, and she resents the fact that they qualify for day care when she, who is working so hard, does not.

You know, there should be free day care centers just as there are free schools for older children. If you go to high school nobody asks if you're married or single or how much you earn. It's free and it's for everybody. There should be day care from three or four years on for everybody even if you're not on welfare.[22]

When Richard Nixon vetoed the 1971 Comprehensive Child Care Act, the number of employed mothers in the United States exceeded 12 million. One-third of all mothers with preschool children—4.5 million women—were in the labor force, leaving some 6 million children in need of care. Less than 10 percent, or approximately 625,000 children, were being cared for in licensed centers in 1970.[23] In summer 1970 the National Council of Jewish Women began a study of day care in the United States. Council members in all parts of the country visited 431 licensed and unlicensed centers that cared for approximately 24,000 children.[24] They interviewed day-care workers, working and nonworking mothers, but above all they observed the conditions under which children were spending their days. Their findings are particularly revealing, for they indicate both how good and how bad day care can be in this country.

Using standardized materials prepared by Mary Dublin Keyserling, former director of the Woman's Bureau, an agency within the U.S. Department of Labor mandated by Congress to deal with issues involving women's employment, the interviewers visited profitmaking centers, nonprofit centers, and family day care (day care for up to six children by a caretaker in her own home), and found that only 1 percent of the proprietary or profitmaking centers were "superior," 15 percent "good," 35 percent "essentially custodial" or "fair," and nearly half were considered "poor."[25] Among the nonprofit centers—which included Head Start projects, centers operated by churches, voluntary community agencies, community action groups, and other nonprofit auspices—9 percent were rated "superior," 28 percent were "good," 51 percent "fair," and 11 percent were considered "poor."[26] Perhaps a few illustrations will indicate the enormous variation among the centers and the appalling conditions in many of them. The study reported on three of the worst proprietary centers:

If ever there was a way to close a day care center, this one should be the first to go. The proprietor is not interested in child care but only in making a profit. She wants to get out of the business and will sell to anyone who will buy it. Back in a dark room, a baby was strapped in an infant's seat inside a crib and was crying pitifully.

They were kept in "cages"—cribs of double-decker cardboard—in one room with open gas heaters.

This is an abominable center [caring for 40 to 50 children, some of them infants]. Couldn't be much worse. One worker washed every child's face with a cloth dipped in a bucket of water one-tenth full. No decent toys. The center was run by high school girls without any adults present. The children were not allowed to talk. . . . Rat holes were apparent.[27]

An example from the other end of the scale was a nonprofit center under Head Start auspices located in a city in the Pacific Northwest. The center was staffed by a director, a college graduate who was professionally trained in early childhood education, four full-time workers, a part-time aide, and four volunteers. "There were thus fewer than five children to each adult. The services of a nutritionist, cook, nurse, and social worker were shared with a public school to which the center was related." The observer reported that there was "a good playground as well as good indoor and outdoor space and equipment" and that there was an "excellent educational program."[28]

Council members also visited family day-care homes. It was estimated in the early 1970s that "as many as 2 million children may be receiving care in homes other than their own while their mothers are away at work." Fewer than 5 percent were estimated to be licensed or supervised. The council's study found that 6 percent of the homes they observed were giving "superior" care, 29 percent "good" care; 51 percent were custodial in nature, providing "fair" care; and 14 percent were providing "poor" care.[29] In one Midwestern city:

This interviewer can still recall quite vividly one particular home she visited where she counted a total of eleven children—five infants and six other small children from about one to four years old of both sexes and almost naked, running and screaming in the four-room house. The strong urine smell, the stale odor of uneaten food everywhere, and the bugs crawling around made one nauseous. There was one very obese, sullen, unpleasant woman in charge. . . .[30]

And in a Northern city, the study found:

Mrs. ——— has great understanding . . . love and warmth. . . . Very clean home, adequate to the needs of the children. Takes children out for play, to parks, local excursions. She shows tremendous interest in children. . . . Mrs. ——— shows great imagination in handling the children in her care. She explained to us how important it is to give these children the feeling that they are wanted and loved.[31]

This study was completed over a decade ago, but there is no reason to believe that conditions have changed significantly since then—if anything, they are likely to have deteriorated. One of the most shocking findings of this study and of others similar to it is the lack of societal monitoring of these centers. Many of the family day-care homes that were found most objectionable in the council's study were being supported financially by local welfare departments. Welfare departments were, in many cases, paying for a child's care in a home that was not licensed and, furthermore, was not fit to provide such care. There is no doubt that welfare departments and day-care accrediting departments do not have the resources to visit, to observe, and to evaluate each and every setting providing care for more than one child. They could, however, have these resources and, moreover, they could put some of the very people whom they are now supporting through an inadequate, stigmatizing welfare system to work to protect the physical, emotional, and intellectual well-being of our children. Our societal ambivalance toward day care, toward working mothers, and possibly even toward children, permits this abdication of responsibility. It is, of course, the children and, in the long run, all of us who suffer.

Many who learn of the deplorable conditions in some U.S. day-care facilities blame the parents. "How can a mother leave her child in a place like that?" is a common response. Parents must, I believe, bear some of the responsibility for the environment in which their children are cared for when they cannot care for them themselves. Parents must learn what conditions are necessary for their children's healthy development and then demand those conditions. But what are parents to do when adequate care does not exist? What are they to do when adequate care exists but they cannot afford it? Perhaps in an era in which the extended family is rarely a viable, functioning institution—even in the black community, where there is a long tradition of grandmothers caring for grandchildren, the grandmothers today are often in the labor force and unable to help the young working mother; at a time when the traditional nuclear family is frequently not a viable, functioning unit, either; in an era in which communities offer few if any supports, the society must accept the role of monitoring services for children and other dependent groups. Just as we expect the Department of Public Health to monitor conditions in restaurants and health facilities, just as we expect the Board of Education to monitor what goes on in our schools, don't we have the right to expect comparable agencies to monitor the conditions in day-care facilities?

As of March 1984, according to the Children's Defense Fund, almost half of all mothers with children under three and almost 52 percent of mothers with children under six were in the labor force. More than 9 million children under six have working mothers, and 67 percent of these mothers work full time.[32] There is grossly insufficient day care for these children; it is estimated, for example, that 7 million children ages thirteen and under may be spending part of each day without adult supervision.[33]

During the first three years of the Reagan administration, federal programs that supported child care were cut dramatically. Title XX, the largest program providing federal support for child care, was cut 21 percent; the Public Service Employment Program of the Comprehensive Employment and Training Act (CETA), which helped to provide staff for child-care centers, was abolished. As a result, thirty-two states provided care to fewer poor children in 1983 than in 1981, and thirty-three states cut child-care spending. In 1981 Illinois served 28,100 children; in 1983, 18,000. In 1981 Delaware served 2,039 children; in 1983, 995.[34] One estimate is that the Reagan administration's budget cuts in the first three years resulted in eliminating child care for at least 150,000 children.[35] The group most severely hurt by these cutbacks are poor families headed by women. According to the Children's Defense Fund, "Most of the families using Title XX are headed by single women who need to work out of economic necessity."[36]

Yet another group hurt by the budget cuts is the working poor. Since 1980 ten states have tightened their requirements, and consequently fewer children of low-income working families are eligible for child care. Nineteen states have either increased their fees for child care or imposed new ones. The working poor have also been hurt by being eliminated from AFDC, thereby entirely losing their eligibility for publicly funded day care.[37]

But it is not only quantity that has been cut; quality has been affected as well. According to the Children's Defense Fund's analysis of the president's fiscal-year 1985 budget, "In the past three years, 24 states have reduced funds for training child care workers, 33 have lowered the standards for Title XX child care programs, and 32 have cut back on the number of child care staff."[38]

While eleven states increased their child-care expenditures between 1983 and 1984, in most cases the gains were not sufficient to make up for the cuts made in 1981. Consequently, many parts of the country report a serious gap between the need and the availability of child care. For example, New Mexico is serving approximately 3,700 children but estimates that more than 50,000 need child care; Georgia's Title XX-funded program serves approximately 8,200 children and has a waiting list of 5,000 for its funded centers; in Los Angeles County, California, there is no licensed child care available for the 135,000 children who need such programs.[39]

President Reagan has, however, continued to claim that his administration supports women's aspirations, including those of working women. As evidence of this support, the administration points to the recent increase in the federal income-tax credit for taxpayers who require child care in order to work or look for work. While this is an important development for many working parents, it clearly does not benefit the poor and the near poor who are most desperate for help with child care.

Perhaps the most significant development over the past few years has been the emergence of employer-supported child care. According to the Conference Board, a nonprofit business research organization, more than 1,800 companies are providing some form of child-care assistance to workers.[40] Child-care support by employers takes many forms. It includes providing or participating in the provision of direct services. The Conference Board study estimates that some 120 companies and 400 hospitals and public agencies sponsor day-care centers.[41] The range includes in-house facilities, such as that provided by Wang Laboratories in Massachusetts; facilities run by profitmaking chains, such as the Campbell's Soup operation, which is run by Kindercare; facilities run by nonprofit organizations, such as the employee-run center of Merck Pharmaceuticals. Some companies join together to form a consortium to run a center; others sponsor family day-care arrangements.

A second form of employer participation in their employees' child-care concerns is the provision of information and referral services, either offered on the work premises or through an existing community agency. Yet another form of involvement is employer-financed subsidy. The establishment of a Dependent Care Assistance Plan was made possible by the Economic Recovery Tax Act of 1981, making child care a nontaxable benefit for employees. The fourth mechanism whereby employers help their employees with child care is through more flexible working hours— flextime, job sharing, part-time work, or home work, also called "flexiplace."[42]

Is employer participation in child care the wave of the future? It has been estimated that, by 1990, 64 percent of all families will have working mothers and that these families will include 10.4 million children under six. Will private industries increasingly feel it is in their best interests to help families solve their personal problems, particularly the problems of child care? For more businesses to move into this area, they must see it as profitable in some way. As Dana Friedman has stated, "The fact that children

are our nation's greatest resource is not the most convincing argument for bottom-line oriented business managers."[43]

There is no doubt that employer involvement in child care is a positive development; it has, for example, undoubtedly legitimized day care in the eyes of many who may have felt doubt or even antipathy. But there are problems with relying on employers to be major providers of child care. One major difficulty is that the current wave of employer-sponsored activity is generally voluntary. Most firms or unions or institutions that move into the area of day care do it because they need to recruit and retain skilled employees, because they feel their employees will, in the long run, have more stable work histories if some of their family problems are solved, or because they feel it is good public relations. As Friedman points out, industries that cater to the family market, such as Gerber Foods and Stride Rite children's shoes, feel a greater commitment to family issues.[44] But what of other working people in the country? Most of the companies that offer child-care options are non-unionized. Child-care benefits are, therefore, often not a right won through negotiation and guaranteed through a contract but rather a result of enlightened self-interest on the part of industry. But what happens when the industry's self-interest changes—if its profit margin shrinks and executives feel such services can be eliminated?

Which segment of the population is most likely to benefit from industry involvement in child care? Will this be yet another way of separating services for the poor from services for working people, many of whom are middle class? Corporate child-care programs are usually found in high-technology companies, insurance companies, banks and hospitals. Are we moving simultaneously toward improved child care for the fortunate few and reduced, often inferior care for the poor, the unemployed, and those workers unfortunate enough to work for companies that are either unenlightened or not making sufficient profit to consider breaking new ground in the area of child care? In addition, many of the companies now offering child-care services offer them as part of a "cafeteria" plan, whereby the worker must choose one benefit over another. Should a parent have to choose dental coverage over child care or vice versa?

Child care is still a two-class system in the United States. Those with adequate income can generally purchase first-rate care for their preschool children;

those without adequate income are left at the mercy of the political and economic forces that determine social policy. While the poor, the near poor, and the working class sometimes have access to good care, more often than not they are faced with long waiting lists, inadequate teacher–child ratios, and a rapid turnover of caregivers.

Statistics from the National Center of Education show that 53 percent of children ages three to four whose families had incomes of $25,000 and above attended a preschool program in 1982, while less than 29 percent of children whose families had incomes below $25,000 were in preschool. In addition, approximately half of the three-year-olds and 72 percent of the four-year-olds whose mothers were college graduates were in such programs in 1982.[45] For child care, as for other human services, affordability and accessibility have become key issues.

That we still have extremely limited access to child care in the 1980s, twenty years after the War on Poverty and the initiation of Head Start, is particularly shameful since a study has recently been released indicating that a first-rate preschool experience may be of particular value to disadvantaged children. Conducted in Michigan by the High/Scope Educational Research Foundation, it found that poor black children with low IQs who received preschool education from the age of three "have grown up with markedly greater success in school and in their personal lives than a comparable group without early childhood education. . . ."[46] Following the children from age three through age nineteen, the researchers found that they had better work histories, completed more years of schooling, were involved in less crime, and had fewer teenage pregnancies than a comparable group that did not have early childhood education. Sixty-seven percent of the preschool education group had graduated from high school by the age of nineteen, compared to 49 percent of the control group.[47]

While the preschool education was not inexpensive—the cost adjusted for inflation at 1981 prices was $4,818 per child per year—the long-term savings to the educational system and to society were far greater.[48] But the financial savings is the least important aspect of this project. As Fred Hechinger has stated, "Neglect at an early age has been shown to mean wasted lives, with mounting costs to individuals and society, and the creation of a permanent underclass."[49]

There is little doubt that the absence of a high-quality, coherent, comprehensive day-care policy is a key factor in the perpetuation of poverty among women and children. Without access to affordable day care, women with young children are frequently unable to enter the labor force. Without adequate day care, how can a mother receiving AFDC hope to acquire skills or get a job in order to get off welfare? If we as a society are serious about economic equity for women, about stemming the feminization of poverty, and about giving every child a fair chance educationally, emotionally, and economically, one of our first priorities must be accessible, affordable, high-quality day care.

Notes

[1] Pamela Roby, "Young Children: Priorities or Problems? Issues and Goals for the Next Decade," in *Child Care—Who Cares? Foreign and Domestic Infant and Early Childhood Development Policies*, Pamela Roby, ed. (New York: Basic Books, 1973), 125–126.

[2] Marion Blum, *The Day-Care Dilemma: Women and Children First* (Lexington, Mass.: Lexington Books, 1983), 2.

[3] Ibid., 5–18.

[4] Ibid., 19–23.

[5] Ibid., 67–76.

[6] Ibid., 41.

[7] *Child Care: The States' Response: A Survey of State Child Care Policies, 1983–1984*, White Paper prepared by Helen Blank (Washington, D.C.: Children's Defense Fund, 1984), 7.

[8] Lela B. Costin and Charles A. Rapp, *Child Welfare*, 473.

[9] Ibid.

[10] Virginia Kerr, "One Step Forward—Two Steps Back: Child Care's Long American History," in *Child Care—Who Cares?*, 160.

[11] Ibid., 161.

[12] Ibid., 162.

[13] Ibid.

[14] Ibid., 163.

[15] Ibid., 165.

[16] Ibid.

[17] Ibid., 166–167.

[18] Ibid., 167.

[19] Costin and Rapp, *Child Welfare*, 478.

[20] Ibid., 478–479.

[21] Ibid., 479.

[22] For additional material on Maria Perez, see Ruth Sidel, *Urban Survival*, 93–106.

[23] Mary Dublin Keyserling, *Windows on Day Care* (New York: National Council of Jewish Women, 1972), 1–3.

[24] Ibid., 3.

[25] Ibid., 120.

[26] Ibid., 119.

[27] Ibid., 64.

[28] Ibid., 123.

[29] Ibid., 155.

[30] Ibid., 135.

[31] Ibid.

[32] *Child Care: The States' Response*, 13.

[33] *A Children's Defense Budget: FY 1984*, 133.

[34] *A Children's Defense Budget: An Analysis of the President's FY 1985 Budget and Children* (Washington, D.C.: Children's Defense Fund, 1984), 161–162.

[35] Dana E. Friedman, "Employer-Supported Child Care: How Does It Answer the Needs and Expectations of Workers?" *Vital Issues* (a service of the Center for Information on America) 32 (1983): 1–6.

[36] *A Children's Defense Budget: FY 1985*, 161.

[37] Ibid., 162.

[38] Ibid., 163.

[39] *Child Care: The States' Response*, 10–11.

[40] Glenn Collins, "More Corporations Are Offering Child Care," *New York Times* (21 June 1985).

[41] Ibid.

[42] Friedman, "Employer-Supported Child Care."

[43] Ibid.

[44] Ibid.

[45] Sheila B. Kamerman, "The Child-Care Debate: Working Mothers vs. America," *Working Woman* (November 1983): 131–135.

[46] Fred M. Hechinger, "Blacks Found to Benefit from Pre-schooling," *New York Times* (11 September 1984).

[47] Ibid.

[48] Ibid.

[49] Fred Hechinger, "Society's Stake in Preschool Teaching of Poor," *New York Times* (9 October 1984).

Women and Law From a Feminist Perspective

Susan Gluck Mezey

*Susan Gluck Mezey was educated at Brooklyn College
and Syracuse University. She has taught in the
departments of political science and government in
eight institutions, including Thammasat University
in Bangkok, the University of Hawaii, and Wesleyan
University in Connecticut. She currently teaches at
Loyola University of Chicago. Her special research
interests include minority group politics and
American politics; she has researched women's political
and legal status since 1974 and has written articles for
several political journals and law reviews.*

*Mezey outlines for us here the current major legal
issues for women and explains the relevant concepts
and terms. She recounts the history of women's fight
for legal equality in the nineteenth century and
concludes that legal reform has only a limited ability to
erase gender injustice. We still have a long way to go.*

Susan G. Mezey wrote this article for this edition of
Issues in Feminism.

WESTERN CULTURE IS TYPIFIED BY A DIVISION OF
human life into public and private spheres. The
public sphere is associated with government, politics, and the community; the private sphere
includes the individual and the family.[1] This separation is reinforced by legal institutions that
maintain male dominance in both sectors by iso-
lating women from the public arena and insulat-
ing family life from governmental regulation.

The legal status of women in the United States
reflects deeply held beliefs about the subordination of women to men in both public and private
worlds. Women have been excluded—by law—
from the public sector through denial of the vote
and restrictions on economic participation. Conversely, the law has excluded itself from the private realm by refusing to interfere in ongoing
marital relationships and even, until very recently,
acquiescing in male brutality toward women by
exempting husbands from charges of battery and
rape.[2]

Because law has served to perpetuate male
domination, the relationship between law and
feminism is tenuous. Some feminists question
whether law can be used to achieve equality and
whether legal equality can be equated with gender equality.[3] On the whole it would appear that
the marriage between feminism and law, while
uneasy, has been a useful weapon in the fight for
social, political, and economic equality. However,
as demonstrated by changes in laws regulating
divorce, employment conditions, and rape, legal
solutions alone, that is, laws prohibiting discrimination or proclaiming women's equality with
men, will not by themselves transform the roles
women play in society.[4]

Employment Discrimination Law

Equal Pay

The modern era of the role of women in American
society can be traced to the early 1960s as women

undertook the slow—and as yet unfinished—task of achieving equality with men. In response to continuing pressure from women's advocates, in the 1960s and 1970s, federal laws were passed to prohibit pay disparity between men and women as well as to bar sex discrimination in employment, credit, housing, and education. Additionally, women increasingly turned to the courts for validation of their rights. The first steps toward a more meaningful equality for women were taken with the passage of the 1963 Equal Pay Act, an act requiring employers to pay men and women working at essentially the same jobs an equal salary. The Equal Pay Act, passed during the administration of John F. Kennedy, commanded employers to provide "equal pay for equal work."

Early Pay Act challenges frequently succeeded in court as judges found that companies were paying women less than men for performing essentially the same work. Thus, the wage difference between male and female "selector-packers" who inspected glass bottles was not justified even though the men also performed the additional job of "snap-up boy." The court ruled that the extra work occasionally performed by the men—essentially unskilled labor—did not merit the 21-½ cents per hour pay differential. Similarly, a court ruled that male night shift workers in another glass factory could not be paid more than female day shift workers since the company did not treat the shifts differently in its own job classification scheme.

Despite these victories, the Equal Pay Act has not solved the problem of the earnings gap between men and women in America because it left the problem of sex segregation in employment virtually untouched. Sex segregation means that women work in jobs predominantly held by women that generally command lower wages than occupations primarily held by men. This issue has become known as the comparable worth, or pay equity, issue.

Comparable worth cases are typically brought by women nurses or clerical workers. And in these cases, the courts are asked to compare the jobs held by the women to jobs of "similar skill, effort, responsibility, and working conditions" held by men and to decide whether the jobs should command comparable pay.

Unlike Equal Pay Act cases, comparable worth cases frequently fail as plaintiffs fall prey to the Equal Pay Act's exception that justifies a wage differential based upon a "factor other than sex." The cases lose because courts have ruled that market conditions, such as the supply of available workers, the wages workers can command from other employers, and the rate of unionization of workers, generally constitute "factor[s] other than sex." Although advances have been made in this area, the identification and correction of pay discrimination still remain elusive goals.

Equal Employment Opportunity

Title VII of the 1964 Civil Rights Act makes it unlawful for employers, labor unions, and employment agencies "to discriminate against any individual with respect to his compensation, terms, conditions or privileges of employment, because of such individual's race, color, religion, sex, or national origin."

Passage of this Act meant that women's employment opportunities were finally guaranteed by federal legislation. The bill was originally intended only to ban racial discrimination in employment, but in the final vote on the floor of the House of Representatives, Congresswoman Martha Griffiths of Michigan proposed an amendment to include sex discrimination within its purview. Accepted in part by the bill's opponents in the hopes that it would torpedo the entire bill, the prohibition on sex discrimination was included in the final version. Despite its early lackluster support, Title VII of the 1964 Civil Rights Act became the single most important piece of legislation in the battle against employment discrimination.[5]

In 1967, President Lyndon Johnson signed Executive Order 11375 which added sex as a protected category to earlier executive orders banning discrimination on the basis of race, color, creed, and national origin. Following the example of its predecessors, Executive Order 11375 prohibited discrimination in federal contracts as well as required federal contractors to adopt affirmative action programs to promote equal employment goals.

The parameters of Title VII have been fleshed out by the courts in cases challenging employment practices as well by the Equal Employment Opportunity Commission, a federal agency authorized to make rules concerning enforcement. But because members of Congress were not convinced that sex differences in employment were *wholly* bad, the statute itself created several exceptions to the ban on sex discrimination. Title VII allows employers to draw distinctions among employees on the basis of sex where it is a "bona fide occupational qualification" for the job, that is, when the business depends upon having an employee of a certain sex. Here, the question is asked whether the job requires that the employee be a certain sex, and whether this requirement is "reasonably necessary" to the essence of the business.

An industry much affected by this interpretation of Title VII was the airline industry. In one of the first Title VII cases a court ruled that customer preference for female stewardesses was not a bona fide occupational qualification and that Pan American Airlines could not refuse to hire male flight attendants. In a later case involving Southwest Airlines, the airline argued that its image, expressed in such ads as "At last there is somebody else up there who loves you" and "We're spreading love all over Texas," demanded the hiring of female flight attendants and customer service people only. The courts disagreed.

When companies make employment decisions, they often select employees on the basis of so-called neutral rules, such as a height and weight minimum. On their face, these selection procedures do not discriminate on the basis of sex, but they frequently have the *effect* of keeping women out of jobs. The courts have ruled that this practice is illegal under Title VII unless the employer can show that the requirement is related to the employee's ability to do the job.

Height and weight requirements were predominantly used as job qualifications by police and fire departments, and, as a result, women were denied access to these jobs. In a 1977 Alabama case, the Supreme Court found that the minimum requirement of 120 pounds and 5 feet 2 inches for the job of prison guard violated Title VII; these conditions had the effect of excluding women from prison jobs, and the state could not show that they were required for the job. In the same case, however, the Court ultimately concluded that the state did not have to hire women because they posed a "substantial" security problem in light of their vulnerability to sexual assault.

Pregnancy in the Workplace

One of the most important debates about women and employment is over the rules governing the activities of pregnant women. Some believe that exceptions for the special condition of pregnancy denies equality between the sexes. Others contend that because pregnant women have special needs, employers *must* treat them differently to allow them to achieve equality with men.

The debate over pregnancy legislation is set against the backdrop of "protective" legislation that diminished the woman's ability to work. In the past, pregnancy-related policies restricted options for working women: they were forced to take unpaid maternity leaves and denied seniority if they were allowed to return to the job. Opposition to such laws led feminists to argue for eliminating all laws relating to pregnancy and for treating pregnancy like other "disabilities," that is, like other physical conditions affecting workers.

Other feminists argue that this hands-off approach to pregnancy fails to acknowledge that pregnancy imposes special obstacles on women in the workforce. They maintain that treating men and women equally with respect to pregnancy minimizes the physical and financial burden that childbearing imposes on working women. An equality approach that urges pregnancy benefits to be equated to disability benefits sends the wrong message; it portrays pregnancy as a workplace oddity rather than as a brief interlude in a woman's employment.

In a series of pregnancy cases beginning in 1983, the Supreme Court seems to have moved toward an approach that denies the specialness of pregnancy and to have rejected the preferential treatment of pregnancy in the workplace.[6]

Sexual Harassment

A relatively recent development in employment discrimination law is the use of Title VII to combat sexual harassment in the workplace. Two models of sexual harassment have been identified, although the two tend to blend into each other. The first, called *quid pro quo*, is when a demand is made to a woman to exchange sexual favors for employment benefits. The second, called "condition of work," is when sexual advances exist as part of the job but are not explicitly tied to a condition of employment.[7] Both models, according to the Supreme Court, constitute sexual harassment.

Women filing sexual harassment charges under Title VII have had difficulty convincing the courts to accept the legitimacy of their claims. The first obstacle lies in the definition itself: is sexual harassment a form of discrimination based upon sex? Although some courts said no because both sexes *could* be harassed, the prevailing view is that sexual harassment should be equated to sex discrimination in employment because it has a negative effect upon the "terms and conditions" of a woman's job. Another thorny issue concerned the extent to which a company, such as a bank, should be held liable when a male employee, such as a bank manager, harasses a female employee, such as a bank teller, especially when the company has a policy against sexual harassment and is unaware of the harassing behavior.

The Equal Employment Opportunity Commission has urged the adoption of a broad interpretation of employer liability for the sexual harassment of an employer. But in 1986, in its only sexual harassment case, the Supreme Court refused to decide the issue of employer liability in a definitive way. The Court ruled that while the company is not automatically liable, claiming ignorance of the harassment will not necessarily shield it from responsibility, nor does an antiharassment policy absolve it from liability.

Constitutional Review

Early Decisions

The United States Supreme Court plays an important part in structuring the legal status of women in America, and its decisions are influenced by the prevailing attitude toward the public and private roles of women in society.

Until the early 1970s, the Supreme Court's interpretation of the Constitution allowed states to bar women from a variety of occupations, including lawyers and bartenders, permitted states to make it more difficult for women to serve on juries, and even acquiesced when states prohibited women from voting.

The Court's early approach to judging the constitutionality of laws affecting women was exemplified by Justice Bradley in an 1873 case involving a challenge to an Illinois statute limiting the practice of law to men only. Bradley stated that:

the constitution of the family organization . . . indicates the domestic sphere as that which properly belongs to the domain and functions of womanhood. The harmony . . . of interests and views which belong or

should belong to the family institution, is repugnant to the idea of a woman adopting a distinct and independent career from that of her husband.

This image of women, easily dismissed today as a relic of the nineteenth century, was again expressed by justices of the Supreme Court in 1961. In this Florida case, the Court was asked to decide on the constitutionality of a jury selection system that produced virtually all-male juries. The Court held that the state could allow women—but not men—to decide whether to register for jury duty because women are "still the center of home and family life."

Equal Protection

The equal protection clause of the Fourteenth Amendment of the U.S. Constitution prohibits a state from "deny[ing] to any person within its jurisdiction equal protection of the laws." This clause tells states that they must justify legislative decisions to treat individuals as legally different; different treatment is permissible when it is based upon *relevant* distinctions among people. The courts have interpreted this to mean that "similarly situated" persons must be treated alike.

The modern phase of equal protection for women was ushered in with two signals from Congress: enactment of federal antidiscrimination legislation and congressional approval of the Equal Rights Amendment.[8] Another factor that led to the establishment of a new judicial doctrine was the rise of litigation activity sponsored by feminist law firms, the NAACP Legal Defense and Education Fund, the American Civil Liberties Union, as well as organized women's groups such as the National Organization of Women and the Women's Equity Action League.[9]

In 1971, for the first time in the history of the Supreme Court, a law that distinguished between men and women was struck down. Since that time the Court has invalidated most of the gender-classifications that have come before it, striking down laws that are based upon "archaic or overbroad generalizations" about men and women.

Five years after this breakthrough, in 1976, the Supreme Court insisted that gender classifications must be "substantially related" to the achievement of an "important" governmental interest. And in 1982 the Court added that the state must establish an "exceedingly persuasive justification" for such a classification.

Based upon these criteria, the Supreme Court has invalidated an Idaho law that preferred male administrators of estates over female administrators, a U.S. armed forces regulation in which female officers had to prove spousal dependency in order to receive benefits, a social security regulation that limited survivor's benefits only to widows (not widowers) taking care of children, an Alabama law that allowed alimony payments to women only, and a Mississippi law that restricted admission in a state nursing college to women only.

Nevertheless, despite this apparent commitment to gender equality, the Court has still approved of a significant number of laws promoting legal differences between the sexes. It has allowed sex-based laws designed to rectify the effects of societal discrimination against women; for the most part, these laws were justified by the economic disparity between males and females. To this end the Court accepted two social security regulations allowing women a more favorable method of computing social security benefits, a Navy regulation permitting women more time in rank than men before being removed for nonpromotion, and a Florida law granting widows only a property tax exemption.

The majority of the laws upheld by the Court are directly or indirectly related to physical differences between the sexes because the Court is persuaded that states may classify in areas where men and women are not "similarly situated." On these grounds the Court approved a law limiting military registration to men only, a law punishing men only for the crime of statutory rape, and several laws creating distinctions between mothers and fathers of illegitimate children.

The Supreme Court also accepted a California law that denied working women pregnancy benefits on the grounds that differentiating on the basis of pregnancy was *not* an impermissible sex classification; in a now-famous footnote the Court explained that "the [California] program divides potential recipients into two groups—pregnant women and nonpregnant persons. While the first group is exclusively female, the second includes members of both sexes." This rather novel characterization of the relationship of women to pregnancy was ultimately reversed by the 1978 Pregnancy Discrimination Act.

Reproductive Rights

In 1969 when Norma McCorvey, an unmarried itinerant carnival worker, learned she was pregnant, she sought an abortion in the state of Texas and discovered that, like most states, Texas allowed legal abortions only in cases where the woman's life was in danger. Within the next few months, McCorvey met with two women lawyers anxious to challenge the Texas law and the result, four years later, was the famous *Roe* v. *Wade* decision.[10]

In *Roe*, the Supreme Court proclaimed that the constitutional right to privacy, formalized in *Griswold* v. *Connecticut* in 1965, was "broad enough to encompass a woman's decision whether or not to terminate her pregnancy." Giving with one hand and taking away with the other, Justice Blackmun immediately reined in this right by announcing that it was not "unqualified." The decision to terminate a pregnancy, he said, could be restricted by the state in furtherance of its goals of protecting maternal health and potential life. Weighing the woman's right to choose against the state's interest in regulation, the Court held that the state cannot impose criminal penalties for abortion during the first six months of pregnancy.

Roe established a formal set of regulations based upon the trimester system of pregnancy. During the first three months (first trimester), because mortality in abortion may be less than mortality in childbirth, the state has no compelling reason to ban abortion. During the next three months (second trimester), the state is permitted to make rules and regulations that reasonably relate to maternal health; the state can regulate the qualifications of the person performing the abortion as well as the facility in which it will be performed. Only during the last three months of pregnancy (third trimester), because of the medical likelihood that the fetus can exist outside the mother's womb, can the state prohibit abortion entirely except when the mother's life or health is at risk.

Roe v. *Wade* has been criticized extensively from both sides of the abortion controversy. Antiabortion groups are opposed because it elevated abortion to a constitutional right. Prochoice (those in favor of a woman's right to choose) groups are grateful to the Court for interposing the Constitution between themselves and restrictive state legislation. Yet they argue that the woman's right to choose is too restricted, allowing too much control to the medical profession. They also contend that focusing on privacy rather than equality loses sight of the fact that a ban on abortion falls more heavily on women than on men and thus perpetuates the "subordination of women to men through the exploitation of pregnancy."[11]

Opposition to *Roe* v. *Wade*, erupting in Congress and state legislatures, resulted in two victories for antichoice forces: restrictions on government funding of abortions for indigent women and requirements for minors to obtain parental consent. The Supreme Court accepted the funding restrictions but refused to allow parents to exercise full veto power over a minor's decision to have an abortion. States can require parental consent, but the law must allow the minor woman to seek judicial consent if the parents refuse to give theirs. The antiabortion forces won as well when the Court upheld a Utah statute requiring physicians to notify parents of a minor before performing an abortion.

Aside from the restrictions on minors and funding, the Supreme Court has continued to adhere to the principles established in *Roe*. In two major abortion cases, in 1983 and 1986, the Court struck down regulations requiring second trimester abortions to be performed in hospitals, specifying that the physician must provide the pregnant woman with information regarding fetal development and the risks and harmful effects of abortion, establishing waiting periods between the time consent is given and the procedure is performed, and requiring the presence of a second physician at abortions performed late in the pregnancy.

Roe was decided by a 7 to 2 vote; the 1983 decision was decided by a 6 to 3 vote, the 1986 decision by a 5 to 4 vote. Since the 1986 decision, two new justices were added to the Court, nominated by a president committed to reversing *Roe* v. *Wade*. All attention was turned to the Court for its next ruling in this turbulent area of law.

Since 1973, abortion opponents have continually asked the Supreme Court to reverse *Roe*. Their wish was partially granted in 1989 when the Court decided a case that imposed significant restrictions on women's reproductive rights. Although the Supreme Court did not take the ultimate step of overturning *Roe* v. *Wade*, in *Webster* v. *Reproductive Health Service*, it moved closer to the antiabortion position than it had ever been since 1973.

In a 5–4 opinion, the Court upheld provisions of a Missouri law that restricted the availability of abortions. The *Webster* decision was primarily concerned with the use of public facilities for abortions. Its major significance, however, was its promise for the future of allowing states greater leeway in imposing limitations upon women's reproductive rights. With five justices agreeing, the Court permitted the state to bar public employees from encouraging or counseling abortions and to prohibit abortions from being performed in public hospitals even if the woman paid all expenses. Additionally, the Court upheld a provision of the law that required additional medical tests on women after twenty weeks of pregnancy.

The implications of *Webster* are not fully known. In his decision, Chief Justice Rehnquist seemed to invite states to pass restrictive laws that would lead to future cases. It appears likely that the five justices who voted to uphold the Missouri law will support the constitutionality of similar legislation: the pendulum is clearly swinging in the other direction. One member of the Court, Justice Scalia, expressed disappointment that the Court did not overturn *Roe*. Justice O'Connor merely said that *this* case did not require the Court to reconsider *Roe*.

By chipping away at *Roe*, *Webster* has expanded the state's authority to regulate and restrict abortions. Whatever position the Court adopts in later cases, both sides of the controversy agree that major battles will be fought in the races for state office as candidates vie with each other for the support of the anti- and prochoice voters. One thing is clear: *Roe* had taken this highly divisive issue out of the political process; *Webster* thrust it back.

Education

In the historic *Brown* v. *Board of Education* decision in 1954, the Supreme Court announced that "separate but equal" has no place in public education and that schools segregated on the basis of race are unconstitutional. Apparently believing that this principle does not apply to sex-segregated education, the Court has refused to rule that "separate but equal" on the basis of sex is unconstitutional.

In 1972, Congress addressed the question of gender inequality in education by passing Title IX of the Educational Amendments, an act providing that "no person in the United States shall, on the basis of sex, be excluded from participation in, be denied the benefits of, or be subjected to discrimination under any education program or activity receiving Federal financial assistance."

Title IX banned discriminatory treatment in vocational, professional, and graduate schools; it encompassed physical education classes, extracurricular activities, scholarships, and counseling. While the law represented an important step toward equality in education, it allowed exceptions to sex equality in two major areas: admissions and athletics. Single-sex admissions remained legal in most elementary and secondary schools, private undergraduate schools, traditionally single-sex public undergraduate institutions, as well as schools claiming the need for a single-sex environment on religious grounds.

Although the problem of athletics was not highlighted during its passage, perhaps the major Title IX battles were fought over the issue of sex equality in athletics. While Title IX encourages schools to offer athletic activities to all students, it allows the exclusion of women from male sports teams, such as football, basketball, and ice hockey, that require body contact among the players. Similarly, a school may restrict a team's membership to one sex only as long as it offers a team for the other sex—regardless of the difference in quality of play or the level of funding allocated to the two teams: "separate but equal" lives.

In its first two Title IX cases, in 1979 and 1981, the Supreme Court expanded the scope of the act by allowing individual discrimination suits and including employees as well as students within the ban on sex discrimination.[12] The Court then executed an about-face in its 1984 decision, *Grove City College* v. *Bell*, by narrowing the definition of a "program or activity" subject to the ban on discrimination.

Grove City College argued that it was not covered by Title IX because it received no direct aid from the federal government and, even if covered, Title IX's prohibition on sex discrimination only applied to the program receiving the indirect aid—in this case, Grove City's financial aid office.

While ruling that educational institutions receiving indirect aid through student grants and loans were subject to Title IX, the Court agreed with Grove City that Title IX only applied to the specific program receiving the federal aid; other units within the college were not under the auspices of Title IX and hence not subject to the nondiscrimination rule.

In 1988, over President Reagan's veto, Congress enacted the Civil Rights Restoration Act to reverse the Court's *Grove City* decision. This Act defined "program or activity" to include the whole institution if any part of it received federal funds.

Family Law

Marriage

Women's lives have always been subject to the legal, economic, and physical constraints of the family. The subordination of married women to their husbands was reflected in the English common law doctrine of coverture—a doctrine that denied married women property and contractual rights and designated their husbands as the legal heads of the household with title to the marital property.

The Married Women's Property Acts, passed individually by states beginning in the 1830s, were the first halting steps to establish a separate legal identity for married women. Although these acts did not produce legal equality for women, they did remove the worst of the restrictions on owning property and making contracts. Women, however, remained burdened with the primary responsibility for the family and received little encouragement to move outside that arena. Indeed, on the contrary, women were constantly reminded throughout the 1800s and 1900s to stay in their place—at home.

Because the family has tended to be sheltered from the reach of law, married women were—and still are to a great extent—subject to their husband's dominion. Under the common law, women were obligated to perform domestic and sexual services as well as care of the children and, in return, were entitled to receive basic necessities of food, clothing, and shelter from their husbands; the level of support to which the wife was entitled was irrelevant to this "contract." This principle was demonstrated in a 1953 Nebraska case, *McGuire* v. *McGuire*, in which the Nebraska Supreme Court stated that:

> *the living standards of a family are a matter of concern to the household, and not for the courts to determine, even though the husband's attitude toward his wife, according to wealth and circumstances, leaves little to*

be said in his behalf. As long as the home is maintained and the parties are living as husband and wife, it may be said that the husband is legally supporting his wife and the purpose of the marriage relation is being carried out.

More than thirty-five years later, this decision is still cited as the legal standard for cases challenging inadequate support by husbands.

Divorce

The law's reluctance to get involved in the private relationship between women and men fades when the marriage is being dissolved.

American divorce laws are creatures of the states, and residency requirements, grounds for divorce, and distribution of property are governed individually by each state.[13] By the 1970s, a rising tide of no-fault divorce laws swept through the states and, by 1985, all states except South Dakota established a variation of a no-fault system; some states simply added no-fault provisions to their pre-existing fault grounds. No-fault divorces are granted on the basis of "irreconcilable differences" or "irretrievable marital breakdown," which means that neither party has to prove the other guilty of breaking one of the rules of marriage. Most states also require a period of time, often six months, to lapse before granting a divorce decree. While the no-fault divorce was hailed as a liberating force because it freed women (and men) from remaining trapped in unwanted marriages, there is a debate about whether it has been an unalloyed blessing for the divorced woman.

Following divorce, wives are usually more economically disadvantaged than their husbands and must earn their own income. Moreover, "divorce may push them into the labor market under unfavorable circumstances."[14] One of the less happy circumstances of the no-fault approach is that ex-husbands have been relieved of much of the responsibility of support. Alimony, as a means of providing financial support for divorced women, has virtually disappeared; among other things, it is now referred to as *maintenance,* a term suggesting limited scope and duration. Because of this shift in attitudes, in most cases, alimony no longer serves as a longterm support mechanism for ex-wives. Additionally, with the adoption of no-fault divorce, women lost much of their bargaining power in settlement negotiations.[15]

The concept of spousal maintenance exemplifies this new approach to divorce; maintenance is only awarded to a small fraction of divorced women and is regarded as an interim measure to allow women to gain skills necessary to support themselves with appropriate employment.[16] Because fault has virtually disappeared as a factor in determining maintenance awards, courts base their maintenance decisions on such factors as the length of the marriage, the age, health, and earning capacity of the parties, as well as the possibility of each party returning to the standard of living enjoyed during the marriage.

While this restructuring of divorce rules is consistent with the feminist philosophy of women taking responsibility for themselves, the reality is that women are often unprepared to assume financial responsibility for themselves and their children because their work experience has been limited to unpaid labor in the home or underpaid labor outside the home.

Along with changes in no-fault divorce and spousal support, states also adopted new procedures for dividing property at divorce. The Married Women's Property Acts had ended the husband's explicit legal dominion over property by changing state laws to allow the spouse who earned or held title to the property to manage and control it. These acts did little to change the fact that, in most states, men were the primary wage earners who held title to the bulk of the property obtained during marriage and retained the right to control it. Women's work in the home received no official recognition in the law.

As with other rules of divorce, property distribution is determined by the state of residence. The fifty states of the United States fall into two categories: community property states and separate property states, the latter also known as common law states.

In the separate property states (forty-two states and the District of Columbia), separately owned property is not divided at divorce; only marital property, held jointly by both marriage partners, is divided between them. In community property states (seven western states plus Louisiana), husband and wife jointly own property acquired during the marriage, and this property is distributed at divorce. Most separate property states now follow a community property model for dividing assets at divorce. Under this system, a spouse who made an economic contribution to the property, regardless of ownership, may claim a share of that property upon divorce.

A number of states have also moved toward a system that allows a spouse, typically the woman, who has made a noneconomic contribution to the marriage to make a claim upon assets at divorce. The major difficulty with this approach lies in the calculation of noneconomic contributions, that is, how to put a market value on the homemaking and parenting services of a stay-at-home spouse. In arriving at their decisions, judges are guided by such factors as the length of the marriage, the age, health, occupation and employability of the parties, as well as the amount and sources of income available.

Increasingly one of the battlegrounds over what constitutes a "fair" divorce involves the problem known as the "medical school syndrome."[17] This situation arises when one spouse, again typically the wife, has supported her husband through medical school and is presented with a request for a divorce when he is presented with his diploma. She wants part of the increased earning power he *will* have; he wants property divisions and maintenance determined by their resources at the time of the divorce. Wrestling with this dilemma, courts have issued conflicting opinions, some favoring the wife, some favoring the husband. This is clearly an area of law in a state of flux.

Violence Against Women

The crime of rape was commonly defined as "unlawful sexual intercourse with a woman by a man, not her husband, by force and without her consent." The prevailing view of rape was that it was triggered by feelings of male passion and frequently provoked by the victim through her behavior, her provocative clothing, or simply by being in the "wrong place at the wrong time." Rape undoubtedly is the only crime in which the victim is accused of inviting the act or at least enjoying its performance.[18]

Because of the widely held myths about this crime, the legal system distinguished it from other crimes of violence and imposed special rules on rape prosecutions. Unlike other crimes, rape convictions required proof of resistance by the victim, demanded that the testimony of the victim be supported by independent (corroborative) evidence, and allowed the introduction of the victim's sexual history as evidence at trial.

Following the view that rape charges were "easily made and once made, difficult to defend against," a rape trial often ended with the judge cautioning the jury about the need to closely examine the victim's version of the events. Thus, rape was unique in focusing upon the behavior and state of mind of the victim—rather than upon the behavior and state of mind of the defendant as other crimes do. Moreover, most states, operating on the assumption that marriage implies continuing consent to sexual intercourse, exempted the crime of marital rape altogether, that is, husbands could not be prosecuted for raping their wives.

Not surprisingly, victims were reluctant to subject themselves to the trauma of a rape trial, and rape was consistently one of the most underreported crimes. Also, not surprisingly, given the stringent proof requirements, rape prosecutions had a notoriously low conviction rate.

During the 1970s, feminists directed their efforts toward changing societal perceptions of rape. Their success can be measured in part by the passage of rape reform legislation in a number of states that redefined the crime and altered evidentiary rules.[19] Along with legal reform came the creation of rape crisis centers to counsel victims of rape and increasing police and prosecutor sensitivity to the injury suffered.

Reformers attacked one of the major misconceptions about rape as a crime of passion and, by redefining rape as sexual assault, made it clear that rape was a crime of violence. Some states as well created a range of illegal behavior dealing with criminal sexual conduct to allow for greater flexibility in prosecution of sex crimes. A number of states eliminated the phrase "against her will" or "without her consent" from the definition of the crime thus eliminating the necessity of proving resistance in circumstances where force is used. Many states also altered those evidentiary rules, unique to rape trials, that made prosecution so difficult. Additionally, most states removed the absolute bar to prosecuting husbands for raping their wives and now, under some circumstances, permit prosecution for spousal rape.[20]

Although the attention focused on this crime has not reduced its rate of occurrence or lessened its impact upon the victim, it has made the public more aware that rape is a *crime* of violence against women and not a sexual interlude in their lives.

Conclusion

Feminists seeking gender equality espouse a variety of methods ranging from reforming political and legal institutions to eliminating patriarchy and dismantling capitalism. While they may disagree over the usefulness of legal reform to accomplish their goals of gender equity, they undoubtedly would agree that changes in the law have produced at least minimum access to equality of education, jobs, and privacy.

This article has discussed some of the highlights of the efforts to achieve these goals through legal means. While the advances won over the past twenty to twenty-five years have been significant, they have certainly not been sufficient to eradicate gender inequality. One can respect the law as an important instrument of reform while recognizing that more work needs to be done: that is the lesson to be learned here.

Notes

[1] Jean Bethke Elshtain, *Private Man, Public Woman* (Princeton: Princeton University Press, 1981); Arlene Saxonhouse, *Women in the History of Political Thought: Ancient Greece to Machiavelli* (New York: Praeger, 1985).

[2] Nadine Taub and Elizabeth Schneider, "Perspectives on Women's Subordination and the Role of Law," in *The Politics of Law*, ed. David Kairys (New York: Pantheon Books, 1982), pp. 117–139. Men were also immune from private suits brought by their wives for intentional and negligent harm caused by them; see Liane Kosaki and Susan Gluck Mezey, "Judicial Intervention in the Family: Interspousal Immunity and Civil Litigation," *Women and Politics* 8(1988):69–87.

[3] Ava Baron, "Feminist Legal Strategies: The Powers of Difference," in *Analyzing Gender*, eds. Beth Hess and Myra Marx Ferree (Beverly Hills: Sage, 1987), p. 475.

[4] See Rosemarie Tong, *Feminist Thought: A Comprehensive Analysis* (Boulder: Westview Press, 1989) for analysis of types of feminist theories. The feminist who sees legal solutions as the key to equality between men and women is a "liberal feminist." Her slightly more radical sister, the welfare feminist agrees on the need for legal solutions but also wants to see increased attention paid to class differences in society.

[5] See Charles Whalen and Barbara Whalen, *The Longest Debate* (New York: New American Library, 1985) for history of the passage of the 1964 Civil Rights Act.

[6] See Wendy Williams, "The Equality Crisis: Some Reflections on Culture, Courts and Feminism," *Women's Rights Law Reporter* 7(Spring 1982):175–200 and Sylvia Law, "Rethinking Sex and the Constitution," *University of Pennsylvania Law Review* 132(1984):955–1040 for opposing sides of the pregnancy and work debate.

[7] See Catherine MacKinnon, *Sexual Harassment of Working Women* (New Haven: Yale University Press, 1979).

[8] Ruth Bader Ginsburg, "The Burger Court's Grapplings with Sex Discrimination," in *The Burger Court*, ed. Vincent Blasi (New Haven: Yale University Press, 1983), pp. 132–133.

[9] See Karen O'Connor, *Women's Organizations' Use of the Courts* (Lexington: Lexington Books, 1980); Ruth Cowan, "Women's Rights Through Litigation: An Examination of the American Civil Liberties Union Women's Rights Project, 1971–1976," *Columbia Human Rights Law Review* 8(Spring–Summer 1976):373–412; Jo Freeman, *The Politics of Women's Liberation* (New York: David McKay, 1975).

[10] See Marian Faux, *Roe v. Wade* (New York: Macmillan, 1988).

[11] See Law, "Rethinking Sex and the Constitution"; Laurence Tribe, *Constitutional Choices* (Cambridge: Harvard University Press, 1985), pp. 243–245.

[12] Joyce Gelb and Marian Lief Palley, *Women and Public Policies* (Princeton: Princeton University Press, 1982); Rosemary Salomone, *Equal Education Under Law* (New York: St. Martin's Press, 1986).

[13] See Doris Jonas Freed and Timothy Walker, "Family Law in the Fifty States: An Overview," *Family Law Quarterly* 18 (Winter 1985):369–471.

[14] Herbert Jacob, "No-Fault Divorce and Finances of Women," *Law and Society Review* 23(1989), p. 98.

[15] See Lenore Weitzman, *The Divorce Revolution: The Unexpected Social and Economic Consequences for Women and Children in America* (New York: The Free Press, 1985).

[16] Herbert Jacob, *Law and Politics in the United States* (Boston: Little Brown and Company, 1986), p. 71.

[17] Freed and Walker, "Family Law in the Fifty States," p. 411.

[18] See Susan Brownmiller, *Against Our Will* (New York: Simon and Schuster, 1975).

[19] Ronald Berger, Patricia Searles, and W. Lawrence Neuman, "The Dimensions of Rape Reform Legislation," *Law and Society Review* 22(1988):329–357.

[20] See Jacob, *Law and Politics*, pp. 17–18, n.18.

References

Baron, Ava
    1987 "Feminist Legal Strategies: The Powers of Difference." In *Analyzing Gender,* edited by Beth Hess and Myra Marx Ferree, pp. 474–503. Beverly Hills: Sage.

Berger, Ronald, Patricia Searles, and Lawrence W. Neuman
  1988 "The Dimensions of Rape Reform Legislation."
  Law and Society Review 22:329–357.

Brownmiller, Susan
  1975 *Against Our Will*. New York: Simon and Schuster.

Cowan, Ruth
  1976 "Women's Rights Through Litigation: An Examination of the American Civil Liberties Union Women's Rights Project, 1971–1976." *Columbia Human Rights Law Review* 8(Spring–Summer):373–412.

Elshtain, Jean Bethke
  1981 *Private Man, Public Woman*. Princeton: Princeton University Press.

Faux, Marian
  1988 *Roe v. Wade*. New York: Macmillan.

Freed, Doris Jonas, and Timothy Walker
  1985 "Family Law in the Fifty States: An Overview." *Family Law Quarterly* 18(Winter):369–471.

Freeman, Jo
  1975 *The Politics of Women's Liberation*. New York: David McKay.

Gelb, Joyce, and Palley, Marian Lief
  1982 *Women and Public Policies*. Princeton: Princeton University Press.

Ginsburg, Ruth Bader
  1983 "The Burger Court's Grapplings with Sex Discrimination." In *The Burger Court*, edited by Vincent Blasi, pp. 132–56. New Haven: Yale University Press.

Jacob, Herbert
  1989 "No-Fault Divorce and Finances of Women." *Law and Society Review* 23:95–115.

———
  1986 *Law and Politics in the United States*. Boston: Little Brown and Company.

Kosaki, Liane, and Susan Gluck Mezey
  1988 "Judicial Intervention in the Family: Interspousal Immunity and Civil Litigation." *Women and Politics* 8:69–87.

Law, Sylvia
  1984 "Rethinking Sex and the Constitution." *University of Pennsylvania Law Review* 132:955–1040.

MacKinnon, Catherine
  1979 *Sexual Harassment of Working Women*. New Haven: Yale University Press.

O'Connor, Karen
  1980 *Women's Organizations' Use of the Courts*. Lexington: Lexington Books.

Salomone, Rosemary
  1986 *Equal Education Under Law*. New York: St. Martin's Press.

Saxonhouse, Arlene
  1985 *Women in the History of Political Thought: Ancient Greece to Machiavelli*. New York: Praeger.

Taub, Nadine, and Elizabeth Schneider
  1982 "Perspectives On Women's Subordination and the Role of Law." In *The Politics of Law*, edited by David Kairys, pp. 117–139. New York: Pantheon Books.

Tong, Rosemarie
  1989 *Feminist Thought: A Comprehensive Analysis*. Boulder: Westview Press.

Tribe, Laurence
  1985 *Constitutional Choices*. Cambridge: Harvard University Press.

Weitzman, Lenore
  1985 *The Divorce Revolution: The Unexpected Social and Economic Consequences for Women and Children in America*. New York: The Free Press.

Whalen, Charles, and Barbara Whalen
  1985 *The Longest Debate*. New York: New American Library.

Williams, Wendy
  1982 "The Equality Crisis: Some Reflections on Culture, Courts and Feminism." *Women's Rights Law Reporter* 7(Spring):175–200.

The Equal Rights Amendment: What Is It, Why Do We Need It, and Why Don't We Have It Yet?

Riane Eisler
Allie C. Hixson

Riane Eisler was born in Vienna and studied anthropology, sociology, and law at the University of California at Los Angeles where she also taught. Author of numerous articles and books, among them The E.R.A. Handbook *(Avon, 1978) and* The Chalice and the Blade *(Harper and Row, 1987), she is an international activist for women's and peace issues. She is also the founder of the Center for Partnership Studies in California.*

Dr. Allie Corbin Hixson holds a master's degree in humanities and was the recipient of an American Association of University Women College Faculty Program Award leading to her doctorate in English from the University of Louisville (1969). She is the author of A Critical Study of Edwin Muir, Orcadian Poet. *After a fifteen-year teaching career, Hixson retired from academia to become a full-time volunteer activist for women's rights. She led the Kentucky International Women's Year (IWY) delegation to the 1977 Houston First National Women's Conference, served as one of the vice chairs for that conference, and currently serves as cochair of the IWY continuing committee, the National Women's Conference Committee.*

The Equal Rights Amendment was first introduced in Congress in 1923 under the leadership of Alice Paul, not three full years after the passage of the Nineteenth Amendment, which guaranteed women the right to vote. After a well-organized and well-financed campaign by conservative and radical right forces such as the John Birch Society, Phyllis Schlafly's Eagle Forum, and many fundamentalist religious sects, the ERA was defeated in 1982.

Down but not out, ERA was reintroduced in Congress on January 3, 1985. It is currently out of the news but not off the feminist agenda.

SECTION 1. EQUALITY OF RIGHTS UNDER THE LAW shall not be denied or abridged by the United States or by any State on account of sex.

Section 2. The Congress shall have the power to enforce, by appropriate legislation, the provisions of this Article.

Section 3. This Amendment shall take effect two years after the date of ratification.

The Statue of Liberty is the symbol of American opportunity, of the promise of equality and justice for all. For American women, in this year of 1986 when we celebrate her hundredth anniversary, our Statue of Liberty has a very special meaning. As she too is female, she has always stood for compassion, caring, and other qualities associated with women's great contribution to our nation, with our love for our country and our service to it. But at this time, when the promise of constitutional protection for the half of our nation born female has not yet been fulfilled—when the United States is the only major industrialized nation other than South Africa that does not yet have a constitutional clause guaranteeing women equal rights with men—she is also our inspiration: the emblem of our *inalienable* rights.

Throughout the world, the Statue of Liberty is the symbol of democracy. In our nation, the modern cradle of democracy, this noble female figure is also a reminder to all American women and men of good will that we cannot countenance any failure of the democratic process: that in a nation where poll after poll shows that the majority of the people favor the proposed Equal Rights Amendment to our Constitution, it is our responsibility as American citizens to see that the people's will is done.

The Moral Imperative: Justice and Equality for All Citizens

We hold this truth to be self evident: that all Americans are entitled to the equal protection of our laws. This is the American creed, the best and finest of the American spirit, the promise of the American dream. For over half a century, this promise has been expressed in twenty-four simple words: "Equality of rights under the law shall not be denied or abridged by the United States or by any state on account of sex."

That is the text of the proposed Equal Rights Amendment to the U.S. Constitution. When Americans are asked whether they approve or disapprove of these words, in poll after poll over 60% express approval. Until 1980, both the Democratic and the Republican Party platforms endorsed the ERA. Every major American women's organization from the National Organization for Women to the YWCA, the American Association of University Women, the National Federation of Business and Professional Women's Clubs, the National Council of Negro Women, the League of Women Voters, the National Women's Political Caucus, Federally Employed Women, the Older Women's League, the National Woman's Party and hundreds more support the ERA. So do the American Bar Association, the United Auto Workers, the AFL-CIO, the National Council of Churches, the National Assembly of Women Religious, the National Association of Social Workers, the American Federation of Governmental Employees, the American Jewish Congress, the National Council of Senior Citizens, and most other mainstream American organizations. Four American first ladies—Lady Bird Johnson, Patricia Nixon, Betty Ford, and Rosalyn Carter—backed the ERA. Why? Because, as Lady Bird Johnson said, "everyone in our democracy deserves to be treated with fairness and justice, and to have that right assured in our Constitution."

How, then, is it that we do not yet have an Equal Rights Amendment? As Betty Ford put it in 1981, when the ERA was only three states short of the thirty-eight states needed for ratification, "as a woman and as a Republican, I do not understand how we, as a people, can continue to hold our heads high and be proud of what this nation stands for if we have not guaranteed the rights of half our nation." When, as Ford summed it up, "all we are asking is that our rights be protected under the law," how could a handful of men in a handful of states deprive all American women of the constitutional protection that is our rightful due?

The answer is that these men voted their prejudices, aided and abetted by a well-financed campaign of slanderous lies against women and the ERA.

The Truth About Five Big Lies

Big Lie Number One: The ERA Should Not Be in the Constitution Because Women Are Not Equal

This is the oldest and most hackneyed of the five Big Lies. In 1860, when American universities did not yet admit women and we were fighting for the very right to equal consideration for a higher education, an article in the *Saturday Review* asserted that there was a simple reason why only American men should have the right to a university education. Appealing to age-old prejudices, this prestigious publication asserted: "The great argument against the existence of this equality of intellect in women is that it does not exist." It then contemptuously added: "If that does not satisfy a female philosopher, we have not better to give." Although responsible publications would no longer dream of printing such ridiculous libels about the half of humanity born female, many of those who oppose the Equal Rights Amendment still argue the same absurdity: that women are intellectually, biologically, or "divinely ordained" inferior, and therefore subordinate to, men.

The Truth Hundreds of scientific studies have shown that women are equal human beings. Just plain common sense, as well as the overwhelming evidence of our day-to-day experience, further demonstrates that men are not superior to women.

Big Lie Number Two: We Don't Need the ERA Because Women Are Already Treated Equally

In 1845, when American women like Ernestine Rose were circulating petitions protesting laws that deprived married women of the right to hold or manage property—even property they had brought to their marriages—they were told that women "had rights enough, if not too many rights already." Today, those who oppose ERA make the same false claim.

The Truth Official statistics as well as the living experience of women of all races, ages, and occupations, be they homemakers or workers in the paid labor force, show that American women are by no means treated equally. The five representative cases that follow—a widow, a married woman, a divorced mother, a high-school girl, and a college graduate—prove the pure falsehood of the Big Lie that we are already being "treated equally."

The Widowed Homemaker Mary S is a widowed homemaker. After twenty-eight years of marriage as a devoted mother and wife, she rightfully looked forward to a well-earned and secure old age. Raised on a farm in Nebraska, she married a rancher, raised their son, and often worked from dawn to dark cooking, cleaning, haying and raising hogs. For many years the ranch prospered and everything seemed to be going well. Then came the first blow. Mary's son was killed in an automobile accident. The second and third blows followed shortly thereafter. Unable to compete with big corporate cattle growers, Mary and her husband lost their ranch, and a few months later Mary's husband died of a sudden heart attack. Mary was unable to find a job, and soon the proceeds from her husband's life insurance, which they took out before inflation became a fact of economic life, were also gone. And—like *90% of American women over retirement age*—Mary *had no pension because she was an unpaid homemaker all her life.*

Despite the claims of ERA opponents that women, especially traditional housewives, are honored and taken care of for life, the fact is that there are millions and millions of women like Mary in America today. The truth is that *85% of elderly Americans are poor women.* The majority of them are widowed homemakers, many of whom depend *solely* on

Social Security payment for survival. And yet, in 1983, the average Social Security payment for women sixty-five or older *was $1,259 below the average payment for men—$4,476 compared to $5,725.* In 1983 18.6% of all elderly women and 43.5% of elderly black women had incomes below the poverty line.

The Married Homemaker Antonia S got married when she was eighteen years old, just out of high school. She has four small children, two girls and two boys, and like many mothers she often works twelve hours a day, seven days a week. Her husband Manuel is a truckdriver, who makes a pretty good income. A former high school football player, he is an amicable fellow who still loves his sports and a good time. And, though he likes to think of himself as a good provider, when Antonia says that he spends too much time out with the boys and too much money on beer and sports, he accuses her of being a "nag." Since he believes that if a man is going to "wear the pants in the family," he has to have financial control, Antonia has had to make-do with a small and often inadequate "allowance" to feed and clothe herself and all four children. When out of desperation Antonia asked an attorney for help, she was told that as a wife living with her husband, she has no legal recourse *except divorce* to ensure herself and her family a fair and reasonable portion of her husband's earnings.

As it now stands, there is no effective legal way to enforce a married man's obligation to provide adequately for his wife and children as long as he is still married and living with them. This traditional rule of law was summed up by the Nebraska State Supreme Court in the case of *McGuire v. McGuire*. This was a lawsuit brought by a wife who—after *thirty-four* years of marriage, during which she "worked in the fields . . . cooked and attended to her household duties, raised as high as 300 chickens, sold poultry and eggs"—still could not get her husband to provide enough money to put a simple heater or inside plumbing in their home, even when she became ill. The court dismissed Mrs. McGuire's request for help on the grounds that "to maintain an action such as the one at bar, *the parties must be separated or living apart from each other.*"

The message to the millions of Antonia S's and Mrs. McGuires of America is that they can legally get adequate support only if they give up completely and move out or if they *first divorce their husbands*. Yet, for most American women today, getting a divorce does *not* make things any more equal.

The Divorced Mother Before Joan M's divorce, she lived in a three-bedroom home in a nice Los Angeles suburb with her husband and two children, Janie and Randy. The children went to a good neighborhood school and Joan was active in the local PTA and other community service organizations. When Joan and her husband, Don, got a divorce—as do half of all couples who get married in America—Joan was awarded custody of the children. She also got the house, child support until the kids reached eighteen, and spousal support for five years so that, as the judge put it, she could go back to school to be "retrained." Joan immediately enrolled in a nearby state college to complete her education for teaching certification, which she had interrupted to get married, and carefully arranged her schedule so that she could be home when the children got back from school. For a while, everything seemed to be going well. Then, after a year and a half, Don stopped paying spousal support. Joan went to court to get relief, and the judge ordered Don to pay. Instead, he left town, leaving no forwarding address. Unable to trace him, and now with no spousal *or* child support, Joan had to sell the house, quit school, and get a low-paying job as a file clerk. Since the job was not enough both to support her family and pay for the child care she needed while working, when the money from the house sale ran out, Joan had no choice but to go on welfare. *Like millions of formerly middle-class American women who once enjoyed a comfortable standard of living and did not realize that the ERA was important to them, Joan has now joined the one-fifth of America, mostly women and children, who live in poverty.*

A California study of 300 divorced couples found that a year after a typical divorce, the wife's income dropped 73%, while the husband's actually rose significantly. Sixty-five percent—nearly two thirds—of American women now raising their children alone are, like Joan, doing so without any financial assistance from a husband and father. Only 15% of divorced American women are awarded alimony or spousal support, and less than a quarter of these receive their court-ordered payments. And, while the traditional prescription for curing poverty is to "get a job," this often does not work for a woman the same as for a man because women—especially dis-

placed homemakers like Joan—have been steered into traditionally "female" jobs, most of them dead-end and low-paying. As a consequence, over one-third of families headed by women in 1982 had incomes below the poverty line, even though many of the women who headed them had jobs. And, according to a report prepared by a California State task force commissioned by Lt. Governor McCarthy, by 1985 this number had risen to nearly one-half!

The High-School Girl In the third grade, Carole N. had the highest grade in her class in math. She was also an outstanding student in algebra and geometry. But, like many of her girlfriends, Carole never thought of becoming an engineer or a physicist. Now Carole is in the eleventh grade and is thinking about going to college. Her brother is planning to go into pre-med, and Carole is wondering if she ought to try this too. But to do that, she would have to start taking courses in trigonometry and calculus, which none of her girlfriends are doing, and which everybody says are really tough. Recently, Carole tried out as cheerleader, and if she gets accepted—and she thinks she has a good chance—that will mean a lot of after-hours practicing. And, of course, there are the household chores she has to help her mother with and she does not want to miss out on a social life, either. So Carole does not know what to do—particularly since there is a really cute guy on the football team, who did not pay any attention to her when she had the reputation as a "brain," but is finally beginning to notice her.

A study by the Council of Chief State School Officers (CCSSO) and the National Association of State Boards of Education (NASBE) in December 1980 found that the portrayals of boys and girls in school textbooks perpetrate the very sexual stereotypes that Carole will have to overcome to have an equal chance—thereby channeling boys and girls into very different kinds of professional and life choices. Not only do elementary school readers and texts predominantly portray boys as independent leaders and achievers, and girls as passive dependents watching from the sidelines, but boy-centered stories outnumber girl-centered stories *five to one*, as if to say that girls are that much less important. Similarly, a study of state-adopted textbooks found that, in 1974, only *one* out of 500 to 800 pages in the average U.S. history text was devoted to the contributions and experiences of women. Lack of role models within our school systems, such as an underrepresentation of women in administrative jobs like principal and superintendent (there has actually been a *drop* in female elementary school principals, from 55% in 1928 to only 20% by 1973) further helps to perpetuate very different and more limited kinds of life tracks for girls than for boys. The different way girls and boys are treated by teachers and career counselors also continues to channel girls into low-paid service jobs traditionally associated with women. The same situation prevails in vocational schools, where 35% of all girls enroll in consumer and homemaking courses that prepare them for no paid employment except as domestic servants, and one-half enroll in traditionally low-paid office skills courses. Similarly, among college-bound high-school seniors, boys outnumbered girls two-to-one in having completed three or more years of physical science and were much more likely to have completed the math courses that are prerequisites for college calculus and admission to a large number of scientific and technical majors. Even in computer programming courses, boys overwhelmingly outnumber girls, so that all along the way girls' career and life options become narrower and narrower rather than wider and wider.

The College Graduate When Elizabeth E. graduated from Northwestern University in 1965, the want ads were still segregated by sex, with most of the good, high-paying jobs in the "Help Wanted—Male" section. But Elizabeth, who had avoided learning how to type because she did not want to end up in a secretarial job like many of the bright young women she knew, was an unusually resourceful person. She found a job with an educational testing firm, and eventually worked her way up to a managerial position. Elizabeth knew she was very lucky both as a woman and as a black person to have a good job. But it still rankled her when she accidentally discovered one day that one of her coworkers, a man with far fewer years of experience or education than she, was earning over $3,000 more each year. At first, Elizabeth took this personally. But then, when she looked into the statistics and started asking around, she realized that this was true for almost *all* women in the workplace. According to the U.S. Department of Labor, *American women who have graduated from college earn less on average than men who have only finished the eighth grade!*

Women comprise about 40% of the American work force. Yet, only 18,000 of us—in the entire nation—earn over $60,00 a year. By contrast, almost a million men—885,000—are in this over-$60,000 income bracket. One major reason for this difference is that, even when a woman does enter a traditionally "male" occupation, she still tends to be paid less than her male counterpart. (For example, in 1981, women doctors averaged $401 per week in pay, compared with $561 for male doctors.) But the main reason is that, whatever becomes labeled "women's work"—whether it takes high skill or not—is paid less. This is true even in demanding female-dominated occupations, such as nursing and teaching, which pay less than plumbers, sign painters, or tire servicemen earn. An indication of how severe such job segregation still is for women workers is that, of the 441 jobs classified by the 1980 U.S. Census, only sixty categories had significant percentages of women; all the others were predominantly male. Moreover, in 1981, men outnumbered women two-to-one in managerial jobs.

With all this sex segregation and underpayment in the marketplace built into the "System," it's little wonder that American women earn on average fifty-nine cents to sixty-one cents for each dollar men do. It is most sobering to recall that sixty-cents-on-the-dollar works out to be exactly three fifths—the very percentage a *slave* was once "worth" relative to a Free Man for purposes of determining a state's population for Congressional representation—even though, of course, slaves, like all women, did not have the vote. So what women are still paid today is essentially slave-percentage wages!

Fundamental changes in sex-based discrimination will not take place until the Equal Rights Amendment becomes part of the U.S. Constitution.

Big Lie Number Three: Women Don't Need the ERA Because the Fourteenth Amendment Already Protects Us from Discrimination

ERA opponents contend that we should not "clutter up" the Constitution with another Amendment. They claim the Equal Rights Amendment is unnecessary because the Fourteenth Amendment already provides that no State shall "deny any person within its jurisdiction the equal protection of the laws," so that women already have all the constitutional protection they need.

The Truth The Fourteenth Amendment was enacted in 1868, but for *over a century* American courts refused even to consider women under the protected category of "persons"! Even though women's rights advocates asserted that for women to be denied the right to vote was a violation of the Fourteenth Amendment, it took until 1920—*and the 19th Amendment to the Constitution*—for us finally to get the right to vote. In fact, when in 1874 a New York judge found feminist leader Susan B. Anthony guilty of the "crime" of voting, he declared explicitly that "under the Fourteenth Amendment, which Miss Anthony claims protects her, she was not protected in a right to vote."

It was not until a mere fifteen years ago, in 1971, that the U.S. Supreme Court for the first time included women under the classification of "persons." And this was in a case where sexual discrimination was so blatant that it was found to be "totally arbitrary and wholly unrelated to the objectives of the state statute involved." Since then, the Supreme Court has continued to vacillate, refusing to apply to cases of sex discrimination the same strict test it uses in civil rights cases where race, instead of sex, is involved: namely, that there must be proof of a "compelling state interest" to justify any kind of legal discrimination. Three Supreme Court justices—Burger, Blackmun, and Powell—have actually stated for the record that whether the Supreme Court applies this strict test in sex discrimination cases or not—in other words, whether or not women's rights will be vigorously protected and consistently enforced—depends on whether the ERA is ratified and becomes part of the Constitution.

Big Lie Number Four: Women Don't Need the ERA Because Federal and State Laws Are Enough to Ensure That They Have Equal Rights

ERA foes would have us believe that discrimination against women is a "thing of the past"—if it ever occurred at all. They would have us believe that there are no laws that discriminate against us, and, in fact, that there are lots of laws protecting us from discrimination.

The Truth During the 1960s and 1970s, due to the heroic efforts of women's rights advocates, a number of important laws protecting women from discrimination *were* passed—despite the efforts of ERA opponents. For example, when Title VII of the Civil Rights Act of 1964 was passed, it marked the first time that American women working for companies or agencies that receive federal money could seek relatively quick redress for discrimination. Another example of a good law is Title IX of the Higher Education Act of 1972, prohibiting discrimination against women in college and university academic and sports programs. The enforcement of this law was one of the main reasons American women did so well in the 1984 Olympics.

But, without the constitutional protection of the ERA, good laws like Title VII and Title IX are not necessarily enforced. They may be ignored, weakened through narrow court interpretation or lack of funding, or even repealed. And this is precisely what has been happening since 1980, which, not coincidentally, marked the end of a forty-year-long commitment by the Republican Party to the ERA.

Indeed, it is a supreme irony of modern history that the very president who argued that women do not need the ERA by his own actions and inactions, *conclusively proved* that American women *must* have the constitutional protection that only ERA can provide.

Ronald Reagan promised that, once elected, he would see to it that existing laws protecting women from sex discrimination were more vigorously enforced—in lieu of the ERA. Instead, his administration systematically ensured that good laws like Title VII and Title IX were *weakened* or *not enforced*. For example, instead of giving more support to the Department of Labor office charged with promoting equal rights and employment opportunities for women, the Reagan Administration deliberately slashed the budget of this crucial office, the Women's Bureau, *far more* than all the others—28%. This cut compared with only 5.5% average cuts for other Department of Labor offices—or almost 600 percent higher!

Another element of Ronald Reagan's highly touted "ERA Alternative"—the elimination, law by law, of 114 federal statutes that still blatantly discriminate on the basis of sex—was, to quote the project's former director, Barbara Honnegger, a "complete sham." Since this brave woman resigned in protest, there has been *no* effort to eliminate or correct the many sections of the U.S. Code that adversely affect women's jobs and educational opportunities in such broad areas as welfare, Social Security, Indian affairs, homesteading, transportation, agriculture, immigration and naturalization, the military, annuities, pensions, and retirement provisions—many of which actually enforce inequities against women.

Perhaps most ironic, and destructive, is that far from seeing to it, as promised, that the Fourteenth Amendment was used to prevent sex-based discrimination, the Reagan Justice Department—under the direction of a Solicitor General who opposed both the ERA and Title IX—took advantage of the absence of the ERA to substantially weaken *all* legal prohibitions against government discrimination.

In the now-famous case of *Grove City University v. Bell,* instead of intervening to obtain *stronger* enforcement of Title IX—the federal law enacted in 1972 forbidding discrimination in our nation's colleges and universities—the Reagan Justice Department instead asked the Supreme Court to radically *reduce* its scope of enforcement. By narrowing this once-important law's application from entire colleges to only the specific program within a college that receives federal funds, the Reagan Administration effectively removed all requirements that colleges and universities that receive your tax dollars must not discriminate against you throughout the school.

This decision, which would never have been possible had the ERA been in our Constitution, in effect made Title IX, though technically still on the books, a meaningless document. Even beyond this, is that the door has been opened to undermine all laws against discrimination. The key words in Title IX's language against sex discrimination weakened by the court are *identical* to the language in fifty-two *other* federal civil rights laws protecting all Americans against not only sex discrimination but also discrimination based on race, national origin, religion, physical handicap and age. So, *precisely because it first successfully opposed the ERA, the Reagan Administration in 1984 was able to gut fifty-two other critical civil rights laws—because there was this one vulnerable link in the entire fabric of civil rights laws: an insufficiently protected law against sex discrimination.*

Big Lie Number Five: The ERA is "A Radical Communist Plot" to Harm the Nation, the Family—and Women

According to ERA foes like the radical-right John Birch Society and Phyllis Schlafly's Eagle Forum, *whatever* one's hidden prejudice, pet peeve, or worst fear, the ERA is to blame.

The Truth Despite absurd charges of rightist-fundamentalist ERA opponents like Jerry Falwell and Fred Schwartz that the ERA will lead America down the "slippery slope to Communism," the truth is that the Communist Party U.S.A. actually went on record in 1970 *against* the Equal Rights Amendment!

Despite the fanning of ridiculous and false fears that ERA would result in unisex toilets, higher taxes, homosexual marriages, the spread of AIDS, and every other conceivable—and inconceivable—social disruption, the extensive Congressional hearings on the original intent of the ERA (which are many thousands of pages long) make it crystal clear that this simple Amendment to our Constitution is intended to do only what it *says* it will do. That is to require that our state and federal laws and regulations treat women as equal citizens, and not discriminate against them simply because they are women.

Despite all the inflammatory rhetoric about the ERA hurting family stability and swelling divorce rates in America, the truth is that in those states where equality between men and women is *more,* not less, valued—as evidenced by their ratification of the ERA—there is *stronger,* not weaker, family cohesion. According to the National Center for Health Statistics, the divorce rate is higher in states which did *not* ratify the ERA. For instance, in Massachusetts, which ratified the ERA, the divorce rate in 1981 was 2.9 per 1,000 marriages per year; whereas, in Utah, which did not ratify the Amendment, and which is the stronghold of the fiercely anti-ERA Mormon Church, the divorce rate was 5.5 percent per 1,000 marriages per year! Similarly, in New York and Pennsylvania, which both ratified the Amendment, the divorce rates in 1981 were only 3.3 and 3.2 per 1,000 marriages per year, respectively. But in Oklahoma and Arkansas, which did not ratify the ERA, they were as high as 7.9 and 9.2 per 1,000 marriages per year!

Despite all the untrue statements about how the ERA would "deprive married women of the right to support," "rob divorced women of alimony," or "require mothers to be sent into combat duty," the Equal Rights Amendment will in reality *vastly improve,* rather than in any way hurt, the lives of just such women, and of *all* American women.

For example, the extensive Congressional hearings on the ERA established that the ERA would be a major step toward providing American homemakers with fairer Social Security payments (instead of receiving only 85% of what their husbands would have received), as well as requiring that public employees' pensions and welfare programs meet the ERA's mandate of fairness. It would also require that laws and regulations which currently discriminate against women—for example, laws that deny unemployment insurance to women unable to work during pregnancy or require pregnant workers to take unpaid leaves, and regulations permitting health and life insurance premiums that are substantially higher for women—be replaced by fair laws.

The experience with State ERAs further shows how the federal ERA would benefit women in all the States. For example, in Pennsylvania, which is one of six states that have their own state ERAs substantially identical to the proposed federal ERA, the old legal presumption that a husband is the owner of all household goods was struck down as violating that State's ERA. In New Mexico, another State with its own ERA, a law which allowed a judge to give instructions to the jury in a rape trial suggesting that the victim's testimony should be less credible because of "the nature of the crime," was struck down as violating the State's ERA.

But the battle for fair and equal treatment of American women cannot be, and will not be, won on a state-by-state basis. We have neither the years nor the resources for such a long, cumbersome and costly fight. Moreover, such a strategy would do nothing to correct or eliminate discriminatory federal laws and regulations, or discriminatory educational and employment practices funded by federal money (that is, our *own* money), essentially forcing women to subsidize discrimination against themselves.

As the Executive Committee of the Congressional Caucus for Women's Issues wrote in 1983, American women need the ERA to secure equal justice under the law. It is as simple as that. *Only* the Equal Rights Amendment can and will enshrine in our Constitution the fundamental principle that equality under the law, regardless of the gender of American citizens, is and should be a basic assumption—*an inalienable right and a moral imperative*—under which we live and work together as a Nation.

Public Information Facts, Strategies, and Tactics

Proponents of the ERA sometimes have difficulty getting across the fact that women are legally "second class" citizens, particularly when those who feel threatened by the ERA are declaring vociferously that they do not "feel" second-class! A major reason is that until very recently there has been a dearth of *facts* about women, with most of what is taught us presenting primarily data about men.

Until the advent of "Women's Studies" departments on college campuses in the 1970s, the writing of history has been, by and large, the work of men. For nearly two centuries, female school children have suffered the drawing of a veil over their mind's eye as they have been fed a carefully controlled diet of the exploits of "great men" of history, interspersed only briefly with an anecdote about Betsy Ross sewing the flag or Molly Pitcher carrying water to the battlefield.

Not a word was there ever to enlighten a young girl when she was taught to recite the Declaration of Independence that the glowing words of "all men are created equal" did not include her. Nor did she hear about the long and bitter struggle of our foremothers to gain their property rights and the right to vote.

Too many of these young girls have first had to grow up from being "cheerleaders" to "displaced homemakers" before the veil of illusion was pierced and they understood all too painfully the real status of females in the United States.

It is a sad fact that still today too many females, of all ages, cannot name the year or the number of the amendment to the Constitution that won for women the vote. Nor do they know about the long struggle women had even to obtain this most elementary of all political rights.

In June 1982, during the close contest over the ERA in the Illinois Legislature, the campaign for ratification was brought to a point of intensity with the arrival of the little band of "hunger fasters." Under the leadership of Sonia Johnson, the ex-communicated Mormon who wrote the story of her life and battle with the Mormon hierarchy in the book *From Housewife to Heretic* (Doubleday, 1981), these women gained attention for ERA by announcing they would fast until the critical vote. But, as she recounts in the film documentary about the Illinois campaign ("Fighting for the Obvious"), former Illinois Representative Susan Catania had to explain to her "shocked" colleagues in the Illinois Assembly—both pro-ERA women and men—that these tactics were hardly new. Quite the contrary, the "fast" and the incident of women chaining themselves to the chamber galleries were strictly in the tradition of the tactics used by the suffragists who had gone to jail, had fasted and were force-fed, beaten, with at least one woman dying in a dungeon for the right of women to go to the polls. Still, not one of these Illinois legislators was familiar with this story of the bitter struggles of the suffragists.

The general ignorance about our real history was undoubtedly a major factor behind the failure of the proposed twenty-seventh amendment to the Constitution. The next campaign in Illinois and elsewhere will be successful only if the American public has the indisputable historical facts about the necessity for the Equal Rights Amendment to perfect a flawed democratic blueprint. More women and men will be spokespersons for the Equal Rights Amendment when they have it clear in their own minds how women got into the current dilemma. And when this information is more widely spread, ERA opponents will no longer be able to delude our countrywomen and men with the myth that American women are—and have traditionally been—truly honored both in law and life. . . .

Impact of ERA on Current Federal Laws That Sanction Inequality

Many an ERA supporter has had the frustrating experience of having a neighbor, friend, or opponent say, "Just tell me one good reason why we need the ERA." Of course, the massive injustice that women have suffered and continue to experience in this society cannot be summed up in "one good reason." But it is helpful to have a ready knowledge of specific laws that discriminate against women.

In a briefing paper prepared by the staff of the Congressional Caucus for Women's Issues in November 1983, the Caucus succinctly identified inequalities and discriminatory provisions under current laws and illustrated the remedies the ERA would provide in six major categories: Homemakers, Working Women, Education, Retirement, Insurance, and the Military.

We may also note here that what the ERA will mean depends on the "legislative history" made during consideration of the next ERA by Congress. When called upon to interpret this Amendment after its passage, the Supreme Court will look to the intent of Congress in passing the Amendment. Committee reports, the debates, and other official documents are the main components of the legislative history.

The Supreme Court will also consider the interpretations that state courts have made of ERAs in state constitutions. The Caucus briefing paper represents generally what the organizations supporting the ERA want expressed in the legislative history. . . .

ERA and the Homemaker

The ERA will recognize the economic partnership of marriage and will acknowledge the homemaker as an equal contributor to the family.

Background

Many laws and practices operate to deprive homemakers of economic security during marriage, upon divorce, or at widowhood, by failing to recognize their valuable contribution to their families and society. The homemaker's contribution is not viewed as economically equal to the breadwinner's. . . .

Homemakers lack basic legal rights concerning ownership, possession and control of marital property. In many states a married homemaker cannot obtain credit in her own name because it is assumed that only the wage-earning spouse controls assets. Some states will follow common-law practices that household goods purchased during marriage belong only to the husband unless the wife can show her monetary contribution to the purchase. . . .

Under the ERA, laws and court orders relating to domestic relations will be based on the principle that each spouse contributes equally to the marriage. The ERA will afford women a basis in law that entitles them to equal management and ownership of property acquired during the marriage.

Questions

Q. What effect would the ERA have on alimony and support awards?

A. Under the ERA, gender-neutral rules will require monetary and non-monetary contributions from both spouses in accordance with their means.

Q. Would men still have to support their wives under the ERA?

A. Many courts have refused to enforce the support obligations of husbands during marriage because of a reluctance to invade the privacy of marriage. (*Note from authors:* Florida is the only state that authorizes enforcement of support by the wife during marriage. The support laws have generally been used to enforce claims by third parties, such as funeral homes, state mental hospitals, and other hospitals.) As a result, even if a husband denies his wife money for her most basic needs—food, health care, clothes—she cannot, as long as she continues to live with him, expect a court to order him to provide reasonable expenses. ERA will have little impact on this unfortunate situation. However, in the event the marriage dissolves, the homemaker's nonmonetary contributions to the family will receive fair recognition in dividing marital property.

Q. Would the ERA force a divorced mother to work in order to meet her obligation of equal support for the children?

A. No. This issue has been litigated in Pennsylvania under the state ERA. The court recognized the importance of the custodial parent's role in staying home with the children. Defining rights and responsibilities in sex-neutral terms means that both breadwinners and homemakers are entitled to legal and economic recognition, not that each must perform both functions.

Sexist assumptions in Social Security work against the homemaker in various ways:

★ The unpaid homemaker receives absolutely no disability protection for herself or her family; her survivors receive no benefits. The assumption is that homemakers do not work.

★ If divorced before ten years of marriage, homemakers have no coverage for those years. Since approximately one-third of all marriages dissolve before the tenth year, a significant number of women lose financial security.

★ If an employed married woman leaves the paid labor force to care for her family, she is penalized by having zero earnings entered into her savings history and her benefits are reduced.

Q. How would ERA affect homemaker's Social Security benefits?

A. Social Security provisions harm women because they are premised on sex-based assumptions that fail to recognize the economic value of work in the home, the discriminatory wage structure in the labor force, and the unique work patterns of women as they temporarily drop out of the labor force to raise children. ERA would require the reexamination of sexist assumptions that underlie the Social Security system.

ERA and Working Women

The ERA will strengthen existing prohibitions against sex discrimination in the work place and require uniform enforcement of current laws which outlaw bias in wages, fringe benefits, hiring practices, and other conditions of employment.

Background

The increased labor force participation of women is one of the most important labor market trends of this century. Forty-three percent of all women are working outside the home today, more than ever before. In 1981, over half of all married women were working, up from 24% in 1950. Forty-eight percent of women with children under six, and 63% of women with children between the ages of six and seventeen were in the labor force.

Growth in the number of single women heading households has been dramatic. Accompanying this trend has been a phenomenon known as the feminization of poverty—more than half of the total number of poor families in this nation are maintained by women. Almost three-quarters of minority children in female-headed households live in poverty. If this trend continues, it is estimated that 100% of the poverty-striken in the year 2000 will be women and their children.

If wives and female heads of households were paid in the wages that similarly qualified men earn, about half of the families now mired in poverty would not be poor.

Discrimination against women in the market place has not been eradicated, despite laws on the books to protect them. Title VII of the Civil Rights Act of 1964 prohibits employment discrimination and the Equal Pay Act of 1963 requires wage equity, but in 1983 women continue to earn only 59% of men's income. (*Authors' note:* The National Commission on Working Women reports that in 1983 women constituted almost 80% of all clerical workers. Their wages were 68.8% of men's. Even when men and women worked in the same job category, male earnings were still higher than female earnings.) These equal employment laws and affirmative action policies are simply inadequate, unevenly applied, and often loosely enforced. And, as with all statutes, they can be repealed or weakened at any time, or simply not be enforced by the agencies charged with that responsibility.

Moreover, even statutes such as Title VII and the Equal Pay Act are inadequate to address one of the most powerful forces against economic equity for women—occupational segregation. Most working women are concentrated in a small number of relatively poorly paid occupations. Studies show that jobs viewed as "women's work" are lower paid simply because they are "women's work," regardless of the skill, responsibility, or training required to do them.

A statute-by-statute approach to remedying economic bias does not work. Only a constitutional guarantee of equal employment opportunities for women can get at the root of the problem. . . .

The ERA would prohibit sex discrimination by public employers, prompt state legislatures to repeal discriminatory laws, and guide the courts when enforcing the laws. So-called "protective legislation" restricting the types of jobs women can hold and the hours they can work would be repealed. Loopholes and exceptions in equal employment laws would be closed.

Questions

Q. What effect would the ERA have on veterans' preference in public employment?

A. It should be noted, first of all, that public employment has always been an important source of jobs for women. There are currently some veterans' preference schemes so extreme that women have been virtually excluded from the upper levels of state employment, relegated to clerical and support positions, no matter how qualified. Programs to reward our veterans reentering the work force would have to be more narrowly tailored and carefully weighed against the ERA's prohibitions against sex discrimination so as not to unduly limit employment opportunities for women.

Q. How would the ERA affect seniority systems?

A. Genuine nondiscriminatory seniority systems would not be struck down by the ERA. However, in cases where these systems mask actions which exclude women from jobs or job advancement, deny them adequate pay, or make them more likely to be laid off, seniority would be subject to challenge. Every major labor union in the nation supports the ERA.

Q. How would the ERA affect employment and pregnancy?

A. Work policies prohibiting pregnant women from working, laws denying unemployment benefits to pregnant women, and plans revoking accrued seniority and fringe benefits following temporary leaves of absence due to pregnancy have created powerful obstacles to women in the work place. Current law offers protection against some of these practices, but are subject to the threat of repeal and less than aggressive enforcement. The constitutional guarantees of the ERA would ensure that pregnant workers continue to be treated as individuals—sick leave, disability pay, and other health benefits would be granted to them on the same basis as to other disabled workers.

ERA and Education

The ERA will require that all publicly supported schools at all levels eliminate practices which discriminate against women. It will not tell schools what to do, but only that whatever they do, they must do fairly.

Background

Sex discrimination in education reflects and perpetuates the discrimination women face throughout their adult lives. It begins in grade school with sex stereotyped texts that portray boys as leaders and achievers and girls as followers and watchers, continues through high schools where boys learn to operate machines and girls learn to keep house, and culminates in universities with weighted admissions policies, limited women's athletic programs and courses of study.

No one can deny the importance of education in determining life and employment opportunities. One-half of all women work; two-thirds work out of economic necessity. Yet women's educational preparation for the job market is heavily weighted in favor of low paying, dead-end jobs. In vocational courses, women have been concentrated in home economics, health, office occupations and consumer and home-making programs, while men have dominated technical, agricultural, trade and industrial programs that lead to higher paying jobs. At a time when our society is moving into an advanced technological era, when math and science training is essential for jobs in high technology and other growing employment fields, 83% of home economics students are female, while 94% of trades and industry students are male.

Questions

Q. What impact would the ERA have on single-sex public schools?

A. The ERA would mandate that public schools could not continue discriminatory practices—they would have to integrate. . . .

Q. Would sports teams have to be integrated?

A. The ERA would accommodate the maintenance of all-female teams where necessary to guarantee equality of athletic opportunity. But women qualified to play on all-male teams would be allowed to do so.

Q. Would ERA outlaw fraternities, sororities and other private clubs and associations at colleges and universities?

A. Purely private and social organizations would not be affected by the ERA. If such organizations were supported with public funds or were so interwoven with the academic life of an institution as to represent official action, the ERA would apply. (See *Iron Arrow Honor Society v. Heckler*, 51 U.S.L.W. 2649, 11th Cir. 4-11-83.)

Q. Would sleeping facilities and bathrooms have to be integrated?

A. No. The right to privacy is not in conflict with the ERA. Privacy cannot be a subterfuge for providing unequal opportunity, however.

ERA and Retirement

The ERA will strike overt discriminatory laws from the books and open the door to challenge superficially sex neutral laws that have a discriminatory impact on women.

Background

The "pension game" is one that the American woman almost always loses. Most retirement systems, designed to reward the long-term, steady worker with low mobility and high earnings, do not reflect modern work and family patterns, and do not apply to most women. . . .

The presumption of dependency works against all women, especially in the Social Security system. If a husband and wife jointly own a business or farm, benefits accrue in his name. If the wife is disabled, she has no credits on which to seek benefits. Because of the principle of only paying one worker in a couple, a two-earner couple with the same income as a one-earner couple receives lower benefits. In 1979, 2.3 million retired women who paid Social Security taxes were no better off than had they never worked for pay and never contributed to Social Security. The net result is a growing population of elderly, poor women. Eighty-five percent of the elderly poor are single women; 60% of them depend solely on Social Security for their income. Yet, in 1983 the average Social Security payment for women sixty-five or older was $4,476, compared to $5,725 for men.

Inequities in pension systems compound the problem. Regulations which ignore women's typical work patterns, such as minimum participation age and vesting requirements, coupled with inadequate provision for survivor benefits, mean that in 1981 only 10% of retirement age women received a pension, compared to 28% of retirement age men. Even if a woman does have a pension based on her own earnings, the average benefit is only 59% of a man's average benefit, reflecting continuation of the wage gap into old age.

Pensions must accommodate today's work patterns and needs of women in order to offer a decent standard of living after retirement.

Questions

Q. Since most women live longer than most men, isn't it fair to have a different contribution and payout schedule under pension plans?

A. Most older women do *not* live longer than most men of the same age. In a random sample of 1,000 men and 1,000 women age sixty-five, 86% of men and women matched in death ages. Life expectancy differences between men and women reflect nothing more than group averages applied to individuals. Moreover, a recent National Research Council study has revealed that the overwhelming reason for the difference in life expectancy at birth between men and women is smoking: the life expectancy figures for non-smoking men and non-smoking women were identical. Other factors, more reliable and specific than sex, should be used in annuity and pension calculations.

Q. Won't the elimination of sex-based actuarial tables, now widely used in pension plans, impose a tremendous administrative burden on companies?

A. Under Title VII of the Civil Rights Act, the Supreme Court has already determined that sex-based actuarial tables cannot be used to force women to contribute more to a pension plan for equal benefits (*Manhart*) or to receive lower benefits for the same contribution (*Norris*). However, these decisions affect only employer-sponsored pension plans and many women are not covered by such plans. The ERA is necessary to expand and cement these principles in all pension plans.

Q. Won't it cost millions to equalize pension payouts?

A. The industry estimates that $2 billion will be required to equalize pension payouts. While that seems like a lot of money, it is only three-tenths of 1% of current pension fund assets.

ERA and the Military

The ERA will prohibit denying women entry, promotion, education, and training in the service branches solely and exclusively on the basis of gender.

Background

The military is the largest employer and educator in the nation and yet is virtually immune from policies and laws prohibiting sex discrimination. These restrictions jeopardize the women who must serve in dangerous military situations without the training and support essential to survival. Further, they perpetrate harmful, archaic, and overboard stereotypes about the capabilities of women and the role of women and men in society. Exclusion from full participation in military service also means lost opportunities for college scholarships, veterans' education benefits, veterans' preference in government employment, veterans' insurance and loan programs, and limited access to the revolving door of the military/industrial connection—where the private sector pays well for the defense-related skills of former service members.

Exclusion of women from the military is an economic issue. The Texas Population Research Center has just released data showing that among employed women of all races, those who have served in the Armed Forces are almost twice as likely to earn salaries at least $300 per week better than those women who have not.

Questions

Q. Would women be eligible for the draft under the ERA?

A. Under the ERA, women would be treated equally with men with regard to registration for the draft. However, certain women, like certain men, may be exempted from the draft as conscientious objectors, the parents of dependent children, or because of medical reasons. Once inducted, men and women would be assigned responsibilities on the basis of service needs and individual qualifications, not gender.

Q. If the ERA is *not* enacted, are women protected from the draft?

A. No. The Department of Defense has already prepared legislation designed to alter existing law so that both sexes can be subject to future conscriptions.

Q. Would the ERA result in women being assigned to combat duties?

A. There is no current statute or policy that defines "combat." Combat exclusion rules are often inconsistent among the service branches and have been altered many times over the years. These rules reflect the needs of each service; they are not designed to protect women. Women, like men, will be assigned to those jobs for which they are qualified.

Q. Would the ERA eliminate job-related qualifications in the military?

A. No, just the reverse. Under the ERA, all military positions, including combat positions, would be filled by the most qualified individuals available. Women and men who are physically or psychologically unsuited for a combat-related job would be excluded from such an assignment.

Q. What effect would the eligibility of women for combat have on military effectiveness?

A. Despite repeated studies to establish the limits of our military women's capabilities, no such limitation has been demonstrated. Army studies show that increasing the proportion of women in combat support and combat service support units has no measurable effect on unit performance in field training exercises.

[End of excerpts from 1983 Congressional Caucus for Women's Issues Briefing Paper.]

Short History of the Equal Rights Amendment

1848   First Women's Rights Convention in Seneca Falls, New York, marks official birth of movement for equal rights in the United States. Elizabeth Cady Stanton proclaims all men *and women* are created equal.

1868   Fourteenth Amendment, including clause guaranteeing all persons equal protection under the law, becomes part of U.S. Constitution. Clause 2 provides for lowered representation for states that restrict right to vote of any qualified *male* citizen.

1870   Fifteenth Amendment guaranteeing black males right to vote becomes part of U.S. Constitution. Despite efforts by feminists, provision guaranteeing white and black women right to vote is not included.

1920   After more than three quarters of a century of struggle, Nineteenth Amendment guaranteeing women right to vote becomes part of U.S. Constitution.

1923   Because U.S. courts consistently fail to include women under the definition of persons protected under Equal Protection clause of the Fourteenth Amendment, under leadership of Alice Paul, Equal Rights Amendment is first introduced in U.S. Congress. Called the "Lucretia Mott Amendment," original version authored by Alice Paul reads: "Men and women shall have equal rights throughout the United States and in every place subject to its jurisdiction."

1943   Convinced that amendment would not pass with original wording, Alice Paul consents to rewording: "Equality of rights under the law shall not be denied or abridged by the United States or any state on account of sex."

1972   After introduction in Congress for forty-nine years, with numerous Congressional hearings, ERA is passed by U.S. Congress.

1973   ERA has been ratified by thirty-one states; only seven more states are needed.

1974   Two more states ratify ERA. The total is now thirty-three, so that only five more states are needed. But a well-financed, slanderous anti-ERA campaign is launched. John Birch Society, Phyllis Schlafly, and Christian Anti-Communist Crusade call ERA a subversive communist plot—even though Communist Party USA went on record in 1970 opposing ERA!

1975   North Dakota ratifies the ERA. Four more states are needed.

1977   January 18—Indiana becomes 35th state to ratify ERA. November 18–21-First National Women's Conference held in Houston, Texas, attended by 20,000 women, including Rosalyn Carter, Betty Ford, and Lady Bird Johnson. Conference is part of formal U.S. participation in First United Nations Decade for Women. It adopts a National Plan of Action which has passage of ERA as its first priority. National Women's Conference Committee is charged with implementation of National Plan of Action.

1978   Anti-ERA campaign has successfully blocked further state ratifications. As March 22, 1979 deadline approaches, ERA is still three states short of ratification. ERA Extension March for Equality of 100,000 in Washington, D.C. is spearheaded by NOW. U.S. Congress approves bill introduced by Representative

Elizabeth Holtzman (D.N.Y.) extending ratification deadline to June 30, 1982.

1979 ERA opponents file suit in Federal Court challenging the constitutionality of the ERA deadline extension. Case is assigned to Judge Marion Callister, a high official in the Mormon Church, which that same year excommunicates Sonia Johnson for her activities in support of ERA.

1980 Republican Party platform and presidential candidate Ronald Reagan reverse Republican Party's traditional pro-ERA position.

Democratic National Convention reaffirms support for ERA and adds platform pledge to withhold campaign funds and assistance from candidates who do not support ERA.

1981 Judge Callister rules ERA extension void, but Supreme Court stays ruling pending ERA ratification.

1982 Despite close votes in Florida, Illinois, and North Carolina, no more states ratify and ratification deadline expires.

Although ERA has been ratified by states representing the numerical majority of American population and polls show majority of Americans favor proposed amendment, it fails to be ratified by three additional states needed for it to become part of the United States Constitution. July 14, ERA is reintroduced in Ninety-seventh Congress.

1983 Equal Rights Amendment is again reintroduced in Congress (Ninety-eighth) on January 3rd with 230 co-sponsors in the House, but passage falls six votes short in November 1983 House vote.

1984 First woman in American history to be nominated for Vice President, Geraldine Ferraro runs on Democratic ticket, strongly endorsing ERA.

1985 Equal Rights Amendment is reintroduced in both houses of Ninety-ninth Congress on January 3, first day of new legislative session.

8

Distortions in Understanding: How Patriarchy Affects Our Minds

Mind Control as an Instrument of Patriarchy

Despite the incredible injustice done to women, few people of either sex take the whole business seriously. In fact, many find the conflict ridiculous if not meaningless. Such people point out that women as well as men are in the nonfeminist or antifeminist camp. Don't they, too, laugh at the jokes? Don't they back legislators and legislation against so-called women's rights? And even if all this nonsense has anything to it, women are their own worst enemies, now, aren't they?

It is true that women have acted side by side with men in the control of women by patriarchy. If one thinks for a minute of the tremendous feat involved in the subjugation of one half of the world's population by the other half, one sees that it would have to be so. Women are and always have been more than half the human population, and there could have been great power in that numerical superiority had it been tapped. Women can be creative, resourceful, and courageous, and we could have stood on our own behalf. Yet for centuries women have typically

supported the patriarchal status quo, have "backed our men," and have demanded that our daughters and granddaughters do so as well, binding their feet and their minds and instructing them in the duties of being good women. How are we to account for that? Could there be something to the charge that we women are our own worst enemies or that there is simply nothing to bother about? Or does the answer lie elsewhere?

Students of politics and government often talk of the impossibility of world domination by a monolithic power on the grounds of size and space. It would be unlikely, they argue, that any power could draw a policing network so encompassing or an executive agency so vast that it could maintain worldwide control. And yet, although patriarchal societies are not themselves a monolith, patriarchy per se is, and for centuries it has maintained a grip of control over women and over the substructures that guide the political, economic, and cultural arrangements governing our lives. How does it do this?

It is neither a new nor a surprising idea that the most potent form of control is one that reigns not over the body but over the mind. Science fiction and cold war drama are full of stories about brainwashing and mind control. To place into the belief system of an individual the idea that the restraints governing her or him are inevitable, right, proper, and desirable is to place a perpetual sentry at the door to a free existence. Given this, there is no need for external guards. So long as the belief remains, the job is done and the control is intact.

Some time ago, at a conference of the Society for Women in Philosophy, as the members were discussing the nature of domination and control, one woman suggested that the most stable and effective form of slavery was one in which the oppressed group were socialized to love their slavery. A second woman countered that an even more perfect form of slavery was one in which the slaves were *unaware* of their condition, unaware that they were controlled, believing instead that they freely chose their life and situation. The control of women by patriarchy is effected in just such a way, by mastery of beliefs and attitudes through the management of all the agencies of thought formation.

For the most part, without counterbalancing ideas and perspectives, most women (and men) are unaware that their behavior, opportunities, and life possibilities are controlled by the gender system and that women do not freely come to choose "femininity" and its trappings. Women and men really live and move in two different conceptual universes. We see the world, value systems, and ourselves differently because in the most pointed ways patriarchy has arranged for the agencies of thought (for example, education, art, and the media) to foster and maintain two separate conceptual environments in which to learn, grow, and act; our world has two separate images of reality to absorb. Not only are women and men trained to divergent perspectives on the world, but we also come to have divergent postures to life and to the inner reality. We come to answer differently the questions, Who am I? What am I? What shall I be?

If patriarchy is to prevail, it must instill its consciousness into the minds of its subjects, particularly women, since the rebellion of women would mean its demise. Let us sharpen our awareness of the many ways that patriarchal culture exerts control over our understanding. Let us look at some of the more powerful agencies of idea formation, their means and their products.

Education

One learns patriarchal consciousness in many ways, from formal teaching environments to informal or subliminal messages. Schools, from the primary grades through college, do not promote teaching only the three Rs and the officially recognized "knowledge" in books and curricula. Self-consciously or not, they also foster values, attitudes, expectations, and world views. In functioning both as trainer for participation in the wider society and as a reflection of that society, the schools transmit the rather traditional views on sexual identity and very early convey, create, and reinforce in females and males the segregated conceptual systems of the sexes.

The Environment

Consider the administrative hierarchy of the typical primary school and high school. Parallel to the arrangement of women and men in most institutions (male doctor to female assistants, male manager to clerks or secretaries, male pilot to his hostesses, male always in charge), the school presents to the students the traditional picture of masculine power. On the front lines, in the classrooms and in the outer offices behind typewriters, one finds women—accessible, concrete, "live" personnel. In the inner office, apart from the common folk, distant and powerful, resides the principal, who, in more than 95 percent of the cases in the United States, is a male. Further removed and even more powerful are the school boards and the superintendents, of whom approximately 97 percent are male.

Female teachers often function with regard to the principal in the same way that female parents at home appear to function with regard to male parents. They maintain policy set by the authority figure, but when children are very difficult, they are sent to that ultimate power for more "meaningful" discipline. When, on occasion, the principal visits the classroom, students are aware that something special is happening. The effect on both female and male children is potent and enduring. The arrangement says something very different to boys and girls about what they may become, what they can expect of people in life, and what they can do and accomplish. Given such environmental cues, the consciousness of the two sexes forms rather differently.

The cues gain credence and depth as they are played out in the same environment among the children themselves. Children are separated and reminded that they are different: *Boys on this side of the room, girls over there*. Their sense of competition is deepened: *Let's have a contest, boys against the girls*. Their place on the power-strength continuum is fixed: *I want three boys to carry the projector for me*. Little girls are taught to "behave like ladies": *Keep your legs down. Don't be rowdy*. Boys are told to be nice young *men* or to help little Suzy. In my daughter's kindergarten room, toys were arranged against two walls—dolls, cradle, ironing board, brooms, and cupboards on one side; trucks, blocks, and a horse on the other. Circumstances do not change in high school. Boys gravitate to science and technology, girls to literature. Boys begin to excel, and girls to channel their interest away from study and toward pleasing the boys. In my high school, girls were required to take shop, but we spent that semester making jewelry while the boys made wooden cabinets.

Physical education with different expectations train differently not only the body but also the mind. Boys' team sports—competitive, aggressive and demanding—teach the participants teamwork, the value of practice and readiness, the effectiveness of perseverance and determination, the willingness to face risk for gain. Girls interested in sports are poorly supported, financially or emotionally. The super femmes lead cheers. They win their kudos standing on the sideline in abbreviated frocks, tossing their bodies and shouting, "Come on, men!"

Consider for a moment the effects of those two different vantage points and the self-perceptions, abilities, and lessons gleaned from them. Think about those two so different sets of perceptions—*I, player* and *I, cheerleader; I, center* and *I, periphery*—and how they will function twenty years later.

The Curriculum

The school system, through its structures and patterns of education, says different things to female and male students because it evolves out of a sexist society. So do the people within them. Teachers, principals, authors, and scientists who grow and work in a sexist environment quite naturally develop sexist world views, beliefs, and perspectives. What they say and teach is therefore also sexist. Books, films, magazines, pamphlets, and papers are usu-

ally sexist; they are used by teachers who rarely notice or question that perspective and so are presented as truth. Sexist theories presented as truth in books have the weight of all history behind them. Even more than propositions about women and men that are consciously and pointedly spoken, the unspoken or subliminal statement has power because it is not even available for comment or critique.

From nursery school through college, then, the learning experience—both formal and supportive—is different for females and males. Traditional behaviors for each sex are taught, rewarded, and required, usually unconsciously. Different images of what women and men are and should be are communicated by the people in institutions and validated by the history of "truth" as maintained in the books.

Females are presented with the same vision of themselves that we meet in the culture at large. From books, teachers, counselors, extracurricular activities, and aptitude tests, we learn to be passive, quiet, nurturing, surreptitiously bossy, incompetent ladies, wives, and mothers and all the rest of the baggage that makes up the content of sexism. Given the power of the school experience—and given its early, continuous, and pervasive entry into our lives—it is hardly surprising that we should imbibe its formulations, believe them, and internalize them.

Education is, therefore, one of the major contributors to the fixing of a "feminine" (that is, masculist) consciousness in women, the consciousness that allows patriarchy to prevail in our own private worlds because it appears "right." If the schools, the teachers, and textbooks say it is right, who then are we to say it is wrong?

Change

Since the impetus of the women's movement and Title IX, sensitivity to sex imbalance is increasing at the college level, in high schools, even in Parent-Teachers Associations and school boards. For teachers now in training, courses on sexism in education are frequently available. Book publishers, newly sensitized to the issue by groups such as the National Organization for Women (NOW) and the Women's Equity Action League (WEAL), are setting new guidelines for language and expression. Schools are integrating the gym classes and the playing teams. Universities and professional schools are under pressure to add women to their faculty and staff not only for their own benefit but also as role models for the next generation of contributors.

In any society the educational process, both formal or otherwise, is a primary effector of enculturation and a major arm of social control and stability. We must expect it, on the one hand, to reflect the beliefs of the wide culture and thus to be basically conservative. On the other hand, in our times, education presents itself as well in another image—as the purveyor of knowledge and truth, as a foil to hardening of the intellectual arteries, as the proponent of constructive growth and change. That is an impressive image, believed by many, that carries with it an impressive responsibility: the duty to ensure that, however difficult the task, new insights and understanding will be absorbed and integrated into the existing body of knowledge and passed on to the next generation. In that duty lies the hopeful optimism of women's studies and contemporary feminists. It is the reason for treating the educational system as a primary target for vigilance and activity.

The Media

A medium, in the sense referred to here, is a mode or agency of public thought communication. In our culture, the important media include newspapers, radio and television, magazines, advertising, books, and films. They are the primary means of carrying ideas among the various segments of the population. Media not only carry information, they are also very powerful in framing attitudes and forming opinions. In a word, media teach, and they teach not only with what they say but also with how they say it.

Television, Magazines, News Reporting

One of the most pervasive elements of media in our lives, especially for children, is television. More than any other modern invention, television has affected the content of our thought because it so thoroughly pervades our conscious waking time, for some people as much as five or six hours a day, starting so early in life for many. During those hours, we see programs and advertising replete with the traditional stereotypes and images, the age-old misogynistic attitudes. On the sitcoms and weekly dramas are the long-suffering wives, the manipulative young beauties, the wronged lovers, the mindless females pursuing husbands, lovers, or other fantasies. In the West, women are dance-hall queens (prostitutes) or damsels in distress. In crime drama, they are the victims of bizarre crimes of murder and rape or perhaps the neglected wives of policemen or bad guys. Sometimes women manage to get on the police force, but they can usually be counted on to mess things up or become victimized in some way and to require saving by the male heroes. Exceptions now exist, thanks to the women's movement, but they are rare. The occasional single women, even the self-sufficient ones, tend to appear in light comedy. Seldom seen are staunch women, realistically presented, wrestling with the simple human problems and issues that we are all heir to.

Advertising, more insidious than even programming because it is more covert in its statements, offers the same fare. Here we see women still groaning over which laundry soap will work best on their teenager's dirt, twittering to one another over the joys of some toilet paper, and decaffeinating their husbands. Now and again we are presented with a professional woman, but she is generally a wife or mother madly juggling her time with the aid of product X so as not to neglect her family. On the other hand are the straight sexual ads: this perfume, hair color, soap, or toothpaste will give you the sex appeal you now lack; if you buy it, you will finally capture your elusive prince. Worse yet are the ads that use female bodies as a shill to the male buyer: semiclad sexpots smiling seductively, draped across automobiles or cooing over shaving cream.

Where are the real women, the millions of working women, the divorced and widowed women, the professional women, the intelligent competent women? Where are the items truly important to us, truly meaningful: dramas about women trying to break into professions; working to stay intact; struggling to hold down jobs, care for children, and maintain peace of mind all at the same time? Where are the products truly useful to us, those that really might save work rather than create it?

Magazines and newspapers are no better. Most women's magazines are typically owned and published by men. It is they who select the articles and the advertising. It is they who decide *and tell us* what women want to see or think about. Women's magazines are most commonly found at the checkout counter of supermarkets and discount stores. They are easily identifiable. On their covers one generally finds pictures of food, artistically presented, side by side with the scoop on the latest quick weight loss diet, or pictures of semi-naked women or pictures of movie and television stars. Inside one finds details on how to fix the wonderful recipes and make the family sit up and take notice (finally); details on how to do that diet, lose pounds and inches, look young again, and make one's husband sit up and take notice (finally); and failing that, how to get lost in the lives of others who were able to get people to sit up and take notice.

The problem of what is "real" and what is not is rather complex in terms of social presentation. The media not only reflect cultural images, but they also create, teach, and reify them as well. Girls and young women, constantly bombarded with certain images of beauty, are being taught that those images *are* beauty, that they should and must have it. Women who see themselves portrayed only as homemakers (happy or otherwise) or hip, sexy bombshells like the women of the soaps are being taught that women really are such things and are anomalous in any other guise. The woman who sees those images and does not fit them rarely says to herself, "Those images aren't real." Because she comes to those images with the unconscious working assumption that the media offer true representations of reality, she believes the images. For her, the images are real; thus, it is she who is not. She must either accept herself as anomaly (with all the attendant conflict) or change to conform. Until alternative visions are given realistic treatment by the mass media, until they are given social reification and approval by that treatment, they remain subversive, alien, or abnormal. Media treatment of alternative visions, however, has been sparse at best and generally well within the bounds of acceptable images. Women work, but they are models, highly paid executives in suits, or chic detectives. Unskinny women show up, but they are clowns, not lovers, with very few exceptions.

Language, of course, is central. The repeated, politically directed use of certain language, particularly words in juxtaposition, can either hide the real meaning of a concept or distort it radically. Consider the term *beauty pageant*. The name alone proclaims that the contestants are beautiful, that they repre-

sent beauty per se. But standards of beauty are not absolute. In 1956, my nineteenth-century European grandmother, for example, worried endlessly that my size 9 frame was far too skinny ever to lure a husband; would she find the undernourished contestants of today's pageants beautiful? And I wonder, after coming to terms with the artifice and plasticity of contemporary feminine makeup and mannerisms, after spending time with and learning to admire very different kinds of women, whether most women would indeed find the pageant contestants beautiful. Can the term itself be wrong? The power of language is such that it can distort reality to its own image. That is why the language and images the media employ have been such a focal point of the movement.

Art and Films

In a university where I taught, a young art instructor was made to remove his painting from a student-faculty art exhibit because his subject was a nude male with full portrayal of genitals. Several nudes (female nudes are always referred to simply as "nudes") remained aloft without comment, their breasts and pubes in plain view.

An avant-garde festival of erotic film at another university advertised itself with a poster picturing the face of the devil superimposed on the nude lower torso of a woman. Complaints to the administration by female faculty and students did not, however, bring it down.

Pop music, rock particularly, has become intensely misogynistic and savagely aggressive. Many all-male rock groups wear their sexuality as costume and chant diatribes against "silicone sisters" and delectable poison. Album covers have appeared depicting chained women, half-clad or sexually expressive, their chests to the floor, their heads beneath the shoe of some arrogant male, the leader of the group. The girls in the audience, "liberated" and "modern," scream for more, pay for the concerts, and buy the albums. The number of female rock groups or females in the groups is minuscule.

The sexism of current rock music is particularly destructive today. Modern technology, with its plug-yourself-in, take-anywhere radios and its high-gloss videos, has made the popular music culture an even more prominent and more attitude-forming phenomenon than it has been for generations past. It is ever present, totally penetrating, and inside the head. Thus its images come to pervade our awareness.

A popular video of the late 1980s, for example, *Addicted to Love,* presented a conservatively suited, well-dressed young man surrounded by several women, all identical. The women—each alike in costume, size, and thin, angular shape—were bizarrely made up so that only their lips, darkened eyes, and hairlines were prominent. Undulating in unison to the rhythm of the music, they were completely without expression or any sign of emotion. They were "sexy." The effect, in its way mesmerizing, was to depict the women not as persons but as caricatures, as clonelike robots, without individuality, identity, thought, or will. They had no humanity. They were props—interesting, decorative, seductive but not fully alive. What lesson does such an image teach men about women? What lesson does it teach women about ourselves? What behaviors does it justify, does it create?

The point of these representative instances is that the perspective is male. Nude women are respectable because men find them "beautiful," like to look at them, and are accustomed to employing them. Nude males are not respectable because the blatant presentation of the unadorned male body removes the aura of godliness, distance, and power from their persons and reduces them to the common, as women have been reduced. It is fashionable today for women to dress so as to display their bodies, and modern chic decrees that those who object are just not "with it." Women who deplore videos because of contemptuous treatment of women are simply dismissed as prudes and poor sports.

The male hegemony of consciousness sets the rules and standards. This is art; this is not. This is presentable; this is not. The depiction of naked women, invitingly arranged, is presentable art; the same depiction of men is irresponsible (and probably perceived as antimale). Literature relating to war, manhood, and mayhem is grandeur and art; that relating to childbirth, families, or women's experiences is petty craft of marginal interest.

The same circumstances obtain in the movies, that great shaper of American attitudes. In her study of the treatment of women in the movies, Molly Haskell explained that as the film industry has grown more and more to resemble an "art," with production of a film in the hands of one great "artist" (such as Bergman or Antonioni), the films increasingly reflect that (male) artist's point of view, and women's images have plunged.[1] Increasingly, the camera's eye is male; the film presents a man's view of reality, but, as de Beauvoir pointed out, in patriarchy maleness equals universality. Both men and women fail to realize that the film reflects a masculine consciousness. What effect does this have on society? What is the effect on men and women respectively?

Social Science

Science is an extremely important factor in the lives of twentieth-century people. Side by side with its data, procedures, and theories stands the scientific world view, an entire way of looking at truth and reality and of relating to life. Some social analysts have suggested that in contemporary times science functions much as a god or as a substitute for God, providing a basis for truth and knowledge, an agent to be trusted and depended on for salvation, even a ground of value.

Placing very high trust in the judgments of science and scientists is part of our cultural ethos. A large segment of the public maintains the belief that Science *is* Truth, the only dependable, sane truth for up-to-date, rational, right-minded people. The corollary to the Science-is-Truth theme is the notion that we should all live our lives in accordance with the truths of Science. Although the idea is rarely articulated in quite this way, a close appraisal of the new intellectual scene reveals the "modern" imperative: Live your life in such a way that Science would be proud of you. As medievals yearned to please God and stand in a state of grace, moderns yearn for a state of "health."

Because today's people want so badly to be judged "healthy," social science—that part of the investigative spectrum that focuses specifically on human behavior—has become very much like a faith. On at least two levels, as a technical-academic enterprise and as a "philosophy" of life for popular culture, social science—and especially psychology—serves as a kind of religion. It forms eternal verities about human nature and goals, decrees standards of perfection (health) toward which one is advised to strive, separates the "good" people (healthy, normal, "okay") from the bad (unhealthy, abnormal, "not okay"), determines social priorities both for individuals and for the state, and carries sufficient esteem in the community to socialize the population according to a certain vision of behavior.

Clearly the impact theories of social science have on the conduct of our lives is tremendous. For women that spells disaster because both the technical enterprise of the social sciences and the contemporary ethic that has evolved from it are rabidly sexist.

The Formal Enterprise

For a variety of reasons—the newness of the study, the complexity of its subject matter, and the absence of clearly articulated concepts and procedures—social science, at least for now and possibly forever, requires a far greater degree of interpretive latitude than its natural-science counterparts. That is a polite way of saying that social science is still quite subjective and thus resistant to the traditional forms of verification. Because of this, theories of the social sciences generally bear the mark of the people who develop them, and they tend to be "culture bound," reflective of both their time and place.

The culture and the greatest part of the personnel of the social sciences have always been predominantly male. For the most part, it was men who developed the methods of research and the procedures for verification; they also originated the earliest axioms and perspectives from which current developments have evolved, and they ultimately fixed the application of those perspectives, carrying theory out of the laboratory into the streets. With few exceptions, the women who gained some recognition for their work were adherents and popularizers of the existent male-identified systems rather than creators of their own models. In fact, their female support lent those antifemale systems greater weight not only in academe but also in the minds of the people who received them. Theories from the pens of men immersed in the Victorian world view brought all the familiar misogynistic stereotypes into greater respectability and enshrined them as science, or truth. At last it was not only taught by experience but was also explained by science that women are petty, self-centered, and unprincipled. Sigmund Freud, for example, had shown how such traits followed from penis envy and the castration complex.

Although some of the most blatant expressions of misogyny have changed (the expression, not the beliefs), the situation is little better today. Sexism in the social sciences is absolutely crucial to the formation and character of women's consciousness in contemporary society. The precepts of science and social science have become the theoretical underpinnings of the public-serving institutions of our culture—education, social service, or medicine—and through them misogynistic doctrines masquerading as scientific truth are being formally infused into our entire conceptual environment. Every teacher, social worker, nurse, and doctor has received the rudiments of elementary psychology and has been properly oriented to the importance of social "adjustment," strong male models, and clear sexual identity distinction. It is a rare child who escapes Erikson or Piaget, a rare ob-gyn patient who eludes Freud. Women are getting extra doses of distortion, officially sanctioned and therefore extremely powerful and convincing.

The other branch of the formal enterprise, the so-called helping professions, is similarly suffused with sexist ideology and perspective. As Phyllis Chesler has pointed out in her book *Women and Madness*, the helping professions may turn out to be more hindrance than help for the woman staggering under the collective weight of patriarchy's consciousness-shapers.

In the nineteenth century, science taught women that "self-abuse" (masturbation) was so damaging that it warranted removal of the clitoris if no other way could be found to stop the sinner-victim from practicing this foul habit. It taught that "ladies" (if not women) never had orgasms and would not want to. Using the label "ladies nostrums," it dosed women up with morphine and barbiturates so that they would not mind their boredom or their overwork or their frustration or their resentment at being controlled. For those few who would not be so easily cured and who could afford it, science recommended lobotomies or incarceration in "rest homes" or mental asylums.

The twentieth century brought us Freud, Spock, and the responsibility for our family's mental health—as if responsibility for their physical health was not enough! Any slip in toilet training, any lack of vigilance in answering questions immediately as they arise, and *wham*, mother makes a crazy child. The scientific and pop literature of the 1950s was full of warnings about the hazards for children whose mother worked outside the home. "Latch-key kids" were likely to be maladjusted at best, prone to crime and drugs at worst. Today, as the economy *requires* mothers and wives to work, studies are emerging that document the unreliability of any evidence that children reared in homes where mothers work are at all different from children of the Beaver Cleaver model home. In fact, evidence shows a slightly higher inclination to autonomy and adaptability in children whose moms work, not bad traits altogether. But how much guilt have women suffered and are still suffering because "science" scared them to death?

Today science tells us that comparable worth programs are unfeasible, that fetuses are babies, that healthy people are heterosexual (and preferably married), and that physical fitness requires us to be skinny. All of us must turn a critical eye to anything we are taught and certainly to received opinion. That is the heart of learning and wisdom. But women must be especially wary because so often we are barred from participating in the creation of "received opinion." So often that opinion is an amalgam of flimsy data and a political agenda created by men.

Religion

Religion as it is practiced through or by the social institutions of a people is as much a reflection and expression of that culture's ideals, attitudes, and needs as it is their creator. The Judeo-Christian tradition of the West is, of course, no exception. As Western culture is patriarchal, so is its religion, and so is its god.

Although most major religions argue that God is without sex, neither female nor male, that contention is contradicted by a host of beliefs indicating the maleness of their anthropomorphic gods. Currently some fathers of the various Christian churches have opposed the ordination of women on the grounds that it would be sacrilegious because the maleness of Christ proves that only men were meant for the priestly office. In medieval times the Church explained that women rather than men were likely to be witches because, among other things, men had been saved from that most awful danger by the fact that Christ was male. Today the use of feminine pronouns, *she* or *her*, to refer to the deity brings a very hostile response. Certainly the Catholic imagery of the Church standing analogously to Christ as a wife stands to a husband once more supports the identification of the deity as male.

So in our culture we traditionally conceive of the god as male. What can we make of that? A great deal. The relationships among the concrete, material conditions of a culture, including its social organization and its myths, mores, and ideals, are intricate and close. The maleness of the Western god, his character and behavior, is as much a source of the content of our culture's masculist perspectives as it is an indicator. If men are to be gods, their god must be male. Likewise, if God in His heaven is male, then on earth men can be the only true gods. The entire conceptual system of Martial thought is elevated and deified by its incarnation in the person of the "One True God," ultimate male, just as the sociopolitical structures of patriarchy are reinforced by their justification through theology. The relationship between masculist theology and patriarchal society is the reason why it is both possible and necessary to insist on the masculinity of the priesthood or the authority of the hierarchy. It is the source of the masculine cast to biblical imagery and to male privilege in church doctrine.

Once again, consider the Genesis story of Adam and Eve, a story whose theme appears in numerous patriarchal mythologies. We can understand it through feminist analysis to function both as an expression of male psychological conflict resolved through myth and as a masculist construct justifying male domination of women. Early in the creation, Adam appears, formed *in the likeness and image of God* (a concept, though unclear, frequently employed to support the ascendancy of maleness). Pure and happy, Adam spends his hours exercising his divinely given dominion over the earth until God decides that he needs a helpmeet. As Adam sleeps, Eve is taken by God from Adam's rib, from his body, formed into a "woman" (so called because she was "taken out of man") and presented to him. Shortly thereafter, Eve is beguiled by a serpent into disobedience, and taking Adam along with her into disfavor with God, she causes the expulsion from the Garden of Eden, the downfall of all humankind, and death. The serpent is henceforth sentenced to the dust, Eve to her husband's yoke, and Adam, because he "hearkened to the voice of [his] wife," condemned to labor, sweat, and sorrow.

People have pulled many meanings from this story. Freud made much of the phallic symbolism of the serpent, building around the tale a sexual inter- pretation. Others have focused on the matter of hu- man growth through separation from parental protection and subsequent trial by life. As feminists, however, we can see other, more pragmatic, applica- tions.

We can see the masculist myth of Adam, the man, created "in the image of God" (in appearance? in power?), the first progenitor, the first earthly par- ent. So what if women and not men are able to con- ceive and bear young? Man did it *first* and produced woman, who produces young only secondarily. And man did it best—cleanly and neatly while he slept, without the fuss and mess of human conception, labor, and childbirth. We can see Eve, the woman— second in creation, an afterthought, a helpmeet— first approached by the snake, easily seduced, equally seducing, placed for sinfulness and stupid- ity under the yoke of her husband, condemned to painful childbirth and suffering. In a single stroke, the awesome female power of procreation is dis- counted (as punishment for sin); supreme parent- ing is comfortably settled upon the male (God and Adam, a theme reiterated and developed in the doc- trine of the Virgin Birth); the man is firmly fixed in a position of dominance over women (his wife and, one assumes, other females); and the exploitation and subjection of woman is justified—she sinned, she was stupid and led humanity into disgrace and misery, she was condemned to the yoke by God. Men go out and work (albeit in sweat), and women bring forth children. Men rule and leave off hear- kening to their wives, whereas woman's desire is to her husband. All is conveniently explained and jus- tified.

As one might expect, the impact of the masculist character of theology and religion is vast, not only on women's lives and perspectives but on the entire culture as well.

Patriarchal Religion and Women

If the religion into which we are given and by which we are expected to live is masculist and misogynist, what would it mean to be a "religious" woman in that context? Although we may rarely focus on them, we are all aware of certain realities of Western religious tradition.

- The god of this tradition (Judaism or Christian- ity) is male. So are its priests, its potentates and hierarchies, its power centers; so are its philoso- phers, apologists, and policymakers; so are its fa- vorite sons. Encyclicals of the Pope to this day are addressed: Honored Brothers and Dear Sons . . .

- The latest savior and messiah of the tradition, Jesus, was himself male; so were the apostles and his disciples. Never did the question arise of his faithful female followers becoming disciples; it was outside the realm of consideration.

- In the tradition, women are conspicuously absent from power, from participation in theory or pol- icy, from full human status. (Aquinas, remember, pointed out that women's souls were not fully developed, and a Jewish male begins his morn- ing prayers with thanksgiving for not having been born a woman.)

- In both Judaism and Christianity, the ideal woman is a fecund animal who tends to her young, to her husband's home and service, and who "humbly" accepts the dominion of her hus- band and the male hegemony. Docile, quiet, pas- sive, obedient, and meek, she neither questions nor challenges.

- The Christian ideal, Mary, perfect in submission ("Thy will be done") and sexual purity, took no active part in the drama of Christ. Receptacle only of God's seed, she nurtured her young male god; she herself neither directed nor taught nor hazarded an intrusion into the march of events. She is the female model.

- According to the tradition, woman's progenitor was Eve, mother of evil, precipitator of the Fall. She resides in each of us.

- According to the early fathers, women's bodies are evil, seductive, damning, dirty. Women are carnal; men are spiritual. Women are body; men are mind. Women are sex, and sex is evil. Women are pleasure and passion, and that too is con- demned.

Consider the impact on your self-image of being "in the likeness of God," like Jesus, the Pope, and the "Brothers of the Church" and contrast it with never finding yourself expressed in the sacred pro- noun. Utter: God, He . . . ; God, Him. Now say: God, She . . . Imagine the experience of seeing one- self reflected in the sacred images of power, Christ walking on clouds, God forming Adam with His powerful arm. Imagine, instead, modeling after the suffering Mary or shamefully hiding one's inner Eve, one's sexuality. Think of looking high into the pulpit, seeing the Man proclaiming the Word of Him, knowing that this is ever out of the grasp of oneself or any of one's kind because of one's lesser excellence and status. Ask again: If one's religion is sexist, masculist, and misogynist, what does it mean to be a religious woman?

No wonder victimization is a sacred principle of womanhood, sacrifice a magic contribution, self-effacement a high.

Patriarchal religion adds to the problem by intensifying the process through which women internalize the consciousness of the oppressor. The males' judgment having been metamorphosed into God's judgment, it becomes the religious duty of women to accept the burden of guilt, seeing the self with male chauvinist eyes. What is more, the process does not stop with religion's demanding that women internalize such images. It happens that those conditioned to see themselves as "bad" or "sick" in a real sense become such. Women who are conditioned to live out the abject role assigned to the female sex actually appear to "deserve" the contempt heaped upon "the second sex."

—Mary Daly[2]

God, Mars, and Culture

To speak of a patriarchal religion and its effect on culture is to consider the cultural impact that the deification of the masculist perspective has, for as pointed out earlier, the forms of institutional religious worship are a reflection of cultural ideals expressed in a different language. What makes the religious expression of those ideals so important and powerful is its claim to absolute cosmic validity and its subsequent persuasive force over society.

What we find when we analyze, with a sensitivity to masculist conceptualizations, the patriarchal Western tradition is precisely what we would expect to find: a Martial god, an authoritarian ethic, and a warrior personality and/or consciousness.

In patriarchy, God rules. He creates out of nothing. Superior and external to the rest, He orders, fixes, requires, commands, and does unto. He gets angry at disobedience, "loves" on condition, rewards and punishes according to the meeting of His standards, and trains His followers through a series of trials and challenges. Jesus was supposed to have

been the "completion" of the person of God—gentle, merciful, and forgiving; but outside of His ultimate sacrifice and readiness to accept us (provided that . . .), one may not experience His sweetness in excess of His power, not practically. Put together, this means that the Trinity as the One generally functions in the Church more as the Power than as the Lamb.

That claims of the gentleness or lovingness of God are unconvincing among the laity is underscored smartly by the popular centrality of Mary as the image of mercy and kindness. In Catholicism, it is the female who captures the heart and serves the needs of the people. The Queen of Heaven, to whom most of the finest churches are dedicated, is the Mother, free from the angry, frightening qualities of Mars/God—forgiving where He is stern, understanding where He is legalistic, accessible where He is distant. It is no accident that Mary is absent from Protestantism, which has been both more ascetic than Catholicism and more unrelenting in its emphasis on sin and punishment.

God is good, we are told, although there are no standards outside of His own will against which we may judge Him. He is good (right) because He is God; that is, He is the Chief. Everybody else is expected to be good, too; that is, obedient to the will of the Chief, not merely through coercion but through choice—ultimate obedience. If one is not good, God punishes. If one suffers sufficiently, one might be redeemed (forgiven), but that, too, is solely up to God. The pattern of the God-person relationship is clearly disciplinarian and authoritarian.

Other relationships in which God resides are equally authoritarian although in a different context. The relationships are generally expressed as dualistic oppositions in which God has ascendancy: God against nature, spirit against body, life against death, God vis-a-vis humanity. The relations are ones of strain, either of striving or of contention.

And of course the ethos of strain and contention permeates the lives of the people who are both its subject and its instigators. One strives constantly to "be good," to conform, to measure up to an image that is not in harmony with what it is to be human because it is derived from only one aspect and one segment of humanity: maleness. One strives and strains, but usually fails, and follows with guilt and penitence and atonement and forgiveness and striving and failing again.

The tone is antihumanistic. You sinned, it bellows. You are bad. Your body is bad; sex is bad; pleasure is bad. You should be ashamed. Try harder, ever harder. Salvation is possible only through vicarious identification with the Sacrificial Lamb. Even the treatment of love is formally rather heavy, generally ascetic, weighted with obligation and prohibitions, not particularly self-affirming. Certainly the qualities of mirth and gaiety have not been extant or even a consideration until recently, and then only under pressure of the new ethic. Levity, in fact, has usually been treated with suspicion and disdain if not outright suppression.

The character of this perspective permeates our culture conceptually and spiritually, expressing itself in our thoughts, institutions, attitudes, and expectations. It is difficult to be self-affirming, constructively self-confident, healthily self-loving in the face of an image of humanity that is "sinful and debased." It is difficult to put into positive ethical perspective the needs and directions of one's natural self in a context that is condemnatory and almost hysterically antinature. It is nearly impossible for self-affirming people to comprehend the healthy possibility of worship, to know what or how or whether to worship when official worship is composed of self-abnegation.

The worship of Mars, the religion of masculism, means for culture an obeisance to all the warrior values we saw in Chapter 2. That is so harmful for a people because it gives them a distorted value base on which to build their society.

Feminist Alternatives

There are other ways to treat religion than as the submission of one's will and understanding to the prescriptions and doctrines of a powerful authority. There are those who view worship as a total emotional, rational, and physical experience of life's elements, so beautiful, meaningful, and profound that they transcend temporary matters and deserve our most concentrated attention and respect. Perhaps such an experience may be possible through a very sensitive portrayal of the Western tradition, through Judaism or Christianity, but certainly not through the secularized, garden variety, patriarchal projections to which we are accustomed.

Many feminists question whether a reformed, nonsexist portrayal of the Judeo-Christian religions is possible, whether the historical identification of God as male can be reversed, whether its hierarchical, authoritarian character can be purged without obliterating its nature altogether.[3] Feminists ask whether women can or should relate to a religion that worships male gods and ideals in male language, demeans women's full humanity, and prohibits the full exercise of women's potentials. Can or should we participate in religious institutions that have historically been misogynistic and that even now form policy for our lives while blocking our power to contribute to those formulations? Is reform possible or even worthwhile?

Feminists both within and outside of the traditional religious institutions raise some rather intriguing questions about "God-talk"[4] and by doing so perhaps point the way to a revitalization of religious experience. Just as conjecture, we might ask whether a feminist theology, projecting a female conceptualization of deity—a female god, or a series of female and male gods—have been less authoritarian, less demanding and constraining than the ones we know? Would the deity Herself, free of masculist ideals, have been visualized as a more tolerant accepting being, and would such a religion have been more affirming? Is there need for a deity of all, or could we, as Mary Daly proposes, think of God not as a person at all, not as a noun, but rather as a verb, the Holy Verb *to be*. Thus life itself and each moment in it are both deity and divine.

Some feminists entirely reject any interest in religion or forms of worship, arguing that religion channels one's energy into the wrong directions, that women's situation requires strong political action, not wasteful dreaming. One can certainly sympathize with such a view, given traditional definitions and the history of religion for women. On the other hand, I perceive feminism to be at base a spiritual movement. Feminists seek increased opportunity for participation and gain not as ends in themselves, not simply for the power they entail, but rather for the growth in the quality of life they represent, and that is a spiritual matter. In such a context, "religion," worship, or reverence may prove fruitful, and it should not be dismissed without careful scrutiny simply because of its past association and its usurpation by patriarchy.

Conclusion

As we critically examine the agencies of thought formation in our culture, we see a network of interlocking and mutually supporting institutions and ideas that form our conceptual environment and thus direct and control the consciousness of society.

Ideas that appear repeatedly in varying forms throughout the network become highly powerful forces of socialization and indoctrination because they are continually reinforced by their pervasiveness and their constant repetition in many languages and contexts. Their repetitiveness alone affords them a cumulative effect on awareness that renders them nearly unquestionable, if not undeniable. We have seen, in case after case, that our culture's agencies of thought promote the traditional misogynistic themes and images of women's inferiority, guilt, and "place" *as truth*. The wonder is not that women absorb and believe them, not that we are prone to participate in our own oppression, but that any of us ever break through to a new vision at all!

And yet we do break through, we do come to recognize the falsehoods and the injustices, and we do strive to live by more accurate, more constructive perspectives. That in a nutshell is what feminism is. However heterogeneous some of the theories, perspectives, methods, or goals, feminism is constant in recognizing the falseness and perversity that distorted masculist images portray of womanhood; it is constant in its affirmation of the worth of women in every sense. The following chapter is a small glimpse at the career of that affirmation.

Notes

[1] Molly Haskell, *From Reverence to Rape: The Treatment of Women in the Movies* (New York: Holt, Rinehart & Winston, 1973).

[2] Mary Daly, *Beyond God the Father* (Boston: Beacon Press, 1973), p. 49.

[3] See particularly the works of Mary Daly: *Beyond God the Father* (1973) and *Gyn/Ecology* (1978).

[4] See the works of Rosemary Radford Ruether, Carol Christ, Starhawk, Merlin Stone, Margot Adler, Anne Kent Rush, Charlene Spretnak, Naomi Goldenberg, Judith Plaskow, Penelope Washbourn, Nelle Morton, Barbara G. Walker, Carol Ochs, Elaine Pagels, Elisabeth Fiorenza, and many other women now participating in the feminist "Womanspirit" movement.

Myth America Grows Up

Rita Freedman

Rita Freedman, author of Beauty Bound *(1986) and more recently* Bodylove: Learning to Like Our Looks—and Ourselves *(1988), has long been concerned with the place of appearance in the formation of women's self-concept. In this selection she details how little girls learn to please with their looks and mannerisms, indeed how we all learn the trappings of femininity.*

My mother was pregnant,
She grew enormously large,
And then I was born—
A perfectly normal baby,
Attached to the fingers of my right hand
Was a typewriter,
And attached to the fingers of my left hand
Was a Brillo pad.
On my body was a bra,
And my cute baby blue eyes
Had a pair of false eyelashes attached to them.
The doctor said
"Congratulations, it's a girl!"

—Sandi Shepard[1]

I COMBED THE BEACHES LAST SUMMER COUNTING topless toddlers. Few could be found. On the Riviera, women freely bare their breasts to the Mediterranean sun. Here at home, the uncomplicated chests of little girls are discreetly covered. In this way young bodies are draped in gender, poured into the female mold, to be shaped, reshaped, and misshapen by it. Three-year-olds veiled behind bikini tops learn a small lesson in body awareness, one that often leads to heightened self-consciousness and sometimes to tormenting obsessions.

In every society, certain behaviors are considered more appropriate for one sex than for the other. Gender divergence includes occupational, recreational, and legal distinctions, as well as decorative and ornamental ones. How do children acquire this complex set of gender rules? A five-year-old confidently tells me that "girls play at being pretty, but boys play cars. . . ." How did she learn these components of masculinity and femininity so soon?

The socialization of gender begins in infancy, continues through adolescence, and involves almost every aspect of experience, including toys, clothes, media images, and, of course, parental

384

expectations and behavior. Although studies of infants reveal few sex-based differences in emotional and cognitive functions, parents believe that their sons and daughters are quite different right from birth. Girls and boys do grow up in different "climates of expectation."

During pregnancy, parents prepare not just for a new baby but for a strong masculine son or a beautiful feminine daughter. Consequently, these are the qualities that they project onto their newborns. As noted . . . earlier . . . when parents rated firstborn infants, they saw their daughters as beautiful, soft, pretty, cute, and delicate, whereas they viewed their sons as strong, better coordinated, and hardier, even though the male and female infants had been carefully matched for equivalent physical characteristics.[2] People who played with a three-month-old dressed in yellow more often judged it a boy because of "the strength of his grasp and his lack of hair." Those who thought the baby was a girl remarked on her "roundness, softness, and fragility."[3] The cuter the baby, the more likely it is to be judged a girl.

Long before birth, babies are imagined through fantasies that devalue girls even while idealizing their appearance. In a song from the show *Carousel*, Bill ponders his unborn child. First a son "with head held high, feet planted firm"; a boy who, in his father's daydream, "grows tall and tough as a tree." Then, in the softer tones of an afterthought, Bill considers a daughter, "pink, and white as peaches and cream"; a girl with "ribbons in her hair, brighter than girls are meant to be," yet still needing to be "sheltered and dressed in the best that money can buy."

Old autograph books sometimes "wish you hope, wish you joy, wish you first a baby boy." A widespread preference for male offspring persists. In a recent American sample, over 90 percent of the couples wanted a firstborn son. Nearly all the men and three-fourths of the women said they would want a boy if they were to have only one child.[4] A frequent reason given by those few women who did prefer a girl was that "it would be fun to dress her and fuss with her hair."[5] When asked what kind of a person they want their child to become, parents mentioned "being attractive" far more often for daughters than for sons.

Imagine a growing girl who represents the collective experiences of many youngsters whose lives were studied for this chapter. The composite experiences of Linda typify the socialization process which teaches girls their role as members of the fair sex. Linda is initiated into the beautified female world through the subtle lessons of daily life. Her few strands of baby hair are swept into a curl in the hospital nursery. Her ears are pierced before her first birthday, her nails polished for her second. She is securely wrapped in a strawberry-shortcake universe: roses on her walls, ribbons in her hair, ruffles on her shirts. "Early in life, the pink world starts to process the girls to value it."[6]

Intuitively, children sense when and how they are touched or avoided, admired or ignored, complimented or criticized. Girls are initially sturdier than boys and developmentally ahead of them, but are perceived as more fragile. Handled more delicately, they receive less physical stimulation and less encouragement for energetic or exploratory behavior. Parents show greater anxiety about a girl's safety even while she is still in diapers. Fathers begin by engaging in more rough-and-tumble play with sons and by spending nearly twice as much time with sons as with daughters.[7] As Bill concludes in his song, "You can have fun with a son, but you gotta be a father to a girl."

Interestingly, fathers seem to sex-type youngsters even more consciously than mothers do, for example by giving children toys that are more gender-stereotyped. Men show greater anxiety over effeminate behavior in sons, while actively encouraging it in daughters. Fathers seem to want their little girls to fit their own personal image of an attractive female, within the bounds of what is appropriate for a child. Wives report that husbands urge them to keep their daughters' hair long and to "doll them up" even when the mothers themselves don't feel that these things are very important. Linda's father echoes the voices of many dads who describe their preschool daughters as "a bit of a flirt": "she cuddles and flatters in subtle ways"; "she's coy and sexy."[8]

Whether such descriptions of "daddy's little girl" are accurate, fathers enjoy and encourage seductive appearance in their daughters, which in turn enhances these Oedipal flirtations. In this way, Linda is more or less explicitly directed toward a kind of "predatory coquetry." Her enactment of the beauty role is therefore shaped by the way her father reinforces Linda's appearance, independently of how her mother may model feminine beauty.

According to Piaget's theory of intellectual growth, children strive to adapt to life by trying to understand their experiences. We are biologically programmed, says Piaget, to mentally reconstruct the world by forming concepts about ourselves and our surroundings. Mental file cards are written and rewritten to conform ever more closely to social "reality." Concepts of masculinity and femininity are learned as part of this general process of intellectual growth.

In acquiring her sense of gender, Linda first develops a rudimentary idea that people come in two separate forms. Her mental file cards are scribbled with vague notions of mommy/daddy, boy/girl, man/woman, along with perceptions about clothing, hair styles, and other gender markers. By her third birthday, she is well aware that girls and boys look and act differently, apart from any underlying genital structure. An anecdote describes two toddlers looking at a statue of Adam and Eve. "Which is which?" asks one. "I could tell if only they had their clothes on," replies the other.

Though she does not yet understand gender constancy (once a girl, always a girl), Linda knows her own gender membership. Confidently she asserts, "I'm a girl," because she has written "me" on the file card that is filled with "feminine" concepts. Once gender has been established internally, Linda begins to strive for consistency between what she knows about herself and what she knows about girls in general. The dialogue in her head runs something like this: "Since I'm a girl, and since girls look and act in certain ways, then I, too, should look and act the way they do." And so she begins to enact her feminine role. The need to establish consistency between oneself and one's gender role is the same for the toddler as for the adult. The problem for Linda (as for all women) is how to bring together her self-perception as a female with an understanding of gender role.

Femininity soon becomes associated with beauty, and to the internal dialogue a subtheme is added. "Since I'm a girl," Linda thinks intuitively, "and since girls are pretty, then I, too, should be (will be, must be) pretty, just like Mommy." In this way, beauty becomes part of her self-perception as a female. When she confirms the belief that she is a girl by enacting some part of the beauty role (such as putting ribbons in her hair), she achieves a sense of cognitive consistency that in turn feels satisfying. Hence, the inner dialogue concludes with the sentiment "I enjoy being a girl!" By maintaining harmony between two concepts (self-image and feminine image), Linda keeps her mental file cards in order, and in this way makes the world more comfortable and predictable.

Piaget explains that knowledge of one's gender role is partly imposed from within, that is, self-motivated through the basic drive to create intellectual order out of chaotic experiences. But gender role is also externally imposed. It is culturally conditioned through the direct experience of hearing Cinderella tales, dressing Barbie dolls, watching Miss America, Miss Teen, Miss Hemisphere. It is also overtly reinforced. Throughout the elementary school years, girls receive more compliments than boys on their appearance. They are given a bigger wardrobe to choose from and are admired especially when they wear dresses.[9] Linda repeatedly hears others say "You look so pretty," and eventually greets her own reflection with "I'm so pretty" or "Am I pretty? . . . as pretty as other girls? . . . as pretty as others expect me to be?" Finally she begins to wonder, "How can I be prettier?" *Pretty* becomes a framework within which she paints her feminine self-image.

Although parents are beginning to treat sons and daughters more similarly, they still give their children sex-typed clothing, toys, and books. These act as powerful conditioning agents that socialize the importance of female beauty. Emphasis on feminine attractiveness is obvious in fairy tales and in picture books for preschoolers, in which female animals are depicted with long curly eyelashes and ribbons on their tails. A study of school texts found that these books traditionally portrayed women as mothers who wear aprons and who "seem to want and do nothing personally for themselves." The notable exception was cited of a mother who "treated herself to some earrings on a shopping trip."[10]

Before 1970, textbooks rarely showed females engaged in independent activities. When the occupational world of women was presented, it consisted of either service jobs (nurse, teacher) or "glamour" jobs (model, dancer, actress), in which body display is an important component. A popular children's book of the 1970s shows a small boy and girl fantasizing about their future: when the boy becomes a jungle explorer and captures a lion, the girl "curls the lion's mane in her beauty shop for animals"; when he dreams of being a deep-sea diver, she becomes "a mermaid who serves him tea and ice cream."[11]

Books are somewhat less stereotyped today, although children's toys remain highly gender-typed.

While boys are given action dolls equipped to capture the enemies of outer space, girls are given fashion dolls equipped with exotic outfits for capturing attention. Over 250 million Barbies have been sold in the past twenty-five years, a doll population that equals the number of living Americans. Over 20 million outfits a year are bought for Barbie and her friends, as the seeds of clothing addiction are sown. One collector concludes that Barbie remains the most popular fashion doll simply because she is the prettiest. (Barbie is both thinner and "sexier looking" than when first created in 1959.) Fashions for Barbie in 1984 featured her in elegant gowns because "glamour is back." Toy stores also sell makeup for dolls. With "Fashion Face," Linda can "put on Barbie's face, wash it off, change her look again and again." A single tube costs several dollars, and remember, this is makeup for a doll!

On Christmas morning, Linda eagerly unwraps her very own superdeluxe makeup set, "just like Mommy's." Here, packaged innocently with fun titles like "Fresh and Fancy" and "Pretty Party" are the sugar and spice that feed the beauty myth. These high-priced glamour rehearsal kits contain the essential tools of the trade. For Linda's hair there are rollers, styling combs, curling irons, "falls," wash-in color, and sparkles. For her face there are paints, gloss, frosting, liners, blush, shadow, and mascara. For her hands there are lotions, polish, nail crayons, and decals. Also included is gold foil for "beauty accents" and glitter for "today's metallic look." The tubes smell like candy and taste like soda pop. They come complete with magnifying mirror in a convenient carrying case so that she can take it anywhere and check her looks perpetually. Here is the making of a mirror junkie. The box covers of cosmetic kits carry reassuring messages to parents. "These toys are suitable for children as young as three"; they will help your child "personalize her own pretty face"; help her "create dozens of fashion looks and become a beauty consultant for her friends"; teach her the "fun way to learn beauty secrets."

What else do they teach Linda about herself and her role in society? That feminine beauty requires many faces and she can cultivate them all; that the easy way to impersonate a real grown-up lady is to put on the same disguise that Mommy wears; that playtime means narcissistic preening; that fantasy fun means enacting Cinderella; that spending time and money on beautifying oneself is approved by parents; that others like her to look fresh, fancy, and seductive; that her own face, though pretty, is some-

how inadequate and needs to be made even lovelier—a double message that fosters negative body image and self-doubt.

For some girls, "glamouring up" is not just child's play. There has been a phenomenal growth in children's beauty contests since those protestors picketed the Miss America Pageant in 1968. Paradoxically, during the very years when the women's movement became a pervasive social force, beauty pageants for children . . . also gained in popularity. The Miss Hemisphere Pageant, with numerous divisions for girls ages three to twenty-seven, has mushroomed in size from a few hundred contestants in 1963 to hundreds of thousands of participants today. It is billed as the largest single beauty pageant in the world. Toddlers barely out of diapers (sometimes wearing false eyelashes and tasseled bikinis) are paraded before judges who scrutinize their "beauty, charm, poise and personality." The separate "masters" division for boys up to age nine attracts far fewer contestants.

Why do parents pay sizable entrance fees, invest in elaborate outfits, and drive hundreds of miles to these contests? Besides seeking prizes and modeling opportunities, many sincerely believe that they are helping girls to develop into "ambitious but feminine women, like Bess Myerson." Some experience a strong element of vicarious achievement. They describe the thrill of seeing their daughters on display. One father remarked, "Taking my girls around to pageants is my activity, like a hobby. The contests are flashier than Little League and the children don't get hurt."[12]

But perhaps they do get hurt, in ways less obvious yet more odious than a sprained ankle in a ballgame. Pediatrician Lee Salk warns that children's beauty contests do more harm than good. He describes them as perfect setups for failure, as girls experience tremendous pressure to accept and identify with exaggerated physical stereotypes. Realizing that they lack the winning look, many suffer deep feelings of inadequacy.

"Girls Like Rainbows, Boys Don't"

Although children start with only rudimentary concepts of masculinity and femininity, they soon fill in the details. Awareness of gender dualism expands and crystallizes with age, as cognitive file cards are refined. Each day, children learn from their books and toys, from parental reaction to their behavior, and from models that constantly surround them, that beauty is a critical part of femininity. When asked how boys and girls are different from each other, children's compositions show a clear understanding that beauty belongs to females. Although genital and reproductive differences are rarely mentioned, youngsters universally say that girls wear makeup, have pretty hair, "don't get as dirty and aren't as tough" as boys. It is tempting to think that times have changed, that the next generation is already liberated from gender stereotypes and is no longer bound by beauty myths. But consider this response written in 1982 by a fifth-grader:

Because I am a girl I am different in many ways. Girls put on eye shoudo and boys ware nothing like eye shoudo. And girls ware gowns and shoes and take a pocket book around. Boys don't do that. Alls they have to do is put on a tie and shine shoes. Girls put lipstick on their lips and girls put on earings, then they put on stockings and put thier hair in a bun or fix up the hair. Girls do housework and take care of a baby if they have one. Boys just sit around and watch football games and other sports.

The following comments from seven- and eight-year-olds are cited because they particularly reflect an awareness that beauty is central to the female role.[13]

"How are Boys and Girls Different?"

—Girls play at being pretty but boys play cars. Boys' voices are louder. Girls wear more jewelry.

—Girls like pink, boys like blue. Boys take their shirts off when it's hot but girls don't.

—Girls are prettier and boys are bossy. Boys stay outside as long as they want, but girls can't.

—Boys don't clean house and girls don't get dirty. Most girls do not get hit by their mothers because girls are more beautiful.

—Girls are cute and harmless, don't get as muddy as boys. Girls like rainbows, but boys don't.

—Boys don't dance, or play hopscotch. Girls don't play rough or get sweaty (but they have the same rights as us).

More articulate ten- and eleven-year-olds made the following observations:

—Girls are very sensitive and delicate. They like perfume and like looking good and sweet. Boys are rough, tough, and insensitive.

—Girls can wear anything they like, but boys can only wear pants. Girls have more clothes. They are more into pink rooms and looking pretty.

—Girls put on makeup and boys don't because they don't want to look pretty. Girls like to stay clean and neat. Some boys say they don't want to take a bath and they want to stay smelly and dirty.

—Girls don't have a mustache, boys don't have a baby. Boys have short hair and drive better than girls. Girls can cook better but boys are stronger.

—Girls are soft like cotton but boys are rough like a truck. But we are nice to each other—that's what counts.

Clearly, these children believe that the male body is to be strengthened and developed, while the female body is to be protected and beautified. In fact, young children evaluate physical attractiveness in much the same way as adults do.[14] In nursery school, they can reliably judge the attractiveness of classmates and prefer to play with those who are better-looking.[15] Preschoolers also connect sex-related personality traits to appearance. They rate unattractive boys as more "scary and aggressive" but rate unattractive girls as more "fearful of things." (Good looks may inhibit assertive behavior in pretty girls who feel out of character when behaving more actively or aggressively than others expect.)

Children sex-typed a pretty face as feminine and a strong muscular physique as masculine. These stereotypes in turn influence the self-concepts of boys and girls in different directions. In a survey of eight- to fifteen-year-olds, girls at each age level worried more about their appearance than boys. Over half the fifth-grade girls in another sample ranked themselves as the least attractive person in their class. Follow-up interviews showed they were not simply motivated by modesty but were truly troubled by their "poor appearance."[16] The older the girl, the greater the influence of attractiveness on her popularity, as if children's understanding of the disproportionate social value of beauty to females gradually increases.

Linda grows up dressing and undressing Barbie, playing with her "Pretty Party" glamour kit, watching the selection of Miss Universe each year. She believes that beauty is something that happens at adolescence. Patiently she awaits it. While marking time, Linda may try on the role of the tomboy. Why do so many tomboys appear only to disappear? What can they teach us about the growing of little Myth America?

Tomboyism is a temporary detour on the road to female development, a last adventure before the final commitment to womanhood. Tomboys are familiar figures. Bred in every neighborhood, they roam like tomcats over the noisy, competitive, outdoor masculine turf. High on energy, they use their bodies freely to explore the world of people and things. The term *tomboy* traces back to the 1600s, when it was first directed at boys to censure them for "rude, boisterous or forward behavior." Soon the label was transferred to "girls who behave like unruly boys," and girls have worn it ever since.[17]

Tomboys not only act the part, they look it as well. We recognize them by their smudged faces and ragged clothes. The frills of Miss Muffet are not for them. Patched, scruffy, and unkempt, they need shoes they can run in, pants they can climb in. A tomboy's appearance enables the very behavior it proclaims. For packaging can create both the image *and* the limits of a person. A female is what she looks like as much as what she does.

One of the most striking aspects of tomboyism is its current popularity. A majority of female college students describe themselves as former tomboys. With bright eyes and a tinge of nostalgia, they recount their tomboy adventures without shame or embarrassment. Tomboyism is the rule rather than the exception. More than half the adult women surveyed recall having been tomboys. Among growing girls, nearly three out of four currently place themselves in the tomboy category.[18]

Although tomboyism is almost universal in western cultures, it has no counterpart among males. Parents, especially fathers, react strongly against effeminate appearance in sons. A young boy in mommy's high heels, pearls, and nail polish, makes parents fidgety, to say the least. Such adornments remain a gender distinction reserved for the other sex. The term *sissy* is sometimes suggested as a parallel to *tomboy*, although the two are not really equivalent. Any child, whether boy or girl, who is noncombative, fearful, prim, and proper can be dubbed a sissy and ridiculed for possessing such "effeminate" qualities. Whereas *sissy* is clearly perjorative for both sexes, the term *tomboy* confers little stigma before puberty; it is never directed at boys and is often considered a tacit compliment for girls. Differences between the two terms clearly reflect the bias that male attributes are normative.

Why does our culture produce so many tomboys? Why do we first dichotomize gender roles and then permit and even encourage girls to "cross over" temporarily? Why do we set them apart with a distinct label?

Answers to these questions lead back to the belief in female deviance. Recall that one strategy women use to normalize their social position is to become one of the boys. Tomboyism has survived for centuries because it serves a purpose: to defer the full impact of being just another girl. As a tomboy, Linda straddles two gender roles and thereby expands the territory of the self into the valued male domain.

Both boys and girls internalize the cultural devaluation of females. Even preschoolers are aware that masculine traits are accorded higher value and yield greater rewards. In tests where children can express a preference for being one sex or the other, only one boy in ten chooses to be female, whereas one girl in three chooses to be male.[19] Similar results are found in age groups ranging from toddlers to adults. Fewer boys than girls believe it would be better to have been born the opposite sex. As one boy remarked, "If I'd been born a girl, I would have to be pretty and no one would be interested in my brains." Nearly a quarter of adult women surveyed recall a conscious desire to be a boy during childhood, but fewer than 5 percent of adult men remember ever wanting to be female.[20] At twelve Linda writes:

I am a female. I play football and baseball with a lot of boys. They sometimes beg me to play with them. I don't think it is fair that boys can do everything and girls can't. Boys have a baseball league but girls can't. . . . Nobody knows if girls could do more than boys or if boys could do more than girls. . . . Girls have to wash the dishes and suffer by doing everything while the boys have all the fun. One day, I want it to be fair.

Tomboys gain temporary access to the valued masculine world. As "one of the boys," they shake off the girlish stigma and enjoy membership in a privileged club. In fact, rejection of personal adornment and adoption of a boyish look accomplishes for the prepubertal girl very much what beauty rituals accomplish for the adult woman. Both facilitate access to male company; both influence body image and self-esteem; and both defend against an underlying feeling of inferiority. Adopting tomboyism, like cultivating beauty, brings similar tangible rewards: visibility, attention, adventure.

Some young girls (like their mothers) maintain a dual repertoire of tomboy togs along with more coquettish drag, using one or the other as events require. In fact, such role diversity and flexibility may epitomize the best of an androgynous gender model. However, a time comes during adolescence when tomboyism evokes more anxiety than satisfaction, and its rewards no longer balance its costs. Though tolerated before puberty, tomboyism becomes increasingly threatening and is usually abandoned as gender file cards are updated. By the late teens, few girls continue to wear the title. When asked why they gave it up, college students replied:

> I just outgrew it. It was more or less a natural process that happened over a long period of time. . . . I started wearing more dresses because I like them and because Mom decided I should look nice. . . . When dating, it was difficult to be myself, so I had to change my image in dressing and mannerisms.

Their responses convey an underlying feeling of loss. Some young women are searching for new labels that can link them to their former selves. At age nineteen Linda says, "If a tomboy is a woman who is very assertive or aggressive, I guess I'm still a tomboy. . . . I don't use the term *tomboy* because that connotes being very young, but I'm still very active, though less athletic, and still consider myself androgynous." The effects of tomboyism reach into adulthood. A survey showed that women who had been overtly tomboyish as children preferred a more tailored style of dress, wore more muted colors, and decorated their homes with a nonfrilly, functional design. Women who had never been tomboys preferred more ruffly clothes, were more marriage-oriented and less career-minded.

Attracting an Identity

"A boy expands into a man; a girl contracts into a woman." So goes an old saying. With each contraction Linda sheds a piece of her comfortable old skin to emerge naked and pink into the pastel shades of womanhood. Transforming into the fair sex, she delivers a new self. Yet labor is painful. Adolescence marks a major crisis in gender acquisition. Puberty rings out, sounding the death knell for a tomboy. Gentle curves on breast and hip expose her. In poetry, Anne Sexton assures her daughter: "There is nothing in your body that lies / All that is new is telling the truth."[21] Revealed as woman, Linda can no longer masquerade as an impostor in a tomboy's costume. Contracting, she abandons the ballfield for the prince's ball, trades in her old uniform, learns to play new games and to compete in new arenas. Contracting, she must outfit herself with the eleven traits that professionals in the Broverman study judged as feminine and must gradually abandon the long list of thirty-eight attributes they rated as masculine.

Puberty arrives uninvited—sometimes prematurely, other times long overdue. Many girls experience it as a turning point in their self-image. At age eleven, Linda was asked to describe herself by making a series of statements starting with "I am a . . ." She began: "I am a human being, I am a girl, I am a truthful person, I am not pretty. . . ." One of the striking sex differences to emerge at adolescence is a greater self-consciousness in females. Girls find it harder than boys do to measure up against the idealized norms for their own sex. In a study of fourth-through tenth-graders, the oldest girls had the poorest self-image of any group in the sample.[22] Nearly half the girls in a survey of twenty thousand teenagers reported they frequently felt ugly.[23] To the extent that adolescent girls dislike their bodies, they also dislike themselves.

Twice as many high school girls as boys want to change their looks. Girls are dissatisfied with a greater number of body parts than boys. They generally see themselves as less attractive than other girls, whereas boys tend to rate themselves as better-looking than their peers.[24] A correlation exists between intelligence and body satisfaction in boys, that is, the brighter the boy, the more satisfied he is with his appearance. No such relationship is found in girls, possibly because bright girls are all too aware that they can never attain the beauty ideal.[25]

By college age, 75 percent of males report they feel good about their overall looks and facial features, as compared with only 45 percent of females.[26] Adolescent girls are tormented by poor body image, partly because they have learned during childhood to overvalue, display, and mistrust their appearance. They enter puberty with a strong need to feel attractive, and therefore suffer greater insecurity than boys do when their developing bodies feel awkward and out of control. Moreover, girls are socialized to search for self-identity through male attention. To transform from tomboy to Tom's girl, Linda must depend in large part on being pretty.

Since good looks are stereotypically associated with desirable personality traits, an "unattractive" changing body threatens self-esteem. The connection between appearance and worthiness for females can become so deeply ingrained during puberty that it remains throughout a woman's life, making her continuously insecure about her appearance and, consequently, about herself. Looking back, women describe their teens as a time filled with awkwardness, embarrassment, feelings of inadequacy, fear of sexuality and of separation. Some become frozen into the negative body images that develop during this transitional stage and are never able to accept themselves as attractive women.

Even those girls who are naturally well endowed with beauty (or who manage to achieve it) report that good looks can be a mixed blessing. Pretty is nice but not always better. Nubile beauties become vulnerable to sexual exploitation, sometimes at a very young age. They may be shown off by parents or "used" by peers who seek social prestige through contacts with them. Many begin to resent attention that is based solely on looks and that disregards who they are as people. Good-looking boys rarely suffer from these special hazards. . . .

In their quest for a separate identity, adolescent girls become especially vulnerable to beauty problems that threaten their health and well-being. For example, sophisticated medical techniques now lure girls into cosmetic surgery even before they are fully grown. Nose jobs, chin implants, and breast reductions are being performed on minors as modern medicine perpetuates the myth of female beauty. The vast majority of teenage aesthetic surgery patients are girls, not boys. Before they can adjust to their own changing profiles, growing girls are considered suitable candidates for cosmetic overhaul. Parents are paying for it; professionals are providing it.

Girls as young as age fourteen are now undergoing breast alterations. This is a good example of how beauty stereotypes interact with the maturational process, producing adjustment problems that in turn prompt cosmetic surgery. Because breasts are so symbolic of feminine beauty (in western cultures), many physically normal girls experience an almost paralyzing self-consciousness during breast development. Advertisements for bust "improvement" products abound in teen magazines. Breast development begins early in puberty, often by age ten. Girls start to mature before boys, and can be several years ahead of boys in the same grade. Full-breasted girls must carry the burden of their early maturation "up front." They suffer embarrassment, ostracism, and overt ridicule. (In fact, large-breasted females of any age are stereotyped as unintelligent, incompetent, immoral, and immodest.)[27] To these young girls, surgical correction of their breast problem seems to be a wonderful solution. In rare cases such a solution may be justifiable; usually it is pre-mature. . . .

The use of cosmetics is another beauty transformation that poses a special health hazard for adolescents. Makeup serves as a critical initiation rite into womanhood. It is an essential fashion prop that helps to exaggerate gender differences. An estimated one-third of the girls who regularly use cosmetics will develop a condition dermatologists are now calling acne cosmetica. Genetic in origin, acne is triggered by increasing hormone production during puberty. The potent ingredients used in cosmetics can induce serious skin problems even in girls who are not genetically prone. Since it takes several months for cosmetic acne to develop, the cause may go unsuspected. Once the acne has developed, a vicious cycle ensues: as it becomes worse, more makeup is used to cover it, which only further escalates the condition.[28] . . .

Pursuit of mythical beauty turns the adolescent girl into an active consumer. Giant industries create, define, and cater to her special beauty "needs" and siphon her babysitting money into the purchase of bust developers and Ultralash. A New York Times editorial asked, "Why does a fourteen-year-old Brooklyn girl need to spend $40 on a manicure and $700 on pants, sweaters, headbands and makeup to complete her back-to-school wardrobe?"[29] The very next day this newspaper carried a full back-page ad directed at potential advertisers for *Seventeen* magazine: "*Seventeen* readers don't love you and leave you. As adults 34% still rinse with the same mouthwash and 33% use the same nail polish. Talk to them in their teens and they'll be customers for life."

After analyzing magazine ads aimed at female adolescents, a researcher concludes that girls are bombarded with one essential message about their purpose in life: "learning the art of body adornment through clothing, cosmetics, jewelry, hair products, perfumes."[30] In these ads cosmetic transformations are made to seem a natural accentuation of what already exists. "I look myself, only better," says the young model, confiding the secret formula that brought out the highlights of her hair. Narcissism is fostered by ads that focus again and again on appearance as the primary source of female identity. Cosmetic advertisements have been shown to affect the "conception of social reality" of teenage girls. A single fifteen-minute exposure to a series of beauty commercials increased the degree to which they perceived beauty as being "important to their own personality and important to being popular with boys."[31]

Ads attempt to convince Linda that she must make up and make over in order to make it in life. She is directed to her mirror to discover herself. In effect, the question "Who am I?" is translated into "What should I look like?" Her natural adolescent drive to attain a personal identity is distorted into a need to package herself as a product. In the end, costly and painful beauty rituals do not produce a sense of individuality. Just the opposite occurs: girls wind up all looking the same and are thus more easily stereotyped. "They look alike, think alike, and even worse . . . believe they are not alike."[32]

Notes

[1]Shepard, S., "My Mother Was Pregnant," in Stanford, B., 1974, 42.

[2]Rubin, J. et al., 1974.

[3]Seavy, C. et al., 1975.

[4]Hoffman, L., 1977.

[5]Coombs, C. et al., 1975.

[6]Bernard, J., 1981, 479.

[7]Lamb, M., 1976.

[8]Maccoby, E., & Jacklin, C., 1974, 329.

[9]Joffe, C., 1971.

[10]Weitzman, L. et al., 1972.

[11]Williams, J., 1977, 176.

[12]Vespa, M., 1975 and 1976.

[13]Author's unpublished data.

[14]Unger, R., & Madar, T., as cited in Unger, R., 1985.

[15]Dion, K., 1973.

[16]Simmons, R., & Rosenberg, F., 1975.

[17]Fried, B., 1979, 37.

[18]Hyde, J. et al., 1977.

[19]Williams, J., 1983, 161.

[20]Ibid., 161.

[21]Sexton, A., "Little Girl, My String Bean, My Lovely Woman," 1966.

[22]Bohan, J., 1973.

[23]Offer, D. et al., 1981.

[24]Musa, K., & Roach, M., 1973.

[25]Offer, D. et al., 1981.

[26]Dacey, J., 1979.

[27]Kleinke, C., & Staneski, R., 1980.

[28]Fulton, J., & Black, E., 1983.

[29]*New York Times*, Sept. 13, 1983, editorial page.

[30]Umiker-Sebeok, J., 1981, 226.

[31]Tan, A., 1977.

[32]Firestone, S., 1970, 151.

Bibliography

Bernard, J.
  1981 *The Female World.* New York: Free Press.
Bohan, J.
  1973 Age and sex difference in self-concept. *Adolescence, 8*, 379–384.
Coombs, C., Coombs, L., & McClelland, G.
  1975 Preference scales for number and sex of children. *Population Studies, 29*, 273–298.
Dacey, J.
  1979 *Adolescents Today.* Santa Monica, Calif.: Goodyear.
Dion, K.
  1973 Young children's stereotyping of facial attractiveness. *Developmental Psychology, 10*, 772–778.
Firestone, S.
  1970 *The Dialectic of Sex.* New York: William Morrow.

Hoffman, L.
   1977 Changes in family roles, socialization and sex dif-
        ferences. *American Psychologist, 32,* 644–657.

Hyde, J., Rosenberg, B., & Behrman, J.
   1977 "Tomboyism." *Psychology of Women Quarterly, 2,*
        73–75.

Joffe, C.
   1971 Sex role socialization and the nursery school: As
        the twig is bent. *Journal of Marriage and the Family,
        33,* 467–475.

Kleinke, C., & Staneski, R.
   1980 First impressions of female bust size. *Journal of So-
        cial Psychology, 10,* 123–124.

Lamb, M.
   1976 (Ed.), *The Role of the Father in Child Development.*
        New York: Wiley.

Maccoby, E., & Jacklin, C.
   1974 *The Psychology of Sex Differences.* Stanford, Calif.:
        Stanford University Press.

Musa, K., & Roach, M.
   1973 Adolescent appearance and self-concept. *Adoles-
        cence, 8,* 385–394.

Offer, D., Ostrov, E., & Howard, K.
   1981 *The Adolescent: A Psychological Self-Portrait.* New
        York: Basic Books.

Rubin, J., Provenzano, F., & Luria, Z.
   1974 The eye of the beholder: Parents' views on sex of
        newborns. *American Journal of Orthopsychiatry, 44,*
        512–519.

Seavey, C., Katz, P., & Zalk, S.
   1975 Baby X: The effect of gender labels on adult re-
        sponses to infants. *Sex Roles, 1,* 103–110.

Sexton, A.
   1966 *Live or Die.* Boston: Houghton Mifflin.

Simmons, R., & Rosenberg, F.
   1975 Sex, sex-roles, and self-image. *Journal of Youth and
        Adolescence, 4,* 229–258.

Tan, A.
   1977 TV beauty ads and role expectations of adolescent
        female viewers. *Journalism Quarterly, 56,* 283–288.

Umiker-Sebeok, J.
   1981 The seven ages of women. In C. Mayo & N. Henley
        (Eds.), *Gender and Non-Verbal Behavior* (pp. 220–
        239). New York: Springer-Verlag.

Unger, R., Hilderbrand, M., & Madar, T.
   1982 Physical attractiveness and assumptions about so-
        cial deviance: Some sex-by-sex comparisons. *Per-
        sonality and Social Psychology Bulletin, 8,* 293–301.

Vespa, M.
   1975, Feb. 9 The littlest vamps. *New York Sunday News.*

Vespa, M.
   1976, Sept. A two year old in false eyelashes. *Ms.,* pp.
        61–63.

Weitzman, L., Eifler, D., Hokada, E., & Ross, C.
   1972 Sex role socialization in picture books for preschool
        children. *American Journal of Sociology, 77,* 1125–
        1150.

Williams, J.
   1977 *Psychology of Women* (First Edition). New York:
        W. W. Norton.

————.
   1983 *Psychology of Women* (Second Edition). New York:
        W. W. Norton.

Womanspeak and Manspeak: Sex Differences and Sexism in Communication, Verbal and Nonverbal

Nancy M. Henley
Mykol Hamilton
Barrie Thorne

Nancy M. Henley is professor of psychology at the University of California, Los Angeles (UCLA). With interests in cognitive, social, and gender psychology, she specializes in issues of communication and gender. She is the author of Body Politics: Power, Sex, and Nonverbal Communication *(1977) and of many journal articles and book chapters on language, nonverbal communication, and gender. She is coeditor with Barrie Thorne of* Language and Sex: Difference and Dominance *(1975); with Clara Mayo of* Gender and Nonverbal Behavior *(1981); and with Barrie Thorne and Cheris Kramarae of* Language, Gender and Society *(1983).*

Mykol Hamilton teaches psychology at Centre College in Kentucky. She has authored several articles on language, gender, and sex roles and has a particular interest in the masculine generic which, she says, has impact on women's self-image as well as on political and social institutions.

Sociologist Barrie Thorne teaches in the Program for the Study of Women and Men in Society at the University of Southern California. In addition to her joint works with Nancy Henley and Cheris Kramarae, she edited Rethinking the Family: Some Feminist Questions *with Marilyn Yalom. She is currently completing a study of children's gender relations in elementary school, tentatively titled* The Girls and the Boys.

Language is not only a medium for communication. In very real ways it both reflects and creates culture. Because of its ability to direct our thinking and form our attitudes, language has been a major focus of feminist critique.

A WOMAN STARTS TO SPEAK BUT STOPS WHEN A man begins to talk at the same time; two men find that a simple conversation is escalating into full-scale competition; a junior high school girl finds it hard to relate to her schoolbooks, which are phrased in the terminology of a male culture and refer to people as "men"; a woman finds that when she uses the gestures men use for attention and influence, she is responded to sexually; a female college student from an all-girl high school finds a touch or glance from males in class intimidating.

What is happening here? First, there are differences between female and male speech styles, and the sexes are often spoken about in different ways. Male nonverbal communication also has certain elements and effects that distinguish it from its female counterpart. Moreover, females and males move in a context of sexual inequality and strongly differentiated behavioral expectations. Because interaction with others always involves communication of some sort, verbal and nonverbal, it is through communication that much of our pattern of sexist interaction is learned and perpetuated. Our ideas of how this happens are vague and sometimes misinformed. Do women talk more than men? Contrary to popular opinion, they do not. Is it "natural" for female voices to be high-pitched and to sound less authoritative than male voices? In actuality, even in childhood female voices are pitched higher, and male voices lower, than the structures of their vocal cords could indicate. Are the "generic" he and the frequent masculine references to humans ("mankind," "the common man") simply innocuous linguistic conventions? Does referring to females as Ms. really make any difference? Research has shown that sexist language does indeed affect people's reactions.

These are a few examples of questions raised in the study of sexism and sex differences in language. These "trivia" of everyday interaction play an important part in determining the larger structure of our lives: They belong to the micropolitical structure that helps maintain and defend their structure. The social status quo is preserved intact by patterns of interaction which define and declare a person's status, role, social value, and expectations. The minutiae of interaction are the first line of defense for the political and economic system, and they deserve our attention and serious investigation, despite any nagging feelings that they can't possibly affect us.

Most of us are largely unaware of the nuances of expression and gesture that identify and stereotype sex; but studies over the past few years, inspired by the resurgence of feminism, now make it possible to examine the nature of female and male communicative interaction and to consider ways to change it if need be. Yet, most of this research, reflecting the biases of our society, ignores the effects of race and class at the juncture of sex and language. As a result, this survey focuses largely on details of white, middle-class life although many findings of communications research apply across race and class. We will start by examining sexism and sex differences in verbal communication, then go on to consider nonverbal communication.

There are two aspects of language we can examine: how the sexes use language differently, and how language uses the sexes differently (though the two aspects also interact with each other). The latter topic, how the English language treats women, is one which our society is becoming increasingly aware of. To understand the importance of linguistic sexism, we must understand the important role language

plays in influencing our thoughts and acts, by naming, defining, describing, and ignoring. Language has been used in the past, and is still used, to dehumanize a people into submission; it both reflects and shapes the culture in which it is embedded.

The Sexist Bias of English

Sexism in the English language takes three main forms: It ignores; it defines; it deprecates.

Ignoring

Most of us are familiar with ways in which our language ignores females. The paramount example of this is the masculine "generic,"[1] which has traditionally been used to include women as well as men. We are taught to use he to refer to someone whose sex is unspecified, as in the sentence, "Each entrant should do his best." We are told that using they in such a case ("Everyone may now take their seat") is ungrammatical; yet Bodine (1975) reports that prior to the eighteenth century, they was widely used in this way. Grammarians who insist that we use he for numerical agreement with the antecedent overlook the disagreement in gender such usage may entail. Current grammars condemn "he or she" as clumsy, and the singular "they" as inaccurate, but expect pupils to achieve both elegance of expression and accuracy by referring to women as he. Despite the best efforts of grammarians, however, singular *they* has long been common in informal conversation and is becoming more frequent even in formal speech and writing.

Many people who claim they are referring to both females and males when they use the word *he* switch to the feminine pronoun when they speak of someone in a traditionally feminine occupation, such as homemaker or schoolteacher or nurse, raising questions about the inclusion of females in the masculine pronoun. Although compared to specific masculine reference the masculine "generic" occurs infrequently, it has a high occurrence in many of our lives; MacKay estimates that highly educated Americans are exposed to it a million times in their lifetimes.

What does the ubiquitous masculine "generic" trigger in our minds? Is it in fact generic at all? Words such as *he* and *man*, when presented without context, are judged unambiguous (MacKay, 1983) and are primarily associated with males. Even in context, the masculine "generic" is likely to have a masculine bias. It tends to elicit male imagery (Hamilton and Henley, 1982) and to be associated more with male-related occupations than with neutral or female-related ones (Martyna, 1978). When asked to supply names for persons referred to in sentences, people given the masculine "generic" tend to exclude females from the meaning of the sentences and to give only masculine names.[2] The overall findings from studies of the masculine "generic" support MacKay's (1983) conclusion that this form has all the advantages of the best propaganda in its potential for influencing people: frequency of occurrence, covertness, and association with high-prestige sources.

Defining

Language both reflects and helps maintain women's secondary status in our society, by defining her and her "place." Man's power to define through naming is illustrated in the tradition of a woman's losing her own name, and taking her husband's, when she marries; the children of the marriage also have their father's name, showing that they too are his possessions. The view of females as possessions is further evidenced in the common practice of applying female names and pronouns to material possessions such as cars ("Fill 'er up!") machines, and ships.

While men are often referred to in occupational terms, women are more often referred to in relation to males. In one study of children's books, although references to men outnumbered references to women by seven to one, the word *mother* occurred more frequently than the word *father,* and the word *wife* appeared about three times as often as the word *husband* (Graham, 1975). The usual titles of respect for females (*Miss, Mrs.*) denote whether or not they have sanctified relationships with males, that is, whether or not they are male possessions; the title of respect for males (*Mr.*) does not denote anything about their relationship to females.

Women are also defined by the groupings we put them in: The phrase "women and children" virtually rolls off the tongue. Women are also frequently classified with the infirm and the incompetent. When grouped with males, females are clearly the second sex. Males are almost universally mentioned first, as in "men and women," "his and hers," "he or she," rather than "women and men," "hers and his," and "she or he." This order is not coincidental, but was urged in the sixteenth century as a proper way of putting the worthier party first (Bodine, 1975).

The fact that our language generally ignores women also means that when it does take note of them, it often defines their status. Thus "lady doctor," "lady judge," "lady professor," "lady pilot" all indicate exceptions to the rule of finding males in these occupations. Expressions like "male nurse" are much less common, because many more occupations are typed as male and because fewer men choose to enter female-typed occupations than vice versa. Even in cases in which a particular field is female-typed, males who enter it often have a term of their own, with greater prestige, such as *chef* or *couturier.* Of course, patterns of usage subtly reinforce our occupational stereotypes; and deeper undertones further reinforce stereotypes concerning propriety and competency.

Another way in which status differences are emphasized is with terms of address. Higher-status people are most frequently addressed in our society with a title and last name; for example, *Mrs.* Jackson, *Professor* Smith. Lower-status persons are often addressed in our society by first names only.

Linguists have observed that women are more readily addressed by their first names than men are. Also, men seem to feel freer to use terms of impersonal endearment with women than women do with men, a practice which may function to trivialize women by depriving them of a name (McConnell-Ginet, 1978). Female first names are also sometimes used to ridicule boys or to identify males as homosexual, the latter an example of how sexism and homophobia may be used to reinforce each other.

Deprecating

The deprecation of women in the English language can be seen in the connotations and meanings of words applied to male and female things. The very word *virtue* comes from an old root meaning *man;* to be *virtuous* is, literally, to be "manly." Different adjectives are applied to the actions or productions of the different sexes: Women's work may be referred to as *pretty* or *nice;* men's work will more often elicit adjectives like *masterful, brilliant.* While words such as *king, prince, lord, father* have all maintained their elevated meanings, the similar words *queen, madam,* and *dame* have acquired debased meanings.

A woman's sex is treated as if it were the most salient characteristic of her being; this is not the case for males. This discrepancy is the basis for much of the defining of women, and it underlies much of the accompanying deprecation. Sexual insult is applied overwhelmingly to women; Stanley (1977), in researching terms for sexual promiscuity, found 220 terms for a sexually promiscuous woman, but only 22 terms for a sexually promiscuous man. Furthermore, trivialization accompanies many terms applied to females. While male-based terms suggest concerns of importance, like *fraternalism* and *mastermind*, female-related terms tend to refer to unimportant or small things, such as *ladyfingers*, *ladybird*, *maidenhair fern* (Nilsen, 1977). The feminine endings *-ess* and *-ette*, and the female prefix *lady*, are added to many words which are not really male-specific. Thus we have the trivialized terms *poetess*, *authoress*, *aviatrix*, *majorette*, *usherette*. Male sports teams are given names of strength and ferocity: "Rams," "Bears," Jets." Women's sports teams often have cute names like "Rayettes," "Rockettes." As Alleen Nilsen (1972) has put it,

> *The chicken metaphor tells the whole story of a girl's life. In her youth she is a* chick, *then she marries and begins feeling* cooped up, *so she goes to* hen parties *where she* cackles *with her friends. Then she has her* brood *and begins to* henpeck *her husband. Finally she turns into an* old biddy. *(p. 109.)*

Breaking the Hold of Sexist Language

Identifying linguistic sexism is easier than eliminating it. The women's movement has already developed or increasingly popularized such terms as *Ms.*, *chairperson*, and *spokesperson*; the use of *woman* rather than *girl* for adult females; and the use of "he or she" and "her or his," in place of the masculine pronoun used generically. New terms have been coined to raise consciousness and assert femaleness even when maleness is not consciously understood or intended, such as *ovarian* for *seminal*, *herstory* for *history*.

Several new pronoun systems have been proposed to replace or supplement "he, him, his" and "she, her, hers." Among them are "co, cos"; "she, herm, heris"; and "tey, tem, ter(s)." While such dramatic linguistic changes do not seem imminent and would require a concerted program of action they are not completely out of the question. On a less dramatic scale, simple changes are being encouraged by teachers, editors, and other arbiters of language.

Many publishing houses encourage or require authors to use nonsexist language, and some scholarly associations require nonsexist language in their journals (e.g. American Psychological Association, 1983). While changing to unbiased language may be awkward for some at first, it is usually readily learned when there is motivation and before long becomes "natural."

There are a number of changes we can make in our own usage. For example, there is no need to use masculine terms if we wish to speak of human beings: we can call them *human beings, people, humankind, humanity, persons,* etc., rather than man or mankind. We can use both pronouns together (*she/he, he or she*), or if we find that awkward, we can use *they* as a singular pronoun. Sentences can be reworded in the plural: "We all remember our first day at school," rather than "Everybody remembers his first day at school." We can refer to both sexes when we're speaking about *people,* and we can break down some expectations by referring to people in female-male order, rather than vice versa. We can guard against referring to women as possessions, relations, or appendages of males, or as individuals whose sexuality is primary.[3] Now let us move from sexism to sex differences in language.

Sex Differences and Similarities in Speech

Early research and folk wisdom both supported the idea that there are large differences between the "languages" of women and men. More recent evidence suggests that many sex differences claimed in the past were entirely imagined, or even reversed from reality. Most were at least exaggerated, and differences which do exist are generally more complex than was thought. Much clarification has been achieved in recent years through careful study using new conceptualizations and methods. The following sections summarize current knowledge in major areas of research on sex differences and similarities in language.

Amount of Speech—Do Women Talk Too Much?

One persistent stereotype asserts that women talk too much—more and longer than men. This is simply not so. In study after study, women have rarely been found to speak more than men. Rather, the two sexes have been found equal in quantity of speech, or men have been found to speak more often and at greater length than women and to interrupt other speakers more than women do. This finding applies to people in all kinds of social situations—alone, in single-sex or mixed-sex pairs, and in groups. Descriptions of some of these studies follows.

In an investigation that used mock jury deliberations, men constituted two-thirds of the juries but contributed almost four-fifths of the talk (Strodtbeck and Mann, 1956). A similar study of mock juries found that at all occupational levels, males talked more than females (Strodtbeck, James, and Hawkins, 1957). In a laboratory study in which individuals were asked to describe a stimulus picture (with no explicit time limitations), females took an average of three minutes, while males averaged thirteen minutes—in fact, some of the males talked beyond the half-hour length of the researcher's recording tape and could only be counted as having half an hour (Swacker, 1975). In a laboratory study of married couples, in 52% of the cases the husband did most or more of the talking; for the rest of the couples, the time was either equally divided or the wives did more talking (Kenkel, 1963). Hilpert, Kramer, and Clark (1975) report a study of male-female dyads in which males spoke more than 59% of the time. Another study that set up husband-wife discussions found that the husband talked more in nineteen cases, and the wives more in fifteen cases (Strodtbeck, 1951).

Several studies have shown that males interrupt more than females (see West and Zimmerman, 1983). In one study, for example, same-sex or mixed-sex two-party conversations were taped in natural settings. In same-sex conversations interruptions were distributed nearly equally between partners; in mixed-sex conversations men initiated 96% of all interruptions. There is another type of male vocal intrusion on female activity: the voice-overs which appear on TV commercials that portray women doing tasks around the house. A study of these found that about 89% of voice-overs in television commercials are male.

(Mis)Perception of Women's and Men's Speech

Given that men actually talk more than women, how is the speech of the two sexes perceived? Researchers

have found that in some cases, similar speech by females and males is perceived differently; for example, an infant's cry was interpreted as anger when listeners were told the baby was a boy, and as fear when they were told it was a girl (Condry and Condry, 1976). Sally McConnell-Ginet (1983) observed that the same intonation patterns may be differently evaluated depending on whether the speaker is a woman or a man—our hearing is sex-typed. Patricia Bradley (In Press) found that in small decision-making groups, women when using qualifying phrases were judged adversely, while men were not.

Intonation and Pronunciation

There is obviously a difference in vocal pitch between women and men, but is this due to anatomical difference alone? The answer is a sonorous "no." While it is true that anatomical differences between males and females produce a slightly higher pitch in females' voices, the difference in anatomy is not nearly great enough to produce the variation that is heard. Recent investigators have concluded that at least some of the vocal differences are learned and constitute a linguistic convention. Females and males talk at greatly different pitches because that is a requirement of their social roles, a requirement so strong that the differences in pitch outstrip the anatomical differences even in children, before the male voice-change at puberty (see Sachs, 1975). There is such a universal expectation that male voices should be low and female voices high that any deviation from this expectation produces a powerful effect on other people's impressions of one's personality. Men with high-pitched voices may be taken for women in phone conversations (and treated accordingly), disregarded in group conversation, and ridiculed behind their backs. But female newscasters with lower pitch are preferred and are hired; since lower pitch is associated with males, who have more authority in our society, it carries more authority in a female also (Hennessee, 1974).

There are other sex differences in speech sounds. For boys in our culture, masculinity and toughness are projected by a slightly nasal speech; girls and "gentlemanly" boys have oral, or non-nasal, speech. Males also speak with greater intensity than females. There are differences in the intonation patterns used by each sex: Women have more variable intonations (contrasting levels) than men do; women are said to have more extremes of high and low intonation than men, and to speak with long rapid glides that are absent in men's speech (McConnell-Ginet, 1983).

The variability of women's speech sounds is interpreted in our culture as intonation patterns of insecurity, ones of whining, questioning, and helplessness. It might also indicate greater emotional expressiveness of a positive sort.

One area where sex differences have consistently been found is in the choice of phonetic variations. Women more frequently choose "proper" forms, pronouncing the g in *running* rather than saying *runnin'*; pronouncing *th* "correctly" rather than as *d, t,* or *f* (e.g., in *with*); pronouncing a final consonant cluster (as in *strengths*); or pronouncing the *r* that follows a vowel at the end of a word (as in *mirror*).

Several careful studies of how people choose among these patterns have found that females, more than males, tend to use the prestigious or "proper" forms of speech generally associated with high-status persons. This pattern has been found among black and white, young and old, in England and in the U.S., in North Carolina, Detroit, New York, and Chicago. Women's greater use of prestige patterns has been attributed to their insecure social position, which has made them more status-conscious, and to males' valuing of "nonstandard" speech because of its association with masculinity (Trudgill, 1975). Women are also often seen as conservators rather than innovators in language; however, Nichols (1983) has demonstrated that women's choice of standard or innovative forms is affected, like men's choice, by their occupations and daily activities.

Word and Phrase Choice

Most stereotypes about sex differences in vocabulary have turned out to be untrue. Women are said to be euphemistic and to "prefer" refined, veiled, and indirect expressions; but if so, this may be because linguistic taboos have made such usage a necessity more than a preference. There *are* vocabulary differences in certain domains, however. One study found that males used more words implying time, space, quantity and destructive action, while females used more words related to feeling, emotion, and motivation, and more self-references, auxiliaries, and negations (Gleser, Gottschalk, and Watkins, 1959). Such findings reflect obvious sex stereotypes and probably also the division of labor (and of interests and

preferences) in our society, which assigns men responsibility for spatial and quantitative manipulation and destruction, and assigns women responsibility for interpersonal relationships.

Studies of topics of conversation in the 1920s similarly found the most frequent topic for men was business and money; for women, people. Women are more likely than men to have elaborated terminology in the areas of sewing, cooking, child care, and colors. Men's elaborated vocabularies center around such areas as sports, autos, and mechanical things. Several researchers have found greater use among men of hostile terms and slang, which contains many sexual references.

Unfortunately, the conclusions regarding these differences in vocabulary are often detrimental to women, since men's work domains (and consequently their speech topics) are viewed as more important than women's, and because men's aggressiveness and hostility are seen as strengths contrasting with women's "weaker" modes of expression.

No consistent differences have been found in choice of adjectives or adverbs, refuting the stereotyped claim that women are prone to overuse intensifiers such as *so, awfully,* and *quite,* and extravagant adjectives such as *heavenly* and *divine* (Kramarae, 1981); nor have consistent sex differences been demonstrated in the use of syntactic forms, such as patterns of question-asking. The complex findings that emerge from research of this kind are illustrated by studies of men's and women's use of tag questions, described in the following section.

Conversational Interaction

There are differences in the conversational patterns of females and males in addition to the tendency for males to talk and interrupt more than females. In an influential and intriguing series of speculations about "women's language," Robin Lakoff (1973) claimed that women more often use tag questions ("Hilda arrived, *didn't she?*"), and that such questions are part of a nonassertive speech pattern. Two studies—one of college students assigned to discussion groups and the other of heterosexual couples conversing at home—did confirm that women used more tag questions than men; but another study found that in a classroom setting, women and men used about the same number of tag questions. Still another study found that in informal conversations men used twice as many tag questions as women; and another, that the male participants in a professional conference had used thirty-three tag questions, while the women had used none. Finally, an analysis of meetings of engineers and designers in a corporation disclosed that the male leader used the majority of tag questions.

It is hard to draw conclusions from such inconsistent findings, except to note that the initial claim was phrased too simply. The study of isolated variables almost without exception leads to further questions about the effects of setting, topic, roles, and other social factors that may interact with gender. It also raises questions about language function and use (McConnell-Ginet, 1980). For example, Lakoff claims that tag questions convey uncertainty; but other researchers demonstrate that women may also use tags to elicit responses from uncommunicative male conversational partners to sustain interaction and (when used in an overbearing way) to forestall opposition.

Recent research on conversational interaction reflects the attempt to conceptualize language not in terms of isolated variables nor as an abstract code, but within contexts of use, looking at features of conversation within the give-and-take of actual talk. Pamela Fishman (1983) analyzed recurring patterns in many samples of the household conversations of three heterosexual couples. Although the women tried more often than the men to initiate conversations, the women succeeded less often because of minimal responses from their male companions. In contrast, the women pursued topics the men raised, asked more questions, and did more verbal support-work than the men. Fishman concluded that the conversations were under male control, but were mainly produced by female work.

Self-Disclosure

Self-disclosure is another variable that involves language but goes beyond it. Research studies have found that women disclose more personal information to others then men do. Subordinates (in work situations) are also more likely to self-disclose than superiors. People in positions of power are required to reveal little about themselves, yet typically know much about the lives of others—perhaps the ultimate exemplar of this principle is the fictional Big Brother.

According to the research of Jack Sattel (1983), men exercise and maintain power over women by withholding self-disclosure. An institutional example of this use of power is the psychiatrist (usually male), to whom much is disclosed (by a predominantly female clientele), but who classically maintains a reserved and detached attitude, revealing little or nothing of himself. Nonemotionality is the "cool" of the professional, the executive, the poker player, the street-wise operator. Smart men—those in power, those who manipulate others—maintain unruffled exteriors.

Women who obtain authoritative positions may do likewise, but most women have been socialized to display their emotions, thoughts, and ideas. Giving out this information about themselves, especially in a context of inequality, is giving others power over them. Women may not be more emotionally variable than men, but their emotional variability is more visible. This display of emotional variability, like that of variability of intonation, contributes to the stereotype of instability in women. Self-disclosure is not in itself a weakness or negative behavior trait; like other gestures of intimacy, it has positive aspects—such as sharing of oneself and allowing others to open up—when it is voluntary and reciprocal.

Silence and Women's Voices

Poets, feminists, theorists, and sociolinguists have recognized, as Adrienne Rich (1978) wrote, that *silence* "is a presence/it has a history and a form. Do not confuse it with any kind of absence." A look at the functions and causes of silence may reveal much about talk.

Women may be stereotyped as talkative because they are expected to be more silent than men (Kramarae, 1981) and in mixed-sex conversations women *are* more silent, with men tending to take more and longer turns at talk. Mechanisms such as interruption and inattention to topics women raise are used by men to construct women's silence in mixed-sex talk. Women's use of silence as a subversive strategy has also been explored.

Men, especially those with class and race privilege, remain the chief gatekeepers and public users of language: the editors, publishers, rhetoricians, lexicographers, broadcasters, educators. In a related vein, Tillie Olsen (1979) wrote of "unnatural silences," brought about by circumstances of sex, race, and social class, which systematically obstruct literary creativity and remove the voices of the oppressed from poetry and fiction.

But women's voices *can* be found if we look in unusual places. There is new, imaginative research on women's gossip, humor, and story-telling as verbal art. These studies point to recurring patterns which distinguish talk among women from that in mixed-sex or all-male groups: mutuality of interaction work (active listening, building on the utterances of others): collaboration rather than competition; and flexible leadership rather than the strong dominance patterns found in all-male groups (Aries, 1976; Kalcik, 1975; Goodwin, 1980; Penelope and Wolfe, 1983).

Change

In the past, speech has too often been studied as a norm, as illustrative of the speech of people in general. Studies were (and are sometimes still) done on all-male groups, without the realization that such groups are selected samples. Any sex differences researchers found were usually used to imply that "women speak differently" (from the norm), not that "women and men speak differently" (from each other). Anthropological reports on cultures which have sex-differentiated languages have often referred to "women's languages" in the cultures as the deviation, assuming that the "men's language" is *the* language. On the contrary, we must insist whenever this practice arises that women's speech forms are every bit as "standard" as men's.

Also, it has often been suggested explicitly or implicitly that women should speak with more forcefulness and assertion, i.e., should speak "more like men." Feminists, however, have recently come to reassess the value of strategies and styles associated with women. The collaborative patterns which are central to talk among women—the drawing out of other speakers, supportive listening and head nods, mutual sharing of emotions and personal knowledge, respect for one another's conversational space—are weak or "powerless" only when contrasted with their opposites. When only women are told to change their behavior, and essentially to adopt "male forms," the characteristics of male speech are ignored; speech as something interactive rather than individually emitted is overlooked; and the notion of power as domination is reproduced.

A feminist definition of power—power as energy, effective interaction, or empowerment—contrasts with and challenges the notion of power as domination or control (Hartsock, 1981). The feminist challenge, Nancy Hartsock observes, is to develop forms derived from this alternative vision, as a way of transforming institutions based on dominance. This vantage point suggests an alternative strategy for transforming gender asymmetries in talk. The new strategy affirms, rather than denies, the patterns often found in women's talk, using them to transform the larger world of speech, empower subordinates, and challenge the communication patterns used by dominants.

Males can obviously gain as well by adopting these patterns; they should be encouraged to do so in order to become better, less oppressive conversationalists. Women can benefit from exploring the positive side of their speaking culture, as well as from eliminating those forms which are self-deprecating and self-limiting. To "speak like a man" may command authority and be valued at this time, but we should work towards the time when all speakers will be attended to and valued.

Nonverbal Communication

Although we are taught to think of communication in terms of spoken and written language, nonverbal communication has much more impact on our actions and reactions than does verbal. One psychological study concluded, on the basis of a laboratory study, that nonverbal messages carry over four times the weight of verbal messages when both are used in interaction. Yet, there is much ignorance and confusion surrounding the subtler nonverbal form, which renders it a perfect avenue for the unconscious manipulation of others. Nonverbal behavior is of particular importance for women, because their socialization to docility and passivity makes them likely targets for subtle forms of social control, and their close contact with men—for example as wives and secretaries—entails frequent verbal and nonverbal interaction with those in power. Additionally, women have been found to be more sensitive than men to nonverbal cues, perhaps because their survival depends upon it. (Blacks have also been shown to be better than whites at interpreting nonverbal signals.)

Sex differences in nonverbal communication—especially those gestures, postures, body movements, etc., which make one's sex visible and salient—have been termed "gender display." Many such differences (e.g., in carrying schoolbooks, walking, holding cigarettes, drinking beverages) are commonly observed and considered "natural," as if arising somehow from "innate" personality tendencies and anatomical differences between the sexes. While there are some physical differences between women and men which contribute to sex differences in behavior, their influence is miniscule compared to that of learned differences. As the well-known kinesicist Ray Birdwhistell has pointed out (1970), compared to other animals human beings do not differ greatly by gender: We are a weakly dimorphic (two-sexed) species and therefore organize much of our gender display in such learned behaviors as body positioning and movement. This sex differentiation in nonverbal behavior varies, like other sex differentiation, from place to place, culture to culture, and through time. According to Marianne Wex (1979), who compared depictions of the body in sculpture from as long ago as four thousand years with today's photographs and advertisements, the ideals of body language and form for the sexes have never been more different than they are today.

In addition to communicating gender and the emotion and attitudes so often associated with it, body language communicates status and power; it is the avenue through which many gestures of dominance and submission are exchanged. Certain nonverbal behaviors are associated in both sexes with subordinate position; many of these same behaviors are often associated exclusively with females (Henley, 1977). Because women often occupy subordinate positions in our society, the status aspect and the sex aspect are frequently confounded. If we ask whether women avert their eyes (a gesture of submission) because they're status subordinates or because they're women, the answer might as well be "both": either way, they are less powerful. Let us look at several types of nonverbal behavior that differ by sex.

Demeanor

Persons of higher status have certain privileges of demeanor that their subordinates do not: the boss can put his feet on the desk and loosen his tie, but workers must be more careful in their behavior. Also, the boss had better not put her feet on the desk; women are restricted in their demeanor. Goffman (1967) observed that in hospital staff meetings, the

doctors (usually male, and always of high status) had the privilege of swearing, changing the topic of conversation, and sitting in undignified positions. They could lounge on the (mostly female) nurses' counter and initiate joking sessions. Attendants and nurses, of lower status, had to be more circumspect in their demeanor. Women are also denied privileges of swearing and sitting in the undignified positions allowed to men; in fact, women are explicitly required to be more cautious than men by all standards, including the well-known double one. This requirement of propriety is similar to women's use of more proper speech forms, but the requirement for nonverbal behavior is much more compelling.

Body tension is another sex-differentiated aspect of demeanor. In laboratory studies of conversation, communicators are more relaxed with lower-status addressees than with higher-status ones, and they are more relaxed with females than with males. Also, males are generally more relaxed than females; females' somewhat tenser postures are said to convey submissive attitudes (Mehrabian, 1972).

Use of Space

Women's general bodily demeanor must be restrained and restricted; their femininity is gauged, in fact, by how little space they take up, while masculinity is judged by males' expansiveness and the strength of their flamboyant gestures. Males control both greater territory and greater personal space, a situation associated with dominance and high status in both human beings and animals. Both field and laboratory studies have found that people tend to approach females more closely than males, to seat themselves closer to females and otherwise intrude on their territory, and to cut across their paths. In the larger aspect of space, women are also less likely to have their own room or other private space in the home.

Looking and Staring—Eye Contact

Eye contact is greatly influenced by sex. It has been repeatedly found that in interactions, women look more at the other person than men do and maintain mutual eye-contact longer. Some researchers have interpreted this finding in terms of women's traditional orientation toward the social world and interpersonal relations. It has also been demonstrated, however, that people maintain more eye contact with those from whom they want approval. Women may depend on this social approval for survival (since they are often economically dependent) and may use this looking to obtain cues from others about the appropriateness of their behavior.

Other writers have observed that rather than stare, women tend more than men to avert the gaze, especially when stared at by men. Although there has been no specific research on this pattern, several studies support the notion that the stare is a dominant and aggressive gesture in human beings, as it is in animals. It is also likely that women are stared at more and hence reciprocate more often by averting their gaze. Our language even has specific words— such as *ogling* and *leering*—for this phenomenon of visual aggression. Public staring, clothing designed to reveal the contours of the body, and public advertising which lavishly flashes women across billboards and through magazines, all make females a highly visible sex. Visual information about women is readily available, just as their personal information is available through greater self-disclosure.

Smiling

The smile is women's badge of appeasement. Many feminists have pointed out that women engage in more smiling than men do, whether they are truly happy or not. Research has confirmed this. Susan Frances (1979) analyzed same-sex and mixed-sex interactions and found that women smiled and laughed more than men. Erving Goffman (1979) analyzed the depiction of gender in U.S. print advertising and concluded that women's smiles are ritualistic mollifiers; women smile more, and more expansively, than men. The smile is a requirement of women's social position and is used as a gesture of submission. Monkeys and apes also smile to indicate submission: The smile is generally thought to signal to an aggressor that the subordinate individual intends no harm. In many women, and in other subordinate persons, smiling has reached the status of a nervous habit.

Touching

Touching is another gesture of dominance, and cuddling to the touch is its corresponding gesture of submission. Touching is reportedly used by primates to maintain a dominance order, and it is likely that it is used by human beings in the same way. Just as the boss can put a hand on the worker, the master on the servant, the teacher on the student, the business executive on the secretary, so men more frequently put their hands on women, despite a folk mythology to the contrary. Both questionnaire and observational studies (Henley, 1977; Major, 1981) have found that females are touched by others more than males are, even at the age of six months. Much of this touching goes unnoticed because it is expected and taken for granted, as when men steer women across the street, through doorways, around corners, into elevators, and so on. The male doctor or lawyer who holds his female client's hand overlong, and the male boss who puts his hand on the female secretary's arm or shoulder when giving her instructions, are easily recognizable examples of such everyday touching of women by men. There is also the more obtrusive touching: the "pawing" by sexually aggressive males; the pinching of waitresses and female office and factory workers; and the totally unexpected and unwelcomed tactual familiarity women are subjected to from complete strangers on the street.

Many interpret this pattern of greater touching by males as a reflection of sexual interest and of a greater level of sexuality among men than women. This explanation, first of all, ignores the fact that touching is a status and dominance signal for human and animal groups, and parsimony of explanation suggests it could be between males and females too. It also ignores the findings of sexual research, which gives us no reason to expect any greater sexual drive in males than in females. Rather, males in our culture have more freedom and encouragement to express their sexuality, and they are also accorded more freedom to touch others. Touching carries the connotation of possession when used with objects, and the wholesale touching of women carries the message that women are community property. They are tactually accessible, just as they are visually and informationally accessible.

Intimacy and Status in Nonverbal Gestures

There is another side to touching, one which is much better understood: Touching symbolizes friendship and intimacy. To speak of the power dimension of touching is not to rule out the intimacy dimension. A particular touch may have both components and more, but it is the *pattern* of touching between two individuals that tells us most about their relationship. When touching is symmetrical—that is, when both parties have equal touching privileges—it conveys information about the *intimacy* dimension of the relationship: much touching indicates closeness, and little touching indicates distance. When one party is free to touch the other but not vice versa, we gain information about the *status*, or power, dimension: the person with greater touching priviliges is of higher status or has more power. Even when there is mutual touching between two people, it is most likely to be initiated by the higher status person; e.g., in a dating relationship it is usually the male who first puts an arm around the female or begins holding hands.

Other gestures are meaningful on both these levels, intimacy and status (Henley, 1977). Staring, intruding on personal space, and loosening of demeanor are all practiced mutually between intimates, but are also privileges accorded more to those with power and to men. When used by women with regard to men, however, these gestures—staring, coming closer, relaxing the demeanor, or touching—are likely to be taken not as dominance gestures but as sexual invitation. Gestures of power are out of context when used by the powerless. It is possible to interpret such gestures in sexual terms because of their duality—in another context they do symbolize intimacy, associated with sexuality. Furthermore, the attribution of sexual invitation to a woman both compliments the man and disarms the woman, placing her back in her familiar, unthreatening role as sex object.

Gestures of Dominance and Submission

We have named several gestures of dominance (invasion of personal space, touching, staring) and of submission (allowing oneself to be touched, averting the eyes, and smiling). Pointing may be interpreted as another gesture of dominance, and the corresponding submissive action is to stop talking or acting. In conversation, interruption often functions as a gesture of dominance, and allowing interruption signifies submission. Often mock play between males and females also carries strong physical overtones of dominance: the man squeezing the woman too hard, "pretending" to twist her arm, playfully lifting her and tossing her from man to man, chasing, catching and spanking her. This type of "play" is also frequently used to control children and to maintain a status hierarchy among male teenagers.

Breaking the Mold—A First Step

Women can reverse these nonverbal interaction patterns with probably greater effect than can be achieved through deliberate efforts to alter speech patterns. Women can stop smiling unless they are happy, stop lowering their eyes, stop getting out of men's way on the street, and stop letting themselves be interrupted. They can stare people in the eye, be more relaxed in demeanor (when they realize it is more a reflection of status than of morality), and touch when they feel it is appropriate. Men can likewise become aware of what they are signifying nonverbally. They can restrain their invasions of personal space, touching (if it is not mutual), and interrupting. They may also benefit by losing their cool and feeling free to display their more tender emotions. Males and females who have responsibility for socializing the next generation—that is, parents and teachers particularly—should be especially aware of what they are teaching children about dominance, power, and privilege through nonverbal communication.

Manipulating the *indicators* of power in our society will not be enough in itself to change the fundamental power structure, but it can have profound effects on power relationships. How far these effects can reach we have no way of knowing at this point. At the very least, knowing how we are affected by these patterns gives us the tools to resist them, tools that women can put to use in gaining control over their lives and creating new structures. We believe that someday the language of a free and equal society will shed all vestiges of patriarchy and express its speakers' ideas and emotions directly and without nuances of inferiority.

Notes

[1] What grammarians have called the "generic masculine" has been variously relabeled the "pseudo-generic," the "false generic," and "prescriptive he." We use the term "masculine 'generic'" to indicate intended generic reference in masculine form, and also to question whether the masculine is generic when so used.

[2] For a review and discussion of the research on the effects of the masculine "generic," see Silveria (1980) or MacKay (1983).

[3] For more complete guidelines for eliminating sexism in language, see Miller and Swift (1980).

References

We would like to acknowledge the influence of Cheris Kramarae on this paper, through her writing and other collaboration with us.

There are many studies which could not be cited here because of space limitations; for further information on any of the topics mentioned in this chapter, see the comprehensive annotated bibliography in Thorne, Kramarae, and Henley (1983).

American Psychological Association.
1983 *Publication Manual.* Washington, D.C.: Author.

Aries, E.
1976 "Interaction Patterns and Themes of Male, Female and Mixed Groups." *Small Group Behavior* 7: 7–18.

Birdwhistell, R. L.
1970 "Masculinity and Femininity as Display." In *Kinesics and Context.* Philadelphia: University of Pennsylvania Press, 39–46.

Bodine, A.
1975 "Androcentrism in Prescriptive Grammar: Singular "They," Sex-indefinite "He," and "He or She."" *Language in Society* 4: 129–146.

Borden, G.
1974 "The Perceived Sexuality of Passages Written in Predominantly Masculine or Feminine Language." Paper presented at the meeting of the Speech Communication Association, Chicago.

Bradley, P.
In Press "The Folklinguistics of Women's Speech: An Empirical Examination." *Communication Monographs.*

Condry, J., and S. Condry.
1976 "Sex Differences: A Study of the Eye of the Beholder." *Child Development* 7: 812–819.

Fishman, P.
1983 "Interaction: The Work Women Do." In *Language, Gender and Society,* edited by B. Thorne, C. Kramarae, and N. Henley. Rowley, Mass.: Newbury House.

Frances, S. J.
1979 "Sex Differences in Nonverbal Behavior." *Sex Roles* 5: 519–535.

Gleser, G. C., L. A. Gottschalk, and J. Watkins.
1959 "The Relationship of Sex and Intelligence to Choice of Words: A Normative Study of Verbal Behavior." *Journal of Clinical Psychology* 15: 182–191.

Goffman, E.
1967 "The Nature of Deferences and Demeanor." In *Interaction Ritual.* New York: Anchor, 47–95.

———.
1979 *Gender Advertisements.* New York: Harper & Row.

Goodwin, M. J.
1980 "Directive-Response Speech Sequences in Girls' and Boys' Task Activities." In *Women and Language in Literature and Society* edited by S. McConnell-Ginet, R. Barker, and N. Furman. New York: Praeger, 157–173.

Graham, A.
1975 "The Making of a Nonsexist Dictionary." *Language and Sex: Difference and Dominance* edited by B. Thorne and N. Henley. Rowley, Mass: Newbury House.

Hamilton, N., and N. Henley.
1982 "Detrimental Consequences of Generic Masculine Usage." Paper presented at the meeting of the Western Psychological Association, Sacramento, Calif.

Hartsock, N.
1981 "Political Change: Two Perspectives on Power." In *Building Feminist Theory* edited by *Quest* Staff and Book Committee. New York: Longman, 3–19.

Henley, N.
1977 *Body Politics: Power, Sex and Nonverbal Communication.* Englewood Cliffs, N.J.: Prentice-Hall.

Hennessee, J.
July 1974 "Some News is Good News." *Ms.* 3: 25–29.

Hilpert, F., C. Kramer, and R. A. Clark.
Spring 1975 "Participants' Perception of Self and Partner in Mixed-sex Dyads." *Central States Speech Journal* 26, no. 5: 2–56.

Kalcik, S.
1975 ". . . Like Ann's Gynecologist or the Time I Was Almost Raped": Personal Narratives in Women's Rap Groups. *Journal of American Folklore* 88: 3–11.

Kenkel, W. F.
1963 "Observational Studies of Husband-Wife Interaction in Family Decision-Making." In *Sourcebook in Marriage and the Family* edited by M. Sussman. Boston: Houghton-Mifflin.

Kramarae, C.
1981 *Women and Men Speaking.* Rowley, Mass.: Newbury House.

Lakoff, R.
1973 "Language and Woman's Place." *Language in Society* 2: 45–79.

MacKay, D. G.
1980 "On the Goals, Principles, and Procedures for Prescriptive Grammar." *Language in Society* 9: 349–367.

———.
1983 "Prescriptive Grammar and the Pronoun Problem." In *Language, Gender and Society* edited by B. Thorne, C. Kramarae, and N. Henley, Rowley, Mass.: Newbury House Publishers.

Major, B.

1981 "Gender Patterns in Touching Behavior." In *Gender and Nonverbal Behavior* edited by C. Mayo and N. Henley. New York: Springer-Verlag.

Martyna, W.

1978 *Using and Understanding the Generic Masculine: A Social-Psychological Approach to Language and the Sexes.* Ph. D. diss. Stanford University.

McGonnell-Ginet, S.

1978 "Address Forms in Sexual Politics." In *Women's Language and Styles* edited by D. Butturff and E. L. Epstein. Akron, Ohio: L & S Books, 23–35.

———.

1983 "Intonation in a Man's World." In *Language, Gender, and Society* edited by B. Thorne, C. Kramarae, and N. Henley. Rowley, Mass.: Newbury House.

———.

1980 In *Language and Women in Literature and Society* edited by S. McGonnell-Ginet, R. Borker & N. Furman. New York: Praeger, pp. 3–25.

Mehrabian, A.

1972 *Nonverbal Communication.* Chicago: Aldine Atherton.

Miller, C. and K. Swift.

1980 *Handbook of Nonsexist Writing.* New York: Lippincott & Cromwell.

Nichols, P. C.

1983 "Linguistic Options and Choices for Black Women in the Rural South." In *Language, Gender, and Society* edited by B. Thorne, C. Kramarae, and N. Henley. Rowley, Mass.: Newbury House.

Nilsen, A. P.

1977 "Sexism as Shown through the English Vocabulary." In *Sexism and Language* edited by A. P. Nilsen, H. Bosmajian, H. L. Gershuny, and J. P. Stanley. Urbana, Ill.: National Council of Teachers of English.

———.

1972 "Sexism in English: A Feminist View." In *Female Studies VI* edited by N. Hoffman, C. Secor, and A. Tinsley. Old Westbury, N.Y.: Feminist Press, 102–109.

Olsen, T.

1979 *Silences.* New York: Delacorte Press.

Penelope (Stanley), J., and S. J. Wolfe.

1983 "Consciousness as Style: Style as Aesthetic." In *Language, Gender, and Society* edited by B. Thorne, C. Kramarae, and N. Henley. Rowley, Mass.: Newbury House.

Rich, A.

1978 "Cartographies of Silence." In *The Dream of a Common Language: Poems 1974–1977.* New York: W. W. Norton, 16–20.

Sachs, J.

1975 "Cues to the Identification of Sex in Children's Speech." In *Language and Sex: Difference and Dominance* edited by B. Thorne and N. Henley. Rowley, Mass.: Newbury House.

Sattel, J.

1983 "Men, Inexpressiveness, and Power." In *Language, Gender and Society* edited by R. Thorne, C. Kramarae, and N. Henley. Rowley, Mass.: Newbury House.

Silveira, J.

1980 "Generic Masculine Words and Thinking." *Women's Studies International Quarterly* 3: 165–178.

Stanley, J. P.

1977 "Paradigmatic Woman: The Prostitute." In *Papers in Language Variation* edited by D. Shores and C. P. Hines. University, Ala.: University of Alabama Press, 303–321.

Strodtbeck, F. L.

1951 "Husband-Wife Interaction over Revealed Differences?" *American Sociological Review* 16: 468–473.

Strodtbeck, F. L., and R. D. Mann.

1956 "Sex Role Differentiation in Jury Deliberations." *Sociometry* 19: 3–11.

Strodtbeck, F. L., R. M. James, and C. Hawkins.

1957 "Social Status in Jury Deliberations." *American Sociological Review* 22: 713–719.

Swacker, M.

1975 "The Sex of the Speaker as a Sociolinguistic Variable." In *Language and Sex: Difference and Dominance* edited by B. Thorne and N. Henley. Rowley, Mass.: Newbury House.

Trudgill, P.

1975 "Sex, Covert Prestige, and Linguistic Change in the Urban British English of Norwich." In *Language and Sex: Difference and Dominance* edited by B. Thorne and N. Henley. Rowley, Mass.: Newbury House.

West, C., and D. H. Zimmerman.

1983 "Small Insults: A Study of Interruptions in Cross-sex Conversations between Unacquainted Persons." In *Language, Gender, and Society* edited by B. Thorne, C. Kramarae, and N. Henley. Rowley, Mass.: Newbury House.

Wex, M.

1979 *Let's Take Back Our Space: "Female" and "Male" Body Language as a Result of Patriarchal Structures.* Hamburg: Frauenliteraturverlag Hermine Fees.

Restoring Women to History

Renate Bridenthal
Claudia Koonz
Susan M. Stuard

Renate Bridenthal was born in Leipzig, Germany, in 1935 and was educated in New York at City College and Columbia University. She now teaches history and coordinates the Women's Studies Program at Brooklyn College. With Claudia Koonz, she edited Becoming Visible *in 1977 and again in 1987. In 1984, she published* When Biology Became Destiny: Women in Weimar and Nazy Germany. *Claudia Koonz has also studied women in Germany in* Mothers in Fatherland: Women, the Family, and Nazi Politics *(1987). She is now at Duke University. Susan Stuard, professor of history at Haverford, works in the area of women's social and economic circumstances. She has written* Women in Medieval Society *(1976). She edited* Women in Medieval History and Historiography *(1987) and* Witnesses for Change *(1989), writings on the activism and thoughts of Quaker women.*

In this discussion, from the introduction to Becoming Visible, *Bridenthal, Koonz, and Stuard show how new, more accurate understanding of women's experience (in this case, history) proceeds from research with a feminist perspective. This work and others like it serve both to erase distorted and derogatory information and to construct better models within which to analyze the information we have. Feminist research may employ categories that traditional male-centered sources omit entirely. In this case, the authors have paid particular attention to two factors almost always overlooked and yet crucial to understanding women: gender, itself, and changes in the perception of women's sexuality. The result is more accuracy and far deeper understanding of subjects involved.*

TWO MAIN TRENDS HAVE SHAPED WOMEN'S HISTORY. One is an accelerating rate of economic and bureaucratic differentiation, that is, a breakdown of tasks and responsibilities into more and simpler ones coordinated by centralized authority. As societies become more complex, power flows to the top and generally into the hands of a few men; most women remain at the bottom. The second historical trend is the attempt to justify women's loss of power and authority by simplifying gender difference into a system of appositions labeled male and female. "Feminine" qualities are counterposed to "masculine": women are labeled passive, men active; women are defined as emotional, men described as intellectual; women are assumed to be "naturally" nurturant, men "naturally" ambitious.

In societies where the division of labor became more refined, gender categories (and eventually notions about race and ethnicity) served to assign the less desirable and remunerative tasks to people stigmatized as "inferior." By contrast, earlier, less differentiated societies, such as those at the dawn of civilization or in the early medieval period (fifth to tenth centuries, A.D.), demanded flexibility in task assignment and valued the ability of people to replace one another easily in case of need. In those eras, survival depended on recognizing women's and men's likeness to each other.

. . . Five thousand years of women's documented history is chronicled in these pages. The essays . . . fit into generally accepted historical periods: the emergence of civilization; the rise and decline of empires; the emergence of a new Christian religion; the agricultural, commercial, industrial, and scientific revolutions in Europe; the wave of social and political revolutions; the world wars. Has the system of gender polarization separated women's experience from men's in these diverse historical eras? How do the contours of women's history correspond to the course men's history has taken? . . .

Such a sweep of time frequently tempts historians and their audiences to read the course of history as progress, but women's historical experience will not fit neatly into that mold. To the extent that women share the same history as men, progress may benefit both equally. For example, women may gain as men do from improved agricultural cultivation, paved roads, and the discovery of penicillin. However, when the system of gender separates women's experience from men's, benefits do not necessarily accrue to women. For example, as centralized monarchies replaced feudal courts, noblewomen lost access to direct political power. Vastly improved opportunities for men to control their environment did not automatically benefit women. The general level of nutrition among European working people, for example, declined from the thirteenth century onward, that is, during the centuries of dynamic change that we associate with capitalism and the Industrial Revolution. The loss of essential nutrients however, was greater in the diet of working women than in the diet of working men.[1] On the other hand, in eras traditionally considered periods of decline, it appears that the status of women did not decline relative to men's. In so-called progressive eras, benefits were distributed unequally by class and gender. Finding women's experience so out of phase with that of men means that the old divisions of history into periods must be reinterpreted.

In the five thousand years, from prehistory to the 1980s . . . we have ample opportunity to observe gender relations in highly developed premodern societies as well as in industrial settings. Often it seems that in simpler times societies depended upon looser definitions of masculine and feminine, which were themselves not always consistent or authoritative. The few surviving texts from those eras provide rare glimpses of dramatically different worlds. Fuller understanding of the differences depends on a sophisticated reading of scarce sources. As political scientists and anthropologists engage in heated debates about the emergence of tyrannical states, feminist scholars also speculate about the sources of patriarchy. . . .

. . . Women's lives during the last century generally showed areas of improvement when compared to earlier generations. So, even though the women of more recent generations may have experienced losses relative to the men of their age, their lives reflected the benefits of improved material conditions. This amelioration came at a price. With the industrialization of the last two centuries, much of the social cost of progress has been exported to the Third World.

Eleanor Leacock indicates that women and men shared roughly equal opportunities before the emergence of civilized institutions. By analogy to more recent stateless societies, she suggests that in prehistoric times women and men readily exchanged tasks and duties and participated in a wide range of productive and administrative roles in religious, political, and economic life. Leacock critically examines historical evidence recorded by male visitors to a stateless society in the context of her own anthropological research and feminist insights into the ways in which prehistoric communities developed methods to regulate aggressive instincts without creating a strong patriarchy. Barbara Lesko demonstrates that a rough parity between the sexes lasted long into the first millennia of civilized life in the Nile and Tigris-Euphrates river valleys. By the end of the Bronze Age, that parity had disappeared. Lesko explains how competition for scarce resources, warfare, and the increasing importance of private property in trade made conditions worse for women. She notes as well that Egypt and Sumer, acting against new trends, preserved women's status for centuries on end.

Marilyn Arthur charts women's status over the course of the Classical era in Greece and Rome. A rigid system of gender (in which men saw women as "naturally" opposite) characterized *polis* life in Greece and represented part of its legacy to Rome and to subsequent European intellectual and cultural life. So totally did the tradition of an earlier *parity* disappear that the Greek historian Herodotus called Egyptian customs "contrary to nature." Arthur reminds us, however, that this brief era of extreme prejudice in Greece was followed by the longer Hellenistic period (323–19 B.C.) in which women assumed a greatly expanded role in cultural and social life.

Christianity and other late antique mystery cults offered women a new empowering sense of self and either directly or obliquely denied the inherited Classical gender system, the legacy from fifth-century

Greece. "In Christ there is no male or female," only the radical equality of all souls before God—or so early Christian women believed when they espoused the new faith. Previously closed out of public life by the polarities popular with the ancient Greeks, women, according to Jo Ann McNamara, opted for a new faith that ignored gender oppositions. Thus, the late Classical world (first through the fifth centuries, A.D.), far from having been one long era of unrelieved decline as historians often depict it, provided important opportunities for women. Improved rights in Roman law and women's central role in the mystery cults inspires us to rethink our basic assumptions about the age. From this perspective, the late antique world represents a new beginning rather than a decline into decadence.

Women made some of their most consequential and lasting contributions to European culture in the early medieval centuries. Christianity and a decentralized economic and political system provided a less gender-dominated world than either the Classical age that preceded it or the modern age that followed. Suzanne Wemple depicts women and men cooperating in the challenging work of creating a new society. To them, their universal, shared human capacities as children of God seemed more consequential than differences between male and female. However, these fluid assumptions about gender gave way in the High Middle Ages (between the twelfth and thirteenth centuries) to a rigid system of gender that revived Classical Greek notions of polarity. Susan Stuard points out that this revival occurred at the very time when economic systems became increasingly complex and centralized bureaucracies more powerful.

The revived system of gender featured in the Scholastic thought of the thirteenth century, with its polarities of female to male, became part of the mental equipment of Europeans and has remained so until relatively recent times. When Joan Kelly asks if women had a Renaissance and answers that they did, but not, on balance, as men did, she calls into question the rigid system of gender that characterized humanist culture. Although a powerful new idea of man emerged in the Renaissance, no comparable rigorous and logical rethinking produced new concepts about the "Renaissance Woman." Assumptions about women remained bound by prejudices and unexamined notions based on inherited classical texts. As William Monter shows, Classical notions

about women were not re-examined in the Reformation era by either the Protestant or Catholic parties. On the contrary, the polarized notions of human nature lay behind the wave of witch-hunts that swept across Reformation Europe. Men were defined as perfectible and created in the image of God, women as weak and prone to the Devil's temptations. With these polar definitions, witch-hunters overwhelmingly identified women as the possessed in the sixteenth and seventeenth centuries. The polarities ruled thought and action in almost all aspects of life. During festivals, however, especially in Catholic regions, when ribald humor turned the world upside down in carnival (or mardi gras), men and women could cross-dress. At least temporarily, revelers could express forbidden feelings and play with the roles that constrained them in the real world.

Simplifying the system of gender had unquestionable advantages for those men whose control of economic resources placed them in positions of power. Women remained highly productive members of families and communities throughout the early modern era, but a rigid gender system denied them positions of authority and, as often as not, the fruits of their labor. Merry Wiesner shows how the new stratification affected women's work in the early modern economy and undervalued much of the work done by women. The most enduring polarity in the West has been the belief in woman's incapacity and imperfectibility in contrast to man's capacity and perfectability. Wages, which came more and more to define the value of work, fell more "naturally" to those found capable and perfectible. These same assumptions eliminated women from positions of authority.

Polar notions of gender also influenced thinking and attitudes toward sexuality. Both ancient and early medieval writers allotted to women an active role in sexual reproduction. But once the Greek polarity of man's capacity and woman's incapacity became fashionable in the High Middle Ages, authors began depicting woman as a mere vessel for sexual reproduction. According to this system, an infertile woman was responsible for her failure to produce offspring; but a mother could take no credit for success in childbearing. In the same way, in terms of sexuality, late Classical authorities had recognized women's orgasmic response in sexual intercourse and associated it with the clitoris. This was confirmed by other authorities until the vogue of polarities came to dominate Western thought in the High

Middle Ages. Then writers on sexuality defined man as active, therefore orgasmic, and woman as passive, capable of arousing men's desire but not of experiencing pleasure themselves. Furthermore, men were thought to be diminished by the sex act, to suffer a "little death." Even the belief in insatiable sexual needs of sixteenth-century witches fit this system since the witch's insatiability was believed to arise not from her desire for pleasure but from a diabolic urge to be filled to compensate for her deprived and passive nature. Over the centuries, European thinkers went so far as to downplay women's role in childbearing, defining them as merely the carriers of the fetuses created by men.

By the time of the Enlightenment, as Elizabeth Fox-Genovese points out, the middle-class woman had become defined as an unattainable object of men's erotic desires. Leisured young women participated in what was almost a cult of virginity, enhancing their suitors' passions by inaccessibility. After marriage—a woman's only respectable option—women were to become maternal, without having ever experienced sexual pleasure. Victorian writers later transformed these simplistic notions into complex codes of behavior for the "proper lady," and biologists developed sophisticated theories about women's innate intellectual inferiority. By the nineteenth century, the message was clear. The bourgeois "lady" was too pure for sexual pleasure and too inferior for emancipation. Meanwhile, poverty drove thousands of poor women into brothels that made a mockery of bourgeois men's pious attempts to keep womanhood on the proverbial pedestal. Male lust, become prurient through the frustration built into Victorian ideology, found an outlet among prostitutes, who were drawn from the ranks of violated domestics and other destitute women.

The most important economic event of the late eighteenth and early nineteenth centuries was the Industrial Revolution, an accelerated change in the production of commodities which was centralized in factories and fueled by investment in new sources of energy and new forms of technology. In the process of capital accumulation, increasing numbers of people became dependent wage laborers, while a few moved upward into highly diversified middle strata in the services, professions, and clerical work. In this new and more highly differentiated social structure, Laura Frader shows, most women fell toward the

bottom as new divisions of labor continued to widen the gender gap. Although most women continued to work in the countryside, increasing numbers of young girls came into towns and cities to work in the new factories.

Ultimately, the overwhelming majority of women employed in industry and services married, and often these working-class women had to continue working for a wage, usually in their own homes for even lower rates. The development of industrial capitalism brought an expansion of subcontracted work done at home, for example making artificial flowers, sewing lingerie, rolling cigars, and producing other luxury items for the increasingly wealthy bourgeoisie. By the end of the nineteenth century, the pattern of men working outside the home and women remaining in the home, although not universal, was well established as a model for working-class as well as middle-class people. Since economic dependency contributes to powerlessness in personal relations as well, the myth of women's weakness came to be grounded in hard economic fact. Nevertheless, family survival often depended upon women's ability to "pinch hit" or "make ends meet" in the unstable economic environment of industrializing Europe.

By the twentieth century, as Renate Bridenthal shows, industrialization had assumed the features we recognize today. Especially during World War I, more young women entered industry, among them many former domestic servants. After that war, the level of women's employment in industry stabilized, although it shot up sharply in the service sector when World War II broke out. The gradual acceptance of birth control freed most women from the exhausting cycle of continuous pregnancy, although not from major responsibility for homemaking, which now became more demanding because of new standards of hygiene and psychology.

However, it would be misleading to conclude that all women remained meekly in their homes. As essays on the premodern period show, women as artisans' or merchants' wives and daughters, as nuns, and as noblewomen had a long tradition of public activity. Several of the essays on the nineteenth and twentieth centuries explore the ways in which women forged new public identities and struggled for equal rights in industrialized societies. Among the diversity of organizations and personalities, three sources of women's newfound sense of entitlement emerge. One source was women's traditional identification with their family responsibilities. A second source was the result of women claiming the "natural" rights extolled by Enlightenment thinkers. The third source was the socialists' more comprehensive analysis that showed both oppression and the hope of emancipation to be vitally connected to economic change.

Elizabeth Fox-Genovese points out that noblewomen of the eighteenth century still played a strong public role, often advancing their families' and husbands' interests in cultural or economic activities and occasionally acting as intellectual facilitators in salons and other gatherings where progressive ideas were formed. After the onset of the Industrial Revolution women of all classes were active in public life as a part of their family responsibilities. During the French Revolution, as Darlene Levy and Harriet Applewhite show, women demonstrated, petitioned, and participated in political discussions. In the course of acting on their ancient rights as family provisioners, women protested against food shortages in peremptory demonstrations that escalated to demands for popular sovereignty and in some cases led to successful revolutions. Temma Kaplan argues that "female consciousness" has often taken women out of their homes and into the public arena during times of political instability or economic disaster. When food is scarce, prices high, and politics chaotic, women depart from the normally accepted domestic models and violently demand their due.

At times, too, women have exercised a decisive impact on the course of modern revolutions. Richard Stites suggests that under the extreme repression of Tsarist Russia women played a vital role in terrorist, revolutionary organizations. Thus, in dire circumstances, received notions about masculine and feminine responsibilities may be reinterpreted by women as justification for entering into the "masculine" public arena. However, only long-term sustained, concerted organization produced legal and economic gains for women.

Among the more leisured middle classes, the women Karen Offen calls "relational feminists" demanded expansion of their narrow "feminine" roles. Accepting the family or the private world as the appropriate sphere for women, they enlarged traditional definitions of femininity to include participation in corresponding areas of public life. For ex-

ample, they argued that, as mothers, women could demand better formal education so they could raise their children to become good citizens; as nationalists or pacifists, women could argue that their familial responsibilities entitled them to speak out on war and peace, and perhaps even to vote. In liberal England, many women's energies went into imperial conquest. Margaret Strobel describes how a class of privileged women, acting in the name of Victorian womanhood, upheld the interests of white rule and their identity as mothers and wives. Some forged new careers for themselves in missionary work, anthropology, and social reform. Women operating in authoritarian or bureaucratized institutions (like the Catholic church or the British Empire) faced formidable opposition. Demanding a special status within the masculine order, they hoped to share the glory of the larger enterprise—and enhance their own influence. Rather than demanding equal rights as citizens, these women asked to share equal burdens as subjects.

In the twentieth century, women in Mussolini's Italy and Hitler's Germany continued that strategy. Claudia Koonz points to the paradox that while no modern governments have so explicitly relegated women to inferiority, none have as energetically recruited women into national organizations. Fascist societies, structured on rigid racial and gender divisions, offered ambitious and nationalistic women the chance to organize their separate sphere for "racially acceptable" women. These powerful dictatorships harnessed women's energies rather than overtly repressing them with either a "back to the home" agenda or a "feminine mystique."

The women who used their claims to uniquely feminine traits as a wedge into public life discovered limits on their aspirations because the priorities of male-dominated institutions invariably took precedence over women's needs. However, contemporary feminist movements have a wider heritage. Two other powerful ideologies, liberalism and socialism, inspired women to act on their own behalf in the nineteenth and twentieth centuries. These women framed their claim to rights not only "in relation" to men and children, but in universal terms.

Over the centuries a few educated women and men, in the tradition of Christine de Pisan, had defended women against misogynist attacks. Philosophically, in praising women's inherent worth, they laid the basis for modern feminism. Only after industrialization restructured society, however, could masses of women turn to the state with demands for equality. During the nineteenth and twentieth centuries, an historically unique movement brought hundreds of thousands of women together in all European nations in the quest for equal rights.

Especially in industrializing Protestant nations, the heritage of the Enlightenment inspired women's claim to equality. Although the reformers reinforced marriage and the patriarchal family by removing convent life as an option, their theology offered an emancipatory potential for women. The elimination of the clergy as a special caste, together with the mandate that every Protestant should read and interpret his or her own Bible, laid down the potential for seeing all human beings as equal in God's eyes. However, as William Monter points out, because in practice literacy among Protestants did not increase rapidly, this potential was only realized in the nineteenth and twentieth centuries.

Enlightenment theories of individualism, although not applied to women at the time, further advanced the notion that human potential should be fulfilled. Applewhite and Levy describe the few educated women who moved beyond the sporadic protests of wives and market women to lay claim to their natural rights as woman and citizen. In the short term, they met resounding defeat. But even as the Napoleonic Code made French women's situation in some ways worse than before 1789, Mary Wollstonecraft's *Vindication of the Rights of Women* affirmed the double heritage of women in the French Revolution with its insistence on women's special status as mothers and its demands for women's equal rights as citizens.

Sharing with the Liberals the conviction that the elimination of unjust laws would usher in an era of liberty, English feminists began to win major reforms in divorce and property law and, in many localities, achieved the right to hold local office by the middle of the nineteenth century. In response to laws regulating prostitution in seaport cities and requiring state inspection of prostitutes, Josephine Butler launched a successful crusade to repeal the hated legislation. Feminists in Germany and Russia launched similar antivice campaigns, but met with less success.

Bourgeois women mobilized to share in the power and privileges held by the men of their class. Such women, enjoying more leisure for political activism than working-class women, organized around a growing sense of gender-based injustice, an early form of feminism. Ironically, suffragists' campaigns made little headway in Europe until after World War I, when many nations granted women the vote more as a reward for patriotic service than as recognition of women's fundamental human equality.

"Success" nearly killed middle-class feminism. However, as Bridenthal notes, the gender gap in income, political power, and family responsibility remained wide. World War II intensified pressure on women for the double duty of producing armaments and reproducing the population, reduced by 50,000,000 people during the war. After the war the myth of women's place in the home was restored, though it corresponded even less to reality than it had before.

The achievement of political equality marked the highwater mark of liberal feminism. But throughout the nineteenth century, working-class women struggled for a very different concept of emancipation. Socialist feminists located the source of their exploitation in the economic system, capitalism, instead of in the legal system. From their broader vision, they developed strategies distinct from those of liberal feminists. Urbanization, new economic ties to employers and husbands, demographic changes, and increasing literacy made new forms of collective action both possible and necessary. By the twentieth century, labor union efforts had reduced the wage gap between women and men and won maternity provisions and protective laws. However, the worldwide Depression of the 1930s crippled all union efforts. Competition for scarce jobs revived male hostility to women workers, and many governments curtailed women's access to jobs and welfare benefits. World War II temporarily engaged more women in unionized manufacturing jobs, but after the war the steady relocation of female workers into traditionally nonunionized white-collar jobs set back labor organization among women until very recently.

Moving beyond immediate work-related reforms, socialists aimed to eliminate capitalism. Socialist leaders, as Charles Sowerwine demonstrates, varied widely in their reactions to women's claim to equality, but women themselves forged their own organizations under the larger rubric of International Socialism. Women succeeded within the predominately male socialist parties when they formed semi-autonomous associations, published their own periodicals, and held separate congresses, even as they joined with their male comrades in the struggle against capitalism. Marxists provided powerful new analyses of women's oppression. They argued that it was reinforced by capitalism, which made women dependent on and therefore subservient to male wage earners. This allowed employers to pay women a "supplementary," that is, much lower, wage when they did enter the labor force. The logical political corollary was that women should join men in fighting capitalism. Nevertheless, because male-dominated socialist parties did not always welcome women's full participation, it took militant women to compel their parties' attention. Although international feminist socialist solidarity never recovered from the divisive impact of World War I, in every European nation Socialist parties have led in demanding not only suffrage and equal legal status, but maternity benefits, access to abortion and birth control, family subsidies, divorce reform, and improved pay for women workers.

A totally different course was followed in the Soviet Union after the Russian Revolution of 1917. Richard Stites shows how here, for the first time in history, across-the-board legislation proclaimed equality between the sexes: in voting, education, in marriage, property rights, and in birth control. This program proved to be too radical for most people, and too costly for a government facing civil war and staggering economic crises. Finally, Stalin's emphasis on rapid and forced industrialization in the 1930s, while consciously advancing some women professionally, nevertheless reimposed a traditional family structure. With the approach of World War II, natal-

ist policies encouraged women to fulfill their patriotic duty by bearing more children and taking up strategically vital jobs in defense industries.

Jane Jenson's essay underscores the complexity of the woman question in the contemporary welfare state. Comparing the role of their respective governments in supporting families and liberating women, Jenson explains how French and British feminists have evolved two different agendas for emancipation. French feminists tend to regard the state as a potential ally while British feminists view it as the inevitable source of patriarchial power. Looking back over the centuries, we see that both viewpoints had their roots in concrete situations and in the social construction of gender.

A continual tension arises from women's double identity. On the one hand, women in most ages have had less access to public power and economic status than men; on the other hand, women have evolved distinctive values within male-dominated societies that in crucial ways diminished their status. How, generations of women have asked, can one integrate claims to full equality with a sense of women's special identity? In the history of women's consciousness we see a steadily expanding vision. The diversity of strategies for women's rights and the rich array of futuristic visions attest to the vitality of feminism.

Notes

[1]H. J. Teuteberg, "The General Relation Between Diet and Industrialization," in Elborg and Robert Forster, eds., *European Diet from Pre-industrial to Modern Times* (New York: Harper, 1975), pp. 61–109.

The Spiritual Significance of the Self-Identified Woman*

Elsa Gidlow

Elsa Gidlow (1898–1986), poet, essayist, activist, philosopher, was called the Poet Warrior. Her autobiography, ELSA: I Come With My Songs *(1986) was the first explicitly lesbian full-life autobiography published.*

Religion, traditional and institutionalized, has been one of the foremost enemies of liberation for women. Yet, Gidlow argues, without inner wholeness, without a spiritual center, life can become directionless and lack zest. Women must regain spiritual autonomy, must in fact become spiritually self-identified.

Reprinted from *Woman of Power*, Issue Twelve, Winter 1989, pp. 15–17. By permission of *Woman of Power* and Celeste West, Booklegger Publishing, San Francisco. Originally published in *Maenad*, Spring 1981, Vol. 1, No. 3, pp. 73–79.

START WITH THE PREMISE THAT SPIRITUAL POWER grows from a ground of personal wholeness. Next, each human born comes into life as a whole being. Third, if the inner sense of wholeness is lost or discouraged from maturing, the individual becomes maimed and susceptible to indoctrination, manipulation and mastery.

I have made no mention of gender; persons are born as women or men. Are their prospects equal for realizing their spiritual personhood?

From earliest childhood a boy's sense of his wholeness is reinforced, encouraged. As he grows, the integrity of his personhood is emphasized. He probably learns he will have to fight for it, but it is his to fight for. Advancing in awareness, he absorbs the conviction that his maleness is the earthly manifestation of deity. He was "*created*" in God's image. Almost all of God's representatives are male. Even if he is atheistic, he is a beneficiary of the religious and philosophical climate of male supremacy. Most religious leaders are male, as are practically all the power figures in the secular world. However humble his social position or role, a man may take for granted that there is someone of lesser importance who can be called upon to serve him: a female someone. His mother was the first model for that and, with rare exceptions, was the instiller of that expectation.

A little girl, on the other hand, from her earliest years and throughout each phase of her education and development, receives both active and subliminal messages of her subsidiary role, of her incompleteness as a person, hence her need to realize and complete herself through others: children, a husband. Her identification with "god" is not one of being created in his image. Impossible. She is female. The alternative is to serve him, as she is expected to serve the needs, works and concerns of men at the secular level. It seems curious that the simple correlation between identifying deity with maleness and subservience with femaleness has not received more emphasis.

Ultimate spirituality, the Source, the creative energy that is incommunicable in words, obviously is beyond gender. Every human may be presumed to reflect equally that spiritual energy, by whatever name and in whatever image it is presented. The fact that nearly every figure embodying spiritual transcendence and human wisdom has been presented as male could hardly leave women unaffected. It is easy and natural for men to seek and find their spiritual selves reflected in these figures, and to draw on their power for worldly enterprise. But since the preemption or destruction of the Goddess religions, there has been no embodiment of woman's spirituality for like identification and power. Is it far-fetched to see in this exclusion from identification with and direct participation in the sacred at least one cause of women's sense of mental and physical limitations and dependence, the feeling of incompleteness pushing her to ally herself with a man in an attempt by indirection to benefit from the male repository of power?

That is how it has been and to a great extent continues to be. But change is well underway. Thoughtful women have come to realize that we must seek individually and collectively—for our survival and perhaps even the survival of the planet—our spiritual path guided by our own inner light. How and where do we begin?

Some start with a personal declaration of independence, as I did at an early age; this impulse culminated in celebration of my eightieth birthday on December 29, 1978, with what I called "*Creed for Free Women*." Here is a passage from that poem:

As no free-growing tree serves another or requires to be served,
As no lion or lamb or mouse is bound or binds,
No plant or blade or grass nor ocean fish,
So I am not here to serve or be served.

I am Child of every Mother,
Mother of each daughter,
Sister of every woman,
And lover of whom I choose or chooses me.[1]

Yes, once we get down to the roots of our power-in-wholeness, our roots can split rock. Clear-eyed on the path to full personhood, we do not ignore the presence of obstacles and seductive temptations. There are women, however, who acquiesce in subsidiary-sex roles in the hope of escaping the struggles of independence or because they fear they may fail to be equal to those struggles, just as some men, more than might admit it, join the Army with a sense of relief at being freed from daily decisions and even long-term responsibilities. The challenges are formidable; the inducements to give up are ever present. It is not and never has been easy to maintain our vision of freedom, but the rewards in selfhood are worth the pains and the risk.

Always, the first step for a woman to determine is whether she wants full personhood in freedom, to decide with her whole being whether she needs autonomy and is willing to pay the price. Not every woman does—yet. There is a useful exercise for determining if one is ready to start on the path of *self-possession*. For fifteen minutes or so before retiring, stand quietly, with inward attention, and ask: "What do I *really* want?" Resist any impulse to give answers. Such usually come from "out there," from the authorities, spiritual and secular, clamoring to enter and make us theirs. Remember, we are not asking, "What *should* I want?" but what do I *really* want? Need? Repeat the exercise night after night and go to sleep empty of answers. As I know from my own experience, sooner or later, almost magically, the answer will come of itself from our own depth.

Then the work begins—work that empowers one as the discoveries unfold. The woman in her revolt realizes that she is not an auxiliary, not a partial being needing to be completed by alliance with a male—not a womb, a pair of breasts, legs, a cunt—but that she emerged into life as a whole human person who was robbed of the recognition of her wholeness to one degree or another. The knowledge comes with a surge of energy. She sees that the source of spiritual autonomy is in herself and may be tapped for whatever course she may choose to pursue. Wide awake to that knowledge, she is flooded with wonder and delight at what she has known in her depths yet hidden from herself: spirituality is relationship—collaboration and interaction with the energies of the universe and with all other women coming into that knowledge.

She realizes what Sappho, the poet, the maker, the archetype of the independent, spiritually creative woman, knew twenty-five centuries ago (and women forgot): "I am forever virgin." One can hardly doubt that she meant being, thinking and acting autonomously, in her own right. As Esther Harding reminded us, virgin originally meant "one-in-herself," not necessarily abstaining from sex or marriage, but remaining independent.[2]

At this point of initial euphoria, many women choose to "become" Lesbian. That surely is one path, a rewarding one for those whom it fulfills. It was my choice because from childhood it appeared to be my original nature. But Lesbianism and liberation from stereotypes are not synonymous. There are millions of Lesbians, declared and undeclared, but multi-millions more of women eager to achieve full personhood whose way of realising their vision need not and will not require a choice between celibacy and erotically loving women. Nor will it require rejection of motherhood for women who genuinely desire to have and nurture children, as opposed to reproducing because of pressure from ecclesiastical or secular authorities who would convince her that childbearing is her sole destiny. A woman's control over her own body is a requisite of autonomy on all levels of her existence. She is not the property or means of production for the interests of church or state. We can see here an extended meaning of "I am virgin: one-in-myself."[3]

Having made the declaration signifying her resolve to reclaim spiritual identity and autonomy on all levels of her life, a woman must be willing to follow through on it. Obviously this involves purging herself of all the false, debilitating images of what a woman is supposed to be: weak, passive, incomplete without male insemination, both spiritual and physical, to give birth to anything of flesh or spirit.

Because she aims at reclaiming full and authentic womanhood, she will come into full realization and acceptance of her erotic capabilities. She discovers the regenerative and recreative powers of her sexuality. This too is an aspect of the knowledge that she has within herself all that is necessary for strength, creativity, autonomy and spiritual relatedness. In salvaging the role of pleasure from repressive puritanism, she discovers the satisfaction inherent in one more victory over stereotypes, in this case the myth of women's "frigidity" or weak libido. Yet, the contrary has been well documented.

Although we use the words "victory" and "battle," we are not speaking about war but leaps in evolution. No banners or fanfares are needed. The women's revolt is fundamentally a quiet one, as quiet and inevitable as a plant bursting into bloom when a long, inner growth has reached culmination. This evolution was necessary not only for women but for our whole society. Much of the clamor over "women's lib" has come from those deploring, contesting, or exploiting it. Those who prefer to think in terms of a "war" are mainly extremists who execute spasmodic and isolated guerrilla attacks. The majority of women aiming at spiritual/political wholeness disavow and avoid the causes of polarization, either between women and men and, even more important, between women, individually and collectively.

Surveying human existence with the needs of a whole person, I hope, I see no opposition between the spiritual and the political. They must permeate, even define, one another. If the political excludes the deep human awe induced by the mysteries of existence and our visions of human perfectability, it is hollow. When the spiritual is intolerant of political necessity and activity, it is ungrounded, a "blue sky" indulgence. Actually, each is rooted in the other. Whole persons know the strength of integrating both into their lives and actions.[4]

Ignoring this, much harm has been done—fortunately short-range and reversible—by some of the bitter feuds between groups whose members would not or could not come into accord on tactics despite a common aim. Stridency, even cruelty, and acts of aggression that debilitate in the long run, have sometimes aped the least attractive qualities of the worst males. There is always the tendency of those involved in a "cause" to assume the masks and adopt the weapons of those who attack them and may be seen as stronger. But it would be fatal for a woman to lose her authentic womanhood in the process of retrieving it. There need be no repression or denial of a woman's gentler, receptive, compassionate qualities. Wholeness consists of integrating all of these within her strengthening Self. It is extremely important that this be recognized. Not only Western society but the entire world is suffering from a submergence of these female qualities, although they exist in all beings who have not been terminally twisted by patriarchal indoctrination.[5]

The future of humankind may depend on acceptance of the gentler, womanly qualities as a key to survival on this miraculously evolved and evolving Earth. Our gentler qualities in the service of the wholeness and strength we are reclaiming is the secret umbilical between all women who share our struggle toward wholeness. Our bond grows from the achievements and ecstasies that accompany acting out of fully realized personhood. And let us never forget that it is also the umbilical linking us to our long heritage of foremothers reaching back to a hardly imaginable past. We are the heirs to their sufferings, arduously won achievements and unrecorded triumphs. Many years ago, in a sort of ecstatic vision during a still dark early morning, lighting my fire, I felt the need to express gratitude to those women. I wrote a poem from which I quote now in the hope that our inner light and fire may lead—with work, hope and laughter—to women's fully human future:

Each dawn, kneeling before my hearth,
Placing stick, crossing stick
On dry eucalyptus bark,
Now the larger boughs, the log
(With thanks to the tree for its life)
Touching the match, waiting for creeping flame,
I know myself linked by chains of fires
To every woman who has kept a hearth.

In the resinous smoke
I smell hut and castle and cave,
Mansion and hovel,
See in the shifting flame my mother
And grandmothers out over the world
Time through, back to the paleolithic
In rock shelters, where flint struck first sparks
(Sparks aeons later alive on my hearth).
I see mothers, grandmothers back to the beginnings,
Huddled beside holes in the earth
Of iglu, tipi, cabin,
Guarding the magic no other
being has learned.
Awed reverent, before the sacred
fire . . .[6]

Notes

*I have chosen the term "*self*-identified woman" for two reasons: "Woman-identified woman" has served well for years, but has come to connote Lesbianism only. "*Self,*" as used here, is more inclusive, applicable to all women. *The American College Dictionary* says that in philosophical terminology it means "the individual consciousness in relationship to itself." Until we know our own selfhood, we are not ready to relate to the selfhood of other women. Ungrounded ideals and visions are not enough.

[1] Elsa Gidlow, "A Creed for Free Women," *The Pacific Sun,* Mill Valley, Ca., December 29, 1978. This was published for my eightieth birthday.

[2] Esther Harding, *Women's Mysteries, Ancient and Modern* (London: Rider and Co., 1971).

[3] Unless the human race is faced with extinction, no female of our species should feel that she has an obligation to reproduce. The sole reason to decide affirmatively to lend herself to procreation must be her own will to motherhood and child nurturing and women's assessment of the ensuing benefit to society.

[4] Speaking personally, in the fifties my own political activities were investigated by the California Un-American Activities Committee (known as The Tenney Committee, after the McCarthy-type senator of that name). In 1962, with Alan and Mary Jane Watts and one or two others, I helped found the Society for Comparative Philosophy; was its first vice-president, later treasurer, and in that capacity have continued to the present on its board of directors.

[5] Males are also victims of stereotypes, although they derive benefits personally and on the world stage. While in the spiritual sense, they too have been robbed of wholeness by the over-emphasis on masculinity, they receive the constant reinforcement that they are the prototypes of humanness; hence, all but a few are spared recognition of their own maimed condition.

[6] Elsa Gidlow, "Chains of Fires," in *Moods of Eros,* Druid Heights Books, Mill Valley, Ca., 1970, p. 20.

III

Women Move

"So—against odds, the women inch forward."
–ELEANOR ROOSEVELT, 1946

AS WE LOOK AT SOME OF WOMEN'S PAST AND present activities on behalf of women, it is worthwhile to consider afresh a point made earlier—that the "history of history" has been prevailingly male. Given the masculist emphasis on political and national power and its contempt for things female, it is clear why women are by and large absent from history books and why the few appearances women do make are trivialized or distorted. If, as in this final chapter, we conceive of the women's movement as primarily a centuries-old process of women coming to awareness of themselves as women, we can recognize that it is not enough to have learned about the past. To know and to understand the women's movement requires of us all that we search for the totality of women's experience throughout history, seek out previously hidden facts, look at old information in new ways, keep our minds open to reinterpretations of traditional recountings, and be ready for surprises from the lost past of women on the move.

9

Feminist Activism: Issues, Events, Documents

When Did the Women's Movement Begin?

It is often asked: When did the women's movement begin? Many discussions attempt to fix origins in relatively recent activity, specifically in the Enlightenment and the French Revolution, in the drive for the abolition of slavery, or in the American civil rights and war resistance movements. These attempts have a certain logic, but they can be misleading. They tend to focus attention not on one movement but on many: on eighteenth-, nineteenth-, or twentieth-century movements, each with a discernible starting point, each built around distinct needs and goals, and each with separate and characteristic political attitudes, personalities, and strategies. A traditional reading in this vein of pinpointed origins might be summed up as follows:

The first stirrings of the women's movement were felt with the publication of Mary Wollstonecraft's A Vindication of the Rights of Women *in 1792. The Women's Rights Movement in the United States was born during the drive for abolition, particularly in the activities and writings of the Grimké sisters in the 1830s. It culminated in the winning of the vote in 1920; and then, because*

women had exhausted themselves in the fight for suffrage, it died, until Betty Friedan's The Feminine Mystique *brought it back to life in 1963.*

A conceptualization of the women's movement that strikes me as more constructive is simply that of women *moving toward greater strength and freedom both in their awareness and in their sociopolitical position.* Development in this direction has been happening through the centuries, often for individuals, sometimes collectively. It has progressed, and it has receded; it has sometimes been subterranean, and sometimes it crests into waves of activism. It has expressed itself in many ways—in poetry, in marches on courthouses, or in the quiet but sturdy resistance of women in their households. It has been conceptualized in varying contexts—political, economic, psychological, or even physical—and it is not easily confined to one model. From this perspective, no discernible "beginning" or cutoff point to the women's movement exists. We need not exclude the Roman women demonstrating in the forum in 195 B.C. for repeal of the antifemale Oppian laws or the poems of Sappho or the struggles for survival of a thirteenth-century group of women called the Beguines (who chose to abjure marriage, live and work together, help the poor in the name of Christianity but maintain independence from the control of the male church). We can include in our understanding of the women's movement the egalitarian ideals of the Quakers, of Anne Hutchinson, or of "Constantia."

Such an approach has manifold value. First, it reveals the universality of women's concerns. It also emphasizes the sisterhood of women. In addition, it reveals the startling continuity over time of feminist issues, values, goals, and challenges and in so doing allows us to see that each wave of activism is not separate and anomalous, destined for an end or for limited achievement at best but is rather an integral part of a progressive development. Finally, this approach affords us a context for evaluating challenges not only to feminist goals but also to the very legitimacy of feminism as a world movement.

Key Themes of Women's Movement

For centuries, in groups and as individuals, women have spoken out consistently on certain key issues. Although they may reflect the character of the times and the attitudes and issues prominent in their age, the products of feminist women's efforts have been remarkably consistent in their direction: They have to do with the *quality* of life for women and for the entire human community.

It is also interesting to note that opponents' reactions have been consistent as well. Adversaries generally attack feminists' "femaleness," good sense, and morality, and they charge activism on women's behalf with triviality or destructiveness or both (however inconsistent that may seem).

Major Issues for Women

It is a revelation to read, "The time has come to take this world muddle that men have created and strive to turn it into an ordered, peaceful, happy abiding place for humanity,"[1] and discover that those words, which sound so like the women's liberation movement of the '60s, '70s, and '80s were spoken by Alva Belmont in 1922. Mary Wollstonecraft chides the affectations and destructive results of traditional "femininity," and were it not for the habits of language current in her time, she would sound quite like Gloria Steinem or Germaine Greer.

Again and again in poetry, political treatises, personal letters, speeches, and social analyses, we see these themes reiterated: the folly of grossly distorting women's physical, emotional, and intellectual development; the injustice of denying to half the world's population their rights, opportunities, and contributions; the great need for humanitarian treatment of the young, the sick, and the powerless in the face of the insensitive and selfish values of traditional masculist institutions; the unlikeliness of peace and harmony in a world suffused with the aggressiveness and arrogance of martial power values.

The consistency of themes and purposes in our history underscores the continuity of the movement, the character of feminist concerns, and, it would appear, the legitimacy of our claims. Feminist analysis is not transitory and culture-bound but rather is part of the mainstream of ongoing political thought and liberation philosophy, although it has not been perceived that way.

Charges and Countercharges

Feminist women all say to the masculists: You misunderstood and malign us: you thwart us; you deny to the world our abilities and contributions; you distort the quality of life; you cause war and unrest; you are arrogant, foolish, and mean. Opponents answer: You, feminists, are misled and confused; your goals are contrary to reason, nature, and order; your behavior is unnatural and unseemly; you are either ill (unfeminine) or evil; your actions will cause your own downfall and that of your family, *the* family, the nation, and the world; you are unable to see this, or you don't care.

It crystallizes one's own sense of place and helps to resolve certain personal conflicts to realize that activist women in any age have met the same misogynist accusations. Cato exclaimed of the Roman women, "It is complete liberty, or rather complete license they desire. If they win in this, what will they not attempt? The moment they begin to be your equals, they will be your superiors."[2] Doesn't that sound like: Give them an inch and they'll take a mile; they want to dominate men? Mary Wollstonecraft commented in 1792: "From every quarter have I heard exclamations against masculine women."[3] The same charge of "masculinity" was made against nineteenth-century activists, and what contemporary feminist has not been called masculine or "queer"? Lucy Stone reported in 1855: "The last speaker [at the National Convention, Cincinnati] alluded to this movement as being that of a few disappointed women."[4] How modern! Feminists today are called "disappointed" (that is, frigid, jilted, or crabby) and are always taken to task for being "in the minority," not in the mainstream of female life.

Just a Disappointed Few

The contention that feminists are not of the majority of women or are not like "normal" women bears looking at, first, because it is an attack so often made and, second, because it raises the question of how accurately feminists may claim to represent women's concern. The argument is phrased in various ways: "'Libbers' are just a bunch of losers who couldn't make it in the man-woman world." "Feminism is just a white middle-class movement." "Feminists are just bored women trying to get their own when there is *real* oppression in the world that affects millions of people." Let us consider those charges one by one.

A Bunch of Losers

To the charge that her movement was that of a few disappointed women, Lucy Stone answered, "In education, in marriage, in religion, in everything, disappointment is the lot of woman! It shall be the business of my life to deepen this disappointment in every women's heart until she bows down to it no longer."[5] That, of course, is the proper answer. Women *are* losers in a patriarchal society, not losers in ourselves, as the epithet implies, not losers because of some personal inadequacy, but losers in a game where the rules and the rewards are so heavily stacked against us. It is the business of the movement to clarify to all women what we are losing and to help us understand that we are the victims and not the perpetrators of loss.

A White Middle-Class Movement

To a movement that proposes to speak to all women, a movement in which the term *sisterhood* is of first priority, the charge that we are composed of and concerned with only a small part of the female community, and that part the more privileged segment, would be a serious matter.

For a period in feminism in the early part of the twentieth century, in seeking the vote, activist groups put aside their original convictions and exploited themes of ethnic, racial, and class bigotry. It was a period in feminist history that bears scrutiny for the lessons it reveals, yet I believe that it does not represent the greatest part of feminist history and thought but rather the smallest. Eighteenth-century analysis, growing as it did out of the Enlightenment, was strongly egalitarian. The next wave of activism, in the nineteenth century, developed out of abolition and the theory of human rights. The first contemporary feminists came out of the civil rights and antiwar movements of the 1950s and 1960s. Their work, *in its intention,* is both internationalistic and egalitarian in its treatment of class, sex, and race.

Certainly we see a great deal of writing and activism that originated with middle-class women (some from working-class backgrounds). An examination of history reveals, however, that almost all movements for liberation and change have originated among those people who would appear privileged beyond the means of those most sorely oppressed. It was they who had the education and training to see beyond their condition to reasons and alternatives, they who could articulate issues and instigate strategies for change, and it was they who had the time and the wherewithal to act. The themes *liberté, egalité* and *fraternité* of the French Revolution originated among the well-educated, well-placed philosophers of the Enlightenment, not among the wretched poor who suffered most and most needed change, and to whom help eventually flowed. Marx and Lenin were intellectuals, and although they hoped for a rising of the masses, Lenin ultimately came to believe in the necessity of an educated vanguard of leadership.

Although the movement may appear to have been instigated by the white middle class (and even this appearance is misleading), it was not meant to be a movement *of* the white middle class. That is, it was not about only the white middle class nor is it today. The drive for jobs and occupational equity certainly concerns working-class and poor women as much as it does middle-class women. Opening skilled and semiskilled unions to women, reforming clerical and secretarial occupations, and expanding women's place in government-funded poverty relief projects are all goals of the feminist movement.

Securing the right of women to control our own bodies affects poor women even more than it does the affluent. Welfare reform has long been a feminist goal. The extinction of racism is a major feminist target.

Where the women's movement originally erred was not in its intentions, but in its own failure to see; this was a result of its youth and lack of development. Like much of the society around them, early feminists did not have sufficient sensitivity to *difference* and to the difference in our lives that difference makes. This led many to lump all women into one category—woman—and to assume that female experience is always the same. Hester Eisenstein described the error as:

> *a false universalism that generalized about the experience of women, ignoring the specificities of race, class, and culture. A feminist perspective assumed that all women in the world, whatever their race, religion, class, or sexual preference, had something fundamentally in common. Some versions of feminism took this assumption a step further: they insisted that what women had in common, by virtue of their membership in the group of women, outweighed all of their other differences, or (to put this another way) that the similarity of their situation as female was more fundamental than their economic and cultural differences. The second step in this argument is what I term "false" universalism. To some extent, this habit of thought grew inevitably from the need to establish gender as a legitimate intellectual category. But too often it gave rise to analysis that, in spite of its narrow base of white, middle-class experience, purported to speak about and on behalf of all women, black or white, poor or rich.*[6]

Feminists, like the wider society, suffered from ethnocentrism, or heterosexism, or classism, or agism, and so on, and it had the same effect as this always does: it was destructive.

Notable, however, is the seriousness of purpose with which the movement has responded to the problem. Efforts are made to increase our sensitivity, to *listen*, to refrain from speaking for others, to make it possible for each to speak and act for herself, and for all to act for each other.

To the question, What are the central challenges for feminist scholars in the future? Catharine Stimpson replied:

> *To end stupid oversimplifications about "all women" and to speak of the differences among women created by race, class, religion, sexuality, nationality, region and age. I believe that the study of differences among women, which I have named "heterogeneity," is a laboratory in which we can learn how to think about and live with "human differences" themselves.*[7]

Tension arises over strategies and issues and between black and white, gay and straight, moderate and radical feminists, but diversity and interchange are creative. The ultimate values have stood.

A Diversion From "Real" Oppression

Feminists have been told that the movement, only about "peripheral" and "trivial" matters, dangerously diverts resources away from "real" problems that are far more serious than ours. That charge is neither new nor unique to our times, as you will see in the selections ahead. When Abigail Adams—young, intelligent, spunky woman of the emerging republic—wrote to her husband to "remember the ladies," she met with little success. Husband John, at that time a young firebrand in the cause of liberty but eventually the second president of the United States, cautioned her to be patient, for *more important matters* were at stake. In a letter to his compatriot James Sullivan, Adams revealed that although good reasons existed to consider the rights of "the ladies," it was consciously decided *not* to insure the rights of women citizens in the new society because it would be impractical and raise too many problems.[8] The egalitarian founders of the new republic were too busy to open such a messy can of worms as women's rights. After the Civil War, when Congress forged the new constitutional amendments for human rights, feminists who had worked tirelessly for abolition asked that women be included among the newly protected persons. They were denied their request, told that it was the negro's day. Paradoxically, only black men, not black women, were guaranteed their rights. You will see in the debate over ERA that the omission of women from those civil rights amendments (13–15) continues to haunt us into the present. During the early 1920s, the new government of the USSR revoked gains made by women in the 1918 revolution on the grounds that Russia was under siege and other needs must take priority over women's rights. Last, women always come last.

Earlier, feminists were chided for "muscling in" to affirmative action, federal programs, and educational opportunities; female activists in political parties are even now ridiculed for harping on "trivia" (women's issues) while men worry about "important" things like Star Wars and B-2 bombers.

Today some would go to prison for the protection of fetuses, but they would cheerfully sacrifice the liberty, autonomy, and quality of life of the women who bear them. The right of a fetus to develop is important. The right of a woman to live well as she sees fit is considered trivial.

The charge of triviality is a constant in women's history and should not surprise us. Reducing women's suffering to trivia is not only an enduring masculist perspective but a misogynist strategy as well. To the sane and right-minded, it is self-evident that denial of autonomy and freedom, denial of political, economic, and educational equity, and daily exploitation are as destructive in women's lives as in men's. A revolution that only advanced the position of men could not justly be called a revolution for human rights. Similarly, "affirmative action" that guarantees jobs for men but not for women cannot claim to be a program for "equal" human rights. When political activists demand parity for the poor, the colonized, and the oppressed, they must remember that more than half of those poor, colonized, and oppressed are female, and that women are doubly tyrannized in being exploited even within their own subgroups, *as women*, by men. History shows that, when all is said and done, women's movement has been a drive to free all women from the tyranny of misogyny and all humanity from the tyrannies of masculism—hardly trivial.

Earlier Sisters, Ongoing Themes

The widest treatment of history and anthropology is called for to begin constructing accurate images of women's movement toward awareness of ourselves as women and of our position in the society. Cave paintings exist in France believed to have been executed by women recording their social organization; poems by ancient Sumerian and African mothers, letters written by a Renaissance woman to her daughter entering marriage, speeches attributed to condemned witches (practitioners of the "old religion"), psychological tracts and social treatises all

carry powerful political messages and implications. By rights, a student of women's experience should see them all. Space, however, precludes so wide a sample. What this chapter presents is just a small segment of women's material, limited for the most part to the United States and to the last two centuries, selected primarily for its representativeness, in period or attitude, and for its fame.

As you sample the writings of foremothers at the end of this chapter, notice how the analyses and arguments of each woman reflect the currents and ideas of her time yet maintain the continuity of concern discussed above. Many of the arguments remain powerful and timely today. Consider, too, how drives for progress in women's affairs have often emanated from human liberation movements, economic or racial, and how necessary it has been for women in every age to remind (male) society that its altruism must be extended to include women in its understanding of "humanity."

Enlightenment Themes

The eighteenth century was a period of tremendous upheaval and change both in the character of its social organization and in the philosophical themes that developed out of it. Major issues of consideration flowed around the concept of rights that human beings could be said to have vis-a-vis society and government. Certain ideals, although hotly debated and often maintained more in principle than in fact, came to occupy a central position in political philosophy. For a variety of reasons, new importance was given to the notion of *natural* human worth, individual value, which was held to be somehow cosmic in its source and prior to any privilege or status that could be bestowed by "civilized" society. Men were said to be equal in that value, brothers to one another, rational and good. Education, free opportunity, and the exercise of reason were seen as supplying the major ingredients of progress and harmonious community. Privilege, hereditary wealth and power, and unearned status were represented as villainous. Authority unchecked and exercised without consent was tyranny. Human excellence was composed of rationality, responsibility, emotional and physical health, independence, and tolerance. These were the major ideals of the political thought that we later called the Enlightenment. Although great diversity arose in how these ideals might be instituted, the values themselves were taken as fundamental by a very large portion of the intelligentsia.

Note that *men* were said to be equal in worth. "All *men* are created equal"—not women. It was left to thinkers like Mary Wollstonecraft to remind the great liberal egalitarians that all they had said regarding worth, rights, opportunity, and freedom, as well as the condition and potential of the poor and oppressed, the uneducated, and unwashed, could and should be applied to women also. Although Abigail Adams's letter to her husband may have been, in her own words, "saucy," it revealed an important truth. The framers of the great experiment in political rights were themselves guilty of the same tyranny against which they had just rebelled in righteous indignation.

Human Rights and Abolition

A saying and belief among radical activists of the 1960s professed that the best way to attract people to the New Left was not to preach or cajole but rather to let people just once confront the police, that establishment barbarity would radicalize them. That indeed in large measure was what happened to women activists in the nineteenth century. Incensed by the injustice of slavery, they moved to correct that social sin; then, finding themselves equally sinned against, they became radicalized on their own behalf.

The women learned much from their work in the abolition movement. It was the Enlightenment commitment to human rights that they brought against slavery, and it was not a far distance from the rights of blacks to the rights of women. (The analogy between blacks and females runs as a recurring theme through feminist analysis right into the twentieth century.) Women learned about the effectiveness of organization and experienced for the first time the potential and joy of female unity and assertiveness. They learned to say openly, "me too." As women came to see clearly the hypocrisy and cruelty of black oppression, they gained the insight to recognize it in their own lives and the strength to reject the absurdity and meanness of masculist values, behavior, and rules.

Representing so well the relationship of black and female oppression and of black and female liberation is the speech of Sojourner Truth at a rights

convention in Ohio in 1851. An ex-slave who had become a lecturer and preacher, Truth was described by the convention's president, Frances Gage, as an "almost Amazon form, which stood nearly six feet high, head erect, and eyes piercing the upper air like one in a dream." Truth's "Ain't I A Woman?" speech is a most powerful and stirring statement of masculist irrationality.

Themes of the First Half of the Twentieth Century

The first half of the twentieth century saw the people of the world drawing closer together, albeit painfully. The rise of industrialism, the need for increased trade, the Great War, the rise of Marxism, and other factors all brought internationalistic questions to the foreground and forced reexamination of many issues. People had to place themselves in a wider context and reconsider the limits of authority; the sources of government; the uses of knowledge; the concepts of community, social responsibility, and freedom; and even the nature of happiness. During this period the social sciences were evolving—sociology, psychology, and anthropology—and they, too, were creating new ideas and questions for consideration: the proper limits of science as well as new forms for the study and control of human behavior or radically altered possibilities for the future of life and society.

The debate over women's issues was affected by the emerging intellectual models. A belief, prevalent among many feminists and nonfeminists alike, is that the women's movement simply died in 1920 with the passage of the Nineteenth Amendment. It is claimed that since the movement narrowed in the latter part of the nineteenth century from very wide-ranging concerns to a total involvement in suffrage, and since the winning of that goal required a Herculean effort, when it was won activists simply folded in exhaustion. This argument has some basis. Certainly political activity organized on a scale like that of the preceding seven decades did diminish. One could look for reasons in the Depression of the 1930s, in the political turmoil of the entire world during that decade, and in the vast energy output in World War II during the 1940s. Such monumental events coupled with the belief that the vote created the opportunity to cure all women's ills might indeed lead to a decrease in organized activism.

Yet we can bring the idea that the movement died (or even went to sleep) into different focus by placing it in the context of events from the wider intellectual and cultural scene. As general political activism and dialogue in the thirties centered mainly in socialism and Marxism, so did feminism. Many of the questions raised by the original American feminists in the nineteenth century were debated by female socialists of this time—the isolation of housework, the opportunity for work, the right to an independent identity, the oppressive elements of marriage and romance. (In fact, feminist groups of all kinds during these years were accused of Bolshevist tendencies.)

Just as the impetus for general social change during this time often arose from within the newly developing social sciences, so, too, speculation about new possibilities for women's personal lives centered there. In the 1920s, Freud's hypotheses regarding female sexuality (among others, that females *had* sexuality) touched off a whole set of issues that were carried into the thirties and forties by psychologists like Karen Horney and her contemporaries. Reinforced by the research of various feministically inclined anthropologists, like Margaret Mead and Ruth Benedict, more positive attitudes toward women's sexuality occasioned lively activism on behalf of biological freedom. The birth control and planned parenthood movement was born and flourished between the 1920s and the 1950s.

In the 1920s, the suffragist Alice Paul and her coworkers of the radical Congressional Union introduced the Equal Rights Amendment and lobbied for its passage. The National Council of Women, the Women's International League for Peace and Freedom, the League of Women Voters, and other organizations like these, each with its own political purpose and agenda, came into existence during this period. Many still function today.

In the first half of the twentieth century, America's economic system underwent tremendous changes as did women's participation in it. After World War I, women moved into the public work place in growing numbers on every level. Frequently, as they grew in numbers, they organized. Women were particularly active in the trade union movement. In the professions, organizations such as Business and Professional Women (BPW) not only supported women in gaining better educational and business opportunities, but they also lob-

bied—and still do—for other women's issues in the legislatures and with presidential commissions.

Given all this activity, it seems shortsighted to insist that exhausted women let their movement die. More accurate is to point out that many suffrage activists moved into divergent areas of activity, that new feminist women expressed their values through these different models. The movement— less organized or centralized, less political, less visible in some ways, even less numerous—was nonetheless alive.

The Second Half and the Second Wave

Although women's issues as a major item of public discussion receded in importance during the 1940s, conditions that would change this continued to ferment. The Depression had had a negative effect on women's position in the economy. What jobs existed had gone to men, and women lost ground in education, professional status, work rights, and salary. During World War II, however, conditions changed. Positions left empty by men gone to war and jobs in the burgeoning industrial sector had to be filled by women. In factories, offices, and industry, managing small businesses, running farms, teaching college, and building tanks, women did very well. Situations until then deemed "for men only" were effectively accommodated by women, and they learned an unforgettable lesson: There is no masculine or feminine occupation.

From 1945 on, even after the war when many women lost their jobs to returning veterans, the number and percentage of working women of all kinds—married and unmarried, young and mature, parent and nonparent—increased dramatically. Their numbers grew, and the realities of women's lives expanded and changed. What did not change, and what eventually was to cause much of the conflict that crystallized in the fifties and exploded in the sixties, was the cultural mythology, the projected ideals of femininity. Except for the brief wartime appearance of the patriotic Rosie the Riveter, America's dream-girl image never adjusted to women's new realities and changing needs. In fact, the gap between myth and reality widened. In the late forties and fifties, popular culture stressed the visions of the virginal, naive girl-next-door and the softly pliant housewife in cotton dress and three-inch spikes tending single-mindedly to family and home. On the surface, at least, it was a time of traditional values and "togetherness."

Betty Friedan, in *The Feminine Mystique,* credits the wars, especially the Korean War, for this period of retrenchment. Disillusioned and emotionally exhausted, people (particularly men) craved the security and nurturance of a stable family and home, and they retreated to the familiar comforting arrangements of marriage, or at least the image of it, and to the concept of the nurturing, tender wife-mother. This is at least partly true.

Again, however, one must be careful not to oversimplify, and one must seek explanations for women's situation with an eye to events in the wider culture. Although the fifties was a period of apparent quiescence, it harbored the seeds of turmoil. Although the decade was known for a kind of apathy toward political and national events, it also saw the cold war, the second "red scare," McCarthy and McCarthyism. It may have had "the corporation man" and the man in gray flannel, but it also had Jack Kerouac and anticonformist Beatniks. It was a day in 1955 when Rosa Parks refused to go to the back of the bus and touched off the civil rights movement, the true beginnings of the New Left. These and other events were as much a part of the personal history of the new feminist women of the sixties as were the television images of superwife.

Somewhere between the opposing realities, between prom gowns and Rosa Parks, between affluence and Vietnam, between maternal admonitions of purity and displaced homemakers, the feminists of the Second Wave emerged alive and kicking.

Contemporary Feminism: The Second Wave— Themes and Theories

Although we have issues on which a high degree of consensus exists among feminists, on some others great divergence arises in general philosophic orientation, strategy, or treatment. These issues, which can generate conflict, are internal themes of contemporary feminism that have developed during and since the early sixties. Because they have a strong effect on the strategies and actions movement leaders choose, because they often determine how we articulate our concerns, and because opponents of feminism often seize on them to split unity among women, these issues deserve our careful attention.

In the introduction to the first edition of their book *Feminist Frameworks,* Alison Jaggar and Paula Rothenberg (Struhl) outline four basic feminist frameworks or theoretical orientations: *liberal* feminism (some call it *moderate* feminism), which essentially seeks opportunities for women's advancement in the existent society through institutional changes in education and the work place; *Marxist* feminism, which locates the source of women's oppression in the general problems of a capitalist society and the remedy, therefore, in its dissolution; *radical* feminism, which locates the source of women's oppression not in any particular economic system but in the nature and implications of gender (perhaps even sex) itself; and *socialist* feminism, an amalgam of the last two, which holds both economic and gender/sex factors equally responsible.[9]

This approach represents one viable classification; others are possible. Some feminists believe that it is better not to classify, arguing that labels are misleading, restrictive, difficult to apply, and so counterproductive. This view has merit, for categorization is always risky. And yet configurations do present themselves, and distinctions that can be helpful in placing ideas into perspective and rendering them more understandable are possible.

Differences in Orientation: Moderate Versus Radical Feminism

To be sure, the word *radical* is a relative term. Where anyone is placed on the radical-to-conservative spectrum is probably at least as much a function of the one doing the placing as of the one described. Yet there have been strong differences of opinion and splits among feminists regarding general approach: choices of strategy (for example, militancy, demonstrations, guerilla theater, and strikes versus painstaking political-legal activism), procedural rules (for example, complete separatism versus male participation), and even language and conceptualization (for example, reform versus revolution).

Some commentators on the movement have associated moderation or conservatism with the women's rights organizations aimed basically at institutional reform. They have reserved the term *radical* for those determined to go beyond institutional reform, which would create *equality* for women, to far-reaching cultural redefinition involving profound changes for both women and men in the entire construction of society. It has been said that moderate feminists want to secure for women a piece of the pie; radical feminists want to change the pie. We must, however, use even this characterization with care, for clearly some overlap of these perspectives exists. Radical feminists usually support institutional reform, and moderate or conservative activists realize that even small changes in social arrangements and institutions engender profound alterations and adjustments in the patterns of social and private life.

The differences between radicals and moderates are based in their general philosophical orientation, ethical priorities, interpretation of causes, cultural vision, and even temperament. Compare, for example, the sharp differences in the tone, attitudes, explanatory constructs, strategies, and goals of the following documents.

> *Radical feminism recognizes the oppression of women as a fundamental political oppression wherein women are categorized as an inferior class based upon their sex. It is the aim of radical feminism to organize politically to destroy this sex class system. . . .*
>
> *A political power institution is set up for a purpose. We believe that the purpose of male chauvinism is primarily to obtain psychological ego satisfaction, and that only secondarily does this manifest itself in economic relationships. For this reason we do not believe that capitalism, or any other economic system, is the cause of female oppression, nor do we believe that female oppression will disappear as a result of a purely economic revolution. The political oppression of women has its own class dynamic; and that dynamic must be understood in terms previously called "nonpolitical"—namely the politics of the ego.*[10]

—from Ann Koedt's *Politics of the Ego*, a manifesto for New York Radical Feminists, 1969[11]

> *We, men and women who hereby constitute ourselves as the National Organization for Women, believe that the time has come for a new movement toward true equality for all women in America, and toward a fully equal partnership of the sexes, as part of the worldwide revolution of human rights now taking place within and beyond our national borders.*

> *The purpose of NOW is to take action to bring women into full participation in the mainstream of American society now, exercising all the privileges and responsibilities thereof in truly equal partnership with men. . . .*
>
> *We realize that women's problems are linked to many broader questions of social justice; their solution will require concerted action by many groups. Therefore, convinced that human rights for all are indivisible, we expect to give active support to the common cause of equal rights for all those who suffer discrimination and deprivation, and we call upon other organizations committed to such goals to support our efforts toward equality for women.*

—from the National Organization for Women's *Statement of Purpose*, 1966[12]

Into the Future: The Next Wave

Feminists must decide many issues for the future. We are feeling the full brunt of an antifeminist, antiwoman backlash, not only in the United States but all over the world. A strong wave of political and economic conservatism has reversed many of the hard-won victories of the past: affirmative action, comparable worth, professional upward mobility programs lie almost in tatters. The religious right has vowed absolute enmity to women's reproductive liberty, and they are making progress. Increasing numbers of women and their children are poor, homeless, and hungry. The Earth we have vowed to protect progressively is being devoured for its resources. All over the world, war, famine, and political repression hit women worst.

Fewer young women today are actively involved in politics or social activism. Indeed, they seem less aware, less concerned, than they were twenty years ago.

Yet, some observers of social life, myself included, see the possibilities of the worm turning: consider the renewed discussion of civil rights protection in Congress; renewed awareness of social discrimination on American campuses, renewed vigor of prochoice activities in response to the relentless attacks upon our personal freedom. It is possible to see seeds of rebirth in the '80s that will flourish in the '90s, just as the worst repressions of the '50s gave birth to the energy of the '60s. This is already visible. A major factor in the last gubernatorial elections of the '80s was the abortion issue—giving the edge to prochoice candidates. As the decade closes on movements for political liberation in China, Korea, and all over Eastern Europe, one can only guess when and how, not if, that drive will affect the United States.

We are the ones who can decide how the energy of the '90s will be employed. What shall we do? Where shall we put our greatest efforts? What should be our priorities? How can we revitalize the energy, optimism, and power of women's movement, and where shall we take it?

These questions are put to all of us. Ultimately they are personal questions. What is *your* response?

For serious feminists, these tough questions should be asked and kept ever in mind as we go about our business. As we grow in sophistication and influence, we need a better sense of our ultimate direction, sharper strategies, more unity. We need themes and constructs more carefully defined and strongly supported in order to communicate with one another, to persuade the outsider, and to counter our challengers.

Notes

[1]*Ladies' Home Journal,* September 1922, p. 7; quoted in Judith Papachristou, ed., *Women Together* (New York: Knopf, 1976), p. 203.

[2]Quoted in Vern L. and Bonnie Bullough, *The Subordinate Sex* (Baltimore: Penguin, 1974), p. 88.

[3]Author's Introduction to Mary Wollstonecraft, *A Vindication of the Rights of Woman* (New York: Dutton, Everyman Library, 1929), p. 3.

[4]Quoted in Judith Papachristou, *Women Together* (New York: Alfred A. Knopf, 1976), p. 32.

[5]Ibid.

[6]Hester Eisenstein, *Contemporary Feminist Thought* (Boston: G. K. Hall & Co., 1983), p. 132.

[7]Catharine R. Stimpson, "Setting Agendas, Defining Challenges," *The Women's Review of Books* VI, No. 5, February 1989: 14.

[8]See the Adams Letters in this chapter.

[9]Alison M. Jaggar and Paula Rothenberg Struhl, eds., *Feminist Frameworks* (New York: McGraw-Hill, 1978), pp. xii–xiii. The second edition of *Feminist Frameworks*, published by McGraw-Hill in 1984, maintains the concept of "frameworks" or categories but develops and deepens them.

[10]ego: We are using the classical definition rather than the Freudian: that is, the sense of individual self as distinct from others. [Footnote in original source.]

[11]*Politics of the Ego* was written by Anne Koedt and adopted as the manifesto of New York Radical Feminists at its founding meeting in December 1969.

[12]Reprinted in Aileen S. Kraditor, ed., *Up From the Pedestal* (Chicago: Quadrangle, 1968), pp. 363ff.

Rediscovering American Women: A Chronology Highlighting Women's History in the United States *and* Update—The Process Continues

The first part of this chronology was included in the Spirit of Houston, *the report to President Carter following the conference in Texas of the National Commission on the Observance of International Women's Year, the First National Women's Conference. No doubt it was meant to remind us that women have been a force in American history, sometimes against all odds.*

The update following the Houston Chronology was compiled by Kim Blankenship, a young feminist activist, a leader, now studying law at Washington University School of Law in St. Louis. It is women like Blankenship who give us all hope that we will continue to be a positive force, for ourselves and for the future.

The reformation which we propose, in its utmost scope, is radical and universal. It is not the mere perfecting of a progress already in motion, a detail of some established plan, but it is an epochal movement—the emancipation of a class, the redemption of half the world, and a comforming reorganization of all social, political, and industrial interests and institutions.

—Paulina Wright Davis
Woman's Rights Convention
Worchester, Massachusetts, 1850

Reprinted from *The Spirit of Houston: The First National Women's Conference.* An Official Report to the President, the Congress and the People of the United States, March, 1978. Washington, D.C.: National Commission on the Observance of International Women's Year, U.S. Department of State, 1978.

1587 VIRGINIA DARE, A GIRL, WAS THE FIRST BABY born to English colonists in the New World. The daughter of Elenor White Dare and Ananias Dare, she was born on August 18 in Roanoke Island, Virginia.

circa 1600 The Constitution of the Iroquois Confederation of Nations guaranteed women the sole right and power to regulate war and peace. The women also selected tribal leaders.

1607 Princess Pocahantas saved the life of Captain John Smith, one of the founders of the Jamestown Colony, by interceding with her father, king of the Powhatan Confederacy.

1620 The Mayflower Compact was signed aboard ship by 39 men and male servants among the 102 passengers aboard the Pilgrim vessel. Women, who were not considered free agents, were not asked to sign. Only five of the 18 wives who arrived in Plymouth on the *Mayflower* survived the first harsh winter in the new land.

1638 Anne Hutchinson was excommunicated by the Puritan church in Boston for challenging its religious doctrines. One of her followers, Mary Dwyer, later became a Quaker and was hanged in 1660 in Boston for refusing to accept a sentence of banishment. Another woman who fought for freedom of conscience was Lady Deborah Moody, who moved from Massachusetts to Gravesend, Long Island where she and her companions established a community based on religious tolerance and self-government.

1648 The first attempt by a white woman to obtain political power in America originated with

Margaret Brent. In a petition to the Colony of Maryland House of Delegates she requested two votes in the Assembly. She believed she merited one vote as a landowner, a vote a man would have obtained without question, and one vote as the executrix for the deceased brother of Lord Baltimore. Her request was denied.

1652 Elizabeth Poole formed a joint stock company in Taunton, Massachusetts to manufacture iron bars. This was one of the first successful iron production plants in the colonies.

1717 Twenty young women sent by King Louis XIV aboard a "brides' ship" to Louisiana to marry French settlers there refused to do so when they arrived in the primitive colony. Their revolt became known as the "petticoat rebellion."

1735 During the eight months that printer Peter Zenger was in jail in New York awaiting trial on charges of printing seditious materials, his wife, Catherine, kept his printshop running. She set type, read proof, wrote, and continued publication of his *New York Weekly Journal.* After her husband's death in 1746, Catherine Zenger continued to publish the newspaper.

The first woman publisher in the Colonies was believed to be Elizabeth Timothy, who took over her late husband's paper, the weekly *South Carolina Gazette,* in Charleston, South Carolina. An estimated 30 women were newspaper publishers in the 18th century Colonies.

1761 The first black poet whose work was to be preserved arrived in Boston harbor on a slave ship from western Africa. Then seven years old, Phyllis Wheatley was taught to read and write English and Latin, and her poetry became a focus for antislavery forces.

American Revolution Women's groups, such as the Daughters of Liberty, organized to boycott tea and later to provide clothing and supplies for the Army. Deborah Sampson served as a soldier, for which she received a military pension, and Molly Pitcher assisted in the battlefield.

Groups of New Jersey women took vigorous action against husbands who abused their wives. Entering the home of a known wife-beater in the evening, they stripped the man and spanked him with sticks, shouting, "Woe to the men that beat their wives."

1777 Abigail Adams wrote to her husband, John Adams, and suggested, ". . . in the code of laws . . . I desire you to remember the ladies and be more generous and favorable to them than your ancestors. Do not put such unlimited power into the hands of the husbands. Remember all men would be tyrants if they could. If particular care and attention is not paid to the ladies, we are determined to foment a rebellion and will not hold ourselves bound by any laws in which we have no voice or representation." The future President replied: "Depend upon it, we know better than to repeal our Masculine systems."

In the years immediately following the American Revolution, women had the right to vote in some parts of Virginia and New Jersey. Later, the adoption of State constitutions limited the franchise to white males and excluded women.

1788 Mercy Otis Warren, the first American woman historian, a political satirist and playwright, wrote her *Observations on the New Constitution* in which she deplored the absence of a Bill of Rights. The first 10 Amendments (the Bill of Rights) were added to the Constitution in 1791.

1800–1820 Deborah Skinner operated the first power loom. In the first two decades of the 19th century, factories were established employing large numbers of women and children, particularly in the New England textile industry.

1804 Sacajawea, a young Indian woman, accompanied the Lewis and Clark expedition to the West. Her skill and courage were credited with helping to make the exploration a success.

1805 Mercy Otis Warren published a three-volume history of the American Revolution which is still used by historians.

1810 Mother Elizabeth Bayley Seton founded and became head of the first sisterhood in America, the Sisters of Charity of St. Joseph's. She was canonized as the Catholic Church's first U.S.-born Saint by Pope Paul VI in 1975.

1821 Emma Willard founded a female seminary at Troy, N.Y., the first effort to provide secondary education for women. In 1837 Mary Lyon founded Mt. Holyoke Seminary (later College), which provided education similar to that offered to men at the better men's colleges.

1828 The first known strike of women workers over wages took place in Dover, N.H. Similar strikes were waged in Lowell, Mass., in 1834 and 1836 by women textile workers protesting reduced real wages.

1833 Prudence Crandall opened a school for black girls in her Connecticut home. She was arrested, persecuted, and forced to give up the school to protect her pupils from violence.

1837 First national Anti-Slavery Convention of American Women met in New York City. This was the first national gathering of women organized for action without the assistance or supervision of men.

1839 After this time, most states began to recognize through legislation the right of married women to hold property. In New York State, Ernestine Rose and Susan B. Anthony led a petition campaign for women's rights. Mrs. Rose, Polish-born daughter of a rabbi, addressed the New York state legislature on at least five occasions until the body enacted a married women's property law in 1848.

1841 The first woman graduated from Oberlin College, having completed an easier "literary" course. At Oberlin, female students were required to wash male students' clothing, clean their rooms, serve them at meals, and were not permitted to recite in public or work in the fields with male students.

1845 *Woman in the Nineteenth Century,* written by Margaret Fuller, was an early and influential publication urging women's rights. Fuller wrote: "We would have every path laid open to Woman as freely as to Man."

1847 Trained by her father as an astronomer, Maria Mitchell at age 29 discovered a comet while standing on a rooftop scanning the sky with a telescope. In 1848 she became the first woman elected to the American Academy of Arts and Sciences in Boston.

1848 The first Women's Rights Convention was held in Seneca Falls, N.Y., led by Lucretia Mott and Elizabeth Cady Stanton. Its Declaration of Sentiments, paraphrased from the Declaration of Independence, stated that "all men and women are created equal." Eleven resolutions were approved, including equality in education, employment, and the law. A resolution advocating the right to suffrage passed by a narrow margin, with some delegates feeling that it was too daring a proposal.

The first issue of *The Lily,* a temperance paper, appeared with an editorial by Amelia Bloomer, later known for her experiment in clothing reform.

1849 Elizabeth Blackwell received her medical degree at Geneva, N.Y., becoming the first woman doctor in the United States.

1851 Sojourner Truth, ex-slave, electrified an audience in Akron, Ohio by drawing a parallel between the struggle for women's rights and the struggle to abolish slavery. In answer to arguments that women were delicate creatures who necessarily led sheltered lives, she described the hard physical labor she had done as a black woman slave and demanded, "And ain't I a Woman?"

1854 The first American day nursery opened in New York City for children of poor working mothers. In later years, licensing standards were established, but only minimal Federal funding was provided, except during the Depression and World War II.

1860 Elizabeth Peabody, a teacher, writer, and associate of the Transcendentalists, organized in Boston the first formal kindergarten in the United States. It was modeled on the Froebel kindergarten system in Germany.

Civil War Women were responsible for the establishment of the U.S. Sanitary Commission. Dorothea Dix, Clara Barton, and Mother Bickerdyke served as nurses and trained others. Dr. Mary Walker was one of several women who served as doctors and surgeons at the front.

Susan B. Anthony organized the National Women's Loyal League to collect signatures for passage of the 13th amendment abolishing slavery. Women's rights leaders were prominent in the struggle to end slavery.

Women entered government offices to replace clerks who went to war. This established women not only in Government service but in clerical work. After the invention of the typewriter in 1867, women flocked to white collar office work, which began to be considered a women's specialty.

1864 Working Women's Protective Union was founded in New York to ensure fair treatment for women wage earners. Thousands of women were working in factories.

1865 Vassar College opened, offering the first college-level curriculum for women. Five years later, Wellesley and Smith Colleges were founded. Although women were admitted to some coeducational institutions, their opportunities to study with men were limited until the University of Michigan admitted women in 1870 and Cornell University became coeducational in 1872.

1866 Elizabeth Cady Stanton became the first woman candidate for Congress, although women could not vote. She received 24 votes.

1868 The first women's suffrage amendment to the Constitution was introduced by Senator S. C. Pomeroy of Kansas. In 1878 another proposal for woman suffrage, which came to be known as the Anthony Amendment, was introduced.

1869 After passage of the 14th and 15th amendments granting suffrage to all males, both black and white, leaders of the women's movement determined to press their own claims more vigorously. Because of differences over strategy, two organizations were formed. The National Woman Suffrage Association was led by Elizabeth Cady Stanton and Susan B. Anthony while the more conservative American Women Suffrage Association was directed by Lucy Stone and Julia Ward Howe. Unification of these two groups was not achieved until 1890.

1870 Women gained the right to vote and to serve on juries in the Territory of Wyoming.

1872 Susan B. Anthony attempted to vote in Rochester, N.Y. She was tried and convicted of voting illegally but refused to pay the $100 fine.

1873 Belva Lockwood was admitted to the bar of the District of Columbia and in 1879 won passage of a law granting women lawyers the right to practice law before the U.S. Supreme Court. She ran for President in 1884 as candidate of the National Equal Rights Party and got 4,149 votes.

1874 Under the leadership of Frances Willard, the Women's Christian Temperance Union became the largest women's organization in the Nation. During this same period, the Young Women's Christian Association evolved to meet the needs of working women away from home. Other women organized for cultural purposes and by 1890 the General Federation of Women's Clubs was formed. The Association of Collegiate Alumnae, organized in 1882 to investigate the health of college women, eventually became the American Association of University Women.

1878 The Knights of Labor advocated equal pay for equal work, the abolition of child labor under age 14, and in 1881 opened their membership to working women. By 1886, 50,000 women were members.

1880's Lucy Gonzalez Parson, a labor organizer, traveled in 16 states to raise funds to help organize women garment workers and others. She founded *The Alarm* newspaper and edited *The Liberator*.

1890 Elizabeth Cady Stanton was elected first president of the unified suffrage organization, the National American Woman Suffrage Association. She also studied organized religion as a major source of women's inferior status and in 1895 published *The Woman's Bible*.

1893 Rebelling against an invitation to organize a Jewish women's committee to serve at receptions during Chicago's big Columbian Exposition, Hannah Greenbaum Solomon invited Jewish women from all over the country to attend a conference at the same time as the Exposition. The result was formation of the National Council of Jewish Women, dedicated to education, social reform, and issues of concern to women.

1896 The National Association for Colored Women, the first national organization of black women, was established, and Mary Church Terrell served as first president.

1898 Charlotte Perkins Gilman published *Women and Economics*, in which she decried the wasted efforts and the low economic status of the housewife. Gilman advocated the industrialization of housework and the socialization of child care.

1899 Florence Kelley became general secretary of the National Consumers League and worked for legislation in behalf of working women and children.

1900 The first decade of the 20th century showed the greatest increase in the female labor force of any period prior to 1940. New groups were formed to protect women and children from exploitation by industry. Several unions were organized at this time composed largely of women in the garment trades. Mother Jones, a labor organizer, led a march of children who worked in the Pennsylvania textile mills to the home of President Roosevelt in Oyster Bay, Long Island to call public attention to their plight.

1902 Carrie Chapman Catt organized the International Suffrage Alliance to help establish effective women's groups in other countries.

1904 Mary McLeod Bethune founded Bethune-Cookman College in Daytona Beach, Florida.

1907 The landmark case, *Muller* v. *Oregon*, established sex as a valid classification for protective legislation. The sociological type of evidence assembled by Florence Kelley and Josephine Goldmark to convince the court that overlong hours were harmful to the future of the race provided a model brief for later laws. While labor laws applying only to women were on the whole beneficial to women in the early part of the century, when jobs were largely sex segregated, the laws did result in loss of job opportunities for those seeking "male" jobs.

1908 A poem, "The New Colossus," written by Emma Lazarus, a poet who had died in 1887, was inscribed on a tablet in the pedestal of the Statue of Liberty in New York harbor. Its most famous lines: "Give me your tired, your poor, Your huddled masses yearning to be free . . ."

1909 The first significant strike of working women, "The Uprising of the 20,000," was conducted by shirtwaist makers in New York to protest low wages and long working hours. The National Women's Trade Union League (founded in 1903) mobilized public opinion and financial support for the strikers.

1911 The Triangle fire on March 25, in which 146 women shirtwaist operators were killed, dramatized the poor working conditions of immigrant women. A report of the Senate Investigation of the Condition of Women and Child Wage Earners led to establishment of the Children's Bureau (1912) and later the Women's Bureau of the Department of Labor (1920).

Liga Feminil Mexicanista was founded in Laredo, Texas to insure that the Mexican American culture and heritage would be preserved and transmitted.

1913 Harriet Tubman, ex-slave and most famous "conductor" on the Underground Railroad, died in poverty. Before the Civil War, she made 19 rescue trips to save hundreds of slaves. During the war, she served as a nurse, spy, and scout and led daring raids into the South.

1914 The Alaska Native Sisterhood was formed as an auxiliary of the Alaska Native Brotherhood, the most powerful union of native peoples in Alaska.

1915 Jane Addams, "the angel of Hull House," Carrie Chapman Catt and other women leaders held a meeting of 3,000 women in Washington, D.C. on January 10 which organized the Women's Peace Party. They called for the abolition of war.

Margaret Sanger, having studied birth control clinics abroad, returned home to campaign against the legal barriers to the dissemination of contraceptive information. She and other women, including Emma Goldman, were jailed for their efforts.

1916 Impatient with the slow pace of the woman suffrage campaign, Alice Paul organized the National Woman's Party to conduct a more militant strategy. Its followers organized suffrage parades, picketed the White House, and chained themselves to its fence. Repeatedly arrested and imprisoned, the women protested their illegal and harsh confinement by going on hunger strikes. They were force-fed by prison authorities. Their suffering aroused widespread public outrage and was credited with hastening ratification of the suffrage amendment.

1917 Jeannette Rankin, a Republican from Montana, was the first woman elected to serve in Congress. The first vote she cast opposed American entry into World War I. She was the only woman to serve in Congress before adoption of the Federal suffrage amendment.

1919 An outgrowth of women suffrage organizations, the League of Women Voters was set up to educate women for their new political and social responsibilities. The National Federation of Business and Professional Women's Clubs was also organized.

1919 Jane Addams led a delegation of American women to a Women's Conference in Zurich, which paralleled the official peace conference in Paris. They formed the Women's International League for Peace and Freedom, with Jane Addams as president and Emily Green Balch as secretary-treasurer.

1920 On August 26, the 19th amendment was ratified and 26 million women of voting age finally gained the right to vote.

1923 The Equal Rights Amendment, advocated by Alice Paul and the National Woman's Party, was introduced in Congress for the first time. Most women did not support this effort because they feared it would threaten protective legislation for women workers who labored in sweatshop conditions.

In the following years, the momentum of women's campaigns for access to equal education, employment, and professional achievement waned. Discrimination against women intensified. From 1925 to 1945 medical schools placed a quota of five percent on female admissions. Columbia and Harvard law schools refused to consider women applicants.

1928 Doris Stevens became the first president of the Inter-American Commission of Women, the Organization of American States.

1930 The Depression encouraged reaction against any change in women's traditional domestic role. Legislation restricted the employment of married women, and there was strong public disapproval of women working when men were unable to find employment. Nevertheless, many women performed low-paid labor to support their families. Opportunities for women to obtain college educations and graduate training were limited by lack of financial support.

1931 Suma Sugi, the first Nisei lobbyist (American born of Japanese ancestry), succeeded in amending the Cable Act of 1922 to permit American-born Asian women to regain their American citizenship upon termination of their marriage to an alien.

1933 Frances Perkins, the first woman to hold a Cabinet post, was appointed to head the Department of Labor by President Roosevelt and served in his cabinet for 12 years.

Eleanor Roosevelt turned her 12 years in the White House into a model of activism and humanitarian concern for future First Ladies.

1935 The National Council of Negro Women was founded in New York, with Mary McLeod Bethune as its first president.

1940 The percentage of working women was almost the same as it had been in 1900, when one of every five women worked for wages. After the U.S. entered World War II, wartime needs required the employment of large numbers of women. "Rosie the Riveter" became a national symbol. After the war, many women remained in the labor force, although many were displaced by returning veterans. Between 1940–60, the number of working women and the proportion of working wives doubled. More women over 35 were employed in rapidly expanding business and industry. Inequities in pay and advancement opportunities became more obvious limitations affecting large numbers of women. Economic conditions produced a favorable environment for the increasing demands for equity voiced by the women of the 1960's.

1950 A repressive decade for Chicana activists. Several were deported for their attempts to organize communities. Also deported was film actress Rosaura Revueltas, featured in the film, "Salt of the Earth," about striking miners in the Southwest.

1952 The Constitution of the Commonwealth of Puerto Rico was enacted, embodying the Equal Rights Amendment.

1953 Simone de Beauvoir's *The Second Sex*, a scholarly and historical analysis of the inferior status of women, was published in the United States.

1956 Rosa Parks, a black seamstress, refused to give up her bus seat to a white man and was arrested, touching off the Montgomery, Alabama, bus boycott.*

1957 Daisy Bates, coeditor with her husband of a black newspaper and president of the Arkansas National Association for the Advancement of Colored People, acted as spokesperson and counselor for the nine black youths who desegrated Little Rock Central High School.

1960 Women Strike for Peace was formed as an outgrowth of protests against resumption of nuclear testing by the Soviet Union and United States.

1961 The President's Commission on the Status of Women, chaired by Eleanor Roosevelt, was established by Executive Order 10980, with a charge to study seven areas: education, private and Federal employment, social insurance and tax laws, protective labor laws, civil and political rights and family law, and home and community. Esther Peterson, Director of the Women's Bureau, was the moving force in its establishment, with the assistance of then Vice President Lyndon Johnson.

1962 In Michigan, the Governor's Commission on the Status of Women became the first State commission. Union women Mildred Jeffrey and Myra Wolfgang were the leaders in obtaining its establishment.

1962 Acting on a recommendation of his Commission on the Status of Women, President Kennedy issued an order requiring Federal employees to be hired and promoted without regard to sex. Prior to this order, Federal managers could restrict consideration to men or women.

1963 The National Federation of Business and Professional Women's Clubs adopted as its top priority the nationwide establishment of State commissions on the status of women. By June 1964 when the first national conference was held, there were

24 commissions, and by the end of the year there were 33.

The Equal Pay Act was passed in June, effective June 1964, after formation of a coalition of women's organizations and unions to support it in Congress.

The Feminine Mystique by Betty Friedan was published. Describing social pressures that sought to limit women to roles as wives and mothers, it became a national and influential best seller.

The Interdepartmental Committee on the Status of Women and Citizens Advisory Council on the Status of Women were established by Executive Order 11126, with Margaret Hickey as its first chairperson. The Committee and Council sponsored national meetings of the State commissions, issued annual reports on issues affecting women, and made legislative and administrative recommendations. Subsequent chairpersons were Maurine Neuberger and Jacqueline Gutwillig. (The Council was terminated on August 22, 1977 by Executive Order 12007.)

1964 The Spring issue of *Daedalus,* Journal of the American Academy of Arts and Sciences, devoted an entire issue to "The Woman in America," enhancing the academic respectability of the subject. Alice Rossi's "Equality Between the Sexes: An Immodest Proposal," probably the most widely reproduced article in the women's movement, first appeared here.

Title 7 of the Civil Rights Act, enacted in 1964, prohibited discrimination in employment because of sex, race, color, religion, and national origin.

The first meeting of the First National Institute on Girls' Sports was held "to increase the depth of experience and expand opportunities for women."

1965 The U.S. Supreme Court found that a Connecticut law banning contraceptives was unconstitutional because it violated the right to privacy. *Griswold* v. *State of Connecticut,* 381 U.S.C. 479.

1966 A Federal court declared that an Alabama law excluding women from State juries was in violation of the equal protection clause of the 14th amendment, the first time in modern times a Federal court had found a law making sex distinctions unconstitutional. *White* v. *Crook,* 251 F. Supp. 401.

The National Organization for Women (NOW) was organized at the Third National Conference of Governors' Commissions on the Status of Women as a culmination of dissatisfaction with the failure to enforce Title 7 of the Civil Rights Act. Among the 28 women who founded NOW were: Betty Friedan,

Aileen Hernandez, Dr. Kathryn Clarenbach, Dr. Pauli Murray, Marguerite Rawalt, Catherine Conroy, Dorothy Haener, and Dr. Nancy Knaak.

1967 The first "women's liberation" group was formed in Chicago, partially in rebellion against the low status of young women in civil rights and "new left" campus movements. Similar groups were independently organized in New York, Toronto, Detroit, Seattle, San Francisco, and other cities. Initially concerned with analyzing the origins, nature, and extent of women's subservient status in society, some groups used the technique of "consciousness-raising" sessions to help women liberate themselves from restricting inferior roles. Most of the groups were small, egalitarian and opposed to elitism. They called for far-reaching and radical change in almost all aspects of American society.

Executive Order 11246, prohibiting discrimination by Federal contractors, was amended to include sex discrimination, with an effective date of October 1968.

A law repealing arbitrary restrictions on military rank held by women was signed by the President.

1968 *The Church and the Second Sex* by Dr. Mary Daly, a scholarly critique of Catholic Church doctrine, influenced Protestant as well as Catholic women. The first stirrings of Catholic feminist dissent occurred at the Second Vatican Council. The American branch of St. Joan's Alliance, an international Catholic feminist organization, had been formed in 1965 by Frances McGillicuddy.

Beginning in 1968, a number of distinguished Native American women, including Lucy Covington (Colville), Ramona Bennett (Puyallup), Joy Sundberg (Yurok), and Ada Deer (Menominee), were elected as tribal chairs.

Federally Employed Women was organized in September to press for equality in Federal employment, with Allie Weedon, a black attorney, as first president.

The Women's Equity Action League was organized in December by Dr. Elizabeth Boyer and other members of the National Organization for Women and concentrated on attacking sexism in higher education.

Women liberationists picketed the Miss America beauty pageant in Atlantic City. Contrary to myth, they did not burn bras. They carried signs that said: Women Are People, Not Livestock.

1969 Shirley Chisholm, Democrat of New York City, was the first black woman elected to Congress.

Weeks v. *Southern Bell Telephone Co.*, 408 F. 2d 228, was the first appeals court decision interpreting sex provisions of Title 7 of the Civil Rights Act of 1964. The lawsuit was brought by a blue collar union woman protesting discriminatory effects of State labor laws applying only to women. Marguerite Rawalt, NOW legal counsel, located a Louisiana lawyer, Sylvia Roberts, to represent Mrs. Weeks, and NOW paid court costs. The excellent decision, the great courage of the plaintiff, and the important victory of a volunteer woman lawyer and a women's organization over highly paid corporation lawyers were a great boost to the women's movement.

An equally important Title 7 case was decided by the Seventh Circuit Court of Appeals, *Bowe* v. *Colgate Palmolive*, 416 F. 2d 711. Union women and volunteer women attorneys were the pattern in this case, too. These and later Title 7 cases illustrated the real effects of State labor laws applying only to women and led to their early demise and broadened support for the Equal Rights Amendment.

The first Commission on the Status of Women appointed by a professional association began to function inside the Modern Language Association. In its early years, that Commission assumed responsibility for collecting and disseminating data on women's studies courses and programs. In December 1970 the Commission published a list of 110 women's studies courses taught at 47 colleges and universities. There were by then two Women's Studies Programs at Cornell University and San Diego State University.

In Fall 1972, the *Women's Studies Newsletter*, edited by Florence Howe, began to appear quarterly on the SUNY College at Old Westbury campus, published by The Feminist Press. *Annually*, the newsletter lists Women's Studies Programs; in 1977, there were 276. There are also groups of women's studies courses on more than 1,000 other campuses. The total number of courses now offered exceeds 15,000.

A women's caucus was organized at the Chicano Liberation Conference held in Denver.

The Boston Women's Health Collective was organized, one of a number of women's self-help groups that emerged in various parts of the country. The group researched and wrote *Our Bodies, Ourselves*, which later became a worldwide bestseller.

The four Republican Congresswomen—Florence

Dwyer, Margaret Heckler, Catherine May, and Charlotte Reid—asked for an unprecedented audience with President Nixon to discuss women's issues. They presented a letter which outlined a proposed administration program and provided data on discrimination. Their program became the agenda of the President's Task Force on Women's Rights and Responsibilities, which the President later established with Virginia Allan as chair.

Women in the American Sociological Association formed the first caucus within a professional association, after presentation of a survey by Dr. Alice Rossi on the status of women in graduate departments of sociology. By the end of 1971 every professional association had an activist women's caucus or official commission to study the status of women.

1970 Women's Equity Action League officer, Dr. Bernice Sandler, filed the first formal charges of sex discrimination under Executive Order No. 11246 against the University of Maryland. The charges were well documented. By the end of 1971 women professors had filed formal charges of sex discrimination against more than 300 colleges, largely through the efforts of Dr. Sandler and WEAL.

The first statewide meeting of AFL-CIO women was held in Wisconsin in March. The women endorsed the ERA, opposing AFL-CIO national policy. The next month the United Auto Workers became the first major national union to endorse ERA. Later the AFL-CIO executive council changed its position and announced its support for the ERA.

The Subcommittee on Constitutional Amendments of the Senate Judiciary Committee, chaired by Senator Birch Bayh, held three days of hearings on the ERA in May. Leaders of women's organizations and unions, women lawyers, and Members of Congress testified.

The NAACP adopted a women's rights platform at its annual national convention in June.

The first national commercial newsletters to serve the women's movement—*Women Today*, published in Washington by Myra and Lester Barrer, and *Spokeswoman*, published in Chicago by Susan Davis—were issued.

The Interstate Association of Commissions on the Status of Women were organized to provide a national voice and greater autonomy for the State commissions. Elizabeth Duncan Koontz, newly appointed Director of the Women's Bureau, arranged the organized meetings, and Dr. Kathryn Clarenbach was elected first president.

The Women's Bureau held its 50th anniversary conference, attended by more than 1,000 women. The Conference endorsed the ERA and other recommendations of the President's Task Force on Women's Rights and Responsibilities.

On the first day of the Women's Bureau Conference, Congresswoman Martha Griffiths filed a petition to discharge the ERA from the House Judiciary Committee, where it had rested without hearings since 1948. The petition was successful, and the ERA was debated in the House on August 10, passing overwhelmingly. It was then defeated in the Senate by the addition of unacceptable amendments.

Hearings on discrimination in education were held in June and July by Congresswoman Edith Green, chairing a special House Subcommittee on Education. The two-volume report is a classic in documenting discrimination against women in education.

The Women's Affairs Division of the League of United Latin American Citizens was organized at the convention in Beaumont, Texas, with Julia Zozoya and Ada Pena in the forefront.

The National Conference of Commissioners on Uniform State Laws published the Uniform Marriage and Divorce Act, based on the assumption that marriage is an economic partnership and recognizing homemakers' contributions as having economic value.

A nationwide celebration of the 50th anniversary of the suffrage amendment, including a mammoth parade in New York City, was held in all major cities on August 26 by a wide spectrum of organizations and individual women. The parade became an annual event.

Sixty-three Native American women from 43 tribes and 23 States met at Colorado State University to discuss their common concerns. They organized the North American Indian Women's Association.

Patsy Mink, Democrat of Hawaii, was the first and only Asian woman elected to Congress. In New York City, Democrat Bella Abzug was the first woman elected to Congress on a women's rights platform. They were among only 11 women in the 435-member House of Representatives.

The Women's Action Organization of State, AID and ICA, the first women's caucus in the federal government, was formed to eliminate discrimination and promote equality of opportunity for women in the foreign affairs agencies.

1971 The National Women's Political Caucus was organized at a meeting in Washington in July, with Congresswoman Bella Abzug, Gloria Steinem, Aileen Hernandez, Fannie Lou Hamer, Edith Van Horn, Liz Carpenter, Koryne Horbal, Congresswoman Shirley Chisholm, Brownie Ledbetter, Betty Friedan, Bobby Kilberg, Jo Ann Gardner, LaDonna Harris, and Virginia Allan among the early leaders.

The U.S. Supreme Court held in *Reed* v. *Reed* that an Idaho law giving preference to males as executors of estates was invalid under the 14th amendment, the first in a series of Supreme Court cases expanding the application of the 5th and 14th amendments to sex discrimination, 404 U.S. 71, 1971.

A preview issue of *Ms.* magazine was published in December with Gloria Steinem as editor. Established to give voice to the ideas of the women's movement, it was an immediate success.

The Women's National Abortion Coalition was organized to work for repeal of anti-abortion laws.

1972 The Equal Rights Amendment was overwhelmingly approved by the Congress and submitted to the States for ratification. Hawaii was the first State to ratify.

The Equal Employment Opportunity Act of 1972, extending coverage and giving the EEOC enforcement authority, passed. The EEOC issued greatly improved sex discrimination guidelines.

Title 9 of the Education Amendments of 1972 was passed, prohibiting discrimination on account of sex in most Federally assisted educational programs. The Equal Pay Act was extended to cover administrative, professional, and executive employees, and the Civil Rights Commission was given jurisdiction over sex discrimination.

The Democratic and Republican Party platforms endorsed the ERA and vigorous enforcement of anti-discrimination laws. As a result of campaigns by the National Women's Political Caucus, the participation of women as convention delegates was higher than in previous conventions. At the Democratic convention, women were 40 percent of the delegates; at the Republican convention, 30 percent.

The National Conference of Puerto Rican Women was organized in Washington, with Carmen Maymi and Paquito Viva in leading roles.

The November elections brought more women into elective office. The number of women elected to State legislatures was 28.2 percent higher than those serving in the preceding year. In the House of Representatives, the number of Congresswomen increased to 16, but with the retirement of Margaret Chase Smith, the U.S. Senate once again became all-male.

Members of the National Council of Jewish Women conducted a study of day-care facilities in 176 areas. The NCJW report, written by Mary Keyserling, concluded that while the need for day-care centers was enormous, facilities were nonexistent in most places or were of poor quality, underfunded, and understaffed.

1973 AT&T signed an agreement with the EEOC and the Labor Department providing goals and timetables for increasing utilization of women and minorities. About $15 million in back pay was paid to some 15,000 employees.

In a historic decision on January 22, the U.S. Supreme Court held that during the first trimester of pregnancy, the decision to have an abortion must be left solely to a woman and her physician. The only restriction a State may impose is the requirement that the abortion be performed by a physician licensed by the State. In the second and third trimesters, the Court held, the States may impose increasingly stringent requirements. Lawyers for the plaintiffs were Sarah Weddington and Marjorie Hames. *Doe* v. *Bolton* and *Roe* v. *Wade,* 93 S. Ct. 739 and 755.

The National Black Feminists Organization was formed. Eleanor Holmes Norton, leading attorney and head of the New York City Human Rights Commission, was one of the leaders.

The Foreign Assistance Act (Public Law 93-189, 87 Stat. 714) included the Percy Amendment providing that in administering financial aid, particular attention be given to "programs, projects, and activities which tend to integrate women into the national status and assisting the total development effort." Dr. Irene Tinker and the Federation of Organizations for Professional Women were leading proponents.

Billie Jean King beat Bobby Riggs in straight sets in their "Battle of the Sexes" tennis match.

1974 The Coalition of Labor Union Women was organized in Chicago with over 3,000 women in atten-

dance. Olga Madar, former UAW vice president, was elected president.

More than 1.5 million domestic service workers were brought under the coverage of the Fair Labor Standards Act by Public Law 93-259, approved April 8. A rate of $1.90 per hour was effective May 1, 1974, with increases slated for later periods.

The Wisconsin Commission on the Status of Women, chaired by Dr. Kathryn Clarenbach, inaugurated a series of six regional conferences to examine the status of the homemaker.

A national newsletter, *Marriage, Divorce and the Family,* edited by Betty Blaisdell Berry, began publication.

The Mexican American Women's Association (MAWA) was founded.

A study by Dr. Constance Uri, a Cherokee/Choctaw physician, revealed the widespread use and abuse of sterilization of Native American women in Indian health care facilities. The exposé led to the investigation of excessive sterilization of poor and minority women and to the 1977 revision of the Department of Health, Education, and Welfare's guidelines on sterilization.

Congresswoman Bella Abzug's bill to designate August 26 "Women's Equality Day" in honor of the adoption of the Suffrage Amendment became Public Law 93-392.

The Housing and Community Development Act of 1974, Public Law 93-383, prohibited sex discrimination in carrying out community development programs and in making federally related mortgage loans. The Civil Rights Act of 1968 was also amended to prohibit sex discrimination in financing, sale or rental of housing, or the provision of brokerage services.

The Equal Credit Opportunity Act became Public Law 93-495 after Congresswomen Bella Abzug, Margaret Heckler, and Leonor Sullivan led the fight for it in the House. It prohibited discrimination in credit on the basis of sex or marital status. Later, Congresswoman Abzug led a delegation of women members of Congress to meet with Chairman Arthur Burns of the Federal Reserve Board to protest unsatisfactory regulations designed to implement the new law. The regulations were revised.

The Screen Actors Guild reported a nationwide survey of 10,000 viewers on their opinions of women in the media. The majority wanted a more positive image of women, wanted to see women appearing on TV in positions of authority and in leading roles, and felt the media did not encourage young girls to aspire to a useful and meaningful role in society.

Following a "Win With Women" campaign by the National Women's Political Caucus, 18 women were elected to the 94th Congress. A 19th member was elected in a special election in early 1975. In the State legislatures there was a 29.5 percent increase in the numbers of women (465 to 604). The first woman governor to be elected in her own right, Ella Grasso, was elected Governor of Connecticut. Mary Anne Krupsak was elected Lieutenant Governor of New York, and many more women were elected to state-wide offices.

1975 The U.S. Supreme Court held in *Wiesenfeld* v. *Wineberger* that a widower with minor children whose deceased wife was covered by social security is entitled to a social security benefit under the same circumstances as a widow would be. The Court held unanimously that the fifth amendment prohibited the present difference in treatment. 43 USLW 4393.

The Supreme Court also held that, in the context of child support, a Utah statute providing that the period of minority extending for males to age 21 and for females to age 18 denies equal protection of the laws guaranteed by the 14th amendment. *Stanton* v. *Stanton,* 43 USLW 4167.

Ms. magazine published a petition for sexual freedom signed by 100 prominent women. They pledged to work for repeal of all laws and regulations that discriminate against homosexuals and lesbians.

The National Commission on the Observance of International Women's Year, 1975, was appointed by President Ford with Jill Ruckelshaus as presiding officer. Elizabeth Athanasakos became presiding officer in 1976. Members of the Commission represented the United States at the United Nations International Women's Year Conference in Mexico City in June.

The First American Indian Women's Leadership Conference met in New York City, sponsored by the International Treaty Council in conjunction with IWY.

A bill introduced by Congresswoman Bella Abzug directed the National Commission to organize and convene a National Women's Conference, preceded by State meetings. The bill was passed by both Houses, was signed by President Ford and became Public Law 94-167.

1976 The number of women delegates to the political party conventions rose to 31.4 percent at the Re-publican convention and declined to 34 percent at the Democratic convention. A large and effective women's caucus at the Democratic convention in New York met with Presidential nominee Jimmy Carter and obtained pledges from him to appoint significant numbers of women to his administration, to take other steps to improve the position of women, and to campaign for ratification of the ERA.

The major parties nominated 52 women for the House of Representatives, eight more than in 1974, but 31 ran against incumbents. Eighteen were elected, one less than in the previous Congress. Although women won seats in Maryland and Ohio and all incumbents won reelection, Congresswomen Bella Abzug and Patsy Mink gave up their seats to make unsuccessful campaigns for the Senate, and Congresswoman Leonor Sullivan retired. The number of women in State legislatures increased to 685, representing nine percent of legislative seats.

1977 President Carter named a new National Commission on the Observance of IWY and appointed Bella Abzug presiding officer. He named two women, Patricia Harris and Juanita Kreps, to his Cabinet and made other major appointments of women. An analysis of the Presidential personnel plum file appointments list in October, however, showed that of 526 top positions in the Carter administration, only 60 (11 percent) were held by women.

The drive for final ratification of ERA was stalled at 35 States, with three more States needed to meet the 1979 deadline for ratification.

The National Women's Conference met in Houston, Texas, November 18–21, attracted almost 20,000 people, including 2,005 delegates, adopted a National Plan of Action, and was acclaimed a success.

Editor's Note: In highlighting some of the notable women and events affecting women in American history, this chronology makes no pretense to being complete or even comprehensive. It is intended rather to remind readers that the role of women in America has too often been overlooked and that the struggle for equality for women is as old as our Nation.

Among the books which the editors found particularly useful in compiling this chronology were:

Chafe, William. The American Woman: Her Changing Social, Economic and Political Roles, 1920–1970. *Oxford University Press.*

DePauw, Linda Grant. Fortunes of War, New Jersey Women and the American Revolution. *New Jersey Historical Commission.*

Flexner, Eleanor. Century of Struggle. *Antheneum.*

Freeman, Jo. Women: A Feminist Perspective. *Mayfield.*

Hole, Judith, and Ellen Levine. Rebirth of Feminism. *Quadrangle.*

Lerner, Gerda. "The Lady and the Mill Girl: Changes in the Status of Women in the Age of Jackson." American Studies Journal, *Spring 1969.*

Lerner, Gerda. Black Women in White America. *Vintage.*

O'Neill, William. Everyone Was Brave. *Quadrangle.*

Papachristou, Judith. Women Together, A History in Documents of the Women's Movement in the United States. A *Ms.* Book.

Wertheimer, Barbara. We Were There: The Story of Working Women in America. *Pantheon.*

Special thanks to Catherine East for compiling the original chronology on which this is based, which appeared as an IWY publication in 1975.

*Rosa Parks' action took place in December of 1955, setting off the boycott, which came to fruition in 1956.

Update—The Process Continues

Kim Blankenship

1978 President Carter nominated Col. Margaret A. Brewer, forty-seven, as the first female general of Marine Corps. She became the Director of Information.

Sea duty was opened to Navy women after a court battle. A U.S. district judge in Washington ruled a federal law unconstitutional which prohibited women from serving on anything other than transport and hospital ships. A few months later in November 8 women reported to serve on Navy ships. They were the first of 5,130 the Navy planned to assign over the following five years.

1979 The Jaycees ousted chapters which retained women as members. Their national executive board revoked the charters of six units, five of which were in Alaska, for noncompliance with the bylaws that restricted the membership to men.

The first woman rabbi headed a congregation. Rabbi Linda Joy Holtzman became a recognized spiritual leader of Conservative Beth Israel Congregation in Coatesville, Pennsylvania. Rabbi Holtzman was a graduate of Reconstructionist Rabbinical College in Philadelphia.

Diana Nyad swam from the Bahamas to Florida. Nyad, a New Yorker, reached Juno Beach after a 60-mile swim in 27 hours and 38 minutes from North Bimini Island off the Bahamas. The thirty-year-old woman fought currents, sharks, and jellyfish.

1980 Firefighter Linda Eaton quit her job in Iowa City, alleging harrassment after she had won a 16-month legal battle for the right to breastfeed her baby at the firehouse. The Iowa Civil Rights Commission found her the victim of sex discrimination. Eaton was the fire department's only female firefighter. Eaton received from the case back pay of $145, $2,000 in damages, and $26,000 in legal fees.

The first women graduated from service academies in May. The Coast Guard commissioned 14 women and 142 men at the New London academy's ninety-eighth graduation ceremony.

The U.S. Military Academy graduated 61 women in a class of 809.

At the Naval Academy, 55 women were a part of the graduating class of 938 midshipmen.

The Air Force Academy graduated 97 women and 970 men.

Women were placed on the AFL-CIO Executive Board for the first time. Joyce Miller, the president of the Coalition of Labor Union Women, was the first female to serve on the council since the federation's formation twenty-five years ago.

1981 The first woman Supreme Court justice was seated. On September 21 the Senate, with a 99–0 vote, confirmed Sandra Day O'Connor as a Supreme Court justice. O'Connor, a judge from Arizona, was the 102nd justice to sit on the Supreme Court. She was confirmed on September 25.

The first test-tube baby was born in a U.S. hospital. Elizabeth Jordan Carr—5 pounds, 12 ounces and healthy—was delivered at Norfolk General Hospital in Virginia. She was conceived in a laboratory dish. She was the fifteenth born in this manner; the others were born in Britain and Australia.

1982 The new edition of the Roget's Thesaurus eliminated sexism from its publication. This edition of the 130-year-old book of synonyms and antonyms barred categories that the woman editor said were biased. "Mankind" became "humankind," and "countryman" was referred to as a "country dweller." The category heads were edited to be as neutral as possible.

The Equal Rights Amendment was defeated. It was three states short of the thirty-eight needed to ratify it as the twenty-seventh amendment to the Constitution. The supporters vowed to fight on.

1983 The first U.S. woman traveled in space. Sally Ride became the first U.S. woman to travel in space in June when the space shuttle *Challenger* was launched from Cape Canaveral, Florida. The *Challenger*, on its second flight, also carried four men in its crew. Ride, a physicist, held the position of mission specialist. The crew members deployed a Canadian communications satellite to hover over the Pacific Ocean at an altitude of 22,000 miles, and a similar satellite was deployed for Southeast Asian nations.

The House of Representatives defeated a plan to revive the proposed Equal Rights Amendment by only six votes short of the two-thirds majority needed.

1984 The thirty-ninth Democratic National Convention nominated former Vice President Walter F. Mondale of Minnesota as candidate for president. He then chose Rep. Geraldine A. Ferraro of Queens, N.Y., by acclamation for vice-president. She was the first woman to be named for the office on a major party ticket.

The Jaycees finally admitted women members. The all-male civic organization bowed to the Supreme Court decision which opened up male-only organizations to female membership.

Marital rape was outlawed in New York. The State Court of Appeals, the highest tribunal, ruled that married men could be prosecuted for raping their wives.

1985 The Equal Rights Amendment was introduced in both houses of the Ninety-Ninth Congress in January.

The first woman conservative rabbi was ordained. Amy Eilberg entered the clergy with a ceremony in New York.

1987 A surrogate mother contract was tested in court for the first time in 1987, and the custody decision handed down favored the biological father and his wife over the surrogate. The case, known as the "Baby M" case, held that the contract was "constitutionally protected" and that the father was better able to care for the child than the biological mother.

In October, lesbian and gay rights supporters marched on Washington. Over 500,000 people attended the march, but major news sources opted not to report the event.

1988 The New Jersey Supreme Court overturned a lower court ruling on the "Baby M" case. The court in its ruling prohibited a natural parent from being deprived of parental rights absent any proof that the parent had neglected or abandoned the child. The court also ruled that surrogacy contracts were legal if there was no fee, and they had no binding agreement forcing the natural mother to give up the child.

1989 Rev. Barbara Harris was consecrated as the first female bishop in the Angelican Church.

In April a march on Washington supported a pro-choice stand on reproductive freedom. One of the largest such marches in U.S. history, it brought over 500,000 people to the Capitol steps.

The Bush administration attorneys requested the Supreme Court to overturn *Roe* v. *Wade*.

In *Webster* v. *Reproductive Health Services*, the Supreme Court upheld states' rights to regulate abortion, gutting much of *Roe* v. *Wade* and leaving abortion rights at risk. Feminists vowed never to give up the right to reproductive freedom.

Source: *The World Almanac,* 1978–1989

A Vindication of the Rights of Woman

Mary Wollstonecraft

It is not uncommon to begin the history of the nineteenth-century wave of feminism and women's rights movements with the work of the eighteenth-century British writer and radical thinker Mary Wollstonecraft. After all, her work had great influence in Europe and the United States, and The Rights of Woman *was read as inspiration by the founders of Seneca Falls, Lucretia Mott, Elizabeth Cady Stanton, and others.*

Born in Spitalfields, a poor district near London, in 1759, Wollstonecraft was destined to live a hard and extraordinary life for women of her time and to learn from experience both the value and the elusiveness of strength and independence in the lives of women. Her father became a drunkard after financial failure and periodically beat his wife and family and trifled away their remaining money. To escape conditions at home, her sister Eliza had married badly while still in her teens, and Wollstonecraft believed she had to spirit Eliza away to safety. On their own, the two sisters found it very hard to earn a living. All but two or three occupations were closed to them as women, and Eliza was not well. With a friend, Fanny Blood, they opened a school for girls; but, ill prepared and untrained, they failed financially, and the school closed.

Having educated herself, Wollstonecraft moved to London and began earning a living at writing—at first books about educating girls and stories for children. But through her publisher, she began to move in intellectual and radical circles and to grow in insight and awareness. In 1792 she published the Vindication of the Rights of Woman, *which was well read and earned her some fame. Later in that year, she moved to Paris to observe firsthand the revolution in France. There she began a history of the French Revolution, later published, and met the American Gilbert Imlay, with whom she lived and had a daughter, Fanny. After Imlay left her in 1795, she returned to London, depressed and heartbroken, to rebuild her life and move in once again with the friends she had known. Soon she met the radical philosopher William Godwin, whom she agreed to marry when she became pregnant. In 1797, shortly after the birth of her daughter Mary, she died at the age of thirty-eight.*

The following excerpts from The Rights of Woman *are from the introduction and the dedication, in which Wollstonecraft sets forth her main principles: Women are turned into weak, petty creatures—mere "alluring objects" (sex objects?)—by neglected education, by manners and morals (what we today would probably call sex-role socialization), and by flattery and dependence. She chides M. Talleyrand-Périgord, and with him the nation of men, to apply to women the same concern and commitment for "human" rights and freedom that they hold for men.*

Author's Introduction

After considering the historic page, and viewing the living world with anxious solicitude, the most melancholy emotions of sorrowful indignation have depressed my spirits, and I have sighed when obliged to confess that either Nature has made a great difference between man and man, or that the civilisation which has hitherto taken place in the world has been very partial. I have turned over various books written on the subject of education, and patiently observed the conduct of parents and the management of schools; but what has been the result?—a profound conviction that the neglected education of my fellow-creatures is the grand source of the misery I deplore, and that women, in particular, are rendered weak and wretched by a variety of concurring causes, originating from one hasty conclusion. The conduct and manners of women, in fact, evidently prove that their minds are not in a healthy state; for, like the flowers which are planted in too rich a soil, strength and usefulness are sacrificed to beauty; and the flaunting leaves, after having pleased a fastidious eye, fade, disregarded on the stalk, long before the season when they ought to have arrived at maturity. One cause of this barren blooming I attribute to a false system of education, gathered from the books written on this subject by men who, considering females rather as women than human creatures, have been more anxious to make them alluring mistresses than affectionate wives and rational mothers; and the understanding of the sex has been so bubbled by this specious homage, that the civilised women of the present century, with a few exceptions, are only anxious to inspire love, when they ought to cherish a nobler ambition, and by their abilities and virtues exact respect.

In a treatise, therefore, on female rights and manners, the works which have been particularly written for their improvement must not be overlooked, especially when it is asserted, in direct terms, that the minds of women are enfeebled by false refinement; that the books of instruction, written by men of genius, have had the same tendency as more frivolous productions; and that, in the true style of Mahometanism, they are treated as a kind of subordinate beings, and not as a part of the human species, when improvable reason is allowed to be the dignified distinction which raises men above the brute creation, and puts a natural sceptre in a feeble hand.

Yet, because I am a woman, I would not lead my readers to suppose that I mean violently to agitate the contested question respecting the quality or inferiority of the sex; but as the subject lies in my way, and I cannot pass it over without subjecting the main tendency of my reasoning to misconstruction, I shall stop a moment to deliver, in a few words, my opinion. In the government of the physical world it is observable that the female in point of strength is, in general, inferior to the male. This is the law of Nature; and it does not appear to be suspended or abrogated in favour of woman. A degree of physical superiority cannot, therefore, be denied, and it is a noble prerogative! But not content with this natural preeminence, men endeavour to sink us still lower, merely to render us alluring objects for a moment; and women, intoxicated by the adoration which men, under the influence of their senses, pay them, do not seek to obtain a durable interest in their hearts, or to become the friends of the fellow-creatures who find amusement in their society.

I am aware of an obvious inference. From every quarter have I heard exclamations against masculine women, but where are they to be found? If by this appellation men mean to inveigh against their ardour in hunting, shooting, and gaming, I shall most cordially join in the cry; but if it be against the imitation of manly virtues, or, more properly speaking, the attainment of those talents and virtues, the exercise of which ennobles the human character, and which raises females in the scale of animal being, when they are comprehensively termed mankind, all those who view them with a philosophic eye must, I should think, wish with me, that they may every day grow more and more masculine.

This discussion naturally divides the subject. I shall first consider women in the grand light of human creatures, who, in common with men, are placed on this earth to unfold their faculties; and afterwards I shall more particularly point out their peculiar designation.

I wish also to steer clear of an error which many respectable writers have fallen into; for the instruction which has hitherto been addressed to women, has rather been applicable to *ladies*, if the little indirect advice that is scattered through "Sandford and Merton" be excepted; but, addressing my sex in a firmer tone, I pay particular attention to those in the middle class, because they appear to be in the most natural state. Perhaps the seeds of false refinement, immorality, and vanity, have ever been shed by the great. Weak, artificial beings, raised above the common wants and affections of their race, in a premature unnatural manner, undermine the very foundation of virtue, and spread corruption through the whole mass of society! As a class of mankind they have the strongest claim to pity; the education of the rich tends to render them vain and helpless, and the unfolding mind is not strengthened by the practice of those duties which dignify the human character. They only live to amuse themselves, and by the same law which in Nature invariably produces certain effects, they soon only afford barren amusement.

But as I purpose taking a separate view of the different ranks of society, and of the moral character of women in each, this hint is for the present sufficient; and I have only alluded to the subject because it appears to me to be the very essence of an introduction to give a cursory account of the contents of the work it introduces.

My own sex, I hope, will excuse me, if I treat them like rational creatures, instead of flattering their *fascinating* graces, and viewing them as if they were in a state of perpetual childhood, unable to stand alone. I earnestly wish to point out in what true dignity and human happiness consists. I wish to persuade women to endeavor to acquire strength, both of mind and body, and to convince them that the soft phrases, susceptibility of heart, delicacy of sentiment, and refinement of taste, are almost synonymous with epithets of weakness, and that those beings who are only the objects of pity, and that kind of love which has been termed its sister, will soon become objects of contempt.

Dismissing, then, those pretty feminine phrases, which the men condescendingly use to soften our slavish dependence, and despising that weak elegancy of mind, exquisite sensibility, and sweet docility of manners, supposed to be the sexual characteristics of the weaker vessel, I wish to show that elegance is inferior to virtue, that the first object of laudable ambition is to obtain a character as a human being, regardless of the distinction of sex, and that secondary views should be brought to this simple touchstone.

This is a rough sketch of my plan; and should I express my conviction with the energetic emotions that I feel whenever I think of the subject, the dictates of experience and reflection will be felt by some of my readers. Animated by this important object, I shall disdain to cull my phrases or polish my style. I aim at being useful, and sincerity will render me unaffected; for, wishing rather to persuade by the force of my arguments than dazzle by the elegance of my language, I shall not waste my time in rounding periods, or in fabricating the turgid bombast of artificial feelings, which, coming from the head, never reach the heart. I shall be employed about things, not words! and, anxious to render my sex more respectable members of society, I shall try to avoid that flowery diction which has slided from essays into novels, and from novels into familiar letters and conversation.

These pretty superlatives, dropping glibly from the tongue, vitiate the taste, and create a kind of sickly delicacy that turns away from simple unadorned truth; and a deluge of false sentiments and overstretched feelings, stifling the natural emotions of the heart, render the domestic pleasures insipid, that ought to sweeten the exercise of those severe duties, which educate a rational and immortal being for a nobler field of action.

The education of women has of late been more attended to than formerly; yet they are still reckoned a frivolous sex, and ridiculed or pitied by the writers who endeavour by satire or instruction to improve them. It is acknowledged that they spend many of the first years of their lives in acquiring a smattering of accomplishments; meanwhile strength of body and mind are sacrificed to libertine notions of beauty, to the desire of establishing themselves—the only way women can rise in the world—by marriage. And this desire making mere animals of them, when they marry they act as such children may be expected to act—they dress, they paint, and nickname God's creatures. Surely these weak beings are only fit for a seraglio! Can they be expected to govern a family with judgment, or take care of the poor babes whom they bring into the world?

If, then, it can be fairly deduced from the present conduct of the sex, from the prevalent fondness for pleasure which takes place of ambition and those nobler passions that open and enlarge the soul, that the instruction which women have hitherto received has only tended, with the constitution of civil society, to render them insignificant objects of desire—mere propagators of fools!—if it can be proved that in aiming to accomplish them, without cultivating their understandings, they are taken out of their sphere of duties, and made ridiculous and useless when the short-lived bloom of beauty is over,[1] I presume that *rational* men will excuse me for endeavouring to persuade them to become more masculine and respectable.

Indeed the word masculine is only a bugbear; there is little reason to fear that women will acquire too much courage or fortitude, for their apparent inferiority with respect to bodily strength must render them in some degree dependent on men in the various relations of life; but why should it be increased by prejudices that give a sex to virtue, and confound simple truths with sensual reveries?

Women are, in fact, so much degraded by mistaken notions of female excellence, that I do not mean to add a paradox when I assert that this artificial weakness produces a propensity to tyrannise, and gives birth to cunning, the natural opponent of strength, which leads them to play off those contemptible infantine airs that undermine esteem even whilst they excite desire. Let men become more chaste and modest, and if women do not grow wiser in the same ratio, it will be clear that they have weaker understandings. It seems scarcely necessary to say that I now speak of the sex in general. Many individuals have more sense than their male relatives; and, as nothing preponderates where there is a constant struggle for an equilibrium without it has naturally more gravity, some women govern their husbands without degrading themselves, because intellect will always govern.

To M. Talleyrand-Périgord
Late Bishop of Autun

Sir,—Having read with great pleasure a pamphlet which you have lately published, I dedicate this volume to you—the first dedication that I have ever written, to induce you to read it with attention; and, because I think that you will understand me, which I do not suppose many pert witlings will, who may ridicule the arguments they are unable to answer. But, sir, I carry my respect for your understanding still farther; so far that I am confident you will not throw my work aside, and hastily conclude that I am in the wrong, because you did not view the subject in the same light yourself. And pardon my frankness, but I must observe, that you treated it in too cursory a manner, contented to consider it as it had been considered formerly, when the rights of man, not to advert to woman, were trampled on as chimerical—I call upon you, therefore, now to weigh what I have advanced respecting the rights of woman and national education; and I call with the firm tone of humanity, for my arguments, sir, are dictated by a disinterested spirit—I plead for my sex, not for myself. Independence I have long considered as the grand blessing of life, the basis of every virtue; and independence I will ever secure by contracting my wants, though I were to live on a barren heath.

It is then an affection for the whole human race that makes my pen dart rapidly along to support what I believe to be the cause of virtue; and the same motive leads me earnestly to wish to see woman placed in a station in which she would advance, instead of retarding, the progress of those glorious principles that give a substance to morality. My opin-

ion, indeed, respecting the rights and duties of woman seems to flow so naturally from these simple principles, that I think it scarcely possible but that some of the enlarged minds who formed your admirable constitution will coincide with me.

In France there is undoubtedly a more general diffusion of knowledge than in any part of the European world, and I attribute it, in a great measure, to the social intercourse which has long subsisted between the sexes. It is true—I utter my sentiments with freedom—that in France the very essence of sensuality has been extracted to regale the voluptuary, and a kind of sentimental lust has prevailed, which, together with the system of duplicity that the whole tenor of their political and civil government taught, have given a sinister sort of sagacity to the French character, properly termed *finesse*, from which naturally flow a polish of manners that injures the substance by hunting sincerity out of society. And modesty, the fairest garb of virtue! has been more grossly insulted in France than even in England, till their women have treated as *prudish* that attention to decency which brutes instinctively observe.

Manners and morals are so nearly allied that they have often been confounded; but, though the former should only be the natural reflection of the latter, yet, when various causes have produced factitious and corrupt manners, which are very early caught, morality becomes an empty name. The personal reserve, and sacred respect for cleanliness and delicacy in domestic life, which French women almost despise, are the graceful pillars of modesty; but, far from despising them, if the pure flame of patriotism have reached their bosoms, they should labour to improve the morals of their fellow-citizens, by teaching men, not only to respect modesty in women, but to acquire it themselves, as the only way to merit their esteem.

Contending for the rights of woman, my main argument is built on this simple principle, that if she be not prepared by education to become the companion of man, she will stop the progress of knowledge and virtue; for truth must be common to all, or it will be inefficacious with respect to its influence on general practice. And how can woman be expected to cooperate unless she knows why she ought to be virtuous? unless freedom strengthens her reason till she comprehends her duty, and see in what manner it is connected with her real good. If children are to be educated to understand the true principle of patriotism, their mother must be a patriot; and the love of mankind, from which an orderly train of virtues spring, can only be produced by considering the moral and civil interest of mankind; but the education and situation of woman at present shuts her out from such investigations.

In this work I have produced many arguments, which to me were conclusive, to prove that the prevailing notion respecting a sexual character was subversive of morality, and I have contended, that to render the human body and mind more perfect, chastity must more universally prevail, and that chastity will never be respected in the male world till the person of a woman is not, as it were, idolised, when little virtue or sense embellish it with the grand traces of mental beauty, or the interesting simplicity of affection.

Consider, sir, dispassionately these observations, for a glimpse of this truth seemed to open before you when you observed, "that to see one-half of the human race excluded by the other from all participation of government was a political phenomenon that, according to abstract principles, it was impossible to explain." If so, on what does your constitution rest? If the abstract rights of man will bear discussion and explanation, those of woman, by a parity of reasoning, will not shrink from the same test; though a different opinion prevails in this country, built on the very arguments which you use to justify the oppression of woman—prescription.

Consider—I address you as a legislator—whether, when men contend for their freedom, and to be allowed to judge for themselves respecting their own happiness, it be not inconsistent and unjust to subjugate women, even though you firmly believe that you are acting in the manner best calculated to promote their happiness? Who made man the exclusive judge, if woman partake with him of the gift of reason?

In this style argue tyrants of every denomination, from the weak king to the weak father of a family; they are all eager to crush reason, yet always assert that they usurp its throne only to be useful. Do you not act a similar part when you *force* all women, by denying them civil and political rights, to remain immured in their families groping in the dark? for surely, sir, you will not assert that a duty can be binding which is not founded on reason? If, indeed, this be their destination, arguments may be drawn from reason; and thus augustly supported, the more understanding women acquire, the more they will be attached to their duty—comprehending it—for unless they comprehend it, unless their morals be fixed on the same immutable principle as those of man, no authority can make them discharge it in a virtuous manner. They may be convenient slaves, but slavery will have its constant effect, degrading the master and the abject dependent.

But if women are to be excluded, without having a voice, from a participation of the natural rights of mankind, prove first, to ward off the charge of injustice and inconsistency, that they want reason, else this flaw in your NEW CONSTITUTION will ever show that man must, in some shape, act like a tyrant, and tyranny, in whatever part of society it rears its brazen front, will ever undermine morality.

I have repeatedly asserted, and produced what appeared to me irrefragable arguments drawn from matters of fact to prove my assertion, that women cannot by force be confined to domestic concerns; for they will, however ignorant, intermeddle with more weighty affairs, neglecting private duties only to disturb, by cunning tricks, the orderly plans of reason which rise above their comprehension.

Besides, whilst they are only made to acquire personal accomplishments, men will seek for pleasure in variety, and faithless husbands will make faithless wives; such ignorant beings, indeed, will be very excusable when, not taught to respect public good, nor allowed any civil rights, they attempt to do themselves justice by retaliation.

The box of mischief thus opened in society, what is to preserve private virtue, the only security of public freedom and universal happiness?

Let there be then no coercion *established* in society, and the common law of gravity prevailing, the sexes will fall into their proper places. And now that more equitable laws are forming your citizens, marriage may become more sacred; your young men may choose wives from motives of affection, and your maidens allow love to root out vanity.

The father of a family will not then weaken his constitution and debase his sentiments by visiting the harlot, nor forget, in obeying the call of appetite, the purpose for which it was implanted. And the mother will not neglect her children to practise the arts of coquetry, when sense and modesty secure her the friendship of her husband.

But, till men become attentive to the duty of a

father, it is vain to expect women to spend that time in their nursery which they, "wise in their generation," choose to spend at their glass; for this exertion of cunning is only an instinct of nature to enable them to obtain indirectly a little of that power of which they are unjustly denied a share; for, if women are not permitted to enjoy legitimate rights, they will render both men and themselves vicious to obtain illicit privileges.

I wish, sir, to set some investigations of this kind afloat in France; and should they lead to a confirmation of my principles when your constitution is revised, the Rights of Woman may be respected, if it be fully proved that reason calls for this respect, and loudly demands JUSTICE for one-half of the human race.

I am, Sir,
Yours respectfully,
M. W.

Notes

[1] A lively writer (I cannot recollect his name) asks what business women turned of forty have to do in the world?

The Adams Letters

Abigail and John Adams

Abigail Adams (1744–1818) was born in Massachusetts the daughter of an upper-middle-class woman and her husband, who was a minister. Typical of her day, she received no formal education. Her husband, John, of course, fared differently. The son of a respected farmer, he graduated from Harvard in 1755, taught school for a while, studied law, and was admitted to the bar in 1758. Finally he carried on an active political life culminating in his becoming the second president of the United States in 1796.

How different, how predictably different, their lives were; how much opportunity to express his intelligence and energy John had and how little Abigail had. No wonder she had to request of him in 1776 that he "remember the ladies" as John Adams, together with Jefferson and Franklin, was composing the Declaration of Independence. No wonder he quite purposely (as his letter to Sullivan shows) turned her down, calling her a "saucy" girl.

It would be nearly three-quarters of a century later before another such declaration could be written—in Seneca Falls.

The first two letters reprinted with permission from *The Book of Abigail and John: Selected Letters of the Adams Family, 1762–1784,* ed. L. H. Butterfield. Cambridge: Harvard University Press, 1975. Copyright © Harvard University Press, 1975. Third letter (to Sullivan) from Charles Francis Adams, ed. Works of John Adams, Vol. ix. Boston: Little, Brown and Co., 1854, p. 375.

From Abigail to John

Braintree
March 31, 1776

—I long to hear that you have declared an independancy—and by the way in the new Code of Laws which I suppose it will be necessary for you to make I desire you would Remember the Ladies, and be more generous and favourable to them than your ancestors. Do not put such unlimited power into the hands of the Husbands. Remember all Men would be tyrants if they could. If perticuliar care and attention is not paid to the Laidies we are determined to foment a Rebelion, and will not hold ourselves bound by any Laws in which we have no voice, or Representation.

That your Sex are Naturally Tyrannical is a Truth so thoroughly established as to admit of no dispute, but such of you as wish to be happy willingly give up the harsh title of Master for the more tender and endearing one of Friend. Why then, not put it out of the power of the vicious and the Lawless to use us with cruelty and indignity with impunity. Men of Sense in all Ages abhor those customs which treat us only as the vassals of your Sex. Regard us then as Beings placed by providence under your protection and in immitation of the Supreem Being make use of that power only for our happiness.

From John to Abigail

April 14, 1776

As to your extraordinary Code of Laws, I cannot but laugh. We have been told that our Struggle has loosened the bands of Government every where. That Children and Apprentices were disobedient—that schools and Colledges were grown turbulent—that Indians slighted their Guardians and Negroes grew insolent to their Masters. But your Letter was the first Intimation that another Tribe more numerous and powerfull than all the rest were grown discontented.—This is rather too coarse a Compliment but you are so saucy, I wont blot it out.

Depend upon it, We know better than to repeal our Masculine systems. Altho they are in full Force, you know they are little more than Theory. We dare not exert our Power in its full Latitude. We are obliged to go fair, and softly, and in Practice you know We are the subjects. We have only the Name of Masters, and rather than give up this, which would compleatly subject us to the Despotism of the Peticoat, I hope General Washington, and all our brave Heroes would fight.

From John Adams to James Sullivan

Philadelphia, 26 May, 1776.

. . . It is certain, in theory, that the only moral foundation of government is, the consent of the people. But to what an extent shall we carry this principle? Shall we say that every individual of the community, old and young, male and female, as well as rich and poor, must consent, expressly, to every act of legislation? No, you will say, this is impossible. How, then does the right arise in the majority to govern the minority, against their will? Whence arises the right of the men to govern the women, without their consent? Whence the right of the old to bind the young, without theirs?

But let us first suppose that the whole community, of every age, rank, sex, and condition, has a right to vote. This community is assembled. A motion is made, and carried by a majority of one voice. The minority will not agree to this. Whence arises the right of the majority to govern, and the obligation of the minority to obey?

From necessity, you will say, because there can be no other rule.

But why exclude women?

You will say, because their delicacy renders them unfit for practice and experience in the great businesses of life, and the hardy enterprises of war, as well as the arduous cares of state. Besides, their attention is so much engaged with the necessary nurture of their children, that nature has made them fittest for domestic cares. And children have not

judgment or will of their own. True. But will not these reasons apply to others? Is it not equally true, that men in general, in every society, who are wholly destitute of property, are also too little acquainted with public affairs to form a right judgment, and too dependent upon other men to have a will of their own? If this is a fact, if you give to every man who has no property, a vote, will you not make a fine encouraging provision for corruption, by your fundamental law? Such is the frailty of the human heart, that very few men who have no property, have any judgment of their own. They talk and vote as they are directed by some man of property, who has attached their minds to his interest. . . .

Your idea that those laws which affect the lives and personal liberty of all, or which inflict corporal punishment, affect those who are not qualified to vote, as well as those who are, is just. But so they do women, as well as men; children, as well as adults. What reason should there be for excluding a man of twenty years eleven months and twenty-seven days old, from a vote, when you admit one who is twenty-one? The reason is, you must fix upon some period in life, when the understanding and will of men in general, is fit to be trusted by the public. Will not the same reason justify the state in fixing upon some certain quantity of property, as a qualification?

The same reasoning which will induce you to admit all men who have no property, to vote, with those who have, for those laws which affect the person, will prove that you ought to admit women and children; for, generally speaking, women and children have as good judgments, and as independent minds, as those men who are wholly destitute of property; these last being to all intents and purposes as much dependent upon others, who will please to feed, clothe, and employ them, as women are upon their husbands, or children on their parents. . . .

Depend upon it, Sir, it is dangerous to open so fruitful a source of controversy and altercation as would be opened by attempting to alter the qualifications of voters; there will be no end of it. New claims will arise; women will demand a vote; lads from twelve to twenty-one will think their rights not enough attended to; and every man who has not a farthing, will demand an equal voice with any other, in all acts of state. It tends to confound and destroy all distinctions, and prostrate all ranks to one common level.

Historical Precedent: Nineteenth-Century Feminists

Judith Hole
Ellen Levine

At the time Rebirth of Feminism *was being written, Judith Hole was a producer for CBS television news. Her credits included shows on the value of homemaking, stepparents, mother-daughter profiles, and the politics of cancer. Ellen Levine, a writer, photographer, and lawyer, participated in the publication of* Notes from the Third Year *and the anthology* Radical Feminism. *She also published a book of her feminist cartoons,* All She Needs. *Here Hole and Levine introduce us briefly to the characters and events of nineteenth-century movement for suffrage and women's rights.*

Introduction: Historical Precedent

The contemporary women's movement is not the first such movement in American history to offer a wide-ranging feminist critique of society. In fact, much of what seems "radical" in contemporary feminist analysis parallels the critique made by the feminists of the 19th century. Both the early and the contemporary feminists have engaged in a fundamental re-examination of the role of women in all spheres of life, and of the relationships of men and women in all social, political, economic and cultural institutions. Both have defined women as an oppressed group and have traced the origin of women's subjugation to male-defined and male-dominated social institutions and value-systems.

When the early feminist movement emerged in the 19th century, the "woman issue" was extensively debated in the national press, in political gatherings, and from Church pulpits. The women's groups, their platforms, and their leaders, although not always well received or understood, were extremely well known. Until recently, however, that early feminist movement has been only cursorily discussed in American history textbooks, and then only in terms of the drive for suffrage. Even a brief reading of early feminist writings and of the few histories that have dealt specifically with the woman's movement (as it was called then) reveals that the drive for suffrage became the single focus of the movement only after several decades of a more multi-issued campaign for women's equality.

The woman's movement emerged during the 1800's. It was a time of geographic expansion, industrial development, growth of social reform movements, and a general intellectual ferment with a philosophical emphasis on individual freedom, the "rights of man" and universal education. In fact, some of the earliest efforts to extend opportunities to women were made in the field of education. In 1833, Oberlin became the first college to open its doors to both men and women. Although female education at Oberlin was regarded as necessary to ensure the development of good and proper wives and mothers, the open admission policy paved the way for the founding of other schools, some devoted entirely to women's education.[1] Much of the groundbreaking work in education was done by Emma Willard, who had campaigned vigorously for educational facilities for women beginning in the early 1820's. Frances Wright, one of the first women orators, was also a strong advocate of education for women. She viewed women as an oppressed group and argued that, "Until women assume the place in society which good sense and good feeling alike assign to them, human improvement must advance but feebly."[2] Central to her discussion of the inequalities between the sexes was a particular concern with the need for equal educational training for women.

It was in the abolition movement of the 1830's, however, that the woman's rights movement as such had its political origins. When women began working in earnest for the abolition of slavery, they quickly learned that they could not function as political equals with their male abolitionist friends. Not only were they barred from membership in some organizations, but they had to wage an uphill battle for the right simply to speak in public. Sarah and Angelina Grimké, daughters of a South Carolina slaveholding family, were among the first to fight this battle. Early in their lives the sisters left South Carolina, moved North, and began to speak out publicly on the abolition issue. Within a short time they drew the wrath of different sectors of society. A Pastoral letter from the Council of the Congregationalist Ministers of Massachusetts typified the attack:

> The appropriate duties and influence of woman are clearly stated in the New Testament. . . . The power of woman is her dependence, flowing from the consciousness of that weakness which God has given her for her protection. . . . When she assumes the place and tone of man as a public reformer . . . she yields the power which God has given her . . . and her character becomes unnatural.[3]

The brutal and unceasing attacks (sometimes physical) on the women convinced the Grimkés that the issues of freedom for slaves and freedom for women were inextricably linked. The women began to speak about both issues, but because of the objections from male abolitionists who were afraid that discussions of woman's rights would "muddy the waters," they often spoke about the "woman question" as a separate issue. (In fact, Lucy Stone, an early feminist and abolitionist, lectured on abolition on Saturdays and Sundays and on women's rights during the week.)

In an 1837 letter to the President of the Boston Female Anti-Slavery Society—by that time many female anti-slavery societies had been established in response to the exclusionary policy of the male abolitionist groups—Sarah Grimké addressed herself directly to the question of women's status:

> All history attests that man has subjugated woman to his will, used her as a means to promote his selfish gratification, to minister to his sensual pleasures, to be instrumental in promoting his comfort; but never has he desired to elevate her to that rank she was created to fill. He has done all he could to debase and enslave her mind; and now he looks triumphantly on the ruin he has wrought, and says, the being he has thus deeply injured is his inferior. . . . But I ask no favors for my sex. . . . All I ask of our brethren is, that they will take their feet from off our necks and permit us to stand upright on that ground which God designed us to occupy.[4]

The Grimkés challenged both the assumption of the "natural superiority of man" and the social institutions predicated on that assumption. For example, in her "Letters on the Equality of the Sexes," Sarah Grimké argued against both religious dogma and the institution of marriage. Two brief examples are indicative:

> . . . Adam's ready acquiescence with his wife's proposal, does not savor much of that superiority in strength of mind, which is arrogated by man.[5]

> . . . man has exercised the most unlimited and brutal power over woman, in the peculiar character of husband—a word in most countries synonymous with tyrant. . . . Woman, instead of being elevated by her union with man, which might be expected from an alliance with a superior being, is in reality lowered. She

*generally loses her individuality, her independent
character, her moral being. She becomes absorbed into
him, and henceforth is looked at, and acts through the
medium of her husband.*[6]

They attacked as well the manifestations of "male
superiority" in the employment market. In a letter
"On the Condition of Women in the United States"
Sarah Grimké wrote of:

> . . . *the disproportionate value set on the time and la-
> bor of men and of women. A man who is engaged in
> teaching, can always, I believe, command a higher
> price for tuition than a woman—even when he teaches
> the same branches, and is not in any respect superior
> to the woman. . . . [Or] for example, in tailoring, a
> man has twice, or three times as much for making a
> waistcoat or pantaloons as a woman, although the
> work done by each may be equally good.*[7]

The abolition movement continued to expand,
and in 1840 a World Anti-Slavery Convention was
held in London. The American delegation included a
group of women, among them Lucretia Mott and
Elizabeth Cady Stanton. In Volume I of the *History of
Woman Suffrage,* written and edited by Stanton, Susan B. Anthony and Matilda Joslyn Gage, the authors
note that the mere presence of women delegates produced an ". . . excitement and vehemence of protest
and denunciation [that] could not have been greater,
if the news had come that the French were about to
invade England."[8] The women were relegated to the
galleries and prohibited from participating in any of
the proceedings. That society at large frowned upon
women participating in political activities was one
thing; that the leading male radicals, those most concerned with social inequalities, should also discriminate against women was quite another. The events
at the world conference reinforced the women's
growing awareness that the battle for the abolition of
Negro slavery could never be won without a battle
for the abolition of woman's slavery:

> *As Lucretia Mott and Elizabeth Cady Stanton wended
> their way arm in arm down Great Queen Street that
> night, reviewing the exciting scenes of the day, they
> agreed to hold a woman's rights convention on their
> return to America, as the men to whom they had just
> listened had manifested their great need of some educa-
> tion on that question.*[9]

Mott and Stanton returned to America and continued their abolitionist work as well as pressing for
state legislative reforms on woman's property and
family rights. Although the women had discussed
the idea of calling a public meeting on woman's
rights, the possibility did not materialize until eight
years after the London Convention. On July 14, 1848,
they placed a small notice in the *Seneca* (New York)
County Courier announcing a "Woman's Rights Convention." Five days later, on July 19 and 20, some
three hundred interested women and men, coming
from as far as fifty miles, crowded into the small
Wesleyan Chapel (now a gas station) and approved a
Declaration of Sentiments (modeled on the Declaration of Independence) and twelve Resolutions. The
delineation of issues in the Declaration bears a startling resemblance to contemporary feminist writings. Some excerpts are illustrative:

> *We hold these truths to be self-evident: that all men
> and women are created equal; that they are endowed
> by their Creator with certain inalienable rights; that
> among these are life, liberty, and the pursuit of
> happiness;*
>
> *. . . . The history of mankind is a history of repeated
> injuries and usurpations on the part of man toward
> woman, having in direct object the establishment of an
> absolute tyranny over her. To prove this, let facts be
> submitted to a candid world. . . .*
>
> *He has compelled her to submit to laws, in the forma-
> tion of which she has no voice. . . .*
>
> *He has made her, if married, in the eye of the law,
> civilly dead. . . .*
>
> *He has monopolized nearly all the profitable employ-
> ments, and from those she is permitted to follow, she
> receives but a scanty remuneration. He closes against
> her all the avenues to wealth and distinction which he
> considers most honorable to himself. As a teacher of
> theology, medicine, or law, she is not known.*
>
> *He allows her in Church, as well as State, but a subor-
> dinate position, claiming Apostolic authority for her
> exclusion from the ministry, and, with some excep-
> tions, from any public participation in the affairs of the
> Church.*
>
> *He has created a false public sentiment by giving to the
> world a different code of morals for men and women,
> by which moral delinquencies which exclude women
> from society, are not only tolerated, but deemed of little
> account in man.*

He has usurped the prerogative of Jehovah himself, claiming it as his right to assign for her a sphere of action, when that belongs to her conscience and to her God.

He has endeavored, in every way that he could, to destroy her confidence in her own powers, to lessen her self-respect, and to make her willing to lead a dependent and abject life.

Included in the list of twelve resolutions was one which read: "*Resolved,* That it is the duty of the women of this country to secure to themselves their sacred right to the elective franchise."

Although the Seneca Falls Convention is considered the official beginning of the woman's suffrage movement, it is important to reiterate that the goal of the early woman's rights movement was not limited to the demand for suffrage. In fact, the suffrage resolution was included only after lengthy debate, and was the only resolution not accepted unanimously. Those participants at the Convention who actively opposed the inclusion of the suffrage resolution:

. . . feared a demand for the right to vote would defeat others they deemed more rational, and make the whole movement ridiculous. But Mrs. Stanton and Frederick Douglass seeing that the power to choose rulers and make laws, was the right by which all others could be secured, persistently advocated the resolution. . . .[10]

Far more important to most of the women at the Convention was their desire to gain control of their property and earnings, guardianship of their children, rights to divorce, etc. Notwithstanding the disagreements at the Convention, the Seneca Falls meeting was of great historical significance. As Flexner has noted:

. . . [The women] themselves were fully aware of the nature of the step they were taking; today's debt to them has been inadequately acknowledged. . . . Beginning in 1848 it was possible for women who rebelled against the circumstances of their lives, to know that they were not alone—although often the news reached them only through a vitriolic sermon or an abusive newspaper editorial. But a movement had been launched which they could either join, or ignore, that would leave its imprint on the lives of their daughters and of women throughout the world.[11]

From 1848 until the beginning of the Civil War, Woman's Rights Conventions were held nearly every year in different cities in the East and Midwest. The 1850 Convention in Salem, Ohio:

. . . had one peculiar characteristic. It was officered entirely by women; not a man was allowed to sit on the platform, to speak, or vote. Never did men so suffer. They implored just to say a word; but no; the President was inflexible—no man should be heard. If one meekly arose to make a suggestion he was at once ruled out of order. For the first time in the world's history, men learned how it felt to sit in silence when questions in which they were interested were under discussion.[12]

As the woman's movement gained in strength, attacks upon it became more vitriolic. In newspaper editorials and church sermons anti-feminists argued vociferously that the public arena was not the proper place for women. In response to such criticism, Stanton wrote in an article in the Rochester, New York *National Reformer:*

If God has assigned a sphere to man and one to woman, we claim the right to judge ourselves of His design in reference to us, and we accord to man the same privilege. . . . We have all seen a man making a jackass of himself in the pulpit, at the bar, or in our legislative halls. . . . Now, is it to be wondered at that woman has some doubts about the present position assigned her being the true one, when her every-day experience shows her that man makes such fatal mistakes in regard to himself?[13]

It was abundantly clear to the women that they could not rely on the pulpit or the "establishment" press for either factual or sympathetic reportage; nor could they use the press as a means to disseminate their ideas. As a result they depended on the abolitionist papers of the day, and in addition founded a number of independent women's journals including *The Lily, The Una, Woman's Advocate, Pittsburgh Visiter* [sic], etc.

One of the many issues with which the women activists were concerned was dress reform. Some began to wear the "bloomer" costume (a misnomer since Amelia Bloomer, although an advocate of the loose-fitting dress, was neither its originator nor the first to wear it) in protest against the tight-fitting and singularly uncomfortable cinched-waisted stays and layers of petticoats. However, as Flexner has noted, "The attempt at dress reform, although badly needed, was not only unsuccessful, but boomeranged and had to be abandoned."[14] Women's rights advocates became known as "bloomers" and the movement for equal rights as well as the individual women were subjected to increasing ridicule. Elizabeth Cady Stanton, one of the earliest to wear the more comfortable outfit, was one of the first to suggest its rejection. In a letter to Susan B. Anthony she wrote:

> We put the dress on for greater freedom, but what is physical freedom compared with mental bondage? . . . It is not wise, Susan, to use up so much energy and feeling that way. You can put them to better use. I speak from experience.[15]

When the Civil War began in 1861, woman's rights advocates were urged to abandon their cause and support the war effort. Although Anthony and Stanton continued arguing that any battle for freedom must include woman's freedom, the woman's movement activities essentially stopped for the duration of the War. After the War and the ratification of the 13th Amendment abolishing slavery (for which the women activists had campaigned vigorously), the abolitionists began to press for passage of a 14th Amendment to secure the rights, privileges and immunities of citizens (the new freedmen) under the law. In the second section of the proposed Amendment, however, the word "male" appeared, introducing a sex distinction into the Constitution for the first time. Shocked and enraged by the introduction of the word "male," the women activists mounted an extensive campaign to eliminate it. They were dismayed to find no one, neither the Republican Administration nor their old abolitionist allies, had any intention of "complicating" the campaign for Negroes' rights by advocating women's rights as well. Over and over again the women were told, "This is the Negroes' hour." The authors of *History of Woman Suffrage* analyzed the women's situation:

> During the six years they held their own claims in abeyance to the slaves of the South, and labored to inspire the people with enthusiasm for the great measures of the Republican party, they were highly honored as "wise, loyal, and clear-sighted." But again

> when the slaves were emancipated and they asked that women should be recognized in the reconstruction as citizens of the Republic, equal before the law, all these transcendent virtues vanished like dew before the morning sun. And thus it ever is so long as woman labors to second man's endeavors and exalt his sex above her own, her virtues pass unquestioned; but when she dares to demand rights and privileges for herself, her motives, manners, dress, personal appearance, character, are subjects for ridicule and detraction.[16]

The women met with the same response when they campaigned to get the word "sex" added to the proposed 15th Amendment which would prohibit the denial of suffrage on account of race.[17]

As a result of these setbacks, the woman's movement assumed as its first priority the drive for woman's suffrage. It must be noted, however, that while nearly all the women activists agreed on the need for suffrage, in 1869 the movement split into two major factions over ideological and tactical questions. In May of that year, Susan B. Anthony and Elizabeth Cady Stanton organized the National Woman Suffrage Association. Six months later, Lucy Stone and others organized the American Woman Suffrage Association. The American, in an attempt to make the idea of woman's suffrage "respectable," limited its activities to that issue, and refused to address itself to any of the more "controversial" subjects such as marriage or the Church. The National, on the other hand, embraced the broad cause of woman's rights of which the vote was seen primarily as a *means* of achieving those rights. During this time Anthony and Stanton founded *The Revolution* which became one of the best known of the independent women's newspapers. The weekly journal began in January, 1868, and took as its motto, "Men, their rights and nothing more; women, their rights and nothing less." In addition to discussions of suffrage, *The Revolution* examined the institutions of marriage, the law, organized religion, etc. Moreover, the newspaper touched on ". . . such incendiary topics as the double standard and prostitution."[18] Flexner describes the paper:

> . . . [It] made a contribution to the women's cause out of all proportion to either its size, brief lifespan, or modest circulation. . . . Here was news not to be found elsewhere—of the organization of women type-

setters, tailoresses, and laundry workers, of the first women's clubs, of pioneers in the professions, of women abroad. But The Revolution *did more than just carry news, or set a new standard of professionalism for papers edited by and for women. It gave their movement a forum, focus, and direction. It pointed, it led, and it fought, with vigor and vehemence.*[19]

The two suffrage organizations coexisted for over twenty years and used some of the same tactics in their campaigns for suffrage: lecture tours, lobbying activities, petition campaigns, etc. The American, however, focused exclusively on state-by-state action, while the National in addition pushed for a woman suffrage Amendment to the federal Constitution. Susan B. Anthony and others also attempted to gain the vote through court decisions. The Supreme Court, however, held in 1875[20] that suffrage was not necessarily one of the privileges and immunities of citizens protected by the 14th Amendment. Thus, although women were *citizens* it was nonetheless permissible, according to the Court, to constitutionally limit the right to vote to males.

During this same period, a strong temperance movement had also emerged. Large numbers of women, including some suffragists, became actively involved in the temperance cause. It is important to note that one of the main reasons women became involved in pressing for laws restricting the sale and consumption of alcohol was that their legal status as married women offered them no protection under the law against either physical abuse or abandonment by a drunken husband. It might be added that the reason separate women's temperance organizations were formed was that women were not permitted to participate in the men's groups. In spite of the fact that temperance was in "women's interests," the growth of the women's temperance movement solidified the liquor and brewing industries' opposition to woman suffrage. As a result, suffrage leaders became convinced of the necessity of keeping the two issues separate.

As the campaign for woman suffrage grew, more and more sympathizers were attracted to the conservative and "respectable" American Association which, as noted above, deliberately limited its work to the single issue of suffrage. After two decades "respectability" won out, and the broad-ranging issues of the earlier movement had been largely subsumed by suffrage. (Even the Stanton-Anthony forces had somewhat redefined their goals and were focusing primarily on suffrage.) By 1890, when the American and the National merged to become the National American Woman Suffrage Association, the woman's movement had, in fact, been transformed into the single-issue suffrage movement. Moreover, although Elizabeth Cady Stanton, NAWSA's first president, was succeeded two years later by Susan B. Anthony, the first women activists with their catholic range of concerns were slowly being replaced by a second group far more limited in their political analysis. It should be noted that Stanton herself, after her two-year term as president of the new organization, withdrew from active work in the suffrage campaign. Although one of the earliest feminist leaders to understand the need for woman suffrage, by this time Stanton believed that the main obstacle to woman's equality was the church and organized religion.

During the entire development of the woman's movement perhaps the argument most often used by anti-feminists was that the subjugation of women was divinely ordained as written in the Bible. Stanton attacked the argument head-on. She and a group of twenty-three women, including three ordained ministers, produced *The Woman's Bible,*[21] which presented a systematic feminist critique of woman's role and image in the Bible. Some Biblical chapters were presented as proof that the Scripture itself was the source of woman's subjugation; others to show that, if reinterpreted, men and women were indeed equals in the Bible, not superior and inferior beings. "We have made a fetish [sic] of the Bible long enough. The time has come to read it as we do all other books, accepting the good and rejecting the evil it teaches."[22] Dismissing the "rib story" as a "petty surgical operation," Stanton argued further that the entire structure of the Bible was predicated on the notion of Eve's (woman's) corruption:

> *Take the snake, the fruit-tree and the woman from the tableau, and we have no fall, nor frowning Judge, no Inferno, no everlasting punishment,—hence no need of a Savior. Thus the bottom falls out of the whole Christian theology. Here is the reason why in all the Biblical researches and higher criticisms, the scholars never touch the position of women.*[23]

Not surprisingly, *The Woman's Bible* was considered by most scandalous and sacriligious. The Suffrage

Association members themselves, with the exception of Anthony and a few others, publicly disavowed Stanton and her work. They feared that the image of the already controversial suffrage movement would be irreparably damaged if the public were to associate it with Stanton's radical tract.

Shortly after the turn of the century, the second generation of woman suffragists came of age and new leaders replaced the old. Carrie Chapman Catt is perhaps the best known; she succeeded Anthony as president of the National American Woman Suffrage Association, which by then had become a large and somewhat unwieldy organization. Although limited gains were achieved (a number of western states had enfranchised women) no major progress was made in the campaign for suffrage until Alice Paul, a young and extremely militant suffragist, became active in the movement. In April, 1913, she formed a small radical group known as the Congressional Union (later reorganized as the Woman's Party[24]) to work exclusively on a campaign for a *federal* woman's suffrage Amendment using any tactical means necessary no matter how unorthodox. Her group organized parades, mass demonstrations, hunger strikes, and its members were on several occasions arrested and jailed.[25] Although many suffragists rejected both the militant style and tactics of the Congressional Union, they nonetheless did consider Paul and her followers in large part responsible for "shocking" the languishing movement into actively pressuring for the federal Amendment. The woman suffrage Amendment (known as the "Anthony Amendment"), introduced into every session of Congress from 1878 on, was finally ratified on August 26, 1920.

Nearly three-quarters of a century had passed since the demand for woman suffrage had first been made at the Seneca Falls Convention. By 1920, so much energy had been expended in achieving the right to vote, that the woman's movement virtually collapsed from exhaustion. To achieve the vote alone, as Carrie Chapman Catt had computed, took:

> . . . *fifty-two years of pauseless campaign.* . . .
> *fifty-six campaigns of referenda to male voters;*
> *480 campaigns to get Legislatures to submit suffrage amendments to voters; 47 campaigns to get State constitutional conventions to write woman suffrage into state constitutions; 277 campaigns to get State party conventions to include woman suffrage planks;*

> *30 campaigns to get presidential party conventions to adopt woman suffrage planks in party platforms, and 19 campaigns with 19 successive Congresses.*[26]

With the passage of the 19th Amendment the majority of women activists as well as the public at large assumed that having gained the vote woman's complete equality had been virtually obtained.

It must be remembered, however, that for most of the period that the woman's movement existed, suffrage had not been seen as an all-inclusive goal, but as a means of achieving equality—suffrage was only one element in the wide-ranging feminist critique questioning the fundamental organization of society. Historians, however, have for the most part ignored this radical critique and focused exclusively on the suffrage campaign. By virtue of this omission they have, to all intents and purposes, denied the political significance of the early feminist analysis. Moreover, the summary treatment by historians of the 19th and 20th century drive for woman's suffrage has made that campaign almost a footnote to the abolitionist movement and the campaign for Negro suffrage. In addition, the traditional textbook image of the early feminists—if not wild-eyed women waving placards for the vote, then wild-eyed women swinging axes at saloon doors—has further demeaned the importance of their philosophical analysis.

The woman's movement virtually died in 1920 and, with the exception of a few organizations, feminism was to lie dormant for forty years.

Notes

[1]Mount Holyoke opened in 1837; Vassar, 1865; Smith and Wellesley, 1875; Radcliffe, 1879; Bryn Mawr, 1885.

[2]Quoted in Eleanor Flexner, *Century of Struggle: The Woman's Rights Movement in the United States* (Cambridge, Mass.: The Belknap Press of Harvard University Press, 1959), p. 27.

[3]*History of Woman Suffrage* (Republished by Arno Press and *The New York Times*, New York, 1969). Vol. I, p. 81. Hereafter cited as *HWS*. Volumes I to III were edited by Elizabeth Cady Stanton, Susan B. Anthony and Matilda Joslyn Gage. The first two volumes were published in 1881, the third in 1886. Volume IV was edited by Susan B. Anthony and Ida Husted Harper and was published in 1902. Volumes V and VI were edited by Ida Husted Harper and published in 1922.

[4]Sarah M. Grimké, *Letters on the Equality of the Sexes and the*

Condition of Woman (Boston: Isaac Kanapp, 1838, reprinted by Source Book Press, New York, 1970), p. 10 ff.

[5] *Ibid.*, pp. 9–10.

[6] *Ibid.*, pp. 85–86.

[7] *Ibid.*, p. 51.

[8] *HWS*, p. 54.

[9] *HWS*, p. 61.

[10] *HWS*, p. 73.

[11] Flexner, p. 77.

[12] *HWS*, p. 110.

[13] *Ibid.*, p. 806.

[14] Flexner, p. 83.

[15] *Ibid.*, p. 84.

[16] *HWS*, Vol. 2, p. 51.

[17] The 13th Amendment was ratified in 1865; the 14th in 1868; the 15th in 1870.

[18] Flexner, p. 151.

[19] *Loc. cit.*

[20] *Minor v. Happersett*, 21 Wall. 162, 22 L. Ed. 627 (1875).

[21] New York, European Publishing Company, 1895 and 1898, Two Parts.

[22] *Ibid.*, II, pp. 7–8.

[23] Stanton, letter to the editor of *The Critic* (New York), March 28, 1896, quoted from Aileen S. Kraditor, *The Ideas of the Woman Suffrage Movement, 1890–1920* (New York: Columbia University Press, 1965), n. 11, p. 81.

[24] See Chapter 2, National Women's Rights Organizations.

[25] A total of 218 women from 26 states were arrested during the first session of the 65th Congress (1917). Ninety-seven went to prison.

[26] Carrie Chapman Catt and Nettie Rogers Shuler, *Woman Suffrage and Politics* (New York, 1923), p. 107. Quoted from Flexner, p. 173.

Declaration of Sentiments and Resolutions

Seneca Falls Convention of 1848

The "woman question" had been bubbling heatedly among the intelligentsia and great reformers of the times and in the press at least since women had begun to emerge as strong and active movers in the antislavery societies. A major precipitating factor of clearly feminist activism occurred in 1840 in London at the World Anti-Slavery Convention attended by many Americans, among them Lucretia Mott, a strong, intelligent Quaker minister and delegate of the American Anti-Slavery Society, and Elizabeth Cady Stanton, then the bride of Henry Stanton, delegate of the American and Foreign Anti-Slavery Society. Although debate over the issue of women's participation in the abolition movement had been sharp in the United States, women had gained some degree of tolerance, if not wholehearted acceptance. Furthermore, the women involved here were educated, spirited women, accustomed to speaking out. They were not prepared for their reception in London: After a full day of debate on the question, on the grounds of morality and propriety (not to mention incompetence), women were finally allowed only to attend, not to participate actively in the discussion. Barred from the central gathering, they were required to sit in a separate curtained gallery, hidden from view, forbidden to speak. Humiliated and furious at the hypocrisy of liberals who could see one brand of oppression but not another, the American women determined to call their own convention on their own issue upon their return home.

Although diverted for nearly eight years, they made good their plan on July 19, 1848, at Seneca Falls, New York. The convention brought forth the following document, written primarily by Stanton and ultimately adopted by the gathering. The decision to use the language of the Declaration of Independence was done pointedly to remind all that women had been omitted from the concerns and safeguards of the original U.S. Constitution. The arguments are clearly in the tradition of eighteenth-century Enlightenment liberalism and nineteenth-century reformism. Notice the breadth of concerns voiced here, suffrage being only a part (and not a well-supported one!) of the commitment. Notice, too, the parallels between these ideas and those of today's women's liberation movement.

WHEN, IN THE COURSE OF HUMAN EVENTS, IT BE-comes necessary for one portion of the family of man to assume among the people of the earth a position different from that which they have hitherto occupied, but one to which the laws of nature and of nature's God entitle them, a decent respect to the opinions of mankind requires that they should declare the causes that impel them to such a course.

We hold these truths to be self-evident: that all men and women are created equal; that they are endowed by their Creator with certain inalienable rights; that among these are life, liberty, and the pursuit of happiness; that to secure these rights governments are instituted, deriving their just powers from the consent of the governed. Whenever any form of government becomes destructive of these ends, it is the right of those who suffer from it to refuse allegiance to it, and to insist upon the institution of a new government, laying its foundation on such principles, and organizing its powers in such form, as to them shall seem most likely to effect their safety and happiness. Prudence, indeed, will dictate that governments long established should not be changed for light and transient causes; and accordingly all experience hath shown that mankind are more disposed to suffer, while evils are sufferable, than to right themselves by abolishing the forms to which they

Stanton, Elizabeth Cady, Susan B. Anthony, and Matilda Joslyn Gage, eds. *History of Women Suffrage,* 2nd ed., Vol. 1, Rochester, N.Y.: Charles Mann, 1889.

were accustomed. But when a long train of abuses and usurpations, pursuing invariably the same object evinces a design to reduce them under absolute despotism, it is their duty to throw off such government, and to provide new guards for their future security. Such has been the patient sufferance of the women under this government, and such is now the necessity which constrains them to demand the equal station to which they are entitled.

The history of mankind is a history of repeated injuries and usurpations on the part of man toward woman, having in direct object the establishment of an absolute tyranny over her. To prove this, let facts be submitted to a candid world.

He has never permitted her to exercise her inalienable right to the elective franchise.

He has compelled her to submit to laws, in the formation of which she had no voice.

He has withheld from her rights which are given to the most ignorant and degraded men—both natives and foreigners.

Having deprived her of this first right of a citizen, the elective franchise, thereby leaving her without representation in the halls of legislation, he has oppressed her on all sides.

He has made her, if married, in the eye of the law, civilly dead.

He has taken from her all right in property, even to the wages she earns.

He has made her, morally, an irresponsible being, as she can commit many crimes with impunity, provided they be done in the presence of her husband. In the covenant of marriage, she is compelled to promise obedience to her husband, he becoming, to all intents and purposes, her master—the law giving him power to deprive her of her liberty, and to administer chastisement.

He has so framed the laws of divorce, as to what shall be the proper causes, and in case of separation, to whom the guardianship of the children shall be given, as to be wholly regardless of the happiness of women—the law, in all cases, going upon a false supposition of the supremacy of man, and giving all power into his hands.

After depriving her of all rights as a married women, if single, and the owner of property, he has taxed her to support a government which recognizes her only when her property can be made profitable to it.

He has monopolized nearly all the profitable em-

ployments, and from those she is permitted to follow, she receives but a scanty remuneration. He closes against her all the avenues to wealth and distinction which he considers most honorable to himself. As a teacher of theology, medicine, or law, she is not known.

He has denied her the facilities for obtaining a thorough education, all colleges being closed against her.

He allows her in Church, as well as State, but a subordinate position, claiming Apostolic authority for her exclusion from the ministry, and, with some exceptions, from any public participation in the affairs of the Church.

He has created a false public sentiment by giving to the world a different code of morals for men and women, by which moral delinquencies which exclude women from society, are not only tolerated, but deemed of little account in man.

He has usurped the prerogative of Jehovah himself, claiming it as his right to assign for her a sphere of action, when that belongs to her conscience and to her God.

He has endeavored, in every way that he could, to destroy her confidence in her own powers, to lessen her self-respect, and to make her willing to lead a dependent and abject life.

Now, in view of this entire disfranchisement of one-half the people of this country, their social and religious degradation—in view of the unjust laws above mentioned, and because women do feel themselves aggrieved, oppressed, and fraudulently deprived of their most sacred rights, we insist that they have immediate admission to all the rights and privileges which belong to them as citizens of the United States.

In entering upon the great work before us, we anticipate no small amount of misconception, misrepresentation, and ridicule; but we shall use every instrumentality within our power to effect our object. We shall employ agents, circulate tracts, petition the State and National legislatures, and endeavor to enlist the pulpit and the press in our behalf. We hope this Convention will be followed by a series of Conventions embracing every part of the country.

WHEREAS, The great precept of nature is conceded to be, that "man shall pursue his own true and substantial happiness." Blackstone in his Commentaries remarks, that this law of Nature being coeval with mankind, and dictated by God himself, is of course superior in obligation to any other. It is binding over all the globe, in all countries and at all times; no human laws are of any validity if contrary to this, and such of them as are valid, derive all their force, and all their validity, and all their authority, mediately and immediately, from this original; therefore,

Resolved, That such laws as conflict, in any way, with the true and substantial happiness of woman, are contrary to the great precept of nature and of no validity, for this is "superior in obligation to any other."

Resolved, That all laws which prevent woman from occupying such a station in society as her conscience shall dictate, or which place her in a position inferior to that of man, are contrary to the great precept of nature, and therefore of no force or authority.

Resolved, That woman is man's equal—was intended to be so by the Creator, and the highest good of the race demands that she should be recognized as such.

Resolved, That the women of this country ought to be enlightened in regard to the laws under which they live, that they may no longer publish their degradation by declaring themselves satisfied with their present position, nor their ignorance, by asserting that they have all the rights they want.

Resolved, That inasmuch as man, while claiming for himself intellectual superiority, does accord to woman moral superiority, it is pre-eminently his duty to encourage her to speak and teach, as she has an opportunity, in all religious assemblies.

Resolved, That the same amount of virtue, delicacy, and refinement of behavior that is required of woman in the social state, should also be required of man, and the same transgressions should be visited with equal severity on both man and woman.

Resolved, That the objection of indelicacy and impropriety, which is so often brought against woman when she addresses a public audience, comes with a very ill-grace from those who encourage, by their attendance, her appearance on the stage, in the concert, or in feats of the circus.

Resolved, That woman has too long rested satisfied in the circumscribed limits which corrupt customs and a perverted application of the Scriptures have marked out for her, and that it is time she should move in the enlarged sphere which her great Creator has assigned her.

Resolved, That it is the duty of the women of this country to secure to themselves their sacred right to the elective franchise.

Resolved, That the equality of human rights results necessarily from the fact of the identity of the race in capabilities and responsibilities.

Resolved, therefore, That, being invested by the Creator with the same capabilities, and the same consciousness of responsibility for their exercise, it is demonstrably the right and duty of woman, equally with man, to promote every righteous cause by every righteous means; and especially in regard to the great subjects of morals and religion, it is self-evidently her right to participate with her brother in teaching them, both in private and in public, by writing and by speaking, by any instrumentalities proper to be used, and in any assemblies proper to be held; and this being a self-evident truth growing out of the divinely implanted principles of human nature, any custom or authority adverse to it, whether modern or wearing the hoary sanction of antiquity, is to be regarded as a self-evident falsehood, and at war with mankind.

Resolved, That the speedy success of our cause depends upon the zealous and untiring efforts of both men and women, for the overthrow of the monopoly of the pulpit, and for the securing to woman an equal participation with men in the various trades, professions, and commerce.

Ain't I A Woman?

Sojourner Truth

Sojourner Truth (1795–1883)—born Isabella, a slave, in New York State—became a well known antislavery speaker some time after gaining her freedom in 1827. This speech, given extemporaneously at a woman's rights convention in Akron, Ohio, 1851, was recorded by Frances Gage, feminist activist and one of the authors of the huge compendium of materials of the first wave, The History of Woman Suffrage. *Gage, who was presiding at the meeting, describes the event:*

The leaders of the movement trembled on seeing a tall, gaunt black woman in a gray dress and white turban, surmounted with an uncouth sunbonnet, march deliberately into the church, walk with the air of a queen up the aisle, and take her seat upon the pulpit steps. A buzz of disapprobation was heard all over the house, and there fell on the listening ear, "An abolition affair!" "Woman's rights and niggers!" "I told you so!" "Go it, darkey!" . . . Again and again, timorous and trembling ones came to me and said, with earnestness, "Don't let her speak, Mrs. Gage, it will ruin us. Every newspaper in the land will have our cause mixed up with abolition and niggers, and we shall be utterly denounced." My only answer was, "We shall see when the time comes."

The second day the work waxed warm. Methodist, Baptist, Episcopal, Presbyterian, and Universalist minister came in to hear and discuss the resolutions presented. One claimed superior rights and privileges for man, on the ground of "superior intellect"; another, because of the "manhood of Christ; if God had desired the equality of woman, He would have given some token of His will through the birth, life, and death of the Saviour." Another gave us a theological view of the "sin of our first mother."

There were very few women in those days who dared to "speak in meeting"; and the august teachers of the people were seemingly getting the better of us, while the boys in the galleries, and the sneerers among the pews, were hugely enjoying the discomfiture as they supposed, of the "strong-minded." Some of the tender-skinned friends were on the point of losing dignity, and the atmosphere betokened a storm. When, slowly from her seat in the corner rose Sojourner Truth, who, till now, had scarcely lifted her head. "Don't let her speak!" gasped half a dozen in my ear. She moved slowly and solemnly to the front, laid her old bonnet at her feet, and turned her great speaking eyes to me. There was a hissing sound of disapprobation above and below. I rose and announced, "Sojourner Truth," and begged the audience to keep silence for a few moments.

The tummult subsided at once, and every eye was fixed on this almost Amazon form, which stood nearly six feet high, head erect, and eyes piercing the upper air like one in a dream. At her first word there was a profound hush. She spoke in deep tones, which, though not loud, reached every ear in the house, and away through the throng at the doors and windows.

One cannot miss that there were those who were staunch for women's rights but yet were racist. It was not until later, much later, that there was much sophisticated analysis linking sexism, racism, and expressions of other kinds.

Truth's speech is reproduced here exactly as Gage recorded it in History of Woman Suffrage.

"WALL, CHILERN, WHAR DAR IS SO MUCH racket dar must be somethin' out o' kilter. I tink dat 'twixt de niggers of de Souf and de womin at de Norf, all talkin' 'bout rights, de white men will be in a fix pretty soon. But what's all dis here talkin' 'bout?

"Dat man ober dar say dat womin needs to be helped into carriages, and lifted ober ditches, and

Elizabeth Cady Stanton, Susan B. Anthony, & Matilda Joslyn Gage eds. *History of Woman Suffrage,* 2nd ed. Vol. 1. Rochester, NY: Charles Mann, 1889.

to hab de best place everywhar. Nobody eber helps me into carriages, or ober mud-puddles, or gibs me any best place!'' And raising herself to her full height, and her voice to a pitch like rolling thunder, she asked. ''And a'n't I a woman? Look at me! Look at my arm! (and she bared her right arm to the shoulder, showing her tremendous muscular power). I have ploughed, and planted, and gathered into barns, and no man could head me! And a'n't I a woman? I could work as much and eat as much as a man—when I could get it—and bear de lash as well! And a'n't I a woman? I have borne thirteen chilern, and seen 'em mos' all sold off to slavery, and when I cried out with my mother's grief, none but Jesus heard me! And a'n't I a woman?

''Den dey talks 'bout dis ting in de head; what dis dey call it?'' (''Intellect,'' whispered some one near.) ''Dat's it, honey. What's dat got to do wid womin's rights or nigger's rights? If my cup won't hold but a pint, and yourn holds a quart, wouldn't ye be mean not to let me have my little half-measure full?'' And she pointed her significant finger, and sent a keen glance at the minister who had made the argument. The cheering was long and loud.

''Den dat little man in black dar, he say women can't have as much rights as men, 'cause Christ wan't a woman! Whar did your Christ come from?'' Rolling thunder couldn't have stilled that crowd, as did those deep, wonderful tones, as she stood there with outstretched arms and eyes of fire. Raising her voice still louder, she repeated, ''Whar did your Christ come from? From God and a woman! Man had nothin' to do wid Him.'' Oh, what a rebuke that was to that little man.

Turning again to another objector, she took up the defense of Mother Eve. I can not follow her through it all. It was pointed, and witty, and solemn; eliciting at almost every sentence deafening applause; and she ended by asserting: ''If de fust woman God ever made was strong enough to turn de world upside down all alone, dese women togedder (and she glanced her eye over the platform) ought to be able to turn it back, and get it right side up again! And now dey is asking to do it, de men better let 'em.'' Long-continued cheering greeted this. '''Bleeged to ye for hearin' on me, and now ole Sojourner han't got nothin' more to say.''

Amid roars of applause, she returned to her corner, leaving more than one of us with streaming eyes, and hearts beating with gratitude. She had taken us up in her strong arms and carried us safely over the slough of difficulty turning the whole tide in our favor. I have never in my life seen anything like the magical influence that subdued the mobbish spirit of the day, and turned the sneers and jeers of an excited crowd into notes of respect and admiration. Hundreds rushed up to shake hands with her, and congratulate the glorious old mother, and bid her God-speed on her mission of ''testifyin' agin concerning the wickedness of this 'ere people.''

Speech Before the Legislature 1860

Elizabeth Cady Stanton

Elizabeth Cady was born in Johnstown, New York, in 1815. As the daughter of a judge of comfortable means, she encountered people and situations that afforded her more than the usual opportunities for education allowed girls of her time. Having displayed an earnest zest and ability for learning, she was granted special permission to attend the Boys Academy in Johnstown. Prevented by her sex from attending college, she was graduated from the rather conservative Emma Willard Seminary in Troy, New York. Afterward she studied law with her father but, again because of her sex, was prevented from gaining admission to the bar. She had learned, however, precisely how the law burdened women and wives.

Elizabeth's family and friends included many of the brightest thinkers of the Northeast, all of whom taught and influenced her. Her marriage to the activist Henry Stanton in 1840, their trip to the World Anti-Slavery Convention in London, and their move in 1842 to Boston further developed her social sensitivities, knowledge, and thirst for intellectual stimulation. After the family returned from Boston in 1846 to settle in Seneca Falls, New York, Elizabeth became isolated from friends and society. She became immersed in the duties and experiences of a housewife and mother of seven. It suffocated her. Only her visits to her friend Lucretia Mott in Waterloo, New York, revived her. There, with Lucretia and her sister Martha Wright, with Jane Hunt and Mary Ann McClintock, in what could only be called consciousness-raising sessions, seated around a table for tea, the women talked, vented their frustration, and finally planned the convention at Seneca Falls.

After that time, Elizabeth Cady Stanton worked determinedly for the whole range of women's freedoms—from discrimination in marriage and divorce to freedom from the misogyny of traditional religion (she published the Woman's Bible *in 1895), to suffrage, and more. In 1851, she met Susan B. Anthony, with whom she worked until the end. They founded a radical magazine,* The Revolution, *in 1868, and in 1869 Stanton was elected president of the National Woman's Suffrage Association, an organization she served for over twenty years. Stanton was always brave, outspoken, often ahead of her time, and sometimes considered too radical even for many of the feminists. She died still at work in New York City in 1902.*

Early in 1860, Stanton was invited to address the New York legislature on a pending bill (subsequently passed) for an enlargement of women's property rights. Her speech, presented here, expressed the themes of natural human rights, the necessary limits of authority, and the parallels between blacks and females. Here she introduced, furthermore, another extremely important concept, one that should be carried into the present, that of woman as citizen. We are, after all, citizens of the United States, and our inalienable right is full participation in all the opportunities of this country.

GENTLEMEN OF THE JUDICIARY:—THERE ARE CERtain natural rights as inalienable to civilization as are the rights of air and motion to the savage in the wilderness. The natural rights of the civilized man and woman are government, property, the harmonious development of all their powers, and the gratification of their desires. There are a few people we now and then meet who, like Jeremy Bentham, scout the idea of natural rights in civilization, and pronounce them mere metaphors, declaring that there are no rights aside from those the law confers. If the law made man too, that might do, for then he could be made to order to fit the particular niche he was designed to fill. But inasmuch as God made man in His own image,

Elizabeth Cady Stanton, Susan B. Anthony, and Matilda Joslyn Gage, eds. *History of Woman Suffrage*, 2nd ed., vol. 1. Rochester, NY: Charles Mann, 1889. Currently available from Ayer Company Publishers, POB 958, Salem, NH 03079.

with capacities and powers as boundless as the universe, whose exigencies no mere human law can meet, it is evident that the man must ever stand first; the law but the creature of his wants; the law-giver but the mouthpiece of humanity. If, then, the nature of a being decides its rights, every individual comes into this world with rights that are not transferable. He does not bring them like a pack on his back, that may be stolen from him, but they are a component part of himself, the laws which insure his growth and development. The individual may be put in the stocks, body and soul, he may be dwarfed, crippled, killed, but his rights no man can get; they live and die with him.

Though the atmosphere is forty miles deep all round the globe, no man can do more than fill his own lungs. No man can see, hear, or smell but just so far; and though hundreds are deprived of these senses, his are not the more acute. Though rights have been abundantly supplied by the good Father, no man can appropriate to himself those that belong to another. A citizen can have but one vote, fill but one office, though thousands are not permitted to do either. These axioms prove that woman's poverty does not add to man's wealth, and if, in the plenitude of his power, he should secure to her the exercise of all her God-given rights, her wealth could not bring poverty to him. There is a kind of nervous unrest always manifested by those in power, whenever new claims are started by those out of their own immediate class. The philosophy of this is very plain. They imagine that if the rights of this new class be granted, they must, of necessity, sacrifice something of what they already possess. They can not divest themselves of the idea that rights are very much like lands, stocks, bonds, and mortgages, and that if every new claimant be satisfied, the supply of human rights must in time run low. You might as well carp at the birth of every child, lest there should not be enough air left to inflate your lungs; at the success of every scholar, for fear that your draughts at the fountain of knowledge could not be so long and deep; at the glory of every hero, lest there be no glory left for you. . . .

If the object of government is to protect the weak against the strong, how unwise to place the power wholly in the hands of the strong. Yet that is the history of all governments, even the model republic of these United States. You who have read the his-

tory of nations, from Moses down to our last election, where have you ever seen one class looking after the interests of another? Any of you can readily see the defects in other governments, and pronounce sentence against those who have sacrificed the masses to themselves; but when we come to our own case, we are blinded by custom and self-interest. Some of you who have no capital can see the injustice which the laborer suffers; some of you who have no slaves, can see the cruelty of his oppression; but who of you appreciate the galling humiliation, the refinements of degradation, to which women (the mothers, wives, sisters, and daughters of freemen) are subject, in this the last half of the nineteenth century? How many of you have ever read even the laws concerning them that now disgrace your statute-books? In cruelty and tyranny, they are not surpassed by any slaveholding code in the Southern States; in fact they are worse, by just so far as woman, from her social position, refinement, and education, is on a more equal ground with the oppressor.

Allow me just here to call the attention of that party now so much interested in the slave of the Carolinas, to the similarity in his condition and that of the mothers, wives, and daughters of the Empire State. The negro has no name. He is Cuffy Douglas or Cuffy Brooks, just whose Cuffy he may chance to be. The woman has no name. She is Mrs. Richard Roe or Mrs. John Doe, just whose Mrs. she may chance to be. Cuffy has no right to his earnings; he can not buy or sell, or lay up anything that he can call his own. Mrs. Roe has no right to her earnings; she can neither buy nor sell, make contracts, nor lay up anything that she can call her own. Cuffy has no right to his children; they can be sold from him at any time. Mrs. Roe has no right to her children; they may be bound out to cancel a father's debts of honor. The unborn child, even by the last will of the father, may be placed under the guardianship of a stranger and a foreigner. Cuffy has no legal existence; he is subject to restraint and moderate chastisement. Mrs. Roe has no legal existence; she has not the best right to her own person. The husband has the power to restrain, and administer moderate chastisement.

Blackstone declares that the husband and wife are one, and learned commentators have decided that that one is the husband. In all civil codes, you will find them classified as one. Certain rights and immunities, such and such privileges are to be secured to white male citizens. What have women and negroes to do with rights? What know they of government, war, or glory?

The prejudice against color, of which we hear so much, is no stronger than that against sex. It is produced by the same cause, and manifested very much in the same way. The negro's skin and the woman's sex are both *prima facie* evidence that they were intended to be in subjection to the white Saxon man. The few social privileges which the man gives the woman, he makes up to the negro in civil rights. The woman may sit at the same table and eat with the white man; the free negro may hold property and vote. The woman may sit in the same pew with the white man in church; the free negro may enter the pulpit and preach. Now, with the black man's right to suffrage, the right unquestioned, even by Paul, to minister at the altar, it is evident that the prejudice against sex is more deeply rooted and more unreasonably maintained than that against color. As citizens of a republic, which should we most highly prize, social privileges or civil rights? The latter, most certainly.

To those who do not feel the injustice and degradation of the condition, there is something inexpressibly comical in man's "citizen woman." It reminds me of those monsters I used to see in the old world, head and shoulders woman, and the rest of the body sometimes fish and sometimes beast. I used to think, What a strange conceit! but now I see how perfectly it represents man's idea! Look over all his laws concerning us, and you will see just enough of woman to tell of her existence; all the rest is submerged, or made to crawl upon the earth. Just imagine an inhabitant of another planet entertaining himself some pleasant evening in searching over our great national compact, our Declaration of Independence, our Constitutions, or some of our statute-books; what would he think of those "women and negroes" that must be so fenced in, so guarded against? Why, he would certainly suppose we were monsters, like those fabulous giants or Brobdignagians of olden times, so dangerous to civilized man, from our size, ferocity, and power. Then let him take up our poets, from Pope down to Dana; let him listen to our Fourth of July toasts, and some of the sentimental adulations of social life, and no logic could convince him that this creature of the law, and this angel of the family

altar, could be one and the same being. Man is in such a labyrinth of contradictions with his marital and property rights; he is so befogged on the whole question of maidens, wives, and mothers, that from pure benevolence we should relieve him from this troublesome branch of legislation. We should vote, and make laws for ourselves. Do not be alarmed, dear ladies! You need spend no time reading Grotius, Coke, Puffendorf, Blackstone, Bentham, Kent, and Story to find out what you need. We may safely trust the shrewd selfishness of the white man, and consent to live under the same broad code where he has so comfortably ensconced himself. Any legislation that will do for man, we may abide by most cheerfully. . . .

But, say you, we would not have woman exposed to the grossness and vulgarity of public life, or encounter what she must at the polls. When you talk, gentlemen, of sheltering woman from the rough winds and revolting scenes of real life, you must be either talking for effect, or wholly ignorant of what the facts of life are. The man, whatever he is, is known to the woman. She is the companion, not only of the accomplished statesman, the orator, and the scholar; but the vile, vulgar, brutal man has his mother, his wife, his sister, his daughter. Yes, delicate, refined, educated women are in daily life with the drunkard, the gambler, the licentious man, the rogue, and the villain; and if man shows out what he is anywhere, it is at his own hearthstone. There are over forty thousand drunkards in this State. All these are bound by the ties of family to some woman. Allow but a mother and a wife to each, and you have over eighty thousand women. All these have seen their fathers, brothers, husbands, sons, in the lowest and most debased stages of obscenity and degradation. In your own circle of friends, do you not know refined women, whose whole lives are darkened and saddened by gross and brutal associations? Now, gentlemen, do you talk to woman of a rude jest or jostle at the polls, where noble, virtuous men stand ready to protect her person and her rights, when, alone in the darkness and solitude and gloom of night, she has trembled on her own threshold awaiting the return of a husband from his midnight revels?—when, stepping from her chamber, she has beheld her royal monarch, her lord and master—her legal representative—the protector of her property, her home, her children, and her person, down on his hands and knees slowly crawling up the stairs? Behold him in her chamber—in her bed! The fairy tale of "Beauty and the Beast" is far too often realized in life. Gentlemen, such scenes as woman has witnessed at her own fireside, where no eye save Omnipotence could pity, no strong arm could help, can never be realized at the polls, never equaled elsewhere, this side the bottomless pit. No, woman has not hitherto lived in the clouds, surrounded by an atmosphere of purity and peace—but she has been the companion of man in health, in sickness, and in death, in his highest and in his lowest moments. She has worshiped him as a saint and an orator, and pitied him as madman or a fool. In Paradise, man and woman were placed together, and so they must ever be. They must sink or rise together. If man is low and wretched and vile, woman can not escape the contagion, and any atmosphere that is unfit for woman to breathe is not fit for man. Verily, the sins of the fathers shall be visited upon the children to the third and fourth generation. You, by your unwise legislation, have crippled and dwarfed womanhood, by closing to her all honorable and lucrative means of employment, have driven her into the garrets and dens of our cities, where she now revenges herself on your innocent sons, sapping the very foundations of national virtue and strength. Alas! for the young men just coming on the stage of action, who soon shall fill your vacant places—our future Senators, our Presidents, the expounders of our constitutional law! Terrible are the penalties we are now suffering for the ages of injustice done to woman.

Again, it is said that the majority of women do not ask for any change in the laws; that it is time enough to give them the elective franchise when they, as a class, demand it.

Wise statesmen legislate for the best interests of the nation; the State, for the highest good of its citizens; the Christian, for the conversion of the world. Where would have been our railroads, our telegraphs, our ocean steamers, our canals and harbors, our arts and sciences, if government had withheld the means from the far-seeing minority? This State established our present system of common schools, fully believing that educated men and women would make better citizens than ignorant ones. In making this provision for the education of its children, had they waited for a majority of the urchins of this State to petition for schools, how many, think you, would have asked to be transplanted from the street to the school-house? Does the State wait for the criminal to ask for his prison-house? the insane, the idiot, the deaf and dumb for his asylum? Does the Christian, in his love to all mankind, wait for the majority of the benighted heathen to ask him for the gospel? No; unasked and unwelcomed, he crosses the trackless ocean, rolls off the mountain of superstition that oppresses the human mind, proclaims the immortality of the soul, the dignity of manhood, the right of all to be free and happy.

No, gentlemen, if there is but one woman in this State who feels the injustice of her position, she should not be denied her inalienable rights, because the common household drudge and the silly butterfly of fashion are ignorant of all laws, both human and Divine. Because they know nothing of governments, or rights, and therefore ask nothing, shall my petitions be unheard? I stand before you the rightful representative of woman, claiming a share in the halo of glory that has gathered round her in the ages, and by the wisdom of her past words and works, her peerless heroism and self-sacrifice, I challenge your admiration; and, moreover, claiming, as I do, a share in all her outrages and sufferings, in the cruel injustice, contempt, and ridicule now heaped upon her, in her deep degradation, hopeless wretchedness, by all that is helpless in her present condition, that is false in law and public sentiment, I urge your generous consideration; for as my heart swells with pride to behold woman in the highest walks of literature and art, it grows big enough to take in those who are bleeding in the dust.

Now do not think, gentlemen, we wish you to do a great many troublesome things for us. We do not ask our legislators to spend a whole session fixing up a code of laws to satisfy a class of most unreasonable women. We ask no more than the poor devils in the Scripture asked, "Let us alone." In mercy, let us take care of ourselves, our property, our children, and our homes. True, we are not so strong, so wise, so crafty as you are, but if any kind friend leaves us a little money, or we can by great industry earn fifty cents a day, we would rather buy bread and clothes for our children than cigars and champagne for our legal protectors. There has been a great deal written and said about protection. We, as a class, are tired of one kind of protection, that which leaves us everything to do, to dare, and to suffer, and strips us of all means for its accomplishment. We would not tax man to take care of us. No, the Great Father has endowed all his creatures with the necessary powers for self-support, self-defense, and protection. We do not ask man to represent us; it is hard enough in times like these for man to carry backbone enough to represent himself. So long as the mass of men spend most of their time on the fence, not knowing which way to jump, they are surely in no condition to tell us where we had better stand. In pity for man, we would no longer hang like a millstone round his neck. Undo what man did for us in the dark ages, and strike out all special legislation for us; strike the words "white male" from all your constitutions, and then, with fair sailing, let us sink or swim, live or die, survive or perish together.

At Athens, an ancient apologue tells us, on the completion of the temple of Minerva, a statue of the goddess was wanted to occupy the crowning point of the edifice. Two of the greatest artists produced what each deemed his masterpiece. One of these figures was the size of life, admirably designed, exquisitely finished, softly rounded, and beautifully refined. The other was of Amazonian stature, and so boldly chiselled that it looked more like masonry than sculpture. The eyes of all were attracted by the first, and turned away in contempt from the second. That, therefore, was adopted, and the other rejected, almost with resentment, as though an insult had been offered to a discerning public. The favored statue was accordingly borne in triumph to the place for which it was designed, in the presence of applauding thousands, but as it receded from their upturned eyes, all, all at once agaze upon it, the thunders of applause unaccountably died away—a general misgiving ran through every bosom—the mob themselves stood like statues, as silent and as petrified, for as it slowly went up, and up the soft expression of those chiselled features, the delicate curves and outlines of the limbs and figure, became gradually fainter and fainter, and when at last it reached the place for which it was intended, it was a shapeless ball, enveloped in mist. Of course, the idol of the hour was now clamored down as rationally as it had been cried up, and its dishonored rival, with no good will and no good looks on the part of the chagrined populace, was reared in its stead. As it ascended, the sharp angles faded away, the rough points became smooth, the features full of expression, the whole figure radiant with majesty and beauty. The rude hewn mass, that before had scarcely appeared to bear even the human form, assumed at once the divinity which it represented, being so perfectly proportioned to the dimensions of the building, and to the elevation on which it stood, that it seemed as though Pallas herself had alighted upon the pinnacle of the temple in person, to receive the homage of her worshippers.

The woman of the nineteenth century is the shapeless ball in the lofty position which she was designed fully and nobly to fill. The place is not too high, too large, too sacred for woman, but the type that you have chosen is far too small for it. The woman we declare unto you is the rude, misshapen, unpolished object of the successful artist. From your stand-point, you are absorbed with the defects alone. The true artist sees the harmony between the object and its destination. Man, the sculptor, has carved out his ideal, and applauding thousands welcome his success. He has made a woman that from his low stand-point looks fair and beautiful, a being without rights, or hopes, or fears but in him—neither noble, virtuous, nor independent. Where do we see, in Church or State, in school-house or at the fireside, the much talked-of moral power of woman? Like those Athenians, we have bowed down and worshiped in woman, beauty, grace, the exquisite proportions, the soft and beautifully rounded outline, her delicacy, refinement, and silent helplessness—all well when she is viewed simply as an object of sight, never to rise one foot above the dust from which she sprung. But if she is to be raised up to adorn a temple, or represent a divinity—if she is to fill the niche of wife and counsellor to true and noble men, if she is to be the mother, the educator of a race of heroes or martyrs, of a Napoleon, or a Jesus—then must the type of womanhood be on a larger scale than that yet carved by man.

In vain would the rejected artist have reasoned with the Athenians as to the superiority of his production; nothing short of the experiment they made could have satisfied them. And what of your experiment, what of your wives, your homes? Alas! for the folly and vacancy that meet you there! But for your club-houses and newspapers, what would social life be to you? Where are your beautiful women? your frail ones, taught to lean lovingly and confidingly on man? Where are the crowds of educated dependents—where the long line of pensioners on man's bounty? Where all the young girls, taught to believe that marriage is the only legitimate object of a woman's pursuit—they who stand listlessly on life's shores, waiting, year after year, like the sick man at the pool of Bethesda, for some one to come and put them in? These are they who by their ignorance and folly curse almost every fireside with some human specimen of deformity or imbecility. These are they who fill the gloomy abodes of poverty and vice in our vast metropolis. These are they who patrol the streets of our cities, to give our sons their first lessons in infamy. These are they who fill our asylums, and make night hideous with their cries and groans.

The women who are called masculine, who are brave, courageous, self-reliant and independent, are they who in the face of adverse winds have kept one steady course upward and onward in the paths of virtue and peace—they who have taken their gauge of womanhood from their own native strength and dignity—they who have learned for themselves the will of God concerning them. This is our type of womanhood. Will you help us raise it up, that you too may see its beautiful proportions—that you may behold the outline of the goddess who is yet to adorn your temple of Freedom? We are building a model republic; our edifice will one day need a crowning glory. Let the artists be wisely chosen. Let them begin their work. Here is a temple to Liberty, to human rights, on whose portals behold the glorious declaration, "All men are created equal." The sun has never yet shone upon any of man's creations that can compare with this. The artist who can mold a statue worthy to crown magnificence like this, must be god-like in his conceptions, grand in his comprehensions, sublimely beautiful in his power of execution. The woman—the crowning glory of the model republic among the nations of the earth—what must she not be?

Constitutional Argument

Susan B. Anthony

Susan B. Anthony was born in Adams, Massachusetts, in 1820. Her father, a Quaker steeped in that religion's historic principle of sexual equality, held Susan in high regard. He educated her as he would a son, taught her responsibility and self-reliance, entrusted her with the management of his farm, and introduced her to the people and ideas of the liberal reform movements current in Rochester, New York, where they had come to live about 1839. In her teens, Susan taught at the Canajoharie Institute, but teaching was not a sufficient challenge for her. Later, having returned to Rochester, she became active in a reform movement to which several of her friends belonged—temperance. It was through the Rochester Daughters of Temperance that she met Amelia Bloomer of Seneca Falls who, in 1851, introduced her to Elizabeth Cady Stanton.

The women quickly became friends. Anthony was soon invited to Stanton's home to discuss ideas, and Anthony's views developed rapidly to coalesce with Stanton's. The two lectured, worked together, and founded The Revolution, *a radical magazine. In 1872, to bring to the test of the Supreme Court her conviction that as a citizen she was guaranteed by the Fourteenth Amendment the right to vote, Anthony "knowingly, wrongfully, and unlawfully" cast a vote in the election in Rochester. Arrested, convicted, and fined, she refused to pay, hoping for an appeal path, but the fine was not pursued. Nonetheless, she brought her principle into view and gained considerable sympathy. Later she was to lecture on coeducation (deemed radical at the time) and on all the various women's issues and to serve in the National American Woman's Suffrage Association and on the International Council of Women. In 1902, shortly after her retirement, she died.*

Like Stanton, Anthony was one of the strongest models in feminist history. The following selection is from a speech delivered during a tour of New York State prior to her trial in 1873. In it Anthony argued her thesis that both the original conception and the current law of the U.S. Constitution guaranteed her a citizen's right to vote.

Delivered in twenty-nine of the post-office districts of Monroe, and twenty-one of Ontario, in Miss Anthony's canvass of those counties prior to her trial in June, 1873.

Friends and Fellow-Citizens:—I stand before you under indictment for the alleged crime of having voted at the last presidential election, without having a lawful right to vote. It shall be my work this evening to prove to you that in thus doing, I not only committed no crime, but instead simply exercised my citizen's right, guaranteed to me and all United States citizens by the National Constitution beyond the power of any State to deny.

Our democratic-republican government is based on the idea of the natural right of every individual member thereof to a voice and a vote in making and executing the laws. We assert the province of government to be to secure the people in the enjoyment of their inalienable rights. We throw to the winds the old dogma that government can give rights. No one denies that before governments were organized each individual possessed the right to protect his own life, liberty and property. When 100 or 1,000,000 people enter into a free government, they do not barter away their natural rights; they simply pledge themselves to protect each other in the enjoyment of them through prescribed judicial and legislative tribunals. They agree to abandon the methods of brute force in the adjustment of their differences and adopt those of civilization. Nor can you find a word in any of the grand documents left us by the fathers which assumes for government the power to create or to confer rights. The Declaration of Independence, the United States Constitution, the constitutions of the several States and the organic laws of the Territories, all alike propose to *protect* the people in the exercise of their

Ida H. Harper, *Life and Work of Susan B. Anthony,* Indianapolis: Bowen-Merrill Co., 1898. Vol. II.

God-given rights. Not one of them pretends to bestow rights.

All men are created equal, and endowed by their Creator with certain inalienable rights. Among these are life, liberty and the pursuit of happiness. To secure these, governments are instituted among men, deriving their just powers from the consent of the governed.

Here is no shadow of government authority over rights, or exclusion of any class from their full and equal enjoyment. Here is pronounced the right of all men, and "consequently," as the Quaker preacher said, "of all women," to a voice in the government. And here, in this first paragraph of the Declaration, is the assertion of the natural right of all to the ballot; for how can "the consent of the governed" be given, if the right to vote be denied? Again:

Whenever any form of government becomes destructive of these ends, it is the right of the people to alter or abolish it, and to institute a new government, laying its foundations on such principles, and organizing its powers in such form, as to them shall seem most likely to effect their safety and happiness.

Surely the right of the whole people to vote is here clearly implied; for however destructive to their happiness this government might become, a disfranchised class could neither alter nor abolish it, nor institute a new one, except by the old brute force method of insurrection and rebellion. One-half of the people of this nation today are utterly powerless to blot from the statute books an unjust law, or to write there a new and a just one. The women, dissatisfied as they are with this form of government, that enforces taxation without representation—that compels them to obey laws to which they never have given their consent—that imprisons and hangs them without a trial by a jury of their peers—that robs them, in marriage, of the custody of their own persons, wages and children—are this half of the people who are left wholly at the mercy of the other half, in direct violation of the spirit and letter of the declarations of the framers of this government, every one of which was based on the immutable principle of equal rights to all. By these declarations, kings, popes, priests, aristocrats, all were alike dethroned and placed on a common level, politically, with the lowliest born subject or serf. By them, too, men, as such,

were deprived of their divine right to rule and placed on a political level with women. By the practice of these declarations all class and caste distinctions would be abolished, and slave, serf, plebeian, wife, woman, all alike rise from their subject position to the broader platform of equality.

The preamble of the Federal Constitution says:

We, the people of the United States, in order to form a more perfect union, establish justice, insure domestic tranquillity, provide for the common defence, promote the general welfare and secure the blessings of liberty to ourselves and our posterity, do ordain and establish this Constitution for the United States of America.

It was we, the people, not we, the white male citizens, nor we, the male citizens; but we, the whole people, who formed this Union. We formed it not to give the blessings of liberty but to secure them; not to the half of ourselves and the half of our posterity, but to the whole people—women as well as men. It is downright mockery to talk to women of their enjoyment of the blessings of liberty while they are denied the only means of securing them provided by this democratic-republican government—the ballot. . . .

But I submit that in view of the explicit assertions of the equal right of the whole people, both in the preamble and previous article of the constitution, this omission of the adjective "female" should not be construed into a denial; but instead should be considered as of no effect. Mark the direct prohibition, "No member of this State shall be disfranchised, unless by the law of the land, or the judgment of his peers." "The law of the land" is the United States Constitution; and there is no provision in that document which can be fairly construed into a permission to the States to deprive any class of citizens of their right to vote. Hence New York can get no power from that source to disfranchise one entire half of her members. Nor has "the judgment of their peers" been pronounced against women exercising their right to vote; no disfranchised person is allowed to be judge or juror—and none but disfranchised persons can be women's peers. Nor has the legislature passed laws excluding women as a class on account of idiocy or lunacy; nor have the courts convicted them of bribery, larceny or any infamous crime. Clearly, then, there is no constitutional ground for the exclusion of women from the ballot-box in the

State of New York. No barriers whatever stand today between women and the exercise of their right to vote save those of precedent and prejudice, which refuse to expunge the word "male" from the constitution. . . .

For any State to make sex a qualification, which must ever result in the disfranchisement of one entire half of the people, is to pass a bill of attainder, an ex post facto law, and is therefore a violation of the supreme law of the land. By it the blessings of liberty are forever withheld from women and their female posterity. For them, this government has no just powers derived from the consent of the governed. For them this government is not a democracy; it is not a republic. It is the most odious aristocracy ever established on the face of the globe. An oligarchy of wealth, where the rich govern the poor; an oligarchy of learning, where the educated govern the ignorant; or even an oligarchy of race, where the Saxon rules the African, might be endured; but this oligarchy of sex which makes father, brothers, husband, sons, the oligarchs over the mother and sisters, the wife and daughters of every household; which ordains all men sovereigns, all women subjects—carries discord and rebellion into every home of the nation. This most odious aristocracy exists, too, in the face of Section 4, Article IV, which says: "The United States shall guarantee to every State in the Union a republican form of government."

What, I ask you, is the distinctive difference between the inhabitants of a monarchical and those of a republican form of government, save that in the monarchical the people are subjects, helpless, powerless, bound to obey laws made by political superiors; while in the republican the people are citizens, individual sovereigns, all clothed with equal power to make and unmake both their laws and lawmakers? The moment you deprive a person of his right to a voice in the government, you degrade him from the status of a citizen of the republic to that of a subject. It matters very little to him whether his monarch be an individual tyrant, as is the Czar of Russia, or a 15,000,000 headed monster, as here in the United States; he is a powerless subject, serf or slave; not in any sense a free and independent citizen.

It is urged that the use of the masculine pronouns *he*, *his* and *him* in all the constitutions and laws, is proof that only men were meant to be included in their provisions. If you insist on this version of the letter of the law, we shall insist that you be consistent and accept the other horn of the dilemma, which would compel you to exempt women from taxation for the support of the government and from penalties for the violation of laws. There is no *she* or *her* or *hers* in the tax laws, and this is equally true of all the criminal laws.

Take for example the civil rights law which I am charged with having violated; not only are all the pronouns in it masculine, but everybody knows that it was intended expressly to hinder the rebel men from voting. It reads, "If any person shall knowingly vote without *his* having a lawful right." It was precisely so with all the papers served on me—the United States marshal's warrant, the bail-bond, the petition for habeas corpus, the bill of indictment—not one of them had a feminine pronoun; but to make them applicable to me, the clerk of the court prefixed an "s" to the "he" and made "her" out of "his" and "him;" and I insist if government officials may thus manipulate the pronouns to tax, fine, imprison and hang women, it is their duty to thus change them in order to protect us in our right to vote.

So long as any classes of men were denied this right, the government made a show of consistency by exempting them from taxation. When a property qualification of $250 was required of black men in New York, they were not compelled to pay taxes so long as they were content to report themselves worth less than that sum; but the moment the black man died and his property fell to his widow or daughter, the black woman's name was put on the assessor's list and she was compelled to pay taxes on this same property. This also is true of ministers in New York. So long as the minister lives, he is exempted from taxation on $1,500 of property, but the moment the breath leaves his body, his widow's name goes on the assessor's list and she has to pay taxes on the $1,500. So much for special legislation in favor of women! . . .

The only question left to be settled now is: Are women persons? I scarcely believe any of our opponents will have the hardihood to say they are not. Being persons, then, women are citizens, and no State has a right to make any new law, or to enforce any old law, which shall abridge their privileges or immunities. Hence, every discrimination against women in the constitutions and laws of the several States is today null and void, precisely as is every one against negroes. . . .

If once we establish the false principle that United States citizenship does not carry with it the right to vote in every State in this Union, there is no end to the petty tricks and cunning devices which will be attempted to exclude one and another class of citizens from the right of suffrage. It will not always be the men combining to disfranchise all women; native born men combining to abridge the rights of all naturalized citizens, as in Rhode Island. It will not always be the rich and educated who may combine to cut off the poor and ignorant; but we may live to see the hard-working, uncultivated day laborers, foreign and native born, learning the power of the ballot and their vast majority of numbers, combine and amend State constitutions so as to disfranchise the Vanderbilts, the Stewarts, the Conklings and the Fentons. It is a poor rule that won't work more ways than one. Establish this precedent, admit the State's right to deny suffrage, and there is no limit to the confusion, discord and disruption that may await us. There is and can be but one safe principle of government—equal rights to all. Discrimination against any class on account of color, race, nativity, sex, property, culture, can but embitter and disaffect that class, and thereby endanger the safety of the whole people. Clearly, then, the national government not only must define the rights of citizens, but must stretch out its powerful hand and protect them in every State in this Union.

If, however, you will insist that the Fifteenth Amendment's emphatic interdiction against robbing United States citizens of their suffrage "on account of race, color or previous condition of servitude," is a recognition of the right of either the United States or any State to deprive them of the ballot for any or all other reasons, I will prove to you that the class of citizens for whom I now plead are, by all the principles of our government and many of the laws of the States, included under the term "previous condition of servitude."

Consider first married women and their legal status. What is servitude? "The condition of a slave." What is a slave? "A person who is robbed of the proceeds of his labor; a person who is subject to the will of another." By the laws of Georgia, South Carolina and all the States of the South, the negro had no right to the custody and control of his person. He belonged to his master. If he were disobedient, the master had the right to use correction. If the negro did not like the correction and ran away, the master

had the right to use coercion to bring him back. By the laws of almost every State in this Union today, North as well as South, the married woman has no right to the custody and control of her person. The wife belongs to the husband; and if she refuse obedience he may use moderate correction, and if she do not like his moderate correction and leave his "bed and board," the husband may use moderate coercion to bring her back. The little word "moderate," you see, is the saving clause for the wife, and would doubtless be overstepped should her offended husband administer his correction with the "cat-o'-nine-tails," or accomplish his coercion with blood-hounds.

Again the slave had no right to the earnings of his hands, they belonged to his master; no right to the custody of his children, they belonged to his master; no right to sue or be sued, or to testify in the courts. If he committed a crime, it was the master who must sue or be sued. In many of the States there has been special legislation, giving married women the right to property inherited or received by bequest, or earned by the pursuit of any avocation outside the home; also giving them the right to sue and be sued in matters pertaining to such separate property; but not a single State of this Union has ever secured the wife in the enjoyment of her right to equal ownership of the joint earnings of the marriage copartnership. And since, in the nature of things, the vast majority of married women never earn a dollar by work outside their families, or inherit a dollar from their fathers, it follows that from the day of their marriage to the day of the death of their husbands not one of them ever has a dollar, except it shall please her husband to let her have it.

In some of the States, also, laws have been passed giving to the mother a joint right with the father in the guardianship of the children. Twenty-five years ago, when our woman's rights movement commenced, by the laws of all the States the father had the sole custody and control of the children. No matter if he were a brutal, drunken libertine, he had the legal right, without the mother's consent, to apprentice her sons to rumsellers or her daughters to brothel-keepers. He even could will away an unborn child from the mother. In most of the States this law still prevails, and the mothers are utterly powerless.

I doubt if there is, today, a State in this Union where a married woman can sue or be sued for slander of character, and until recently there was not one where she could sue or be sued for injury of person. However damaging to the wife's reputation any slander may be, she is wholly powerless to institute legal proceedings against her accuser unless her husband shall join with her; and how often have we heard of the husband conspiring with some outside barbarian to blast the good name of his wife? A married woman can not testify in courts in cases of joint interest with her husband. . . .

I submit the question, if the deprivation by law of the ownership of one's own person, wages, property, children, the denial of the right as an individual to sue and be sued and testify in the courts, is not a condition of servitude most bitter and absolute, even though under the sacred name of marriage? Does any lawyer doubt my statement of the legal status of married women? I will remind him of the fact that the common law of England prevails in every State but two in this Union, except where the legislature has enacted special laws annulling it. I am ashamed that not one of the States yet has blotted from its statute books the old law of marriage, which, summed up in the fewest words possible, is in effect ''husband and wife are one, and that one the husband.''

Thus may all married women and widows, by the laws of the several States, be technically included in the Fifteenth Amendment's specification of ''condition of servitude,'' present or previous. The facts also prove that, by all the great fundamental principles of our free government, not only married women but the entire womanhood of the nation are in a ''condition of servitude'' as surely as were our Revolutionary fathers when they rebelled against King George. Women are taxed without representation, governed without their consent, tried, convicted and punished without a jury of their peers. Is all this tyranny any less humiliating and degrading to women under our democratic-republican government today than it was to men under their aristocratic, monarchial government one hundred years ago? . . .

Is anything further needed to prove woman's condition of servitude sufficient to entitle her to the guarantees of the Fifteenth Amendment? Is there a man who will not agree with me that to talk of freedom without the ballot is mockery to the women of this republic, precisely as New England's orator, Wendell Phillips, at the close of the late war declared it to be to the newly emancipated black man? I admit that, prior to the rebellion, by common consent, the right to enslave, as well as to disfranchise both native and foreign born persons, was conceded to the States. But the one grand principle settled by the war and the reconstruction legislation, is the supremacy of the national government to protect the citizens of the United States in their right to freedom and the elective franchise, against any and every interference on the part of the several States; and again and again have the American people asserted the triumph of this principle by their overwhelming majorities for Lincoln and Grant. . . .

It is upon this just interpretation of the United States Constitution that our National Woman Suffrage Association, which celebrates the twenty-fifth anniversary of the woman's rights movement next May in New York City, has based all its arguments and action since the passage of these amendments. We no longer petition legislature or Congress to give us the right to vote, but appeal to women everywhere to exercise their too long neglected ''citizen's right.''

Marriage and Love

Emma Goldman

Anarchist, author, lecturer, and activist, Emma Goldman was born in Lithuania in 1869 and emigrated to the United States in 1886, settling in Rochester, New York. After working in a factory there for a short time, she moved to New York City and began her lifelong participation in radical political activity. Militantly involved in the labor movement, accused of complicity in the assassination of President McKinley, and active in the antidraft-antiwar movement of World War I, she was jailed twice, was deported to Russia in 1919, and spent the rest of her life traveling, writing, lecturing, and agitating on a variety of social issues. From 1906 to 1917, she copublished a radical American journal, Mother Earth, *and she wrote several books, among them* Anarchism and Other Essays *(1910), excerpted here, and* Living My Life *(1934), an autobiography. She died in Toronto, Canada, in 1940.*

As an anarchist, Goldman opposed any state interference in personal life. As a feminist, therefore, she opposed institutional marriage, the dependency it fostered, and laws relating to contraception and abortion. The following essay considers the relationship of love, sex, marriage, and parenthood and calls for the freeing of women from the "insurance pact" of state-sanctioned wedlock. Goldman's issues are classic in the women's movement, although she treats them in the context of her own particular political beliefs. She is an excellent example of the twentieth-century shift in feminist activism from a purely women's movement to more comprehensive organizations or models.

From ANARCHISM AND OTHER ESSAYS by Emma Goldman. Port Washington, NY: Kennikat Press, 1910, pp. 233–242. By permission of Gordon Press Publishers, New York, NY.

THE POPULAR NOTION ABOUT MARRIAGE AND LOVE is that they are synonymous, that they spring from the same motives, and cover the same human needs. Like most popular notions this also rests not on actual facts, but on superstition.

Marriage and love have nothing in common; they are as far apart as the poles; are, in fact, antagonistic to each other. No doubt some marriages have been the result of love. Not, however, because love could assert itself only in marriage; much rather is it because few people can completely outgrow a convention. There are today large numbers of men and women to whom marriage is naught but a farce, but who submit to it for the sake of public opinion. At any rate, while it is true that some marriages are based on love, and while it is equally true that in some cases love continues in married life, I maintain that it does so regardless of marriage, and not because of it.

On the other hand, it is utterly false that love results from marriage. On rare occasions one does hear of a miraculous case of a married couple falling in love after marriage, but on close examination it will be found that it is a mere adjustment to the inevitable. Certainly the growing-used to each other is far away from the spontaneity, the intensity, and beauty of love, without which the intimacy of marriage must prove degrading to both the woman and the man.

Marriage is primarily an economic arrangement, an insurance pact. It differs from the ordinary life insurance agreement only in that it is more binding, more exacting. Its returns are insignificantly small compared with the investments. In taking out an insurance policy one pays for it in dollars and cents, always at liberty to discontinue payments. If, however, woman's premium is a husband, she pays for it with her name, her privacy, her self-respect, her very life, "until death doth part." Moreover, the marriage insurance condemns her to life-long dependency, to parasitism, to complete uselessness, individual as well as social. Man, too, pays his toll, but as his sphere is wider, marriage does not limit him as much as woman. He feels his chains more in an economic sense.

Thus Dante's motto over Inferno applies with equal force to marriage. ''Ye who enter here leave all hope behind.''

That marriage is a failure none but the very stupid will deny. One has but to glance over the statistics of divorce to realize how bitter a failure marriage really is. Nor will the stereotyped Philistine argument that the laxity of divorce laws and the growing looseness of woman account for the fact that: first, every twelfth marriage ends in divorce; second, that since 1870 divorces have increased from 28 to 73 for every hundred thousand population; third, that adultery, since 1867, as ground for divorce, has increased 270.8 per cent.; fourth, that desertion increased 369.8 per cent.

Added to these startling figures is a vast amount of material, dramatic and literary, further elucidating this subject. Robert Herrick, in *Together*; Pinero, in *Mid-Channel*; Eugene Walter, in *Paid in Full,* and scores of other writers are discussing the barrenness, the monotony, the sordidness, the inadequacy of marriage as a factor for harmony and understanding.

The thoughtful social student will not content himself with the popular superficial excuse for this phenomenon. He will have to dig down deeper into the very life of the sexes to know why marriage proves so disastrous.

Edward Carpenter says that behind every marriage stands the life-long environment of the two sexes; an environment so different from each other that man and woman must remain strangers. Separated by an insurmountable wall of superstition, custom, and habit, marriage has not the potentiality of developing knowledge of, and respect for, each other, without which every union is doomed to failure.

Henrik Ibsen, the hater of all social shams, was probably the first to realize this great truth. Nora leaves her husband, not—as the stupid critic would have it—because she is tired of her responsibilities or feels the need of woman's rights, but because she has come to know that for eight years she had lived with a stranger and borne him children. Can there be anything more humiliating, more degrading than a lifelong proximity between two strangers? No need for the woman to know anything of the man, save his income. As to the knowledge of the woman—

what is there to know except that she has a pleasing appearance? We have not yet outgrown the theologic myth that woman has no soul, that she is a mere appendix to man, made out of his rib just for the convenience of the gentleman who was so strong that he was afraid of his own shadow.

Perchance the poor quality of the material whence woman comes is responsible for her inferiority. At any rate, woman has no soul—what is there to know about her? Besides, the less soul a woman has the greater her asset as a wife, the more readily will she absorb herself in her husband. It is this slavish acquiescence to man's superiority that has kept the marriage institution seemingly intact for so long a period. Now that woman is coming into her own, now that she is actually growing aware of herself as a being outside of the master's grace, the sacred institution of marriage is gradually being undermined, and no amount of sentimental lamentation can stay it.

From infancy, almost, the average girl is told that marriage is her ultimate goal; therefore her training and education must be directed towards that end. Like the mute beast fattened for slaughter, she is prepared for that. Yet, strange to say, she is allowed to know much less about her function as wife and mother than the ordinary artisan of his trade. It is indecent and filthy for a respectable girl to know anything of the marital relation. Oh, for the inconsistency of respectability, that needs the marriage vow to turn something which is filthy into the purest and most sacred arrangement that none dare question or criticize. Yet that is exactly the attitude of the average upholder of marriage. The prospective wife and mother is kept in complete ignorance of her only asset in the competitive field—sex. Thus she enters into life-long relations with a man only to find herself shocked, repelled, outraged beyond measure by the most natural and healthy instinct, sex. It is safe to say that a large percentage of the unhappiness, misery, distress, and physical suffering of matrimony is due to the criminal ignorance in sex matters that is being extolled as a great virtue. Nor is it at all an exaggeration when I say that more than one home has been broken up because of this deplorable fact.

If, however, woman is free and big enough to learn the mystery of sex without the sanction of State or Church, she will stand condemned as utterly unfit to become the wife of a ''good'' man, his goodness consisting of an empty brain and plenty of money. Can there be anything more outrageous than the idea that a healthy, grown woman, full of life and passion, must deny nature's demand, must subdue her most intense craving, undermine her health and break her spirit, must stunt her vision, abstain from the depth and glory of sex experience until a "good" man comes along to take her unto himself as a wife? That is precisely what marriage means. How can such an arrangement end except in failure? This is one, though not the least important, factor of marriage, which differentiates it from love.

Ours is a practical age. The time when Romeo and Juliet risked the wrath of their fathers for love, when Gretchen exposed herself to the gossip of her neighbors for love, is no more. If, on rare occasions, young people allow themselves the luxury of romance, they are taken in care by the elders, drilled and pounded until they become "sensible."

The moral lesson instilled in the girl is not whether the man has aroused her love, but rather is it, "How much?" The important and only God of practical American life: Can the man make a living? can he support a wife? That is the only thing that justifies marriage. Gradually this saturates every thought of the girl; her dreams are not of moonlight and kisses, of laughter and tears; she dreams of shopping tours and bargain counters. This soul poverty and sordidness are the elements inherent in the marriage institution. The State and the Church approve of no other ideal, simply because it is the one that necessitates the State and Church control of men and women.

Doubtless there are people who continue to consider love above dollars and cents. Particularly is this true of that class whom economic necessity has forced to become self-supporting. The tremendous change in woman's position, wrought by that mighty factor, is indeed phenomenal when we reflect that it is but a short time since she has entered the industrial arena. Six million women wage workers; six million women, who have the equal right with men to be exploited, to be robbed, to go on strike; aye, to starve even. Anything more, my lord? Yes, six million wage workers in every walk of life, from the highest brain work to the mines and railroad tracks; yes, even detectives and policemen. Surely the emancipation is complete.

Yet with all that, but a very small number of the vast army of women wage workers look upon work

as a permanent issue, in the same light as does man. No matter how decrepit the latter, he has been taught to be independent, self-supporting. Oh, I know that no one is really independent in our economic treadmill; still, the poorest specimen of a man hates to be a parasite; to be known as such, at any rate.

The woman considers her position as worker transitory, to be thrown aside for the first bidder. That is why it is infinitely harder to organize women than men. "Why should I join a union? I am going to get married, to have a home." Has she not been taught from infancy to look upon that as her ultimate calling? She learns soon enough that the home, though not so large a prison as the factory, has more solid doors and bars. It has a keeper so faithful that naught can escape him. The most tragic part, however, is that the home no longer frees her from wage slavery; it only increases her task.

According to the latest statistics submitted before a Committee "on labor and wages, and congestion of population," ten per cent. of the wage workers in New York City alone are married, yet they must continue to work at the most poorly paid labor in the world. Add to this horrible aspect the drudgery of housework, and what remains of the protection and glory of the home? As a matter of fact, even the middle-class girl in marriage can not speak of her home, since it is the man who creates her sphere. It is not important whether the husband is a brute or a darling. What I wish to prove is that marriage guarantees woman a home only by the grace of her husband. There she moves about in *his* home, year after year, until her aspect of life and human affairs becomes as flat, narrow, and drab as her surroundings. Small wonder if she becomes a nag, petty, quarrelsome, gossipy, unbearable, thus driving the man from the house. She could not go, if she wanted to; there is no place to go. Besides, a short period of married life, of complete surrender of all faculties, absolutely incapacitates the average woman for the outside world. She becomes reckless in appearance, clumsy in her movements, dependent in her decisions, cowardly in her judgment, a weight and a bore, which most men grow to hate and despise. Wonderfully inspiring atmosphere for the bearing of life, is it not?

But the child, how is it to be protected, if not for marriage? After all, is not that the most important consideration? The sham, the hypocrisy of it! Marriage protecting the child, yet thousands of children destitute and homeless. Marriage protecting the child, yet orphan asylums and reformatories overcrowded, the Society for the Prevention of Cruelty to Children keeping busy in rescuing the little victims from "loving" parents, to place them under more loving care, the Gerry Society. Oh, the mockery of it!

Marriage may have the power to bring the horse to water, but has it ever made him drink? The law will place the father under arrest, and put him in convict's clothes; but has that ever stilled the hunger of the child? If the parent has no work, or if he hides his identity, what does marriage do then? It invokes the law to bring the man to "justice," to put him safely behind closed doors; his labor, however, goes not to the child, but to the State. The child receives but a blighted memory of its father's stripes.

As to the protection of the woman,—therein lies the curse of marriage. Not that it really protects her, but the very idea is so revolting, such an outrage and insult on life, so degrading to human dignity, as to forever condemn this parasitic institution.

It is like that other paternal arrangement—capitalism. It robs man of his birthright, stunts his growth, poisons his body, keeps him in ignorance, in poverty, and dependence, and then institutes charities that thrive on the last vestige of man's self-respect.

The institution of marriage makes a parasite of woman, an absolute dependent. It incapacitates her for life's struggle, annihilates her social consciousness, paralyzes her imagination, and then imposes its gracious protection, which is in reality a snare, a travesty on human character.

If motherhood is the highest fulfillment of woman's nature, what other protection does it need, save love and freedom? Marriage but defiles, outrages, and corrupts her fulfillment. Does it not say to woman, Only when you follow me shall you bring forth life? Does it not condemn her to the block, does it not degrade and shame her if she refuses to buy her right to motherhood by selling herself? Does not marriage only sanction motherhood, even though conceived in hatred, in compulsion? Yet, if motherhood be of free choice, of love, of ecstasy, of defiant passion, does it not place a crown of thorns upon an innocent head and carve in letters of blood the hideous epithet, Bastard? Were marriage to contain all the virtues claimed for it, its crimes against motherhood would exclude it forever from the realm of love.

Love, the strongest and deepest element in all life, the harbinger of hope, of joy, of ecstasy; love, the defier of all laws, of all conventions; love, the freest, the most powerful moulder of human destiny; how can such an all-compelling force be synonymous with that poor little State and Church-begotten weed, marriage?

Free love? As if love is anything but free! Man has bought brains, but all the millions in the world have failed to buy love. Man has subdued bodies, but all the power on earth has been unable to subdue love. Man has conquered whole nations, but all his armies could not conquer love. Man has chained and fettered the spirit, but he has been utterly helpless before love. High on a throne, with all the splendor and pomp his gold can command, man is yet poor and desolate, if love passes him by. And if it stays, the poorest hovel is radiant with warmth, with life and color. Thus love has the magic power to make of a beggar a king. Yes, love is free; it can dwell in no other atmosphere. In freedom it gives itself unreservedly, abundantly, completely. All the laws on the statutes, all the courts in the universe, cannot tear it from the soil, once love has taken root. If, however, the soil is sterile, how can marriage make it bear fruit? It is like the last desperate struggle of fleeting life against death.

Woman and the New Race

Margaret Sanger

Nothing has contributed so much to women's growing liberation as the increasing control women can exercise over their reproductive capacities. Although some forms of birth control had been practiced in antiquity, it did not become a major force in the lives of ordinary women, especially poor women, until the twentieth century. In this country, into the 1930s, the so-called Comstock Laws of 1873 forbade the distribution of birth control information through the mails, and many states had laws prohibiting the use and sale of contraceptives. The efforts of the Birth Control League and particularly Margaret Sanger eventually resulted in the social acceptance of "planned parenthood."

Sanger was born in Corning, New York, in 1883. She studied nursing in White Plains and New York City. Early in her first marriage, she worked as an obstetrical nurse on New York's impoverished Lower East Side, where she saw the destructive burdens unchecked reproduction imposed on the poor and underprivileged. After studying contraception in Europe in 1913, she returned to New York, where she founded the magazine Woman Rebel *and, in 1916, opened her first clinic with her sister, Ethel Byrne, and a friend, Fania Mindell. All were arrested, and Byrne was subsequently jailed and mistreated. The episode brought this until-then rarely discussed issue into public view, and 1917 saw the founding of the National Birth Control League, with a growing membership.*

Although the birth control campaign did not have the support of many of the established women's rights organizations, who feared the controversy, various reform groups (including some trade unions) and women activists, many from the suffrage movement, pressed vehemently for birth control. Circumstances were in many ways analogous to today's abortion debate. Then, as now, opposition was highly charged and well organized in both religious and political circles; the poor were in even greater need of the reform than were the more affluent; and issues centered on matters of morality and "nature." Sanger ultimately won her fight. By 1952 in Bombay, she was well respected and was named first president of the International Planned Parenthood Federation. She died in Arizona in 1966. She had founded various journals and leagues and had written six books, including Woman and the New Race *(1920). In the section reprinted here, Sanger argues the claims of women's right to personal freedom and autonomy in procreative decisions, points out the implications for the world community of unchecked reproduction, and focuses on the centrality of women alone in carrying the burdens and responsibilities of having and rearing children. These remain contemporary themes.*

Woman's Error and Her Debt

The most far-reaching social development of modern times is the revolt of woman against sex servitude. The most important force in the remaking of the world is a free motherhood. Beside this force, the elaborate international programmes of modern statesmen are weak and superficial. Diplomats may formulate leagues of nations and nations may pledge their utmost strength to maintain them, statesmen may dream of reconstructing the world out of alliances, hegemonies and spheres of influence, but woman, continuing to produce explosive populations, will convert these pledges into the proverbial scraps of paper; or she may, by controlling birth, lift motherhood to the plane of a voluntary, intelligent function, and remake the world. When the world is thus remade, it will exceed the dream of statesman, reformer and revolutionist.

Only in recent years has woman's position as the gentler and weaker half of the human family

Margaret Sanger, *Woman and the New Race*. New York: Brentano's Publishers, 1920. By permission of Pergamon Press.

been emphatically and generally questioned. Men assumed that this was woman's place; woman herself accepted it. It seldom occurred to anyone to ask whether she would go on occupying it forever.

Upon the mere surface of woman's organized protests there were no indications that she was desirous of achieving a fundamental change in her position. She claimed the right of suffrage and legislative regulation of her working hours, and asked that her property rights be equal to those of the man. None of these demands, however, affected directly the most vital factors of her existence. Whether she won her point or failed to win it, she remained a dominated weakling in a society controlled by men.

Woman's acceptance of her inferior status was the more real because it was unconscious. She had chained herself to her place in society and the family through the maternal functions of her nature, and only chains thus strong could have bound her to her lot as a brood animal for the masculine civilizations of the world. In accepting her rôle as the "weaker and gentler half," she accepted that function. In turn, the acceptance of that function fixed the more firmly her rank as an inferior.

Caught in this "vicious circle," woman has, through her reproductive ability, founded and perpetuated the tyrannies of the Earth. Whether it was the tyranny of a monarchy, an oligarchy or a republic, the one indispensable factor of its existence was, as it is now, hordes of human beings—human beings so plentiful as to be cheap, and so cheap that ignorance was their natural lot. Upon the rock of an unenlightened, submissive maternity have these been founded; upon the product of such a maternity have they flourished.

No despot ever flung forth his legions to die in foreign conquest, no privilege-ruled nation ever erupted across its borders, to lock in death embrace with another, but behind them loomed the driving power of a population too large for its boundaries and its natural resources.

No period of low wages or of idleness with their want among the workers, no peonage or sweatshop, no child-labor factory, ever came into being, save from the same source. Nor have famine and plague been as much "acts of God" as acts of too prolific mothers. They, also, as all students know, have their basic causes in over-population.

The creators of over-population are the women, who, while wringing their hands over each fresh horror, submit anew to their task of producing the multitudes who will bring about the *next* tragedy of civilization.

While unknowingly laying the foundations of tyrannies and providing the human tinder for racial conflagrations, woman was also unknowingly creating slums, filling asylums with insane, and institutions with other defectives. She was replenishing the ranks of the prostitutes, furnishing grist for the criminal courts and inmates for prisons. Had she planned deliberately to achieve this tragic total of human waste and misery, she could hardly have done it more effectively.

Woman's passivity under the burden of her disastrous task was almost altogether that of ignorant resignation. She knew virtually nothing about her reproductive nature and less about the consequences of her excessive childbearing. It is true that, obeying the inner urge of their natures, *some* women revolted. They went even to the extreme of infanticide and abortion. Usually their revolts were not general enough. They fought as individuals, not as a mass. In the mass they sank back into blind and hopeless subjection. They went on breeding with staggering rapidity those numberless, undesired children who become the clogs and the destroyers of civilizations.

To-day, however, woman is rising in fundamental revolt. Even her efforts at mere reform are, as we shall see later, steps in that direction. Underneath each of them is the feminine urge to complete freedom. Millions of women are asserting their right to voluntary motherhood. They are determined to decide for themselves whether they shall become mothers, under what conditions and when. This is the fundamental revolt referred to. It is for woman the key to the temple of liberty.

Even as birth control is the means by which woman attains basic freedom, so it is the means by which she must and will uproot the evil she has wrought through her submission. As she has unconsciously and ignorantly brought about social disaster, so must and will she consciously and intelligently *undo* that disaster and create a new and a better order.

The task is hers. It cannot be avoided by excuses, nor can it be delegated. It is not enough for woman to point to the self-evident domination of man. Nor does it avail to plead the guilt of rulers and the exploiters of labor. It makes no difference that she does not formulate industrial systems nor that she is an instinctive believer in social justice. In her submission lies her error and her guilt. By her failure to withhold the multitudes of children who have made inevitable the most flagrant of our social evils, she incurred a debt to society. Regardless of her own wrongs, regardless of her lack of opportunity and regardless of all other considerations, *she* must pay that debt.

She must not think to pay this debt in any superficial way. She cannot pay it with palliatives—with child-labor laws, prohibition, regulation of prostitution and agitation against war. Political nostrums and social panaceas are but incidentally and superficially useful. They do not touch the source of the social disease.

War, famine, poverty and oppression of the workers will continue while woman makes life cheap. They will cease only when she limits her reproductivity and human life is no longer a thing to be wasted.

Two chief obstacles hinder the discharge of this tremendous obligation. The first and the lesser is the legal barrier. Dark-Age laws would still deny to her the knowledge of her reproductive nature. Such knowledge is indispensable to intelligent motherhood and she must achieve it, despite absurd statutes and equally absurd moral canons.

The second and more serious barrier is her own ignorance of the extent and effect of her submission. Until she knows the evil her subjection has wrought to herself, to her progeny and to the world at large, she cannot wipe out that evil.

To get rid of these obstacles is to invite attack from the forces of reaction which are so strongly entrenched in our present-day society. It means warfare in every phase of her life. Nevertheless, at whatever cost, she must emerge from her ignorance and assume her responsibility.

She can do this only when she has awakened to a knowledge of herself and of the consequences of her ignorance. The first step is birth control. Through birth control she will attain to voluntary motherhood. Having attained this, the basic freedom of her sex, she will cease to enslave herself and the mass of humanity. Then, through the understanding of the intuitive forward urge within her, she will not stop at patching up the world; she will remake it.

Birth Control—A Parents' Problem or Woman's?

The problem of birth control has arisen directly from the effort of the feminine spirit to free itself from bondage. Woman herself has wrought that bondage through her reproductive powers and while enslaving herself has enslaved the world. The physical suffering to be relieved is chiefly woman's. Hers, too, is the love life that dies first under the blight of too prolific breeding. Within her is wrapped up the future of the race—it is hers to make or mar. All of these considerations point unmistakably to one fact—it is woman's duty as well as her privilege to lay hold of the means of freedom. Whatever men may do, she cannot escape the responsibility. For ages she has been deprived of the opportunity to meet this obligation. She is now emerging from her helplessness. Even as no one can share the suffering of the overburdened mother, so no one can do this work for her. Others may help, but she and she alone can free herself.

The basic freedom of the world is woman's freedom. A free race cannot be born of slave mothers. A woman enchained cannot choose but give a measure of that bondage to her sons and daughters. No woman can call herself free who does not own and control her body. No woman can call herself free until she can choose consciously whether she will or will not be a mother.

It does not greatly alter the case that some women call themselves free because they earn their own livings, while others profess freedom because they defy the conventions of sex relationship. She who earns her own living gains a sort of freedom that is not to be undervalued, but in quality and in quantity it is of little account beside the untrammeled choice of mating or not mating, of being a mother or not being a mother. She gains food and clothing and shelter, at least, without submitting to the charity of her companion, but the earning of her own living does not give her the development of her inner sex urge, far deeper and more powerful in its outworkings than any of these externals. In order to have that development, she must still meet and solve the problem of motherhood.

With the so-called "free" woman, who chooses a mate in defiance of convention, freedom is largely a question of character and audacity. If she does attain to an unrestricted choice of a mate, she is still in a position to be enslaved through her reproductive powers. Indeed, the pressure of law and custom upon the woman not legally married is likely to make her more of a slave than the woman fortunate enough to marry the man of her choice.

Look at it from any standpoint you will, suggest any solution you will, conventional or unconventional, sanctioned by law or in defiance of law, woman is in the same position, fundamentally, until she is able to determine for herself whether she will be a mother and to fix the number of her offspring. This unavoidable situation is alone enough to make birth control, first of all, a woman's problem. On the very face of the matter, voluntary motherhood is chiefly the concern of the woman.

It is persistently urged, however, that since sex expression is the act of two, the responsibility of controlling the results should not be placed upon woman alone. Is it fair, it is asked, to give her, instead of the man, the task of protecting herself when she is, perhaps, less rugged in physique than her mate, and has, at all events, the normal, periodic inconveniences of her sex?

We must examine this phase of her problem in two lights—that of the ideal, and of the conditions working toward the ideal. In an ideal society, no doubt, birth control would become the concern of the man as well as the woman. The hard, inescapable fact which we encounter to-day is that man has not only refused any such responsibility, but has individually and collectively sought to prevent woman from obtaining knowledge by which she could assume this responsibility for herself. She is still in the position of a dependent to-day because her mate has refused to consider her as an individual apart from his needs. She is still bound because she has in the past left the solution of the problem to him. Having left it to him, she finds that instead of rights, she has only such privileges as she has gained by petitioning, coaxing and cozening. Having left it to him, she is exploited, driven and enslaved to his desires.

While it is true that he suffers many evils as the consequence of this situation, she suffers vastly more. While it is true that he should be awakened to the cause of these evils, we know that they come home to her with crushing force every day. It is she who has the long burden of carrying, bearing and rearing the unwanted children. It is she who must watch beside the beds of pain where lie the babies who suffer because they have come into overcrowded homes. It is her heart that the sight of the deformed, the subnormal, the undernourished, the overworked child smites first and oftenest and hardest. It is *her* love life that dies first in the fear of undesired pregnancy. It is her opportunity for self expression that perishes first and most hopelessly because of it.

Conditions, rather than theories, facts, rather than dreams, govern the problem. They place it squarely upon the shoulders of woman. She has learned that whatever the moral responsibility of the man in this direction may be, he does not discharge it. She has learned that, lovable and considerate as the individual husband may be, she has nothing to expect from men in the mass, when they make laws and decree customs. She knows that regardless of what ought to be, the brutal unavoidable fact is that she will never receive her freedom until she takes it for herself.

Having learned this much, she has yet something more to learn. Women are too much inclined to follow in the footsteps of men, to try to think as men think, to try to solve the general problems of life as men solve them. If after attaining their freedom, women accept conditions in the spheres of government, industry, art, morals and religion as they find them, they will be but taking a leaf out of man's book. The woman is not needed to do man's work. She is not needed to think man's thoughts. She need not fear that the masculine mind, almost universally dominant, will fail to take care of its own. Her mission is not to enhance the masculine spirit, but to express the feminine; hers is not to preserve a man-made world, but to create a human world by the infusion of the feminine element into all of its activities.

Woman must not accept; she must challenge. She must not be awed by that which has been built up around her; she must reverence that within her which struggles for expression. Her eyes must be less upon what is and more clearly upon what should be. She must listen only with a frankly questioning attitude to the dogmatized opinions of man-made society. When she chooses her new, free course of action, it must be in the light of her own opinion—of her own intuition. Only so can she give play to the feminine spirit. Only thus can she free her mate from the bondage which he wrought for himself when he wrought hers. Only thus can she restore to him that of which he robbed himself in restricting her. Only thus can she remake the world.

The world is, indeed, hers to remake, it is hers to build and to recreate. Even as she has permitted the suppression of her own feminine element and the consequent impoverishment of industry, art, letters, science, morals, religions and social intercourse, so it is hers to enrich all these.

Woman must have her freedom—the fundamental freedom of choosing whether or not she shall be a mother and how many children she will have. Regardless of what man's attitude may be, that problem is hers—and before it can be his, it is hers alone.

She goes through the vale of death alone, each time a babe is born. As it is the right neither of man nor the state to coerce her into this ordeal, so it is her right to decide whether she will endure it. That right to decide imposes upon her the duty of clearing the way to knowledge by which she may make and carry out the decision.

Birth control is woman's problem. The quicker she accepts it as hers and hers alone, the quicker will society respect motherhood. The quicker, too, will the world be made a fit place for her children to live.

The Class Roots of Feminism

Karen Sacks

Karen Brodkin Sacks directs the Women's Studies Program at UCLA and is a member of the Anthropology Department. She is the author of Sisters and Wives, Caring by the Hour *(1988) and coeditor of* My Troubles Are Going To Have Trouble With Me *(1984).*

Generally speaking, we tend to hear most about the political and psychosocial issues raised during the nineteenth century and carried into the twentieth. But one ought to also recall that economic issues were at the heart of both the abolition and the women's rights movements. Karen Sacks traces those issues in the following article. She describes separate trends in the women's movement: black women's drive for legal and economic equality, middle-class women's push for educational opportunity and full legal membership in their class, and working-class women's drive for economic progress. Sacks's discussion reveals some of the sources of tension among those groups today in their differing needs and priorities, but she demonstrates the fallacy of identifying the entire impetus of women's desires for change as a "white middle-class movement."

This paper originally appeared in *Monthly Review*, 27, No. 9 (February 1976). Copyright © 1976 by Monthly Review Inc. Reprinted by permission of Monthly Review Press and the author.

This article is a revised version of a paper read at the University of Connecticut Anthropology Department and at the 1973 meetings of the American Anthropological Association. The following people gave various kinds of assistance and very helpful criticism: Mary Clark, Soon Young Yoon, Bill Derman, Bobbye Ortiz, Rayna Reiter, Susan Reverby, the N.Y. Women's Anthropology Conference, and the librarians at the Archives of Labor History and Urban Affairs at Wayne State University. [K. Sacks' note]

DURING THE NINETEENTH CENTURY (SAY FROM 1820 to 1920) the women's movement in the United States was not a single movement, but rather three movements which were consciously movements for the rights of women. There was an industrial-working-class women's movement for economic improvement and equality which began with the earliest factories in the United States, the New England textile mills of the 1830s. Second, there was a black women's movement made up of working- and middle-class black women against racism and for both economic improvement and legal equality with whites. This also had its roots in the 1830s, in the black convention movements.* And finally, there was the white middle-class movement for legal equality which had its beginnings in women's attempts to become full legal members of their class, also in the 1830s.

While two well-known histories of the women's movement[1] show clearly that the white middle-class movement did not speak for all women, they do not examine the demands, priorities, and alliances of all three movements from the viewpoint of class roots and class interests. I would like to sketch such an analysis.

Class is the key, in the sense that the material conditions of black and working-class women, as well as the social ideology regarding them, have been very different from the material conditions of white middle-class women and their corresponding social ideologies. In both the colonial period and after independence, the only woman whose place was in the home was the woman of property. Neither slave women nor free propertyless women "belonged" there. Before the growth of industry, the United States had a domestic and agrarian economy in which men and women both could play a productive role "at home," so to speak—provided they owned or leased or otherwise had access to a home with farm (means of production), which most whites and some free blacks did. But those without their own household means of production, both men and women, had to work for someone else. Puritan religion and law in the North and slavery in the South were in agreement that those without property, free or slave, male or female, had an obligation to work for those with property. The terrible stigma attached to idleness by the Puritan religion largely served the interests of employers of labor. Efforts to stimulate a cloth-making industry, dating from the colonial period, emphasize the labor of "our own women and children who are now in a great measure idle."[2] Propertyless people who were not working for a master were a "public nuisance," the "public" in this phrase meaning, of course, people with property (especially manufacturing interests). Several New England states had laws compelling the binding out of children of the poor until the age of marriage. Adult poor, female as well as male, could be punished for "idleness." Thus for free as well as slave women, work outside the home was not looked down upon as unfeminine; rather, it was demanded as the only virtuous activity of propertyless women.

Propertied women, on the other hand, were virtuous and productive mistresses of households—until factories operated by propertyless women began to transform the domestic economy into an industrial one. Then they became ladies ("of leisure" being implicit in the word). The Southern transformation from domestic to industrial economy lay earlier, in the development of plantation slavery, with cotton grown partly by black women and a household run by the labor of black women. Thus, a double standard based on class came into being for women.

The self-consciously feminist movements and groups which developed—chiefly in the North during the nineteenth century—reflect the different circumstances of middle- and working-class women in the pre-Civil War years. Goals and tactics differed by class. Working-class women fought for more wages, equal wages with men, shorter hours, health, safety, and protective legislation. These were clearly class demands, and collective action was used to get them: strikes and unions mainly, but electoral pressure too (even without the vote). But working-class women also formed protective societies which got together for the purpose of self-"improvement" or of coping with various facets of a difficult life, rather than for the purpose of fighting to change social conditions.

The middle-class movement used analogous tactics, but in different proportions. Here, struggles of women to obtain and provide professional education and professional jobs for women, and to speak in public as full members of the anti-slavery movement, were, by and large, waged individually by women, rather than as part of a collective movement. It was the Abolition movement which gave birth to a self-conscious women's movement in the middle class, one which engaged in collective action, largely in the form of legislative petitions.

The pre-Civil War struggles were more social and thus collective among working-class women, and more self-help among middle-class women. This was due largely to the nature of the demands themselves and to the identity of the enemy, or obstacle. Education involved attacking no enemies. Likewise, both black and white women's improvement or protective societies were self-help ventures and did not identify enemies. The economic demands of women factory workers, on the other hand, were pursued solely by collective action directed against both mill owners and legislators.

Along with mill work, teaching school was a widespread women's occupation throughout this period. Not only were teachers and mill girls from the same background (farm families), but some women did both, alternating teaching and mill work. Though mill work paid badly, teaching paid worse. Schools were tiny affairs with few teachers, but factories often had several thousand workers. Despite the relatively better pay, it was the collective situation which allowed women to define "relatively better" as absolutely unsatisfactory by forming their own organization. Teachers, isolated and scattered, seem to have suffered in silence.

In the middle-class movement, collective action focused on those aspects of domestic law which prevented married women from having an independent economic status. Women's right to own inherited property was petitioned for and won without much opposition. But such a law had little relevance to working-class women. The situation in New York, the first state to pass such a law (1848), is illuminating. Its moving force was largely propertied males: "Fathers who had estates to bequeath to their daughters," and "husbands in extensive business operations [who could] see the advantage of allowing the wife the right to hold separate property."[3]

Middle-class women led two other important struggles in the legal realm of household affairs which did have relevance to working-class women: for the right of the woman to her own wages and to custody of children. By 1880 these were won in most states. New York was again the first state in which public sentiment for these changes was organized, beginning in 1854 via a petition campaign throughout the state. Middle-class feminists organized a delegation of working-class women to present this petition to the legislature and argue for it.[4] When it failed to move the legislature, Susan B. Anthony campaigned again throughout the state. Precisely what happened between 1855 and 1860 is not clear. But in 1860 the legislature passed a bill giving women property ownership, the right to collect their own wages, to sue in court, and to inherit the husband's property. It seems, though, that the majority of advances in civil law pertained to property law and thus to the middle and upper classes. While legislatures may have had to be persuaded, there were solid class interests for such reforms among propertied males and females.

As regards working-class women, the middle-class women who gathered at the Rochester women's convention in 1848 seem to have been both conscious of their own class and divided on class vs. sex interests. While all other resolutions passed clearly stated beliefs and principles, this one hedged: Resolved "*that those who* believe the laboring classes of women are oppressed, ought to do all in their power to raise their wages, beginning with their own household servants."[5]

Collective action by textile-mill women preceded that of middle-class women. Textile mills, centered in New England and staffed almost totally by women, were the nuclei of pre-Civil War U.S. industry. The first factory strike took place in 1824, just after the birth of the factories themselves, and involved both men and women. The 1830s saw a large number of strikes and the beginnings of many labor organizations, labor parties and papers, all short-lived. In this context, the record is full of male-female labor cooperation and independent women's actions and organizations. One of these labor parties, the Association of Working People of New Castle, Delaware, demanded the vote for women in 1831.[6]

Women were in the forefront and leadership of trade-union development in the 1840s and the focus was in the textile industry. The mills of the 1830s had been staffed by single women, largely daughters of farmers, who worked for a short time or a specific purpose. In the crisis of 1837 many farms were wiped out, and the workers in the mills during the forties and fifties were, by and large, landless native-born and Irish immigrants who could no longer quit if wages and hours were unsatisfactory. Out of this milieu came a whole host of factory-worker papers and organizations. The New England Female Labor Reform Association (FLRA) under its president, Sarah Bagley, a Lowell factory worker, became the main group for factory women. In addition to organizing in New England, this group stimulated and kept in contact with branches of women textile-worker groups in New York and western Pennsylvania. Though officially an affiliate of the New England Workingmen's Association (NEWA), in reality it was the center of it and provided much of its leadership, particularly in the fight for the ten-hour day. The FLRA argued for a ten-hour law in the Massachusetts legislature and, despite the fact that women could not vote, ran a successful campaign to defeat the re-election of Lowell's state representative, a mill owners' man who opposed the ten-hour bill.

Though women workers were centered in New England, the biggest women's struggle took place in the western Pennsylvania textile mills. Here the workers struck in 1845 for a ten-hour day. After a month, some workers began returning to the mills. But women strikers, aided by a "men's auxiliary," stormed the gates of one factory and threw out the strikebreakers. Despite this militancy, the strikers were told that they would get a ten-hour day only when New England workers did. They then appealed to the NEWA and the FLRA for help. Apparently only the women in New England were ready to call a general strike. In the face of the NEWA's hopelessness, they gave it up. Again in 1848 the Pennsylvania workers went out on strike, and again it looked like defeat. This time, the women, armed with axes, stormed the factory, took on a company of police, captured the strikebreakers, and then closed it down again. The leaders were arrested, but the strike continued. Though they finally won a ten-hour day only by accepting a wage cut, it is not clear whether they soon increased their wages to what they had been for twelve hours' work.[7] In any case, these early textile battles show the militance and leadership women gave to the early labor movement.

Though largely separate, the working-class and middle-class movements had a common ground in the anti-slavery movement. Abolition joined white well-to-do and professional people with free black men and women, and in the 1840s with a growing number of white workers, particularly from the New England textile mills. In Abolition one finds the seeds of class and race conflicts which pitted the women's movements against each other. In the 1830s the antislavery movement had split over women's participation, with particularly strong objections coming from the clergy. Middle-class women saw Abolition and women's rights as part of a single movement for extending democracy. In 1832 Lowell factory women formed a Female Anti-Slavery Society, and by 1845 they were fund-raising and circulating anti-slavery petitions, despite hostility on the part of the mill owners.[8] But their reasons for favoring Abolition differed from those of middle-class women. The mill women argued that a labor force in slavery degraded free labor as well as slave labor, and that all labor had a two-faced enemy: "the lord of the loom and the lord of the lash."

Abolition, whether spoken by middle- or working-class people, faced much more organized opposition than women's rights. Mobs in the North were "organized and led by prominent, respected members of the community." And, according to R. B. Nye, the major root of pro-slavery force was economic: fear of displeasing the Southern planter on whom much of New York commerce and rising New England textiles depended.[9] Indeed, H. Josephson has shown how assiduously the New England magnates of the 1840s and 1850s courted the planters and reviled the Abolitionists.[10]

Yet the anti-slavery movement contained much of the racism and class antagonisms which led to three separate and generally antagonistic women's movements after the Civil War. Many white middle-class Abolitionists were violently anti-labor, and most crafts excluded free black workers. While many Abolitionist groups spoke out against job discrimination against black workers in the North, some of their members were at the same time also practicing this same discrimination. In 1852 a number of black men applied for jobs at the businesses of members of the American and Foreign Anti-Slavery Society. Some were rejected outright; others got only menial jobs.[11] The widespread exclusion of black men and women from craft and factory jobs is well known. What has not received adequate treatment is the extent to which employers and workers were responsible for it.

These class and race antagonisms among the Abolitionists (important divisions to be inherited by the women's movement) were deepened by pro-slavery forces. Before the 1830s its defenders rationalized slavery as a necessary evil. To counter anti-slavery forces they developed a whole pseudo-science of white supremacy. Together with nativist corollaries, this became a cornerstone of post-Civil War bourgeois ideology. The war itself gave birth to accelerated industrialization and thus to the development of an industrial working class as well as a more powerful bourgeoisie. The latter took governmental power from the Southern agrarian bourgeoisie. Once in power, the Northern industrialists re-allied themselves with the Southern planters to defeat Reconstruction and entrench their common position against the black and white working class. Economic, political, and legal discrimination against black people was made a virtue through the newly developed national policy of white supremacy; at the same time an anti-foreignism was directed against white working-class immigrants in the North. Racism and nativism were important to the new capitalists because neither black nor white workers passively accepted the conditions of industrial wage slavery. Against this general background, we may better understand the divisions in the developing women's movement.

From the end of the Civil War until 1920, when it collapsed, the white middle-class women's movement defined itself as middle class by excluding black and working-class women. As such women moved from the liberalism of the Reconstruction period to the racist and anti-working-class mainstream of the "progressive era," they took for granted this status quo—a status quo with a sharp division between middle and working classes and with hierarchical divisions within the working class based on race, nationality, and sex. Black men and women were to be confined to agrarian and domestic work; native-born and immigrant white men and women would make up the industrial working class, with skilled crafts largely excluding all save native-born white men.

The Civil War itself led to middle-class women's widespread involvement in a variety of service and professional positions—from nursing and teaching to office work. By and large, the new war opportunities were important for middle-class kinds of jobs, mainly for whites, but some black women also entered, particularly in teaching, through the Freedmen's Bureau. Opportunities were there, but they were not equal. For example, the federal government was delighted to have women replace the male office workers, not least because they worked for half pay. Black women received even less for their work—if they received anything at all. Harriet Tubman had to fight almost until her death before the government would pay her for her very considerable services, both military and civilian, during and after the war. Even then she received a pittance, and that as a pension for her husband. Tubman was nationally famous. It is thus probable that the thousands of less famous black women were treated much worse.

Postwar years, then, saw the growth in numbers of middle-class women as independent earners in largely professional or so-called semi-professional occupations. Materially, they were members of a growing middle class. As such (and like the women factory workers of prewar years) they began developing a stronger class identity. They began to see themselves less as a socially excluded and oppressed segment of humanity and more as second-class members of the white middle class. Black middle-class women were largely prevented from claiming *class* rights by the practice of segregation and white supremacy. As black women they struggled against racial oppression, including the ideological stereotyping of black women as immoral.

The Civil War affected working-class women in some basically different ways than it affected middle-class women, even though there were some superficial similarities. While groups of middle-class women might get together to sew uniforms for the Union army as their patriotic duty, for working-class women taking in sewing of uniforms was wage work for survival in a period of inflation. However, they were often not paid for this work. Apparently the government felt that since middle-class women did not need to be paid, neither did working-class women. The war and postwar years saw working-class women developing their own unions and protective associations, at least in part to combat situations like the above. By and large, these were localized efforts. To some extent, though, they were integrated into the National Labor Union (NLU).

Thus, in 1863, women collar workers in Troy, New York, formed a local union and struck successfully for higher wages. Kate Mullaney, their president, became assistant secretary of the NLU. But this women's local disbanded with the demise of the NLU.

To some extent, women's locals were joined with men's local or national organizations in the same industry. The men and women weavers in Fall River exemplify this pattern. In the face of a pay cut in 1875, the men's union voted to acquiesce; the women, knowing the results of the men's meeting, held their own and voted to strike three mills. The men then followed their lead and they won.[12]

Women workers did form one national organization. The Daughters of St. Crispin, begun by women shoe-stitchers in Lynn, Massachusetts, was an organization parallel to the men's Knights of St. Crispin. New England shoe workers, particularly women, had organized before the Civil War. In 1860 they had gone on strike throughout New England in the most extensive pre-Civil War strike.[13] The Daughters of St. Crispin, formed in 1869, had 24 chapters, most of which were in New England—the center of the shoe industry—and in six other states as well. They demanded equal pay for equal work. Though they affiliated with the NLU, they managed to outlast it, staying in existence through much of the 1873 depression, and continuing in New England until 1876. For those days it was a long-lived organization.

The Knights of Labor, the first enduring national labor organization in the United States, saw women and black people as important parts of the working class, and on this basis supported equality within the organization and demanded it of employers. At its first national convention in 1878, they voted for equal pay for equal work, and began from the outset to include women workers in separate locals as well as in male-female locals. The first all-women local, of Philadelphia shoe workers, joined in 1878. By 1886, at the peak of the Knights of Labor, there were about 194 women's locals and about 50,000 women members (8–9 percent of the total). In Massachusetts the proportion was higher: 1 in 7 members were women.[14] The Knights followed the same direction with regard to black workers, organizing them in the South and the North into both black-white and separate black locals. In 1886 there were about 60,000 black Knights out of about 700,000; in 1887 some 90,000 out of about half a million.[15] The Knights did seem to try in practice as well as rhetoric to fight for equal rights for all workers.

By contrast, the newly formed American Federation of Labor, an association of craft unions, supported few working-class women's issues, even though its membership included male-female as well as all-female locals, especially in the United Garment Workers (UGW). But if the UGW is any example of female participation, the AFL did not take the needs of its women members seriously.[16] The AFL did have some unofficial women organizers in the early years. Hannah Morgan organized some 23 women's locals in a variety of jobs; she also built the Illinois Women's Alliance, which led mass campaigns for protective legislation for women and children (and she organized secondarily for suffrage). Also under the AFL, the collar and shirt workers of Troy pulled together again, struck and won in 1891. The leader of the Working Women's Society of New York City unofficially organized women into the AFL, while the society organized support for strikes and for factory legislation.[17]

Meanwhile, the middle-class movement had become mainly a suffrage movement. But it too was divided. The National Women's Suffrage Association (NWSA) Stanton-Anthony wing, though biased in favor of the middle class by its suffrage focus, was willing to join with labor. Anthony and other suffrage leaders organized women's protective societies, supported and helped organize women's unions. For a time Susan Anthony was a member of the Knights of Labor (which favored suffrage). The rival group of suffragists, the American Women's Suffrage Association (AWSA), was anti-labor, narrowly suffragist, and drew its support from professional and leisured middle-class women, mainly through women's clubs.

Until 1890, then, there was a strong organization in the Knights of Labor fighting for equal rights for all labor, as well as a middle-class organization willing to join its main fight for suffrage with the economic demands of working women. Class determined the priorities, but on these issues there was no necessary conflict between them.

But the balance of forces favoring such inter-class cooperation changed in the 1890s. With the demise of the Knights, the AFL faced no competition and freely moved to organize skilled crafts only, largely the province of white, native-born men. Not only by focusing on skilled labor but also by deliberately excluding black and female skilled and semi-skilled workers, the AFL spread racism and sexism during its long-term domination of trade unionism. (It seems to me that modern-day notions about working-class racism and sexism are based heavily on the AFL's practice.) Women continued to form unions, some independent, which had a hard time, and some affiliated with the AFL, which seem to have faced almost equal difficulties.[18] At the same time that the unity of labor was weakened by this organizational practice, the ruling class stepped up its propaganda to cultivate and fix black-white, native-immigrant divisions and conflicts. The suffrage movement, represented by the National American Women's Suffrage Association (NAWSA, the merger of the two suffrage groups), fell solidly into line with them, abandoning even the divided support they had given working-class women in the 1860s.

In 1892, when the Homestead Steel workers struck and were embroiled in a nearly full-scale war to save job and union from Carnegie, the Pinkertons, and federal troops, Lucy Stone wanted to know why the workers didn't start their own businesses if they didn't like their jobs.[19] And Susan Anthony went to labor asking for suffrage support, but refused to do anything about working women's demands until the vote was won. Likewise, she raised her influential voice to argue that NAWSA should do nothing to fight Jim Crow laws barring black people (including black women) from decent railroad seats.

Their arguments for suffrage, as Kraditor has clearly shown,[20] came explicitly to be arguments for enfranchising white, American-born, and educated women as allies with their male counterparts against black and immigrant workers.

This government is menaced with great danger. . . . That danger lies in the votes possessed by the males in the slums of the cities, and the ignorant foreign vote which was sought to be brought up by each party, to make political success. . . . In the mining districts, the danger has already reached this point—miners are supplied with arms, watching with greedy eyes for the moment when they can get in their deadly work of despoiling the wealth of the country. . . . There is but one way to avert the danger—cut off the vote of the slums and give to woman, who is bound to suffer all, and more than man can, of the evils his legislation has brought upon the nation, the power of protecting herself that man has secured for himself—the ballot.[21]

NAWSA closed ranks against working-class women, not so much by the demand for suffrage itself as by their arguments claiming it should be granted and by their hostility to more pressing needs of women workers and black women of both classes. Thus the 1893 convention of NAWSA passed the following resolution directed against black people in the same way that Catt's speech attacked immigrants and the working class:

Resolved, *that without expressing any opinion on the proper qualifications for voting, we call attention to the significant facts that in every State there are more women who can read and write than all negro* [sic] *voters; more American women who can read and write than all foreign voters; so that the enfranchisement of such women would settle the vexed question of rule by illiteracy, whether of home-grown or foreign-born production.*[22]

They lashed out at "foreigners" not only for being "ignorant" in general, but for being a major force in opposing women's rights. Kraditor summed up suffrage explanations of why voting in wards with large immigrant populations went against suffrage: "Foreign-born men had been brought up in a culture in which women were inferior [here the suffragists forgot earlier arguments and proudly pointed to the respected position of women in their own society]; . . . the ignorance of the foreign born disqualified them from voting wisely; . . . the new voters generally used alcoholic beverages and feared that woman suffrage would bring prohibition; . . . foreign-born workers in cities voted as dictated by saloonkeepers, rich employers, or party machines."[23] Ironically, when New York finally passed its suffrage referendum in 1917, it was working-class and immigrant New York City which carried it over the opposition from non-worker, native-born upstate! By this time, though, some members of NAWSA had begun to overcome their aversion to the working class, and to campaign in working-class districts. As late as 1916, however, NAWSA had made little effort to communicate across class lines.

While the overt anti-working-class, racist, and nativist arguments remained until the end, there were growing numbers of NAWSA members after the turn of the century who believed it important to speak to the working class. Thus Florence Kelley worked hard to fight the exploitation of workers in the sweatshops and to obtain protective legislation for women workers. She even criticized the anti-foreign mouthings of NAWSA. Yet she too resented being forced to campaign among workers: "[It was] an ignominious way to treat us, to send us to the Chinamen [sic] in San Francisco, to the enfranchised Indians of other western states, to the negroes [sic], Italians, Hungarians, Poles, Bohemians and innumerable Slavic immigrants in Pennsylvania and other mining States to obtain our rights of suffrage."[24]

Jessie Ashley, treasurer of NAWSA and a socialist, also criticized the association for its anti-worker attitudes, in particular for not addressing its campaigns to the real needs of working-class women—economic needs. But she did accept some very middle-class stereotypes of working-class women. Remarking on the contrast made in another article between the "handsome ladies" at a suffrage parade and the working girls getting onto the subway, Ashley wrote,

For it is those "handsome ladies," and they alone, who have begun to see that women must stand and think and work together, and they, alas, are not the ones whose need to do so is the greatest. . . . For the most part the handsome ladies are well satisfied with their personal lot, but they want the vote as a matter of justice, while the fluttering, jammed-in subway girls are terribly blind to the whole question of class oppression and of sex oppression. Only the women of the working class are really oppressed, but it is not only the working-class women to whom injustice is done. Women of the leisure class need freedom, too.[25]

Considering that this was written less than two years after the massive women's garment strike in New York (where Ashley lived), her talk of working-class women being blind to class oppression flies in the face of reality, as does her notion that only the "handsome ladies" know they must work together. Essentially, Ashley is reflecting the stereotype of the ignorant and docile working girl.

Along with the general racist stereotyping of black people, which NAWSA accepted and propagated, there existed the stigmatizing of black women as "loose" and "immoral." Sometimes this stereotyping was done "sympathetically":

The negro [sic] *women of the South are subject to temptations, of which their white sisters of the North have no appreciation, and which come to them from the*

days of their race enslavement. They are still the victims of the white man under a system tacitly recognized, which deprives them of the sympathy and help of the Southern white women, and to meet such temptations the negro [sic] women can only offer the resistance of a low moral standard, an inheritance from the system of slavery, made still lower from a life-long residence in a one-roomed cabin.[26]

But it propagates the same false stereotype of the immoral black woman, adding another kind of fuel to racist propaganda.

Black women, led by black middle-class and professional women, had long before formed their own clubs and expressed a desire to work with the white clubs, which in general the latter refused to do. To combat this racism they formed the National Association of Colored Women. The conditions facing black women differed in many ways from those facing white middle-class women. Black women's clubs organized around providing a particular social service, since public facilities were even less available in black communities than in white working-class communities. They also exposed and organized against lynching and terror campaigns directed against black men and women. At least one club maintained a settlement house and served the poor and working-class neighborhoods through militant action as well as services. Moreover, the membership, if not the leadership, of black women's clubs differed from their white counterparts. While the white clubs were middle class and professional, black club members were often workers, tenant farmers, or poor women.[27]

Even though the suffrage movement somewhat weakened its anti-worker attitude and to some extent its anti-immigrant posture, it never publicly mitigated its racism. This was largely due to the strategy of allying with Southern white middle-class women, who wanted the vote at least as much to maintain white supremacy as to have the vote. As a result of this "Southern strategy," black women were all but kept out of the association.[28] While support for racial equality was ruled out of order as an extraneous issue, the numerous white-supremacy speeches never met any such objection, or any other kind of public objection, for that matter.

What little amelioration there was of NAWSA's anti-worker and anti-immigrant stance came about largely because of the growth of city-wide women's strikes, notably in the garment and textile industries, in 1909 in New York, 1910 in Chicago, and 1912 in Lawrence. Prior to that time a number of white middle-class women—radicals, reformers, and socialists like Jessie Ashley, Ella Reeve Bloor, etc.—had urged concentration on working women's needs. But they were mainly rebuffed by NAWSA.

It was largely through the National Women's Trade Union League (NWTUL), formed in 1903, that the suffrage movement saw possible allies in working-class women. Made up of women trade unionists, but run mainly by middle-class reformers, many of whom were active suffragists, the NWTUL tried to serve two functions. First, in the face of AFL indifference to women workers, it organized women to improve their working conditions through trade unionism. Specifically, it organized women into AFL locals and supported AFL strikes. Its second role was to make trade unionism "respectable" through publicity and by winning middle-class support for strikes. It did succeed in organizing women into the AFL and in making *certain kinds* of unions "respectable." But it did not reform the AFL, which sold out the Chicago clothing strike in 1911. And the following year, despite anger over Chicago, the NWTUL actually helped the AFL break a strike, in Lawrence, Massachusetts.

In this case, the AFL had organized only among skilled (white, male, native-born) workers. But the vast majority were unskilled female, as well as male and immigrant, workers. The IWW [International Workers of the World] represented these workers; and when they walked out, it was the IWW that led this Lawrence strike. Together with the AFL, the Boston TUL set up a relief council which aided only those who pledged to go back to work.[29]

So while they did unionize women and ameliorate some of the anti-worker attitudes in the middle class, their role within the working-class movement was to be in the midst of things, to see that events did not get out of control, and to make sure women workers stayed respectable in bourgeois eyes.

Many women in the Boston TUL were disgusted with the role of their own organization in Lawrence. "Are we, the NWTUL, to ally ourselves inflexibly with the 'stand-patters' of the Labor Movement or are we to hold ourselves ready to aid the 'insurgents,' those who are freely fighting the fight of the exploited, the oppressed, and the weak among the workers?"[30] While this may have been a widespread feeling among NWTUL members, publicly they stood pat with the stand-patters of the AFL. Their official stance appeared in *Life and Labor,* the NWTUL paper:[31] the AFL "refused to take any action during the first fortnight of the strike while it was being led by enemies of organized labor [the IWW], but now that it shows every symptom of collapse they do not propose to allow the misled workers to suffer or lose any opportunity to bring them into recognized trade organizations."[32]

Working-class women, the IWW, the radicals reacted to this suffragist and middle-class bias. One working woman wrote to Leonora O'Reilly of her experience at a New York suffrage conference:

I feel as if I have butted in where I was not wanted. Miss Hay gave me a badge and was very nice to me but you know they had a school teacher represent the Industrial workers if you ever herd her it was like trying to fill a barrell with water that had no bottom not a word of labor spoken at this convention so far . . . after the hole thing was over some people came to me and said I had a right to speak for labor but they kept away until it was over. . . . I am not goying to wait for sunday meeting I am goying home satturday.[33]

In the New York shirtwaist strike, two upper-class women rented the Hippodrome for a strike-support rally, attended by approximately 8,000 people. Though much has been made of rich women's generosity, Theresa Malkiel, a striker, wrote another side to it in her diary:

The most of our girls had to walk both ways in order to save their car fare. Many came without dinner, but the collection baskets had more pennies than anything else in them—it was our girls themselves who helped make it up, and yet there were so many rich women present. And I'm sure the speakers made it plain to them how badly the money was needed, then how comes it that out of $300 collected there should be $70 in pennies?[34]

The IWW saw the vote as irrelevant and the suffrage movement as making working women "the tail of a suffrage kite in the hands of women of the very class driving the girls to lives of misery and shame."[35] Yet Elizabeth Gurley Flynn, then an IWW organizer, speaks approvingly of socialists in 1904 organizing working-class women to demand the vote so they can vote on labor issues.[36] Emma Goldman saw suffrage as a "modern fetish" of women who swore

loyalty to every institution which oppresses them. "Else how is one to account for the tremendous, truly gigantic effort set in motion by those valiant fighters for a wretched little bill which will benefit a handful of propertied ladies, with absolutely no provision for the vast mass of working women?"[37]

Through the efforts of middle-class NWTUL women, and to some degree those of the militant suffragists' Women's Party, Wage Earners' Suffrage Leagues did come into being and working-class women did march in suffrage demonstrations. But even where working-class women participated in suffrage demands, they did so separately from the middle-class organizations, in a labor-based organization. Suffrage in this context never had a high priority for working-class women as a whole.

The years 1909–1912 marked a huge upsurge in working-class women's activity. The 1909 New York dressmakers' strike, or the "Uprising of 20,000," was the largest women's strike in history. It was followed by many large and small garment and textile strikes and the formation of enduring unions, steps toward the elimination of sweatshops, cutting hours, and increasing pay for women workers. By and large, women won these victories without the ballot.

As a rule, next to nothing is said of black working-class women in these struggles. Though black women were largely excluded from industry before the First World War, and hence from unions, there were black women working in the packinghouses of Chicago, in tobacco warehouses in the South, and as pressers in the garment industry in New York. In 1902 two packinghouse women organized a women's local which included black women. But more significant is a white garment worker and organizer's account of the beginning of the 1909 New York strike. She writes of her anxiety as to whether the women of the shop would walk out at the appointed time. They did, fifteen minutes early, when the fifty-three black women of the pressing department dropped their work and led the whole shop out.[38] Even where black women were employed during and after the First World War, they were largely in the worst jobs, with little or no chance for advancement, and often paid one half or one third what white women received. For example, pressers in the garment industry had the most physically difficult job in that industry. This was the job given to black women.[39]

Whom the women's movements perceived as the enemy illuminates the primacy of class lines over sex.

In the working-class movement it was clearly the employer. The suffragists saw their enemies mainly as the liquor interests and, to some extent, big-business interests. Only the Women's Party actually saw the President and much of Congress as real enemies of women. For this breach of class loyalty they got the same treatment as working-class women strikers: jail, police brutality, etc.

The working-class women's movement, rather than dying in 1920, continued in the drives of the 1920s and 1930s to organize in Southern textile and tobacco shops. Here, black and white working-class women not only struggled to overcome racism, but had to take on the AFL[40] directly. Neither before nor since 1920 have women won equal pay for equal work, one of the two long-standing working-class women's demands. However, to the extent that women have won union representation, male-female pay scales have made moves in that direction. The other demand, for unionization itself, also continues. As middle-class women's jobs have become collectivized (teaching, white-collar, health, social work, clerical), middle-class women have also moved into union situations, which at least provide a material basis for middle-class women to join working-class women rather than the ruling class.

Notes

*I could find very little information on the class composition of black women's organizations, or on the organizations and struggles of working-class black women. Thus there is a data bias of which the reader should be aware. Though there were national black conventions from 1830, the earliest specific mention of women's rights, support for the Seneca Falls Declaration, is in 1848 (R. E. Paulson, *Women's Suffrage and Prohibition* [Glenview: Scott Foresman, 1973], p. 34). The 1848 convention in Cleveland resolved for equality for women with men and for full citizenship, including the vote for black men and women (H. H. Bell, ed., *Minutes and Proceedings of the National Negro Conventions 1830–1864* [New York: Arno Press and the *New York Times*, 1969]).

[1]A. Kraditor, *The Ideas of the Woman Suffrage Movement, 1890–1920* (New York: Columbia University Press, 1965); E. Flexner, *Century of Struggle* (New York: Atheneum, 1968).

[2]E. Abbott, *Women in Industry* (New York: Appleton and Company, 1913), pp. 21–22.

[3]E. C. Stanton, S. B. Anthony, and M. J. Gage, *History of Women's Suffrage*, vol. 1 (Rochester: Chas. Mann), p. 16.

[4]A. Henry, *The Trade Union Woman* (New York: Appleton and Company, 1915), p. 254.

[5]Stanton, Anthony, and Gage, p. 809. Italics added.

[6]On early struggles by women the major source is J. B. Andrews and W. D. P. Bliss, *History of Women in Trade Unions* (vol. 10 of *Report on Conditions of Women and Child Wage Earners in the U.S.*, in 19 vols., U.S. Senate Doc. 645, 61st Cong., 2d Sess.); see also Flexner; Abbott; P. Foner, *History of the Labor Movement in the United States*, vol. 1 (New York: International, 1947); Henry, 1915; and A. Henry, *Women and the Labor Movement* (New York: Doran, 1923). Flexner claims men feared women's competition but gives no specifics. For this early period, only the printers and cigarmakers manifested the conservative stance, though it was later a strong position among conservative skilled trades unions. The instances of early cooperation between men's and women's unions are more impressive: in 1834 the Lady Shoe Binders of Lynn struck for higher wages and were supported by the men's cordwainers union in the form of money, a pledge not to work for any manufacturer who refused the women's demands, and an attempt to organize a boycott of such (Foner, pp. 108–111). In 1833 the Baltimore seamstresses and tailoresses were supported by the men journeymen tailors (Henry 1923, p. 41). In 1835 the Philadelphia Journeymen Cigarmakers opposed the low wages paid to women and recommended a joint strike. In this city, too, the men cordwainers and Ladies Shoe Binders Society waged a joint strike. In 1831 the New England Farmers, Mechanics and Other Workingmen tried, though without success, to spread unionism from skilled workers to factory women (Foner, pp. 105, 108–111).

[7]For differing accounts see Andrews and Bliss, p. 65; Foner, p. 212; Flexner, p. 56.

[8]Foner, p. 267.

[9]R. B. Nye, *Fettered Freedom: Civil Liberties and the Slave Controversy, 1830–1860* (East Lansing: Michigan State University Press, 1963), p. 194.

[10]H. Josephson, *Golden Threads: New England's Mill Girls and Magnates* (New York: Duell, Sloan and Pearce, 1949), pp. 300–303.

[11]C. H. Wesley, *Negro Labor in the United States, 1850–1925* (New York: Russell and Russell, 1967), pp. 78–79.

[12]In addition to Andrews and Bliss, pt. 2, see Abbott, p. 131; and Henry, 1923, p. 48.

[13]Foner, p. 241; Henry, 1923, p. 47.

[14]Foner, vol. 2, p. 61; Flexner, p. 194.

[15]R. Logan, *The Betrayal of the Negro* (New York: Macmillan, 1970), pp. 150–151.

[16]M. H. Willett, *The Employment of Women in the Clothing Trade* (New York: AMS Press, 1968).

[17]Foner, vol. 2, pp. 189–193.

[18] *Ibid.*, pp. 364–366; Foner, vol. 3, pp. 724–727.

[19] Kraditor, p. 159.

[20] *Ibid.*, chap. 6.

[21] Carrie Chapman Catt, in *The Woman's Journal,* 1894; quoted in Flexner, p. 125.

[22] *Ibid.*, p. 131.

[23] *Ibid.*, p. 128.

[24] *Ibid.*, p. 139.

[25] *The Woman's Journal,* 1911; quoted in Flexner, p. 157.

[26] *Ibid.*, p. 187.

[27] G. Lerner, *Black Women in White America* (New York: Pantheon, 1972), pp. 198, 437.

[28] Kraditor, pp. 170, 212–214; Logan, pp. 239–241.

[29] Foner, vol. 4, pp. 338–339.

[30] Letter from Mrs. Clark to Mrs. Robins; quoted in G. Boone, *The Women's Trade Union Leagues in Great Britain and the United States of America* (New York: AMS Press, 1968), p. 106.

[31] *Life and Labor,* vol. 2, pp. 73, 77, 196.

[32] *Ibid.*, p. 77.

[33] Quoted in Kraditor, p. 160.

[34] Quoted in R. Jacoby, "Feminism and Class Consciousness in the British and American Women's Trade Union Leagues, 1890–1925." Unpublished ms. (History Dept., University of Michigan, 1973), p. 21.

[35] Quoted in Foner, vol. 4, p. 168.

[36] E. G. Flynn, *I Speak My Own Piece* (New York: Masses and Mainstream, 1955), p. 46.

[37] E. Goldman, *Anarchism and Other Essays* (New York: Mother Earth Publishing Association, 1917), p. 212.

[38] A. Hourwich, *I Am a Woman Worker: A Scrapbook of Autobiographies* (New York: Affiliated Schools for Workers, Inc., 1936), p. 110.

[39] On pressers' work: J. Laslett, *Labor and the Left* (New York: Basic Books, 1970), p. 103. On discrimination against black women: Henry 1923, pp. 203–206.

[40] Supported again by a dying NWTUL. See *Life and Labor Bulletin* (July 1928 and January 1931).

Sexual Politics

Kate Millett

Kate Millett, feminist, author, and sculptor, was born in 1934 in St. Paul, Minnesota. She studied English at the University of Minnesota and at Oxford University and finished a doctorate at Columbia University with a dissertation that became the book Sexual Politics. *Millett has taught English and women's studies, worked as a sculptor, and codirected a film,* Three Lives. *An activist early in her career, she served in CORE (Congress of Racial Equality) in the 1950s, supported student strikes while teaching at Barnard, and served in NOW as chair of the Education Committee. During the early days of the Iranian revolution, she traveled to Iran to study the effects of the revolution on women there and to talk to feminist leaders. In addition to* Sexual Politics, *her works include* The Prostitution Papers *(1973),* Flying *(1974),* Sita *(1976), and* Going to Iran *(1982).*

The publication of Sexual Politics *in 1970 was an important development in the current movement. It received wide press attention, focused public attention on women's liberation, and was one of the first books to articulate a broad theoretical base for the ideas of the growing movement. Millett widens the term* politics *(which traditionally means simply "that which pertains to the* polis, *or city") to refer to "power-structured relationships . . . whereby one group of persons is controlled by another" then shows how this concept captures the essence of male-female arrangements. Using literary and historical models to support her thesis, she argues that social and sexual relations between women and men are not-so-nice power arrangements, grounded in misogyny, expressing themselves as a life view (patriarchy), and resulting in the worldwide oppression of women on both an institutional and a personal level.*

Theory of Sexual Politics

. . . In introducing the term "sexual politics," one must first answer the inevitable question "Can the relationship between the sexes be viewed in a political light at all?" The answer depends on how one defines politics.[1] This essay does not define the political as that relatively narrow and exclusive world of meetings, chairmen, and parties. The term "politics" shall refer to power-structured relationships, arrangements whereby one group of persons is controlled by another. By way of parenthesis one might add that although an ideal politics might simply be conceived of as the arrangement of human life on agreeable and rational principles from whence the entire notion of power *over* others should be banished, one must confess that this is not what constitutes the political as we know it, and it is to this that we must address ourselves.

The following sketch, which might be described as "notes toward a theory of patriarchy," will attempt to prove that sex is a status category with political implications. Something of a pioneering effort, it must perforce be both tentative and imperfect. Because the intention is to provide an overall description, statements must be generalized, exceptions neglected, and subheadings overlapping and, to some degree, arbitrary as well.

The word "politics" is enlisted here when speaking of the sexes primarily because such a word is eminently useful in outlining the real nature of their relative status, historically and at the present. It is opportune, perhaps today even mandatory, that we develop a more relevant psychology and philosophy of power relationships beyond the simple conceptual framework provided by our traditional formal politics. Indeed, it may be imperative that we give some attention to defining a theory of politics which treats of power relationships on grounds less conventional than those to which we are accustomed.[2] I have therefore found it pertinent to define them on grounds of personal contact and interaction between members of well-defined and coherent groups: races, castes, classes, and sexes. For it is precisely because certain groups have no representation in a number of recognized political structures that their position tends to be so stable, their oppression so continuous.

In America, recent events have forced us to acknowledge at last that the relationship between the races is indeed a political one which involves the general control of one collectivity, defined by birth, over another collectivity, also defined by birth. Groups who rule by birthright are fast disappearing, yet there remains one ancient and universal scheme for the domination of one birth group by another—the scheme that prevails in the area of sex. The study of racism has convinced us that a truly political state of affairs operates between the races to perpetuate a series of oppressive circumstances. The subordinated group has inadequate redress through existing political institutions, and is deterred thereby from organizing into conventional political struggle and opposition.

Quite in the same manner, a disinterested examination of our system of sexual relationship must point out that the situation between the sexes now, and throughout history, is a case of that phenomenon Max Weber defined as *herrschaft*, a relationship of dominance and subordination.[3] What goes largely unexamined, often even unacknowledged (yet is institutionalized nonetheless) in our social order, is the birthright priority whereby males rule females. Through this system a most ingenious form of "interior colonization" has been achieved. It is one which tends moreover to be sturdier than any form of segregation, and more rigorous than class stratification, more uniform, certainly more enduring. However muted its present appearance may be, sexual dominion obtains nevertheless as perhaps the most pervasive ideology of our culture and provides its most fundamental concept of power.

This is so because our society, like all other historical civilizations, is a patriarchy.[4] The fact is evident at once if one recalls that the military, industry, technology, universities, science, political office, and finance—in short, every avenue of power within the society, including the coercive force of the police, is entirely in male hands. As the essence of politics is power, such realization cannot fail to carry impact.

What lingers of supernatural authority, the Deity, "His" ministry, together with the ethics and values, the philosophy and art of our culture—its very civilization—as T. S. Eliot once observed, is of male manufacture.

If one takes patriarchal government to be the institution whereby that half of the populace which is female is controlled by that half which is male, the principles of patriarchy appear to be two fold: male shall dominate female, elder male shall dominate younger. However, just as with any human institution, there is frequently a distance between the real and the ideal; contradictions and exceptions do exist within the system. While patriarchy as an institution is a social constant so deeply entrenched as to run through all other political, social, or economic forms, whether of caste or class, feudality or bureaucracy, just as it pervades all major religions, it also exhibits great variety in history and locale. In democracies,[5] for example, females have often held no office or do so (as now) in such miniscule numbers as to be below even token representation. Aristocracy, on the other hand, with its emphasis upon the magic and dynastic properties of blood, may at times permit women to hold power. The principle of rule by elder males is violated even more frequently. Bearing in mind the variation and degree in patriarchy—as say between Saudi Arabia and Sweden, Indonesia and Red China—we also recognize our own form in the U.S. and Europe to be much altered and attenuated by the reforms described in the next chapter.

I Ideological

Hannah Arendt[6] has observed that government is upheld by power supported either through consent or imposed through violence. Conditioning to an ideology amounts to the former. Sexual politics obtains consent through the "socialization" of both sexes to basic patriarchal polities with regard to temperament, role, and status. As to status, a pervasive assent to the prejudice of male superiority guarantees superior status in the male, inferior in the female. The first item, temperament, involves the formation of human personality along stereotyped lines of sex category ("masculine" and "feminine"), based on the needs and values of the dominant group and dictated by what its members cherish in themselves and find convenient in subordinates: aggression, intelligence, force, and efficacy in the male; passivity, ignorance, docility, "virtue," and in-effectuality in the female. This is complemented by a second factor, sex role, which decrees a consonant and highly elaborate code of conduct, gesture and attitude for each sex. In terms of activity, sex role assigns domestic service and attendance upon infants to the female, the rest of human achievement, interest, and ambition to the male. The limited role allotted the female tends to arrest her at the level of biological experience. Therefore, nearly all that can be described as distinctly human rather than animal activity (in their own way animals also give birth and care for their young) is largely reserved for the male. Of course, status again follows from such an assignment. Were one to analyze the three categories one might designate status as the political component, role as the sociological, and temperament as the psychological—yet their interdependence is unquestionable and they form a chain. Those awarded higher status tend to adopt roles of mastery, largely because they are first encouraged to develop temperaments of dominance. That this is true of caste and class as well is self-evident.

IV Class

It is in the area of class that the castelike status of the female within patriarchy is most liable to confusion, for sexual status often operates in a superficially confusing way within the variable of class. In a society where status is dependent upon the economic, social, and educational circumstances of class, it is possible for certain females to appear to stand higher than some males. Yet not when one looks more closely at the subject. This is perhaps easier to see by means of analogy: a black doctor or lawyer has higher social status than a poor white sharecropper. But race, itself a caste system which subsumes class, persuades the latter citizen that he belongs to a higher order of life, just as it oppresses the black professional in spirit, whatever his material success may be. In much the same manner, a truck driver or butcher has always his "manhood" to fall back upon. Should this final vanity be offended, he may contemplate more violent methods. The literature of the past thirty years provides a staggering number of incidents in which the caste of virility triumphs over the social status of wealthy or even educated women. In literary contexts one has to deal here with wish-fulfillment. Incidents from life (bullying, obscene, or hostile remarks) are probably another sort of psychological gesture of ascendancy. Both convey more hope than reality, for class divisions are generally quite impervious to the hostility of individuals. And yet while the existence of class division is not seriously threatened by such expressions of enmity, the existence of sexual hierarchy has been re-affirmed and mobilized to "punish" the female quite effectively.

The function of class or ethnic mores in patriarchy is largely a matter of how overtly displayed or how loudly enunciated the general ethic of masculine supremacy allows itself to become. Here one is confronted by what appears to be a paradox: while in the lower social strata, the male is more likely to claim authority on the strength of his sex rank alone, he is actually obliged more often to share power with the women of his class who are economically productive; whereas in the middle and upper classes, there is less tendency to assert a blunt patriarchal dominance, as men who enjoy such status have more power in any case.[7] . . .

One of the chief effects of class within patriarchy is to set one woman against another, in the past creating a lively antagonism between whore and matron, and in the present between career woman and housewife. One envies the other her "security" and prestige, while the envied yearns beyond the confines of respectability for what she takes to be the other's freedom, adventure, and contact with the great world. Through the multiple advantages of the double standard, the male participates in both worlds, empowered by his superior social and economic resources to play the estranged women against each other as rivals. One might also recognize subsidiary status categories among women: not only is virtue class, but beauty and age as well.

Perhaps, in the final analysis, it is possible to argue that women tend to transcend the usual class stratifications in patriarchy, for whatever the class of her birth and education, the female has fewer permanent class association than does the male. Economic dependency renders her affiliations with any class a tangential, vicarious, and temporary matter. Aristotle observed that the only slave to whom a commoner might lay claim was his woman, and the service of an unpaid domestic still provides working-class males with a "cushion" against the buffets of the class system which incidentally provides them with some of the psychic luxuries of the leisure class.

Thrown upon their own resources, few women rise above working class in personal prestige and economic power, and women as a group do not enjoy many of the interests and benefits any class may offer its male members. Women have therefore less of an investment in the class system. But it is important to understand that as with any group whose existence is parasitic to its rulers, women are a dependency class who live on surplus. And their marginal life frequently renders them conservative, for like all persons in their situation (slaves are a classic example here) they identify their own survival with the prosperity of those who feed them. The hope of seeking liberating radical solutions of their own seems too remote for the majority to dare contemplate and remains so until consciousness on the subject is raised.

As race is emerging as one of the final variables in sexual politics, it is pertinent, especially in a discussion of modern literature, to devote a few words to it as well. Traditionally, the white male has been accustomed to concede the female of his own race, in her capacity as "his woman" a higher status than that ascribed to the black male.[8] Yet as white racist ideology is exposed and begins to erode, racism's older protective attitudes toward (white) women also begin to give way. And the priorities of maintaining male supremacy might outweigh even those of white supremacy; sexism may be more endemic in our own society than racism. For example, one notes in authors whom we would now term overtly racist, such as D. H. Lawrence—whose contempt for what he so often designates as inferior breeds is unabashed—instances where the lower-caste male is brought on to master or humiliate the white man's own insubordinate mate. Needless to say, the female of the nonwhite races does not figure in such tales save as an exemplum of "true" womanhood's servility, worthy of imitation by other less carefully instructed females. Contemporary white sociology often operates under a similar patriarchal bias when its rhetoric inclines toward the assertion that the "matriarchal" (e.g. matrifocal) aspect of black society and the "castration" of the black male are the most deplorable symptoms of black oppression in white racist society, with the implication that racial inequity is capable of solution by a restoration of masculine authority. Whatever the facts of the matter may be, it can also be suggested that analysis of this kind presupposes patriarchal values without questioning them, and tends to obscure both the true character of and the responsibility for racist injustice toward black humanity of both sexes. . . .

VI Force

We are not accustomed to associate patriarchy with force. So perfect is its system of socialization, so complete the general assent to its values, so long and so universally has it prevailed in human society, that it scarcely seems to require violent implementation. Customarily, we view its brutalities in the past as exotic or "primitive" custom. Those of the present are regarded as the product of individual deviance, confined to pathological or exceptional behavior, and without general import. And yet, just as under other total ideologies (racism and colonialism are somewhat analogous in this respect) control in patriarchal society would be imperfect, even inoperable, unless it had the rule of force to rely upon, both in emergencies and as an ever-present instrument of intimidation.

Historically, most patriarchies have institutionalized force through their legal systems. For example, strict patriarchies such as that of Islam, have implemented the prohibition against illegitimacy or sexual autonomy with a death sentence. In Afghanistan and Saudi Arabia the adulteress is still stoned to death with a mullah presiding at the execution. Execution by stoning was once common practice through the Near East. It is still condoned in Sicily. Needless to say there was and is no penalty imposed upon the male corespondent. Save in recent times or exceptional cases, adultery was not generally recognized in males except as an offense one male might commit against another's property interest. In Tokugawa Japan, for example, an elaborate set of legal distinctions were made according to class. A samurai was entitled, and in the face of public knowledge, even obliged, to execute an adulterous wife, whereas a chōnin (common citizen) or peasant might respond as he pleased. In cases of cross-class adultery, the lower-class male convicted of sexual intimacy with his employer's wife would, because he had violated taboos of class and property, be beheaded together with her. Upper-strata males had, of course, the same license to seduce lower-class women as we are familiar with in Western societies.

Indirectly, one form of "death penalty" still obtains even in America today. Patriarchal legal systems in depriving women of control over their own bodies drive them to illegal abortions; it is estimated that between two and five thousand women die each year from this cause.[9]

Excepting a social license to physical abuse among certain class and ethnic groups, force is diffuse and generalized in most contemporary patriarchies. Significantly, force itself is restricted to the male who alone is psychologically and technically equipped to perpetrate physical violence.[10] Where differences in physical strength have become immaterial through the use of arms, the female is rendered innocuous by her socialization. Before assault she is almost universally defenseless both by her physical and emotional training. Needless to say, this has the most far-reaching effects on the social and psychological behavior of both sexes.

Patriarchal force also relies on a form of violence particularly sexual in character and realized most completely in the act of rape. The figures of rapes reported represent only a fraction of those which occur,[11] as the "shame" of the event is sufficient to deter women from the notion of civil prosecution under the public circumstances of a trial. Traditionally rape has been viewed as an offense one male commits upon another—a matter of abusing "his woman." Vendetta, such as occurs in the American South, is carried out for masculine satisfaction, the exhilarations of race hatred, and the interests of property and vanity (honor). In rape, the emotions of aggression, hatred, contempt, and the desire to break or violate personality, take a form consummately appropriate to sexual politics. In the passages analyzed at the outset of this study, such emotions were present at a barely sublimated level and were a key factor in explaining the attitude behind the author's use of language and tone.[12]

Patriarchal societies typically link feelings of cruelty with sexuality, the latter often equated both with evil and with power. This is apparent both in the sexual fantasy reported by psychoanalysis and that reported by pornography. The rule here associates sadism with the male ("the masculine role") and victimization with the female ("the feminine role").[13] Emotional response to violence against women in patriarchy is often curiously ambivalent; references to wife-beating, for example, invariably produce laughter and some embarrassment. Exemplary atrocity, such as the mass murders committed by Richard Speck, greeted at one level with a certain scandalized, possibly hypocritical indignation, is capable of eliciting a mass response of titillation at another level. At such times one even hears from men occasional expressions of envy or amusement. In view of the sadistic character of such public fantasy as caters to male audiences in pornography or semi-pornographic media, one might expect that a certain element of identification is by no means absent from the general response. Probably a similar collective *frisson* sweeps through racist society when its more "logical" members have perpetrated a lynching. Unconsciously, both crimes may serve the larger group as a ritual act, cathartic in effect.

Hostility is expressed in a number of ways. One is laughter. Misogynist literature, the primary vehicle of masculine hostility, is both an hortatory and comic genre. Of all artistic forms in patriarchy it is the most frankly propagandistic. Its aim is to reinforce both sexual factions in their status. Ancient, Medieval, and Renaissance literature in the West has each had a large element of misogyny.[14] Nor is the East without a strong tradition here, notably in the Confucian strain which held sway in Japan as well as China. The Western tradition was indeed moderated somewhat by the introduction of courtly love. But the old diatribes and attacks were coterminous with the new idealization of woman. In the case of Petrarch, Boccaccio, and some others, one can find both attitudes fully expressed, presumably as evidence of different moods, a courtly pose adopted for the ephemeral needs of the vernacular, a grave animosity for sober and eternal Latin.[15] As courtly love was transformed to romantic love, literary misogyny grew somewhat out of fashion. In some places in the eighteenth century it declined into ridicule and exhortative satire. In the nineteenth century its more acrimonious forms almost disappeared in English. Its resurrection in twentieth-century attitudes and literature is the result of a resentment over patriarchal reform, aided by the growing permissiveness in expression which has taken place at an increasing rate in the last fifty years.

Since the abatement of censorship, masculine hostility (psychological or physical) in specifically *sexual* contexts has become far more apparent. Yet as masculine hostility has been fairly continuous, one deals here probably less with a matter of increase than with a new frankness in expressing hostility in specifically sexual contexts. It is a matter of release and freedom to express what was once forbidden expression outside of pornography or other "underground" productions, such as those of De Sade. As one recalls both the euphemism and the idealism of descriptions of coitus in the Romantic poets (Keats's *Eve of St. Agnes*), or the Victorian novelists (Hardy, for example) and contrasts it with Miller or William Burroughs, one has an idea of how contemporary literature has absorbed not only the truthful explicitness of pornography, but its anti-social character as well. Since this tendency to hurt or insult has been given free expression, it has become far easier to assess sexual antagonism in the male.

The history of patriarchy presents a variety of cruelties and barbarities: the suttee execution in India, the crippling deformity of footbinding in China, the lifelong ignominy of the veil in Islam, or the widespread persecution of sequestration, the gynacium, and purdah. Phenomenon such as clitoroidectomy, clitoral incision, the sale and enslavement of women under one guise or another, involuntary and child marriages, concubinage and prostitution, still take place—the first in Africa, the latter in the Near and Far East, the last generally. The rationale which accompanies that imposition of male authority euphemistically referred to as "the battle of the sexes" bears a certain resemblance to the formulas of nations at war, where any heinousness is justified on the grounds that the enemy is either an inferior species or really not human at all. The patriarchal mentality has concocted a whole series of rationales about women which accomplish this purpose tolerably well. And these traditional beliefs still invade our consciousness and affect our thinking to an extent few of us would be willing to admit.

Notes

[1]The American Heritage Dictionary's fourth definition is fairly approximate: "methods or tactics involved in managing a state or government." *American Heritage Dictionary* (New York: American Heritage and Houghton Mifflin, 1969). One might expand this to a set of strategems designed to maintain a system. If one understands patriarchy to be an institution perpetuated by such techniques of control, one has a working definition of how politics is conceived in this essay.

[2]I am indebted here to Ronald V. Samson's *The Psychology of Power* (New York: Random House, 1968) for his intelligent investigation of the connection between formal power structures and the family and for his analysis of how power corrupts basic human relationships.

[3]"Domination in the quite general sense of power, i.e. the possibility of imposing one's will upon the behavior of other persons, can emerge in the most diverse forms." In this central passage of *Wirtschaft und Gesellschaft* Weber is particularly interested in two such forms: control through social authority ("patriarchal, magisterial, or princely") and control through economic force. In patriarchy as in other forms of domination "that control over economic goods, i.e. economic power, is a frequent, often purposively willed, consequence of domination as well as one of its most important instruments." Quoted from Max Rheinstein's and Edward Shil's translation of portions of *Wirtschaft und Gesellschaft* entitled *Max Weber on Law in Economy and Society* (New York: Simon and Schuster, 1967), pp. 323–24.

[4]No matriarchal societies are known to exist at present. Matrilineality, which may be, as some anthropologists have held, a residue or a transitional stage of matriarchy, does not constitute an exception to patriarchal rule, it simply channels the power held by males through female descent—, e.g. the Avunculate.

[5]Radical democracy would, of course, preclude patriarchy. One might find evidence of a general satisfaction with a less than perfect democracy in the fact that women have so rarely held power within modern "democracies."

[6]Hannah Arendt, "Speculations on Violence," *The New York Review of Books*, Vol. XII No. 4, February 27, 1969, p. 24.

[7]Goode, *op. cit.*, p. 74.

[8]It would appear that the "pure flower of white womanhood" has at least at times been something of a disappointment to her lord as a fellow-racist. The historic connection of the Abolitionist and the Woman's Movement is some evidence of this, as well as the incident of white female and black male marriages as compared with those of white male and black female. Figures on miscegenation are very difficult to obtain: Goode (*op. cit.*, p. 37) estimates the proportion of white women marrying black men to be between 3 to 10 times the proportion of white men marrying black women. Robert K. Merton "Intermarriage and the Social Structure" *Psychiatry,* Vol. 4, August 1941, p. 374, states that "most intercaste sex relations—not marriages—are between white men and Negro women." It is hardly necessary to emphasize that the more extensive sexual contacts between white males and black females have not only been extramarital, but (on the part of the white male) crassly exploitative. Under slavery it was simply a case of rape.

[9]Since abortion is extralegal, figures are difficult to obtain. This figure is based on the estimates of abortionists and referral services. Suicides in pregnancy are not officially reported either.

[10]Vivid exceptions come to mind in the wars of liberation conducted by Vietnam, China, etc. But through most of history, women have been unarmed and forbidden to exhibit any defense of their own.

[11]They are still high. The number of rapes reported in the city of New York in 1967 was 2432. Figure supplied by Police Department.

[12]It is interesting that male victims of rape at the hands of other males often feel twice imposed upon, as they have not only been subjected to forcible and painful intercourse, but further abused in being reduced to the status of a female. Much of this is evident in Genet and in the contempt homosexual society reserves for its "passive" or "female" partners.

[13]Masculine masochism is regarded as exceptional and often explained as latently homosexual, or a matter of the subject playing "the female role"—e.g., victim.

[14]The literature of misogyny is so vast that no summary of sensible proportions could do it justice. The best reference on the subject is Katherine M. Rogers, *The Troublesome Helpmate, A History of Misogyny in Literature* (Seattle, University of Washington Press, 1966).

[15]As well as the exquisite sonnets of love, Petrarch composed satires on women as the "De Remediis utriusque Fortunae" and *Epistolae Seniles*. Boccaccio too could balance the chivalry of romances (Filostrato, Ameto, and Fiammetta) with the vituperance of Corbaccio, a splenetic attack on women more than medieval in violence.

NOW Bill of Rights

National Organization for Women

The National Organization for Women (NOW) was formed in 1966 by a group of feminist legislators, authors, professionals, labor workers, and academics. Set off by a series of events—the publication of Friedan's Feminine Mystique, *the addition of "sex" to the Civil Rights Act of 1964, the decade's climate of social criticism and change—the formation of the organization was one of the major events responsible for increasing feminist activism of the second wave. Notice that among its goals were passage of ERA and access to day care and to legal abortion, issues that at the time were controversial and yet galvanizing to many women, even those who might not have formerly been politically active.*

Adopted by NOW at their First National Conference, Washington, DC (© NOW), 1967.

Bill of Rights

National Organization for Women (NOW)

I   Equal Rights Constitutional Amendment

II   Enforce Law Banning Sex Discrimination in Employment

III Maternity Leave Rights in Employment and in Social Security Benefits

IV   Tax Deduction for Home and Child Care Expenses for Working Parents

V   Child Care Centers

VI   Equal and Unsegregated Education

VII Equal Job Training Opportunities and Allowances for Women in Poverty

VIII The Right of Women to Control Their Reproductive Lives

WE DEMAND
Exception
   I That the United States Congress immediately pass the Equal Rights Amendment to the Constitution to provide that "Equality of rights under the law shall not be denied or abridged by the United States or by any State on account of sex," and that such then be immediately ratified by the several States.

   II That equal employment opportunity be guaranteed to all women, as well as men, by insisting that the Equal Employment Opportunity Commission enforces the prohibitions against sex discrimination in employment under Title VII of the Civil Rights Act of 1964 with the same vigor as it enforces the prohibitions against racial discrimination.

   III That women be protected by law to ensure their rights to return to their jobs within a reasonable time after childbirth without loss of seniority or other accrued benefits, and be paid maternity leave as a form of social security and/or employee benefit.

IV Immediate revision of tax laws to permit the deduction of home and child care expenses for working parents.

V That child care facilities be established by law on the same basis as parks, libraries, and public schools, adequate to the needs of children from the pre-school years through adolescence, as a community resource to be used by all citizens from all income levels.

VI That the right of women to be educated to their full potential equally with men be secured by Federal and State Legislation, eliminating all discrimination and segregation by sex, written and unwritten, at all levels of education, including colleges, graduate and professional schools, loans and fellowships, and Federal and State training programs such as the Job Corps.

VII The right of women in poverty to secure job training, housing, and family allowances on equal terms with men, but without prejudice to a parent's right to remain at home to care for his or her children; revision of welfare legislation and poverty programs which deny women dignity, privacy and self-respect.

VIII The right of women to control their own reproductive lives by removing from penal codes laws limiting access to contraceptive information and devices and laws governing abortion.

Declaration of American Women, 1977

Mim Kelber

Writer, researcher, and peace activist Mim Kelber was policy adviser and speech writer for Congresswoman Bella Abzug when she became planning coordinator for the National Commission on the Observance of International Women's Year in 1977. She was the chief writer and editor of the report on the National Women's Conference, The Spirit of Houston, *which was delivered to President Jimmy Carter. Since then, she has published many articles on women and on peace and is currently editorial director for the Women's Foreign Policy Council in New York City.*

This declaration is the opening statement of The Spirit of Houston. *It has been more than a decade since the women in Houston, "expecting and entitled to serious attention" to their proposals demanded action. How much has changed? How much has not?*

Mim Kelber, The Spirit of Houston: The First National Women's Conference, ed. Helene Mandelbaum. Washington, DC: National Comm. on Observance of International Women's Year, 1978, DECLARATION OF AMERICAN WOMEN 1977.

WE ARE HERE TO MOVE HISTORY FORWARD.

We are women from every State and Territory in the Nation.

We are women of different ages, beliefs and lifestyles.

We are women of many economic, social, political, racial, ethnic, cultural, educational and religious backgrounds.

We are married, single, widowed and divorced.

We are mothers and daughters.

We are sisters.

We speak in varied accents and languages but we share the common language and experience of American women who throughout our Nation's life have been denied the opportunities, rights, privileges and responsibilities accorded to men.

For the first time in the more than 200 years of our democracy, we are gathered in a National Women's Conference, charged under Federal law to assess the status of women in our country, to measure the progress we have made, to identify the barriers that prevent us from participating fully and equally in all aspects of national life, and to make the recommendations to the President and to the Congress for means by which such barriers can be removed.

We recognize the positive changes that have occurred in the lives of women since the founding of our nation. In more than a century of struggle from Seneca Falls 1848 to Houston 1977, we have progressed from being non-persons and slaves whose work and achievements were recognized, whose needs were ignored, and whose rights were suppressed to being citizens with freedoms and aspirations of which our ancestors could only dream.

We can vote and own property. We work in the home, in our communities and in every occupation. We are 40 percent of the labor force. We are in the arts, sciences, professions and politics. We raise children, govern States, head businesses and institutions, climb mountains, explore the ocean depths and reach toward the moon.

Our lives no longer end with the childbearing years. Our lifespan has increased to more than 75 years. We have become a majority of the population, 51.3 percent and by the 21st century, we shall be an even larger majority.

But despite some gains made in the past 200 years, our dream of equality is still withheld from us and millions of women still face a daily reality of discrimination, limited opportunities and economic hardship.

Man-made barriers, laws, social customs and prejudices continue to keep a majority of women in an inferior position without full control of our lives and bodies.

From infancy throughout life, in personal and public relationships, in the family, in the schools, in every occupation and profession, too often we find our individuality, our capabilities, our earning powers diminished by discriminatory practices and outmoded ideas of what a woman is, what a woman can do, and what a woman must be.

Increasingly, we are victims of crimes of violence in a culture that degrades us as sex objects and promotes pornography for profit.

We are poorer than men. And those of us who are minority women—blacks, Hispanic Americans, Native Americans, and Asian Americans—must overcome the double burden of discrimination based on race and sex.

We lack effective political and economic power. We have only minor and insignificant roles in making, interpreting and enforcing our laws, in running our political parties, businesses, unions, schools and institutions, in directing the media, in governing our country, in deciding issues of war or peace.

We do not seek special privileges, but we demand as a human right a full voice and role for women in determining the destiny of our world, our nation, our families and our individual lives.

We seek these rights for all women, whether or not they choose as individuals to use them.

We are part of a worldwide movement of women who believe that only by bringing women into full partnership with men and respecting our rights as half the human race can we hope to achieve a world in which the whole human race—men, women and children—can live in peace and security.

Based on the views of women who have met in every State and Territory in the past year, the National Plan of Action is presented to the President and the Congress as our recommendations for implementing Public Law 94-167.

We are entitled to and expect serious attention to our proposals.

We demand immediate and continuing action on our National Plan by Federal, State, public, and private institutions so that by 1985, the end of the International Decade for Women proclaimed by the United Nations, everything possible under the law will have been done to provide American women with full equality.

The rest will be up to the hearts, minds and moral consciences of men and women and what they do to make our society truly democratic and open to all.

We pledge ourselves with all the strength of our dedication to this struggle "to form a more perfect Union."

What Will You Reap; What Will You Sow?

Barbara Jordan

Legislator and political leader Barbara Charline Jordan was born in Houston, the daughter of a Baptist minister. She was the first black student to graduate from Boston University Law School, and, after serving for a time in the Texas Senate, she was the first black woman elected to Congress from the deep South. She gained national attention in 1974 when, as a member of the House Judiciary Committee, she distinguished herself during the impeachment hearings of Richard Nixon. In 1976, she delivered an electrifying address as the keynote speaker at the Democratic Convention. That same year, she decided not to run again for Congress and took a position at the University of Texas at Austin. Her books include Local Government Election Systems *(with Terrell Blodgett) and her autobiography (with Shelby Hearon)* Barbara Jordan: A Self Portrait *(1979).*

Jordan told women in 1977, "Not making a difference is a cost we cannot afford." Is it any different now?

Keynote Speech by Congresswoman Barbara Jordan, First Plenary Session, The First National Women's Conference, November 19, 1977. Reported in *The* Spirit of Houston as the foregoing.

. . . IF YOU READ THE 31ST CHAPTER, IT BEGINS A litany of praise for the worthy woman. It begins this way: "Who can find a virtuous woman for her price is far above others." From virtue to power. What we are about here now will require no small amount of virtue and a great deal of power.

The value of women mostly in a narrowly construed fashion has been recognized throughout the ages, but the value of women has been periodically re-evaluated and is sometimes devalued.

American history is peppered with efforts by women to be recognized as human beings and as citizens and to be included in the whole of our national life. . . .

If Americans were asked to differentiate or distinguish between what characterized other countries and what characterizes us, we would say our high regard for the individual. That's the thing which makes us different.

We endorse personal and political freedom as a national right of human pride. Human rights are more than abstractions, particularly when they are limited or non-existent. Human rights apply equally to Soviet dissidents, Chilean peasants and American women.

Women are human. We know our rights are limited. We know our rights are violated. We need a domestic human rights program. . . .

Not making a difference is a cost we cannot afford. . . .

What will you reap?
What will you sow?

Bibliography

Abbott, Franklin, ed.
1987 *New Men, New Minds: Breaking Male Tradition*. Freedom, CA: Crossing Press.

Abbott, Sidney, and Barbara Love
1972 *Sappho Was a Right-on Woman*. New York: Stein & Day.

Adams, Elsie, and Mary Louise Briscoe, eds.
1971 *Up Against the Wall, Mother*. Beverly Hills, CA: Glencoe Press.

Adelstein, Michael E., and Jean G. Pival, eds.
1972 *Women's Liberation*. New York: St. Martin's.

Afshar, Haleh, ed.
1987 *Women, State, and Ideology: Studies from Africa and Asia*. Albany, NY: SUNY Press.

Agonito, Rosemary, ed.
1977 *History of Ideas on Woman: A Source Book*. New York: Putnam.

Aiken, Susan Hardy, Karen Anderson, Myra Dinnerstein, Judy Nolte Lensink, and Patricia MacCorquodale
1988 *Changing Our Minds: Feminist Transformations of Knowledge*. Albany, NY: SUNY Press.

Allen, Jeffner
1986 *Lesbian Philosophy: Explorations*. Palo Alto, CA: Institute of Lesbian Studies.

Altbach, Edith Hoshino, ed.
1971 *From Feminism to Liberation*. Cambridge, MA: Schenkman.

Amundsen, Kirsten
1971 *The Silenced Majority: Women and American Democracy*. Englewood Cliffs, NJ: Prentice-Hall.

Andelin, Helen B.
1975 *Fascinating Womanhood*. New York: Bantam.

Angelou, Maya
1981 *The Heart of a Woman*. New York: Random House.

———
1969 *I Know Why the Caged Bird Sings*. New York: Random House.

Ardrey, Robert
1966 *The Territorial Imperative*. New York: Atheneum.

Ashley, Jo Ann
1976 *Hospitals, Paternalism, and the Role of the Nurse*. New York: Teachers College Press.

Auerbach, Sylvia
1976 *A Woman's Book of Money: A Guide to Financial Independence*. New York: Doubleday.

Babcox, Deborah, and Madeline Belkin, comps.
1971 *Liberation Now!* New York: Dell.

Baeher, Helen, ed.
1980 *Women and Media*. New York: Pergamon Press.

Baetz, Ruth, ed.
1980 *Lesbian Crossroads*. New York: William Morrow Co.

Banner, Lois W.
1983 *American Beauty*. New York: Knopf.

———
1980 *Elizabeth Cady Stanton: A Radical for Women's Rights*. Boston: Little, Brown.

———
1984 *Women in Modern America: A Brief History*, 2nd ed. San Diego: Harcourt Brace Jovanovich.

Bardwick, Judith M.
1979 *In Transition: How Feminism, Sexual Liberation, and the Search for Self-Fulfillment Have Altered America*. New York: Holt, Rinehart, and Winston.

———
1972 *Readings on the Psychology of Women*. New York: Harper & Row.

Barker, Diana Leonard, and Sheila Allen
1976 *Dependence and Exploitation in Work and Marriage.* New York: Longman.

Barker-Benfield, G. J.
1976 *The Horrors of the Half-known Life.* New York: Harper Colophon.

Barry, Kathleen
1985 *Female Sexual Slavery.* New York: New York University Press.

——
1988 *Susan B. Anthony: A Biography of a Singular Feminist.* New York: New York University Press.

Bart, Pauline B., and Patricia H. O'Brien
1985 *Stopping Rape: Successful Survival Strategies.* New York: Pergamon Press.

Baxandall, Rosalyn, Linda Gordon, and Susan Reverby, eds.
1976 *America's Working Women.* New York: Random House.

Beauvoir, Simone de
1953 *The Second Sex.* Trans. and ed. by H. M. Parshley. New York: Knopf.

Belenky, Mary Field, Blythe McVicker Clinchy, Nancy Rule Goldberger, and Jill Mattuck Tarnle
1986 *Women's Ways of Knowing: The Development of Self, Voice, and Mind.* New York: Basic Books.

Bengis, Ingrid
1972 *Combat in the Erogenous Zone.* New York: Knopf.

Benhabib, Seyla, and Drucilla Cornell, eds.
1987 *Feminism as Critique: On the Politics of Gender.* Minneapolis: University of Minnesota Press.

Benstock, Shari, ed.
1987 *Feminist Issues in Literary Scholarship.* Bloomington: Indiana University Press.

Bergmann, Barbara R.
1986 *The Economic Emergence of Women.* New York: Basic Books.

Bernard, Jessie
1973 *American Family Behavior.* New York: Russell & Russell.

——
1981 *The Female World.* New York: Free Press.

——
1987 *The Female World from a Global Perspective.* Bloomington: Indiana University Press.

——
1973 *The Future of Marriage.* New York: Bantam.

——
1974 *The Future of Motherhood.* New York: Dial.

——
1971 *Remarriage.* New York: Russell & Russell.

——
1972 *The Sex Game.* New York: Atheneum.

——
1971 *Women and the Public Interest.* Chicago: Aldine.

——
1975 *Women, Wives, Mothers: Values and Options.* Chicago: Aldine.

Berry, Mary Frances
1986 *Why ERA Failed: Politics, Women's Rights and the Amending Process of the Constitution.* Bloomington: Indiana University Press.

Billings, Victoria
1974 *The Womansbook.* Los Angeles: Wollstonecraft.

Bird, Caroline
1968 *Born Female. The High Cost of Keeping Women Down.* New York: David McKay.

Bleier, Ruth H., ed.
1986 *Feminist Approaches to Science.* New York: Pergamon.

Boston Women's Health Book Collective
1984 *Our Bodies, Ourselves: A Book by and for Women.* 2nd ed. New York: Simon & Schuster.

——
1978 *Ourselves and Our Children: A Book by and for Parents.* New York: Random House.

Braun, Lily
1987 *Selected Writings on Feminism and Socialism.* Trans. and ed. by Alfred G. Meyer. Bloomington: Indiana University Press.

Bridenthal, Renate, Claudia Koonz, and Susan M. Stuard, eds.
1987 *Becoming Visible: Women in European History,* 2nd ed. Boston: Houghton Mifflin.

Brod, Harry, ed.
1987 *The Making of Masculinities: The New Men's Studies.* Boston: Allen and Unwin.

Brookes, Barbara A.
1988 *Abortion in England: 1900–1967.* New York: Croom Helm.

Brown, Rita Mae
1979 *Rubyfruit Jungle.* New York: Bantam Books.

——
1988 *Starting from Scratch: A Different Kind of Writer's Manual.* New York: Bantam Books.

——
1983 *Sudden Death.* New York: Bantam Books.

Brownmiller, Susan
1975 *Against Our Will: Men, Women, and Rape.* New York: Simon & Schuster.

———— 1984 *Femininity*. New York: Simon & Schuster.

Bullough, Vern L., Brenda Shelton, and Sarah Slavin
1988 *The Subordinated Sex*. Athens, Georgia: U. of Georgia Press.

Bunch, Charlotte
1987 *Passionate Politics: Feminist Theory in Action*. New York: St. Martin's Press.

Bunch, Charlotte, and Nancy Myron, eds.
1974 *Class and Feminism: A Collection of Essays from the Furies*. Baltimore: Diana Press.

————, eds.
1975 *Lesbianism and the Women's Movement*. Baltimore: Diana Press.

Bunch, Charlotte, and Sandra Pollack, eds.
1983 *Leaning Our Way: Essays in Feminist Education*. Trumansburg, NY: Crossing Press.

Bynum, Caroline Walker, Stevan Harrell, and Paula Richman
1986 *Gender and Religion: On the Complexity of Symbols*. Boston: Beacon Press.

Cade, Toni, ed.
1970 *The Black Woman: An Anthology*. New York: Signet.

Caine, Lynn
1974 *Widow*. New York: Morrow.

Case, Sue-Ellen
1988 *Feminism and Theatre*. New York: Methuen.

Chafe, William H.
1974 *The American Woman: Her Changing Social, Economic, and Political Roles, 1920–1970*. New York: Oxford University Press.

Chafetz, Janet Saltzman
1986 *Female Revolt: Women's Movements in World and Historical Perspective*. Totowa, NJ: Rowman and Allenheld.

———— 1978 *Masculine/Feminine or Human?: An Overview of the Sociology of Gender Roles*. Itasca, IL: Peacock.

Chernin, Kim
1987 *The Flame Bearers*. New York: Perennial Library, Harper & Row.

———— 1985 *The Hungry Self*. New York: Perennial Library, Harper & Row.

———— 1983 *In My Mother's House*. New Haven, CT: Ticknor & Fields.

———— 1982 *The Obsession: Reflections on the Tyranny of Slenderness*. New York: Harper & Row.

———— 1987 *Reinventing Eve*. New York: Harper & Row.

Chesler, Phyllis
1978 *About Men*. New York: Simon & Schuster. Reissued by Harcourt, Brace, Jovanovich in 1989.

———— 1989 *Sacred Bond: The Legacy of Baby M*. New York: Times Books.

———— 1979 *With Child: A Diary of Motherhood*. New York: Crowell.

———— 1972 *Women and Madness*. New York: Doubleday. Reissued with a new introduction by Harcourt, Brace, Jovanovich, 1989.

Chisholm, Shirley
1971 *Unbought and Unbossed*. New York: Avon.

Chmaj, Betty E.
1971 *American Women and American Studies*. Pittsburgh: Know, Inc.

———— 1974 *Feminist Resources for Schools and Colleges: A Guide to Curricular Materials*. Old Westbury, NY: Feminist Press.

———— 1972 *Image, Myth, and Beyond*. Pittsburgh: Know, Inc.

Chopin, Kate
1972 *The Awakening* (1899). New York: Avon Books.

Christ, Carol P.
1986 *Diving Deep and Surfacing: Women Writers on Spiritual Quest*. 2nd ed. Boston: Beacon Press.

———— 1987 *Laughter of Aphrodite: Reflections on a Journey to the Goddess*. San Francisco: Harper & Row.

Christ, Carol P., and Judith Plaskow, eds.
1979 *Womanspirit Rising: A Feminist Reader in Religion*. San Francisco: Harper & Row.

Cline, Sally, and Dale Spender
1987 *Reflecting Men at Twice Their Natural Size*. New York: Seaver Books/Henry Holt.

Cohen, Sherrill, and Nadine Taub, eds.
1989 *Reproductive Laws for the 1990's*. Clifton, NJ: Humana Press.

Collard, Andree, and Joyce Contrucci
1989 *Rape of the Wild!: Man's Violence Against Animals and the Earth*. Bloomington: Indiana University Press.

Collins, Sheila D.
1974 *A Different Heaven and Earth*. Valley Forge, PA: Judson Press.

Conover, Pamela Johnston, and Virginia Gray
  1983 *Feminism and the New Right: Conflict over the American Family*. New York: Praeger.

Cooke, Joanne, Charlotte Bunch-Weeks, and Robin Morgan, eds.
  1970 *The New Women*. Greenwich, CT: Fawcett.

Corea, Gena
  1985 *The Hidden Malpractice: How American Medicine Mistreats Women*. New York: Harper & Row.

_____
  1985 *The Mother Machine*. New York: Harper & Row.

Corea, Gena, et al.
  1987 *Man-Made Women: How New Reproductive Technologies Affect Women*. Bloomington: Indiana University Press.

Cotera, Martha P.
  1976 *The Chicana Feminist*. Austin, TX: Information Systems Development.

_____
  1976 *Diosa y Hembra: The History and Heritage of Chicanas in the United States*. Austin, TX: Informations Systems Development.

Cott, Nancy F.
  1987 *The Grounding of Modern Feminism*. New Haven, CT: Yale University Press.

Cott, Nancy F., and Elizabeth H. Pleck, eds.
  1979 *A Heritage of Her Own: Toward a New Social History of American Women*. New York: Simon & Schuster.

Daly, Mary
  1973 *Beyond God the Father*. Boston: Beacon Press.

_____
  1975 *The Church and the Second Sex*. New York: Harper Colophon.

_____
  1978 *Gyn/Ecology: The Metaethics of Radical Feminism*. Boston: Beacon Press.

_____
  1984 *Pure Lust*. Boston: Beacon Press.

Daly, Mary and Jane Caputi
  1987 *Webster's First New Intergalactic Wickedary of the English Language*. Boston: Beacon Press.

Darty, Trudy, and Sandee Potter, eds.
  1984 *Women-identified Women*. Palo Alto, CA: Mayfield.

David, Deborah S., and Robert Brannon, eds.
  1976 *The Forty-Nine Percent Majority: The Male Sex Role*. Reading, MA: Addison-Wesley.

Davis, Angela
  1974 *Angela Davis: An Autobiography*. New York: Random House.

_____
  1971 "Reflections on the Black Woman's Role in the Community of Slaves." *The Black Scholar* 3, No. 4 (December):2–16.

_____
  1989 *Women, Culture, and Politics*. New York: Random House.

_____
  1981 *Women, Race and Class*. New York: Random House.

Davis, Elizabeth Gould
  1971 *The First Sex*. New York: Putnam.

Deckard, Barbara
  1983 *The Women's Movement: Political, Socioeconomic, and Psychological Issues*. 3rd ed. New York: Harper & Row.

DeCrow, Karen
  1975 *Sexist Justice*. New York: Vintage.

Decter, Midge
  1972 *The New Chastity and Other Arguments Against Women's Liberation*. New York: Coward, McCann & Geoghegan.

Diamond, Irene, ed.
  1983 *Families, Politics, and Public Policy: A Feminist Dialogue on Women and the State*. New York: Longman.

_____
  1976 *Sex Roles in the State House*. New Haven: Yale University Press.

Ditzion, Sidney
  1978 *Marriage, Morals, and Sex in America: A History of Ideas*. New York: Norton.

Doress, Paula Brown, Diana Laskin Siegal and The Midlife and Older Women Book Project
  1987 *Ourselves Growing Older: Women Aging with Knowledge and Power*. New York: Simon & Schuster.

Dornbusch, Sanford M., and Myra H. Strober, eds.
  1988 *Feminism, Children and the New Families*. New York: Guilford.

Dworkin, Andrea
  1987 *Ice and Fire: A Novel*. New York: Weldenfeld & Nicolson.

_____
  1987 *Intercourse*. New York: Free Press.

_____
  1976 *Our Blood: Prophecies and Discourses on Sexual Politics*. New York: Harper & Row.

_____
  1987 *Pornography: Men Possessing Women*. New York: Free Press.

_____
  1983 *Right-Wing Women*. New York: Putnam.

———
1974 *Woman-Hating*. New York: E. P. Dutton.

Easlea, Brian
1983 *Fathering the Unthinkable: Masculinity, Scientists and the Nuclear Arms Race*. Great Britain: Pluto Press.

Edson, Sakre Kennington
1988 *Pushing the Limits: The Female Administrative Aspirant*. Albany: State University of New York Press.

Eisenstein, Hester
1983 *Contemporary Feminist Thought*. Boston: G. K. Hall.

Eisler, Riane
1987 *The Chalice and the Blade*. New York: Harper & Row.

Ellis, Julie
1970 *Revolt of the Second Sex*. New York: Lancer.

Ellmann, Mary
1968 *Thinking About Women*. New York: Harcourt Brace Jovanovich.

English, Jane, ed.
1977 *Sex Equality*. Englewood Cliffs, NJ: Prentice-Hall.

Epstein, Cynthia Fuchs
1970 *Woman's Place*. Berkeley, CA: University of California Press.

———
1988 *Deceptive Distinctions: Sex, Gender, and the Social Order*. New Haven, CT: Yale University Press.

Erikson, Erik H.
1964 "Inner and Outer Space: Reflexions on Womanhood." *Daedalus* 93:582–606.

Estrich, Susan
1987 *Real Rape: How the Legal System Victimizes Women Who Say No*. Cambridge, MA: Harvard University Press.

Evans, Judith
1986 *Feminism and Political Theory*. Beverly Hills, CA: Sage Publications.

Evans, Sara
1978 *Personal Politics: The Roots of Women's Liberation in the Civil Rights Movement and the New Left*. New York: Knopf.

Evans, Sara M., and Barbara J. Nelson
1989 *Wage Justice: Comparable Worth and the Paradox of Technocratic Reform*. Chicago: University of Chicago Press.

Falk, Ruth
1975 *Women Loving*. New York: Random House.

Farrell, Warren
1986 *Why Men Are the Way They Are*. New York: McGraw-Hill.

Fasteau, Marc Feigen
1974 *The Male Machine*. New York: McGraw-Hill.

Ferguson, Mary Anne, ed.
1986 *Images of Women in Literature,* 4th ed. Boston: Houghton Mifflin.

Figes, Eva
1971 *Patriarchal Attitudes*. Greenwich, CT: Fawcett.

Filene, Peter
1986 *Him/Her/Self: Sex Roles in Modern America*. 2nd ed. Baltimore: Johns Hopkins.

Fillmore, Mary Dingee
1987 *Women MBA's: A Foot in the Door*. Boston: G. K. Hall.

Firestone, Shulamith
1971 *The Dialectic of Sex*. New York: Bantam.

Fisher, Dexter, ed.
1980 *The Third Woman: Minority Women Writers of the United States*. Boston: Houghton Mifflin.

Flexner, Eleanor
1973 *Century of Struggle*. New York: Atheneum.

Frankfort, Ellen
1972 *Vaginal Politics*. New York: Quadrangle.

French, Marilyn
1977 *The Women's Room*. New York: Jove Publications.

Friedan, Betty
1963 *The Feminine Mystique*. New York: Dell.

———
1976 *It Changed My Life: Writings on the Women's Movement*. New York: Random House.

———
1981 *The Second Stage*. New York: Summit.

Frieze, Irene H., Jacquelynne E. Parsons, Paula B. Johnson, Diane N. Ruble, and Gail L. Zellman
1978 *Women and Sex Roles*. New York: Norton.

Fuchs, Victor R.
1988 *Women's Quest for Economic Equality*. Cambridge, MA: Harvard University Press.

Fulenwider, Claire Knoche
1980 *Feminism in American Politics: A Study of Ideological Influence*. New York: Praeger.

Gearhart, Sally, and William R. Johnson
1974 *Loving Women—Loving Men: Gay Liberation and the Church*. San Francisco: Glide.

Gergen, Mary McCanney, ed.
1988 *Feminist Thought and the Structure of Knowledge*. New York: New York University Press.

Gifford, Carolyn De Swarte, and Donald Dayton, eds.
1988 *The American Ideal of the "True Woman" as Reflected in Advice Books to Young Women*. New York: Garland Publishing.

Gilman, Charlotte Perkins
1973 *The Yellow Wallpaper* (1892). New York: Feminist Press.

1979 *Herland: A Lost Feminist Utopian Novel*. New York: Random House.

Githens, Marianne, and Jewel L. Prestage, eds.
1977 *A Portrait of Marginality: The Political Behavior of the American Woman*. New York: David McKay.

Goldberg, Steven
1974 *The Inevitability of Patriarchy*. New York: Morrow.

Goldstein, Leslie Friedman
1988 *The Constitutional Rights of Women: Cases in Law and Social Change*. Madison: University of Wisconsin Press.

Gordon, Linda
1976 *Woman's Body, Woman's Right: A Social History of Birth Control*. New York: Viking.

1988 *Heroes of Their Own Lives: The Politics and History of Family Violence*. New York: Viking.

Gordon, Margaret T., and Stephanie Riger
1989 *The Female Fear*. New York: Free Press.

Gordon, Vivian
1987 *Black Women, Feminism, and Black Liberation: Which Way?* Chicago: Third World Press.

Gornick, Vivian, and Barbara K. Moran
1972 *Woman in Sexist Society*. New York: Basic Books.

Gould, Carol C., and Marx W. Wartofsky, eds.
1976 *Women and Philosophy: Toward a Theory of Liberation*. New York: Putnam.

1984 *Beyond Domination: New Perspectives on Women and Philosophy*. Totowa, NJ: Rowman & Allenheld.

Greer, Germaine
1971 *The Female Eunuch*. New York: McGraw-Hill.

1986 *The Madwoman's Underclothes: Essays and Occasional Writings*. New York: Atlantic Monthly Press.

1979 *The Obstacle Race: The Fortunes of Women Painters and Their Work*. New York: Farrar, Straus & Giroux.

1984 *Sex and Destiny: The Politics of Human Fertility*. New York: Harper & Row.

Griffin, Susan
1981 *Pornography and Silence: Culture's Revenge Against Nature*. New York: Harper & Row.

1979 *Rape: The Power of Consciousness*. San Francisco: Harper & Row.

1987 *Unremembered Country*. Port Townsend, WA: Copper Canyon.

1978 *Woman and Nature: The Roaring Inside Her*. New York: Harper & Row.

Griffiths, Morwenna, and Margaret Whitford, eds.
1988 *Feminist Perspectives in Philosophy*. Bloomington: Indiana University Press.

Grimke, Sarah
1988 *Letters on the Equality of the Sexes and Other Essays*. Ed. Elizabeth Ann Bartlett. New Haven, CT: Yale University Press.

Gubar, Susan, and Joan Hoff, eds.
1989 *For Adult Users Only: The Dilemma of Violent Pornography*. Bloomington: Indiana University Press.

Gurko, Miriam
1976 *The Ladies of Seneca Falls: The Birth of the Women's Rights Movement*. New York: Schocken.

Hall, Kermit L., ed.
1987 *Women, the Law, and the Constitution*. New York: Garland Publishing, Inc.

Haskell, Molly
1973 *From Reverence to Rape: The Treatment of Women in the Movies*. New York: Holt, Rinehart and Winston.

Hays, H. R.
1964 *The Dangerous Sex*. New York: Putnam.

Hite, Shere
1974 *Sexual Honesty*. New York: Warner.

1987 *Women and Love: A Cultural Revolution in Progress*. New York: Alfred A. Knopf.

Hoagland, Sarah Lucia
1988 *Lesbian Ethics: Toward New Value*. Palo Alto, CA: Institute of Lesbian Studies.

Hoch-Smith, Judith, and Anita Spring, eds.
1978 *Women in Ritual and Symbolic Roles*. New York: Plenum.

Hole, Judith, and Ellen Levine
1971 *Rebirth of Feminism*. New York: Quadrangle Books.

Hooks, Bell
1981 *Ain't I A Woman: Black Women and Feminism*. Boston: South End Press.

1984 *Feminist Theory: From Margin to Center*. Boston: South End Press.

Horner, Matina
1969 "A Bright Young Woman is Caught in a Double Bind." *Psychology Today* 3, No. 6 (November).

Howe, Florence, ed.
1975 *Women and the Power to Change*. New York: McGraw-Hill.

Howe, Florence, and Marsha Saxton
1987 *With Wings: An Anthology of Literature by and about Women with Disabilities.* New York: Feminist Press at CUNY.

Hughes, Jean O., and Bernice R. Sandler
1987 *"Friends" Raping Friends: It Could Happen to You.* Washington, DC: Association of American Colleges, Project on the Status and Education of Women.

Hunt, Morton
1975 *Sexual Behavior in the 1970's.* New York: Dell.

_____
1966 *The World of the Formerly Married.* New York: Mc-Graw-Hill.

Hurcombe, Linda, ed.
1987 *Sex and God: Some Varieties of Women's Religious Experience.* New York: Routledge, Chapman and Hall.

Hurston, Zora Neale
1979 *I Love Myself When I am Laughing . . . and Again When I am Looking Mean and Impressive: A Zora Neale Hurston Reader,* ed. Alice Walker. Old Westbury, NY: Feminist Press.

Iglitzin, Lynne B., and Ruth Ross, eds.
1976 *Women in the World: A Comparative Study.* Santa Barbara, CA: Clio Press.

Jacobs, Sue Ellen, and Karen T. Hansen
1977 *Anthropological Studies of Women: A Course for Independent Study.* Seattle: University of Washington.

Jagger, Alison M., and Paula S. Rothenberg, eds.
1984 *Feminist Frameworks,* 2nd ed. New York: McGraw-Hill.

Janeway, Elizabeth
1982 *Cross Sections from a Decade of Change.* New York: William Morrow.

_____
1987 *Improper Behavior.* New York: Morrow.

_____
1971 *Man's World, Woman's Place.* New York: Delta Books.

_____
1980 *Powers of the Weak.* New York: Knopf.

Jaquith, Cindy
1988 *Surrogate Motherhood, Women's Rights, and the Working Class.* New York: Pathfinder Press.

Jardine, Alice, and Paul Smith, eds.
1987 *Men in Feminism.* New York: Methuen.

Jayawardena, Kumari
1986 *Feminism and Nationalism in the Third World.* (New Delhi: Kali for Women) Totowa, NJ: US Distributor, Biblio Distribution Center.

Johnson, Kim
1985 *If You Are Raped.* Holmes Beach, FL: Learning Publications.

Johnson, Robert A.
1974 *He: Understanding Masculine Psychology.* New York: Perennial Library.

_____
1977 *She: Understanding Feminine Psychology.* New York: Perennial Library.

Johnson, Sonia
1987 *Going Out of Our Minds: The Metaphysics of Liberation.* Freedom, CA: Crossing Press.

Johnston, Jill
1973 *Lesbian Nation.* New York: Simon & Schuster.

Jong, Erica
1979 *At the Edge of the Body.* New York: Holt, Rinehart and Winston.

_____
1973 *Fear of Flying.* New York: Holt, Rinehart & Winston.

_____
1976 *Loveroot.* New York: Holt, Rinehart and Winston.

_____
1983 *Ordinary Miracles: New Poems.* New York: New American Library.

_____
1984 *Parachutes and Kisses.* New York: New American Library.

_____
1981 *Witches.* New York: H. A. Abrams.

Kandal, Terry R.
1988 *The Woman Question in Classical Sociological Theory.* Gainsville: University Presses of Florida.

Kaplan, Alexandria G., and Joan P. Bean, eds.
1976 *Beyond Sex-Role Stereotypes.* Boston: Little, Brown.

Kass-Simon, G., and Patricia Farnes, eds.
1989 *Women of Science: Righting the Record.* Bloomington: Indiana University Press.

Kimball, Gayle
1986 *Life After College: Combining a Career and Family.* Chico: Women's Studies, California State University.

Kirkland, Gelsey
1986 *Dancing on My Grave.* New York: Doubleday.

Komarovsky, Mirra
1976 *Dilemmas of Masculinity.* New York: Norton.

Korda, Michael
1972 *Male Chauvinism! How It Works.* New York: Random House.

Kraditor, Aileen S.
1965 *The Ideas of the Woman Suffrage Movement, 1890–1920*. New York: Columbia University Press.

——, ed.
1968 *Up from the Pedestal*. Chicago: Quadrangle.

Kramarae, Cheris, and Paula A. Treichler
1985 *A Feminist Dictionary*. Boston: Pandora Press.

Kreps, Juanita
1971 *Sex in the Marketplace: American Women at Work*. Baltimore: Johns Hopkins Press.

Kuhn, Annette
1988 *Cinema, Censorship and Sexuality, 1909–1925*. New York: Routledge, Chapman and Hall.

Lawless, Elaine J.
1988 *Handmaidens of the Lord: Pentecostal Women Preachers and Traditional Religion*. Philadelphia: University of Pennsylvania Press.

Lederer, Wolfgang
1968 *The Fear of Women*. New York: Grune & Stratton.

Lerner, Gerda
1986 *The Creation of Patriarchy*. New York: Oxford University Press.

——
1977 *The Female Experience*. Indianapolis: Bobbs, Merrill.

——
1979 *The Majority Finds Its Past: Placing Women in History*. New York: Oxford University Press.

Lessing, Doris
1962 *The Golden Notebook*. New York: Simon & Schuster.

Levinson, Daniel
1978 *The Seasons of a Man's Life*. New York: Alfred A. Knopf.

McBride, Angela Barron
1977 *Living with Contradictions: A Married Feminist*. New York: Harper Colophon.

Maccoby, Eleanor E., ed.
1966 *The Development of Sex Differences*. Stanford, CA: Stanford University Press.

Maccoby, Eleanor E. and C. N. Jacklin
1974 *The Psychology of Sex Differences*. Stanford, CA: Stanford University Press.

Mahowald, Mary B., ed.
1983 *Philosophy of Woman: Classical to Current Concepts*, 2nd ed. Indianapolis: Hackett.

Mailer, Norman
1971 *The Prisoner of Sex*. Boston: Little, Brown.

Maio, Kathi
1988 *Feminist in the Dark: Reviewing the Movies*. Freedom, CA: Crossing Press.

Manning, Beverly
1988 *We Shall Be Heard: An Index to Speeches by American Women, 1978–1985*. Metuchen, NJ: Scarecrow Press.

Marine, Gene
1972 *A Male Guide to Women's Liberation*. New York: Avon.

Martin, Del, and Phyllis Lyon
1972 *Lesbian/Woman*. New York: Bantam.

Martin, M. Kay, and Barbara Voorhies
1975 *Female of the Species*. New York: Columbia University Press.

Martin, Wendy, ed.
1972 *The American Sisterhood*. New York: Harper & Row.

A Matter of Simple Justice
1970 Report of the President's Task Force on Women's Rights and Responsibilities. Washington, DC: Government Printing Office.

Mead, Margaret
1928 *Coming of Age in Samoa*. New York: Morrow.

——
1949 *Male and Female*. New York: Dell.

——
1935 *Sex and Temperament in Three Primitive Societies*. New York: Morrow.

Medea, Andrea, and Kathleen Thompson
1974 *Against Rape: A Survival Manual for Women*. New York: Farrar, Straus, and Giroux.

Messer, Ellen, and Kathryn E. May
1988 *Back Rooms: Voices from the Illegal Abortion Era*. New York: St. Martin's Press.

Millett, Kate
1970 *Sexual Politics*. New York: Doubleday.

——
1979 *The Basement: Meditations on a Human Sacrifice*. New York: Simon & Schuster.

Millman, Marcia, and Rosabeth M. Kanter, eds.
1975 *Another Voice: Feminist Perspectives on Social Science*. New York: Doubleday.

Mills, Patricia J.
1987 *Woman, Nature, and Psyche*. New Haven, CT: Yale University Press.

Minh-ha, Trinh T.
1989 *Woman, Native, Other: Writing Postcoloniality and Feminism*. Bloomington: Indiana University Press.

Mitchell, Juliet
1975 *Psychoanalysis and Feminism*. New York: Vintage.

——
1973 *Woman's Estate*. New York: Vintage.

———
1984 *Women: The Longest Revolution*. New York: Pantheon Books.

Mitchell, Juliet, and Ann Oakley, eds.
1986 *What is Feminism?* New York: Pantheon Books.

Mitter, Swasti.
1986 *Common Fate, Common Bond: Women in the Global Economy*. Great Britain: Pluto Press.

Momsen, Janet Henshall, and Janet Townsend, eds.
1987 *Geography of Gender in the Third World*. New York: SUNY Press.

Money, J., and A. A. Ehrhardt
1972 *Man and Woman, Boy and Girl*. Baltimore: Johns Hopkins Press.

Montague, Ashley
1974 *The Natural Superiority of Women*. New York: Collier Books.

Moraga, Cherríe, and Gloria Anzaldúa, eds.
1983 *This Bridge Called My Back: Writings by Radical Women of Color*, 2nd ed. New York: Kitchen Table, Women of Color Press.

Morgan, Elaine
1972 *The Descent of Woman*. New York: Stein & Day.

Morgan, Robin
1984 *The Anatomy of Freedom: Feminism, Physics and Global Politics*. Garden City, NY: Anchor Books/Doubleday.

———
1978 *Going Too Far: The Personal Chronicle of a Feminist*. New York: Vintage Books.

———, ed.
1984 *Sisterhood Is Global: The First Anthology of Writings from the International Women's Movement*. Garden City, NY: Anchor Press/Doubleday.

———, ed.
1970 *Sisterhood is Powerful*. New York: Vintage.

Morris, Desmond
1968 *The Naked Ape*. New York: McGraw-Hill.

Morrison, Toni
1972 *The Bluest Eye*. New York: Washington Square Press.

Moynihan, Patrick
1965 *The Negro Family: The Case for National Action*. Washington, DC: US Department of Labor.

Mueller, Carol M., ed.
1988 *The Politics of the Gender Gap: The Social Construction of Political Influence*. Beverly Hills, CA: Sage Publications.

Murray, Pauli
1989 *Pauli Murray: The Autobiography of a Black Activist, Feminist, Lawyer, Priest, and Poet*. Knoxville: University of Tennessee Press.

Myron, Nancy, and Charlote Bunch, eds.
1975 *Lesbianism and the Women's Movement*. Oakland, CA: Diana Press.

National Commission on the Observance of International Women's Year
1976 *"To Form a More Perfect Union . . .": Justice for American Women*. Washington, DC: U.S. Department of State.

Oakley, Ann
1974 *The Sociology of Housework*. New York: Pantheon.

———
1976 *Woman's Work: The Housewife Past and Present*. New York: Vintage.

Okin, Susan Miller
1979 *Women in Western Political Thought*. Princeton, NJ: Princeton University Press.

O'Leary, Virginia E.
1977 *Toward Understanding Women*. Belmont, CA: Brooks-Cole.

Papachristou, Judith, ed.
1976 *Women Together: A History in Documents of the Women's Movement in the United States*. New York: Knopf.

Parpart, Jane L., and Kathleen A. Standt, eds.
1989 *Women and the State in Africa*. Boulder, CO: Lynne Rienner.

Parrot, A.
1988 *Coping with Date Rape and Acquaintance Rape*. New York: Rosen Publishing Group.

Patton, Cindy, and Janis Kelly
1987 *Making It: A Woman's Guide to Sex in the Age of AIDS*. Spanish trans. Papusa Molina. Ithaca, NY: Firebrand Books.

Penley, Constance, ed.
1988 *Feminism and Film Theory*. New York: Routledge, Chapman and Hall.

Pharr, Suzanne
1988 *Homophobia, A Weapon of Sexism*. Inverness, CA: Chardon Press.

Pizzey, Erin
1974 *Scream Quietly or the Neighbors Will Hear*. Baltimore: Penguin.

Plath, Sylvia
1971 *The Bell Jar*. New York: Harper & Row.

Pleck, J. H. and J. Sawyer
1974 *Men and Masculinity*. Englewood Cliffs, NJ: Prentice-Hall.

Pleck, Joseph
1981 *The Myth of Masculinity*. Cambridge, MA: MIT Press.

Pribram, Deidre, ed.
1988 *Female Spectators: Looking at Film and Television*. New York: Verso.

Rabuzzi, Kathryn Allen
1988 *Motherself: A Mythic Analysis of Motherhood*. Bloomington: Indiana University Press.

Randall, Margaret
1987 *This Is About Incest*. Ithaca, NY: Firebrand Books.

Raymond, Janice
1986 *A Passion for Friends: Toward a Philosophy of Female Affection*. Boston: Beacon Press.

——
1979–80 "Women's Studies: A Knowledge of One's Own." *Union Seminary Quarterly Review* (Fall/Winter):34–48.

Réage, Pauline
1965 *Story of O*. Trans. Sabine d'Estree. New York: Grove Press.

Redfern, Bernice J.
1989 *Women of Color in the United States: A Guide to the Literature*. New York: Garland.

Reed, Evelyn
1971 *Problems of Women's Liberation*. New York: Pathfinder Press.

——
1970 Woman's Evolution. New York: Pathfinder Press.

Reiter, Rayna, ed.
1975 *Toward an Anthropology of Women*. New York: Monthly Review Press.

Rich, Adrienne
1975 *Adrienne Rich's Poetry*. New York: Norton.

——
1986 *Blood, Bread, and Poetry: Selected Prose, 1979–1985*. New York: Norton.

——
1978 *The Dream of a Common Language: Poems, 1974–1977*. New York: Norton.

——
1986 *Of Woman Born: Motherhood as Experience and Institution*. New York: Norton.

——
1979 *On Lies, Secrets, and Silence: Selected Prose, 1966–1978*. New York: Norton.

——
1983 *Sources*. Woodside: Heyeck Press.

——
1986 *Your Native Land, Your Life: Poems*. New York: Norton.

Richardson, Betty
1974 *Sexism in Higher Education*. New York: Seabury.

Rohrlich-Leavitt, Ruby, ed.
1975 *Women Cross-Culturally*. The Hague, the Netherlands: Mouton Press.

Roman, Leslie, and Linda K. Christian-Smith and Elizabeth Ellsworth, eds.
1988 *Becoming Feminine: The Politics of Popular Culture*. New York: Falmer.

Rosaldo, Michelle Z., and Louise Lamphere, eds.
1974 *Women, Culture, and Society*. Stanford, CA: Stanford University Press.

Rosen, Randy, et al.
1988 *Making their Mark: Women Artists Move into the Mainstream, 1970–85*. New York: Abbeville Press.

Ross, Heather L., and Isabel V. Sawhill
1975 *Time of Transition*. Washington, DC: Urban Institute.

Rosser, Sue V., ed.
1988 *Feminism within the Science and Health Care Professions: Overcoming Resistance*. New York: Pergamon Press.

Rossi, Alice S., ed.
1988 *The Feminist Papers: From Adams to de Beauvoir*. Boston: Northeastern University Press.

Rossi, Alice, and Ann Calderwood, eds.
1973 *Academic Women on the Move*. New York: Russell Sage.

Rossiter, Amy
1988 *From Private to Public: A Feminist Exploration of Early Mothering*. Toronto, Ontario: Women's Press.

Rothman, David J., and Sheila M. Rothman, eds.
1988 *Divorce: The First Debates*. New York: Garland.

Rowbotham, Sheila
1976 *Hidden from History*. New York: Vintage.

——
1973 *Woman's Consciousness, Man's World*. Baltimore: Penguin.

——
1974 *Women, Resistance and Revolution*. New York: Vintage.

Ruether, Rosemary Radford, ed.
1974 *Religion and Sexism*. New York: Simon & Schuster.

——
1983 *Sexism and God-Talk: Toward a Feminist Theology*. Boston: Beacon Press.

Ruether, Rosemary, and Rosemary Skinner Keller, eds.
1986 *Women and Religion in America*. San Francisco: Harper & Row.

Ruether, Rosemary, and Eleanor McLaughlin, eds.
1979 *Women of Spirit: Female Leadership in the Jewish and Christian Traditions*. New York: Simon & Schuster.

Russell, Diana
1984 *Sexual Exploitation: Rape, Child Sexual Assault and Workplace Harrassment*. Beverly Hills, CA: Sage.

Russell, Letty M., et al., eds.
1988 *Inheriting Our Mother's Gardens: Feminist Theology in Third World Perspective*. Philadelphia, PA: Westminster Press.

Ryan, Mary P.
1975 *Womanhood in America: From Colonial Times to the Present*. New York: Franklin Watts.

Sapiro, Virginia
1986 *Women in American Society*. Palo Alto, CA: Mayfield.

Sargeant, Alice G., ed.
1984 *Beyond Sex Roles*, 2nd ed. St. Paul, MN: West Publishing Co.

Scanzoni, John
1972 *Sexual Bargaining: Power Politics in the American Marriage*. Englewood Cliffs, NJ: Prentice-Hall.

Scarf, Mimi
1988 *Battered Jewish Wives: Case Studies in the Response to Rage*. Lewiston, NY: E. Mellen Press.

Scharf, Lois, and Joan M. Jensen
1983 *Decades of Discontent: The Women's Movement, 1920–1940*. Westport, CT: Greenwood Press.

Schecter, Susan
1982 *Women and Male Violence: The Visions and Struggles of the Battered Women's Movement*. Boston: South End Press.

Schneir, Miriam, ed.
1971 *Feminism: The Essential Historical Writings*. New York: Random House.

Scott, Hilda
1985 *Working Your Way to the Bottom: The Feminization of Poverty*. Boston: Pandora.

Seaman, Barbara
1972 *Free and Female*. New York: Coward McCann & Geoghegan.

Self, Donnie J., ed.
1977 *Philosophy and Public Policy*. Norfolk, VA: Teagle and Little.

Sharma, Arvind, ed.
1987 *Women in World Religions*. New York: SUNY Press.

Shulman, Alix Kates
1972 *Memoirs of an Ex-Prom Queen*. New York: Knopf.

Simon, Barbara Levy
1987 *Never Married Women*. Philadelphia: Temple University Press.

Sinclair, Marianne
1988 *Hollywood Lolitas: The Nymphet Syndrome in the Movies*. New York: Henry Holt.

Sloan, Irving J.
1988 *The Law Governing Abortion, Contraception and Sterilization*. New York: Oceana Publications.

Smith, Joan, et al., eds.
1988 *Racism, Sexism and the World-System*. Westport, CT: Greenwood Press.

Sochen, June
1974 *Herstory*. Sherman Oaks, CA: Alfred Publishing Co.

——— 1974 *Movers and Shakers: American Women Thinkers and Activists, 1900–1970*. New York: Quadrangle.

Spallone, Patricia, and Deborah Lynn Steinberg, eds.
1987 *Made to Order: The Myth of Reproductive and Genetic Progress*. New York: Athene Series, Pergamon Press.

Spender, Dale
1983 *Feminist Theorists: Three Centuries of Key Women Thinkers*. New York: Pantheon.

——— 1985 *For the Record: The Making and Meaning of Feminist Knowledge*. London: Women's Press.

——— 1985 *Man Made Language*, 2nd ed. Boston: Routledge, Chapman and Hall.

——— 1981 *Men's Studies Modified: The Impact of Feminism on the Academic Disciplines*. New York: Pergamon Press.

——— 1983 *There's Always Been a Women's Movement This Century*. Boston: Pandora.

——— 1988 *Women of Ideas (and What Men Have Done to Them): From Aphra Behn to Adrienne Rich*. Boston: Pandora.

——— 1988 *Writing a New World*. London: Pandora.

Spender, Dale, and Cheris Kramerae
1989 *The Knowledge Explosion*. New York: Athene Series, Pergamon.

Spiegel, Marcia Cohn, and Deborah Lipton Kremsdorf, eds.
1987 *Women Speak to God: The Prayers and Poems of Jewish Women*. San Diego, CA: Women's Institute for Continuing Jewish Education.

Spirit of Houston: The First National Women's Conference
1978 Washington, DC: U.S. Department of State, National Commission on the Observance of Women's Year.

Stacey, Judith, Susan Bereaud, and Joan Daniels, eds.
1974 *And Jill Came Tumbling After: Sexism in American Education*. New York: Dell.

Stannard, Una
    1977 *Mrs. Man*. San Francisco: Germain Books.

Stanton, Elizabeth Cady
    1972 *The Woman's Bible*. New York: Arno Press.

Stanton, Elizabeth Cady, Susan B. Anthony, and Matilda Joslyn Gage, eds.
    1881–1886 *History of Woman Suffrage*. 3 vols. New York: Fowler and Wells.

Stichter, Sharon B., and Jane L. Parpart
    1988 *Patriarchy and Class: African Women in the Home and the Workforce*. Boulder, CO: Westview Press.

Stimpson, Catharine R.
    1988 *Where the Meanings Are*. New York: Methuen.

Stoll, Clarice Stasy
    1974 *Female and Male*. Dubuque, IA: William C. Brown.

Stone, Merlin
    1979 *Ancient Mirrors of Womanhood: Our Goddess and Heroine Heritage*. Vols. I & II. New York: New Sibylline Books.

    ———
    1978 *When God Was a Woman*. New York: Harcourt Brace Jovanovich.

Stromberg, Ann H., and Shirley Harkess, eds.
    1978 *Women Working*. Palo Alto: Mayfield.

Szekely, Eva
    1988 *Never Too Thin*. Toronto, Ontario: Women's Press.

Tanner, Leslie B., ed.
    1970 *Voices from Women's Liberation*. New York: Signet.

Tavris, Carol, and Carole Offir
    1977 *The Longest War*. Part I. New York: Harcourt Brace Jovanovich.

Taylor, Dena
    1988 *Red Flower: Rethinking Menstruation*. Freedom, CA: Crossing Press.

Terborg-Penn, Rosalyn, Sharon Harley, and Andrea Benton Rushing, eds.
    1988 *Women in Africa and the African Diaspora*. Washington, DC: Howard University Press.

Thiam, Awa
    1986 *Black Sisters, Speak Out*. Trans. by Dorothy Blair. Great Britain: Pluto Press.

Thompson, Mary Lou, ed.
    1970 *Voices of the New Feminism*. Boston: Beacon Press.

Thorne, Barrie, and Nancy Henley, eds.
    1975 *Language and Sex: Difference and Dominance*. Rowley, MA: Newbury House.

Tiger, Lionel
    1969 *Men in Groups*. New York: Random House.

Tiger, Lionel, and Robin Fox
    1971 *The Imperial Animal*. New York: Holt, Rinehart and Winston.

Todd, Janet, ed.
    1988 *Women and Film*. New York: Holmes and Meier.

Tolchin, Susan, and Martin Tolchin
    1976 *Clout: Womanpower and Politics*. New York: Capricorn.

Trebilcot, Joyce, ed.
    1984 *Mothering: Essays in Feminist Theory*. Totowa, NJ: Rowman and Allanheld.

Tuchman, Gaye, Arlene K. Daniels, and James Benet, eds.
    1978 *Hearth and Home: Images of Women in the Mass Media*. New York: Oxford University Press.

Tucker, Susan
    1988 *Telling Memories among Southern Women: Domestic Workers and Their Employees in the Segregated South*. Baton Rouge: Louisiana State University Press.

Vetterling-Braggin, Mary, Frederick A. Elliston, and Jane English, eds.
    1977 *Feminism and Philosophy*. Totowa, NJ: Littlefield, Adams.

Vicinus, Martha
    1985 *Independent Women*. Chicago: University of Chicago Press.

Walker, Alice
    1982 *The Color Purple*, New York: Harcourt Brace Jovanovich.

    ———
    1973 *In Love and Trouble: Stories of Black Women*. New York: Harcourt Brace and Jovanovich.

    ———
    1983 *In Search of Our Mother's Gardens: Womanist Prose*. San Diego: Harcourt, Brace, Jovanovich.

    ———
    1989 *The Temple of My Familiar*. New York: Harcourt, Brace, Jovanovich.

    ———
    1981 *You Can't Keep a Good Woman Down: Stories*. New York: Harcourt, Brace, Jovanovich.

Walker, Barbara
    1988 *The Woman's Dictionary of Symbols and Sacred Objects*. San Francisco: Harper & Row.

    ———
    1983 *The Woman's Encyclopedia of Myths and Secrets*. San Francisco: Harper & Row.

Ware, Susan
    1981 *Women in the New Deal*. Cambridge, MA: Harvard University Press.

Warren, Mary Anne
  1980 *The Nature of Woman: An Encyclopedia and Guide to the Literature*. Point Reyes, CA: Edgepress, 1980.

Wegner, Judith Romney
  1988 *Chattel or Person? The Status of Women in the Mishnah*. New York: Oxford University Press.

Weis, Lois, ed.
  1988 *Class, Race, and Gender in American Education*. New York: SUNY Press.

Welter, Barbara
  1966 "The Cult of True Womanhood: 1820–1860," *American Quarterly* 18, No. 2, Pt. 1: 151–174.

Whelehan, Patricia et al.
  1988 *Women and Health: Cross-Cultural Perspectives*. Granby, MA: Bergin and Garvey.

Wilson, Edward O.
  1975 *Sociobiology: The New Synthesis*. Cambridge, MA: Harvard University Press.

Wittig, Monique
  1973 *Les Guérillères*. Trans. by David Le Vay. New York: Avon.

"Women's Studies: Awakening Academe."
  1977 A symposium issue of *The Social Science Journal* 14, No. 2 (April).

Young, Kate, ed.
  1988 *Women and Economic Development: Local, Regional and National Planning Strategies*. New York: St. Martin's Press/Berg/UNESCO.

Yorburg, Betty
  1974 *Sexual Identity*. New York: Wiley.

Zopf, Paul E. Jr.
  1989 *American Women in Poverty*. Westport, CT: Greenwood Press.

Index